Cultural Heritage Issues:
The Legacy of Conquest, Colonization, and Commerce

Cultural Heritage Issues:
The Legacy of Conquest, Colonization, and Commerce

Edited by

James A.R. Nafziger
Ann M. Nicgorski

MARTINUS NIJHOFF PUBLISHERS

2009

The image reproduced on the front cover of this book is the original excavation photo of the famous female head from the ancient Sumerian site of Uruk (modern Warka, Iraq), ca. 3500–3000 BCE, which was looted from the Iraq Museum in Baghdad in April of 2003 but recovered and returned to the museum a few months later. The long history of this "Sumerian Mona Lisa," already a fragmentary survivor of many past wars, civilizations, and the ravages of time, represents all the themes of this volume including the effects of conquest, colonization, and commerce on our shared cultural heritage as well as the important role of museums in preserving it for future generations.

Courtesy of the Deutsches Archäologisches Institut, Orient-Abteilung

Library of Congress Cataloging-in-Publication Data

Cultural heritage issues : the legacy of conquest, colonization, and commerce / edited by James A.R. Nafziger, Ann M. Nicgorski.
p. cm.
Includes index.
ISBN 978-90-04-16036-1
1. Cultural property—Protection—Law and legislation. I. Nafziger, James A. R. II. Nicgorski, Ann M.
K3791.C848 2009
344'.09–dc22

2009023785

PRINTED IN THE NETHERLANDS

CONTENTS

PREFACE AND ACKNOWLEDGMENTS

The chapters in this volume represent a groundbreaking international conference entitled "Cultural Heritage Issues: The Legacy of Conquest, Colonization, and Commerce" that took place October 12–14, 2006, at Willamette University. The conference featured some 30 distinguished panelists who addressed five themes: the legacy of indigenous conquest, the legacy of international conquest and colonization, the legacy of commerce, avoidance and resolution of cultural heritage disputes, and issues related directly to museums and sites. Papers drew on the panelists' expertise in a broad range of disciplines, from archaeology to law enforcement. Two evening lectures explored, respectively, the ownership of culture from a philosophical perspective (Kwame Anthony Appiah) and the recovery of objects stolen from the Iraq National Museum (Matthew Bogdanos). On the final day, the luncheon speaker, Richard M. Leventhal, presented a lively exchange with another museum director whose videotaped remarks were projected on a screen. The constructed dialogue centered on the responsibilities of museums to preserve objects as well as their archaeological contexts, as well as the ethical implications of museum acquisitions whose origins lie in colonized, war-torn, or impoverished source countries.

The conference was organized by a diverse group of Willamette University faculty members that included the editors of this volume and our colleagues Rebecca Dobkins (Anthropology), Ortwin Knorr (Classics), David McCreery (Religious Studies), John Olbrantz (Hallie Ford Museum of Art), and Scott Pike (Geology). During the conference these faculty members also led or co-led discussion groups for the conferees on specific cultural heritage topics of interest including copyright protection for Maori art, the Amber Room, the Dead Sea Scrolls, the R.M.S. Titanic, the Elgin Marbles, and the Seattle Matisse. Other colleagues and students of Willamette University contributed behind the scenes to the success of the 2006 conference. Without their expertise, dedication, and patience, the event would not have been possible.

In extending our thanks beyond Willamette University, we first acknowledge the original people of the Willamette Valley (the Kalapuyans), whose descendants today are members of the Grand Ronde and Siletz Confederated Tribes. They have been vigorous supporters of the arts and contributors to the dialogue about cultural heritage. We also thank our supporting and cooperating professional organizations, which include the Archaeological Institute of America, the American Branch of the International Law Association, the American School of Classical Studies at Athens, the American Schools of Oriental Research, the American Society of Comparative Law, the American Society of International Law, and the German Archaeological Institute.

The conference was made possible in part by grants and donations from the Oregon Council for the Humanities, a statewide non-profit organization that is an independent affiliate of the National Endowment for the Humanities, the Foreign Affairs Canada Grant Program, and the Archaeological Institute of America. Willamette University's Colleges of Law and Liberal Arts as well as the Departments of Art, Art History, History and Religious Studies, and the Dwight and Margaret Lear Chair in American History provided further funding. Deans Carol Long and Symeon Symeonides were supportive throughout the planning and publishing process. We are also grateful for the financial support from the Hallie Ford Museum of Art, Willamette University's Indian Country Conversation Series, and the Lilly Project at Willamette for providing us with this remarkable opportunity to reflect on our collective vocation as well-educated citizens, many of us representing the most powerful nations on earth, to protect and preserve the significant cultural heritage of all peoples.

Several Willamette staff members have been indispensable in making arrangements and designing publicity for the conference as well as in providing assistance for the publication of this volume, in particular, Andrea Foust, Candace Bolen, Kendra Mingo, Carrie Mosar, Linda Nelson, Patricia Alley, Allison Towers, and especially the indispensable Andrea Whalen.

Finally, we thank Heike Fenton, Lindy Melman, Maria Angelini, and Maxine Idakus of Martinus Nijhoff Publishers for their support and assistance in the preparation and publication of this book.

James A.R. Nafziger, College of Law, and

Ann M. Nicgorski, Department of Art and Art History,

Willamette University, Salem, Oregon, July 2009

ABOUT THE EDITORS AND AUTHORS

James A.R. Nafziger is the Thomas B. Stoel Professor of Law and Director of International Programs at the Willamette University College of Law. The author of numerous books and articles on international and comparative law, he is a former Fulbright lecturer at the National Autonomous University of Mexico and Scholar-in-Residence at the Rockefeller Foundation's Study Center in Bellagio, Italy. He chairs both the Cultural Heritage Law Committee of the International Law Association and the executive committee of the ILA's American Branch. A member of the American Law Institute, Professor Nafziger served in 2005 as the English-speaking Director of Research at The Hague Academy of International Law on the theme that year of the cultural heritage of mankind.

Ann M. Nicgorski is professor of art history at Willamette University, where she also serves as faculty curator at the Hallie Ford Museum of Art. She has extensive archaeological field experience in Greece at the sites of Corinth, as well as Halasmenos and Mochlos on Crete. Professor Nicgorski is a founding member and officer of the Salem Society Archaeological Institute of America (1995). Her publications include contributions to the Mochlos excavation series and various articles on Greek sculpture including the Parthenon frieze.

Kwame Anthony Appiah is Laurance S. Rockefeller University Professor of Philosophy and the University Center for Human Values at Princeton University. He was born in London and grew up in Ghana. Among his books are *In My Father's House: Africa in the Philosophy of Culture, Color Conscious: The Political Morality of Race* (with Amy Gutmann) and *The Ethics of Identity*, and *Cosmopolitanism: Ethics in a World of Strangers*. His most recent book is *Experiments in Ethics*.

Catherine Bell is a professor of law at the University of Alberta specializing in Aboriginal legal issues, dispute resolution, property law, cultural heritage law, and interdisciplinary, community-based legal research. Professor Bell is published widely on Métis and First Nation legal issues and has acted as an advisor to First Nation, Canadian government, and Métis organizations. Recent publications relating to cultural heritage include two collections of essays published by UBC Press (2008): *First Nations Cultural Heritage and Law: Case Studies, Voices and Perspectives* (with Val Napoleon) and *Protection of First Nations Cultural Heritage: Laws, Policy and Reform* (with Robert K. Paterson).

Colonel Matthew Bogdanos has been an assistant district attorney in Manhattan since 1988. A colonel in the U.S. Marine Corps Reserves, middleweight boxer, author, and native New Yorker, he holds advanced degrees in law, classics, and military strategy. Recalled to active duty after September 11, 2001, he received a Bronze Star for counter-terrorist operations in Afghanistan, served multiple tours in Iraq and the Horn of Africa, and received a 2005 National Humanities Medal for his work recovering Iraq's treasures. He has returned to the DA's office and continues the hunt for stolen antiquities. Royalties from his book, *Thieves of Baghdad*, go to the Iraq Museum.

Ricardo J. Elia is associate professor and chair of the department of archaeology at Boston University. He teaches archaeological ethics, law, and heritage management, and his research interests include archaeological protection, policy, and the antiquities market.

Margarete van Ess is scientific director at the German Archaeological Institute—Orient Department. She is a member of a UNESCO experts group on Iraq. She was born in Frankfurt/M and grew up in Beirut, Lebanon, and Tübingen. Among her publications are *Uruk. Architektur II. Von der Akkad- bis zur mittelbabylonischen Zeit, Teil I: Das Eanna-Heiligtum zur Ur III- und altbabylonischen Zeit* and most recently "Baalbek/Heliopolis. Results of Archaeological and Architectural Research 2002–2005," in *Bulletin d'archéologie et d'architecture libanaises, hors serie 4.*

Patty Gerstenblith is professor of law at DePaul University College of Law and director of its Center for Art, Museum and Cultural Heritage Law. She is founding president of the Lawyers' Committee for Cultural Heritage Preservation. She previously served as a public representative on the President's Cultural Property Advisory Committee, editor-in-chief of the *International Journal of Cultural Property*, and co-chair of the American Bar Association's Art and Cultural Property Committee. She is the author of *Art, Cultural Heritage and the Law* and co-author of *Iraq Beyond the Headlines: History, Archaeology, and War.*

McGuire Gibson is professor of Mesopotamian archaeology in the Oriental Institute and the department of near eastern civilizations at the University of Chicago. He has conducted archaeological research in Iraq since 1964, mainly at Nippur, and has also worked in Saudi Arabia, Yemen, and Syria, where he directed the investigations of the early city site of Hamoukar. He has authored or edited more than 12 books, including *The City and Area of Kish, Seals and Sealing in the Ancient Near East* and *The Organization of Power: Aspects of Bureaucracy in the Ancient Near East.* Theoretical articles include "Violation of Fallow and Engineered Disaster in Mesopotamian Civilization." He was the founder of the American Institute for Yemeni Studies and the American Academic Research Institute in Iraq. He served on UNESCO and the National Geographic Society fact-finding teams in Iraq in May 2003.

Lawrence M. Kaye is a partner at the New York law firm of Herrick, Feinstein LLP. He is engaged in all facets of international art law and represents a wide range of domestic and international clients. He is noted for his representation of foreign governments, victims of the Holocaust, families of renowned artists, and other claimants in connection with the recovery of art and antiquities. He most recently represented the heir of Jacques Goudstikker, a prominent Jewish art dealer in the Netherlands who died while fleeing the Nazis, in the 2006 restitution by the Dutch government of 200 old masters' paintings looted by the Nazis and the heirs of the famed Russian artist, Kazimir Malevich, in their litigation and 2008 settlement between the City of Amsterdam and the Stedelijk Museum.

Maria P. Kouroupas is director of the Cultural Heritage Center, Bureau of Educational and Cultural Affairs, U.S. Department of State. The center is responsible for the administrative and technical support requirements of U.S. implementation of the 1970 UNESCO Convention on Cultural Property and of the U.S. Ambassadors Fund for Cultural Preservation. The center also oversees State Department efforts in support of cultural preservation in Iraq. Prior to joining the State Department, Kouroupas administered the international program of the American Association of Museums where she developed "International Partnerships Among Museums" and contributed an international column to the AAM journal, *Museum*.

Claire L. Lyons is curator of antiquities at the J. Paul Getty Museum. Her research has focused on the afterlife of antiquity in the visual arts, culture, and politics. She co-authored the exhibition catalogue *Antiquity & Photography: Early Views of Ancient Mediterranean Sites* (2005), and was co-curator of "The Herculaneum Women and the Origins of Archaeology," and "Grecian Taste and Roman Spirit: The Society of Dilettanti." A specialist in ancient Italy, she has excavated at Murlo, Metaponto, Corinth, and Morgantina. Among her publications are *Morgantina: The Archaic Cemeteries* (1996), as well as the edited volumes *The Archaeology of Colonialism* (2002) and *Naked Truths: Women, Sexuality and Gender in Classical Art and Archaeology* (1997). Claire Lyons is a research associate of the Cotsen Institute of Archaeology at UCLA, and sits on the editorial boards of the *International Journal of Cultural Property*, *The Journal of the History of Collections*, and the *American Journal of Archaeology*.

Patrick O'Keefe is semi-retired but holds the positions of adjunct professor at the School of Pacific and Asian Studies, Australian National University and honorary professor at the University of Queensland. He has been awarded the Order of Australia and is a fellow of the Society of Antiquaries of London and the Australian Academy of the Humanities. A specialist in the law and management of cultural heritage, his latest book is the second edition of a commentary on the 1970 UNESCO Convention.

Robert K. Paterson is a professor of law at the University of British Columbia where he teaches and publishes in the area of cultural property law. He received his legal training in New Zealand and also holds a J.S.M. from Stanford Law School. He is the Rapporteur of the Cultural Heritage Law Committee of the International Law Association and an editor of the *International Journal of Cultural Property*. He was recently appointed a member of the advisory board of the University of British Columbia Museum of Anthropology.

Lyndel V. Prott has been responsible for over 260 books, reports, or articles and is currently based at the University of Queensland. She was closely associated with the negotiation of the UNIDROIT Convention on Stolen or Illegally Exported Cultural Objects 1995, the Second Protocol 1999 to The

Hague Convention for the Protection of Cultural Property in the Event of Armed Conflict 1954, and the UNESCO Convention on the Protection of the Underwater Cultural Heritage 2001.

Sabine von Schorlemer, chair of international law and international relations at the University of Dresden since 2000, wrote her Ph.D. thesis on "Cultural Property Law in Peace and Armed Conflict" and obtained her habilitation in International Politics and Public International Law at the University of Munich in 1997. Being a legal advisor on U.N. policy for the German Foreign Ministry, she served both as an independent expert for the UNESCO director general in 2003/2004/2007 and as a member of the German delegation regarding the adoption of the "UNESCO Convention on the Promotion and Protection of Cultural Expressions" (2005). Professor von Schorlemer has been a member of the ILA Cultural Heritage Law Committee since 1993.

Tullio Scovazzi is professor of International Law at the University of Milano-Bicocca, Milan, Italy. He frequently serves as a legal expert for the government of Italy at international meetings relating to law of sea, the environment, cultural properties, and human rights. He is the author or editor of numerous articles and books on topics of international and comparative law, including two co-edited works: *The Protection of the Underwater Cultural Heritage* (2003) and *Biotechnolgy and International Law* (2006). In 2005, Professor Scovazzi served as the French-speaking Director of Research at The Hague Academy of International Law on the theme that year of the cultural heritage of mankind.

Folarin Shyllon is a professor of law at Olabisi Olabanjo University, Ago-Iwoye, Ogun State, Nigeria where he is the dean of the faculty of law. He was also a professor of law at the University of Ibadan, Ibadan, Oyo State, Nigeria where he was the foundation dean of the faculty of law from 1984 to 1991. He was educated at King's College, London. His current teaching and research interests are in the fields of cultural property law and intellectual property law. The author of *Intellectual Property Law in Nigeria* (Munich, Germany, 2004), he was a contributor to UNESCO's maiden issue of *World Culture Report* (1998) and contributed a chapter to Halina Niec's *Cultural Rights and Wrongs* (Paris, UNESCO, 1998), published to mark the 50th anniversary of the Universal Declaration of Human Rights of 1948. He is a member of the Nigerian Bar, a former president of the Nigerian Association of Law Teachers, a former member of the Nigerian Institute of Advanced Legal Studies, and a member (2007–) of the Council of Legal Education (CLE). He is on the editorial board of the *International Journal of Cultural Property* and *Art Antiquity and Law.*

Anastasia Telesetsky is currently Assistant Professor in the School of Law at the University of Idaho. She is a graduate of Boalt Hall School of Law, University of California at Berkeley with legal fieldwork experience in the Philippines and Papua New Guinea. She was a member of the Centre for Studies and Research at The Hague Academy of International Law in 2005 and published a chapter on the protection of traditional knowledge in the resulting volume of reports (2008).

Rebecca Tsosie joined the faculty of the Sandra Day O'Connor College of Law at Arizona State University in 1993 and teaches in the areas of Indian law, property, bioethics, and critical race theory. She has served there as executive director of the Indian Legal Program since 1996 and was appointed as a Willard H. Pedrick Distinguished Research Scholar in 2005. She has published widely on issues related to tribal sovereignty, environmental policy, and cultural rights, resources and pluralism, as well as Native rights to genetic resources. Tsosie, who is of Yaqui descent, also serves as a Supreme Court Justice for the Fort McDowell Yavapai Nation. She is the co-author with Robert Clinton and Carole Goldberg of a federal Indian law casebook entitled *American Indian Law: Native Nations and the Federal System.*

Nancy C. Wilkie is William H. Laird Professor of Classics, Anthropology and the Liberal Arts, and director of the archaeology concentration at Carleton College. She served as president of the Archaeological Institute of America from 1998–2002 and has been a member of the Cultural Property Advisory Committee of the U.S. Department of State since 2003. She has conducted archaeological research in Greece and Egypt and also in Nepal where she was a Senior Fulbright Visiting Lecturer.

INTRODUCTION

The global community, dependent as always on the cooperation of nation states, is gradually learning to address the serious threats to the cultural heritage of our disparate but shared civilizations. The legacy of conquest, colonialization, and commerce looms large in defining and explaining these threats.

The international conference on cultural heritage issues that took place at Willamette University in October 2006 sought to generate fresh ideas about these cultural heritage issues; offer a good sense of their nuances and complexities; and reveal how culture, law, and ethics can interact, complement, diverge, and contradict one another. The chapters that follow in this book, written by conference participants, seek to accomplish these purposes. In 2006, the dramatic looting of the Iraq National Museum, as well as libraries and archaeological sites in that country, following the armed intervention there three years earlier, was still paramount in the minds of many if not most panelists and conferees. But the threats to cultural heritage are nothing new.

Indeed, the Willamette conference marked the centennial of two important developments in the history of threats to the cultural heritage in the United States. The Antiquities Act of 1906 was the first comprehensive legislation to address the plight of the fragile and non-renewable archaeological heritage in this country. Although much of the act was later gutted by the courts and superseded by other federal and state laws, it remains a foundation for national heritage protection, including the designation of national monuments.

The year 2006 also marked the centennial of the controversial donation to the American Museum of Natural History in New York of the Willamette Meteorite (Tomonowos in the Clackamas tribal language). It is the largest meteorite ever found in the United States and the sixth largest in the world. After coming to rest in the Willamette Valley of Oregon thousands of years ago, it eventually endured a questionable series of commercial transactions and litigation early in the last century that resulted in the relocation of most but not all of it in a specially built exhibit area at the museum. Several broken-off pieces migrated elsewhere, including a small piece that Willamette University recently rediscovered and returned to the Confederated Tribes of Grand Ronde community near Salem, Oregon. Since 2000, the meteorite lodged in New York has been subject to an agreement that ensures special access to it by members of the Grand Ronde community for cultural, religious, and historical purposes, including an annual ceremonial visit.

Despite a long history of issues and responses to them, it is only in the last few decades that the global community has acted to construct a specific, comprehensive regime of law for regulating and protecting the cultural heritage of humankind. Among the earliest multilateral agreements was the Roerich Pact of 1935 to protect monuments in western hemispheric states and the 1954 Hague Convention for the Protection of Cultural Property in the Event of Armed Conflict.

In the late 1960s, however, four developments sparked a series of further initiatives to construct an effective regime of supervision and control. First, concerned archaeologists began to blow their whistles on questionable excavations, illegal trafficking in cultural objects, and acquisitions of them by collectors, museums, and other institutions. Second, governments, notably Mexico, brought pressure on import states, particularly the United States, to cooperate in barring the import of significant cultural material and returning such contraband to countries of origin. Third, the Native Peoples Movement inspired efforts to regain possession of indigenous material. And fourth, more sophisticated thefts of cultural material and their growing links with money-laundering as well as other organized crime alerted law enforcement authorities to the need for better policing of transactions involving important cultural objects. It was truly alarming to find that illegal trafficking in cultural material had assumed third place behind drugs and weapons as international contraband. In response to these developments, inter-governmental and non-governmental organizations, particularly the United Nations Educational, Scientific and Cultural Organization (UNESCO), enlisted the cooperation of national governments and private institutions in fashioning and enforcing the rules and procedures that now form the general framework of cultural heritage law.

The emerging regime for protecting the global heritage performs five interrelated functions: *protection, cooperation, rectification, criminal justice,* and *dispute resolution.* Accordingly, the law seeks to protect the physical integrity and contextualization of cultural material; facilitate cooperation in its management, appropriate transfer, and safe return to legitimate claimants; rectify wrongful activity by means of civil remedies and otherwise; impose penal sanctions for illegal activity involving cultural material; and provide formal and informal mechanisms and rules for resolving related disputes.

In particular, claims for the return, restitution, or repatriation of cultural heritage have been of central importance. On the domestic level, for example, the historical and cultural identity of tribal and other indigenous groups is often at stake in efforts to reclaim significant artifacts from museums, art galleries, and private collections. On the international level, the recovery of stolen cultural material, whose value is estimated to be as high as $3 billion annually, requires substantial diligence by customs officials and cooperation among international organizations, governments, private institutions, and individuals. Not surprisingly, the claims can easily beget complexity.

Some claims seek to right the wrongs of conquest and colonialization, particularly by native and colonial peoples seeking to reclaim material looted from them, while other claims address issues of illegal commercial activity. Often all three dimensions of the cultural heritage predicament—conquest, colonialization, and commerce—converge. For example, almost as soon as the British military had looted scores of extraordinary Benin bronze sculptures from West Africa in 1897, they found their way into private collections and museums, primarily in Europe. This combined legacy of conquest, colonialization, and commerce continues to generate tensions and provoke ethical and legal questions, even as the cultural objects at issue continue to excite people's imaginations around the world and encourage notions of cross-cultural pride and human solidarity. In the course of the two years during which this book was in preparation, an unprecedented exhibition of Benin bronzes toured four countries. One sentence in the preface to the exhibition catalogue reflects the characteristic ambiguities of contested heritage derived, in the case of the Benin bronzes, from an "unjustifiable" military acquisition that has nevertheless brought the works of art to "far broader attention."[1]

Until recently, requirements to return cultural material to territories of origin, dating back to Persian, Greek, and Roman times, were addressed almost exclusively to military-related problems of plunder, the spoils of warfare, and occupation. For example, The Hague Conventions of 1899 and 1907 on the laws and customs of war, followed by the reparation provisions of the Treaties of Versailles and Saint-Germain after the First World War, underscored the illegality of military plunder and articulated basic remedies for victim states. The spoils of war and occupation still threaten the world's cultural heritage, as in the wake of the 2003 military intervention in Iraq, but for several decades a booming art market has shifted attention to peacetime trafficking as well.

Because the origins of international cultural heritage law lie in the battlegrounds of conflict and the underworld of crime, it is not surprising that the normative framework to protect the cultural heritage has been essentially adversarial. Historically, efforts to develop an effective body of cultural heritage law have emphasized formal remedies for past wrongs. Considerable emphasis has been placed on exclusive rights of ownership and the elaboration of rules for the restitution of stolen property or return of illegally exported property. In resolving related disputes, litigation has been a preferred means despite the voices of experience that have urged a greater recourse to mediation and other informal means of dispute resolution when that is feasible. Unfortunately, however, the stakes are often too high in the commercial art world to rely on mediation and other informal techniques.

The availability of adjudication and the articulation of applicable rules are essential, of course. Conversely, an absence of detailed rules may inhibit the resolution of cultural property disputes such as those arising out of the confiscation and transfer of cultural treasures during the Holocaust and World War II. But rules and formal processes for applying them are inadequate by themselves. As one of the conference speakers, Folarin Shyllon, has pointed out, a reliance on adversarial processes, particularly litigation, is bedeviled by

---

[1] Barbara Plankensteiner ed., Benin Kings and Rituals: Court Arts from Nigeria 17 (2007).

two intractable problems: evidentiary issues and refusals to recognize or enforce foreign export controls, not to mention the often prohibitive costs of litigation. And in addressing Native American and Native Hawaiian claims, it is likewise apparent that formal rules, scientific theories, and academic practices—the legacy of what Roger Echo-Hawk calls "conquest archaeology"—have inherent limitations in constructing our views of ancient human history and cultural traditions. The will to cooperate and collaborate in equitably sharing the global heritage—it is really a matter of *good*will—is essential.

It seems clear that the global community should seek a balance between rectification of what has gone wrong and advocacy of what seems right. This, however, will require a greater emphasis on a spirit of commonality, a commitment to the principle of sharing, and open, well-informed mechanisms of collaboration. We also need to refurbish our vocabulary and renovate our mind-sets, which have relied too heavily on such dichotomies as art-exporting versus art-importing countries; common heritage versus national patrimony; salvage of underwater wreck versus preservation of underwater heritage; and so on. Dichotomies of this sort are, of course, normal if not essential as analytical constructs in advancing any system of law and governance, but they are apt to blinker our vision of reality and inhibit constructive discourse and action.

A sharp division by some commentators between cultural internationalism and cultural nationalism is particularly questionable. The wordsmiths of the benign-sounding term "cultural internationalism" cleverly pirated a respectable term—internationalism—to justify laissez-faire practices that actually defy the fundamental requirements of cooperation and collaboration underlying internationalism in its normal sense. One of the conference speakers, Lyndel Prott, has effectively debunked this classification as simply a rhetorical construct to justify a perpetual legacy of commerce. It must yield and, indeed, is yielding to more cooperative approaches for accommodating the many diverse interests in the cultural heritage of humankind. An example is the broadly applicable Principles for Cooperation in the Mutual Protection and Transfer of Cultural Material, which were adopted by the International Law Association in 2006.

Bilateral agreements now reflect this trend as well. So do concrete proposals for dispute resolution. For example, William St. Clair, an expert on the endless issue of the Elgin (Parthenon) Marbles, has suggested that the core of an agreement for their return to Greece need not be simply a transfer from one location and one museum management to another, but rather more of a universal trusteeship. Such an approach, in keeping with the more global vision of our times might, for example, impose specific duties on the trustees with regard to conservation, display, access, record keeping, needs of scholars, consultation, and accountability. Collaboration of this sort represents the best of cosmopolitanism, to use Kwame Anthony Appiah's term.

Along with an emerging blend of adversarial and collaborative processes to address cultural heritage issues has come a substantial broadening of the normative framework in recent years. This framework now spans a welter of issues ranging from the creation of cultural safety zones during armed conflict, to the ongoing rectification of genocidal conquest during the European Holocaust and World War II, to the treatment of shipwrecks and their cargo, to the protection of folklore and other intangibles, to the promotion of traditional knowledge in the interest of biological diversity. All of these topics are controversial, as are the legal instruments that incorporate them, but the issues they embrace are vital to us all, whether our viewpoint is in the global arena, a national legislature, a courtroom, a classroom, an archaeological site, or a museum.

PART I

LEGACY OF INDIGENOUS CONQUEST

CHAPTER 1

WHO CONTROLS NATIVE CULTURAL HERITAGE?: "ART," "ARTIFACTS," AND THE RIGHT TO CULTURAL SURVIVAL

Rebecca Tsosie

The protection of Native cultural heritage is closely linked with tribal needs to promote cultural survival. Cultural survival is a concept that resonates with Native peoples but not necessarily with members of the dominant societies that have tried to assimilate them for nearly two centuries. Of course, certain practices—such as the forcible removal of Native children to boarding schools, the prohibitions on speaking Native languages, and the criminalization of Native religion—are now denounced as being inhumane and unconstitutional under contemporary norms. However, the assimilationist tendency of the dominant society persists in court cases that deny protection for sacred sites or Native claims for repatriation of ancestral human remains, citing broader social interests as a means of discrediting specific cultural claims. The resultant cultural harm to Native peoples is dismissed as non-cognizable.

In order to understand why the dominant legal framework for cultural resources protection is insufficient to fully protect tribal rights, it is necessary to understand what the concept of cultural heritage means to Native peoples. Such an "inter-cultural" examination reveals profound conceptual differences. Consequently, because Native peoples' cultural claims are viewed as "different" from those of other litigants, they are often not afforded protection under the structures that protect non-Native interests in "religious freedom" or "cultural property." Similarly, conceptual and linguistic categories of "art" and "artifacts" are employed to limit and qualify Native rights. These conceptual challenges are undergirded by historical themes of "discovery" and "conquest" that have privileged certain values through the establishment of "rights" to certain aspects of cultural heritage, while negating or dismissing corollary rights. This chapter evaluates the limitations of the existing legal framework that applies to Native cultural heritage and highlights the need to develop inter-cultural frameworks that can better protect the core values of tribal cultures.

A. CONCEPTUAL CHALLENGES TO THE PROTECTION OF NATIVE CULTURAL HERITAGE

At the most fundamental level, what is comprised within the scope of tribal "cultural heritage"? How we define cultural heritage has a great deal to do with how it is ultimately protected by the law. Some textbooks on cultural heritage define "heritage resources" as coextensive with "cultural resources," including a "wide range of archaeological sites, historic structures, museum objects, historic shipwrecks, and traditional cultural places."[1] Indeed, this definition is widely used within domestic and international law.

In the United States, federal statutes specifically protect "archaeological resources" and "historic properties." According to the Archaeological Resources Protection Act (ARPA), "archaeological resources" include "any material remains of past human life or activities" that are at least 100 years of age and are of "archaeological interest."[2] Material remains are "physical evidence of human habitation, occupation, use or activity, including the site, location, or context in which such evidence is situated."[3] Such remains are of archaeological interest if they are "capable of providing scientific or humanistic understandings of *past* human behavior."[4] Similarly, the National Historic Preservation Act (NHPA) protects "historic properties" that comprise tangible "districts, sites, buildings, structures, and objects significant in American history, architecture, archaeology, engineering, and culture."[5] Both statutes protect tangible, physical resources that are significant because they have information about who "we" were in the past.

International conventions on cultural resources are similar. The 1970 UNESCO convention on cultural property, for example, includes historic and archaeological sites, antiquities that are more than 100 years old, and artistic property and manuscripts that represent particular historic periods and have significance in documenting history.[6] The 1972 convention on cultural and national heritage addresses the categories of monuments and sites that are of "outstanding universal value" from the point of view of "science, conservation, or natural beauty."[7]

Scholarly work on cultural heritage has identified several key conceptual problems in cultural heritage protection that further illustrate the Euro-American norms underlying these legal categories.[8] The first of these problems is the pervasive inability to distinguish "objects of art" from "cultural objects," though the law distinguishes the two categories. Artists maintain the right to protect their "creative expression" (for example, through copyright), while the government maintains an interest in protecting "historic" or "archaeological"

---

[1] Sherry Hutt, Caroline Blanco & Ole Varmer, Heritage Resources Law 1 (1999).

[2] 16 U.S.C. §§ 470-aa-mm, 470bb(1) (2008).

[3] 43 C.F.R. § 7.3(a)(2) (defining "material remains").

[4] 43 C.F.R. § 7.3(a)(1) (defining "of archaeological interest").

[5] 16 U.S.C. §§ 470-70x-6, 470(a)(1)(A) (2008).

[6] UNESCO Convention on the Means of Prohibiting and Preventing the Illicit Import, Export, and Transfer of Ownership of Cultural Property (Nov. 14, 1970), 22 U.S.T. 19, 823 U.N.T.S. 231, *available at* http://portal.unesco.org/en/ev.php-URL_ID=13039&URL_DO=DO_TOPIC&URL_SECTION=201.html.

[7] UNESCO Convention Concerning the Protection of the World Cultural and Natural Heritage, Nov. 16, 1972, 27 U.S.T. 37, 1037 U.N.T.S. 151, *available at* http://portal.unesco.org/en/ev.php-URL_ID=13055&URL_DO=DO_TOPIC&URL_SECTION=201.html.

[8] Patty Gerstenblith, Art, Cultural Heritage and the Law *passim* (2004).

resources for the public because these objects offer society information about the past. In each case, the scope of the right and the holder of the right are identified by the perceived justification for the right.

The second problem involves competing viewpoints about the significance of "culture" in relation to notions of "ownership" and "access." Is "culture" the "property" of a specific people or nation? Or is it representative of a "universal heritage" for all mankind? Is the value of "cultural property" cognizable outside of the cultural context of an object? Some would say that the value of an object is dependent upon removal of the object from its culture of origin and its ability to freely circulate to the highest bidder. Others would argue that the true value of a cultural object cannot be realized outside of its cultural context. Still others would claim that the "preservation" of an object is the key and that a culture that would allow the natural deterioration of such objects necessarily fails to "value" them appropriately.

As this chapter will demonstrate, these definitions of cultural heritage under domestic and international law are insufficient to capture Native understandings of cultural heritage. Moreover, the basic conceptual problems identified above are responsible for many of the conflicts between Native and non-Native peoples over who has the right to control various aspects of Native cultural heritage.

1. "Art," "Artifacts," and Native Cultural Heritage

In contemporary America, "art" is perceived as a luxury, a commodity, and sometimes, an investment: paintings grace our walls, pottery is displayed on our bookshelves, and jewelry is collected to accentuate our personal attire. Most people consider "art" to be separate from business, governance, the judiciary, and scholarly disciplines such as philosophy and theology. Certainly, there are laws to regulate the economic aspects of art as an enterprise; but art is conceptually distinct from the practical aspects of day-to-day life. Very different laws and worldviews inform the treatment of those aspects of Native culture that are delineated as "art." Within many traditional Native cultures, "art" is closely connected to all aspects of daily life. "Art" may be integrated with theology, with the philosophies that govern cultural worldviews and their expression in institutions of governance, law, and material aspects of daily life. Not surprisingly, Native peoples often require legal protections for culture that differ from those routinely given to "artists" under Anglo-American law.

Language and art both offer an important lens into the cultures of distinctive groups. Language offers an insight into how a people organize their world, the categories, for example, that describe what is animate or inanimate (including what is "alive" or has "volition"), what things are "related" to one another (including kinship terms), and what behavior is considered appropriate or inappropriate. Some Native languages do not have a word that is equivalent to "art" as it is understood in the Western world, for example, as a collector's item or a luxury commodity. Pottery or a woven rug therefore may be described by words that describe the utilitarian function of the object. Art may also have a ritual or ceremonial function, such as sandpaintings for the Navajo, which are associated with healing practices. Alternatively, an object may be described by reference to the aesthetic quality it possesses and offers the owner. For example, jewelry described as "beautiful" may encompass a value and significance to the wearer that is distinctive from the mere aesthetic quality that we would associate with a "pretty" bracelet. In particular traditions, a set of jewelry may prepare the foundation for the wearer to live a life that is good, balanced, and "beautiful." The objects embody the spiritual foundation of a life lived in beauty.

Scholar Gary Witherspoon gives one of the best accounts of the distinctive cultural significance of "art" for the Navajo people in *Language and Art in the Navajo Universe*.[9] Witherspoon notes that the Navajo concept of Hozho incorporates a cultural belief that "the creation of beauty and the incorporation of oneself in beauty represents the highest attainment and ultimate destiny" of human beings.[10] Thus, beauty is not something that can be separated from "good, from health, from happiness, or from harmony."[11] Rather, beauty is the embodiment of all of these qualities. If a person is living in an ideal state of being, he or she experiences these qualities in daily life. In other words, "beauty" is created by the person through their thoughts and their actions. A person *experiences* beauty in this way; it is an internal state that is expressed into the world. Beauty is not a concept that is "external" to the person, that he or she looks at and *perceives* from the outside. Witherspoon says that "for the Navajo, beauty is not so much in the eye of the beholder as it is in the mind of its creator and in the creator's relationship to what is created."[12]

Witherspoon contrasts the approach of Western cultures, which tend to see beauty as a quality of things to be perceived, to be observed, and to be preserved. He says that Navajo society is predominantly one of "artists" (meaning art creators), while Anglo society consists primarily of non-artists who view art (art consumers). These diverse perspectives can lead to conflicts. For example, an Anglo observer of a Navajo sandpainting might be horrified that something so intricate and "beautiful" would be destroyed after the healing ceremony is performed. For the Navajo healer, however, the creation of the painting is tied to its healing function, and the destruction of the painting is likewise part of the entire process embodied in the ritual (which is not merely a sandpainting, but a series of prayers and songs). The Anglo observer might attempt to understand this perspective but would likely try to "preserve" the sandpainting as an *object* by a photograph, which would be completely antithetical to the Navajo understanding of the appropriate function of the sandpainting, including its ultimate disposition.

The current difficulties with the legal protection of Native American art and culture are in many ways related to the conceptual gaps between the cultural understandings of Native peoples and Anglo-American people about "art." To Anglo-American people, the carved poles of Northwest Coast Indians, such as the Haida and Tlingit, are "art," as are Navajo sandpaintings, Hopi Kachinas, and the Zuni "War Gods." American consumers have difficulty understanding

---

[9] Gary Witherspoon, Language and Art in the Navajo Universe (1977).
[10] *Id.* at 151.
[11] *Id.*
[12] *Id.*

that these aspects of Native culture are "sacred" and have a distinctive function, value, and significance. Anglo consumers, in fact, may not differentiate the treatment of cultural objects (Native "artifacts") from the art produced by contemporary Native painters, sculptors, and jewelers (Native "art"). Both are used by non-Indian consumers as "objects" of art, to be collected or displayed. Nor do consumers always distinguish between Native "fine art" and Native "crafts." In fact, due to economic pressures, collectors and consumers tend to collapse those distinctions, which can harm Native artists and infringe upon tribal interests in certain art forms.

These tensions are illuminated by the legal framework for protecting Native culture as it is expressed within the context of "art" or "artifacts." In this chapter, I make a distinction between "*cultural property*"—items that are part of the "cultural heritage" of a tribe and therefore have a distinctive significance necessary to the survival of the culture and the people—and "*commercial products*"—Native art that is intentionally placed into commerce and may be either reflective of an individual artist's unique creation or a tribal design or tradition. Art collectors often seek to appropriate Native cultural property, despite existing legal restrictions, because of the commercial value of these objects. For example, art collectors repeatedly try to take sacred objects, such as ritual masks or medicine bundles, from their Native caretakers. In some cases, collectors are ignorant of the difference between cultural property and commercial products. For example, some Hopi Kachinas are created specifically for tribal ceremonial purposes and may not be sold. On the other hand, there are contemporary Hopi artists who have transformed Kachina-making into a secular artform that is intentionally marketed outside the culture.

2. The Significance of "Culture" in Establishing Rights to Cultural Heritage

One of the central problems with the existing legal framework for cultural resources protection is that it does not correspond to Native understandings of cultural heritage. Rights to "ownership" and "access" within Native and Western cultures are developed according to a set of cultural norms that is markedly different. First, the two sets of cultures do not share a uniform understanding of the "past" and its relationship to contemporary peoples. The American legal system understands heritage resources as belonging to the U.S.'s collective "past." Moreover, the Anglo-American legal system routinely distinguishes between "history" and "prehistory," and assigns different values to cultural resources, depending upon whether they are "historic" or "prehistoric." For example, some scientists claim that no modern group should have a claim to ownership of "prehistoric" human remains.[13] However, most Native peoples, such as the Navajo, do not even have a word for "prehistory." Rather, the history of the Navajo people "begins at the creation of life and at the creation of this world."[14] "Prehistory" is not even a viable conceptual category within cultural

[13] *See, e.g.*, Bonnichsen v. United States, 367 F.3d 864 (9th Cir. 2004).

[14] Richard M. Begay, "The Role of Archaeology on Indian Lands: the Navajo Nation," *in* N. Swidler, K. Dongoske, R. Anyon & Alan Downer, Native Americans and Archaeologists: Stepping Stones to Common Ground 161–66, at 163 (1997).

worldviews that see human history as continuous, with unbroken connections between ancient ancestors and contemporary descendants. On a metaphysical level, many Native cultures understand that the spirits of the ancient peoples are still present and can be of assistance (or harm) to contemporary peoples, depending upon the ability of the descendant groups to appropriately protect and value the physical remains of the ancestors.[15]

There is a very different conception of "relatedness" among Native peoples than among non-Native peoples. Studies have demonstrated, for example, that most white Americans view family histories as the immediate concern of living members.[16] For example, Thomas Jefferson's living white descendants had various reactions to the assertions of his African American descendants who claimed "inclusion" into "their" family. Most white Americans view the history of the "United States," on the other hand, as a common resource that belongs to all Americans. In comparison, most Native peoples understand their primary identity through their tribal nation and the linkages between their extended family or clan and others within the nation. This sense of identity is distinct from one's "ethnic identity" as "Native American" or one's national identity as a "citizen of the United States." Those are descriptive terms that, to some extent, define political or social status. However, they do not have the capacity to define one's true social, cultural, or spiritual identity. The most important thing for children to know is "who their people are, how they came to be here, how we're all related."[17] It is incomprehensible that one would seek to disassociate one's family from the larger tribal nation or treat the ancestors differently from living tribal members. The collective responsibility for the ancestors resides in their descendants, contemporary tribal members.

Not surprisingly, tribal cultural heritage laws tend to adopt a more comprehensive definition of cultural heritage. For example, the code of the Confederated Tribes of the Warm Springs Reservation in Oregon defines tribal cultural heritage protection as a "trust" on behalf of all tribal members, which includes "the management of ancient and contemporary cultural use sites and materials which are fundamental in the recognition of the traditional lifeways, values and histories" of those tribes.[18] The Code pertains to traditional foods, medicines, and other natural resources, as well as significant sites associated with particular habitations, events, and personalities in tribal traditions. It seeks to protect all tribal resources within the traditional territories of the confederated tribes, regardless of the current ownership of those lands or resources. The Eastern Band of Cherokee Indians is among the tribes that have issued specific

---

[15] *See, e.g.*, Na Iwi O Na Kapuna O Mokapu v. Dalton, 894 F. Supp. 1397 (D. Haw. 1995) (Native claimants asserted a cause of action on their own behalf, as well as on behalf of the remains themselves, for the asserted harms arising from mistreatment of ancestral human remains in the custody of the Department of Navy.).

[16] *See* Roy Rosenzweig & David Thelen, The Presence of the Past: Popular Uses of American History in American Life (1998).

[17] *Id.* at 162.

[18] Warm Springs Tribal Code, Chapter 490: Protection and Management of Archaeological, Historical, and Cultural Resources, § 490.001, http:www.warmsprings.com/images/Warmsprings/Tribal Community/Tribal Government/Current Governing Body/Tribal Code Book/Doc Files/490 culturalresources.pdf.

protection for all ancestral human remains. The Code extends to Cherokee remains regardless of where they are found and provides that the graves of Cherokee people and their ancestors are sacred and shall not be disturbed or excavated.[19] Where they are inadvertently disinterred, the Code provides for immediate reburial of the remains and associated funerary objects. The Code further specifies that the remains of Cherokee people shall not be subjected to destructive skeletal analysis.

Second, the two sets of cultures do not share a uniform understanding of the relationship between "tangible" and "intangible" aspects of culture. Under both international and domestic law, cultural heritage is viewed as comprising tangible or material resources. Intangible resources (creative endeavors, for example) are protected as "intellectual property" using concepts of copyright, patent and trademark, depending upon what specific values society seeks to protect. Native cultures, on the other hand, routinely identify the intangible elements of cultural heritage (songs and stories, for example) as necessarily related to the tangible aspects of culture (sacred sites or cultural objects, for example). Every tangible cultural object has a tangible and intangible essence and value. One could not adequately protect one aspect without protecting the other. Existing laws, such as the Native American Graves Protection and Repatriation Act (1990; NAGPRA),[20] tend to protect the tangible aspects of Native culture (for example, ancestral human remains or cultural objects) but not the intangible aspects of culture, unless these can be fit into existing categories of "intellectual property" defined by domestic law.

A good example of this challenge is illustrated by an ongoing case involving the Fallon Paiute-Shoshone Tribe of Nevada in its claim for repatriation of an ancient skeleton, popularly understood as "Spirit Cave Man," now in possession of the Bureau of Land Management (BLM). A NAGPRA claim involves the question of whether the tribe is "culturally affiliated" to the remains and, thus, whether the tribe will have a right to repatriate the skeleton of this ancestor from the custody of the BLM.[21] The Fallon Paiute-Shoshone Tribe hired experts to develop the most current and extensive record of cultural affiliation possible. On the basis of this record, the NAGPRA review committee issued an opinion that the tribe is culturally affiliated to the remains and that the remains should be repatriated to the tribe.[22] Although the BLM initially declined to reconsider its earlier finding that the tribe had not proven cultural affiliation, a federal district court has remanded the matter to the BLM to consider the most recent evidence of affiliation pursuant to its statutory duties under NAGPRA.[23]

---

[19] The Cherokee Code: Published by Order of the Tribal Council of the Eastern Band of Cherokee Indians, Chapter 70: Skeletal Remains and Burial Site Preservation, art. I, § 70-1, http://www.tribalresourcecenter.org/ccfolder/eccodech70preservation.htm.

[20] 25 U.S.C. § 3001 et seq.

[21] Fallon-Paiute Shoshone Tribe v. U.S. Bureau of Land Mgmt., 455 F. Supp. 2d 1207 (D. Nev. 2006) (holding that BLM's determination that remains were not culturally affiliated to any tribe was arbitrary and capricious, and remanding the case for the agency to consider the most recent evidence of cultural affiliation produced by the tribal claimant).

[22] *Id.* at 1212.

[23] Fallon-Paiute Shoshone Tribe v. U.S. Bureau of Land Mgmt., 455 F. Supp. 2d 1207 (D. Nev. 2006).

The debate over the Spirit Cave Man is not limited to the conflict over the cultural affiliation of the remains. There is also a dispute over who owns the digital depictions of the skeleton and a reconstructed bust produced from these images.[24] The Nevada State Museum, which has physical custody of the remains under an agreement with BLM, commissioned physical anthropologist Sharon Long to reconstruct a bust with simulated facial muscles and outer skin. The museum intended to put the reconstructed bust on display because the remains themselves could not be displayed pending the outcome of the legal action. The museum had the skeleton CAT-scanned and used electronic data bits to produce a three-dimensional replica of the skull. Ms. Long then used these images to reconstruct the bust. This reconstructed bust was featured on the cover of *Newsweek* magazine in April 1999, along with the caption of the story: "Who Were the First Americans?"[25] The article emphasized the differences in Spirit Cave Man's facial features from those of so-called "modern Native Americans" and queried whether "Native Americans" were indeed the "first" Americans or whether another group of people (perhaps "Europeans"?) were actually "first." The challenge to Native political status is obvious. "If the discoveries make today's Native Americans just another Ellis Island group, it makes it harder for them to preserve their sovereignty," which, as the authors note, is the basis for Indian gaming and other perceived "special rights" enjoyed by federally recognized tribes.[26]

The Fallon Paiute Shoshone Tribe and other concerned Native peoples protested the display of the bust and its use as "visual evidence" for a speculation that Europeans might be the true "indigenous" peoples of the Americas. Ms. Long asserted a copyright interest in the reconstructed bust of Spirit Cave Man, leading to further protests from Native peoples that, as the rightful claimants to this ancestor, they should have the legal right to preclude any visual rendering of the skeleton. So, who owns the virtual Spirit Cave Man or the tangible works made from this rendering? What values and assumptions will be used in adjudicating ownership? What narratives will be maintained?

There are no clear answers at this point. The repatriation case involves who will own and control the physical remains of this ancient ancestor pursuant to the standard set forth in NAGPRA. The conflict over the images and reconstructed bust of Spirit Cave Man deal with claims of ownership to "intangible" aspects of the skeleton's identity that have not yet been litigated and seem to transcend the standard categories of "intellectual property" law. Significantly, the conceptual challenges to both claims can be traced to a common theme: "discovery." The next part of this chapter discusses the notion of "discovery" as a justification for conquest and colonialism and the role of "discovery" in defining contemporary Native legal rights and political status.

---

[24] *See* Kathryn Milun, *Keeping-While-Giving-Back: Computer Imaging and Native American Repatriation,* 24(2) Pol. & Legal Anthro. Rev. 39 (Nov. 2001).

[25] Sharon Begley & Andrew Murr, *The First Americans: New Digs and Old Bones Reveal an Ancient Land that Was a Mosaic of Peoples—Including Asians and Europeans. Now a Debate Rages: Who Got Here First?,* Newsweek, Apr. 26, 1999.

[26] *Id.*

B. FEDERAL INDIAN LAW AND THE JURISPRUDENCE OF "DISCOVERY"

The conflicts over protection of Native cultural heritage relate to a fundamental difference in beliefs. This cannot simply be understood in the context of a difference in "religious" beliefs or even a difference between categories of belief, say "science" versus "religion." Such simplifications often result from the commitment to "cultural pluralism" within modern democracies and the concomitant tendency to rely upon a set of "secular principles" to adjudicate the differences between citizens with purportedly "equal rights." That language will not fully serve this debate, however, because the debate is much more fundamental: it is the belief about who Native peoples are. Native peoples understand themselves to be the first people of a land that gave birth to their ancestors, with a set of responsibilities and rights that emerge from that relationship. They are the oldest living cultures to have a relationship with these lands that we now call "America," and for Native peoples, that fundamental relationship can and must structure their interaction with the government of the United States. The government of the United States, on the other hand, constantly seeks to articulate Native rights in the context of its perception about who Native peoples "really" are, that is, who they are in relationship to European peoples. Since contact, Native rights have been defined in the context of their encounter with European peoples, according to European norms, values, and perceptions of who Native peoples are and where they "came from." That is the primary legacy of "discovery," which has been used to justify "conquest" and "colonialism" in the Americas. The theme of discovery was pivotal in articulating the foundation for Native rights in the United States, and it continues to have an effect on shaping Native rights.

1. The Rule of Discovery Within Federal Indian Law: Defining Rights to Sovereignty and Property

The political relationship between the federal government and the Indian nations is structured by a complex and somewhat byzantine set of doctrines known as "Federal Indian law." Notably, federal Indian law developed around the premise that the Europeans "discovered" the New World and crafted a unique political and then legal relationship with the purportedly "uncivilized occupants" of this land. The effect of this understanding was to place the paramount rights to property and sovereignty with the European governments, and then with the United States, rather than with the Native peoples. The doctrine of discovery within federal Indian law is best represented by Chief Justice John Marshall's famous 1823 opinion in *Johnson v. McIntosh.*[27] The litigants in that case were two non-Indians, each of whom sought to maintain the paramount claim of title to the same land. The plaintiff's claim of title related back to a pre-revolutionary war purchase of land directly from the Indian tribes who were in "original possession" of the lands. The defendant had received his title at a later time through a grant from the U.S. government. In an opinion authored by Chief Justice John Marshall, the Supreme Court held for the defendant, finding that the character of Native peoples was such

[27] 21 U.S. (8 Wheat.) 543 (1823).

that they could not be recognized as holding the full rights and title to their ancestral lands, as would be the case with landholders in "civilized" nations. Marshall described Native peoples as

> fierce savages, whose occupation was war, and whose subsistence was drawn chiefly from the forest. To leave them in possession of their country, was to leave the country a wilderness; to govern them as a distinct people, was impossible, because they were as brave and as high spirited as they were fierce, and were ready to repel by arms every attempt on their independence.[28]

The "inevitable consequence" of this situation, according to Marshall, was a bifurcated system of legal rights, which stemmed from the international law of "discovery." Normally, the law of discovery was intended to confer title upon the first nation to discover "vacant" (e.g., unoccupied) lands. The law of conquest, on the other hand, governed property rights upon the transition of governance following warfare between civilized nations and generally required the property rights of existing inhabitants to be left intact and respected by the new sovereign. Marshall found that the doctrine of conquest could not apply to "uncivilized nations." Rather, the first European sovereign to "discover" and "take possession" of lands occupied by Indian people received the "title" to those lands. The Native peoples retained a more limited "right of occupancy," which essentially allowed them to maintain their actual use and possession until the discovering sovereign or its successors in interest extinguished that right by "purchase or conquest."[29]

The doctrine of discovery within federal Indian law has been called a "discourse of conquest," confirming the superior rights of Europeans to lands occupied by the "savage" Indians, encouraging white settlement of these lands on the theory that Native peoples were not making productive use of these lands, and vesting "authority in a centralized sovereign to regulate the Indians' dispossession according to national interest."[30] Thus, *McIntosh* institutionalized European racism and colonialism in American law and denied respect to the human rights of Native peoples on the premise that they were not on the same level as "civilized" Europeans.[31]

The rule of *Johnson v. McIntosh* became a cornerstone of federal Indian law, and Chief Justice Marshall drew upon this opinion in two subsequent cases involving the Cherokee nation's struggle to defend itself against the incursions of Georgia, which ultimately defined the unique political status of Indian tribes as "domestic dependent nations" under the protection of the United States. Of course, consistent with the themes of 19th-century colonialism, this status necessarily implied a set of diminished political rights as compared with those of an independent, foreign nation. The Court held, for example, that because it was not a "foreign" sovereign, the Cherokee nation lacked constitutional

---

[28] *Id.* at 590.
[29] *Id.* at 545.
[30] Robert A. Williams, Jr., The American Indian in Western Legal Thought 312, 317 (1990).
[31] *Id.* at 317.

standing to bring a claim into the U.S. Supreme Court to vindicate its treaty rights against incursions by the Georgia state government.[32] When a non-Indian claimant brought a similar case on the merits, however, the Court held that the Cherokee nation occupied a distinct territory under its own sovereign authority and the protection of federal law, and thus the state of Georgia could not exercise jurisdiction within it.[33] Thus, the Cherokee nation had the rights and political status of a "nation" rather than merely a collective of individual "citizens" or "foreign nationals."

This separate political status continues to characterize the relationship between the United States and the federally recognized Native American nations within the United States and serves as a justification for congressional "plenary power" to enact legislation on behalf of Indian nations. The plenary power doctrine is rooted in constitutional sources of authority, such as the Commerce Clause and Treaty Clause, but also in the federal government's duty to protect the Indian nations.[34] During the early years of American history, Indian tribes were deemed not to be incorporated within the polity of the United States and were not recognized as "citizens" absent special circumstances (e.g., detribalization and inter-marriage with a non-Indian) that justified naturalization. In 1924, the U.S. Congress gratuitously conferred blanket citizenship upon Native Americans, and now the courts often deal with Native rights as if they are those of "equal citizens" under a uniform set of secular principles. Thus, aspects of cultural heritage—such as religious practices, cultural objects, sacred sites, and language—are associated with rights to religion, free speech, or property that might pertain to individual citizens under the Bill of Rights. Because group claims to such resources are inherently suspect within our liberal democracy, Native claims to cultural heritage are often subordinated to the broader interests of American society.

Despite the popular tendency to conflate Native rights with individual rights, federal law and policy continues to affirm the unique political and legal status of Native American nations. Today, federal policy has shifted away from "assimilation" and in favor of "self-determination" for Native American nations. This means that the federal government has committed itself to recognize the political sovereignty of Native American nations and their rights to self-governance, which include the right to have tribal laws and to operate tribal court systems, schools, and hospitals on the reservation. Indian nations enjoy considerable autonomy within reservation boundaries. All federally recognized tribes maintain governmental systems with legislative and executive functions. Many tribes also have tribal judicial systems. Thus, for activities occurring on the reservation or significantly involving the tribe or its members, tribal law is an important source of legal rights and responsibilities. The role of federal law is also pervasive within the reservations. In recent years, the federal government has reaffirmed its "trust responsibility" to Native American nations by providing

---

[32] Cherokee Nation v. Georgia, 30 U.S. (5 Pet.) 1 (1831).

[33] Worcester v. Georgia, 31 U.S. (6 Pet.) 515 (1832).

[34] *See, e.g.*, United States v. Kagama, 118 U.S. 375 (1886).

needed services and funding to assist the tribes (e.g., in the areas of health care, education, law enforcement, and infrastructure—roads, buildings, and electricity) and by supporting tribal economic development and enhanced self-sufficiency. The federal government has also committed to respect the right of Native peoples to practice and enjoy their own cultures, and Congress has enacted a variety of laws designed to foster cultural survival, which are selectively discussed in this chapter.[35]

The developments within United States domestic law in favor of Native rights are paralleled by developments within international human rights law. In September 2007, the U.N. General Assembly adopted the Declaration on the Rights of Indigenous Peoples, which outlines several categories of political and cultural rights that ought to be respected by the various nation-states that now exert authority over indigenous peoples.[36] Although the declaration is purely prescriptive for those nation-states who do not implement these guarantees through their domestic legal structures, the declaration is a persuasive consensus-based document that attests to the unique needs and interests of indigenous peoples. Since the end of World War II, countries throughout the world have cooperated in the development of human rights law in order to prevent the type of atrocities that occurred during the Nazi regime in Europe. Today, international agreements govern many important areas that intersect with rights to Native cultural heritage, including the provisions of the U.N. Covenant on Civil and Political Rights that secure cultural and religious rights to minority groups, and the conventions that describe the rights of states to their cultural property and cultural heritage.[37] The Declaration on the Rights of Indigenous Peoples can serve as an interpretive guide to understanding how indigenous rights ought to be harmonized within the various existing covenants on minority rights generally or on cultural heritage specifically.

So, in the enlightened global society that we live in today, is the theme of discovery relegated to the past? As this chapter next discusses, the legacy of the doctrine of discovery continues to frame Native rights interactively and in relationship to the "rights" (or perhaps more appropriately, the interests) of non-Natives. The jurisprudence of discovery continues in the present day, albeit masked in a set of "neutral" constitutional ideals. "Justice" in contemporary society is shaped according to the public interest and further defined by the categories of knowledge that respond to those interests. To develop this idea, I will examine a particular historical account of discovery—the Lewis and Clark expedition—and demonstrate how that narrative influenced a modern court's

---

[35] *See, e.g.,* the Native American Graves Protection and Repatriation Act, 25 U.S.C. § 3001 et seq., the Indian Arts and Crafts Act, 25 U.S.C. § 305 et seq., the Native American Languages Act, 25 U.S.C. §§ 2991–2906 (2000), and the American Indian Religious Freedom Act, 42 U.S.C. § 1996, as amended by 42 § U.S.C. 1996a.

[36] Declaration on the Rights of Indigenous Peoples, G.A. Res. 61/295, U.N. Doc. A/RES/47/1 (Sept. 12, 2007), *available at* http://www.un.org/esa/socdev/unpfii/en/drip/html.

[37] The International Covenant on Civil and Political Rights, G.A. Res. 2200A(XXI), U.N. Doc. A/6316 (1966), *available at* http://www.unhchr.ch/html/menu3/b/a_ccpr.htm; 1970 UNESCO Convention on Cultural Property, *supra* note 6; 1972 Convention on Cultural and National Heritage, *supra* note 7.

decision that a set of ancient remains found in the state of Washington were not "Native American" for purposes of NAGPRA.

2. The Lewis and Clark Expedition and the Historical Narrative of Discovery

The Lewis and Clark expedition is emblematic of the notions of "discovery" and conquest. The two intrepid discoverers and their cohort were commissioned by President Thomas Jefferson to map the newly acquired lands of the Louisiana Purchase and document the scientific and commercial value of these resources for the American public. In addition, their story is one that appeals to the romantic American imagination. As one scholar notes, the act of "reconsidering Lewis and Clark" is important to Americans, because in this process, "we consider ourselves, not as an act of self-indulgence but as an act of self-discovery."[38] The Lewis and Clark expedition symbolizes the birth of a new nation carved out of "foreign soil." In that process, Native peoples became part of the creation story of America, and the narratives that Native peoples have always had to mark their own identity and connection to particular lands became subordinated by the myth of "discovery" embodied within American history and law.

In a material sense, Lewis and Clark mapped and documented the character and extent of a new nation. In a symbolic sense, they appropriated the places, images, and character of the people they "discovered" to construct an American epic, including a new frontier—the American West—that would be vital to the creation of the nation. The result was to incorporate Native peoples into the political and legal structure of America, not as foreign sovereigns or citizens, but as a strange hybrid of the two, denominated as "domestic, dependent nations." By placing the "civilized government" (the United States) into a superior position, the Supreme Court created a hierarchical structure of rights that replicated the pervasive 19th-century ideology that described Native peoples as living "in a state of nature." In the evolutionary process leading to "civilization," they were treated as emergent peoples, who, by necessity, had to rely on the protective paternalism of the federal government for their very survival. However, by studying them, European-Americans could discover the more pristine essence of their identity as children of God. The racialized hierarchy that marked European domination of the "New World" gave rise to a legal structure that encompassed the subordination of both Native and African peoples and legitimated the superiority of white people. As Thomas Jefferson opined in a 1785 letter,

> I am safe in affirming, that the proofs of genius given by the Indians of North America, place them on a level with whites in the same uncultivated state. . . . I believe that the Indian, then, to be in body and mind equal to the white man. I have supposed the black man, in his present state, might not be so; but it would be hazardous to affirm, that, equally cultivated for a few generations, he would not become so.[39]

[38] James Ronda, *Counting Cats in Zanzibar, or Lewis and Clark Reconsidered,* 33(1) W. HIST. Q. 5, 9 (Spring 2002).

[39] *"Thomas Jefferson to the Marquis de Chastellux" (June 7, 1785), in* THOMAS JEFFERSON: WRIT-

This statement seems patently racist when evaluated against the social norms of America in 2008. Yet, the statement reflects the social Darwinism that informed the American Enlightenment: the idea that different races of people were in various stages of evolution and that scientific study of these people could assist civilized nations in furthering their own development. In fact, Jefferson agreed with John Locke's view that "studying people living in a natural state . . . would teach something about the fundamentals of civilization and permit the reformation of society in the name of nature and simplicity."[40] Today, we might seek to distance ourselves from such beliefs. However, have we really outgrown the central tenets of the American Enlightenment: "the triumph of reason, the rightness of nature, and the improvement of society through knowledge"?[41] Under this view, Indians were important to the development of America both as "objects of scientific study and as sources of geographic information."[42]

Jefferson understood that the United States could become a powerful nation only if it could annex the lands west of the Mississippi. There were, however, several significant obstacles to westward expansion, including limited opportunities for transportation and a lack of knowledge about the nature and characteristics of Western lands. The Lewis and Clark Expedition was necessary to give the United States the information necessary to acquire and develop the Western lands "owned" by other European sovereigns by virtue of "discovery." It was also necessary to understand the Native peoples who were in actual possession of the lands before developing appropriate strategies to appropriate their lands and resources.[43] Jefferson understood Indian tribes generally to be increasingly dissatisfied with the diminution of their territory and knew they were reluctant to cede any further lands. In order to counter this resistance, Jefferson observed that federal Indian policy would have to focus on two measures: First, it must encourage the Indians to abandon hunting and turn to agriculture, which would require less land and labor on their part. And second, it was necessary to "multiply trading houses among them" and cultivate a desire for "domestic comforts" (including tools, firearms, pots and pans, and cloth) in order to induce the Indians to give up their traditional lifeways.[44] Of course, Jefferson was careful to express an overall benevolent intent: "In leading them

---

INGS 801 (Merrill D. Peterson ed., 1984), *reprinted in* JUAN F. PEREA ET AL., RACE AND RACES 185 (2000).

[40] STEPHEN DOWN BECKHAM, THE LITERATURE OF THE LEWIS AND CLARK EXPEDITION: A BIBLIOGRAPHY AND ESSAYS 7 (2003).

[41] *Id.*

[42] Ronda, *supra* note 38, at 12–13.

[43] *See, e.g.*, William Nichols, *Lewis and Clark: Probe the Heart of Darkness*, AM. SCHOLAR 94, 96 (1970–80). Professor Nichols quotes Jefferson's instructions to Lewis and Clark to collect information from the Indians, among other things, on their names, their traditionally claimed territories, their number, the articles of commerce that they need, the "peculiarities in their laws, customs and dispositions," and the "diseases prevalent among them and the remedies they use." In addition, Jefferson specified that information on their state of "morality, religion and information" would be vital to later attempts to "civilize and instruct them" on needed social change.

[44] Thomas Jefferson, *Confidential Message Recommending a Western Exploring Expedition* (January 18, 1803), *in* 1 MESSAGES AND PAPERS OF THE PRESIDENTS 1789–1897 352 (James D. Richardson ed., 1899), *reprinted in* PEREA ET AL., *supra* note 39, at 184.

thus to agriculture, to manufacture and civilization; in bringing together their and our settlements, and in preparing them ultimately to participate in the benefits of our Government, I trust and believe that we are acting for their greatest good."[45]

Thus, 19th-century federal Indian policy carefully aligned the economic and political interests of the United States with the supposed interest of the Indians in becoming "civilized." The darker side of this policy is reflected in correspondence from Jefferson that encourages U.S. officials to target "good and influential individuals" among the Indians to "run into debt," observing that only then would they have sufficient motivation to pay their debts "by a cession of lands."[46] For those Indians foolish enough to resist incorporation into America's developing economy, Jefferson foresaw a darker end: "we presume that our own strength and their weakness is now so visible that they must see we have only to shut our hand to crush them."[47]

The material impact of discovery upon Native peoples reflects, to some extent, a political "conquest," understood as political subordination and coercion and the economic pressures of colonialism, both of which fostered dependency as a means to appropriate tribal lands and resources. But what of the symbolic impact of discovery? On this level, the Lewis and Clark Expedition transformed the world of Native peoples by appropriating their places and identities to create "the United States." Native lands, cultures and political identities were claimed, discarded, or transformed into those of "America." The United States employed the legal fiction of "discovery" to claim "title" to Native lands and resources. As those lands were mapped by Lewis and Clark, they were often renamed to commemorate people or events important in the lives of the exploring team. There is a great deal of knowledge embodied in Native peoples' place names, as anthropologist Keith Basso has documented in the context of the Western Apache people.[48] The impact of the re-naming process is therefore profound, transforming indigenous understandings of the land into an "American" understanding of the land, discarding thousands of years of oral history reflecting the creation of Native peoples, their migrations, and their experiences through time, into a written account of an "exploration journey" that gave birth to an American nation. To re-name a place is to attempt to change an entire cultural system of knowledge. What, then, is the overall impact of this journey of "discovery" upon Native peoples?

> In a nutshell, what happened to our people in the years after Lewis and Clark is that we went downhill. In a nutshell, we lost. . . . We started going from a dependency on the environment, on the spiritualism of the land, to a dependency on the traders and the military and everything

[45] *Id.*

[46] *President Jefferson to William Henry Harrison (February 27, 1803), in* 10 Writings of Thomas Jefferson 369–71 (Andrew A. Lipscomb ed., 1904), *reprinted in* Perea et al., *supra* note 39, at 184.

[47] *Id.*

[48] *See* Keith Basso, Wisdom Sits in Places (1996).

> else that came after Lewis and Clark . . . Indian people see the expedition, especially today . . . [as] the beginning of an end . . ."[49]

Today, U.S. domestic law replicates that dynamic by negating the cultural significance of Native lands and resources and emphasizing the overriding importance of American norms and values. To explore a contemporary application of the discovery doctrine in relation to cultural heritage, I will comment on the Ninth Circuit's opinion in *Bonnichsen v. United States.*[50]

3. *Bonnichsen v. United States*: A Contemporary Narrative of Discovery

In *Bonnichsen v. United States,*[51] the Ninth Circuit Court of Appeals found that an ancient skeleton unearthed on the banks of the Columbia river in the state of Washington was not "Native American" for purposes of NAGPRA, and the court therefore denied the ownership claims of the five Indian nations who claimed cultural affiliation. NAGPRA is a federal statute, enacted in 1990, which protects the rights of Native peoples to their ancestral remains, funerary objects, sacred objects, and objects of cultural patrimony.[52] The statute is intended to secure the human rights of Native peoples to claim repatriation of their ancestral remains and cultural property. However, much of the statute is built on a property-rights-based approach, which assigns to culturally affiliated groups the rights to such resources, either when housed in museum collections (thus justifying claims for "repatriation") or when excavated on federal or tribal land (thus justifying claims to "ownership"). As this chapter demonstrates in the next section, Indian nations have successfully used NAGPRA to recover important cultural resources, and thus, the statute has played a significant role in remediating past injustices and securing Native human rights. However, the limitations of NAGPRA became apparent in the litigation over ownership of "Kennewick Man," an ancient skeleton found in the state of Washington that has been estimated to be approximately 9,000 years old. The first archaeologist to examine the remains described them as "Caucasoid" in appearance, thus setting off a media frenzy over whether this Ancient One was really Native American at all.[53] Maybe he was an ancient European instead!

The five Native American tribes indigenous to the area where he was found, on lands now under the jurisdiction of the Army Corps of Engineers, claimed him as their common ancestor under NAGPRA, and the secretary of the interior upheld their ownership claim based on the fact that the skeleton clearly predated documented European contact. The secretary further found that the available cultural and historical evidence (both are expressly identified as relevant categories of evidence under the statute) indicated that the tribes of this area were "culturally affiliated" to the remains. A group of scientists

[49] Gerard Baker (Mandan/Hidatsa), Superintendent of the Lewis and Clark National Historical Trail, *in* Public Broadcasting System, *What Is the Larger Historical Significance of the Expedition?* http://www.pbs.org/lewisandclark/living/idx_9.html.

[50] 367 F.3d 864 (9th Cir. 2004).

[51] *Id.*

[52] 25 U.S.C. § 3001 et seq.

[53] Ann Gibbons, *DNA Enters Dust Up Over Bones*, 274(5285) Sci. 172 (Oct. 11, 1996).

challenged that decision in a federal district court, claiming that the skeleton was a vitally important scientific discovery, and that, because it was so ancient, it should not be classified as Native American for purposes of NAGPRA.[54]

The federal district court held in favor of the scientists, and the Ninth Circuit Court of Appeals affirmed that decision, thereby casting doubt upon the continuing vitality of NAGPRA as a statutory tool to protect Native rights to ancestral human remains that cannot be linked to contemporary Native peoples under the stringent criteria developed by the court in its interpretation of the statute. The court of appeals interpreted NAGPRA as a statute designed to protect the interests of modern tribes in human remains that can be tied directly to them through common "genetic or cultural features."[55] The opinion questions whether Native Americans as a modern group of indigenous people have any scientifically provable connection to the ancient peoples of North America.[56]

The opinion draws firmly on the narratives of discovery and conquest that characterized 19th-century federal Indian law. This ancient skeleton impressed the court as "one of the most important American anthropological and archaeological discoveries of the late twentieth century," leading to the court's conclusion that the skeleton is the property of Western science.[57] This "discovery" is yet another example of the appropriation of Native America for the greater "public good" of the United States.

The court specifically discounted the weight of certain tribal narratives entered into evidence as a method of proving that the ancient and modern tribes were culturally connected, despite the fact that NAGPRA specifically provides that tribal oral histories are to be given the same evidentiary weight as scientific or other cultural data. Finding that the only evidence adduced in support of the tribes' claim came in the form of oral histories, including published folk narratives and statements from individual tribal members, the court concluded that these accounts were not sufficient "to show a significant relationship of the Tribal Claimants with Kennewick Man."[58] Given the problems of "authenticity, reliability, and accuracy" that attach to oral histories, the court determined that the "record as a whole does not show where historical fact ends and mythic tale begins."[59] The court concludes,

> because Kennewick Man's remains are so old and the information about his era is so limited, the record does not permit the Secretary to conclude reasonably that Kennewick Man shares special and significant genetic or cultural features with presently existing indigenous tribes, people, or cultures.[60]

---

[54] Bonnichsen v. United States, 367 F.3d 864, 872 (9th Cir. 2004).

[55] *Id.* at 882.

[56] *Id.* at 880–81.

[57] *Id.* at 868, 882 (because the court finds that the remains are not "Native American" for purposes of NAGPA, they become the property of the federal government under ARPA and may be scientifically studied).

[58] *Id.* at 881.

[59] *Id.* at 882.

[60] *Id.*

What, then, is the ultimate result of this opinion? The court of appeals held that the skeleton was "federal property" available for study by the plaintiff scientists (and potentially others) under ARPA. The Native tribes, who maintain that these ancestral human remains are sacred and must not be submitted to destructive scientific analysis, but rather should be immediately reburied with appropriate respect, are left without any legally cognizable right or means of enjoining the scientific study of the "Kennewick Man."

What values are omitted from consideration under the court of appeals' analysis? Philip Cash Cash, a Umatilla cultural practitioner, has offered a cultural perspective on the case. According to Mr. Cash Cash, ancestral human remains hold paramount spiritual significance for Native peoples in the Pacific Northwest. This is based on an ethical principle that he associated with the sanctity of life and death. He explained,

> The Creator gave us a Great Law and because of that, we took care of our land and our Ancestors. This sacred law establishes how human beings relate to each other, to the human and spiritual worlds. All natural resources are dependent upon animated spiritual forces. If something is disturbed, everything else suffers. To understand this, to adhere to the traditional ways of life, ensures the continuity of the world. In the Nez Perce language, the word for "life" means "as one goes successively in the dawn."[61]

Mr. Cash Cash alludes to the cyclical view of life and death that is reflected among many Native cultural traditions. All living things possess a will or consciousness, an animating force. This essence or life force dissipates upon death, but still pervades the remains, particularly the bones of the deceased. The spiritual essence of a person is not destroyed at death; rather it is transformed. According to Mr. Cash Cash, when Indian people express concern for the Ancient One, they are expressing an ethical commitment to self. To treat ancestral human remains as "federal property," holding them indefinitely for successive invasive and destructive tests, causes a harm to Native peoples, whether understood as a tangible harm (depriving Native peoples of access to ancestral human remains) or an intangible harm (doing things to the remains that interfere with their essence and power).

In any event, the *Bonnichsen* case is probably the best example of why domestic law should develop an inter-cultural approach to cultural resources protection. Such an approach should take note of the conceptual divides between the respective understandings of cultural heritage and attempt to develop a framework that can accommodate the distinctive perspectives and interests expressed by Native cultures. To further engage this point, the next two sections of this chapter evaluate the existing legal frameworks that govern tribal "cultural property" and "Indian art," probing the challenges in each area for Native nations.

---

[61] Narrative of Proceedings, Symposium on *NAGPRA: The Issue of "Culturally Unidentifiable Remains"* held at Arizona State University College of Law, Nov. 30, 2001 (document in possession of author).

C. THE STATUTORY FRAMEWORK FOR PROTECTING NATIVE RIGHTS TO CULTURAL PROPERTY

Developing an inter-cultural approach to cultural resources protection must necessarily be a joint endeavor between Native nations and the U.S. government. To some extent, this is already occurring under NAGPRA in the context of tribal claims to cultural patrimony and sacred objects. Native claims to cultural property stem, in many cases, from egregious conduct by anthropologists and archaeologists throughout much of the 19th and 20th centuries. These individuals routinely looted Native villages, battlefields, and cemeteries to acquire Native peoples' personal effects (e.g., moccasins, shields, and guns), as well as sacred objects (e.g., masks and medicine bundles), funerary objects, and even human remains. They often couched these actions in the "need" to preserve aspects of Native culture in the face of rapid assimilation of Native peoples (as well as their physical demise from disease and warfare) that would ultimately extinguish these groups altogether (the "vanishing redman" ideology). These cultural objects were then sold to artifact collectors or donated to museums. When Native peoples sought to reclaim ownership under state law (e.g., in actions for replevin, conversion, or malicious interference with a human burial), their claims were routinely denied under a variety of theories (e.g., that state cemetery laws only protected marked, Christian burials). These egregious historical circumstances necessitated passage of NAGPRA in 1990. A comparative examination of cases involving Native cultural patrimony and sacred objects prior to and after the statute's enactment illustrates the emerging inter-cultural approach to Native cultural heritage issues within U.S. domestic law.

1. NAGPRA

NAGPRA affirmatively protects Native American rights with respect to four discrete categories of cultural objects: (1) human remains, (2) funerary objects, (3) sacred objects, and (4) objects of cultural patrimony.[62] To the extent that these objects are in the collections of federal agencies or museums that receive federal funds, Native peoples may maintain a claim for repatriation of the objects upon a showing that they are "culturally affiliated" to the item in question and that the museum or agency lacks any "right of possession."[63] In addition, NAGPRA specifically outlaws commercial trafficking in Native American cultural objects. This latter provision is important in order to half the continuing efforts of art collectors to raid the cultural property of Native nations.

NAGPRA narrowly defines the categories of objects that are subject to regulation. "Funerary objects," for example, are objects that, "as part of the death rite or ceremony of a culture, are reasonably believed to have been placed with individual human remains either at the time of death or later."[64] "Sacred

---

[62] 25 U.S.C. § 3001.

[63] 25 U.S.C. §§ 3001(13) (defining "right of possession"), 3005 (describing requirements of repatriation process).

[64] 25 U.S.C. § 3001(3)(A) and (B) (defining "associated funerary objects" and "unassociated funerary objects").

objects" are "specific ceremonial objects which are needed by traditional Native American religious leaders for the practice of traditional Native American religions by their present day adherents."[65] This category includes objects used for currently practiced ceremonies, as well as objects necessary to renew traditional religious ceremonies. The determination of "sacredness" is to be made by the Native American religious leaders themselves and may vary according to the traditions of the particular community. "Cultural patrimony" includes objects "having ongoing historical, traditional, or cultural importance central to the Native American group or culture itself, rather than property owned by an individual Native American, and which, therefore, cannot be alienated, appropriated, or conveyed by any individual Native American."[66] Such objects must have been considered inalienable by the Native American group at the time the object was separated from the group.

NAGPRA does not apply to purely secular objects, including objects made for commercial sale or trade, even though they may have a spiritual context or value to the tribal community.[67] However, many non-Indians have difficulty distinguishing replicas (e.g., Hopi Kachinas) made for commercial sale from those that are sacred objects intended only for tribal ceremonial use. In other cases, the collectors are well aware that they are dealing with cultural patrimony, but they intentionally trade in these cultural objects, which carry great value on the "black market." Thus, the distinctions between "cultural property" and "commercial products" can become blurred by collectors and consumers into the category of "Native art." This can be illustrated best by a comparative evaluation of cases that arose prior to and after the enactment of NAGPRA.

2. Pre-NAGPRA Case Law

a. *Blackfeet Medicine Bundles*

Immediately prior to the enactment of NAGPRA, media attention focused on the actions of a non-Indian collector and artist, Bob Scriver, who sold an extensive collection of early Blackfeet religious and cultural objects to a Canadian museum for over $1 million.[68] Scriver and his family had lived among the Blackfeet people and traded with them for many years. Scriver himself had been initiated into the Blackfeet religion through the transfer of a pipe and name from a Blackfeet religious leader. Much of the collection was comprised of Blackfeet medicine bundles, the contents of which Scriver photographed, documented, and published in a book, prior to the sale. Within the belief system

[65] 25 U.S.C. § 3001(3)(C).

[66] 25 U.S.C. § 3001(3)(D).

[67] *See* Select Committee on Indian Affairs, Providing for the Protection of Native American Graves and the Repatriation of Native American Remains and Cultural Patrimony, S. Rep. No. 101-473, at 7 (1990) ("It has been suggested that some Native American artisans create objects which could be construed as falling within the definition of sacred object and therefore this provision would adversely impact the trade in Native American artwork. The Committee does not intend the definition of sacred object to include objects which were created for purely a secular purpose, including the sale or trade in Indian art.").

[68] William E. Farr, *Troubled Bundles, Troubled Blackfeet: The Travail of Cultural and Religious Renewal*, Montana: The Magazine of Western History 1–17 (Autumn 1993).

of the Blackfeet, the bundles are considered to be living entities with power to heal, or to harm, depending upon whether they were treated appropriately by their human caretakers. The inference in this case was that some Blackfeet had entrusted the bundles to Scriver because they feared that their own family members would not or could not maintain the appropriate care of the bundles and could perhaps bring harm on the family. The spirit entities within the bundles "exacted duties and obligations," and they had to be "guarded and protected, cared for daily like children."[69] In the traditional society, the bundles were circulated throughout the society, so that spiritual responsibilities and knowledge could be shared for the mutual benefit of all tribal members and so that the knowledge would not be concentrated inappropriately or lost. The bundles were associated with certain songs and prayers, ceremonies and rituals. The bundles, in this way of seeing the world, exercised power over their human caretakers.

Scriver maintained that once the traditional knowledge was lost, the bundles ceased to "live" and became inanimate artifacts that could be sold. Scriver maintained that without the traditional knowledge, the bundles were no longer "alive" or "sacred" but were the type of property amenable to private ownership. Under the Anglo property system, of course, the owner has power over the object. He also maintained that the Alberta Provincial Museum was the appropriate repository of the objects, which represented the *past* of the Blackfeet people, mainly located in Canada. When asked by one reporter whether the Montana Blackfeet should feel angered by the sale, Scriver replied: "Why should they be? They didn't own them."[70]

Notably, in this case, the tribe apparently did not have a cultural resources ordinance in place that would have either prevented the tribal owners of these medicine bundles from alienating them to a non-member, or prevented the removal of the bundles from the reservation, regardless of ownership. Either system could have been instituted by the tribe, depending upon the appropriate normative structure for treatment of these bundles. For example, many countries have in place legal restrictions that preclude removal of certain types of cultural property from the country. Although private owners may obtain rights of possession or use, the government retains rights of disposition and control in order to retain such property within the country.

b. Chilkat Indian Village v. Johnson: *The Whale House Artifacts*

The Village of Chilkat (the "Village"), an Alaska Native community, enacted a 1976 ordinance forbidding the sale or removal of "artifacts, clan crests or other traditional Indian artwork owned or held by members of the Chilkat Indian Village," except with the permission of the Chilkat Indian Village Council.[71] The defendant, Mr. Johnson, a non-Indian art collector, made several attempts to convince tribal members to sell him a collection of objects designated as the "Whale House Artifacts." He finally succeeded in 1984, and the artifacts were

[69] *Id.* at 9.

[70] *Id.* at 13.

[71] Chilkat Indian Village, *IRA v. Johnson*, 20 Indian L. Rep. 6127 (Chilkat Tr. Ct. 1993).

removed from the Village and housed in a Seattle warehouse, leading to the legal dispute that resulted in both federal and tribal court causes of action.[72]

The artifacts at issue consisted of four elaborately carved wooden posts, made of spruce and over nine-feet high, and a wooden partition, made of thin cedar boards, called a rain screen. The artifacts, which were created around 1830, are described by a noted expert as "unquestionably the finest example of native art, either Tlingit or Tsimshian, in Alaska, in boldness of conception . . . in execution of detail, and in arrangement of detail."[73] The record indicated that if the artifacts were sold on the open market, they would likely reap a price of several million dollars.

Of course, for the Native peoples, these objects were not "art." They represented the history, culture, and living traditions of the Tlingit people. The four posts represented the four groups that were brought together to form the Whale House. The posts and rain screen tell stories of the clan, not just of the Whale House. The artifacts and the Whale House itself were created and dedicated in the traditional manner, which involved potlatch ceremonies between both the Eagle and Whale clans and the ceremonial dedication of the objects as clan property.

The Village filed an action in federal district court against Johnson, his corporation, and the tribal members who had alienated the objects, for conversion. The Village also attempted to bring a claim under 18 U.S.C. Section 1163, which prohibits embezzlement and theft from Indian tribes, although this claim was dismissed by the district court, which held that this section does not create a private right of action in federal court.[74] The conversion claim proceeded in tribal court, although the federal courts indicated that the question of tribal authority over the non-Indian defendant raised a federal question, and the merits were subject to the exhaustion doctrine.[75]

The tribal court upheld the authority of the Village to enact the 1976 ordinance and enforce it against both the non-Native defendants and the Tlingit Indian defendants. The heart of the case, of course, involved the nature of these particular objects under tribal law and the defendants' claim that they were the property of individual tribal members who had full authority to alienate them.

The court evaluated the testimony of several witnesses who identified the house posts and rain screen as "clan trust property," which has great spiritual significance to a particular clan with custodial rights over the objects. One of the primary witnesses was Rosita Worl, a Tlingit tribal member who was also a professional anthropologist. She testified that the Whale House artifacts were "crest objects" owned by the entire clan and that any member of the clan has the

---

[72] *Id.*; *see also* Chilkat Indian Vill. v. Johnson, 643 F. Supp. 535 (D. Alaska 1986); Chilkat Indian Vill. v. Johnson, 870 F.2d 1469 (9th Cir. 1989).

[73] Chilkat Indian Village, *IRA v. Johnson*, 20 Indian L. Rep. 6127, 6137 (Chilkat Tr. Ct. 1993).

[74] Chilkat Indian Vill. v. Johnson, 643 F. Supp. 535 (D. Alaska 1986), *aff'd*, 870 F.2d 1469 (9th Cir. 1989).

[75] Chilkat Indian Vill. v. Johnson, 870 F.2d 1469 (9th Cir. 1989).

right, under Tlingit law, to use the objects for specific purposes. Under Tlingit law, such objects cannot be sold unless, for some reason (such as restitution for a crime), the entire clan decides to do so. Ms. Worl testified that the traditional penalty for an individual selling artifacts in violation of tribal law was death.

Several witnesses testified that the objects were significant to all tribal members because of the relationship between the clans. The caretaker of the Killer Whale House, Mr. Hotch, testified that the caretaker, or *hitsati*, has the duty under tribal law to care for the property of the house and the clan but has no right to sell or otherwise dispose of clan property. Mr. Hotch described the creation, role, and purpose of the objects for the entire tribe. Certain objects are commissioned and then confirmed as clan trust property through ceremonies that bring both clans of the tribe together.

The purpose of the objects is also consistent with their use by both clans. For example, when a member of the opposite clan died and a potlatch was held as part of the funeral proceedings, members of the grieving clan would be brought before the rain screen and told that it constituted medicine that would relieve the loss of their clan member. Another witness testified that through this type of use, the spirits of the ancestors are honored such that they tend to gather around the objects. Thus, the objects, which in many cases include associated songs and stories, cannot be "owned" because "there is no way to put a price on spirits."[76] Demonstrating that tangible objects can have intangible components, one tribal member testified as to the historical and spiritual significance of the objects:

> The primary significance is knowing who you are . . . with us, these particular artifacts tell a story . . . When you're selling an artifact . . . you're not only getting rid of a piece of wood . . . you're getting rid of the music, the song, the dance, and the good, the bad, and the ugly.[77]

The objects in the *Chilkat* case, much like the Blackfeet medicine bundles, are considered "alive" and embody the spirit entities that assist modern human beings in their daily lives. The objects themselves are thus much more than "material" items of "property." They encompass stories, songs, and rituals necessary for the continued survival of the Native peoples. The removal of these objects from the people jeopardizes the cultural and physical survival of Native communities.

In the *Chilkat* case, it is significant that all of the Tlingit defendants ultimately abandoned their claims of "ownership," expressed regret for their actions, and sought the return of the artifacts to the Village. The tribal court ordered the artifacts to be returned to the Whale House in Klukwan and ordered Johnson and his corporation to pay for the associated expenses, as well as to compensate the plaintiff for the costs and fees in the tribal court action. The court did not award any other damages.

---

[76] Chilkat Indian Village, *IRA v. Johnson*, 20 INDIAN L. REP. 6127, 6134 (Chilkat Tr. Ct. 1993).

[77] *Id.* at 6135.

3. The Anti-Trafficking Provisions of NAGPRA

United States v. Corrow[78] involved the anti-trafficking provision of NAGPRA. The defendant, Richard Corrow, purchased a set of Navajo sacred objects that are used in healing ceremonies. The objects are described by the court as ceremonial adornments used by traditional Navajo practitioners and known as "masks of the gods" (*Yei B'Chei*) and "medicine bundles" (*jish*), although neither term adequately captures their cultural essence as living entities. The *Yei B'Chei* had belonged to a Navajo religious singer (*Hataali*), who had passed away without giving instructions to his family about what to do with the *Yei B'Chei*, which Corrow purchased from the *Hataali*'s widow. According to Navajo tradition, a *Hataali* generally passes the *Yei B'Chei* to a family or clan member, who has studied the ceremonies, but sometimes loans the *Yei B'Chei* to another clan.

In this case, Corrow represented to Mrs. Winnie, the singer's widow, that he would like to purchase the *Yei B'Chei* and deliver them to a young Navajo singer in Utah. He purchased them for $10,000 and then, with the assistance of artifact brokers, entered an agreement with an undercover federal agent, posing as an artifacts collector, to sell the items for $70,000. He was charged with and convicted of trafficking in protected Native American cultural items in violation of NAGPRA. The statute provides that "Whoever knowingly sells, purchases, uses for profit, or transports for sale or profit any Native American cultural items obtained in violation of the NAGPRA" shall be guilty of a misdemeanor (or in the case of a subsequent violation, a felony).[79]

On appeal, Corrow challenged the constitutionality of NAGPRA's definition of "cultural patrimony," which served as the basis for his conviction, on the grounds that it was "unconstitutionally vague." In the prosecution, the definition of cultural patrimony required the government to prove that Mr. Corrow trafficked in an object that (1) was not owned by an individual Native American; (2) could not be alienated, appropriated, or conveyed by an individual; and (3) had an ongoing historical, traditional, or cultural importance central to the Native American group. Mr. Corrow challenged the first and second elements as unconstitutionally vague, in light of conflicting testimony on the nature of the objects.

At the trial, the government relied on testimony from several witnesses, including Navajo medicine men and a cultural anthropologist, in support of its claim that the *Yei B'Chei* constituted "cultural patrimony." One witness described the *Yei B'Chei* as the "heartbeat" of the Navajo people and said that they must remain within the four sacred mountains of the Navajo people.[80] These objects embody a "God given gift to the Navajos," and they have "everything to do with the welfare and the health and wisdom" of the people.[81] The witnesses testified that the *Hataali* is responsible for caring for the *Yei B'Chei* and restoring them in the event of exposure to the wrong people or places. A *Hataali* may give the *Yei*

---

[78] 941 F. Supp. 1553 (D.N.M. 1996), *aff'd*, 119 F.3d 796 (10th Cir. 1997).

[79] 18 U.S.C. § 1170(b).

[80] United States v. Corrow, 119 F.3d 796, 801 (10th Cir. 1997).

[81] *Id.* at 801 n.7.

B'Chei to another chanter, who, in a traditional sense, may offer compensation in recognition of the value in the gift. The Navajo anthropologist, testified that there is "no such thing as ownership of medicine bundles and that these are viewed as living entities."[82] He testified that some aspects of ceremonial use may seem consistent with "ownership," but noted that the cultural items are generally sold only in response to economic pressure.

The defendant's witnesses gave conflicting testimony. One Navajo medicine man testified that if no claim is made by a clan relative or other singer, the objects may pass to the widow, who must care for them. If the widow feels uncomfortable about keeping them, he testified, she may sell them. The other two Navajo witnesses asserted their belief that the objects were "alive," which may deter family members from keeping them, and that the singer's family would have the right of disposition, although no one could really "own" living gods.

The Tenth Circuit upheld the conviction against defendant's challenge, finding sufficient evidence that Corrow had had ample notice that the *Yei B'Chei* were powerfully connected to Navajo religion and culture. Moreover, while it may be true that Navajo practitioners differed in their accounts of alienability, no expert had testified that it was permissible to sell the *Yei B'Chei* to non-Navajos for profit, which is the conduct that 18 U.S.C. Section 1170(b) penalized.

The idea that cultural objects may be "living entities" is one that non-Indians appear to have a great deal of difficulty accepting even though it is that belief, as well as the notion of "sacredness" that demonstrates the impermissibility of treating these items as "property" that is amenable to trade in the market economy. Not surprisingly, the problems associated with this conflict of views are abundant. To the extent that NAGPRA does not cover the conduct in question, important cultural values are in jeopardy. The distinction between "cultural patrimony" and "Indian arts and crafts," therefore, is critical in order to protect the important cultural values associated with Native cultural objects.

D. The Statutory Framework for Protecting Native Rights to Market "Indian Arts and Crafts"

The phrase "Indian arts and crafts" is routinely used to describe a broad category of Native art that is intentionally made for commercial purposes. In the contemporary world, Native artists do create items for sale that are patterned after traditional cultural objects, such as Haida totem poles, Alaska Native masks, and Hopi Kachina dolls. In addition, Native artists incorporate traditional techniques of wood carving, ivory carving, quill work, hide painting, beadwork, and basket weaving to create contemporary art. Finally, some Native artists have attained national and global acclaim in the fine art market for their innovative designs and high quality technical execution.

What are the interests of Native artists and Native communities with respect to "Indian arts and crafts"? First, let us consider the economic interest. The market for Indian art has become a lucrative business that generates millions of

[82] *Id.* at 801.

dollars annually. A 1985 congressionally mandated study by the U.S. Department of Commerce, for example, estimated annual sales of Native American jewelry and crafts at $400–$800 million.[83] Not surprisingly, there are efforts by foreign and other non-Indian entrepreneurs to capture part of this market by creating objects that "look" like Indian art, but are not. The same study estimated that approximately 20 percent of the annual sales were of "fake" Indian art: goods "passed off" as Indian and generally sold for prices that were up to 50 percent lower than legitimate Indian art.[84] In many cases, these goods were imported from countries such as Mexico, the Philippines, and Taiwan, where North American entrepreneurs sent samples and supplies to be duplicated, even in many cases, by reproducing the craftman's signature. Native artists and Indian tribes naturally have a strong interest in preventing such fraudulent misrepresentations of art as "Indian made." Their interest is analogous to that which is protected under trademark law.

Secondly, there are important property interests at stake. Individual artists or Native nations may hold a particular interest in a design, symbol, or art form, such that any attempt to appropriate it would be analogous to a copyright infringement—the unauthorized use of a protected creation—whether the copier is "Indian" or "non-Indian." Although copyright law is the closest analogy, it does not completely protect the interests of Native artists and Indian tribes.

Finally, profound cultural interests of Indian nations and tribal members are significantly involved. To the extent that a particular artform (for example, a Kachina) is associated with a particular tribe and cultural tradition, that tribe has an interest in ensuring that its culture is not misappropriated or misrepresented. The significance of a Kachina within Hopi tradition, for example, may be tied to cultural beliefs that govern who may carve Kachinas, how they must be carved, what may or may not be done with them, and a host of other requirements. How can tribes protect these interests if unauthorized individuals (Native or non-Native) carve Kachinas and sell them or if consumers alter the Kachinas after purchase?

1. Economic Interests

The problem of non-Indian entrepreneurs exploiting Native designs and products started early in the 20th century. In 1935, as part of the New Deal legislation designed to enhance tribal self-government and inspire economic development on reservations, Congress enacted the first version of the Indian Arts and Crafts Act (IACA).[85] The act created the Indian Arts and Crafts Board as an entity to (1) promote the market for Indian arts and crafts and (2) prevent fake goods from entering the market. In terms of enforcement, the 1935 act provided criminal penalties for people who were convicted of intentionally selling goods with the fraudulent misrepresentation that they were Indian-produced. The penalties were a maximum of $500 and/or six months in prison.

---

[83] William J. Hapiuk, *Of Kitsch and Kachinas: A Critical Analysis of the Indian Arts and Crafts Act of 1990*, 53 STAN. L. REV. 1009, 1017 & n.31 (2001).

[84] *Id.*

[85] 25 U.S.C. § 305.

The "willful intent" requirement, coupled with the minimal penalty provisions, proved to be a great deterrent to prosecution. As of 1990, when the law was revised, there had never been a successful conviction under the 1935 statute.

Congress held hearings on the problem of counterfeit "Indian art" in the late 1980s, which documented the harm to both Native artists and consumers caused by the fraudulent production and sale of such art. These hearings also elicited another rationale for expanding the statutory protection for Indian art, which is that, if not protected by law, Native arts and crafts traditions might die out.[86] This perspective is partially based on a notion that the government ought to affirmatively protect Native cultural survival and partially based upon a paternalistic view that Native cultures are an "American" resource.

Congress subsequently enacted a new version of the Indian Arts and Crafts Act in 1990, which made several substantial changes to the statute, and then passed further amendments in 2000 to enhance the reach of the statute.[87] The definition of "Indian" was narrowed under the 1990 act to include federally recognized tribes and their members, state recognized tribes and their members, and persons who may not be tribal members but meet other criteria of lineage and are certified as tribal artisans by the recognized government of the tribal entity. The definition of "Indian product," on the other hand, is very broad and includes "any art of craft product made by an Indian." The amended statute significantly enhances the criminal penalties associated with a violation of the statute and now makes it a felony "to knowingly misrepresent" products as Indian-made.[88] In addition, the IACA now authorizes civil actions to be filed against any person who directly or indirectly commits the proscribed conduct.[89] Such actions may be filed by the attorney general of the United States upon the request of the secretary of the interior or a tribe, tribal member, or tribal organization, or they may be filed directly by the tribe, tribal member, or tribal organization. The statute specifically authorizes the award of damages (including treble damages, punitive damages, and attorneys' fees), injunctive relief, and other equitable remedies.

Not surprisingly, the civil remedies provision of the IACA is getting the most attention in current litigation. The Ho-Chunk Tribe of Wisconsin, for example, has sued several national retailers, including Wal-Mart and J.C. Penney, alleging that the defendants have misrepresented items for sale as "Indian made" when in fact they were not.[90] The suit against J.C. Penney was for over $240 million; the suit against Wal-Mart sought $60 million in compensatory damages and $60 million in punitive damages, plus attorneys' fees. Several of the lawsuits settled for undisclosed amounts.

The IACA is essentially premised upon notions of trademark law that require goods to be identified for the benefit of producers and consumers and

---

[86] Hapiuk, *supra* note 83, at 1022–23.
[87] 25 U.S.C. § 305e.
[88] 18 U.S.C. § 1159.
[89] 25 U.S.C. § 305e.
[90] Hapiuk, *supra* note 83, at 1038–41.

that proscribe the fraudulent misrepresentation of products. It is not a crime for a non-Indian artist to create "Indian style" jewelry so long as it is correctly labeled. Nor is it a crime for an Indian artist of one tribe to create a product that is based on another Indian tribe's traditional work. Nor does the statute require Indian artists to observe any specified standards for the production of their work in order to guarantee the integrity of the product. Although certain interests in intellectual property might be involved in these situations, the IACA is not the statute to address these issues. I will turn to discuss those interests next.

2. Property Interests

Under the IACA, the term "Indian" acts as a "trademark denoting products made by Indians, just as 'Roquefort' denotes a cheese manufactured from sheep's milk cured in limestone caves in the Roquefort region of France."[91] Thus, as a form of trademark law, the IACA fits within the broader category of "intellectual property rights." The IACA, however, is quite limited in its focus, and Native artists or tribes must rely on general principles of intellectual property law for protection of interests beyond the scope of the IACA.

In the United States, intellectual property rights are protected through federal and state laws that focus on patent, trademark, and copyright law. The Constitution allocates the primary authority over intellectual property rights to Congress. Article 1, Section 8, clause 8 provides that "The Congress shall have the power . . . to promote the progress of science and useful arts, by securing for a limited time to authors and inventors the exclusive right to their respective writings and discoveries." By statute, Congress has created protections for artists and inventors through patent law, trademark law, and copyright law. State common law doctrines fill in the gaps by protecting certain aspects of intellectual property rights that are otherwise not protected by federal law.

Patents offer limited protection for new and useful inventions and discoveries. Patent law promotes the development of new technology by offering limited protection to inventors in order to allow them to reap the rewards of their labor. Trademark law originated under the English common law as a device to identify in the marketplace the craftsmen responsible for producing goods for sale. In the United States, the states drew on this common law tradition and developed trademarks to prevent one person from "passing off" his goods as those of another. Federal trademark law provides a structure to enforce the state-derived common law of trademark, which is important for national uniformity and enforceability in interstate commerce. In particular, the Lanham Act recognizes various categories of trademarks to provide protection against unfair competition and prevent deceptive marketing of goods and services that could cause injury to other competitors.

The final category, copyright law, protects original creations that are "fixed" in a tangible medium, such as literature, music, and art. Under the federal copyright statute, the protection arises when the author fixes the expression in

[91] Native Am. Arts, Inc. v. The Waldron Corp., 399 F.3d 871, 873–74 (7th Cir. 2005).

a permanent medium and lasts for the lifetime of the author, plus an additional period of time, depending upon the nature of the work. The copyright protects only the original expression of an idea and does not protect the idea itself. Thus, the author's copyright gives him or her the exclusive right to make copies of the work and to control derivative works. When the copyright expires, the work enters the "public domain" and may be used by others without restriction.

The federal and state laws governing intellectual property rights may be used by any individual artist, craftsman, or inventor. Thus, individual Indians may certainly use these statutes to protect their interests. However, an Indian tribe that seeks to protect tribal intellectual property rights by maintaining that, by tradition, it has the exclusive right to produce Kachinas, for example, or wool rugs with a "Two Grey Hills" pattern, or a "squash blossom necklace," its claim will not be cognizable under federal intellectual property law for several reasons. First, copyrights and patents only protect "new" knowledge (novel inventions, original expressions), not knowledge that already exists and has existed throughout time as "traditional knowledge." Second, copyrights and patents confer property rights on individuals (or corporations, which legally operate as individuals), rather than groups. Indigenous designs or art forms, however, are often connected with group identity rather than being considered as expressions of individual creation. Intellectual property law unfortunately fails to recognize group claims, including rights to control a design, symbol, or art form and exclude others from the use of it. Finally, copyrights and patents establish limited, rather than permanent, protection of the invention or creation. The law does not support perpetual rights in intellectual property because competition is seen as beneficial and monopolies are perceived as socially destructive.

The regime for protecting intellectual property rights is squarely based on Anglo-American property law, which reflects a series of rules that govern the legal relations between individuals with respect to resources. It protects several essential societal values, including certainty of title, fairness, economic efficiency, and investment of productive labor in resources. The law sustains "private property rights," recognizing that owners enjoy a "bundle of rights," including the right to transfer title and the right to "exclude" others from the title. The preference is for free alienability, and restrictions on alienability are quite limited and focused on particular needs and interests.

Native property systems, on the other hand, are quite distinctive as they are based on collective claims to ownership. The collective or group nature of tribal interests in tribal art is characterized as a set of cultural interests, and, yet, these interests are intangible, and so they cannot be protected by laws such as NAGPRA, which protect "cultural property." These interests represent a category that is currently not cognizable under federal law.

3. Cultural Interests in Intellectual Property

Tribal property systems tend to be "group" oriented with aspects of both "collective" and "communal" ownership. Collective ownership systems place "ownership" in the community but may allow individuals to acquire superior rights to or responsibilities for part of the collective property. Communal ownership systems, on the other hand, do not permit individuals to acquire special rights to any part of the property vis-a-vis other community members.

As with the Anglo-American law, Native property systems include a bundle of rights that attach to property, but most often these are couched in terms of certain duties and responsibilities that people have with respect to resources. The notion of alienability is not a core feature of such systems, although many types of property are alienable, either within the society or even outside the society. Other categories of objects, such as the *Yei B'Chei* described in the *Corrow* case, may be strictly inalienable outside the tribe.

Indigenous property systems often encompass notions of the "sacred," reflecting tribal worldviews that see a special relationship between the people and the rest of the universe. The primary value of certain objects may be spiritual, and thus, the purpose of the object and the duties associated with appropriate care of the object may be very incompatible with Western notions of ownership, which tend to center upon material profit and utility. Moreover, Native cultural resources often have a tangible component and an intangible component, which are inseparable. So, for example, the Chilkat artifacts described above had a material essence: the carved rainscreen and poles. But they also had an intangible essence: the songs and stories that went with the images. Together, they represent a category of "spiritual property" necessary to the cultural survival of the Native peoples who use the objects in various ways to deal with aspects of daily life and the relationship of clans and individuals to one another.

Group claims of tribes to intangible cultural property (e.g., songs, symbols, designs) are the most problematic aspects of contemporary law. NAGPRA, however, does not protect these claims, apart from the tangible object covered by the statute. Nor does the IACA protect such claims. The law is still emerging. Currently, tribes are examining international human rights law and provisions of other legal systems to design a model that could be used in the United States to protect their cultural interests.

4. Bulun Bulun Equity

One of the most interesting models is based on a 1998 Australian case, *Bulun Bulun v. R & T Textiles Pty Ltd.*[92] There, the Australian Federal Court recognized an indigenous group's communal ownership interest in the visual depiction of a sacred site and found that a Native artist had a fiduciary responsibility to the group with respect to his copyrighted work.

The case arose when an indigenous Australian artist, John Bulun Bulun, painted a work entitled "Magpie Geese and Water Lilies at the Waterhole" and sold it to an arts and crafts center in Australia. He created the work with the permission of the elders of his tribe, the Ganalbingu people. The painting depicted a Ganalbingu sacred site and drew upon the group's sacred knowledge

[92] 157 A.L.R. 193.

and traditions. Without authorization, a textile company reproduced substantial portions of the painting on fabric and sold them in the form of T-shirts and other clothing items. Bulun Bulun, the legal owner of the copyright, sued the company. The company admitted infringement and immediately withdrew the shirts from sale.

Another representative of the Ganalbingu, George Milpurrurru, also sued the company, claiming equitable ownership of the copyright in the painting. Milpurrurru claimed that the equitable ownership was the result of the Ganalbingu's connection with their traditional lands and that the community's customary law entitled the group to control the reproduction of ritual knowledge. The artist, as a group member, was merely a "fiduciary" or "trustee" owner, on behalf of the group. Milpurrurru sought a declaration from the Australian courts that the group could possess "communal title in their traditional knowledge and in particular in their artwork." When the textile company argued that the representative had no standing to bring such a claim, the issue of equitable ownership proceeded to trial.

Like U.S. law, Australian law had no provision for a communal title in copyright. The judge therefore held that the group could not maintain a statutory copyright claim but found that its fiduciary claim was valid. The court held that Bulun Bulun, as the individual artist, had a fiduciary obligation not to act in violation of laws and custom of the Ganalbingu people in his artistic endeavor and held also that in the event of infringement by a third party, he must take reasonable and appropriate action to restrain and remedy infringement of the copyright in the artistic work. In applying this rule, the court found that Bulun Bulun had acted appropriately in both respects, and that the Ganalbingu therefore had no need for additional remedies.

The case is important because the court found that customary indigenous law can be used in the federal courts as a basis for cognizable legal rights, although the group's right is asserted, if at all, against its own member, rather than the non-Native individual who infringed the copyright. Drawing on earlier cases dealing with Native title claims to traditional lands to define a property right based on indigenous law, the court evaluated the extensive evidence and testimony offered by the Ganalbingu to support their claim to ownership over the subject matter of the painting and the artistic work itself. That evidence demonstrated that the waterhole depicted in Bulun Bulun's bark painting was of a very sacred site in Ganalbingu tradition: it was the birthplace of their human and spiritual ancestors. One witness testified as follows:

> Barnda [the Creator] gave us our language and law. Barnda gave to my ancestors the country and the ceremony and paintings associated with the country. My ancestors had a responsibility given to them by Barnda to perform the ceremony and to do the paintings which were granted to them.[93]

[93] *Id.*

The aboriginal art had a spiritual significance that was manifested through a series of designs. The images, motifs, and stylistic depictions associated with these designs could not be changed but had to be reproduced in the same form throughout subsequent generations. The people believed that if this was not done, the power associated with those designs, which invoked the assistance of the Ancestral Beings, would be lost.[94] In return for the ownership of the land, the Ganalbingu had obligations to honor the customs passed down to them from their ancestors and to create and perform art associated with that land and those customs. Failure to respect this customary law would result in loss of rights to land as well as harm to the community.

This case gave rise to a principle known as the "Bulun Bulun equity,"[95] which does not create a group title in copyright but does assign legal importance to the communal interests of indigenous groups. The principle also grants the traditional owners standing to challenge misuse of the group's sacred images and designs. The cause of action contains important limitations, however: (1) the group's customary law must regulate culturally based artistic creations; (2) the artwork must possess great social and cultural importance to the group; and (3) the individual artist maintains the copyright but is responsible to the group for appropriate use of group symbols, images, and designs. Thus, it remains to be seen how far the courts will expand the jurisprudence in this area beyond these limitations. In addition, as a practical matter, indigenous groups vary in terms of the control they maintain over cultural knowledge and in their views as to whether individual group members should enjoy autonomy as artists to use the group's cultural symbols in their individual artwork.

E. CONCLUSION: WORKING TO RESOLVE CONTEMPORARY CONFLICTS

So far, in this discussion of claims dealing with ownership of Indian art and artifacts, most of the cases have focused on conflicts between Native and non-Native peoples. Jurisdictional considerations have placed the majority of these claims in federal court. As we have seen, however, the applicable federal statutes all contain significant limitations that do not always protect Native peoples' interests. For this reason, I believe that our legal system must be inclusive of *both* tribal courts and federal courts such as to allow for needed structural changes in the administration of justice and needed innovation in the substantive law that applies to cultural conflicts. As *Bulun Bulun* demonstrates, indigenous conceptions of justice, whether embodied in case law generated by tribal courts or in the group's customary law, can provide a basis for domestic and international bodies to recognize indigenous laws governing important resources.

In the United States, tribal courts are in an ideal position to articulate the operative cultural values that frame the tribe's conception of its cultural rights and the rights of its members. The late Claudeen Bates-Arthur, who served

[94] Amina Para Matlon, *Safeguarding Native American Sacred Art by Partnering Tribal Law and Equity: An Exploratory Case Study Applying the Bulun Bulun Equity to Navajo Sandpainting*, 27 COLUM. J. L. & ARTS 211, 220 n.60 (2004).

[95] *Id.* at 212 n.9.

as Chief Justice of the Navajo Nation Supreme Court, emphasized that it is important for Indian tribes to "decide for themselves what is important for their survival as tribal people."[96] For the Navajo people, she said, these are "the fundamental philosophy and laws ordained by the Holy People, which are those concepts that remain unchanged despite the intrusions that come from the outside and those things that were there when we came to our homeland between the four sacred mountains and that will distinguish us as *Dine* ("the People") forever."[97]

The "law" of any people is dependent upon a moral and philosophical framework to distinguish "right" from "wrong" conduct. NAGPRA and the IACA provide a good start in protecting Native peoples' cultural and artistic rights within United States domestic law, but tribal law also contains great potential to generate different jurisprudential frameworks to govern the conception of rights. All Native nations possess traditional systems for determining appropriate conduct, individual and governmental. However, those systems are largely neglected in contemporary society because of the prevalence of Anglo-American concepts of justice that are embodied within the state and federal legal systems.

Former Justices of the Navajo Nation, Tom Tso and Robert Yazzie, have both written widely about Navajo concepts of justice.[98] The Navajo Nation court system possesses both modern and traditional structures. The modern court system consists of a set of district courts which hear various civil and criminal actions and a Supreme Court. The traditional system is composed of the Peacemaker Court, which is organized around customary dispute resolution techniques that tend to be less adversarial and coercive in nature than those of the modern court. Even within the modern court system, however, traditional Navajo concepts of justice are often employed as "customary law." Thus, the Navajo Nation justice system is an excellent example of an approach to community justice that integrates traditional and modern sources of law.

In explaining the jurisprudential framework that underlies the Navajo justice system, Justice Yazzie writes that the Navajo word for law (*beehaz/aanii*) means something "fundamental, and something that is absolute and exists from the beginning of time."[99] In the beginning, he says, the Holy People put these principles into operation for human beings to guide and plan their lives. These laws are "the source of a healthy, meaningful life, and thus 'life comes from it.'"[100] The precepts of Navajo law, which are stated in prayers and ceremonies, tell the people of "*hozho*"—the perfect, or ideal state.

As Justice Yazzie describes it, the Navajo justice system is set up to protect this understanding of the role of law. He describes Anglo-American justice systems,

---

[96] Claudeen Bates-Arthur, *The Role of the Tribal Attorney*, 34 Ariz. St. L.J. 21, 23 (2001).

[97] *Id.* at 23.

[98] *See, e.g.,* The Hon. Tom Tso, *The Process of Decision-Making in Tribal Courts*, 31 Ariz. L. Rev. 225 (1989); The Hon. Robert Yazzie, *Life Comes from It: Navajo Justice Concepts*, 24 N.M. L. Rev. 175 (1994).

[99] Yazzie, *supra* note 98, at 175.

[100] *Id.*

which he terms "vertical" systems of justice," as hierarchical, authoritarian, and based upon an adversarial "win-lose" ethic of justice. In comparison, he says, the Navajo justice system is a "horizontal" system, in which all parties are treated with equal respect, group solidarity is stressed (as opposed to force and coercion), and the goal is to promote healing and good relations. Whereas the Anglo system often results in permanently impaired interpersonal relations, the Navajo system seeks to re-establish the "perfect state" of harmony that ought to govern individuals within human societies. The difference is between an adversarial, punitive system of justice and a restorative or reparative justice system.

It is time to heal the cultural conflicts that have long divided Native and non-Native peoples. These conflicts perpetuate the ongoing dichotomy between legal categories that protect or do not protect Native interests in "Native art" and Native "artifacts." To generate new categories of law that can successfully protect the multiple and distinctive interests expressed by Native peoples requires a thoughtful inter-cultural dialogue and a willingness to make structural changes to the law in order to achieve justice for Native peoples. Native law will be pivotal to the creation of these new legal categories, and international human rights law can provide guidance on the necessary structural changes to enable indigenous rights to be realized within U.S. domestic law. Native peoples have expressed important cultural, religious, and spiritual interests in their cultural and intellectual expressions and property, and they continue to exist as separate governments within the United States. These attributes provide a firm foundation for the necessary legal innovation that must occur in order to fully protect Native cultural heritage.

CHAPTER 2

PROTECTION AND REPATRIATION OF INDIGENOUS CULTURAL HERITAGE IN THE UNITED STATES

James A.R. Nafziger*

In the United States, federal and state statutes largely define the legal regime for protection and repatriation of indigenous heritage. This study summarizes the legislation, with a focus on the Native American Graves Protection and Repatriation Act (1990; NAGPRA),[1] its regulations, and interpretations of it. NAGPRA's gradual maturation as a human rights instrument may not always be apparent from discourse about the indigenous heritage in the United States. It will be seen, however, that NAGPRA has worn well, having become effective and well accepted over time. Provisions in NAGPRA for review of issues related to it and for avoiding and resolving disputes are particularly noteworthy. These provisions have given rise to ongoing processes of consultation, significant interpretations of the law, and refinements in it. The minutes of the NAGPRA review committee's meetings, in particular, disclose the law's efficacy. Still, NAGPRA has its problems. After a review of the general legal regime for protecting the indigenous heritage in the United States, a concluding section of this study will identify strengths and weaknesses of NAGPRA that have become apparent in its first decade and a half.

A. THE STATUTORY FRAMEWORK

1. Federal Laws

The Antiquities Act[2] (1906) provides a permit system for examination of ruins, excavation of archaeological sites, and gathering of artifacts on federally owned or controlled lands. Further, this legislation made it a crime to "appropriate, excavate, injure, or destroy any historic or prehistoric ruin or monument, or any object of antiquity," found on federally owned or controlled

---

* Earlier versions of this chapter appear in PROTECTION OF FIRST NATIONS CULTURAL HERITAGE: LAWS, POLICY AND REFORM (Catherine Bell & Robert K. Paterson eds., 2008) and 14 WILLAMETTE J. INT'L L. & DISP. RES. 175 (2006). The author thanks Larion Barsukoff and Kristin Hausler for their invaluable research assistance.

[1] 25 U.S.C. §§ 3001–3013 (2000).

[2] 16 U.S.C. §§ 431–433 (2000). This summary of federal legislation is an updated and otherwise adapted version of James A.R. Nafziger, *The Underlying Constitutionalism of the Law Governing Archaeological and Other Cultural Heritage*, 30 WILLAMETTE L. REV. 581, 582–85 (1994).

lands, without a permit from the federal government. Penalties for violations of the law are minor, however.[3]

The National Historic Preservation Act[4] (1966; NHPA) is rooted in scattered, often site-specific legislation originating in the 19th century. It requires federal agencies to manage heritage resources under their control and establishes a National Register of historically significant buildings, sites, and areas, providing special tax benefits, such as income tax credits, deductions, and accelerated depreciation of designated property. The NHPA also creates special historic easements, provides for transferability rights, and authorizes federal matching grants to the states to support local survey and preservation efforts. All federally directed, funded, or licensed projects—public or private—must be evaluated to determine a project's impact on archaeologically significant resources and take account of non-binding comments by an Advisory Council on Historic Preservation. Amendments in 1980 and 1992 require substantial participation of Native Americans in policymaking and decisionmaking under the NHPA.[5]

The Archaeological Resources Protection Act[6] (1979; ARPA) refines and largely supersedes the Antiquities Act. It reasserts federal control over archaeological resources on federal lands, requiring a permit for any excavation, removal, or alteration of such resources. ARPA also provides stiff penalties for persons who knowingly excavate, sell, purchase, transport, exchange, receive, or remove those resources without a federal permit. The term "archaeological resources" is defined to include "any material remains of past human life or activities which are of archaeological interest" and are at least 100 years old. To summarize, ARPA has helped guide an ongoing successful effort by federal agencies to protect Native American sites on public land.[7]

---

[3] *See* United States v. Diaz, 499 F.2d 113 (9th Cir. 1974) (where the Ninth Circuit Court of Appeals, whose jurisdiction encompasses a major part of the indigenous cultural heritage, largely eviscerated the penal provisions of the Act. As a matter of due process, the court declared unconstitutional the vague definitions of the terms "ruin," "monument," and "object of antiquity."); *but see* United States v. Smyer, 596 F.2d 939 (10th Cir. 1979) (declaring that the act is not unconstitutionally vague and uncertain, and upholding penalties for wrongful appropriation of ancient objects which, unlike the objects at issue in *Diaz*, were ancient). Despite the *Diaz* decision, the 1906 act continues to have profound effects in protecting cultural heritage. For example, the act authorizes the president, without legislative enactment, to establish national monuments in order to preserve "objects of historic or scientific interest that are situated upon the lands owned or controlled by the Government of the United States." Under this authority, for example, Theodore Roosevelt established the Grand Canyon National Monument in 1908, Franklin D. Roosevelt designated the Jackson Hole National Monument in 1913, Jimmy Carter added 15 more national monuments in Alaska in 1978, and, in 1996, Bill Clinton created the Grand Staircase-Escalante National Monument, which is the largest outside Alaska.

[4] 16 U.S.C. §§ 470–470w-6 (2000).

[5] For a brief summary, see Patty Gerstenblith, Art, Cultural Heritage and the Law: Cases and Materials 677 (2004).

[6] 16 U.S.C. §§ 470aa-470mm (2000).

[7] *See* Marcia Yablon, *Property Rights and Secret Sites: Federal Regulatory Responses to American Indian Claims on Public Land*, 113 Yale L.J. 1623 (2004).

The first prosecution under ARPA based on trafficking in archaeological objects removed from private land was *United States v. Gerber*.[8] In a landmark opinion by Judge Richard Posner, the Seventh Circuit Court of Appeals ruled that ARPA applies to private land. The decision rested on an interpretation of ARPA's provision against trafficking in archaeology resources "in violation of any provision, rule, regulation, ordinance, or permit in effect under State or local law."[9] The defendant had unsuccessfully argued that ARPA was inapplicable to archaeological objects removed from lands not owned by either the federal government or Indian tribes. The defendant had further argued, also unsuccessfully, that any state or local law to which ARPA refers is limited to provisions expressly protecting archaeological objects or sites, as distinct from laws of general application such as those forbidding trespass, theft, and trafficking.

The Cultural Property Implementation Act[10] (1983; CPIA) executes the obligations of the United States under a 1970 UNESCO convention against illegal trafficking in cultural property that will be summarized in Section B. Unlike other parties, the United States entered a reservation to the convention through which it has refused to enforce export controls of foreign countries that are based solely on illicit trafficking of cultural property. Instead, under another provision of the convention, the United States has agreed that other parties to the convention can call upon it to embargo designated classes of items from their national patrimony if such items are in jeopardy. The president then may unilaterally impose restrictions on such imports or may enter into executive agreements with individual nations to restrict the importation from them of archaeological or ethnological materials threatened with "pillage."

The National Museum of the American Indian Act[11] (1989; NMAIA) established, within the Smithsonian Institution, a "living memorial to Native Americans and their traditions [to] be known as the 'National Museum of the American Indian.'"[12] The NMAIA is a precursor to NAGPRA and, as amended, adopts NAGPRA's scheme for protection, supervision, and repatriation of indigenous human remains and cultural objects.

NAGPRA,[13] which will be discussed later in detail, vests Indian tribes and Native Hawaiian organizations with ownership and control of Native American remains and cultural objects on federal and tribal lands. It also regulates excavation and removal of human remains and objects from federal or tribal lands, subject to criminal sanctions. NAGPRA requires federal agencies and federally funded museums to furnish inventories of Native American human remains and associated funerary objects, as well as summaries of unassociated cultural objects. The law provides for the repatriation of such objects to lineal descendants of Native Americans or, by default, to tribes or groups, according

---

[8] 999 F.2d 1112 (7th Cir. 1993).

[9] 16 U.S.C. § 470ee(c) (2000).

[10] 19 U.S.C. §§ 2601–2613 (2000).

[11] 20 U.S.C. § 80q (2000).

[12] 20 U.S.C. § 80a-1(a) (2000).

[13] 25 U.S.C. §§ 3001–3013 (2000).

to prescribed criteria and procedures. A review committee supervises its implementation. Alternatively, claims under NAGPRA may be brought in a federal district court.

In contrast, other federal laws seek to protect archaeological resources only secondarily. For example, the National Environmental Policy Act[14] (1969; NEPA) requires federal agencies to prepare an environmental impact statement whenever a proposed project might affect the quality of the environment. NEPA specifically includes the historical and cultural heritage within the federal government's scope of responsibility under the act.

The periodic Department of Transportation Acts[15] and related regulations seek to avoid harm to historical sites threatened by federal highway and related projects and to permit states to use federal highway funding for archaeological salvage. They also provide a means for recovery of archaeological material at impacted sites. The Historic Sites, Buildings, and Antiquities Act of 1935[16] seeks to ensure the preservation for public use of historic structures and objects of national significance. In a single paragraph, the American Indian Religious Freedom Act[17] (1978) enunciates federal policy to protect and preserve access to sites, use and possession of sacred objects, and the freedom to worship through ceremonies and traditional rites. This act is largely precatory, but in 1996 it incorporated an executive order that requires protective implementation by federal agencies, including measures to avoid adversely affecting the physical integrity of protected sites.

The Indian Arts and Crafts Act[18] was initially enacted in 1935, during the Great Depression, to encourage a legitimate market for Native American arts and crafts. Later amendments updated the purpose and scope of the act to establish a procedure for certification of authentic work created by an enrolled member of a recognized tribe. The main purpose of the act is to foil counterfeit or bogus Native American art. The authenticity of a work refers not to its cultural representation, but to the tribal status of its creator. In other words, certified works eligible for protection under the act need not bear any association with a particular tribe or its tradition.

Because of the dominance of NAGPRA in specifically protecting and providing for repatriation of indigenous heritage, further evaluation of federal law will be deferred to Section E, which addresses its strengths and weaknesses, with a focus on NAGPRA.

2. State Laws

State laws that bear on the protection and repatriation of indigenous heritage fall into four categories, as follows.

---

[14] 42 U.S.C. §§ 4321–4370a (2000).
[15] *See, e.g.*, 23 U.S.C. §§ 138, 305 (2000).
[16] 16 U.S.C. §§ 461–470x-6 (2000).
[17] 42 U.S.C. § 1996 (2000).
[18] 25 U.S.C. §§ 305–310 (2000).

a. Protection of Designated Archaeological Sites

All states have laws protecting designated archaeological sites.[19] The majority that specifically address excavation on these sites rely on either *registration* of sites by landowners, with stipulated benefits to them, or *regulation* of any activity on designated sites regardless of a landowner's consent.[20]

b. General Burial Protection

All states and most local governments protect burial sites, criminalize desecration of them or unapproved interference with them, regulate the excavation and re-interment of human remains, and provide for re-interment or other disposition of excavated remains.[21] Forty-one states permit closure of cemeteries and re-interment of human remains, subject to a variety of conditions on procedure.[22] Thirty-five states require notice to a deceased person's next-of-kin or friends of planned closure or re-interment of a burial.[23]

The applicability of this general category of protective legislation to indigenous remains is greatly limited, of course, because such remains are often isolated, unmarked, or both. The consequent lack of protection from general burial legislation has encouraged a type of exceptionalism in the past whereby Native American remains, but ordinarily not other remains, were subject to excavation, scientific inquiry, and display, in violation of the constitutional right of equal protection.[24]

c. Specific Protection of Ancient or Historic Remains

All states specifically protect ancient or historic remains in marked or unmarked burial sites.[25] A majority or near majority of these laws extends protection to burials on private land.[26] Such laws, the majority of which impose

---

[19] *See* United States v. Gerber, 999 F.2d 1112, 1112 (7th Cir. 1993).

[20] *See* Richard B. Cunningham, Archaeology, Relics, and the Law 338 (1999).

[21] *See* John Alan Cohan, *An Examination of Archaeological Ethics and the Repatriation Movement Respecting Cultural Property (Part One)*, 27 Environs Envt'l L. & Pol'y J. 349, 401 (2004).

[22] *See* State *ex rel.* Comm'r Transp. v. Medicine Black Bear White Eagle, 63 S.W.3d 734, 751 n.11 (2001).

[23] *Id.*

[24] Gerstenblith, *supra* note 5, at 677.

> The differences in legal treatment of the burials of Native Americans and that of burials of the dominant European-derived culture is probably the most striking area of inequality and presents an unresolved clash in cultural values. Native Americans have suffered the desecration of their dead in the interests of science and the antiquities market for over two hundred years. Archaeologists and anthropologists have long studied the Native American civilizations, excavated their archaeological sites, and placed their human and material cultural remains on exhibit and in storage in museums. These practices often failed to recognize that these remains are part of continuing extant cultural and religious traditions.

[25] State *ex rel.* Comm'r Transp. v. Medicine Black Bear White Eagle, 63 S.W.3d 734, 752 n.17 (2001). *But see* Christopher A. Amato, *Digging Sacred Ground: Burial Site Disturbance and the Loss of New York's Native American Heritage*, 27 Colum. J. Envtl. L. 1, 24 (2002) (only 46 states have such legislation).

[26] *See, e,g.*, Gerstenblith, *supra* note 5, at 683. References in the text to a "majority" or a "minority" imply slight variations in available tabulations and commentaries.

criminal penalties, typically prohibit intentional disturbance of unmarked burials, regulate excavations and inadvertent disturbance, and require re-burial of excavated remains within specified time limits.[27]

A majority of states requires notice to tribal groups of intended excavation of burial sites or inadvertent discovery of remains.[28] Most of these laws provide for oversight commissions or boards with Native American representation.[29] A minority of states requires actual consent by tribal representatives concerning the disposition of intentionally excavated or inadvertently discovered Native American remains.[30]

d. Repatriation of Human Remains and Cultural Objects

Eleven states have "little NAGPRA" laws that require repatriation of Native American remains to tribal representatives.[31] Five of these states also require repatriation of stipulated classes of cultural objects.[32] The state laws that most comprehensively protect and provide for repatriation of indigenous remains appear to be those of Montana[33] and Utah.[34]

It is difficult to evaluate the efficacy of the various state laws because of a lack of published data. A few general observations may be helpful, however. Not surprisingly, there is some evidence that the state legislation requiring substantial Native American participation in policy development and decisionmaking works best, and that careful management of remains and cultural objects enhances broader collaboration and consultation between Native Americans and archaeologists.[35] Nonetheless, there is other evidence that open-textured language of protection, however appealing it might seem, all too easily leads to denials of protection to unrecognized tribes without judicial intervention.[36] It is also evident that extension of legislation to activity on or related to private lands may be fruitless without active governmental initiatives and enforcement.[37]

B. The Origins of the NMAIA and NAGPRA

Unfortunately, this general framework of pertinent laws was either non-existent (especially the NMAIA, NAGPRA, and state laws), incipient (ARPA), or inadequate when heated controversies concerning Native American heritage emerged during the 1970s and 1980s. The controversies swirled around the

---

[27] Amato, *supra* note 25.

[28] *Id.* at 26.

[29] *Id.*

[30] *Id.*

[31] *Id.*

[32] *Id.*

[33] MONT. CODE ANN. §§ 22-3-901 to 22-3-921 (2005).

[34] UTAH CODE ANN. §§ 9-9-401 to 9-9-406 (2003).

[35] *See, e.g.*, ROBERT A. BIRMINGHAM & LESLIE E. EISENBERG, INDIAN MOUNDS IN WISCONSIN 59, 60, 183 (2000).

[36] *See, e.g.*, Steve Cusick, *Giving the Abenaki Dead Their Due: A Proposal to Protect Native American Burial Sites in Vermont*, 28 VT. L. REV. 467 (2004).

[37] *See* Amato, *supra* note 25 (reporting that after 30 years, the state of New York had designated only one private burial site as historically significant upon which special protection could be based).

status and return of indigenous human remains and cultural objects, particularly those reposing and subject to study in museums and scientific institutions. It was a momentous era. Even today, some protagonists on both sides of controversies about the indigenous heritage base their arguments on the bygone legal premises that existed when the controversies began to emerge.

For the most part, archaeologists and others in the scientific and museum communities used to expect substantial if not unlimited access to, and control over, "found" or "discovered" remains and cultural objects for purposes of more or less permanent study and public display. Scientists emphasized the extraordinary contributions of bone studies to historical and medical research and the universal heritage of ancient remains.[38] However, Native Americans sharply contested this established practice. To them, "unredeemed artifacts and the bones of their ancestors had become potent symbols of conquest and cultural rape."[39] Repatriation of remains and culturally significant objects often became an issue of religious freedom involving the "'liberation' of still-living things that have been trapped in museum basements, in a limbo between the spirit world and the human."[40] Mounting skepticism among Native Americans concerning scientific inquiry also stemmed from a fear of technological complexity, scientific error, erosion of traditional values, and misuse of data specifically resulting from DNA analysis.[41]

Some Native Americans and scientists broadened the critique of established scientific practices into an appeal for the rectification of colonialist wrongs. Museum collections

> were not representations of reality, they were "hostages" and constant reminders of the nation's new imperial power. One way alien territory was reconfigured to fit into the national imagination was through the removal of objects from the conquered landscape. The idols, masks, baskets and clothing that were carried back to Eastern museums were the 19th-century equivalents of the dancing bears and barbarian slave girls that conquering generals paraded through the streets of ancient Rome. Things were ripped out of their context in a simultaneous exercise of political and aesthetic will. The most prized objects of all were the most secret.[42]

---

[38] On the scientific uses of human remains, see Ryan M. Seidemann, *Bones of Contention: A Comparative Examination of Law Covering Human Remains from Archaeological Contexts in Former Colonial Countries*, 64 La. L. Rev. 545, 550 (2004). On contributions that have been made to medical research by studies of ancient bones and bodies, see, e.g., Kevin Krajick, *The Mummy Doctor*, New Yorker, May 16, 2005, at 66. On the scientific argument for free access to remains and unlimited retention of them, see David Hurst Thomas, Skull Wars: Kennewick Man, Archaeology, and the Battle for Native American Identity 209–10 (2000).

[39] Fergus M. Bordewich, Killing the White Man's Indian 172 (1996).

[40] *Id.*

[41] K. TallBear, Genetics, Culture and Identity of Indian Country (Oct. 23–27, 2000) (unpublished, presented at the Seventh International Congress of Ethnology, on file with author).

[42] Remarks of Southwest historian Curtis Hinsley, *quoted in* Bordewich, *supra* note 39, at 172.

In the words of a Chippewa commentator, the "bone robber barons . . . are academic neocolonialists and racial technocrats who now seem to posture as liberal humanists."[43]

In its starkest portrayal, the emerging clash of values between scientific-institutional and indigenous communities became one of tradition versus science. This is not the place to rehash that rather stale dialectic. Suffice it to say that indigenous concerns about the confiscation of ancestral remains and associated objects fueled an Indian burial rights movement. Tribal leaders decided it was time for political and legal action. They were emboldened by the dramatic social movements of the 1960s and early 1970s associated with civil rights demonstrations, anti-Vietnam War protests, counter-cultural non-conformity, and demands for environmental protection.[44] Their efforts culminated in NMAIA and NAGPRA, as well as a proliferation of state law. The same consciousness-raising pressures from tribal communities also led to progressive judicial decisions, particularly in extending federal and state regulations of remains and cultural objects to private land and related transactions.

The reformist challenge to scientific-institutional practices could not have succeeded, however, without foundations in international practice. In particular, the rapid development in the 1970s of cooperation to protect the global cultural heritage helped set the stage for the enactment of the NMAIA and NAGPRA. During the 1970s, for example, the International Council of Museums (ICOM) confirmed that

> [T]he reassembly of dispersed heritage through restitution or return of objects which are now of major importance for the cultural identity and history of countries having been deprived thereof, is now considered to be an ethical principle recognized and affirmed by the major

---

[43] Gerald Vizenor, Crossbloods: Bone Courts, Bingo and Other Reports 67 (1990).

[44] Birmingham & Eisenberg, *supra* note 35, at 181.

Social changes stemming from the social upheavals of the 1960s and early 1970s promised for many a new age, one that would be harmonious, environmentally conscious, and tolerant of many lifeways and belief systems. Racism came under attack and was exposed in many areas of life, including established histories that excluded whole classes of people or distorted their contributions to the grand sweep of human history. Out of that era came some very positive social changes in American society and ideology, including an emphasis on social justice, a respect for the environment, and the rewriting of histories to include, for example, the roles played by Native Americans. Native Americans themselves reasserted their status as sovereign nations, claiming long-denied rights under treaties and demanding respect for their cultures, beliefs, and traditions.

But the era also produced a mistrust of science, the apparent cause of some modern problems, and many turned instead to mysticism, religious movements, and alternative realities associated with paranormal and psychic phenomena. It also spawned alternative histories written by people skeptical of mainstream science and history and excited by the flirtation with mythology, mysticism, and even notions of extraterrestrial contacts.

international organizations. This principle will soon become an element of jus cogens of international relations.[45]

Such soft-law pronouncements contributed to and crystallized a new spirit of international cooperation, including acceptance, in principle, of the need for repatriation of cultural heritage. That spirit was then codified in domestic legislation and regulations, as well as international agreements.[46] The United States took the lead in these initiatives during the 1970s and early 1980s. Its new legislation, regulations, and entry into international agreements responded primarily to appeals from Latin American governments alarmed by the plunder and marketing of their pre-Columbian heritage.

In 1982, the United States followed Canada in ratifying the UNESCO Convention on the Means of Prohibiting and Preventing the Illegal Import, Export and Transfer of Ownership of Cultural Property.[47] The United States thereby became the first major importer and market of cultural property to ratify the treaty. Significantly, the United States, continuing to focus on pre-Columbian heritage, developed a confidence in the collaborative processes of repatriation. Seeing that such processes could work well and appreciating their diplomatic merits, the United States realized the value of cooperating more generally in the repatriation of cultural material. It was therefore a small step in 1989 (NMAIA) and 1990 (NAGPRA) for Congress to extend such cooperation, still focused on the Mesoamerican heritage, to kindred Native Americans.

In the very year that Congress enacted the NMAIA, and the year before it enacted NAGPRA, two supportive regimes emerged. First, Native American leaders and the scientific community reconciled their interests in an important document, the Vermillion Accord on Human Remains.[48] Above all, this agreement restored to Native Americans control of their heritage. Although the accord was the product of only limited indigenous representation, it remains the leading agreement between indigenous and scientific communities on principles regarding the control and disposition of human remains. The Dakota-Lakota-Nakota Human Rights Advocacy Coalition notes, in particular, the essential role of the Vermillion Accord in paving the way to the enactment of NAGPRA.[49] As such, the accord is an important source for interpreting NAGPRA.

Also in 1989, the General Conference of the International Labor Organization adopted and opened for signature a Convention Concerning Indigenous

---

[45] *See Return and Restitution of Cultural Property* (Special Issue), 31 MUSEUM 62, ¶ 38 (1979).

[46] For a summary of these early developments, *see* NAFZIGER, *supra* note 2, at 588–89.

[47] UNESCO Convention on the Means of Prohibiting and Preventing the Illegal Import, Export and Transfer of Ownership of Cultural Property (Nov. 14, 1970), 823 U.N.T.S. 231, 10 I.L.M. 289.

[48] Vermillion Accord on Human Remains, The World Archaeological Inter-Congress, Jan. 15, 2006, http://www.wac.uct.ac.za/archive/content/vermillion.accord.html.

[49] *See Dakota-Lakota-Nakota Human Rights Advocacy Coalition on Burial and Repatriation* (Jan. 15, 2006), http://www.dlncoalition.org/dln_issues/burial_and_repatriation .htm.

and Tribal Peoples in Independent Countries.[50] Convention 169, as it is known, does not specifically address issues of cultural heritage, but does require the adoption of "special measures . . . as appropriate for safeguarding the persons, institutions, property, labor, cultures and environment of the peoples concerned."[51]

Finally, it should be noted that, by the mid-1980s, a preliminary text had been prepared of the Draft U.N. Declaration on the Rights of Indigenous Peoples.[52] The draft declaration was revised and adopted by the U.N. General Assembly on September 13, 2007.

Article 11 of the U.N. Declaration on the Rights of Indigenous Peoples[53] provides as follows:

> 1. Indigenous peoples have the right to practise and revitalize their cultural traditions and customs. This includes the right to maintain, protect and develop the past, present and future manifestations of their cultures, such as archaeological and historical sites, artefacts, designs, ceremonies, technologies and visual and performing arts and literature.
>
> 2. States shall provide redress through effective mechanisms, which may include restitution, developed in conjunction with indigenous peoples, with respect to their cultural, intellectual, religious and spiritual property taken without their free, prior and informed consent or in violation of their laws, traditions and customs.

Article 12 provides, more explicitly, that

> 1. Indigenous peoples have the right to manifest, practice, develop and teach their spiritual and religious traditions, customs and ceremonies; the right to maintain, protect, and have access in privacy to their religious and cultural sites; the right to the use and control of their ceremonial objects; and the right to the repatriation of their human remains.
>
> 2. States shall seek to enable the access and/or repatriation of ceremonial objects and human remains in their possession through fair, transparent and effective mechanisms developed in conjunction with indigenous peoples concerned.

All of these obligations and soft-law norms (the U.N. declaration in the form of a similar draft[54] at the time) paved the way for the adoption of the NMAIA and

---

[50] Convention Concerning Indigenous and Tribal Peoples in Independent Countries, 28 I.L.O. 1382 (1989).

[51] *Id.*, art. 4.

[52] *See* Draft Declaration on the Rights of Indigenous Peoples, U.N.ESCOR, 1994, Annex, U.N.HCR Res. 1994/45, U.N. Doc. E/CN.4/1995/2, E/CN.4/Sub.2/1994/56.

[53] U.N. Declaration on the Rights of Indigenous Peoples, G.A.Res. 295, U.N.GAOR, 61st Sess., U.N. Doc. A/RES/61/295 (2007).

[54] *Supra* note 52.

NAGPRA. More importantly, however, they stabilized expectations concerning both the substance and procedures regarding claims for repatriation of Native American heritage.

C. NAGPRA[55]

1. Purposes and General Contents

NAGPRA is, first and foremost, human rights legislation. It is *not* property legislation. Nor is it a legislative framework for balancing interests, although it was intended to operate within a collaborative framework that included such instruments as the Vermillion Accord. Congress clearly intended the legislation to repair past wrongs and ensure present and future rights. As such, it must be seen and interpreted against the backdrop of modern human rights legislation at both domestic and international levels. NAGPRA also conforms to a general theory for repatriation. Accordingly, it can be fairly described as an instrument of decolonization, self-determination and reparation; as a vindication of Native American religious and other cultural freedoms; as a means of enhancing cultural revival and transmission of cultural knowledge among tribes and Native Hawaiian groups; as a contributor to self-identity and community solidarity; and as a means for restoring Native American control over pertinent culture.[56]

But whose human rights does NAGPRA protect? The law makes clear that it operates to vindicate the rights of disinterred persons, their lineal descendants, Native American tribes, and Native Hawaiian organizations. The rights of the disinterred include, of course, the right to be buried (or not) according to their own cultural traditions and not those of an unrelated, surrogate people or organization. The dead should be protected from claims of culturally unaffiliated peoples or groups. At the same time, however, the remains themselves are not legally recognized persons and therefore have no standing to assert the rights of the deceased as has sometimes otherwise been conceded by courts to animals and sacred material.

NAGPRA's general contents may be summarized as follows.[57] It first confirms indigenous ownership or control over native cultural items found on federal and tribal lands. The governing body of a pertinent Indian tribe or Native Hawaiian organization may, however, relinquish title or control to such items.[58] Ancillary provisions restrict the availability of permits for excavation

[55] 25 U.S.C. §§ 3001–3013 (2000). For an extensive bibliography on NAGPRA, see Nancy Carol Carter, *Native American Graves, Protection and Repatriation Act: Law, Analysis and Context*, 8 Int'l J. Cultural Prop. 285 (1999).

[56] *See* Catherine Bell, Restructuring the Relationship: Repatriation and Canadian Law Reform, Presentation and Paper Outline (unpublished report on file with the author).

[57] This summary is drawn from James A.R. Nafziger & Rebecca J. Dobkins, *The Native American Graves and Repatriation Act in Its First Decade*, 8 Int'l J. Cultural Prop. 77, 73–79 (1999).

[58] 25 U.S.C. § 3002 (2000). In this and other respects, NAGPRA is closely related to ARPA, *supra* note 6. ARPA reasserts federal control over archaeological resources on federal and tribal lands and provides stiff penalties for persons who knowingly excavate, remove, or engage in transactions involving those resources without a federal permit.

and removal of Native American[59] human remains or cultural items and require notification of inadvertent discoveries of such material.[60] To enforce these provisions, NAGPRA amends the federal code by criminalizing illegal trafficking in Native American human remains and cultural items obtained in violation of the law's provisions.[61]

The most innovative part of NAGPRA is a scheme for repatriation of Native American human remains and other cultural items from museums and federal agencies.[62] They are required to compile inventories or provide summaries[63] of Native American remains and cultural items[64] in their possession. A lineal descendant of a deceased Native American may then request material listed in an inventory or summary. In the absence of such a person, a culturally affiliated[65]

---

[59] 25 U.S.C. § 3002(c) (2000). "'Native American' means of, or relating to, a tribe, people or culture that is indigenous to the United States." 25 U.S.C. § 3001(9) (2000). The term therefore embraces Indian tribes and Native Hawaiian organizations. The statute primarily protects the interests of *recognized* Indian tribes and Native Hawaiian organizations. The latter designation merits further explanation. NAGPRA defines "Native Hawaiian organization" as "any organization that serves and represents the interests of Native Hawaiians, has a primary and stated purpose of the provision of services to Native Hawaiians, and has expertise in Native Hawaiian affairs." 25 U.S.C. § 3001(11) (2000). "Native Hawaiian" is defined as "any individual who is a descendant of aboriginal people who, prior to 1778, occupied and exercised sovereignty in [Hawaii]." 25 U.S.C. § 3001(10) (2000). Some concern has been expressed that the definition of a "Native Hawaiian organization" is broad enough to include organizations without regard to whether their membership is Native Hawaiian. *See* William S. Richardson, *Native Prospects: Symposium on Challenges Facing the Hawaiian Community Today*, 4 ASIAN-PAC. L. & POL'Y J. 598, 607 (2003).

[60] 25 U.S.C. § 3002(d) (2000).

[61] 18 U.S.C. § 1170 (2000). Penalties include fines and imprisonment up to five years, in the case of a second or subsequent offense, for knowingly engaging in commercial transactions without the right of possession to human remains of a Native American or otherwise in violation of NAGPRA. It is unclear what constitutes a criminal "violation of NAGPRA." Presumably, violations would be limited to commercial transactions in material either taken without permit and against specific federal law from federal or tribal land or obtained from museums or federal agencies after NAGPRA's enactment.

[62] 25 U.S.C. § 3005 (2000). NAGPRA does not provide for the repatriation of cultural items from individuals or enterprises that are not museums, as very broadly defined, but the law's terms and process of repatriation have helped define claims beyond its scope. *See, e.g.*, Margaret Loke, *Aleut Sacred Objects to be Auctioned at Sotheby's Despite Protests by the Tribe*, N.Y. TIMES, Nov. 30, 1998, at B5.

[63] The statute requires a simple (but detailed and itemized) *inventory* of all human remains and associated funerary objects in a collection. 25 U.S.C. § 3003(a) (2000). The statute also requires a more general *summary* of unassociated funerary objects, sacred objects, or objects of cultural patrimony. The summary is to describe the collection as a whole, its size, and the circumstances of its acquisition. 25 U.S.C. § 3004(a) (2000).

[64] Although the statutory definition of the term "cultural items" includes all material for which an inventory or summary is required, including human remains, NAGPRA regulations, reflecting objections to the classification of human remains as cultural items, eliminate the generic term "cultural items" and refer only to "human remains" and other specific categories of materials. 43 C.F.R. § 10.1 (1998).

[65] The statutory definition of "cultural affiliation" refers to "a relationship of shared group identity which can be reasonably traced historically or prehistorically between a present-day Indian tribe or Native Hawaiian organization and an identifiable earlier group." 25 U.S.C. § 3001(2) (2000).

Indian tribe, a culturally affiliated Native Hawaiian organization, or a tribe or organization that can show ownership or control of an item may request such material.[66] Under pain of civil penalty,[67] museums and federal agencies must expeditiously return any such material to a claimant that has established the requisite link of lineal descendancy, cultural affiliation, or ownership or control, as the case may be.[68]

Determination of whether an object is properly classified, especially whether it is a "sacred object"[69] or an "object of cultural patrimony,"[70] may pose particular difficulties. Such issues of classification have often been resolved by consultation and collaboration between native groups and museums or federal agencies. Aside from understandable delays that may result from having to resolve these kinds of issues, there are four statutory qualifications on the requirement of expeditious return of material. First, if an inventory or summary does not itself establish cultural affiliation of the item with a requesting tribe or organization, a federal agency or museum may retain the item until the requesting party can demonstrate cultural affiliation by a preponderance of evidence based on several factors, including "geographical, kinship, biological, archaeological, anthropological, linguistic, folkloric, oral traditional, historical or other relevant information or expert opinion."[71] Second, if a cultural item is "indispensable for completion of a specific scientific study, the outcome of which would be of major benefit to the United States," repatriation may

---

[66] 25 U.S.C. § 3005(a)(1), (2) (2000).

[67] 25 U.S.C. § 3007 (2000) allows the secretary of the interior to assess a civil penalty against "[a]ny museum that fails to comply with the requirements of this Act." *See* 43 C.F.R. § 10.12 (1998).

[68] 25 U.S.C. § 3005(a)(1), (2), (4), (5) (2000).

[69] The statutory definition of "sacred objects" includes "specific ceremonial objects which are *needed* by traditional Native American religious leaders for the practice of traditional Native American religions by the *present day* adherents." 25 U.S.C. § 3001(3)(C) (2000) (emphasis added).

[70] NAGPRA defines "cultural patrimony" as

> an object having ongoing historical, traditional, or cultural importance central to the Native American group or culture itself, rather than property owned by an individual Native American, and which, therefore, cannot be alienated, appropriated, or conveyed by any individual regardless of whether or not the individual is a member of the Indian tribe or Native Hawaiian organization and such object shall have been considered inalienable by such Native American group at the time the object was separated from such group.

25 U.S.C. § 3001(3)(D) (2000). This initially appeared to be "NAGPRA's most difficult definition." Thomas H. Boyd & Jonathan Haas, *The Native American Graves Protection and Repatriation Act: Prospects for New Partnerships Between Museums and Native American Groups*, 24 ARIZ. ST. L.J. 253, 265 (1992). "[I]dentifying cultural patrimony may require extensive inquiry into both the circumstances surrounding the alienation and the state of traditions and customs as they existed at the time of transfer." *Id.* at 266. Arguably, the result is to create a rebuttable presumption that an object belongs to a claimant's cultural patrimony. Sarah Harding, *Justifying Repatriation of Native American Cultural Property*, 72 INDIANA L.J. 723, 738 (1997). Regardless of this presumption, the interpretive task appeared to be demanding but has not turned out to be so, and the term itself not so controversial.

[71] 25 U.S.C. § 3005(a)(4) (2000).

be delayed until no later than 90 days after completion of the study.[72] Third, the claimant of an unassociated funerary object, sacred object or object of cultural patrimony may present evidence "which, if standing alone (before the introduction of evidence to the contrary), would support a finding that the federal agency or museum did not have the right of possession."[73] In response, the particular museum or federal agency is given an opportunity to prove its right of possession to the item.[74] Finally, a museum or federal agency may retain in its possession any item disputed by multiple (competing) claimants until such time as they may agree to the terms of its disposition or until the dispute is otherwise resolved under either internal NAGPRA procedures or a court of competent jurisdiction.[75] This provision is, of course, particularly significant as long as remains cannot be culturally identified according to the statutory criteria.

Ordinarily, lineal descendants, Indian tribes, and Native Hawaiian groups pursue their rights informally. NAGPRA therefore serves more as a safety net to protect those rights than as a necessary instrument of that protection. Partly to help avoid and resolve disputes involving the exercise of those rights, NAGPRA establishes a review committee within the U.S. Department of the Interior (DOI) to monitor and review implementation of the inventory-and-identification process and of repatriation activities.[76] Concluding sections of the legislation provide for grants of assistance by the federal government to Indian tribes, Native Hawaiian organizations, and museums;[77] require the secretary of the interior to promulgate regulations to carry out the law;[78] and establish the jurisdiction of federal district courts over alleged violations of NAGPRA.[79]

2. Review Committee

NAGPRA provides for a seven-person review committee with nine responsibilities, namely, to

1. appoint one of its members as chair;
2. monitor the inventory-and-identification process;
3. on request of "any affected party," review and make findings related to the identity or cultural affiliation of cultural items or the return of such items;
4. facilitate the resolution of disputes relating to the return of cultural items, "including convening the parties to a dispute if deemed desirable";

---

[72] 25 U.S.C. § 3005(b) (2000).

[73] 25 U.S.C. § 3005(c) (2000). The statutory definition of a "right of possession" is elaborate. Essentially, it requires "possession obtained with the voluntary consent of an individual or group that had authority of alienation." 25 U.S.C. § 3001(13) (2000).

[74] 25 U.S.C. § 3005(c) (2000).

[75] 25 U.S.C. § 3005(e) (2000).

[76] 25 U.S.C. § 3006 (2000).

[77] 25 U.S.C. § 3008 (2000).

[78] 25 U.S.C. § 3011 (2000). The review committee is given the responsibility of consulting with the secretary of the interior in the development of regulations to carry out the law. 25 U.S.C. § 3006(c)(7) (2000). Current regulations appear at 43 C.F.R. § 10 (2005).

[79] 25 U.S.C. § 3013 (2000).

5. compile an inventory of culturally unidentifiable human remains in the possession of federal agencies and museums and develop a process for disposing of them;
6. consult with Indian tribes, Native Hawaiian organizations, and museums on pertinent matters;
7. consult with the Secretary of the Interior in developing regulations to implement the law;
8. perform other functions assigned by the Secretary of the Interior; and
9. make recommendations regarding future care of repatriated items.[80]

The U.S. secretary of the interior appoints the review committee on the basis of a statutory formula: three from nominations by indigenous communities, three from nominations by national museums and scientific organizations, and one by cooptation from a list developed and consented to by the six other appointees.[81] In its first six years, 1992–1998, the review committee, meeting 15 times, focused on organizing itself and its agenda, refining NAGPRA definitions and a process for the disposition of culturally unidentifiable remains, monitoring NAGPRA implementation by museums and agencies, as well as developing and reviewing regulations under the law. The review committee attempted with only marginal success to facilitate the resolution of some five disputes.[82]

In its second six years, 1998–2004, the review committee met 11 times.[83] It again worked to refine NAGPRA definitions and to improve government implementation and enforcement of the law. The review committee's work on culturally unidentifiable remains culminated in developing Draft Principles of Agreement Regarding the Disposition of Culturally Unidentifiable Remains ("Draft Principles"). The review committee approved innovative arrangements for shared re-burial of culturally unidentifiable remains in several national parks and other federal land. The review committee also developed and applied policies to protect sacred tribal information, addressed issues arising out of the circumstances of re-burial of repatriated remains on certain federal land, recommended against the imposition of a number of different conditions on repatriation, and supported plans for repatriation to unrecognized tribes.

During its second six years, the review committee facilitated the resolution

---

[80] 25 U.S.C. § 3006(c) (2000).

[81] 25 U.S.C. § 3006(b) (2000).

[82] See the discussion of the review committee's first six years in Nafziger & Dobkins, *supra* note 57, at 93–96.

[83] *See* Minutes, Native American Graves Protection and Repatriation review committee, March 2, 2006, http://www.cr.nps.gov/nagpra/REVIEW/meetings/MINUTES.htm. The meetings were as follows: Sixteenth Meeting, Dec. 10–12, 1998 (Santa Fe, NM); Seventeenth Meeting, May 3–5, 1999 (Silver Spring, MD); Eighteenth Meeting, Nov. 18–20, 1999 (Salt Lake City, UT); Nineteenth Meeting, Apr. 2–4, 2000 (Juneau, AK); Twentieth Meeting, Dec. 11–13, 2000 (Nashville, TN); Twenty-First Meeting, May 31–June 2, 2000 (Kelseyville, CA); Twenty-Second Meeting, Nov. 17–19, 2001 (Cambridge, MA); Twenty-Third Meeting, May 31–June 2, 2002 (Tulsa, OK); Twenty-Fourth Meeting, Nov. 8–9, 2002 (Seattle, WA); Twenty-Fifth Meeting, May 9–10, 2003 (St. Paul, MN); Twenty-Sixth Meeting, July 19, 2004 (Teleconference).

of at least four disputes. To be sure, it is difficult to establish the exact number of more or less formally resolved disputes because of the problem of distinguishing them from a much larger number of review committee-directed discussions leading to agreements among participants in the committee meetings. Be that as it may, the review committee's success in helping resolve disputes was again mixed. What is striking, however, is the review committee's emphasis during its second six years on the *avoidance* of disputes by developing clearer definitions, policies, and principles, as well as by encouraging parties to discuss problems openly during the review committee's meetings. Going one step further, the review committee supported innovative agreements within the NAGPRA framework between the tribes, on one hand, and the federal government or private interests on the other.

It is apparent that the review committee made substantial progress during its second six years in fulfilling its nine assigned responsibilities. What follows is a summary of the review committee's work in its second six years, based on the minutes of the review committee meetings.

a. Policymaking and Implementation

i. Contamination

Contamination of human remains and cultural material is a serious problem. Any contamination of remains and sacred objects, in particular, threatens their sanctity and readiness for re-burial. Chemical contamination is unfortunately extensive. For example, tests on indigenous cultural material at San Francisco State University revealed that one-quarter of the 28 samples had pesticide and widespread mercury contamination. Cleaning the artifacts with various agents, including microbes that digest toxins, can be effective, but any such cleaning should have the consent of the tribe or group to whom an object is being returned.

Disease is also a problem. It is especially serious in Alaska, and with respect to Alaskan heritage, where diseases lay dormant in cold permafrost soils until remains and objects were excavated from those soils and introduced into the collections of museums and other institutions. Many diseases from the 1800s and early 1900s, such as encephalitis, meningitis, and tuberculosis, thus pose a continuing danger. The use of dust masks, surgical gloves, and other equipment to handle excavated material is therefore essential.

The NAGPRA regulations require museums and federal agencies to inform the recipients of repatriations of any presently known treatment of cultural items with pesticides, preservatives, or other substances that present a potential hazard to the objects or persons handling the objects.[84] The review committee expressed a need to improve testing for pesticide presence and to identify the concomitant risks for individuals and the environment. Museums were also

[84] 43 C.F.R. § 10.10(e) (2005). A failure to inform recipients of presently known treatment constitutes a "failure to comply" subject to civil penalties. 43 C.F.R. § 10.12(b)(viii) (2005).

urged to prepare histories of pesticide use, even if they cannot always determine the extent of contamination, and to train staff to respond to the problem. One option under consideration by the tribes—if, for example, an object cannot be properly cleaned, in a culturally affiliated tribe's view—is to continue the repatriation process without taking physical possession of a contaminated object, thereby allowing museums to continue to curate the object after its nominal repatriation.

ii. Culturally Unidentifiable Human Remains

The review committee has extensively addressed issues related to three categories of culturally unidentifiable human remains: (1) those whose cultural affiliation with a tribe or specific group can be determined, but the tribe or group is not recognized; (2) those that can be identified only with an extinct tribe or group; and (3) those generating insufficient evidence for a museum or federal agency to make any reliable determination of cultural affiliation. Some of the rhetoric in review committee hearings concerning the disposition of culturally unidentifiable remains has been controversial. For example, a representative of the American Association of Physical Anthropologists (AAPA) observed that "[i]n terms of culturally unidentifiable human remains, NAGPRA does not prohibit studies, even invasive studies." A tribal member objected, however, pointing out that "science needs to recognize that these objects are not just objects but sacred objects."

The review committee developed a set of recommendations[85] regarding the disposition of culturally unidentifiable human remains. These were then formulated as the Draft Principles, which set forth several guidelines for disposition. Most importantly, the Draft Principles mandate the participation of Native Americans in the processes of making decisions about the disposition of their ancestors' remains. The Draft Principles also encourage regional consultations, leading to claims and joint recommendations by federal agencies and museums. Essentially, the resulting "recommendations" represent genuine agreements on the appropriate disposition of culturally unidentifiable remains. Out of respect for secret burial and sacred sites, the Draft Principles allow for the exemption from the public record of sensitive information that otherwise would fall under the Freedom of Information Act (FOIA).

Another initiative supported by the review committee has been to encourage shared burial sites to overcome the problem of uncertain cultural affiliations. Several tribes discussed plans for a common cemetery of culturally unidentifiable human remains, such as the proposed Native American Memorial Park at the Fernald Nuclear Waste Management site in Ohio for "commonly shared ancestors."

[85] *See* Recommendations Regarding the Disposition of Culturally Unidentifiable Native American Human Remains, 65 Fed. Reg. 36,462-03 (June 8, 2000) [hereinafter Recommendations].

The review committee's use of the Draft Principles and its models for disposition has been instrumental in repatriation of culturally unidentifiable remains and cultural objects. In one case, for example, the review committee approved of an arrangement worked out between the DOI's National Park Service (NPS), acting on behalf of Carlsbad Caverns and Guadalupe Mountains National Parks, and 12 Indian tribes for repatriation of archaic human remains to their original location for re-burial. While there was no direct line established through archaeology or anthropology leading from the remains to any of the 12 tribes in the region, the review committee relied on oral history to confirm the arrangement, promoting it as a good model for repatriation of culturally unidentified remains. The review committee emphasized the importance of oral tradition and the need for protective measures after re-burial.

Similarly, Zion National Park and seven Indian tribes gained the review committee's support for the park's proposal to repatriate ten sets of culturally unidentifiable human remains to the tribes. The preponderance of evidence did not confirm a cultural affiliation with any single present-day tribe, band, or clan, but tribal elders directed that it was the tribes' joint responsibility to cooperate in taking care of the remains that needed to be returned, whenever possible, to their original locations. The review committee enthusiastically supported the proposal for shared re-burial according to the Draft Principles' cooperative models for the disposition of culturally unidentifiable human remains.

The encouragement of cooperative management agreements is a particularly significant example of the review committee's role in addressing the problem of culturally unidentifiable remains. Repatriation of remains on this basis presupposes satisfaction of the requirement of cultural affiliation, but broadens terms such as "tribal land" and "closest cultural affiliation" on an inter-tribal or inter-organizational basis.

iii. Protection of Information

The Cochiti Pueblo maintains a ceremonial way of life with a theocratic government. In 1996, the government contemplated repatriation of cultural material under NAGPRA from various sources. However, even after a religious leader had identified items of importance to the Pueblo, they could not actually seek repatriation because NAGPRA regulations require claimants to describe the purpose of the material and circumstances of its use. The Pueblo explained that they would rather walk away from these sacred items than reveal such information. Some of the objects, which were indisputably sacred, could be repatriated without further information from the Pueblo, whereas some of the objects were deemed to be utilitarian and therefore could not be repatriated without rebuttal by information that the Pueblo were unwilling to provide. The review committee recommended repatriation of all of the material to the tribes in this instance but acknowledged its continuing role in refining the definition of "sacred" in NAGPRA.

The NPS has attempted to respect tribal claims of restricted information while fulfilling the requirements of the U.S. Constitution to treat everyone equally by conducting business openly and having a sound basis on record for any decisions. As noted earlier, the FOIA, by insisting that federal agencies operate in the open, calls into question any exceptions to NAGPRA that would relax normal requirements for information from tribes and groups in the interest of confidentiality. In response, the review committee has been instrumental in advocating exemptions from FOIA. For example, under the Draft Principles regarding culturally unidentifiable remains, tribes and groups may refuse to disclose the location of certain sacred burial sites. Congress itself has approved of exemptions in some cases. Amendments to the NHPA in 1992 authorized a federal agency to withhold information when its release could place a historic, sacred, or archaeological site at risk. Also, the National Parks Management Omnibus Act of 1998[86] gave authority to withhold information on the nature and location of objects of cultural patrimony in National Park system units.

iv. Protection of Burial Sites

The review committee has been effective in helping protect burial sites even in the absence of any claim under NAGPRA. In one significant case, the Dineh Nation claimed that burial sites were destroyed by the Peabody Western Coal Company in its mining operations. It operates under the Surface Mining Control and Reclamation Act of 1977,[87] which prohibits coal mining close to cemeteries. The company's permit was therefore revoked, but that decision was overturned on appeal. The review committee expressed its concern about the appellate decision to the secretary of the interior and the assistant secretary for Indian affairs, which received assurances from the company that it would attempt to avoid interfering with any known cultural areas or burial sites, although there appeared to be no basis for concluding that the company had violated NAGPRA or ARPA.

v. Conditions of Repatriation

NAGPRA does not prescribe any specific disposition of remains and objects after repatriation. Moreover, the DOI does not have a department-wide policy concerning re-burial on federal lands. Thus, for example, the NPS permits re-burial if cultural items were originally removed from land within park boundaries, but the Bureau of Land Management (BLM) prohibits re-burial on their lands because of security concerns regarding their large land base. In one hearing of the review committee, the confederated Salish and Kootenai tribes criticized the BLM policy for denying them fundamental rights of re-burial in territory formerly under tribal control. The review committee requested the secretary of the interior to develop uniform policies that would allow re-burial on all federal and federally managed lands.

In another petition, the Ho-Chunk Nation complained that the Field Museum in Chicago wanted to repatriate a war bundle but only on the condition that if it was ever alienated from the nation, the museum could reclaim it.

[86] 16 U.S.C. §§ 5901–6011 (2000).
[87] 30 U.S.C. §§ 1201–1328 (2000).

The review committee concluded that repatriation should occur free of that condition.

vi. Unrecognized Tribes

Although NAGPRA favors federally recognized tribes, museums and federal agencies are not precluded from working with non-federally recognized groups, and some requests involving non-federally recognized groups have come before the review committee. Moreover, unrecognized tribes may enlist the cooperation of federally recognized tribes in pursuing their repatriation claims. For example, repatriation of human remains to a non-federally recognized group in Alaska, the Auk Kwaan, has been effected through the Central Council of the Tlingit and Haida Indian Tribes.

When a non-federally recognized group makes a request, federally recognized tribes in the area must provide written evidence of notification and a record of consultation. One problem, however, is that 19 of the 50 states do not have any federally recognized tribes although some of them have substantial Indian populations. Non-federally recognized tribes in these states cannot readily turn to recognized tribes for assistance and are, therefore, handicapped in bringing claims before the review committee.

However, the review committee has supported voluntary repatriation of remains and cultural objects to non-federally recognized tribes. For example, the Peabody Museum of Archaeology wished to repatriate remains and associated funerary objects that were culturally affiliated with the non-federally recognized Abenaki group. The review committee supported this repatriation, upon receiving letters of support from all of the federally recognized tribes that were potentially interested parties. The same museum also sought to repatriate culturally unidentifiable human remains it possessed to a non-federally recognized Indian group, the Nipmuc Nation. The review committee also endorsed that repatriation.

b. Definitions

i. "Affected Party"

Neither NAGPRA nor its regulations define an "affected party" that is entitled to assert claims under the law. The review committee distinguishes between the broad, judicially created category of an "interested party" and the narrower statutory category of an "affected party" that is entitled to receive a remedy under NAGPRA. An agent may represent an affected party or parties but is itself not considered to be an affected party. A determination by the DOI that a party is not "affected" may be appealed and, if the appeal is successful, the dispute may then come before the review committee for its consideration.

ii. "Indigenous"

An acceptable definition of the term "indigenous" remains elusive despite its use in treaties, statutes, and judicial authority. A lawyer turns to the usual definitional sources in vain. For example, the term does not appear among some 43,000 definitions in *Black's Law Dictionary*. The term does appear, however, in NAGPRA's definition of "Native American" as "of, or relating to, a tribe, people, or culture that is *indigenous* to the United States." A recurring context in which the term has required definition has involved disputes between two tribes, a tribe and a band or other Native American group, or two Native Hawaiian organizations. The latter is a particularly common occurrence for lack of federal recognition of Native Hawaiian organizations, except for NAGPRA's specific designation of the Hui Malama I Na Kupuna O Hawaii Nei and the Office of Hawaiian Affairs. The review committee normally has interpreted the term "indigenous" to describe first arrival in a particular territory to the extent that it is known and relevant.

iii. "Sacred"

As we have seen, the definition of "sacred" may affect both the exigency of repatriation and the extent to which a claimant may be excused from providing specific information about the purpose of a particular object and the circumstances of its use. The review committee, which encourages reliance on tribal or Native Hawaiian designations of an object as sacred or not, nevertheless recognizes its role in further defining the term.

c. Dispute Resolution

i. Hopi Tribe and the Chaco Culture National Historic Park

NAGPRA legislation requires federal agencies and museums to determine cultural affiliation based upon multiple lines of evidence of shared group identity. Chaco Culture National Historic Park (NHP) determined that the Navajo Tribe was most closely affiliated with human remains that had been identified with the Chaco Canyon area. The determination was based on the standard of a preponderance of evidence. The problem was that the Hopi Tribe also claimed exclusive cultural affiliation. Unfortunately, the Chaco Culture NHP did not consult each tribe individually, but only collectively on this crucial issue—a technique of investigation that deeply offended the Hopis. In response, the review committee concluded that the overall process by which the Chaco Culture NHP made determinations of cultural affiliations was flawed. The review committee also agreed with the Hopi that an objective determination of cultural affiliation should be re-evaluated, on a site-by-site basis for each controverted object, based on consultation with each tribe individually. Finally, the review committee undertook to develop guidelines for weighing evidence related to competing claims of this sort so as to make the process more predictable and equitable.

The DOI, on behalf of the Chaco Culture NHP, rejected the review committee's recommendation, however. This was the first time that a party to a NAGPRA dispute had declined to accept the review committee's findings. There the matter ended, rather unsatisfactorily, because the review committee's work is over when it has heard a dispute and issued its recommendation, regardless of whether its recommendation is followed or not.

ii. The Spirit Cave Dispute: Fallon Paiute Shoshone Tribe and the DOI, BLM, and Nevada State Office

Human remains had been unearthed in 1940 by two amateur archaeologists working for the Nevada State Park Commission, well within the territory of the Paiute-Shoshone Tribe. After the tribe had submitted eight reports to prove their cultural affiliation with the remains, the Nevada-based BLM director announced his preliminary determination that the remains were not culturally affiliated with any existing Native American Indian tribe, although they were deemed to be Native American. Despite the Nevada BLM's preliminary determination, the review committee recommended repatriation of the remains to the tribe. It found that the BLM had failed to consult with the tribe and had defined shared group identity and cultural affiliation too narrowly.

iii. Royal Hawaiian Academy of Traditional Arts and Bishop Museum

The Royal Hawaiian Academy of Traditional Arts ("the Academy") requested the review committee's assistance in its dispute with the Bishop Museum regarding the manner in which the museum had transferred cultural items to Native Hawaiians. The museum possessed 83 items that originally had been removed from the Kawaihae Caves on the island of Hawaii in 1905. It loaned the items to Hui Malama I Na Kupuna O Hawaii Nei, a Native Hawaiian organization that is specifically designated by NAGPRA as such. The organization promptly sealed the items in one of the Kawaihae Caves, in compliance, they claimed, with their ancestors' wishes. The Bishop Museum therefore could not reclaim possession of the items. It then wrote the DOI that it had completed the NAGPRA requirements for repatriation. The Academy, however, disputed that assurance because the Bishop Museum did not have control or possession of the 83 items when it purported to repatriate them. Thus, neither the Academy nor some 12 other claimant organizations ever received effective notice of intended repatriation and were therefore denied an opportunity to assert their claims under NAGPRA to any of the sealed items.

The review committee concluded that the Bishop Museum had made an error when it loaned the artifacts; its repatriation process had been flawed and therefore remained incomplete. Some committee members argued that, under NAGPRA, ownership of a cultural object is transferred once a notice of a transfer, apparently including a loan, is published in the *Federal Register* and no objection is made during the 30-day waiting period. But NAGPRA's regulations make it clear that a loan does not in itself transfer ownership. (Later, the Academy and Na Lei Alii Kawananakoa won a civil action in federal court against Hui Malama I Na Kupuna O Hawaii Nei. The judge ordered the defendant to unseal the items in the caves and return them to the Bishop Museum for later disposition in accordance with NAGPRA. When the defendant's executive director refused to comply with the order, he was cited for contempt of court and jailed.[88])

---

[88] *See* USA TODAY, Dec. 30, 2005, at 4A.

iv. *Western Apache Working Group and Denver Art Museum*

Several cultural objects claimed by the Western Apaches are used for ceremonies and are deemed to be spirit-filled. The Denver Art Museum asked for information to prove that the claimed objects were needed for present-day ceremonies. The Apache objected on the basis that such information was secret. The review committee recommended that the museum consider the oral testimony that had been presented, undertake further research on the objects, re-evaluate its preliminary determinations against unconditional repatriation, and report back to the committee.

d. Implementation and Enforcement

The DOI is charged with implementation and enforcement of NAGPRA. Within the DOI, the main areas of concern have involved the completion of inventories and summaries by museums and possible civil penalties against those that fail to complete them, allocation of NAGPRA-based grants to tribes (some of whom had not yet received funding that had been promised to them), compliance by federal agencies with NAGPRA, and possible conflicts of interest in vesting authority in the NPS to administer NAGPRA. For example, several national parks have held collections of human remains and cultural objects subject to repatriation under NAGPRA, and the NPS acts on behalf of parks that are sometimes parties to disputes falling within NAGPRA jurisdiction. The same agency is therefore quite awkwardly both a subject of the law and an enforcer of it. Indeed, the designated federal officer responsible for administering NAGPRA is the NPS's chief of archaeology. Although the review committee supported the idea of moving the NAGPRA program into a central unit of the DOI, it remains within the NPS.

More generally, compliance by federal agencies with NAGPRA has been an ongoing problem requiring vigilant oversight. Some federal land managers still seemed to be years away from completing the summaries and inventories required by the legislation (as of the time of pertinent review committee meetings), while non-federal museums had to meet a November 1995 deadline for inventory completion. Therefore, federal agencies may not always be held to the same standard of accountability as museums, and civil penalties for violations of NAGPRA apply only to museums. Unfortunately, the review committee can only encourage or urge federal agencies to undertake inventories, summaries, and other reports. It has no enforcement powers of its own.

A lack of financial resources has sometimes generated tensions between tribes or groups, on one hand, and the DOI on the other. Auk Kwaan, Tlingit, and Haida groups complained that promises by the U.S. Forest Service made during consultation meetings had been forgotten. Also, the Auk Kwaan group was denied funding for construction of a burial box and a memorial dinner after re-burial, both of which are traditional practices.

3. Federal Court Litigation

NAGPRA provides that U.S. district courts have jurisdiction over "any action brought by any person alleging a violation of this Act and shall have [enforcement authority]."[89] In addition, state courts have competence, in interpreting and applying state law, to address NAGPRA-related issues. During NAGPRA's first eight years, 1990–1998, there were six published opinions by federal courts involving NAGPRA, only four of which addressed substantial issues.[90] No significant state court opinions were reported. During NAGPRA's second six years, 1998–2004, 11 federal court opinions and one state court opinion were published, as follows:

a. Standing Issues

i. Crow Creek Sioux Tribe v. Brownlee[91]

A tribe lacked standing to seek an injunction against a land transfer from the U.S. Army Corps of Engineers to the state of South Dakota. Although the tribe alleged that proposed flooding would injure the tribe by inundating an important indigenous heritage site, the court ruled that NAGPRA, NHPA, and ARPA would explicitly apply to safeguard the heritage and that any claim of diminished federal enforcement was purely speculative.

ii. Bear Lodge Multiple Use Association v. Babbitt[92]

Climbers challenged an essentially voluntary ban on climbing Devil's Tower in the national monument of that name in Wyoming at a time when a tribe was to perform religious activities. The court denied the climbers' standing for failure to show requisite injury to them in responding to the requested ban.

iii. Jacobs v. Pataki[93]

In a skimpy, if not cryptic, opinion, the court ruled that the plaintiff lacked standing to bring a NAGPRA-related claim arising out of the alleged desecration of burial sites in New York.

b. The Federal or Tribal Land Requirement

i. Western Mohegan Tribe and Nation v. New York[94]

Alleging NAGPRA and other statutory and constitutional claims, the plaintiffs sought to enjoin construction of a state park, including an access roadway and bridge, and to obtain a court order for a new archaeological survey of designated land in New York. The court dismissed the NAGPRA claim, as well as an NHPA claim, because no Native American artifacts had yet been found, and the land at issue was neither tribal nor federal even though the state had obtained a construction permit from the U.S. Army Corps of Engineers.

---

89 25 U.S.C. § 3013 (2000).

90 *See* Nafziger & Dobkins, *supra* note 57, at 96–98.

91 331 F.3d 912 (D.C. Cir. 2003).

92 175 F.3d 814 (10th Cir. 1999).

93 68 F. App'x 222 (2d Cir. 2003).

94 100 F. Supp. 2d 122 (N.D.N.Y. 2000), *aff'd in part, vacated and rem'd in part on other grounds*, 246 F.3d 230 (2d Cir. 2001).

ii. Castro Romero v. Becken[95]

The plaintiff, claiming to be the lineal descendent of a Lipan Apache chief, brought a NAGPRA claim, seeking damages for injury arising out of the construction of a golf course on the alleged burial grounds of the Lipan Apache. The court dismissed the claim, ruling that the alleged remains were not on federal or tribal land and that NAGPRA does not allow a money judgment to individuals.

c. Protection of Burial Grounds

i. State of Tennessee ex rel. Commissioner of Transportation v. Medicine Bird Black Bear White Eagle[96]

The Tennessee Transportation Department acquired land to improve a highway. An archaeological examination found two unmarked ancient graves. The department petitioned to relocate the graves. The appellate court ruled that neither the state's Commission of Indian Affairs, its executive director, nor 15 individual Native Americans had standing as "interested persons" to intervene or participate in the action. The commission had no standing because it had no rights or interests of its own entitled to constitutional protection. It also had not alleged that any of its proprietary interests as a state agency would be jeopardized. The Native Americans did not have veto power over disinterment, nor could they be considered to be interested persons without proof of blood relationships with the buried persons or interest in the property.

Also, the court ruled that Tennessee's statutes governing the termination of burial grounds are neutral and uniformly applicable, only incidentally burdening the Native American's religious practices and rights of conscience. These statutes are a reasonable means to promote a legitimate public interest. The opinion contains an extensive and exceptionally interesting discussion of human burial law through history.

ii. Yankton Sioux Tribe v. U.S. Army Corps of Engineers[97]

The court determined that there was sufficient tribal and public interest in protecting remains under NAGPRA to enjoin the U.S. Army Corps of Engineers from continuing construction activities that threatened Native American remains. The court eventually allowed limited construction under certain conditions, upon the recommendation of archaeologists.

iii. San Carlos Apache Tribe v. United States[98]

A tribe sought to enjoin the drawdown of water on its reservation, alleging foreseeable disturbance of ancient graves in violation of NAGPRA. The court ruled that NAGPRA is not prospective and is triggered only upon an inadvertent

---

[95] 256 F.3d 349 (5th Cir. 2001).

[96] 63 S.W.3d 734 (Tenn. Ct. App. 2001).

[97] 258 F. Supp. 2d 1027 (D.S.D. 2003), 209 F. Supp. 2d 1008 (D.S.D. 2002), 194 F. Supp. 2d 977 (D.S.D. 2002) (three phases of the same litigation).

[98] 272 F. Supp. 860 (D. Ariz. 2003).

discovery. Here, unlike the *Yankton* case just discussed, the alleged injury was only speculative.

d. Trafficking

i. United States v. Tidwell[99]

A dealer in Native American art was convicted of conspiracy and illegal trafficking in Native American cultural material and archaeological resources, as well as theft of tribal property. On appeal, the court held that NAGPRA is not unconstitutionally vague—particularly as to the terms "inalienability" of an item and its "ongoing historical, traditional, or cultural importance" to a Native American group—and that the dealer had the background knowledge and burden of due diligence, having been convicted once already under NAGPRA, to avoid the crimes for which he was charged.

ii. United States v. Kramer[100]

In an appeal of a conviction, the court confirmed that NAGPRA criminalizes trafficking by individual traders in Native American remains and cultural items.

e. Temporal Scope of NAGPRA

i. Kickapoo Traditional Tribe v. Chacon[101]

NAGPRA's reference to "human remains" did not contemplate a recently buried corpse that state authorities wished to exhume to determine the cause of death for an inquest. NAGPRA's association with cultural items and ARPA's limitation to archaeological resources helped clarify the temporal scope of the term "human remains" in light of applicable criminal laws.

ii. Bonnichsen v. United States[102]

By far the most significant litigation under NAGPRA, providing definitive interpretations of its terms, was *Bonnichsen v. United States.* The case began with an inadvertent discovery of unusually complete skeletal remains that consist of some 350 bones and bone fragments of what came to be known as "Kennewick Man" or "The Ancient One" (see summary of the facts in the Appendix to this chapter). The remains were preliminarily determined to be some 8,340–9,200 years old. Before *Bonnichsen,* it had been thought that NAGPRA-based litigation

---

[99] 191 F.3d 976 (9th Cir. 1999).

[100] 168 F.3d 1196 (10th Cir. 1999).

[101] 46 F. Supp. 2d 644 (W.D. Tex. 1999).

[102] 367 F.3d 864 (9th Cir. 2004). The federal appeals court specifically upheld the last of three principal district court decisions and generally accepted the findings and conclusions of all the decisions. The published opinions of the district court include *Bonnichsen v. United States,* 969 F. Supp. 614 (D. Or. 1997) (denying the defendants' motion to dismiss based on failure to state a claim and ripeness grounds); Bonnichsen v. United States, 969 F. Supp. 628 (D. Or. 1997) (denying the defendants' motion for summary judgment and vacating the government's decision on disposition of the Kennewick Man's remains); Bonnichsen v. United States, 217 F. Supp. 2d 1116 (D. Or. 2002) (again vacating the government's decision on disposition of the remains and permitting scientific examination of them).

would mostly involve repatriation issues. Instead, *Bonnichsen* involved the issue of properly disposing of ancient remains that had been found on a shoreline of the Columbia River under the supervision of the U.S. Army Corps of Engineers. Leaving aside for now the complicated procedural steps in the litigation itself as well as general questions about the questionable conduct of the U.S. Army Corps of Engineers and the DOI, the salient conclusions of both the trial and appellate courts were these:

1. Where lineal descendants of human remains excavated or discovered on federal or tribal lands cannot be ascertained, NAGPRA mandates a two-part analysis. First, are the remains "Native American"? If not, then NAGPRA does not apply. If the remains are deemed to be Native American, however, a second question is: Which tribe or organization has the closest relationship with the remains (and cultural objects, as well), based on a complex formula that takes account of the statutory category of the material and the existence of territorial and cultural relationships with it?[103]
2. NAGPRA's definition of "Native American"—"of, or relating to, a tribe, people, or culture *that is* indigenous to the United States"[104]—is expressed in the present tense. The *Bonnichsen* opinions therefore confirmed that the tribes, peoples, or cultures with which Native American remains must bear the requisite relationship are those that are *presently existing*. In drafting the NAGPRA regulations, however, the DOI had eliminated the critical words "that is," thereby obscuring the intended limitation to existing tribes.[105] The courts concluded that the DOI had crafted an interpretation of the law that lay outside the bounds of normal judicial deference to administrative regulatory authority under the *Chevron* doctrine.[106] The courts also rejected the DOI's argument at trial that the pivotal phrase "that is" could be used interchangeably with "that was." DOI had therefore acted arbitrarily and capriciously. On the other hand, in treating the definitional issue in terms of burden of proof, the courts carefully refrained from passing any judgment of their own on whether Kennewick Man/The Ancient One was, indeed, Native American.
3. Regarding the appropriate disposition of newly discovered human remains, NAGPRA was enacted with two main goals: to respect the burial traditions of modern-day American Indians and to protect the dignity of the human body after death. NAGPRA was intended

[103] 25 U.S.C. § 3002(a) (2000).

[104] 25 U.S.C. § 3001(9) (2000) (emphasis added).

[105] 43 CFR § 10.2(d) (2007). As of the end of 2008, the regulation still did not include the critical words "that is," even though the definitional section of the regulations (43 C.F.R. § 10.2) was revised in 2005 and 2006. 71 Fed. Reg. 16501 (Apr. 3, 2006); 70 Fed. Reg. 57179 (Sept. 30, 2005).

[106] Chevron U.S.A. v. Natural Res. Def. Council, 467 U.S. 837 (1984) (establishing that if a governmental agency is charged with a statute's implementation, courts must accept the agency's *reasonable* interpretation of the statute).

to benefit modern American Indians by sparing them the indignity and resentment that would be aroused by the display of *their ancestors'* remains.[107]

4. Congress did not intend for NAGPRA to apply where geography alone established a relationship between a tribe and particular remains. There is some evidence that Kennewick Man/The Ancient One was deliberately deposited where it was found, but, even if that could be established, it would still be unclear when and under what circumstances the remains were put there. Often, too, the current location of remains is fortuitous, resulting, for example, from erosion, natural transport downstream, glacial deposit, or human conveyance. Moreover, tribes have been forcibly relocated and have otherwise migrated over the years. More broadly, Congress clearly did not intend that the mere finding of "any remains in the United States in and of itself would render these remains 'Native American.'"[108]
5. In determining whether the requested identification or relationship of Kennewick Man/The Ancient One with an existing tribe, people, or culture existed, the court borrowed from NAGPRA's prescribed sources for analysis of "cultural affiliation." Cultural affiliation is to be determined "by a preponderance of evidence based upon geographical, kinship, biological, archaeological, anthropological, linguistic, folkloric, oral traditional, historical, or other relevant information and expert opinion."[109] Aboriginal occupation of tribal territory is insufficient by itself to establish the requisite link between ancient remains and a presently existing tribe. More broadly, in applying the statutory matrix of information sources, the record disclosed *no* cognizable link between Kennewick Man/The Ancient One and modern Columbia Plateau Indians as a whole.
6. The third main opinion of the district court, in particular, very carefully analyzed the oral histories upon which the federal government relied in its argument to establish the requisite relationship between the remains and an existing tribe.[110] The appellate court opinion, although less extensive on the issue than the dis-

[107] Bonnichsen v. United States, 367 F.3d 864, 876 (9th Cir. 2004) (emphasis added).

[108] *Id.* at 878 n.17. The court emphasized as follows: "At oral argument, the government urged that its interpretation of remains as Native American when found within the United States would apply even to remains as old as 100,000 or 150,000 years, close to the dawn of *homo sapiens.* Indeed, the government at oral argument even said that if remains of a mythical first man and woman, an 'Adam and Eve,' were found in the United States, those remains would be "Native American" under the government's interpretation of NAGPRA. Thus, the government's unrestricted interpretation based solely on geography, calling any ancient remains found in the United States 'Native American' if they predate the arrival of Europeans, has no principle of limitation beyond geography. This does not appear to us to be what Congress had in mind. Nor does the legislative history support NAGPRA coverage of bones of such great antiquity."

[109] 25 U.S.C. § 3005(a)(4) (2000).

[110] Bonnichsen v. United States, 217 F. Supp. 2d 1116, 1151–55 (D. Or. 2002).

trict court opinion it upheld, also discussed oral histories that presented evidence of ancient floods, volcanic eruptions, and the like. The court concluded, however, that

> [t]he Secretary's only evidence, perhaps, of a possible cultural relationship between Kennewick Man and modern-day American Indians comes in the form of oral histories. . . . [E]vidence in the record demonstrates that oral histories change relatively quickly, that oral histories may be based on later observation of geological features and deduction (rather than on the first teller's witnessing ancient events), and that these oral histories might be from a culture or group other than the one to which Kennewick Man belonged. . . . [They] are just not specific enough or reliable enough or relevant enough to show a significant relationship of the Tribal Claimants with Kennewick Man. . . . As the district court observed, 8340 to 9200 years between the life of Kennewick Man and the present is too long a time to bridge merely with evidence of oral traditions.[111]

While emphasizing the limitations of oral history, the court was careful not to apply strict rules of evidence to the history and accepted the probity of the histories that were offered as evidence of cultural affiliation.

7. Both trial and appellate courts were keenly aware of the substantial burden of proving the requisite tribal affiliation with remains so as to define them as "Native American" and thereby bring them under NAGPRA. The courts readily acknowledged the inevitability of gaps in continuity.[112] Noting that the empirical record did not adequately establish *any* cultural continuities dating back earlier than 5,000 B.C., however, the courts relied on the secretary of interior's own acknowledgment of major discontinuities. Hence, the resulting record was barren of any link between cultural groups existing 8,500–9,500 years ago that might have included Kennewick Man/The Ancient One and the later Columbia Plateau Culture

[111] Bonnichsen v. United States, 367 F.3d 864, 881 (9th Cir. 2004).

[112] The legislative history succinctly articulates a common-sense analysis of cultural affiliation that was adopted by the court, as follows:

> [C]laimants do not have to establish "cultural affiliation" with scientific certainty. . . . Where human remains and funerary objects are concerned, the committee is aware that it may be extremely difficult, unfair or even impossible in many instances for claimants to show an absolute continuity from present day Indian tribes to older, prehistoric remains without some reasonable gaps in the historic or prehistoric record. In such instances, a finding of cultural affiliation should be based upon an overall evaluation of the totality of the circumstances and evidence pertaining to the connection between the claimant and the material being claimed and should not be precluded solely because of gaps in the record.

S. Rep. No. 101-473, at 4, 8–9 (1990).

> with which modern tribes can certainly establish requisite relationships. The secretary of the interior had himself acknowledged a lack of evidence regarding burial practices during the earlier period that would clearly indicate the appropriate disposition of the ancient remains.[113]

D. THE LEGITIMACY AND LEGACY OF *BONNICHSEN*

1. Issues of Legitimacy

As we have seen, the three detailed opinions of the district court and the broader appellate court opinion in the *Bonnichsen* case provide substantial guidance for interpreting several important provisions of NAGPRA. Unfortunately, the *Bonnichsen* decision sparked latent tensions between the Native American and scientific communities that were too often, indeed depressingly, expressed in the grandiose vocabulary of *tradition* versus *science*. The decision's legality did not ensure its legitimacy.

In commenting on *Bonnichsen*, a Choctaw archaeologist's observations are insightful. Emphasizing the "unspoken intersection of the knowledge that is produced by archaeologists and the needs of Native Americans to maintain and continue our own histories,"[114] she lamented the "polarized view of the case."[115] "The resulting caricature," she wrote,

> returns the discourse surrounding repatriation to a previous level in which arguments were made over the question, "who owns the past?" While this may be a rhetorically satisfying problem to wrestle with, it does not capture the true nature of how archaeology can engage with Native people in the process of understanding ancient lives. It presumes that the past exists as a form of property. Under this simplistic construction, human remains can exist as property and can be owned by one group or another.[116]

What went wrong?

a. The Posture of the Dispute Resolution

NAGPRA does not offer a formula for determining whether particular remains are "Native American" beyond the simple definition of that term. To be sure, the review committee had begun to address the issue of culturally unidentifiable remains by the time Kennewick Man/The Ancient One was discovered. But its work on the issue was still preliminary. Moreover, the Draft Principles[117] on culturally unidentifiable remains that eventually resulted from the review committee's work limit the prescribed process of disposition to

---

[113] Bonnichsen v. United States, 367 F.3d 864, 881 (9th Cir. 2004).

[114] Dorothy Lippert, *Remembering Humanity: How to Include Human Values in a Scientific Endeavor*, 12 INT'L J. CULTURAL PROP. 275, 276 (2005).

[115] *Id.* at 275.

[116] *Id.*

[117] *See* Recommendations, *supra* note 85.

"Native American" remains, offering no further definition of the term.

Significantly, when the remains were discovered, the Vermillion Accord,[118] providing for tribal and scientific cooperation, was in effect. So was NAGPRA's fundamental scheme for protecting the human rights of deceased Native Americans and, in that regard, of any Native American tribe or group with whom such persons were related. It should be remembered that NAGPRA was the product of joint drafting and agreement among leaders of tribal, scientific, and museum communities. In other words, the stage was well set for collaboration among Native Americans, museums, and the federal government in making decisions about the disposition of remains and cultural objects. Although NAGPRA is human rights legislation that does not invite interest-balancing, it was intended to operate within a collaborative framework defined by such contemporary instruments as the Vermillion Accord.

Against this background, the process of dispute resolution that followed the discovery of Kennewick Man/The Ancient One was, indeed, disappointing. The process almost immediately assumed a posture of confrontation between scientists and regional tribes, not because of any intrinsic defects in NAGPRA, but because the federal government too quickly and carelessly took a position that was questionable under NAGPRA and its premise in well-defined human rights. The federal government's position also ignored the accommodation of interests that the non-binding Vermillion Accord had prescribed.

b. *The Posture of the Scientists*

The scientists who brought the claim against the federal government in *Bonnichsen* reasonably complained of both procedural irregularities by the U.S. Army Corps of Engineers and the DOI, as well as the arbitrary and capricious nature of the actions by the two agencies. More fundamentally, however, they claimed a questionable right, unfettered by NAGPRA, to scientific examination of the remains prior to their re-burial or whatever other disposition of them would be deemed appropriate. To be sure, the scientists' posture in the case relied on a professional ethos of advancing knowledge not simply for its own sake but, as summarized earlier,[119] for the benefit of humankind.

The posture of the scientists in *Bonnichsen* raises another interesting question. If particular remains are not deemed to be "Native American," should they be allowed to remain in a sort of institutional ossuary not simply for lack of alternatives but, deliberately, in order to await the development of new scientific techniques?[120] NAGPRA, of course, does not speak to that issue.

---

[118] *See* Vermillion Accord on Human Remains, *supra* note 48.

[119] *See supra* text at note 38.

[120] Cohan, *supra* note 21, at 362.

It has been said that [a]rchaeologists, for the most part, are not extremists, and merely wish to have objects properly excavated, studied initially in situ, and preserved at least for a reasonable period of time, perhaps decades, so that they and their colleagues can return with new questions and new techniques and thereby gain more knowledge of past cultures from these materials.

c. The Posture of the Federal Government

The coordinated roles of the U.S. Army Corps of Engineers and the DOI dominated the process for deciding what to do with the remains and how to resolve any related disputes that might arise. Neither federal agency seems to have specifically acknowledged either the human rights of Kennewick Man/The Ancient One himself or the normative significance of the Vermillion Accord in avoiding unnecessary confrontation between tribal and scientific communities. Several developments called into question the military's reliability as a dispassionate manager of the land on which the skeletal remains had been found:[121] the military's seizure of the remains; its custodial claim to them; its negligent custody of the remains, resulting, for example, in a tribal acquisition and secret re-burial of a small quantity of bones; its unannounced burial of the site of discovery; and its concomitant violations of the NHPA. Similarly, the elimination by the DOI of key language in NAGPRA's definition of "Native American"[122] was ill advised, as were DOI's questionable pre-trial practices. These involved secret notifications to the defendants of developments in the case, secret communications and meetings with them, and a refusal to allow plaintiffs to view expert reports and other materials in a timely manner.[123] These tactics raised questions about DOI's impartiality in carrying out its responsibilities under NAGPRA.

d. The Posture of the Regional Tribes

Perhaps the federal government's apparent lack of evenhandedness is attributable to the paternal role that both Indian law and NAGPRA assign to it. An unfortunate consequence of this role, however, was the inability of the regional tribes, as truly interested parties, to present their own evidence during the *Bonnichsen* trial or to participate in establishing post-trial standards for scientific examination of the remains. Unfortunately, by the time of the trial, their interests had been compromised by the federal government's handling of their claim to the remains (not to mention by its handling of the remains themselves, an issue that was not determinative in the judicial proceedings, however). The district court, to its credit, permitted the tribes to intervene in order to appeal its interpretation of NAGPRA. On appeal, therefore, the tribes joined the federal government as appellants, but it was almost too late. The Army Corps of Engineers and DOI had acted and defended their actions, the district court had issued its ruling, the appellate court was soon to affirm the lower court, and the tribe decided not to petition the Supreme Court for protective relief.[124] The claimants of the remains—four Indian tribes and an

---

[121] Bonnichsen v. United States, 367 F.3d 864, 871 n.10 (9th Cir. 2004).

[122] *Id.* at 877.

[123] Bonnichsen v. United States, 217 F. Supp. 2d 1116, 1133 (D. Or. 2002).

[124] *See* Bonnichsen v. United States, 2004 WL 2901287 (D. Or.):

In an Order dated October 21, 2002, this court granted the Tribes' motion to intervene for the purposes of appealing the court's interpretations of [NAGPRA]. After the Ninth Circuit affirmed the decision from which the Tribes appealed, plaintiffs sought an Order formally dismissing the intervenors, and clarifying their obligation to serve materials filed in this matter only on the United States. In an Order dated

Indian band—were given limited standing individually but failed in their joint claim of repatriation under NAGPRA. Understandably, the secondary or even phantom posture assigned to the Indian coalition fueled their frustration with the *Bonnichsen* decision and their unwillingness to accord legitimacy to it.

2. The Legacy

The legacy of *Bonnichsen* may seem unsettling. Although the district and appellate courts opinions are certainly compelling—indeed, models of statutory interpretation—their broader implications beyond NAGPRA raise fundamental questions about human origins and migration. After all, Kennewick Man/The Ancient One is not alone. So far, some 15 skeletons have been found in North America that are more than 8,000 years old. Their divergent cranial and other characteristics suggest the probable complexity of human migration to North America.[125] Certainly the traditional explanation of early migration as exclusively a sort of Asian horde pouring over a land bridge into North America is problematic.[126] Even more problematic, under DNA analysis, is the theory of a spontaneous creation of the first human beings on the continent.[127] To the extent that *Bonnichsen* denied legal effect to such a theory of creationism as a religious tenet, it is consistent with a long line of constitutional interpretation against the governmental establishment of religion in the United States.

Native Americans quite rightly argue that culture, not biology, should determine the status of remains, as NAGPRA makes abundantly clear.[128] But tribal claims to culturally unidentifiable remains must necessarily rely on biological ancestry, even as a matter of oral history.[129] Indeed, the oral history about their ancient origins encapsulates a genetic continuity. Through history, however, ethnic shifting and shopping may have been more the rule than the exception in North America. Put more bluntly, there may simply be "no well-attested, or long-enduring, or pure, or unchanged social or cultural entities."[130] Ethnicity is, indeed, "a tricky thing because it is commonly understood as something fixed and essential rather than what it more likely is: an unarticulated negotiation

August 17, 2004, this court denied the motion to dismiss the intervenors as moot on the grounds [of] the Ninth Circuit's decision.

[125] *See* Eli Sanders, *Custody of Remains is Settled*, INT'L HERALD TRIB., July 22, 2004, at 10.

[126] *See, e.g.*, Evan Hadingham, *America's First Immigrants*, SMITHSONIAN, Nov. 2004, at 90. *See generally* CHARLES C. MANN, 1491: NEW REVELATIONS OF THE AMERICAS BEFORE COLUMBUS (2005).

[127] The Confederated Tribes of the Umatilla articulated this theory in the *Bonnichsen* litigation as follows: "From our oral histories, we know that our people have been part of this land since the beginning of time. We do not believe that our people migrated here from another continent, as the scientists do." Bonnichsen v. United States, 217 F. Supp. 2d 1116, 1121 (D. Or. 2002).

[128] *See* Eric Beckenhauer, *Redefining Race: Can Genetic Testing Provide Biological Proof of Indian Ethnicity?* 56 STAN. L. REV. 161, 186 (2003).

[129] For example, "Indian representatives testified that the spirits of *their ancestors* would not rest until they are returned to their homeland." H.R. REP. NO. 101-877, at 4372 (1990) (emphasis added).

[130] David Lowenthal, *Why Sanctions Seldom Work: Reflections on Cultural Property Internationalism*, 12 INT'L J. CULT. PROP. 393, 405 (2005).

between what you call yourself and what people are willing to call you back."[131]

The skeletal peculiarities of Kennewick Man/The Ancient One only hint at these broad issues. Whatever scientific analysis of the remains reveals, the *Bonnichsen* court's strict interpretation of the term "Native American" helps safeguard the integrity of determinations about tribal relationship and cultural affiliation and in that way protects the human rights of the intended beneficiaries.

E. STRENGTHS AND WEAKNESSES

This study has identified numerous strengths and weaknesses in the statutory effort to protect and repatriate indigenous heritage in the United States. The following summary of these strengths and weaknesses is intended both to encourage improvements in the law and to facilitate comparative analysis.

1. Strengths

1. One strength of the overall regime of protection and repatriation is the multiplicity of mutually enforcing state and federal statutes. ARPA, NHPA, NAGPRA, and other federal legislation often operate in tandem to reinforce each other. The growing roster of "little NAGPRA" laws enacted by state legislatures strengthens the implementation and enforcement of common rules and procedures.
2. The repatriation requirements of the NMAIA and NAGPRA and some state statutes have significantly protected the human right of appropriate re-burial and have also awakened members of Native American tribes and organizations to their cultural traditions. Specifically, the repatriation process has prompted tribes to open new research and display facilities.[132]
3. NAGPRA's uniform statutory criteria, including the requirement of "closest affiliation,"[133] together with the review committee's scrutiny of decisions and claims, help avoid the risk of repatriating the wrong remains to the wrong tribe or group, thereby violating cultural norms and religious beliefs.[134]
4. NAGPRA has mandated enhanced protection of sites and cooperation with Native Americans by restoring ownership to them of remains and cultural material in their territory.

---

[131] *See* Jack Hitt, *The Newest Indians*, N.Y. TIMES, Aug. 21, 2005, at 36, 40.

[132] *See* Patty Gerstenblith, *Acquisition and Deacquisition of Museum Collections and Fiduciary Duties of Museums*, 11 CARDOZO J. INT'L & COMP. L. 409, 427 n.78 (2003) (noting that what may seem to be losses to the public of objects as a result of NAGPRA-based repatriations may represent simply a shift of those objects from mainstream institutions to Native American institutions).

[133] 25 U.S.C. § 3002(a)(2)(B) (2000).

[134] *See* Robert Pickering & R.L. Jantz, *Look Again Before Repatriating: Avoiding a Moral and Legal Morass*, FED. ARCHAEOLOGY, Fall/Winter 1995, at 35 (discussing the risks and consequent need for highly technical cranial analysis to avoid significant errors, particularly involving culturally unidentifiable remains).

5. The NMAIA and NAGPRA have established a coherent framework of consultation, collaboration, and dispute resolution that has helped forge new relationships between Native American tribes and groups, on one hand, and museums and federal agencies, on the other. After just five years of NAGPRA, the NPS had noted already "a dramatic increase in dialogue among tribes, museums, and agencies."[135] Collaboration on specific issues of repatriation has encouraged broader cooperation, often extending well beyond specific cultural issues. "The good part about NAGPRA is that it opens up communication between Native Americans and physical anthropologists that didn't exist before."[136] Native American spokespersons, while acknowledging a continuing clash of values between scientific and Native American communities, have observed the role of NAGPRA in fostering new partnerships and symbolizing "a new treaty of cooperation between Indians and anthropologists."[137] To be sure, there have been many bumps along the path toward mutually productive collaboration—*Bonnichsen* is certainly a case in point—but by now that path is well defined and well-traveled.
6. NAGPRA's requirements have redefined the scope of a museum's fiduciary duties without draining collections, as had been feared, or creating unavoidable liability as a fiduciary.[138] The legislation specifically provides that good-faith repatriation of an item relieves a museum of liability for breach of fiduciary duty, public trust, or violation of conflicting state law.[139]
7. NAGPRA's review committee, charged with nine major responsibilities, has proven to be a vigorous, effective mechanism. The minutes of its meetings reveal much heated controversy, and some failures, but also a growing capacity and sophistication. The small docket of NAGPRA cases in the federal courts may attest in part to the efficacy of the review committee.
8. The review committee and the practice of federal agencies (other than in the case of Kennewick Man/The Ancient One) have been instrumental in developing workable procedures for resolving several important issues. These issues include the accommodation of competing claims (often between rival Indian tribes or Native Hawaiian organizations), the status of claims from non-federally recognized tribal groups, and the disposition of culturally unidentifiable remains.

---

[135] C. Timothy McKeown, *Confessions of a Bureaucrat*, Fed. Archaeology, Fall/Winter 1995, at 5, 9.

[136] Andrew Curry, *Tribal Challenges*, Fed. Archaeology, Sept./Oct. 2005, at 57, 59 (remarks of Philip Walker, a past president of the American Association of Physical Anthropologists).

[137] Rosita Worl, *NAGPRA: Symbol of a New Treaty*, Fed. Archaeology, Fall/Winter 1995, at 28, 29.

[138] *See* Gerstenblith, *supra* note 132, at 433–34, *citing* James A.R. Nafziger, *The New Fiduciary Duty of United States Museums to Repatriate Cultural Heritage: The Oregon Experience*, U.B.C. L. Rev. 37, 41–42 (Spec. Issue 1995).

[139] 25 U.S.C. § 3005(f) (2000).

By contrast, resolution of disputes outside of the NAGPRA frame-work has often been haphazard and troublesome. Take, for example, the problem arising out of the return of Native American remains and cultural objects on a basis other than NAGPRA's "closest affiliation"[140] requirement. Given the diversity of burial practices among tribal claimants, often engaging sensitive religious traditions, getting repatriation right is critical. Getting it wrong ignores human rights, purely and simply.

Competing tribal claimants in New York are a case in point.[141] During a construction project in 1995 not on federal or Indian land, several culturally unidentifiable burials were discovered that may have been 1,000 years old. Officials first notified an Iroquois/Onondaga chief and then initiated negotiations with him for re-burial of the remains in a nearby state park. The Stockbridge Munsee Band of Mohican Indians learned of the development and immediately protested, on the basis that the Mohicans were the original inhabitants of the land on which the remains were unearthed. They wished to bury the remains on an established tribal site. Although the issue of the competing claims even reached the New York governor's office, no deliberate determination of the closest affiliation or stronger cultural relationship, as between the rival tribes, was ever made. Instead, the remains were repatriated to the Onondaga, contrary to the wishes of the aboriginal Mohicans, simply because they were the initial claimants for re-burial.

9. NAGPRA's reporting requirements of summaries and inventories have led to more systematic data collection,[142] broader dissemination of information, and sharing of cultural material.[143]
10. NAGPRA has dovetailed well with other federal laws, such as ARPA and NHPA, which are designed to protect cultural heritage. In addition, NAGPRA has inspired the states to strengthen their own protective legislation and, in some cases, to adopt "little NAGPRAs" that, in effect, can do the work of NAGPRA closer to the grass roots of cultural heritage and its discontents.

[140] 25 U.S.C. § 3002(a)(2)(B) (2000).

[141] Brenda Baker et al., *Repatriation and the Study of Human Remains, in* THE FUTURE OF THE PAST: ARCHAEOLOGISTS, NATIVE AMERICANS, AND REPATRIATION 69, at 76 (Tamara L. Bray ed., 2001).

[142] NAGPRA's database allows for systematic entry, retrieval, and tracking of data and provides a comprehensive and accurate record of files and information related to the law. NAGPRA's Web site provides information to the public on grants, a text of the law and its regulations, guidance, published notices, documents relating to the review committee, and contact information for national NAGPRA program staff. There are also databases on Native American consultations and culturally unidentifiable human remains. The latter database contains information, when known, on such matters as the location of remains and associated funerary objects, their age, and, in a Notes section, the names of sites, accession numbers, and cultures, if known. *See* http://www.cr.nps.gov/nagpra.

[143] *See* Barbara Isaac, *An Epimethean View of the Future at the Peabody Museum of Archaeology and Ethnology at Harvard University*, FED. ARCHAEOLOGY, Fall/Winter 1995, at 19, 21, 22; Nafziger & Dobkins, *supra* note 57, at 83–91.

11. Both state and federal legislation have provided the impetus for public education and awareness of the need for protection and repatriation as human rights.
12. NAGPRA has greatly enhanced the status of Native Hawaiian organizations, particularly in their quest for greater self-determination and standing to assert claims.

2. Weaknesses

1. Terminological ambiguities remain. To be sure, the review committee and courts have done an admirable job of clarifying such terms as "culturally identifiable remains" and "Native American" and have established protocols for avoiding and resolving related definitional disputes. But the terms "sacred" and "oral history," in particular, remain ambiguous, and the term "Native Hawaiian organization," overly broad.

   On the whole, Native American interpretations of those terms are controlling. A fascinating example of this involved the repatriation of sacred buffalo-hide shields from federal land in Utah that had found their way into a collection of the Capitol Reef National Park. They were the oldest leather shields known in the United States, radiocarbon dated to have been produced between 1420 and 1640. Navajo oral history and characterization of the shields as sacred objects settled the repatriation issues despite competing claims by other tribes and the descendants of the original collector-donor.[144] Despite such reliance on Native American oral history and interpretations of the "sacred," however, the applicable rules of evidence are sometimes painfully unclear, as *Corrow*[145] and *Bonnichsen*[146] demonstrate.

2. NAGPRA is silent with regards to several issues. These involve the acceptability of replicas and virtual representations of cultural material (which is, however, addressed by the Indian Arts and Crafts Act of 1990[147]); sanctions to ensure compliance with the terms of repatriation by recipients of repatriated material, including the disposition of remains and use of cultural objects; and the acceptability of audio recordation and other uses of intangible heritage. (The NAGPRA regulations do suggest "photographic documentation, if appropriate"[148] in museum summaries.)

---

[144] Curry, *supra* note 136, at 64–66.

[145] United States v. Corrow, 119 F.3d 796 (10th Cir. 1997), *cert. denied*, 118 S. Ct. 1089 (1998) (affirming a criminal conviction of the defendant for illegally trafficking in Navajo masks and associated objects that constituted a medicine bundle. Despite factual issues concerning them, the masks were never exhibited for the jury to see because of their sacred nature.). *See* discussion in Nafziger & Dobkins, *supra* note 57, at 97–98.

[146] Bonnichsen v. United States, 367 F.3d 864 (9th Cir. 2004); *see supra* notes 102–132.

[147] 25 U.S.C. §§ 305–310 (2000).

[148] 43 C.F.R. § 10.8(e)(3) (2005).

3. It is unclear whether NAGPRA claims may be made by coalitions of tribes or by one tribe on behalf of another. NAGPRA itself, as interpreted by the district court in *Bonnichsen*, seems to require independent showings of cultural affiliations with specific tribal or organizational claimants.[149] On the other hand, the review committee, particularly under its Draft Principles, has supported consolidated plans worked out by multiple tribal or organizational claimants. It is difficult, however, to reconcile the equity and practicality of consolidation with the premise of tribal and group autonomy that inheres, for example, in determinations of the closest cultural affiliation.
4. NAGPRA protects only federally recognized Indian tribes or, as defined, Native Hawaiian organizations. Although the definition of "Native American" sweeps in all indigenous tribes, peoples, or cultures, the operational provisions do not offer such broad protection. It is a problem not only for non-recognized *Indian* tribes or bands who find themselves unable to enlist the assistance for their cause of recognized tribes, but also for other, often "indigenous" ethnic minorities, such as the Taino of Puerto Rico.[150]
5. Despite NAGPRA's strength in fostering cooperation between tribes or groups and museums, it must be noted that NAGPRA is still resented by some museum interests. They hold NAGPRA responsible for having "created a confrontational climate when Indian people and museums were developing positive working relationships."[151] They also fear "its possibly chilling effects on future study of American Indian history and culture."[152]
6. NAGPRA has suffered from a lack of adequate funding, particularly to enable Native American tribes and groups to pursue legitimate claims of repatriation and properly use, display, or dispose of repatriated items. In past years some 60 percent of NAGPRA-related grants went to museums, leaving only 40 percent for tribes and other Native American and Native Hawaiian organizations. Bureaucratic delays and occasional conflicts of interest have also marred the effective implementation of NAGPRA.
7. Unlike many state laws, NAGPRA does not extend to privately owned real or personal property or to "any institution or state or local government agency (including any institution of higher learning) that does [not] receive Federal funds."[153] As it happens, almost all pertinent agencies and institutions of higher learning

---

[149] The appellate court did not reach or review this holding. Bonnichsen v. United States, 367 F.3d 864, 872 n.11 (9th Cir. 2004).

[150] *See* De Anna Marie Rivera, *Taino Sacred Sites: An International Comparative Analysis for a Domestic Solution*, 20 Ariz. J. Int'l & Comp. L. 443 (2003).

[151] *See, e.g.*, Nancy Oestreich Lurie, Wisconsin Indians 81 (2002) (views of a Curator Emerita of the Milwaukee Public Museum).

[152] *Id.* at 82.

[153] 25 U.S.C. § 3001(8) (2000).

do receive federal funding, so the primary limitation of NAGPRA involves its non-extension to such other institutions as auction houses and to privately owned real or personal property. Of course, that may be an inevitable weakness in any comprehensive scheme of human rights protection within legal systems based on essentially private ownership of property.

8. The prospect of repatriation may deter some prospective donors from giving cultural objects to institutions. A possible solution might be to exempt at least designated tribal museums from repatriation claims for such material in the future.
9. Neither the NMAIA nor NAGPRA extends extraterritorially to allow foreign claims, on one hand, or hold accountable foreign museums and government agencies, on the other. Under the NMAIA, however, the Smithsonian has repatriated remains to several countries, including Canada, Ecuador, Peru, and Cuba.[154] Moreover, Canadian First Nation claimants have enlisted the cooperation of related tribal members in the United States as agents to pursue their claims.
10. Although the review committee has found ways to exempt sensitive information from the disclosure requirements of the FOIA—for example, sacred practices and symbolism of tribes or organizations—the parameters of such exemptions remain unclear.
11. Civil penalties for breaches of the NMAIA and NAGPRA or for unwarranted delays in implementing those laws to the detriment of Native Americans apply only to museums, not federal agencies. Extending penalties to federal agencies and thereby exposing them to possible liability might provide an incentive for swifter compliance by agencies with NAGPRA requirements.
12. No uniform rule applies to the right of Indians and Indian tribes to re-bury repatriated remains on federally owned or managed land from which those remains were originally taken. The Bureau of Land Management, for example, denies re-burial, thereby impeding the fulfillment of a fundamental right after transfer of remains.

F. CONCLUSION

The largely statutory regime for protecting and repatriating indigenous cultural heritage in the United States is evolving through an important phase of interpretation and greater emphasis on collaborative implementation. For example, although federal laws primarily govern activity on or related to public and tribal lands, they have been interpreted selectively to extend to private institutions receiving federal funds and to private property and transactions related to cultural resources that are subject to federal regulation. State laws also apply variously and selectively to private property and transactions.

[154] Colleen Popson, *Native Voices*, ARCHAEOLOGY, Sept./Oct. 2004, at 62, 66.

NAGPRA is a crucial statute. An assessment of NAGPRA's strengths and weaknesses demonstrates a law that is thoroughly in action. Its review committee, in particular, has been instrumental in interpreting the law and putting emphasis on collaborative solutions to problems. It has had growing significance in shaping not only protection and repatriation of indigenous heritage, but also broader and more positive relations among scientists, Indian tribes, Native Hawaiian organizations, museums, and federal agencies. Museums have assumed a new fiduciary duty of compliance with repatriation and other requirements of NAGPRA. NAGPRA has provided a sturdy framework of rules and procedures for stabilizing expectations about the possession, ownership, and disposition of Native American cultural heritage and for effecting both change and compromise in the interest of human rights.

APPENDIX

(Excerpted from *Bonnichsen v. United States*, 357 F.3d 962, 967–68 (9th Cir. 2004).[155]

In July 1996, teenagers going to a boat race discovered a human skull and bones near the shore of the Columbia River just outside Kennewick, Washington The remains were found on federal property under the management of the United States Army Corps of Engineers ("Corps") and, at the request of the county coroner, were removed for analysis by an anthropologist, Dr. James Chatters, pursuant to an ARPA permit. Because of physical features such as the shape of the skull and facial bones, anthropologists at first thought the remains were those of an early European settler. But the anthropologists then found a stone projectile point embedded in the skeleton's upper hipbone. The object's design, when viewed with x-rays and CT scans of the hip, resembled a style that was common before the documented arrival of Europeans in the region. Further study of the remains revealed characteristics unlike those of a European settler, yet also inconsistent with any American Indian remains previously documented in the region. A minute quantity of metacarpal bone was radiocarbon dated. The laboratory estimated the age of the bones to be between 8340 and 9200 years old. . . .

Many scientists believed the discovery might shed light on the origins of humanity in the Americas. . . .

Indian tribes from the area of the Columbia River opposed scientific study of the remains on religious and social grounds. Four Indian groups (the "Tribal Claimants") demanded that the remains be turned over to them for immediate burial. The Tribal Claimants based their demand on NAGPRA. The Corps agreed with the Tribal Claimants and, citing NAGPRA, seized the remains on September 10, 1996, shortly before they could be transported to the Smithsonian. The Corps also ordered an immediate halt to DNA testing, which was being done using the remainder of the bone sample that had been submitted earlier for radiocarbon dating. After investigation, the Corps decided to give the remains to the Tribal Claimants for burial. As required by NAGPRA, the Corps published a "Notice of Intent to Repatriate Human Remains" in a local newspaper on September 17, 1996, and September 24, 1996.

The scientists did not convince the Corps to permit them to study the remains, and commenced litigation in the United States District Court for the District of Oregon. In an initial opinion, the district court denied the Corps' motion for summary judgment, finding that the Corps had "acted before it had all of the evidence," "did not fully consider or resolve certain difficult legal questions," and "assumed facts that proved to be erroneous." The district court vacated the Corps' earlier decision on disposition of the remains and remanded the case to the Corps for further proceedings. The district court also denied, without prejudice, Plaintiffs' motion to study the remains and directed the

[155] For a fuller account of the discovery of the skeleton and first stages of the case, see Douglas Preston, *The Lost Man*, NEW YORKER, June 16, 1997, at 70.

Corps to consider, on remand, "whether to grant [P]laintiffs' request [under ARPA] for permission to study the remains."

On March 24, 1998, the Corps and the Secretary of the Interior entered into an agreement that effectively assigned to the Secretary responsibility to decide whether the remains were "Native American" under NAGPRA, and to determine their proper disposition. The Department of the Interior then assumed the role of lead agency on this case.

Almost two years after this matter was remanded, the Secretary's experts began to examine the remains in detail. The experts estimated that Kennewick Man was 5'9" to 5'10" tall, 45 to 50 years of age when he died, and 15 to 20 years old when the projectile point became embedded in his hip. The experts could not determine, from non-destructive examination of the skeleton alone, when Kennewick Man lived. However, analysis of sediment layers where the skeleton was found supported the hypothesis that the remains dated back not less than 7600 years ago and Kennewick Man could have lived more than 9000 years ago (the date indicated by the initial radiocarbon dating of the skeleton). Further study of the sediment was recommended, but the Corps' decision to bury the discovery site in April 1998 prevented completion of those studies.[156]

The experts compared the physical characteristics of the remains—e.g., measurements of the skull, teeth, and bones—with corresponding measurements from other skeletons. They concluded that Kennewick Man's remains were unlike those of any known present-day population, American Indian or otherwise.

The Secretary's experts cautioned, however, that an apparent lack of physical resemblance between the Kennewick Man's remains and present-day American Indians did not completely rule out the possibility that the remains might be biologically ancestral to modern American Indians. Moreover, although Kennewick Man's morphological traits did not closely resemble those of modern American Indian populations, the Secretary's experts noted that Kennewick Man's physical attributes are generally consistent with the very small number of human remains from this period that have been found in North America.

---

[156] The court described this development as follows:

> The Corps buried the discovery site of the remains under approximately two million pounds of rubble and dirt, topped with 3700 willow, dogwood, and cottonwood plants. The lengthy administrative record that Defendants filed with the district court documents only a portion of the process by which the decision to bury the site was made. Nevertheless, that record suggested to the district court that the Corps' primary objective in covering the site was to prevent additional remains or artifacts from being discovered, not to "preserve" the site's archaeological value or to remedy a severe erosion control problem as Defendants represented. Burial of the discovery site hindered efforts to verify the age of Kennewick Man's remains, and effectively ended efforts to determine whether other artifacts are present at the site which might shed light on the relationship between the remains and contemporary American Indians.

Bonnichsen v. United States, 367 F.3d 864, 969 n.10 (9th Cir. 2004).

Relying solely on the age of the remains and the fact that the remains were found within the United States, on January 13, 2000, the Secretary pronounced Kennewick Man's remains "Native American" within NAGPRA's meaning. And on September 25, 2000, the Secretary determined that a preponderance of the evidence supported the conclusion that the Kennewick remains were culturally affiliated with present-day Indian tribes. For this reason, the Secretary announced his final decision to award Kennewick Man's remains to a coalition of the Tribal Claimants. The Corps and the Secretary also denied Plaintiffs' request to study the remains.

Plaintiffs filed an amended complaint in the district court challenging the Secretary's decisions. The district court again ruled in Plaintiffs' favor, [vacating] the Secretary's decisions as contrary to the Administrative Procedure Act, on the ground that the Secretary improperly concluded that NAGPRA applies. The district court also held that, because NAGPRA did not apply, Plaintiffs should have the opportunity to study Kennewick Man's remains under ARPA. Defendants and the Tribal Claimants appealed, and we stayed the district court's order granting Plaintiffs-scientists' study of the remains pending our decision herein.

CHAPTER 3

REPATRIATION OF CULTURAL MATERIAL TO FIRST NATIONS IN CANADA: LEGAL AND ETHICAL JUSTIFICATIONS

Catherine Bell

A. INTRODUCTION

Since its publication in 1991, the report of the joint Canadian Museums Association and Assembly of First Nations Task Force on Museums and First Peoples ("Task Force") has influenced federal and provincial museum policy, particularly in the area of repatriation.[1] So too has the inclusion of repatriation and cultural heritage matters in modern treaty and land claim negotiations.[2] Both have influenced policy in the areas of collection management, care and interpretation and, in some instances, creation and implementation of specific Aboriginal repatriation policies.[3] These policies and, where they do

[1] TASK FORCE REPORT ON MUSEUMS AND FIRST PEOPLES, TURNING THE PAGE: FORGING NEW PARTNERSHIPS BETWEEN MUSEUMS AND FIRST PEOPLES (3d ed. 1994) [hereinafter TASK FORCE REPORT]. It has also influenced policies of government departments, universities, and other institutions holding First Nation and other Aboriginal material. Although the report addresses increased involvement in interpretation, improved access, training, and support for cultural institutions, the most detailed recommendations of the Task Force are concerned with repatriation and optional treatments that fall short of return. For further elaboration of the report and other issues raised in this chapter, see Catherine Bell, *Restructuring the Relationship: Repatriation and Canadian Law Reform* [hereinafter Bell, *Restructuring*], *in* CATHERINE BELL & ROBERT K. PATERSON EDS., PROTECTION OF FIRST NATIONS CULTURAL HERITAGE: LAWS, POLICY AND REFORM 15–77 (2009) [hereinafter BELL & PATERSON FIRST NATIONS CULTURAL HERITAGE].

[2] For example, the Tlicho Agreement signed on August 25, 2003, provides for return of heritage resources through cooperative efforts of the government of Canada, the Northwest Territories and the Tlicho provided that "appropriate facilities and expertise exist . . . which are capable of maintaining such Tlicho heritage for future generations" and that "relocation is compatible with the maintenance of the integrity of public archives and national and territorial heritage resource collections." The Nisga'a treaty also contains repatriation provisions affecting collections of the Royal British Columbia museum and the Canadian Museum of Civilization. For further discussion of these and other examples, see Bell et al., *Survey*, *infra* note 3, at 384–86.

[3] The Aboriginal peoples of Canada are the Inuit, Indians, and Métis. Many Indian nations self-identify as "First Nations." Although this chapter is concerned with First Nations, many of the issues raised are also relevant to repatriation claims by Inuit and Métis. Métis peoples are peoples of mixed European and Aboriginal ancestry recognized as having constitutional rights sourced in the distinctive cultures of Métis communities at the time of ef-

not exist, willingness to address a range of repatriation claims under general deaccessioning procedures, demonstrate a commitment by many institutions holding Aboriginal material to return cultural items of ongoing significance on moral and ethical grounds. In areas such as northern Canada and British Columbia where modern treaties and land claims are being negotiated, repatriation occurs through public negotiation involving federal and provincial governments and institutions, as well as private negotiation. Institutions holding Aboriginal material also continue to be engaged in initiatives preceding the Task Force that demonstrate respect and support for living Aboriginal communities and traditions.

The relationship between museums and First Nations today is quite different from what it was in 1988 when the Lubicon Lake Nation organized a boycott against the "Spirit Sings" exhibition at the Calgary Olympics and the Mohawk sued the Glenbow-Alberta Institute (the "Glenbow") for the return of a False Face Mask that they considered integral to their spiritual practices and that had been obtained in violation of their laws.[4] Out of this controversy the Task Force was born, existing programs and partnerships were expanded, and positive new relationships were forged. This new relationship is also very different from the relationship that existed then, or as existed between Native American Indians and American museums in 1990 when the Native American Graves Protection and Repatriation Act (NAGPRA) was enacted in the United States.[5] Indeed the Glenbow is now one of the most responsive museums to repatriation claims and has worked with the Blackfoot to change Alberta law to enable large scale repatriations of "sacred ceremonial items" to First Nations in Alberta.[6]

Given the evolution in ethics of collecting, museum understandings of public trust, increased appreciation of rationales for repatriation, and the improved

---

fective European control over a particular community and its territory. The CANADIAN MUSEUM ASSOCIATION [hereinafter CMA], ETHICAL GUIDELINES § E.4.4 (1999), http://www.museums.ca/en/info_resources/ reports_guidelines/ (last visited Feb. 6, 2007) provides that museums should be "committed to the return . . . of culturally sensitive objects when requested by communities or groups with a demonstrable claim of historical relationship" and "be prepared to facilitate the return of material which may have been acquired under circumstances that invalidate the museums claim to title." Although some museums have specific repatriation policies, others use general deaccession policies. For examples of policies and processes and other initiatives, see Catherine Bell et al., *First Nation Cultural Heritage: A Selected Survey of Issues and Initiatives* [hereinafter Bell et al., *Survey*], *in* CATHERINE BELL & VAL NAPOLEON EDS., FIRST NATIONS CULTURAL HERITAGE AND LAW: CASE STUDIES, VOICES AND PERSPECTIVES 367, 367–86 (2008) [hereinafter BELL & NAPOLEON, VOICES AND PERSPECTIVES].

[4] Litigation has been used sparingly for repatriation claims in Canada. An exception is *Mohawk Bands of Kahnawake, Akwesasne and Kanesatake v. Glenbow-Alberta Institute,* [1988] 3 C.N.L.R. 70 (Alta. Q.B.). Litigation was also used to increase power in negotiations, for example as between the Nuxalk Nation and an art dealer seeking to export an Echo Mask from Canada. The matter was eventually settled out of court. For further discussion, see Catherine Bell & Robert K. Paterson, *International Movement of First Nations' Cultural Heritage in Canadian Law* [hereinafter Bell & Paterson, *International*], *in* BELL & PATERSON, FIRST NATIONS CULTURAL HERITAGE, *supra* note 1, at 78.

[5] 25 U.S.C. §§ 3001–3013 (West Supp. 2001) [hereinafter NAGPRA].

[6] Legislation referred to here and discussed below is the First Nations Sacred Ceremonial Repatriation Act, R.S.A. 2000, ch. F-14, § 2 [hereinafter Repatriation Act].

relationship noted above, some question the necessity and desirability of engaging in discussions of repatriation rationale and law reform in Canada. However, my research suggests that the flexibility of the existing policy environment can be both a blessing and a curse. For example, a benefit of the current regime is its ability to accommodate diversity in a number of areas. Examples include community preparedness,[7] access requirements and restrictions, levels of interest in repatriation, and First Nations laws and protocols. On the other hand, a one-size-fits-all framework could reduce flexibility by requiring strict adherence to legal burdens of proof and definitions of material culture, generating "either/or" thinking, limiting ability to negotiate outside legal parameters, and applying culturally biased legal evidentiary standards. Shifting to a rights-based approach could also undermine existing positive relationships and over time influence First Nation understandings of their relationship to the material world.[8] For many involved in repatriation negotiations, the issue is not one of legal rights but respect. First Nations largely respect the role museums and other institutions have had in educating the public and preserving cultural items. The need for return varies according to nation and object, with some nations being satisfied with (and sometimes grateful for) materials being retained in museum collections where concerns for physical preservation are shared and appropriate local facilities are not available.

The above arguments assume legislation is incapable of facilitating negotiations based on common interests and must be mandatory in its application to the exclusion of other successful processes. This need not be the case. For example, as elaborated below, Alberta's repatriation law applies only to those First Nations in Alberta who choose to invoke it to obtain transfer of title to sacred ceremonial objects. Procedural details are negotiated on a community-by-community basis and are implemented through regulation to meet the specific needs and protocols of affected communities. Although it is true that emphasis on legal rights can create adversarial relationships and obscure the true nature of the conflict to be resolved, it is equally true that, regardless of attempts to avoid assertion of legal positions, negotiations take place in the shadow of the law. That is, the legal environment affects decisions made by custodians of material culture in assessing their best and worst alternatives to negotiated agreements, obligations and potential liabilities, and parameters

---

[7] This may not only be an issue of physical capacity and museological training where they are considered important to one or both parties to negotiations, but also spiritual readiness to put items back into use and attend to their spiritual needs.

[8] Consider for example the concept of communal property. First Nation property systems are much more complex than simplistic understandings of communal and individual property division. Within a First Nation, cultural items may have individual, familial, and group dimensions. They may also be governed by specific laws of descent or exclusivity that enable alienation by individuals but restrict the class of recipients. Emphasis on communal ownership as a criteria for repatriation may not only impose Western norms on First Nation understandings, but as Harding argues, the need to fit within this and other categories may also encourage "groups to claim their cultural heritage is group owned in the absence of any strong proof that this is the case." Sarah Harding, *Value, Obligation and Cultural Heritage*, 31 ARIZ. ST. L.J. 291, 305 (1999).

for negotiation. Further, the experience of many indigenous peoples is that interest-based negotiation affecting property rights tends to balance in favor of dominant cultures absent recourse to other dispute resolution processes and support in Canadian law, even where sincere attempts are made to give equal consideration to different cultural understandings.[9]

Other problems may potentially arise. These include increased time and costs associated with a lack of uniform procedures from one institution to the next, varying levels of commitment to repatriate, conscious and unconscious bias in favor of documentary evidence, differing perspectives on appropriate conservation and preservation (including the need for museum-like facilities), reliance on personal relationships with staff who take time to educate and who then eventually leave, lack of a centralized system to access information about policies and collections, lack of research support and funding for separate or joint initiatives, and the limited scope of material some institutions are willing to repatriate.[10] In situations where these and other problems are overcome through collaborative negotiation, further barriers may be created by Canadian law, particularly outside of the public treaty and land claim negotiation processes. For example, policies concerning standards of proof, public notification, competing claims, use, preservation, and other conditions placed on return may be influenced by potential liability. This suggests that certain changes in Canadian law could assist repatriation negotiation, albeit not necessarily through enactment of repatriation legislation per se. For example, changes in common law and legislation addressing public ownership by governments or fiduciary obligations of museums to the public they serve may be necessary to facilitate repatriation of a large number of objects from a single collection; items obtained legally in the eyes of Euro-Canadian law but contrary to the laws of the originating First Nation; or material of significant historical, traditional, or cultural importance that is not needed for use in religious or other ceremonies of ongoing importance to a community.

Canadian legislation affecting ownership and control of cultural heritage is also largely dated and fails to take into consideration developments in Aboriginal rights law and the unique interests of, and constitutional obligations to, Aboriginal peoples of Canada. These considerations could implicate

[9] *See* Catherine Bell & David Kahane eds., Intercultural Dispute Resolution in Aboriginal Contexts *passim* (2004) [hereinafter Bell & Kahane, Intercultural].

[10] Specific aboriginal repatriation policies vary among institutions, but all consider return of items or other arrangements concerning access and care of those items, as recommended by the Task Force Report, *supra* note 1. The scope for repatriation claims may be broader under treaty, land claims, and general deaccessioning processes. All of these processes and their outcomes are solely within the discretion of custodial institutions and negotiated on a case-by-case basis. Of particular interest at the time of writing were proposed changes to Manitoba's policy, which take into consideration "cultural duress" in assessing legality of acquisition, do not require that sacred and ceremonial items be needed for use in ongoing practices to be eligible for repatriation, and contemplate negotiations related to "archival written records, audio documentation, films, photographs, and other forms of research information." However, it is not known if these elements will be included in the final version of the policy. The Manitoba Museum, Draft Repatriation Policy 3 (Mar. 2005; unpublished), available from the Manitoba Museum.

reliance on statutory title (for example, title arising from passage of limitation periods or legislation vesting ownership of archaeological property in the Crown), scope of material eligible for return, choice of law in determining the validity of a transfer, conditions for repatriation, consultation on creation and amendment of legislation, and a range of other issues central to repatriation negotiations. In short, the interplay of common law, legislation, and Aboriginal constitutional rights in Canada generates uncertainty of ownership and liability rendering the legal environment for negotiation even more complex.

For these and other reasons I believe it continues to be important to discuss repatriation rationale and reform in Canada. Elsewhere I have explored in greater detail arguments for and against legislated intervention and possibilities for change through amendment and enactment of repatriation legislation.[11] In this chapter I introduce key normative and legal justifications for law reform, drawing in part from the former writings and case studies conducted in collaboration with First Nation partners in Canada. I begin with a discussion of the broader research program of which this research forms a part followed by an overview of the legal environment for repatriation in Canada. I conclude with issues in law reform including a discussion of how repatriation legislation might assist negotiations and fundamental principles in law reform affecting Aboriginal peoples in Canada. I am concerned specifically with material culture of ongoing significant historical, traditional, or cultural importance that is considered by First Nations to be central to their cultural identity,[12] "owned" or controlled by the Crown, in the possession of government funded museums holding public collections, and what Western conceptualizations of cultural heritage understand as cultural objects or artifacts.

B. BROADER RESEARCH PROGRAM

This chapter emerges from a broader research program on protection and repatriation of First Nation cultural heritage in Canada funded by the Social Sciences and Humanities Research Council of Canada and conducted in collaboration with a team of scholars in law, linguistics, archaeology, and anthropology from Canada and the United States. It is informed by a range of sources including case studies designed in collaboration with First Nation partners. First Nation partners are the Hul'qumi'num Treaty Group (HTG), U'mista Cultural Center and 'Namgis Nation, Ktunaxa Kinbasket Tribal Council

---

[11] *See, e.g.*, Bell, *Restructuring*, *supra* note 1. Portions of the discussions on normative and legal justifications are also taken from this work. *See also* Bell & Paterson, *International*, *supra* note 4.

[12] The first part of this definition is taken from the definitions of cultural patrimony adopted by the *Task Force*, *supra* note 1, at 8, and the second reflects judicial tests for identifying Aboriginal constitutional rights in Section 35(1) of the Constitution Act, 1982, enacted as Schedule B to the Canada Act, 1982 (U.K.), 1982, Chapter 11 [hereinafter Constitution Act]. It is also consistent with definitions of cultural patrimony under Section 2(3)D of NAGPRA, *supra* note 5, which defines cultural patrimony as "an object of ongoing historical, traditional, or cultural importance central to the Native American group or culture itself, rather than property owned by an individual." The definition also reflects perspectives of First Nation partners reproduced in BELL & NAPOLEON, VOICES AND PERSPECTIVES, *supra* note 3, but is more liberal than some Canadian repatriation policies.

(KKTC); the Mookakin Cultural Society (Mookakin) of the Kainai Nation (Blood Tribe); the Old Man River Cultural Center (in discussion with the Knut-sum-atak Society) of the Piikani Nation (Peigan); the Gitanyow Hereditary Chiefs and Ganeda (Frog Clan), House of Luuxhon (Luuxhon).[13]

Our research has six primary objectives, which are to (1) provide First Nation participants with an opportunity to identify, define, and articulate their own concepts of property and law as well as their experiences relating to protection, repatriation, and control of their cultural heritage; (2) facilitate greater understanding and respect for diverse First Nation cultures; (3) create reflective case study reports with the potential for diverse uses and means of dissemination; (4) assist First Nation partners to collect data and develop practical resources on cultural heritage issues that are of concern in their communities; (5) disseminate information about the operation, impact, and limits of the existing Canadian legal regime as it applies to First Nations heritage; and (6) critically analyze domestic law within a broader international, social, political, and legal context.

Case studies represent a range of individual perspectives of elders, ceremonialists, spiritual leaders, community members engaged in conservation, repatriation and heritage protection activities, and others considered by their respective communities to be knowledgeable in cultural heritage matters.[14] Case studies are not intended to represent a generalized First Nation perspective, and indeed all our partners have emphasized the need for more resources and extensive consultation across Canada on these issues. However, the studies provide some insight into issues faced by First Nations, and their legal systems and processes concerning cultural heritage, and participant views on strategies for moving forward.

As part of our research, we also prepared several background reports including a review of media reports, case law and other accounts of First Nation experiences across the country and examples of Canadian legislation impacting First Nation tangible and intangible cultural property. Other works flowing from the research program cover a range of topics relating to repatriation and trade in First Nation material culture; protection of heritage sites; repatriation of ancestral remains; intangible cultural heritage and intellectual property laws; international comparisons and contexts; human rights; and First Nation laws, jurisdiction and processes.[15]

---

[13] Details on project objectives and methodology, including problems and lessons learned, are discussed in the introduction to BELL & NAPOLEON, VOICES AND PERSPECTIVES, *supra* note 3, at 1–18.

[14] The *Northwest Coast Adaawk Study* by Susan Marsden, *infra* note 32, draws on the formal written record of the oral history of the Gitksan and Tsimishian. This study and most of the others can be found online at http://www.law.ualberta.ca/research/aboriginalcultural-heritage (last visited Dec. 11, 2006). All case studies have been edited for publication in BELL & NAPOLEON, VOICES AND PERSPECTIVES, *supra* note 3. At the time of writing, decisions had not yet been rendered regarding placement of transcripts in a public archive.

[15] Some of this work is online, *id.* Academic essays are being published in BELL & NAPOLEON, VOICES AND PERSPECTIVES, *supra* note 3, and BELL & PATERSON, FIRST NATIONS CULTURAL HERITAGE, *supra* note 1.

An important aspect of the research has been First Nation participation in all aspects of the research program. Key components include participation in research design; conducting the research and authoring, commenting on and approving case studies; and authoring and commenting on academic papers drawing on case studies. For example, case studies were designed to be of immediate benefit to communities (for example in treaty negotiations, specific claims submissions, and research on heritage site protection). Community members were also hired and trained to conduct research in collaboration with academic partners and in accordance with the protocols of their communities. Partners were also encouraged to conduct research in their own language and, where required, community members were also hired to translate and transcribe.

C. NORMATIVE JUSTIFICATIONS FOR REPATRIATION

Although rationales for repatriation vary among First Nations and depend on particular items in question, several common themes emerge from the case studies and other literature reviewed in this research. Some of these are summarized below.

1. Decolonization and Self-Determination

Repatriation efforts in Canada, as elsewhere, are part of a broader movement of decolonization and reparation of past injustice. Within this context, certain material may be considered so integrally related to group identity that it takes on characteristics of community property, even if it was not considered to be so at the time of removal. Refusal to return may represent a continuation of oppression. Understanding this situation within the Canadian context requires familiarity with the role British and Canadian law and government played in undermining First Nation cultures. Of particular significance was the removal of children from their communities into environments that suppressed indigenous languages and traditions, and laws prohibiting First Nation religious and cultural practices. Some of the most fundamental components of the civilizing policy were residential schools, instruction in Christianity, voluntary and involuntary enfranchisement, dismantling of traditional governments, and banning of ceremonies, such as the potlatch, and practices associated with ceremonies, such as the Blackfoot Sundance and the Cree and Saulteaux Thirst Dance.[16]

---

[16] There are many writings on the impact of residential schools and federal Indian legislation on First Nations. *See, e.g.*, JIM. R. MILLER, TROUBLED LEGACY: A HISTORY OF NATIVE RESIDENTIAL SCHOOLS 357 (2003); JOHN S. MILLOY, A NATIONAL CRIME: THE CANADIAN GOVERNMENT AND THE RESIDENTIAL SCHOOL SYSTEM 1879 TO 1986 (1999); ROYAL COMMISSION ON ABORIGINAL PEOPLES, REPORT OF THE ROYAL COMMISSION ON ABORIGINAL PEOPLES: LOOKING FORWARD, LOOKING BACK, 245–386 (1996) [hereinafter RCAP]; SUZANNE FOURNIER & ERNIE CREY, STOLEN FROM OUR EMBRACE: THE ABDUCTION OF FIRST NATIONS CHILDREN AND THE RESTORATION OF ABORIGINAL COMMUNITIES (1997); KATHERINE PETTIPAS, SEVERING THE TIES THAT BIND: GOVERNMENT REPRESSION OF INDIGENOUS RELIGIOUS CEREMONIES ON THE PRAIRIES (1994); Annabel Crop Eared Wolf, *Protecting Religious Rights and Freedoms: Blood Tribe/Kainai Efforts Through Cultural and Intellectual Properties Policy and Repatriation,* ALBERTA MUS. REV. 38 (Fall 1997). *See also* case studies and Dale Cunningham et al., *Canada's Policy of Cultural Colonization: Indian Residential Schools and the Indian Act, in* BELL & NAPOLEON, VOICES AND PERSPECTIVES, *supra* note 3, at 10.

Items were also acquired in a manner that, under Canadian laws at the time, would have been considered illegal. For example, during the banning of ceremonies, there are accounts of individuals being coerced to surrender regalia under threat of criminal prosecution. As Stan Ashcroft, legal counsel to the 'Na̲mgis Nation explains:

> Halliday [an Indian agent] had amendments made to the *Indian Act* which provided that the conviction could be by way of summary conviction. What that meant is it didn't have to go to a judge. It could go to a magistrate, which happened to be Halliday. So what happened then, of course, is the people go before Halliday, he convicts them, sentences them to prison. But he and Angerman [sergeant] concocted a scheme whereby the individuals and the various bands and chiefs are offered, essentially, an ultimatum. If you turn over your potlatch artifacts and regalia, not only of those persons who have been charged and/or convicted, but all the other, . . . potlatch artifacts and regalia, we won't put these people in jail and we will be lenient in terms of any other prosecutions. In the future, in fact, we won't prosecute if you agree to this. So, effectively, it was coercion. It was duress. It resulted in the giving up of a huge amount of regalia and artifacts, portions of which have only recently been returned.[17]

The impact of discriminatory laws and policies and suffering they caused is resonant in the voice of Emma Tamilin, a *Kwakwa̲ka̲'wakw* elder:

> I hope that someday before I leave this world that I see a lot of—all of our stuff come back. 'Cause I hear we got things all over the world. And why did we lose it? What really happened? Why was the government against us? . . . Was it just to kill our souls? To kill us? Maybe that was one way of getting rid of us? And why was it against the law to have a potlatch? And it's so beautiful, especially when you celebrate the birth of a baby, when you're giving names to your child when it grows up, and when [a] woman becomes a woman and the young man steps into the his father's shoes. . . . [W]hy on earth was it against the law?[18]

The answer is because potlatch ceremonies were the foundation of economic, political, social, spiritual, and legal systems, and the means for transferring cultural knowledge to future generations among West Coast First Nations. Banning them and other practices fulfilled the civilizing policy of the church and state.

---

[17] Interview of Stan Ashcroft by Barb Cranmer, West Vancouver, British Columbia, Nov. 21, 2002. Transcripts of all interviews are located at the U'mista Cultural Centre in Alert Bay, B.C., *quoted in* Catherine Bell et al., *Recovering from Colonization: Perspectives of Community Members on Protection and Repatriation of Kwakwa̲ka̲'wakw Cultural Heritage* [hereinafter Bell et al., *Recovering*], online, *supra* note 14, and *in* Bell & Napoleon, Voices and Perspectives, *supra* note 3, at 54.

[18] Interview of Emma Tamilin by Barb Cranmer, Alert Bay, British Columbia, Jan. 9, 2003. Transcripts of all interviews are located at the U'mista Cultural Center in Alert Bay, B.C., *quoted* online in Bell et al., *Recovering*, *id.* at 33.

In the late 19th and early 20th century, fear that Indian cultures in Canada would vanish also provided an impetus for anthropologists, archaeologists, and other collectors who were carrying out institutional mandates to gather and preserve as much as they could for the benefit of future generations—an action carried out largely in good faith. Items were also gifted, exchanged, and intentionally made for sale. Some items considered inalienable outside the originating community, or of significant intrinsic value to it, were also sold by converts. Other items were sold under situations of mistake or economic and social duress.[19] The legal assault on First Nation culture, restrictions placed on the economic use of reserve lands, and involuntary enfranchisement provisions also contributed to alcoholism, family breakdown, illness, and other forms of social hardship that further stimulated the market in First Nation artifacts and the growth of collections through donations, sometimes for safekeeping, and sale. Depopulation resulting from disease and other factors also meant that there were fewer people around to defend regalia against thieves.

As a result of these various influences, museum and other collections contain not only items sold under illegal, potentially illegal and questionable ethical circumstances, but they also contain an array of tangible and intangible material acquired legitimately under the laws of Canada and affected First Nation communities. Most museums in Canada recognize an ethical obligation to return items obtained illegally. More controversial is the return of so-called "secular" items that have been obtained legally under Canadian law but not under First Nation laws at the time of removal, or under other questionable circumstances such as economic duress.

2. Identity and Well-Being

Emma Tamilin's words also underscore the relationship between material culture, identity, and well-being. Objects may be valued because they represent "extensions of ourselves" or because they are "endowed with special significance because they are spiritual, memory laden, rare, mysterious, or in some other fashion worth treasuring."[20] The disappointment and disempowerment felt by those who suffer loss or theft of such items speaks to their psychological importance. Similar analysis can be applied to many cultural objects sought to be returned—they are tangible expressions of a people. Further, people develop a sense of "self" not only through personal experience, but also relationship to community—their own and others. Cultural context and differentiation is inextricably linked to one's sense of dignity, emotional strength, personal development, and well-being.[21] Material cultural heritage is an important

---

[19] For example, on Canada's west coast, experienced collectors "took measure both of the seasonal employment and of the years when the salmon fishery failed" and had knowledge of those communities under the influence of missionaries most likely to sell. *See* DOUGLAS COLE, CAPTURED HERITAGE: THE SCRAMBLE FOR NORTHWEST COAST ARTIFACTS 297 (1995). Other First Nations sold under similar pressures. *See generally* BELL & NAPOLEON, VOICES AND PERSPECTIVES, *supra* note 3.

[20] BRUCE ZIFF, PRINCIPLES OF PROPERTY LAW 27 (4th ed. 2006).

[21] *See* WILL KYMLICKA, MULTICULTURAL CITIZENSHIP: A LIBERAL THEORY OF MINORITY RIGHTS

expression of not only individual creative processes, but also individual and group spiritual and cultural life. It is for this reason that controlling, removing, and destroying cultural heritage is "such an effective tool of domination."[22]

Whatever its form, material culture is an expression of relationships between individuals, community, the natural, and the spiritual realm. However, some material has a more significant historical and contemporary role in maintaining these relationships, the health of the community, and interacting with the spiritual and supernatural. Emphasis given by many participants in our research on repatriation of spiritual and ceremonial items and inappropriate use of spiritual items, places, and songs underscores this point. Consequently repatriation is sometimes viewed as a duty, not a matter of choice. As Frank Weasel Head, an elder of the Kainai Nation explains, using the example of medicine bundles, "[i]n our way, the old people would say they have become orphans. And those bundles in museums are all orphans waiting for somebody to adopt them and bring them back and get painted for them so they can be put back into use."[23] The obligation to attend to spiritual needs of bundles and to engage bundles in appropriate relations and ceremonies is not alleviated by their removal from the community.

Repatriation can also be a means to improve economic well-being. Some First Nations in Canada seek to develop their own cultural and interpretive centers. Not only do such centers help them ensure local involvement in interpretation, priorities, and protocols for preservation, use, and access by community members, they also generate employment and training opportunities and attract tourists. Such centers, when provided with adequate funding, also incorporate cultural and language education programs. However, few First Nations in Canada have cultural education centers with adequate facilities to meet contemporary museum conservation standards. Where they share similar concerns for physical preservation and museums are willing to assist in training and other areas (which is often the case), limited funding is available for this purpose. The absence of funds and facilities has proven to be a barrier in some repatriation negotiations, particularly in the context of negotiations to return items not needed for ongoing ceremonial or religious purposes.

(New York, 1995); Will Kymlicka, Liberalism, Community and Culture (1989), *cited in* Harding, *supra* note 8, at 334–35.

22 Harding, *id.* at 335.

23 First interview with Frank Weasel Head by Dennis First Rider, Standoff, Alberta, Feb. 25, 2003 (Frank Weasel Head part 1) [translated by Dennis First Rider]. Transcripts for all interviews are held by the Mookakin Society in Standoff, Alberta. *Quoted in* Catherine Bell et al., *Repatriation and Protection: Reflections on the Kainai Experience* [hereinafter Bell et al., *Kainai*], *in* Bell & Napoleon, Voices and Perspectives, *supra* note 3, at 206. Bundles with which this chapter is concerned are those that are transferred to authorized members of societies or are held for the benefit of the community. These bundles contain numerous ceremonial items associated with visions, songs, dances, and other cultural knowledge. Bundles are opened on ceremonial occasions and serve various functions in Blackfoot society including healing, spiritual functions, and transmission of knowledge within sacred Blackfoot societies. They ensure health, harmony and well-being for both the individual bundle holder and the community. They are held by individual caretakers who are an active part of a religious society. They belong to the Creator and are given to the Blackfoot for specific purposes.

3. Respect for First Nation Laws and Human Rights

Seeking recognition of First Nation laws and dispute resolution processes in this and other contexts is not only an aspect of the broader goal of self-determination, but also respect for human rights including cultural, linguistic, and religious freedoms. For example, the Blackfoot have specific practice-based laws concerning control, use, treatment, and transfer of medicine bundles and the knowledge associated with them.[24] Although these types of laws have sometimes been in abeyance, they continue to be integral to First Nation communities whose traditions survived the impact of colonization or are in the process of cultural revitalization. From a Western perspective, title can be acquired through donation or sale from another person with valid legal title. For the Blackfoot, title documents and payment are irrelevant considerations. What is important is who specifically underwent the formal ceremonial transfer processes, whether traditional protocol was adhered to during the process, and whether that party met any relevant qualifications of membership during that process.

Although many custodial institutions recognize an ethical obligation to address violation of First Nation laws of use and transfer, others may point to title documents, written records signed by sellers and donors, familial connection to an object, legislation, and other forms of familiar evidence to support a legal right and obligation to retain control. Abeyance in the exercise of First Nation laws or individuals acting in breach can be taken as evidence that laws that had been allegedly broken did not exist at the time of separation. Unlike in the United States, limitation periods can also operate to cure a defective chain of title by taking away the ability of previous owners to bring their title action before the courts, and provincial legislation may vest title to a range of material in the Crown. These factors can result in solutions that fall short of return such as loans, replicas, co-management, and traveling exhibitions. Sometimes these solutions are satisfactory for the claimants, and sometimes not.

Complications are also created through different understandings of ownership, belonging, and responsibility. As Francis First Charger, another Kainai elder explains,

> For myself, those items [medicine bundles] that were properly transferred to me, I cannot honestly make a statement that I owned these things outright. They are meant to be transferred on to the next. For the ones that were sold to the white communities, institutions, or individuals, the white people, to them, ownership is another thing. They don't necessarily use First Nation peoples' knowledge and un-

---

[24] For a discussion of Blackfoot laws and transfer processes concerning bundles, tee pee designs, and other material, see generally Bell et al., *Kainai*, *in* BELL & NAPOLEON, VOICES AND PERSPECTIVES, *supra* note 3; Brian Noble, *Poomaksin: Skinnipiikan-Nitsiitapii Law, Transfers, and Making Relatives: Practices and Principles for Cultural Protection, Repatriation, Redress, and Heritage Law Making with Canada*, online, *supra* note 14, and *in* BELL & NAPOLEON, VOICES AND PERSPECTIVES, *supra* note 3, at 258.

> derstanding of how these come into the possession of individuals. It is my opinion that these items were born from our own way of life, our own territory. That is my understanding of the origin and their purpose. . . . We cannot state that these belong to an individual or a family. We have joint ownership of these items. They belong to everybody in our tribe. They were meant to be transferred from one to another and a process has to go on sometimes within a family to another family. Part of the reasons why they are transferred to certain people is because these certain people will make specific vows to acquire the rights of that bundle to be transferred to them. Sometimes these reasons relate to illness and other misfortunes. These sacred items were given to us for these purposes.[25]

From the perspective of many First Nations, proper resolution of the conflict between First Nation and Western law and differing concepts of ownership is through respect for laws and treaty jurisdictions of originating First Nations. As argued below, consideration of Aboriginal rights law provides support for a blended approach. It is not necessary to prove an unbroken chain in continuity of laws within a First Nation community nor compliance by all community members in order to consider First Nation laws in the legal analysis.

4. Cultural Loss, Cultural Revival, and Transmission of Cultural Knowledge

Of concern to many First Nations is loss of traditional cultural knowledge and the strengthening and renewal of that knowledge within the community. This loss is facilitated by a separation from material culture and inability to disseminate attending knowledge within the community connected to its accessibility and use. Thus, the value of some forms of material culture may be measured not so much by necessity for use in ongoing activities as for the educational and cultural knowledge it represents so that it may be of equal importance to repatriate everyday items such as clothing, baskets, utensils, and other similar items. Violet Birdstone, a member of the Ktunaxa/Kinbasket repatriation committee explains as follows:

> [W]hen our cultural items were sold and placed into museums, we lost a lot of our cultural knowledge. I'll give you an example of the Lower Kootenay people. When I was in the . . . National Museum of the American Indian in New York, we saw, . . . duck decoys. And they were just in perfect condition. Like whoever made them were really experts . . . because these decoys looked exactly like the living bird. . . . They used the feathers, the head, the feet, everything. . . . I don't know of any people [if] any of our Ktunaxa people today [know] how to make a duck decoy. I mean that is one example. That's . . . a complete loss of our traditions. [W]ith our items, like our cultural work, artwork being held by museums, they've taken away the knowledge from our com-

[25] Interview of Francis First Charger by Dorothy First Rider, Blood Reserve, Alberta, Jan. 30, 2003 [Dorothy First Rider trans.], *in* Bell et al., *Kainai*, *id.* at 224.

munities and you know, placed them far away, where most people will never get to and never see.[26]

Another common theme in the case studies is that knowledge manifested in material form, or derived from the material world, cannot always be conceptually separated from, transmitted, or protected independent of those manifestations. Consider again medicine bundles. They contain numerous ceremonial items and associated songs, dances, and other cultural knowledge necessary for the performance of ceremonies and transmission of knowledge within Blackfoot societies. When bundles are absent, the societies and individuals charged with keeping the knowledge associated with them are unable to perform complete ceremonies, transmit certain knowledge, or train others, and are therefore jeopardized.

All studies emphasize the importance of language retention and revitalization to recovery and preservation of distinctive cultural identities. Repatriation of objects and oral material is considered one of several important strategies in language preservation and revitalization. Access to objects fosters language renewal as elders and other knowledge keepers recall and share associated information using words and concepts that have fallen out of regular use, whether it be through putting objects back into ceremonial use; advice on proper labelling, use, and display; educational, social, or other functions in which material culture plays a role; or sharing memories generated with family and friends. Oral material such as recordings, written forms of language, and research on language is important to help learn and pronounce the language as well as connect listeners to the past.

5. Control Over and Access to Images and Information

Of concern to many First Nations is how their histories and cultures are depicted. Many of these concerns are being addressed through the establishment of advisory committees; cooperative management agreements; recruitment of First Nation board members, volunteers, and personnel; and other initiatives. Attempts have also been made by some First Nations to control future misrepresentation through research protocols, and some, fortunate enough to have sufficient funds, have created their own museum-like facilities and are interpreting their own collections acquired through repatriation, donation, and other means. However, issues of access and control have deeper aspects to them including (1) access to material and associated knowledge needed for ongoing ceremonies and legal and political orders and (2) controlling the use of intangible heritage associated with an object.

---

[26] Interview of Violet Birdstone by Laura McCoy, Cranbrook, British Columbia, Oct. 2, 2002, *quoted in* Catherine Bell & Heather McCuaig, *Protection and Repatriation of Ktunaxa/Kinbasket Cultural Resources: Perspectives of Community Members* [hereinafter Bell & McCuaig, *Ktunaxa*], online, *supra* note 14, and *in* BELL & NAPOLEON, VOICES AND PERSPECTIVES, *supra* note 3, at 316–17. Transcripts of participants who agreed to have their entire interviews made available are located in Cranbrook at the Ktunaxa Kinbasket Tribal Council Archives.

An example of the latter point can be found in the Luuxhon study.[27] Among the Gitksan, the image portrayed on an object may be more important than the object itself. Each House (lineage group) among the Gitxsan holds a unique set of crest images on blankets, rattles, poles, and other regalia. Relationships with land and each other are re-created and affirmed through use and display of these images. Intangible images, words and music, and their tangible depictions on regalia and poles are held in trust by the chief for future generations. The trust property is the right to display the images, sing the songs, perform the dramas, and so on, as these define the relation of the house to another in the group including connection to territories. What is important is not the object so much as use and control of the image on it.

D. ABORIGINAL AND TREATY RIGHTS

Section 35(1) of the Constitution Act, 1982 recognizes the "existing aboriginal and treaty rights of the Aboriginal peoples of Canada." Although there is no case law on point, trends in Aboriginal rights law concerning definition, interpretation, and termination of a wide range of Aboriginal constitutional rights support a general right of cultural integrity. This right has several aspects including the basic right to carry on activities grounded in the central and significant elements of their historical cultures.[28] More specifically, Brian Slattery, an eminent scholar in Canadian Aboriginal rights law, argues this right of cultural integrity includes the right to follow certain spiritual practices, speak certain languages, and perform cultural activities in accordance with the particular customs, practices, and traditions of a specific First Nation.[29]

When we examine various streams of Aboriginal and treaty rights jurisprudence, the following specific arguments, among others, supporting First Nation ownership and control of cultural property emerge:[30]

---

[27] Richard Overstall, *The Law Is Opened: The Constitutional Role of Tangible and Intangible Property in Gitanyow* online, *supra* note 14, and *in* BELL & NAPOLEON, VOICES AND PERSPECTIVES, *supra* note 3, at 92.

[28] This argument is derived in part form the reasoning in *R. v. Van der Peet,* [1996] 2 S.C.R. 507. *See also* discussion of Aboriginal rights and title in *Delgamuukw v. British Columbia,* [1998] 1 C.N.L.R 14 (S.C.C.)

[29] Brian Slattery, *The Generative Structure of Aboriginal Rights,* 38 SUP. CT. L. REV. 595, 605 (2007).

[30] Some of these arguments are elaborated by Catherine Bell & Robert K. Paterson, *Aboriginal Rights to Repatriation of Cultural Property, in* BOX OF TREASURES OR EMPTY BOX? TWENTY YEARS OF SECTION 35, 103, (2003) and in Bell, *Restructuring, supra* note 1. There has been limited litigation in Canada directly on this point. However, *obiter* comments by the Supreme Court of Canada in *Kitkatla Band v. British Columbia (Minister of Small Business, Tourism and Culture),* [2002] 2 C.N.L.R. 143, 168 (S.C.C.) suggest that cultural heritage may in some cases "be a key part of the collective identity of people" and that "some component of cultural heritage" might go to the core of identity in such a way as to affect application of provincial law. *Mohawk Bands of Kahnawake, Akwesasne and Kanesatake v. Glenbow-Alberta Institute,* [1988] 3 C.N.L.R. 70 (Alta. Q.B.), recognized that the Mohawk claim to Aboriginal rights to enforcement of traditional laws concerning use and display of a False Face Mask raised a serious legal issue to be tried.

1. Rights to material culture may form part of a broader claim to Aboriginal title. The *Delgamuukw* case[31] clarifies that we must look to a number of factors to determine the content of title including Aboriginal perspectives, laws, and land tenure systems. So for example, under a First Nation law, an object may be considered part of the land and to be transferred with it, as is the case with heirlooms in Anglo-Canadian law.[32]
2. Rights to use and control may arise if an object is part of historical activity, custom, practice, or tradition that was, and continues to be, integral to the distinctive cultural identity of a First Nation, and either has pre-contact origins or is not pre-contact in origin but is vital to an activity, custom, tradition, or practice that is pre-contact in origin.
3. Rights may also be sourced in pre-contact First Nation laws that continue to be integral to the community concerning their individual or communal nature and proper transfer. Although specific customary laws may have been terminated within the clear and plain intent of federal legislation, customary laws survive the general assertion of Crown sovereignty, introduction of English and French law, division of legislative jurisdiction under the Canadian Constitution, and other general assertions of jurisdiction. Gaps in continuity will not necessarily vitiate a claim.
4. Jurisdiction over ownership and control may be sourced in broader rights of cultural integrity, customary law, and self-government that are recognized and affirmed in treaty relationships between First Nations and the Crown.
5. Rights may also be implied in treaty. For example, prairie treaties are silent on the specific issue of use and control of cultural items. However, emphasis on preserving cultural norms and use of cultural items and representative imagery at the time of treaty negotiation, and within the text of the treaty itself, arguably reflect a common intention not to interfere with cultural and spiritual beliefs and practices.[33] Alternatively, even if such rights cannot be found explicitly or by implication in a treaty, one can still argue that they are not replaced by treaty rights and therefore continue to exist as Aboriginal rights.

---

[31] Delgamuukw v. British Columbia, [1998] 1 C.N.L.R 14 (S.C.C.)

[32] Take, for example, crest poles, which are not only manifestations of the power, history, and identity of a particular chief, but are material representations of land ownership rights. These may be considered part of the land itself wherever they are situated given the unique nature of Aboriginal title and the requirement to incorporate indigenous laws and perspectives in ascertaining its scope. *See* Susan Marsden, *Northwest Coast Adawx Study*, *in* BELL & NAPOLEON, VOICES AND PERSPECTIVES, *supra* note 3, at 114.

[33] This argument is drawn from principles of treaty interpretation found in *R. v. Marshall,* [2005] 2 S.C.R. 220. It should be noted that different rules of interpretation apply to modern treaties and land claims where there is a presumption that these matters have been addressed and there are surrender and release clauses.

6. The treaty relationship, Aboriginal rights, and assumption of federal and provincial jurisdiction over Aboriginal cultural property also create a fiduciary responsibility of protection, or at the very least, a duty of consultation.

Claims to Aboriginal rights can be refuted by arguments that they were extinguished by a valid act of state prior to 1982 when they and treaty rights were recognized in the Canadian Constitution. However, once the right is established, this line of argument becomes harder to maintain, as only the federal government can extinguish Aboriginal rights, and most legislation affecting ownership of cultural heritage is provincial. Further, legislation purporting to extinguish Aboriginal property rights must be clear and plain in its intent.[34] This requirement arguably means consideration must be given to the potential conflict with Aboriginal or treaty rights, and a choice must be made to resolve that conflict through abrogation. Not only is there an absence of federal legislation asserting ownership over Aboriginal cultural property, but Aboriginal rights have not been considered or addressed in federal legislation that affects trade in Aboriginal cultural property such as Section 91 of the Indian Act[35] and the Cultural Property Export and Import Act (CPEI).[36]

Rights that have not been extinguished by statute or treaty are protected by the Canadian Constitution but are not immune from regulation. Provincial and federal governments have the power to regulate such rights provided they can justify their actions by demonstrating a valid legislative objective exercised in a manner consistent with the honor of the Crown and its fiduciary obligations toward Aboriginal peoples.[37] For example, many provinces have legislation originating in the early 1970s that vests ownership of archaeological heritage in the Crown.[38] Such legislation can, of course, interfere with actual or potential Aboriginal and treaty rights. But such legislation can be justified. Otherwise,

---

[34] R. v. Sparrow, [1990] 3 C.N.L.R. 160, 177 (S.C.C.).

[35] R.S.C. 1985, ch. I-5. Ownership of property located on reserve land is governed by the *Indian Act*. The federal government does not claim ownership of movable cultural property on these lands, but certain restrictions have been placed on the care and disposition of material objects. For example, Section 91 of the Indian Act requires that the written consent of the minister of Indian and Aboriginal affairs be obtained to transfer title to Indian grave houses, totem poles, carved house poles, pictographs, and petroglyphs located on reserve lands. Objects listed in this section removed or sold before it came into force or before the land in issue became reserve land would not fall within the scope of this provision. The existence of this section, however, would bolster a claim for return regardless of prior legal standards.

[36] R.S.C. 1985, ch. C-51.

[37] R. v. Sparrow, [1990] 3 C.N.L.R. 160, 177 (S.C.C.). The Section 35 obligation includes a duty to consult. Duties to consult can exist even in the context of potential rights and where a fiduciary relationship in law and the least amount of interference possible has not arisen. *See* Haida Nation v. British Columbia (Minister of Forests), [2004] 3 S.C.R. 511.

[38] Also largely absent in most provincial legislation is express recognition of the rights of Aboriginal people to participate in the management of their archaeological heritage. An exception is the B.C. Heritage Conservation Act, R.S.B.C. 1985, ch. H-4, which enables the designated minster to enter into formal agreements with First Nations concerning conservation and protection of heritage sites and objects, although to my knowledge no such agreements have been entered independent of the B.C. treaty process. Other exceptions are special laws and policies concerning discovery and excavation of human remains.

aboriginal ownership could deprive Canadians as a whole from the opportunity to learn from and about practices, traditions, and people integral to Canada's multicultural society. However, this is a weak argument insofar as American experiences under NAGPRA and the nature of repatriation negotiations in Canada suggest that the threat of significant depletion of museum collections is minimal. Other arguments include these: government interference operates to the benefit of Aboriginal peoples by ensuring the proper care and protection of Aboriginal material that might otherwise be destroyed, and Crown ownership is necessary to facilitate exploitation of natural resources for the economic well-being of all citizens of a province, including Aboriginal peoples. Regardless of the legitimacy of these concerns, they do not justify provincial expropriation of the broad range of Aboriginal material currently affected by provincial heritage conservation legislation.

Canadian governments must also prove that they are accomplishing their objectives in a manner consistent with their fiduciary obligation. Courts will also take into consideration interests of the broader public, including innocent private good faith purchasers of cultural material. However, the government is required to consult if legislation affects the exercise of constitutionally protected Aboriginal and treaty rights. In the repatriation context this could apply to application of laws implicating ownership, disposition, and protection of products of archaeological research and excavation or destruction of sites. Recent decisions of the Supreme Court also suggest that maintaining the honor of the Crown requires some degree of consultation in relation to potential rights not yet recognized by Canadian courts or through agreement.[39]

Taking Aboriginal rights into consideration also means that the journey of an item must be assessed within the cultural context of a particular First Nation, taking into consideration perspectives of the affected First Nation toward the nature of the rights at stake. This process could result in a blending of First Nation and Western property laws in the resolution of a claim. For example, under the common law principle, a person cannot transfer greater rights in property than he or she has. This principle may be considered along with laws of an affected First Nation at the time of separation to determine the capacity of an individual or group to convey title. This approach is adopted in U.S. repatriation law through NAGPRA. Tribal law of the originating group determines what cultural patrimony is capable of individual ownership and is therefore alienable.[40] The consideration of context will also influence a determination of the cultural significance of an item to a particular community. Once title is called into question, other First Nation laws may come into play concerning an item's proper use and preservation.

---

[39] Haida Nation v. British Columbia (Minister of Forests), [2004] 3 S.C.R. 511.

[40] *Supra* note 5. Paragraph 2(3)(D) defines cultural patrimony as

an object having ongoing historical, traditional, or cultural importance central to the Native American group or culture itself, rather than property owned by Native American, and which, therefore cannot be alienated, appropriated, or conveyed by an individual . . . considered inalienable . . . by such Native American group at the time the object was separated from such group.

E. LEGISLATION AND LAW REFORM

1. Amending Existing Legislation

Law reform entails either the amendment of existing legislation or the creation of new legislation. Provincial and federal legislation affecting ownership and trade of Aboriginal material culture is largely dated and has not kept pace with developments in the area of Aboriginal rights law. An example already considered is provincial heritage conservation law, which vests ownership of items excavated or discovered on provincial lands and largely does not include a requirement for consultation (although this is often the practice).

Another example is the CPEI.[41] One of its objectives is to keep objects of national importance within Canada. It does this by export controls that delay permits and provision of repatriation grants, loans, and tax incentives to institutions (mainly museums) to purchase objects being exported or currently located outside of Canada. There is no express accommodation or recognition of unique rights and interests of First Nations. This situation is not surprising as the CPEI emerged before the recognition of Aboriginal rights in the Canadian Constitution and without having in mind the interests of First Nations. For example, although a few First Nation organizations are among those entitled to receive notice of delayed export permits and to apply for repatriation funding under the act, notification is primarily issued to organizations that receive repeated gifts of cultural objects, such as museums. There is no obligation to notify First Nation communities of origin. There is no mechanism under the CPEI for a First Nation to prohibit export of a particular item or for the review board to investigate the legitimacy of title claimed. There is no First Nation representation on the review board. When First Nations have been fortunate enough to find out about an item pending export they consider to be valuable communal property, they have successfully partnered with museums and other institutions to obtain funding under the CPEI and prevent export. However, they must negotiate a purchase price, often inflated, with dealers or exporters.

2. Enacting Repatriation Legislation

The introduction to this chapter raised some of the dangers of enacting repatriation legislation. These opinions about legislation have been influenced to a degree by discussion among museum professionals and indigenous peoples concerning problems in the early administration of NAGPRA. Among these are (1) mandatory provisions in NAGPRA result not only in a strain on resources for some museums, but also tribal museums and governments responding to notifications, collection summaries and inventories, requests for consultation, and other processes generated by NAGPRA; (2) dissent in communities sometimes arising from a non-conformity of federally recognized tribes with tribal law or structures of decision-making authority within a tribal confederation of formerly autonomous tribes; and (3) trying to fit within pre-

[41] Operation of this legislation and problem areas are discussed in detail in Bell & Paterson, *International, supra* note 4.

defined legal categories that are inconsistent with indigenous ways of knowing.[42] Despite its limitations, NAGPRA has also been working well to facilitate repatriation, improve relations, and generate respect for First Nation laws and processes concerning sacred material and other significant cultural patrimony with issues of ambiguity often, but not always, resolved in their favor.[43] Not surprisingly, sufficient funding to implement its objectives continues to be a concern. In short, NAGPRA has many lessons for Canada should Canada proceed with repatriation legislation.

Another complication in Canada is the division of jurisdiction between the federal and provincial governments. Although it can be argued that matters of Aboriginal cultural heritage are areas of core federal jurisdiction over Aboriginal rights, culture per se does not fall within federal jurisdiction. Further, subject to a few exceptions such as regulation of inter-provincial or international trade, provincial governments have jurisdiction over moveable property within their boundaries. Pursuant to this jurisdiction, provinces are able, for example, to enact legislation of general application that affects Aboriginal archaeological heritage.[44] It is more questionable whether a province can enact "property legislation" applicable to First Nations only, such as Alberta's First Nations Sacred Ceremonial Objects Repatriation Act. What is clear is that the provinces do not have jurisdiction to enact repatriation laws applicable to federal collections or affecting federal land.

For many First Nations, cultural heritage is considered a matter of inherent First Nations jurisdiction. Unlike the United States, Canada does not have a body of jurisprudence on rights to internal self-government. However, *obiter* comments and reasoning in various decisions support the conclusion that First Nation jurisdictions co-exist with those of other governments where they have not been clearly extinguished by legislation or treaty. Currently, governmental powers, territory, and membership, including matters of heritage protection and ownership of material culture, are the subject of modern treaty, self-government, and land claim negotiations.[45] First Nations also have differing views on the appropriate role of federal and provincial governments in matters of material culture. Given this environment, legislated responses to repatriation will only be acceptable to most First Nations if they recognize and seek to reconcile First Nation laws and social practices concerning use, disposition, and belonging; are initiated, supported, and shaped by those First Nations affected; and are flexible enough to enable First Nations who choose not to be regulated by external federal or provincial laws to pursue other means or choose application until the contemporary scope of First Nation jurisdictions

---

42 See, for example, discussion of these and other problems and benefits in James D. Nason, *Beyond Repatriation: Cultural Policy and Practice for the Twenty-First Century*, *in* BORROWED POWER: ESSAYS ON CULTURAL APPROPRIATION 291 (Bruce Ziff & Pratima V. Rao eds., 1997). See also various articles arising from a symposium on NAGPRA in 24(1) ARIZ. L. REV. (1992).

43 *See, e.g., id.*; James Nafziger, *The Protection and Repatriation of Indigenous Cultural Heritage in the United States*, *in* BELL & PATERSON, FIRST NATIONS CULTURAL HERITAGE, *supra* note 1.

44 Kitkatla Band v. British Columbia (Minister of Small Business, Tourism and Culture), [2002] 2 C.N.L.R. 143 (S.C.C.).

45 *See, e.g., supra* note 2.

are determined through self-government, treaty, or other processes. Such optional frameworks are not unheard of in Canada in matters that potentially affect powers of self-government.[46]

3. How Can Repatriation Legislation Facilitate Negotiation?

There are numerous ways in which legislation can assist negotiation. I offer two contexts here: dispute resolution and museum or government liability arising from disposal of collections.

a. Dispute Resolution

Reliance on museum policy and goodwill in negotiations raises issues of power and equality of participation. In the main, major Canadian institutions holding First Nation material recognize the importance of addressing "past inequities that have characterized their relationships in the past," treat First Nation parties to negotiation with respect, appreciate the complexities created by different cultural understandings, and consider evidence based on kinship, oral tradition, and other sources, the current regime nevertheless continues to perpetuate colonial relationships of dependency as absolute authority, and final decisionmaking remains with external governments and custodial institutions.[47] The only recourse for First Nations if negotiation fails for these or other reasons is expensive litigation before Canadian courts.

Important in designing an effective resolution process is awareness that familiar forms such as mediation, arbitration, and expert tribunals have taken on specific roles within Western legal culture and are influenced by it. Thus, Michelle LeBaron notes that in designing dispute resolution systems between diverse First Nations and dominant cultural groups, important questions that need to be asked include the following: "Whose values are reflected when there is opposition within or between groups? How do we design processes that accommodate preferences for directness and indirectness, for unrestricted speaking time and tight limits on participation?"[48] These issues increase in complexity when we consider "how the process frames the way that cultural understandings and meanings get listened to during a process—or not."[49] Although it is beyond the scope of this chapter to get into specific challenges of design, the main point is that creating an effective mechanism means more than just adopting familiar forms.

---

[46] An example is the First Nations Land Management Act S.C. 1999, ch. 24. This First Nation initiative empowers signatory First Nations to a framework agreement on land management the power to opt out of the land management of the Indian Act, R.S.C. 1985, Chapter I-5 to establish their own land management regimes and increase decisionmaking at the local level. Land codes enacted pursuant to this legislation may include heritage matters. For greater discussion and examples, see Catherine Bell et al., *A Selected Review of Canadian Legislation Affecting First Nation Cultural Heritage*, online, *supra* note 14 [hereinafter Bell et al., *Legislation*].

[47] Task Force Report, *supra* note 1, at 7.

[48] Michelle LeBaron, *Learning New Dances: Finding Effective Ways to Address Intercultural Disputes*, *in* Bell & Kahane, Intercultural, *supra* note 9, at 1, 20.

[49] *Id.*

A principle for conflict resolution currently respected by many Canadian institutions is that competing claims within a community or between First Nation communities are best resolved within and between those communities. This both respects matters of internal governance and avoids potential liability from returning items, albeit in good faith, to the wrong entity. A more difficult question is whether litigation should be the only recourse if efforts to resolve conflict between claimants fail, given the potential for this situation to indefinitely block a repatriation claim. The number of disputes managed by the NAGPRA review committee involving inter-tribal claims suggests a more accessible and expert mechanism to resolve conflict may be required. Other challenging questions include how to create an effective and inter-culturally legitimate process for resolving impasses in negotiations and whether resort to such processes should be mandatory before repatriation claims can be taken to Canadian courts. Given the importance of respecting autonomous decisionmaking by First Nations in the current legal and political environment, requiring consent of First Nation claimants initiating a claim to alternative processes is likely to get the most support from First Nations. As facilitated mediation and negotiation are dependent upon good faith participation, consent of all affected parties may be preferable.

Numerous generic arguments exist for seeking to resolve conflict outside of the adversarial judicial system. Some of these applied to repatriation claims are lack of First Nation involvement in final decisionmaking when agreements cannot be reached; lack of judicial expertise relating to the needs of scientific, museum, and First Nation communities; formality; strict evidentiary rules; and costs of litigation. Legislation could help address these concerns by establishing a single representative expert decision-making body (such as the NAGPRA repatriation committee) or on a case-by-case basis with members appointed by affected parties. As effective dispute resolution needs to be anchored in the values of those it is intended to serve, and given the diversity of First Nation cultures in Canada, issues of cultural legitimacy may best be addressed by representation of First Nations and institutions directly affected as well as an agreed upon neutral party (as is often the model adopted in Canadian labor disputes). Access to lists of experts and a range of dispute resolution options made available by national or provincial repatriation institutions or foundations would assist in this process. Currently, no such institutions to facilitate claims in this or other ways exists in Canada. At the very least, ultimate decision-making authority should not simply be shifted from custodial institutions to government personnel or ministers, as this sort of arrangement simply perpetuates relationships of power and dependency.

Attention should also be given to flexibility of procedure, incorporation of cultural elements into procedure and decisionmaking, and costs, particularly given the poor economic conditions of most First Nation communities. An example in Canada is the Métis Settlements Appeal Tribunal (MSAT), a bicultural tribunal consisting mainly of elected Métis settlement members. Its role is to interpret and enforce Métis settlement legislation and Métis laws enacted pursuant to that legislation. It has jurisdiction not only over settlement members, but also over oil and gas companies with interests in Métis settlement lands. The concept of justice that informs MSAT operations, decisions, and procedures is influenced by principles of administrative law, Métis custom, traditional Métis dispute resolution values, and Western alternative dispute resolution rationales. The MSAT promotes fair, efficient, and accessible justice in a number of ways including holding public hearings on affected settlement land or locations most accessible to parties affected; eliminating costs for filing and adopting a policy of not awarding costs; employing of research development officers who conduct investigations and provide relevant findings to all affected parties; and fashioning and requiring participation in alternative processes, such as mediation, that are designed to reflect the cultural values of those affected.[50]

b. Liability of Museums and Governments

Museum legislation considered together with common law of negligence and fiduciary obligation may place legal restraints on the ability to repatriate. For example, provincial and federal museums have statutory mandates obliging them to preserve, educate, and promote public access to their collections. By law, their collections are often held for the benefit of the people of a province. Unlike in the United States, museums in Canada are not usually established as trusts, but public mandates could be interpreted to impose "trustee-like" obligations. The common law may also require boards of trustees to "manage the affairs of the museum so that its property will not be diverted from the public purposes for which it was entrusted."[51] This management may include the duty to exercise the care a reasonably prudent person would in dealing with his or her own property.[52] Because of these and other legal obligations, such as those arising under contract or trust conditions with donors, museums in Canada tend to have deaccessioning policies that require approval of the board of directors, and in some cases, ministerial approval is required. Further, it is unclear how statutory and common law responsibilities are to be understood in the context of repatriation, given the diverse public that museums are intended to serve. As a result, a museum may be reluctant to repatriate some forms of First Nation material absent an agreement on certain conditions for proper preservation and access.

---

[50] For a discussion of the tribunal and a collection of decisions, see CATHERINE BELL & MSAT, CONTEMPORARY MÉTIS JUSTICE: THE SETTLEMENT WAY (1999). The MSAT can still be criticized on several levels including on the basis that it is too influenced by Western law, but this was a decision that was considered necessary in order to create their own dispute resolution system, particularly given its jurisdiction over non-settlement members. MSAT has employed Métis custom and practice as well as principles of common law in its decisions. Of 167 decisions, only seven have been appealed, and, of those, only one was successful. See also on MSAT and for other examples, Catherine Bell, *Indigenous Dispute Resolution Systems Within Non-Indigenous Frameworks: Intercultural Dispute Resolution Initiatives in Canada, in* BELL & KAHANE, INTERCULTURAL, *supra* note 9; see also other essays in that volume.

[51] MARILYN PHELAN, MUSEUMS AND THE LAW 154 (1982). This is an American text but analogous arguments can be made in Canadian law.

[52] *Id.* at 155. *See also* PATTY GERSTENBLITH, ART, CULTURAL HERITAGE, AND THE LAW: CASES AND MATERIALS 293 (2004).

Museums and governments also likely have an obligation to take reasonable steps to ensure they are returning the item to the correct First Nation and perhaps even the correct entity within that Nation. Consequently, proof of cultural affiliation, public notification of claims, and resolution of potential competing claims within and outside of the claimant community need to be addressed. Some museums have developed detailed repatriation policies that address these and other concerns.[53]

Potential liability and the desire for a clear and transparent process by government were the primary motivators for Alberta's First Nations Sacred Ceremonial Objects Repatriation Act, (2000). Although enacted in aid of specific repatriation negotiations between the Blackfoot people of Alberta and the Glenbow-Alberta Institute for return of medicine bundles and other ceremonial items, it also applies to the Royal Alberta Museum and all First Nations in Alberta. It is intended to "ensure First Nations communities have full ownership and responsibility [for] spiritual artifacts" and "to harmonize the role of museums in preservation of human heritage with the aspirations of First Nations to support traditional values."[54] Section 1(e) defines sacred ceremonial objects as objects, the title to which is vested in the Crown and which are "vital to the practice of the First Nation's sacred ceremonial traditions."[55] Although not the product of rights-based negotiation, this definition is consistent with judicial definitions of Aboriginal rights as being sourced in customs, practices, and traditions integral to a distinctive Aboriginal culture. It is also consistent with the modern ethics of museums, which held that sacred and ceremonial objects of ongoing importance to a community should be returned. The Alberta legislation recognizes this new ethic in its preamble, which notes that museums have "for several decades held sacred ceremonial objects of great spiritual value to First Nations, preserving them for the benefit of future generations."

Prior to the enactment of Alberta's legislation, returning medicine bundles and other sacred ceremonial items could expose the Glenbow and the government to legal liability as provincial law provided that objects in the Glenbow collection are held by the provincial Crown and Glenbow on behalf of the citizens of Alberta.[56] Even though the Glenbow had the authority

---

[53] Where such policies have not been in place or have not been followed controversies have arisen over return. A recent example is the repatriation of two water drums and two birch bark scrolls to the Three Fire Midewiwin Society by the Anthropology Museum at the University of Winnipeg. A dispute subsequently arose between competing parties. A forensic audit subsequently showed 85 artifacts, including these items, were missing and documentary records of the deaccessions were not always complete. The water drum controversy was eventually resolved and litigation did not ensue. *See* Manitoba Office of the Auditor General, *Investigation of Missing Artifacts at the Anthropology Museum of Winnipeg* (2002); Bell et al., *Survey, in* BELL & NAPOLEON, VOICES AND PERSPECTIVES, *supra* note 3, at 377–80.

[54] Alberta Legislative Assembly, *Hansard*, 01, at 4 (Feb. 17, 2000) (Speech from the Throne); Repatriation Act, *supra* note 6, pmbl.

[55] *Id.*, § 1(e).

[56] The legislation creating the Glenbow-Alberta Institute and outlining rules governing its collections was amended to allow for repatriation and to indicate that except where property has been repatriated, it is held by the Crown on behalf of the people of Alberta. *See* Glenbow Alberta Institute Act, R.S.A. 2000, ch.G-6, §§ 20–21.

to manage its collections, including loans to First Nations' objects from these collections, ministerial approval was required to deaccession. But the ministerial approval was difficult to obtain for a number of reasons including uncertain legal status of band councils and potential conflicts that could be generated by returns to individuals.[57] As the Glenbow and the Royal Alberta Museum were making increasingly extensive loans of ceremonial items that technically "belonged" to the province or were held in trust for the people of the province, the government felt that a consistent and transparent process to guide such decisions was required.[58] The new legislation sought to facilitate return by relieving the Glenbow and the Province of any legal liability arising from a repatriation done in good faith pursuant to the act. As a result, title to 251 cultural items previously on loan to the Blackfoot has been transferred by the Glenbow to Blackfoot communities.

Under the Act, First Nations initiate the repatriation process by negotiating regulations. The minister must grant approval for repatriations in accordance with the regulations unless, in the minister's opinion, it would be considered inappropriate.[59] Repatriation involves transfer to a First Nation of the Crown's title and acceptance by the First Nation on behalf of all of its people. Rules concerning repatriation of sacred ceremonial items not covered by the Blackfoot agreement are governed by regulations.[60]

Reliance on negotiated regulations enables creation of unique community-specific processes but also increases costs and delay. However, Alberta's legislation was drafted under time pressures and in response to a particular request and as such leaves more to regulation than might otherwise have been allowed. The act can also be criticized on many other levels including the assumption of validity of Crown ownership, its limited application to items that under conventional property analysis place title in the Crown, its failure to include private institutions that receive provincial funding, the emphasis on sacred ceremonial property to the exclusion of other forms of cultural property, and its failure to facilitate claims by First Nations located in other provinces. Although enacted with good intentions, the discretion that is placed in the minister to deny claims and the retention of power by non-indigenous governments over the fate of indigenous

---

[57] Personal Communication with Gerald Conaty, Senior Curator of Ethnology, Glenbow Museum (Apr. 30, 2003).

[58] Personal Communication with Jack Ives, former Manager, Archaeology and History (Provincial Archaeologist), Heritage Resources Management (June 25, 2004).

[59] Repatriation Act, *supra* note 6, §§ 2(1), (2). Dr. Ives explains that this would include circumstances such as competing claims or where a replica is being requested.

[60] Currently the only regulation is the Blackfoot First Nations Sacred Ceremonial Objects Repatriation Regulation, Alta Reg. 96/2004 [hereinafter Blackfoot Regulation]. Under this regulation, an application for repatriation must be made by a society incorporated under Alberta law and acknowledged by the elected chiefs and council. The society accepts title on behalf of the First Nation and agrees to ensure the object is used in a manner consistent with its sacred ceremonial nature. Although not suitable for all First Nation communities, these requirements are consistent with Blackfoot systems of authority and traditions concerning the responsibility of bundle holders to use bundles as intended by the Creator. Also the mechanism of a legal society enables repatriation to appropriate community authorities rather than the band council.

cultural items continue to generate power imbalances running contrary to the aspirations for self-determination of many First Nations. The legislation can only be fully understood as a compromise that is based in trust, enabling items vital to the continuity of Blackfoot ceremonies to be returned home. Further, the Blackfoot people see this act as only one step in a broader repatriation effort.

F. FUNDAMENTAL PRINCIPLES FOR LAW REFORM

Given public interests in preservation and access to First Nation material culture, the current legal, political, and ethical environment, and the rationale for repatriation, what fundamental principles should guide law reform? The Canadian Royal Commission on Aboriginal Peoples (RCAP) offers four fundamental principles for forging new relationships between First Nations and the Crown. These are mutual recognition, mutual respect, sharing, and mutual responsibility.[61] As the RCAP's principles aim to assist the process of decolonization, and repatriation is largely concerned with this process, these principles are helpful in shaping regulatory frameworks for repatriation. They call for

- recognition and protection of the integrity and survival of Aboriginal laws, customs, and practices concerning belonging, responsibility, use, and disposition of material culture;
- a review of public institutions, laws, and policies that perpetuate relationships of dependency;
- laws and policies that do not repeat past injustices but instead take into account historical circumstances under which material came into the possession of public institutions;
- difficult burdens of proof born by Aboriginal peoples because of the passage of time;
- understanding the interrelatedness of intangible and material culture, language, land, well-being, and the natural and spiritual realms; and
- protection and preservation of indigenous lands and languages.

Participants in our research recognize the importance of interpreting these principles in a manner that can be given practical effect in a world where different values and systems of law must co-exist. Thus, they speak of

[61] RCAP, *supra* note 16, at 674–97. Similar principles have been recommended by Dr. Erica-Irene Daes, U.N. Special Rapporteur on the Heritage of Indigenous Peoples. These are the principles of integrity (respecting indigenous views on the interrelatedness of the material and non-material world), locality (recognition of laws unique to particular territories and peoples), and effectiveness (choosing effective legal mechanisms to defend and protect heritage and resource rights). Dr. Erica-Irene A. Daes, *Defending Indigenous Peoples' Heritage* (Keynote address, to the conference, Protecting Knowledge: Traditional Resource Rights in the New Millenium, Feb. 2000), http://ubcic.bc.ca/files/PDF/Keynote.pdf (last visited Dec. 11, 2006). These and other recommendations presented to the United Nations were developed with the assistance of many indigenous organizations.

partnerships, parallel systems, dialogues, respect, and cooperation. The RCAP's approach also recognizes the rights and interests of non-Aboriginal peoples and Aboriginal peoples living off reserve. In particular, the principles of sharing and mutual recognition call for reciprocity, recognition of inter-dependency, respect for different cultures and institutions, and action that benefits both partners in the relationship. These principles are not only consistent with views First Nations individuals shared in our research, but also the original relationship between Aboriginal peoples and the broader Canadian public. Applied to repatriation, they call on First Nations to acknowledge the role that museums and other public institutions have played in public education and preservation of First Nation material culture as well as the need to harmonize that role with aspirations to strengthen and renew cultural identity and ensure survival of healthy First Nations communities.

G. CONCLUSION

Many First Nation communities appreciate and respect the roles museums play in preserving cultural heritage and of material culture in educating non-indigenous peoples about indigenous life. Thus, in addition to repatriation efforts, First Nations and museums have entered into lasting relationships of mutual respect. Many museums, governments, and other custodians of First Nation material are committed to maintaining relationships of equality and assisting in programs central to continuity and revitalization of living First Nation communities. However, the current legal regime obscures and threatens development of relationships of true equality because of the lack of clear jurisprudence on the legal rights of First Nations, issues of power in negotiation, dated legislation affecting fundamental issues such as ownership and consultation, and liabilities of public institutions, to name just a few problem areas. Until these issues are resolved, First Nations are unequal partners in the new relationship and remain dependent on the discretion of museums, other public institutions, and the state. Not only does this situation perpetuate relationships of dependency, it fails to recognize that formal recognition by Canadian federal and provincial governments of the injustices suffered by First Nations is important to the process of healing and restructuring inter-governmental relationships between them.

CHAPTER 4

TAONGA MAORI RENAISSANCE: PROTECTING THE CULTURAL HERITAGE OF AOTEAROA/NEW ZEALAND

Robert K. Paterson*

A. INTRODUCTION

Changes in New Zealand society over the last three to four decades have seen the Maori population of the country re-emerge as a people. These changes have been varied, complex, and interrelated. This chapter will summarize some developments as they affect Maori culture in the broad sense. The exercise is an ambitious one and will necessarily omit certain developments. The overall objective is to present a survey and commentary on Maori cultural heritage law and policy that will furnish a useful comparison concerning the cultural heritage of other indigenous peoples.

B. THE TREATY OF WAITANGI IN NEW ZEALAND LAW

For lawyers, the centerpiece of the renaissance of Maori in New Zealand society has been the 1840 Treaty of Waitangi.[1] The treaty marked the establishment of British sovereignty over New Zealand and purported to guarantee Maori possession of their lands and retention of fishing and other rights. For well over 100 years, the provisions of the treaty were not taken seriously by New Zealand courts or lawyers. This ended in 1986 when the Court of Appeal of New Zealand upheld a statutory reference to the treaty, finding that it mandated the executive to safeguard certain Maori interests.[2] The present chief justice of New Zealand, The Right Honorable Dame Sian Elias, has said of the treaty,

* Many people offered valuable assistance in connection with this article, and the author wishes to thank in particular (while granting absolution for any errors contained herein) the following: Piers Davies, Paul Tapsell, Paul Myburgh and Jane Legget (all of Auckland), Kelvin Day (New Plymouth), David Butts (Palmerston North) and Kim Connelly-Stone, Jo Torr, and Lois Searle (all of Wellington).

[1] A facsimile copy of the treaty and other information can be accessed online at http://www.archives.govt.nz/exhibitions/permanentexhibitions/treaty.php. *See also* CLAUDIA ORANGE, THE TREATY OF WAITANGI (1987).

[2] New Zealand Maori Council v. Attorney-General (Lands), [1987] 1 N.Z.L.R. 641 (C.A.).

> Perhaps most importantly [it] impacts upon the exercise of discretions conferred as a matter of statute or prerogative. It is here that a real revolution in attitude to the treaty can be seen. The treaty is part of the context in which New Zealand legislation . . . as well as the common law, is to be interpreted. Thus, the deductibility of tangi expenses and the rights of Maori to cast-up whales have been recognized by the courts. When legislation is ambiguous, an approach consistent with the Treaty is to be preferred.[3]

Without entrenched constitutional protection of indigenous rights, such as that furnished in Canada by Section 35 of its Constitution Act, New Zealand lawyers have had to resort to ingenious strategies to gain judicial recognition of Maori rights.[4] These efforts are ongoing, but they inform the development of the protection of Maori cultural heritage under New Zealand law.

The Treaty of Waitangi also provided the foundation for the establishment, in 1975, of a separate quasi-judicial body, the Waitangi Tribunal. Consisting of 17 persons, it can only make non-binding decisions (except for certain questions relating to Maori land), but its recommendations have usually been responded to in the form of implementing legislation.[5] Thus, when the tribunal concluded that the government had not adequately protected the Maori language (*te reo Maori*), Parliament enacted the Maori Language Act 1987 which recognized Maori as an official New Zealand language.[6]

Some claims brought before the Waitangi Tribunal have concerned the protection of Maori cultural heritage (both tangible and intangible). Thus, the *Te Roroa* claim referred to spiritual places and wooden burial chests in caves and crevices.[7] Several Maori burial chests had been discovered in North Auckland in 1902 and turned over to the then Auckland Institute and Museum, where they had remained. The tribunal concluded that the Crown (government) had violated its Treaty of Waitangi obligations in not upholding Maori rights to preserve and control these *taonga* (or "treasures"), but it declined to say what Maori rights, if any, existed in respect of the burial chests still in the Auckland Museum. There were other claims regarding Maori artifacts in museum collections in the *Te Roroa* claim, but the tribunal found them unsubstantiated

---

[3] *See* Rt. Hon. Dame Sian Elias, C.J.N.Z., *Maori and the New Zealand Legal System*, 76 AUSTL. L.J. 620, at 626 (2002). See, *infra*, *Glossary of Maori Terms* for definition of the Maori term used in this quotation.

[4] *See* Constitution Act, 1982, being Schedule B of the Constitution Act 1982 (U.K.), ch. 11, § 35.

[5] *See* Treaty of Waitangi Amendment Act 1985 and Treaty of Waitangi (State-Enterprises) Act 1988. *See also* GISSELLE BYRNES, THE WAITANGI TRIBUNAL AND NEW ZEALAND HISTORY (2004).

[6] *See* DEPARTMENT OF JUSTICE, REPORT OF THE WAITANGI TRIBUNAL ON THE TE REO MAORI CLAIM (WAI 11) (1986). Under the Maori Language Act 1987, the Maori language can be used in court proceedings (Section 4). The obligation of the New Zealand Crown to protect the Maori language under the Treaty of Waitangi was also recognized by the English Privy Council in *New Zealand Maori Council v. Attorney-General (Broadcasting Assets)*, [1994] 1 N.Z.L.R. 513 [hereinafter *Broadcasting Assets*].

[7] *See* THE TE ROROA REPORT (WAI 38) (1992), at 210.

by the evidence presented. It should be noted that the tribunal is not bound by the conventional rules of evidence applicable in judicial proceedings.

Sometimes *taonga* have been symbolically returned on the occasion of Treaty of Waitangi claim settlements even though they were not the subject of any specific claim themselves. The best known instance is probably the return of *Korotangi*, a stone carving of a bird that was once part of the National Museum collection and is said to have traveled by the *waka* (canoe) *Tainui* on the great Maori voyage of migration to New Zealand.

There is an important claim now pending before the Waitangi Tribunal that covers cultural and intellectual property relating to flora and fauna that are indigenous to New Zealand.[8] This claim will involve issues relating to Maori claims concerning both tangible and intangible cultural heritage and is the first claim to comprehensively address such issues.

C. THE MINISTRY FOR CULTURE AND HERITAGE: *TE MANATU TAONGA*

The late 1990s saw a broad movement to reconsider the role of the government in relation to culture and heritage generally and Maori culture and heritage in particular. The Culture and Heritage Section Review ultimately led to the establishment, in 1999, of the Ministry for Culture and Heritage and a variety of other initiatives. A new Ministry of Maori Development (*Te Puni Kokiri*) was made responsible for matters connected with international repatriations of *taonga Maori*, as well as the protection of the Maori language, and has a role of monitoring Maori heritage issues, including the performance of other government ministries.

The Ministry for Culture and Heritage is responsible for advising the government in specific areas, including arts, culture, and heritage. In relation to Maori culture, the two most recent projects the ministry has been involved with have been the development of amendments to the former Antiquities Act 1975, concerning cultural property export controls, and to the Historic Places Act 1993, to enhance Maori involvement in resource management processes. The ministry also has responsibilities connected with Crown interests in Maori culture and heritage. A Maori reference group facilitates the ministry's discharge of these responsibilities, which include presentations on Maori customs and arranging visiting speakers on Maori issues.

D. *TAONGA MAORI*

The Waitangi Tribunal in its *Te Roroa Report* describes *taonga* as

> an umbrella term, inclusive of a wide range of things upon which Maori in general and whatu-ora (claimants) . . . place great value and regard as treasures. Among them are intangibles like spiritual values as well as tangible objects. They include the land, sea fronts, forests, lakes

[8] The WAI 262 claim is still being considered by the Waitangi Tribunal. *See*, *infra*, text accompanying note 76.

> and rivers: also places associated with life and death. Although the degree of tapu (sacredness) varies, all these toanga touch the 'heart', the manawa pa (desires) and ngakau pa (ends) of the people.[9]

The former president of the New Zealand Court of Appeal has discussed the term, as it appears in the Treaty of Waitangi, as follows: "Taonga, rendered in the [Maori] version as *treasures* is represented in the English text as *other properties* and in Williams [Maori dictionary] as *property, anything highly prized.* The Waitangi Tribunal has treated the word as embracing the Maori language."[10]

Most judicial comment on the concept of *taonga* has involved the Crown's obligation to protect the Maori language. This legal obligation of the Crown (shared with Maori) means that it must take reasonable action to protect Maori *taonga.*[11]

Movable Maori cultural heritage is probably the best known manifestation of *taonga.* Such objects gained international attention in 1984 when major examples from New Zealand collections toured several museum venues in the United States as part of the renowned Te Maori exhibition. For the first time, an international exhibition of Maori material from New Zealand museums involved the participation of Maori elders, as well as the source museums themselves.

Maori material cultural objects are found in vast numbers both in New Zealand and in foreign museums and private collections. A significant amount of Maori material culture left New Zealand, mostly during the 19th century, and is now found mainly in North American and European collections. There were some early attempts to reverse this outflow, the most significant being the 1948 purchase by the New Zealand government of the vast Oldman collection of Maori and Pacific artifacts from England.[12] In 1967, the Maori collection of K.A. Webster, a New Zealander resident in England, was also returned to New Zealand under the terms of Webster's will.

Over the past 30 or so years, there has been a vigorous revival of Maori arts and culture. Changing perspectives about *taonga Maori* have led some to suggest that the New Zealand government should not acquire old examples by purchase in international markets. Instead of outright purchasing, efforts have sometimes been made to convince foreign museums or collectors to voluntarily return such material by way of gift, loan, or exchange. In the future, private philanthropy, along with government funding, may also facilitate the return of Maori artifacts to New Zealand.

---

[9] *Supra* note 7.

[10] *Supra* note 2, at 663.

[11] *See* Broadcasting Assets, *supra* note 6.

[12] *See* Keith W. Thomson, *The Role of the New Zealand Government in Retrieving Cultural Property*, 9 ART GALLERIES ASS'N N.Z. NEWS 12 (1978).

E. THE PROTECTED OBJECTS ACT 1975

1. Introduction

New Zealand's current cultural patrimony law—the newly named Protected Objects Act 1975 (POA)—dates, in its present form, from 2006. Its origins can be traced to the Maori Antiquities Act 1901, but it took its basic form as the Antiquities Act 1975. Starting in 1995 there were a series of attempts to reform or amend the 1975 law, but none of these efforts was successful.[13] The purpose of the new POA is stated in Section 1A as follows:

> The purpose of this Act is to provide for the better protection of certain objects by—
> (a) regulating the export of protected New Zealand objects; and
> (b) prohibiting the import of unlawfully exported protected foreign objects and stolen protected foreign objects; and
> (c) providing for the return of unlawfully exported protected foreign objects and stolen protected foreign objects; and
> (d) providing compensation, in certain circumstances, for the return of unlawfully exported protected foreign objects; and
> (e) enabling New Zealand's participation in—
> (i) the UNESCO Convention; and
> (ii) the UNIDROIT Convention; and
> (f) establishing and recording the ownership of nga taonga tuturu; and
> (g) controlling the sale of nga taonga tuturu within New Zealand."

The achievement of these objectives is undermined by the clumsy way in which the current law has taken shape. Instead of a repeal of the Antiquities Act 1975 and its replacement by the POA, the current law comprises various unrepealed provisions of the 1975 act (renamed the POA) together with extensive new provisions in the form of amendments to the old law. The result is a confusing patchwork of often complex and unwieldy provisions.

The POA focuses on *taonga Maori* and other nationally significant cultural objects and regulates both their collection and sale together with the imposition of controls on their export from New Zealand. The POA also contains provisions intended to give effect to New Zealand becoming party to the two major international agreements concerning the regulation of illicit trade in material cultural property.[14]

2. The Regulation of Collecting

Unlike most Western countries, New Zealand regulates the private collecting and sale of what the POA terms *taonga tuturu*. Section 2 of the POA defines *taonga tuturu* as

---

[13] *See*, for example, the discussion of the use of a trust in Jonathan Keate, *A Proposal to Improve the Protection of New Zealand's Movable Cultural Heritage by Means of a Statutory Trust*, 23 VIC. U. WELLINGTON L. REV. 97 (1993).

[14] See, *infra*, text accompanying note 26.

an object that—
(a) relates to Maori culture, history, or society; and
(b) was or appears to have been,—
 (i) manufactured or modified in New Zealand by Maori; or
 (ii) brought into New Zealand by Maori; or
 (iii) used by Maori; and
(c) is more than 50 years old.

Residents of New Zealand who possess one or more *taonga tuturu* must register as collectors if they wish to acquire more such objects.[15] Collectors must also notify the authorities of changes in the location of their collections. This system has effectively insulated the market for Maori artifacts inside New Zealand from would-be foreign buyers.

The POA also provides that no person may sell *taonga tuturu* to anyone other than a registered collector, a public museum, or through a licensed auctioneer or second-hand dealer.[16] Dealers must also notify museums of the *taonga tuturu* they intend offering for sale, which presumably gives such institutions the opportunity to purchase such objects for their own collections.[17] This system of registration itself is presumably a significant factor in ensuring against the unauthorized export of Maori cultural property from New Zealand.

3. Maori Cultural Property Export Controls

Like many countries (other than the United States) New Zealand has restrictions on the export of certain categories of cultural property. All *taonga tuturu* require government permission in order to be lawfully exported from New Zealand.[18] The discretion as to the granting of an export permit is based on the consideration of whether the restricted object is

(b) (i) associated with or representative of, activities, events, ideas, movements, objects, persons, or places of importance to New Zealand; or
 (ii) important to New Zealand for its technical accomplishment or design, artistic excellence, or symbolic, commemorative, or research value; or
 (iii) part of a wider historical scientific, or cultural collection or assemblage of importance to New Zealand, and
(c) is of such significance to New Zealand or part of New Zealand that its export from New Zealand would substantially diminish New Zealand's cultural heritage.[19]

---

[15] Protected Objects Act 1975, § 14 [hereinafter POA]. A number of Maori tribes and other Maori organizations have registered as collectors under the legislation.

[16] POA, § 13. Section 15 of the act establishes a system of licensing for auctioneers and secondhand dealers.

[17] POA, § 6.

[18] POA, Schedule Four.

[19] POA, § 7A.

These criteria represent a version of the well-known "Waverley criteria" for allowing the export of cultural property, based on the famous recommendations of a 1952 English committee chaired by Lord Waverley.[20] Permission to export can be made conditional on such things as the owner giving permission for copies of the objects being made and the objects being packed and dispatched as required.[21] What is unclear at present is how the criteria for granting export permits are applied to *taonga tuturu*. It does not seem that many permits are currently being granted for protected Maori objects.

The most infamous example of non-compliance with New Zealand cultural property export controls was the removal of the carved wooden Motunui Pataka panels without government permission.[22] The New Zealand government first became aware of the panels when they were offered for sale in London in 1978. New Zealand sued the consignor and the Sotheby Parke Bernet auction house to recover the carvings. The English trial judge was sympathetic to the claim but, at final appeal, the English House of Lords denied a remedy based on its opinion that the carvings had not been forfeited to New Zealand upon being illegally exported.[23] The court did not express any view on the enforceability in England of the New Zealand export controls. At the time of the proceedings in *Attorney General of New Zealand v. Ortiz and Others*,[24] neither the United Kingdom nor New Zealand were parties to the 1970 UNESCO Convention on illicit trafficking in cultural property.[25] If both states had been parties, there might have been a real possibility of an order to return the carvings to New Zealand.[26]

4. Implementation of the UNESCO and UNIDROIT Conventions Into New Zealand Law

One of the primary objectives behind recent revisions to the Antiquities Act 1975 was to amend it in accordance with New Zealand's accession to both the UNESCO convention and the UNIDROIT Convention on Stolen or Illegally Exported Cultural Objects.[27] Under New Zealand law, in order for these agreements to be binding in domestic law, they must be implemented by legislation. New Zealand appears to be the first common law jurisdiction to have implemented both of these multilateral conventions on illicit cultural property trafficking simultaneously, as of May 1, 2007. The implementation of

[20] *See* THE EXPORT OF WORKS OF ART, ETC. REPORT OF A COMMITTEE APPOINTED BY THE CHANCELLOR OF THE EXCHEQUER (1952).

[21] POA, § 8.

[22] *See* KELVIN DAY, MAORI WOOD CARVING OF THE TARANAKI REGION 38–39 (2001).

[23] Attorney General of New Zealand v. Ortiz and Others, [1982] 1 Q.B. 349 (Staughton J.), *rev'd*, [1982] 3 W.L.R. 570 (C.A.), *rev'd*, [1983] 2 W.L.R. 809 (H.L.).

[24] *Id.*

[25] *See* Convention on the Means of Prohibiting and Preventing the Illicit Import, Export and Transfer of Ownership of Cultural Property (Nov. 14, 1970), *reprinted in* 10 I.L.M. 189 (entered into force Apr. 24, 1972).

[26] *See* Robert K. Paterson, *The Legal Dynamics of Cultural Property Export Controls:* Ortiz *Revisited*, U.B.C. L. REV. 241 (Special Issue 1995).

[27] June 24, 1995, *available at* http://www.unidroit.org/english/conventions/1995 culturalproperty/1995culturalproperty-e.htm.

the conventions took somewhat peculiar form in that while certain language of both conventions appears in various sections of the POA itself, the conventions themselves were also appended as schedules to the act—though they were not, as such, given force of law! It has been suggested that while the language of the conventions could still be resorted to clarify the wording of the POA itself, the simultaneous adoption of the language of both conventions in the one law may result in significant problems of interpretation.[28]

The POA defines the term "protected foreign object" in the same way as the UNESCO and the UNIDROIT conventions define "cultural property."[29] The POA then provides for the return of such objects when they are unlawfully exported, subject to limitation periods based on the UNIDROIT convention and on the payment of "fair and reasonable compensation" to bona fide purchasers.[30] The POA also provides for the return of stolen protected foreign objects, but only if they belong to "foreign cultural institutions," which are defined as museums, religious or secular public monuments, or similar institutions in a state other than New Zealand.[31] There are similar provisions regarding stolen objects, as in the case of smuggled objects, concerning payment of compensation.[32] This latter provision represents a significant inroad into New Zealand common law, which does not otherwise oblige owners of stolen goods to pay any form of compensation to bona fide purchasers. Private owners of foreign stolen goods taken to New Zealand are not subject to these rules, however, and will still be free from any compensatory responsibility in a claim in conversion to recover their property.

F. NEWLY FOUND OBJECTS: *TAONGA TUTURU*

The common law of finders does not apply to newly discovered Maori artifacts (*taonga tuturu*). Under the POA, any such objects found after 1975 are "deemed to be *prima facie* the property of the Crown."[33] The Maori Land Court has jurisdiction to resolve competing claims as to the ownership or possession of newly found Maori artifacts, though no such claim appears ever to have been brought before it.[34]

New Zealand courts have found that the Crown is obliged to act in good faith in deciding matters affecting Maori interests. This obligation will, in some cases,

---

[28] *See* Piers Davies & Paul Myburgh, *The Protected Objects Act in New Zealand: Too Little, Too Late?* 15 Int'l J. Cultural Prop. 321 (2008).

[29] POA, § 2.

[30] POA, §§ 10A to 10C.

[31] POA, § 2.

[32] POA, §§ 10D and 10E.

[33] POA, § 11. The term "found" is defined, in Section 2, to mean a situation where there is no reasonable certainty about lawful ownership and where any previous owner is probably deceased.

[34] POA, §§ 11 and 12. The Maori Land Court, which has existed for over 100 years, has specialized jurisdiction over applications concerning the administration of Maori land. Te Ture Whenua Maori Act/Maori Land Act 1993; *see also* Norman Smith, Maori Land Law (1960). Recent assessments put Maori land at 1.3 million hectares. In the *Manukau Report* (WAI 18) (1989), a complaint was made to the Waitangi Tribunal that Maori artifacts found in the lands involved in the claim had been retained by their finders.

require the Crown to consult with Maori regarding *taonga tuturu,* depending on the importance of the issue in question.[35] In light of these requirements, the Ministry for Culture and Heritage has developed processes to involve local Maori (*tangata whenua*) from the area of the find in any decision as to how the artifacts are to be dealt with. Ministry personnel usually take responsibility for the care and conservation of newly found artifacts and ensure that they are properly registered. Prior to the POA coming into force, the practice was that the award of custody of objects to Maori, obviated the need for an application to the Maori Land Court concerning the question of ownership.[36] Current practice under the POA is still evolving.

The new provisions of the POA also clarify the government's obligation to provide for the custody and recording of newly found *taonga tuturu* and to notify any parties that may have an interest in them.[37] A public notice is to be published calling for claims of ownership to be lodged within 60 days. If only one claim is lodged, an application must be made to the Maori Land Court for its confirmation. If competing claims are lodged, the government must consult, and if no resolution can be reached, an application may be made to the Maori Land Court to determine ownership. Thus, the new provisions largely confirm and clarify preexisting law and practice.

G. HERITAGE CONSERVATION LEGISLATION

1. Introduction

New Zealand has long provided legal means for ensuring the protection of lands, sites, and waters that are thought to have archaeological, scientific, or historical significance. For decades, however, there was rarely any attention given to Maori perspectives on heritage conservation priorities. In the *Te Roroa Report* of the Waitangi Tribunal, Sir Tipene O'Regan, chair of the Ngai Tahu Trust Board, is quoted as follows:

> The Maori membership of the [Historic Places] Trust's committees have . . . been concerned and, at times, distressed by the difficulty of securing protection for a huge range of sites of great importance to Maori on grounds of historic, traditional or spiritual association. We have felt that there was well entrenched legislative protection for sites on a [sic] grounds of essentially Pakeha (non-Maori) academic interest but a gross lack of ability to protect sites on Maori grounds. Put simply it has been easier to protect an ancestral rubbish dump than a tuahu or a waka landing site or a maunga whakatauaki. In the 1970s and early 1980s we also experienced considerable resistance from professional archaeologists, including those on the staff of the [New Zealand Historic Places] Trust at the time, to our attempts to secure a similar

---

35 New Zealand Maori Council v. Attorney-General (Lands), [1987] 1 N.Z.L.R. 641, 682–83 (C.A.).

36 *See* Brodie Stubbs, *Newly-Found Maori Artifacts*, 28 TE ARA: MUSEUMS AOTEAROA 41 (2003).

37 POA, § 11(4) to (9).

standard of protection for sites of Maori value to that enjoyed by sites deemed to have archaeological value.[38]

The following is a brief survey of both longstanding and contemporary New Zealand legislation dealing with heritage conservation topics. It is largely in the context of such laws and their interpretation by the courts that a compromise between the sorts of Maori concerns just outlined and other priorities, such as scientific and environmental protection, have been and remain to be worked out.

2. The Historic Places Act 1993

The Historic Places Act 1993 is a comprehensive law dealing with archaeological sites (including artifacts located at such sites), historic places, and Maori sacred places (*wahi tapu*). The 1993 law arose from a 1988 review by the Ministry of Conservation of New Zealand historic places legislation and the role of what in 2005 became a Crown entity, the New Zealand Historic Places Trust. The new law seeks to develop a bicultural guardianship of New Zealand's historic heritage and is a direct response to the sort of criticism made by Sir Tipene O'Regan above.

The Historic Places Act 1993 continues the Historic Places Trust (Pouhere Taonga) with wide powers.[39] The trust (first established in 1954) now has multiple statutory functions, including the recording and conservation of *wahi tapu*.[40] The board of trustees of the trust comprises nine persons, three of whom must have expertise regarding Maori culture.[41] The Historic Places Act 1993 also establishes a Maori Heritage Council comprising eight members, half of whom must be Maori and half of whom must be members of the board of trustees of the Historic Places Trust.[42] The role of the Maori Heritage Council is to seek to ensure that Maori perspectives, and concerns are taken into account in connection with heritage issues, along with protecting places and sites of Maori interest and advocating Maori heritage concerns generally.[43]

The Historic Places Act 1993 carries forward the preexisting system requiring applications for interfering with archaeological sites.[44] Interference applications respecting sites of Maori interest must be referred by the Historic Places Trust to the Maori Heritage Council in order to obtain its recommendations. The trust can carry out its own archaeological investigation of a site, but it cannot do so without the landowner's consent and that of such tribal authority as the Maori Heritage Council considers appropriate.[45]

The Historic Places Act 1993 also maintains a system of registration of

---

[38] The Te Roroa Report, *supra* note 7. See, *infra*, *Glossary of Maori Terms* for definitions of Maori terms used in this quotation.

[39] Historic Places Act 1993, § 38.

[40] Historic Places Act 1993, § 39.

[41] Historic Places Act 1993, § 42, as amended, 2005.

[42] Historic Places Act 1993, § 84, as amended, 2005.

[43] Historic Places Act 1993, § 85.

[44] Historic Places Act 1993, § 18.

[45] Fulton Hogan Ltd. v. Bay of Plenty Regional Council, A106/02,7 NZED 485.

historic places and areas and sacred Maori places.[46] In the case of *wahi tapu* the Maori Heritage Council deals with applications for registration.[47] Many of these procedures were in response to concerns raised in reports of the Waitangi Tribunal and were the subject of 2005 amendments to the act, which establish more detailed procedures to register historic places or *wahi tapu.*

The facts in the Court of Appeal decision in *Quixley Enterprises Ltd. v. Ngati Paoa Development Trust*[48] provide an example of the operation of the statute in relation to Maori concerns. The land involved was a small piece of urban land said to be the site of an ancient burial ground or *urupa.* The whole of the land was designated as an archaeological site under the Historic Places Act 1993 and recognized as such by the Historic Places Trust. The presence of the burial site became known in 1985 to elders of the Ngati Paoa Tribe, who lived in the area in the early 19th century. A development company purchased the land in 1988 and sought the permission of the trust to modify the site. This permission was granted in 1990 but did not extend to the part of the land containing the burial site. The litigation involved an unsuccessful attempt to obtain judicial review of a subsequent ministerial decision that allowed for the modification of the entire site, including the burial site.

3. The Resource Management Act 1991

The Resource Management Act 1991 is a complex law concerned with the sustainable development of New Zealand's natural and physical resources.[49] The statute enumerates seven "matters of national importance" to be advanced in the carrying out of the functions under the law. Included among these is a furthering of Maori interests, stated as follows: "The relationship of Maori and their culture and traditions with their ancestral lands, water sites, *wahi tapu* and other *taonga.*"[50]

Part VIII of the law provides for the establishment of "heritage protection authorities." These can be any corporation possessed of an interest in the protection of any place. Notice may be given by such an authority to any territorial authority under the act of a request for heritage protection of places such as those with spiritual significance to Maori. The owner of the land on which a place sought to be subject to a heritage order under the Resource Management Act 1991 is located may apply for his or her land to be purchased.

In the *Te Roroa Report,* the Waitangi Tribunal expressed concern that the procedures under the Resource Management Act 1991 conflicted with Maori culture and tradition, referring specifically to the payment of compensation to landowners and the impracticability of the corporate form for Maori

---

[46] Historic Places Act 1993, §§ 22–28, 31–37.

[47] Historic Places Act 1993, § 25.

[48] (1992), 275/91 (C.A.) (unreported).

[49] Resource Management Act 1991, § 5.

[50] Resource Management Act 1991, § 6(e). The act also provides for its administration to take into account the principles of the Treaty of Waitangi; Resource Management Act 1991, § 8.

communities. The report cites several issues raised by the statute, but since it had not become law prior to the conclusion of the hearings in *Te Roroa*, the Waitangi Tribunal declined to deal with them.[51]

The rights of Maori under the Resource Management Act 1991 were the subject of extensive discussion in the case of *Takamore Trustees v. Kapiti Coast District Council*.[52] The case involved a decision by a local council to allow the construction of a linkage road in the face of opposition from local Maori (represented by the Takamore Trustees) who claimed the road would be built over a sacred site that included *taonga* and ancestral remains. This council decision was confirmed by the Environmental Court whose decision was then appealed to the High Court.

The High Court found that the Environmental Court had erred in failing to give reasons for its rejection of evidence of the presence of ancestral remains and *taonga* in part of the area affected by the proposed road:

> The Court complains about a lack of 'back-up history' or 'tradition'. Again, it is difficult to understand what this means. Those in the iwi entrusted with the oral history of the area have given their evidence. Unless they were exposed as incredible or unreliable witnesses, or there was other credible and reliable evidence which contradicted what they had to say, accepted by the Court, how could the Court reject their evidence? The Court complained it was bereft of 'evidence' and had 'assertion' only of the presence of koiwi. The evidence was given by kaumatua based on the oral history of the tribe. What more could be done from their perspective? The fact no European was present with pen and paper to record such burials could hardly be grounds for rejecting the evidence. Nor could the kind of geographical precision apparently sought by the Court be reasonably expected. The claim of burials is within a defined area. To require a precise location of burial in such circumstances before satisfaction with the evidence is to potentially reduce many claims of waahi tapu areas to unproven and reduce ss 6(3), 7 and 8 matters accordingly. If the test applied to koiwi presence by the Court was also applied to the presence of taonga, the Court would have logically been required to find their presence not proved. The fact it did not seems difficult to understand.[53]

The High Court went on to say that while a written record might support oral history, its absence could hardly detract from the significance of such history.

The High Court in *Takamore Trustees* also commented on the requirement of consultation set out in the legislation. The Environmental Court was satisfied that the necessary consultation with Maori had occurred, but the High Court was critical of its approach, writing as follows:

---

[51] *Supra* note 7, at 256–57.

[52] [2003] 3 N.Z.L.R. 496 (H.C.).

[53] *Id.* at 512–13. See, *infra, Glossary of Maori Terms* for definitions of Maori terms used in this quotation.

> Consultation by itself without allowing the view of Maori to influence decision making is no more than window dressing . . . This does not mean that . . . Maori exercising guardianship have a right to veto . . . But their view . . . must be paid particular regard to in the balance of factors.[54]

Finally, the High Court looked at whether the Environmental Court had erred in applying the Resource Management Act 1991 by failing, as the act requires, to take into account the principles of the Treaty of Waitangi. Since the High Court had found the Environmental Court had, without reasons, rejected evidence of an important sacred Maori site, it thought it had also failed to perform its statutory duty in regard to the treaty.

The *Takamore Trustees* case is an important milestone in the legal development of Maori cultural heritage rights under New Zealand law. It reveals that New Zealand courts are willing to hold their government to high standards in respect of its statutory responsibilities to consider and protect Maori cultural heritage concerns in the context of other social interests such as land development.

4. The Conservation Law Reform Act 1990

This statute disestablished various parks and reserves boards and advisory committees and replaced them with the New Zealand Conservation Authority and local conservation boards. Two of the 12 members of the authority are appointed by the minister of Maori development. The legislation does not set out in detail how natural and historic resource management is to be integrated; this function is left for statements of general policy to be developed under the law.[55] Local conservation boards have already developed policies for the protection of sacred places after consultation with Maori.

The legislation also requires that it be interpreted so as to give effect to the principles of the Treaty of Waitangi.[56] This provision was subject to interpretation by the New Zealand Court of Appeal in *Ngai Tahu Maori Trust Board v. Director-General of Conservation*.[57] The Court found, consistent with the High Court decision in the *Takamore Trustees* case (see Section G.3), that this sort of statutory direction gave rise to a duty of active protection and could not be limited to consultation or some procedural matters.[58] In the Court of Appeal in *Ngai Tahu*, P. Cooke stated, "it has been established that the principles [of the treaty] require active protection of Maori interests. To restrict this to consultation would be hollow."[59]

There is a significant body of New Zealand case law dealing with similar references to the Treaty of Waitangi to that contained in the Conservation

---

[54] *Id.* at 517.
[55] Conservation Law Reform Act 1990, § 17B.
[56] Conservation Law Reform Act 1990, § 4.
[57] [1995] 3 N.Z.L.R. 553 (C.A.).
[58] *Id.* at 553, 561.
[59] *Id.* at 560.

Law Reform Act 1990.[60] The strength of the obligation to apply treaty principles varies with the language of the statute incorporating a reference to the treaty. The "give effect to" wording discussed in the *Ngai Tahu* case has been seen as creating a mandatory obligation to apply treaty principles, at least insofar as they are not clearly inconsistent with the provisions of the statute itself. If the courts find a breach of legislation as a result of failure to apply the treaty, they have then concluded that any resultant executive action by government is invalid.[61]

5. Conclusion

The legislation summarized here, as interpreted by the New Zealand courts, shows that a significant level of accommodation is developing in relation to Maori cultural heritage interests and countervailing policies. While the protection of Maori cultural and spiritual concerns in the context of such laws remains a "work-in-progress," recent cases suggest that New Zealand courts are increasingly ready to meaningfully address the sorts of concerns referred to by Sir Tipene O'Regan and others.[62]

H. MAORI GRAVES AND ANCESTRAL REMAINS

1. Maori Graves

A major concern regarding the protection of Maori heritage has been the level of legal protection afforded Maori graves and burial sites. As we have seen in relation to heritage legislation, Maori interests have often come in conflict with the economic priorities of property developers and other land users.

The principal New Zealand law dealing with graves is the Burial and Cremation Act 1964, which provides for the establishment, maintenance and regulation of cemeteries and crematoria. Section 3 of this act provides that, unless expressly stated otherwise, it does not apply to Maori burial grounds or bodies buried in such grounds.

Maori burial sites are separately provided for in the Te Ture Whenua Maori/ Maori Land Act 1993. Under this act, the chief executive of the Ministry of Maori Development can set aside any Maori freehold or other land for, among other things, a burial ground.[63] The same dilemma thus arises as in the case of heritage and archaeological sites of choosing between the need to create a reserve to protect Maori burial grounds and pressures to use the same land for other purposes, such as economic development. The Burial and Cremation Act, however, is not premised on this sort of weighing of priorities, suggesting that, despite the need for consultation and other legal protection afforded Maori, non-Maori burial sites receive a higher level of protection under New Zealand law than do Maori sites.

---

[60] *See* HE TIKOHANGA O KAWA KI TE TIRITI O WAITANGI: A GUIDE TO THE PRINCIPLES OF THE TREATY OF WAITANGI AS EXPRESSED BY THE COURTS AND THE WAITANGI TRIBUNAL 20–22 (2001).

[61] New Zealand Maori Council v. Attorney-General (Lands), [1987] 1 N.Z.L.R. 641 (C.A.); *see also* New Zealand Maori Council v. Attorney-General (Forests), [1989] 2 N.Z.L.R. 142 (C.A.).

[62] *Supra* note 38 and accompanying text.

[63] Te Ture Whenua Maori/Maori Land Act 1993, § 338.

2. Repatriation of Maori Ancestral Remains: *Koiwi Tangata Maori*

An early European witness to Maori culture, the Reverend William Yate, described Maori respect for their dead in the following terms:

> Their treatment of the dead may next be noticed. In no country can greater respect be shown for the dead than in New Zealand. Those who, whilst here, were the pest of society—those who for their crimes were almost universally disliked—those to whom no assistance was rendered, if they required it, during life—are wept over and honoured when dead; and all the customary forms, the tapuing, and the feasting, are gone through, as though the departed had been a rich man, a mighty conqueror, a great friend of society, or a person universally beloved.[64]

Many early Maori traditions may have disappeared, but reverence for the dead has not.

For decades now the possession and display of Maori ancestral remains has been a highly sensitive issue for Maori and non-Maori alike. Of special concern have been Maori *toi moko* (preserved tattooed Maori heads) which were originally treasured as memorial relics but began to be collected by Europeans during the 19th century.[65] It may have been this foreign interest that led to the practice of preserving the heads of enemies as objects of trade.[66] These preserved heads were long displayed openly in New Zealand and foreign museums, as well as being sold at auction or privately. This practice came to public attention in the 1988 decision of the High Court of New Zealand in *Re Estate of Tupuna Maori* where letters of administration were granted to enable the president of the New Zealand Maori Council to take possession of a head that had been consigned for sale by auction in London.[67] Following this case and growing outrage at the trade in Maori ancestral remains, leading international auction houses declined to accept *toi moko* for sale and they were withdrawn from open display by many foreign museums.

In 1998, the New Zealand government finally agreed to take a more active role in facilitating the repatriation of Maori ancestral remains (*koiwi tangata Maori*) from foreign institutions. In 2003, the Cabinet approved a repatriation

---

[64] *See* Rev. William Yate, An Account of New Zealand and the Formation and Progress of the Church Missionary Society's Mission in the Northern Island 135 (2d ed. 1835).

[65] The term *mokamokai* was previously used to describe these objects, but this term, which translates as "slave head," has now been replaced in usage because of its derogatory connotation. Communication from Dr. Paul Tapsell (Sept. 1, 2005).

[66] Yate, *supra* note 64, at 130–34.

[67] *Re* Estate of Tupuna Maori, P580/88 High Court of New Zealand, Wellington, May 19, 1988, Greig J. (unreported). A similar result occurred in 1983 when the Marquis of Tavistock agreed to withdraw a head from auction in London after receiving a request from the New Zealand government. Prominent among efforts to repatriate *toi moko* located outside of New Zealand were those of the late Maui Dalvanius Prime. These efforts continue under the auspices of the Mokomokai Education Trust. *See* http://digitalus.co.nz/mokomokai/index1.html.

policy regarding ancestral remains (the Karanga Aotearoa Repatriation Program) and mandated the Museum of New Zealand—Te Papa Tongarewa—to be the authorized Crown agent to undertake this work, which has received $NZ500,000 per year in funding. For the purposes of this repatriation process, the term *koiwi tangata Maori* is defined as "any part of the human body (skeletal or soft tissue) of Maori or Moriori origin, which is in an unmodified state since death. This includes all *toi moko*, which are tattooed, preserved heads of Maori or Moriori origin."[68] The repatriation policy is governed by the following six principles:

1. The government role is mainly one of facilitation—it does not claim ownership of *koiwi*;
2. Repatriation from overseas institutions and individuals is by mutual agreement only;
3. The repatriation policy does not cover Maori remains in war graves maintained by the Commonwealth War Graves Commission or other similar institutions;
4. No payment for *koiwi* will be made to overseas institutions;
5. *Koiwi* must be identified as originating from New Zealand; and
6. Maori are to be involved in the repatriation of *koiwi* and will determine the final resting place, where possible.[69]

The Museum of New Zealand has identified approximately 110 overseas museums and universities that hold collections of Maori ancestral remains.[70]

International repatriation of Maori ancestral remains is continuing. As an interim measure some foreign museums have removed *toi moko* from public display.[71] In October 2007, the mayor of Rouen agreed to return to New Zealand a *toi moko* held in the French city's Museum of Natural History. The French Ministry of Culture then blocked the return on the ground that the object was a work of art and "inalienable" under French law. A French administrative tribunal subsequently ruled that the attempted return was invalid on the grounds that Rouen had failed to consult a scientific committee before withdrawing the head from the Museum's collection. Amidst worldwide publicity about the case, New Zealand remains optimistic that a return of the head from Rouen will still happen.[72]

---

[68] *Koiwi* does not include items that have been modified entirely or partly from human bone (*e.g.* carved or decorated).

[69] *See* Evidence of James McKenzie and Brodie Stubbs on behalf of the Ministry for Culture and Heritage, Urewera District Inquiry (WAI 894), No. L.16, at 24.

[70] *See* TAONGA MAORI CONFERENCE: NEW ZEALAND NOV. 18–27, 1990, at 76 (1990).

[71] Recent returns negotiated by *Te Papa* include three *toi moko* and a leg bone of a Maori warrior chief by the Kelvingrove Art Gallery and Museum in Glasgow, Scotland, and two *toi moko* by the Perth Museum, also in Scotland. At present T*e Papa* holds over 100 Maori ancestral remains awaiting return to descendants or other appropriate persons. *See* N.Z. HERALD (Auckland), Nov. 16, 2005.

[72] *See* Elaine Sciolino, *French Dispute Whether Maori Head is Body Part or Art*, N.Y. TIMES, Oct. 26, 2004; *No Homecoming for Preserved Head*, N.Y. TIMES, Jan. 3, 2008, at B2. It has also been reported that President Sarkozy has asked his minister of culture to discuss the issue of the return of objects in French museum collections. *See* Roxana Azimi & Gareth Harris, *To Sell or Not to Sell?* ART NEWSPAPER, No. 185, Nov. 2007, at 5. For an English translation of the French tribunal's decision, see Robert K. Paterson, *Administrative Tribunal of Rouen, Decisions*

I. INTELLECTUAL PROPERTY: *MATAURANGA MAORI*

There is substantial literature on the relevance of intellectual property law to the protection of indigenous culture.[73] It is beyond the scope of this chapter to examine all aspects of this issue in relation to Maori, but a few specific developments should be referred to.

1. The Mataatua Declaration

In 1993, the Year of Indigenous Peoples, the "First International Conference on the Cultural and Intellectual Property Rights of Indigenous Peoples" was held at Whakatane in New Zealand. The conference produced the well-known Mataatua Declaration on the Cultural and Intellectual Property Rights of Indigenous Peoples, which stressed the inadequacy of existing intellectual property rules to protect indigenous culture and the need for new protective initiatives.[74] Though legally non-binding, the Mataatua Declaration added to emerging pressure on the New Zealand government to address Maori intellectual property-related concerns.

2. The *Toi Iho* (Maori Made) Mark

The Maori made mark (*toi iho*) was developed in response to Maori concerns about protecting traditional Maori cultural expressions, including their misuse by non-Maori. Some see the mark as an interim means of providing protection to traditional Maori cultural expressions by limiting the market for works produced by non-Maori that evoke Maori cultural expressions.

The *toi iho* mark was developed by the Maori Arts Board (Te Waka Toi) of the Arts Council of New Zealand ("Creative New Zealand") and is a registered trade mark. The mark indicates to consumers that the author of a work is of Maori descent and produces work of a particular quality. The trademark is owned by Creative New Zealand, but it is envisaged that its ownership will eventually be transferred to an autonomous Maori entity.

A "Mainly Maori Mark" is also available for groups of artists who work together and are predominantly of Maori descent. The "Maori Co-production Mark" is available for Maori artists who create works collaboratively with persons of non-Maori descent.

No. 702737, Dec. 27, 2007 (Maori Head Case), 15 INTL. J. CULTURAL PROP. 223 (2008).

[73] *See* Christine H. Farley, *Protecting Folklore of Indigenous Peoples! Is Intellectual Property the Answer?* 30 CONN. L. REV. 1 (1997); D. Downs, *How Intellectual Property Could be a Tool to Protect Traditional Knowledge*, 25 COLUM J. ENVTL. L. 253 (2000); B.S. Mandelker, *Indigenous People and Cultural Appropriation: Intellectual Property Problems and Solutions*, 16 CAN. INTEL. PROP. REV. 367 (2000); Robert K. Paterson & Dennis S. Karjala, *Looking Beyond Intellectual Property in Resolving Protection of the Intangible Cultural Heritage of Indigenous Peoples*, 11 CARDOZO J. INT'L. & COMP. L. 633 (2003); *Symposium: Traditional Knowledge, Intellectual Property, and Indigenous Culture*, 11 CARDOZO J. INT'L & COMP. L. (2003).

[74] *See* http://aotearoa.wellington.net.nz/imp/mata.htm.

3. Offensive Marks

Another innovation responding to Maori concerns has been the introduction of legislation dealing with offensive marks.[75] New Zealand's trade marks legislation has been amended to prevent the registration of trademarks whose registration or use is likely to be offensive to a significant section of the community, including Maori. A person who claims to be "culturally aggrieved" can also apply to have a registered mark invalidated. A Maori trademarks advisory committee has been established to advise the commissioner of trademarks on whether trademarks based on Maori text and imagery are likely to be considered as offensive to Maori.

4. The Maori Intellectual Property (WAI 262) Claim

A Waitangi Tribunal claim by six *iwi* filed in 1991 alleges that New Zealand intellectual property laws violate the Treaty of Waitangi in certain respects.[76] The claim (WAI 262) embraces several allegations that include the failure of the Crown to consult with Maori before entering into a number of international intellectual property instruments, the failure of the Crown adequately to protect the Maori language and other intangible *taonga*, the failure adequately to protect Maori artistic works through inadequate laws and neglectful policies, and the failure of the Crown actively to protect Maori *taonga* in general, including moveable cultural property and immovable *taonga*, such as sites of cultural significance to Maori.[77] The claim goes beyond the traditional subject matter of intellectual property, however, by including loss of indigenous flora and fauna.

The claim raises very fundamental and difficult issues concerning the feasibility of the role of central government in protecting all aspects of intellectual property.[78] It also raises questions about the factors that should inform intellectual property law development as a major facet of overall cultural policy. The claims in WAI 262 concern the failure of the Crown to protect Maori culture in diverse respects. If these claims are upheld, it will be interesting to see how far governments are actually willing to change cultural policy in the future. Hearings in WAI 262 started in 1998, and in June 2002 the Crown filed its statement of response with the tribunal, which heard evidence during 2006 and 2007. At the time of writing, the tribunal had not yet released its report.

---

[75] *See* Trade Marks Act 2002; Owen Morgan, *Protecting Indigenous Signs and Trade Marks—The New Zealand Experiment*, 1 Intell. Prop. Q. 58 (2004).

[76] For further information, see the Waitangi Tribunal Web site, http://www.Waitangi-tribunal.govt.nz/research/wai262/7. Since 1991, three other *iwi* have lodged separate statements of claim. See also the Ministry of Economic Development Web site, http://www.med.govt.nz/buslt/int-prop/info-sheets/wai-262.html.

[77] *See* Graeme W. Austin, *Re-treating Intellectual Property? The WAI 262 Proceeding and the Heuristics of Intellectual Property Law*, 11 Cardozo J. Int'l. & Comp. L. 333 (2003); Maui Solomon, *Protecting Maori Heritage in New Zealand*, *in* Art and Cultural Heritage: Law, Policy, and Practice 352 (Barbara T. Hoffman ed., 2006).

[78] Solomon, *supra* note 77, at 357–62.

J. MAORI LANGUAGE PROTECTION

The Maori language was severely compromised during the 20th century, but in the last 20 years a number of initiatives have sought to strengthen the language. Most court decisions dealing with *taonga* have centered on the obligation of the Crown to protect the Maori language (*te reo Maori*). In *New Zealand Maori Council v. Attorney-General (Broadcasting Assets),* the Privy Council in London, England (then New Zealand's highest court) not only accepted the Crown's obligation to protect the Maori language, but also explained that this responsibility was enhanced when the language was in a vulnerable state and that the obligation was one Maori themselves shared.[79] In *New Zealand Maori Council v. Attorney-General (Broadcasting)* the Crown's duty to protect *te reo Maori* as a *taonga* was discussed by the New Zealand Court of Appeal as follows:

> It was not disputed either that the prime objective of the Treaty was to ensure a proper place in the land for the two peoples on whose behalf it was signed. Nothing could be further from that objective than the obliteration of the culture of one of them or its absorption into that of the other. Thus protection of the Maori language, an essential element of Maori culture, was and is a fundamental Treaty commitment on the part of the Crown.[80]

In 1987, the Maori Language Act established the Maori language as an official New Zealand language. This paved the way for the growth of Maori language schools and some 22 Maori radio stations as well as the Maori Television Service. The 1987 statute also created the Maori Language Commission, which supports the growth of the language through developing new terminology and increasing usage standards.

In 2003, the Ministry of Maori Development announced a Maori language strategy aimed at furthering these initiatives. Now efforts will be made to focus on greater use of Maori language in communities by strengthening language use and skills, developing greater education opportunities in the Maori language, and expanding recognition of the language generally. In the first six decades of the 20th century, English language skills were seen by most Maori as a key to their economic and social improvement. Many Maori who knew their own language did not use it among their families at home. These factors marginalized the language and put its survival seriously at risk. New policies have already borne fruit with the numbers of Maori speakers having stabilized between 1996 and 2001, and with approximately 130,000 Maori (about 25 percent of the total Maori population of 520,000) indicating they could speak Maori.

---

[79] New Zealand Maori Council v. Attorney-General (Broadcasting Assets), [1994] 1 N.Z.L.R. 513 (P.C.).

[80] New Zealand Maori Council v. Attorney-General (Broadcasting), [1992] 2 N.Z.L.R. 576, 587 (C.A.) per Hardie Boys J.

K. MUSEUMS AND *TAONGA*

1. Introduction

Given its small size and population, New Zealand has a large number of museums, many of which hold significant collections of *taonga Maori*. These were, however, long sidelined by the attention given to collections of European origin.[81] The scope of the early Maori collections reflected contemporary collecting patterns and resultant gifts (mostly by non-Maori). Significant additions also occurred as a result of the acquisition of Maori material that had earlier left New Zealand. As Professor Hirini Moko Mead has observed, since the staff at the museums were, until recently, all non-Maori, "The Maori people whose traditions were being studied were not an important part of the scholars' world except in the limited sense of being informants. It was assumed that everyone belonged to and believed in the world of the dominant group."[82]

2. The Te Maori Exhibition

One of the most symbolic events affecting the place of Maori culture in modern New Zealand was the 1984 Te Maori exhibition of Maori art from New Zealand collections.[83] This international exhibition involved not only the participation of New Zealand museums whose collections were its subject matter, but also consultation with Maori elders whose consent was seen as necessary in order to secure spiritual and political legitimacy for the tour. This exhibition challenged the status quo and eventually led to a new working relationship between Maori and non-Maori in relation to museum exhibitions and management.

After its tour of the United States, the Te Maori exhibition traveled to Australia in modified format in 1989 and 1990.[84] This was followed by a Taonga Maori Conference in New Zealand where museum professionals from 15 foreign institutions with significant collections of *taonga Maori* met with Maori and other New Zealanders in an attempt to continue cooperation and understanding.[85] This event had more significance than might immediately seem apparent in view of the geographical isolation of New Zealand from most of the foreign institutions represented.

3. Te Papa Tongarewa: The Museum of New Zealand

In 1998, the new Museum of New Zealand (Te Papa Tongarewa) opened in Wellington. The museum ("Te Papa") was a reincarnation of the former National Museum that had been founded in 1865. The new museum is a major

---

[81] *See* KEITH W. THOMSON, ART GALLERIES AND MUSEUMS IN NEW ZEALAND (1981) (hardly even referring to the large collections of Maori material in New Zealand museums).

[82] *See* Hirini Moko Mead, *The Nature of Taonga, in* TAONGA MAORI CONFERENCE, *supra* note 70, at 164.

[83] SIDNEY M. MEAD ED., TE MAORI: MAORI ART FROM NEW ZEALAND COLLECTIONS (1984); David Butts, *Maori and Museums: The Politics of Indigenous Recognition, in* MUSEUMS, SOCIETY, INEQUALITY 228 (Richard Sandell ed., 2002).

[84] *See* TAONGA MAORI: TREASURES OF THE NEW ZEALAND MAORI PEOPLE (2000).

[85] *See supra* note 70.

manifestation of a new spirit of partnership between Maori and non-Maori in connection with museum buildings, collections, and displays. Te Papa had been formally established by the Museum of New Zealand Te Papa Tongarewa Act 1992. The museum is governed by a board of six to eight members who are selected by the minister for arts, culture, and heritage. There is no legislative requirement that any of the board members be Maori (though two are), but the board has established a Maori advisory committee and is required by the act to secure the substantial involvement of Maori as employees.[86] There is also a Maori director (*Kaihautu*) position at Te Papa at the same level as the chief executive officer.

4. Bicultural Governance in New Zealand Museums

For the last 20 years, most New Zealand museums have embraced a concept of biculturalism in relation to governance and other issues. The spark for this development was the success of the Te Maori exhibition in 1984. In the words of Gerard O'Regan (a member of Te Papa's board),

> In the course of *Te Maori*, iwi entered the museums in considerable numbers, so gaining some familiarity with these organizations. In the process, they reaffirmed their relationship to the taonga and asserted some authority over the presentation of 'the Maori story'. Since *Te Maori*, it has no longer been acceptable to embark on a presentation of things Maori within a New Zealand museum without the appropriate approval, support and involvement of Maori people.[87]

No legislation requires New Zealand museums to govern themselves on a bicultural basis. Museums, however, have been influenced by the changes in the New Zealand legal framework concerning Maori rights in developing their particular strategies. While biculturalism remains an amorphous concept, it is usually understood in terms of Maori participation in some form of partnership with non-Maori in connection with not only the management and governance of museums, but also regarding such specific matters as employment, exhibitions, loans, and other museum services. A 1995 report on performance measurements in New Zealand museums by McKinlay Douglas Ltd. found three generic understandings of what a bicultural organization may be:

- The institution itself is bicultural in the sense that power within the institution is exercised in a bicultural manner.
- It is bicultural in the sense that its management practices and the way in which it deals with and recruits, trains and places staff, is bicultural.
- The institution is bicultural in the sense that the focus of its activity, and its relationship with wider community is on acting biculturally.[88]

---

[86] *See* Museum of New Zealand Te Papa Tongarewa Act 1992, Schedule 1, § 1(4)(2)(d).

[87] *See* Gerard O'Regan, Bicultural Developments in Museums of Aotearoa: What Is the Current Status? 6 (1997).

[88] *Id.* at 7.

Whatever definition is adopted, there seems to be consensus that no New Zealand museum can any longer refrain from some kind of engagement with Maori populations.

Te Papa displays a broad range of policies and practices that reveal its commitment to the concept of biculturalism. One example is the *iwi* exhibition program. This is a program of short-term exhibitions that the museum develops with identified *iwi* partners. Through such exhibitions, *iwi* can present *taonga*, art and narratives from their own collections and those at Te Papa or other museums. Thus, the museum acknowledges that cultural knowledge does not always lie with museum experts. Another example of biculturalism in action is Rongomaraeroa, which is a functioning *marae* at Te Papa and within the museum building. While it is a Maori institution, its placement inside the museum is symbolic of the strength of an institutional commitment to the recognition of Maori values and beliefs.

Though a commitment to biculturalism seems to exist on the part of most New Zealand museums, its outcomes for different institutions have been varied. There has been a change in thinking on the part of most New Zealand museums towards almost every aspect of their management and practices. Again, quoting Gerald O'Regan,

> Some Maori communities have expressed an interest in being involved in existing museum operations. Others are seeking to establish their own cultural facilities, thus diminishing the role museums might otherwise have in presenting Maori art and taonga. The 'Maori renaissance' continues to challenge the traditional roles of museums. At the same time, some Maori are pursuing developments that will cater for the tourist industry's interest in things Maori. Iwi in different regions differ both in their approach and in the current levels of their interest in these things. This is mirrored within the museum sector in its diverse approaches and degrees of interest in 'bicultural' developments.
>
> Issues of ownership and trusteeship have dominated some discussions within museums holding taonga. These have been fuelled by an increasing recognition of Indigenous people's mana over their taonga and histories. The *Te Maori Hui* Wananga held at the National Museum, October 1986, called for greater Maori participation in museums and that 'every effort be made to put Maori people in charge of their art heritage in New Zealand museums, art galleries and cultural institutions.' Nonetheless, the resources and will to implement such wide-ranging statements have not necessarily been forthcoming. Further, the statements are seen to impinge on different museums in different ways.[89]

In its role as the national museum of New Zealand, Te Papa also administers Te Paerangi National Services, which is a program supporting regional museums and offering partnership programs with them in areas such as biculturalism and exhibition development. Given the extensive financial and human resources of

---

[89] *Id.*

Te Papa, it is appropriate that it use these to expand the work of museums around New Zealand. Te Paerangi National Services has also organized several conferences on bicultural development in New Zealand museums.

The Auckland War Memorial Museum Act 1996 specifically provides for Maori representation on the board of trustees of the museum—now renamed Tamaki Paenga Hira.[90] The act also establishes a Maori advisory committee (*Taumata-a-Iwi*) that comprises representatives of Maori from the Auckland area.[91] The committee has five members (three of which are from Ngati Whatua, and one each from the Tainui and Ngati Paoa tribes). Unlike Te Papa, the Auckland Museum's version of biculturalism (or what it prefers to call "integrated Maori values") focuses on a relationship with local tribes and relies on them to represent the interests of Maori from outside the Auckland region.[92] It also appears that the Auckland Museum policy stresses that both Maori and non-Maori alike should seek to uphold Maori values and concerns in the governance of the museum.

Other museums in New Zealand have developed different governance structures based on their particular histories and needs. At the Tairawhiti Museum in Gisborne about half the board members are Maori (which is seen as consistent with about half the population of the Gisborne region itself being Maori) so that the representation format is perceived as highly democratic. The issue of relative representation of Maori and non-Maori proved more divisive in Wanganui, where the Whanganui Regional Museum experienced difficulties with a proposal that required approval of new measures from majorities of both Maori and non-Maori representative bodies. This meant one or the other body effectively had a right of veto. There were further difficulties because Maori population in the area of the Whanganui Museum is smaller than is the case in Gisborne.[93]

This brief discussion of governance initiatives in New Zealand museums shows that there is a high level of commitment amongst most New Zealand museum professionals to the spirit of partnership with Maori in one form or another. This commitment appears to be shared nationally by Te Papa and governmental policies.

5. Repatriation of *Taonga* From Museums in New Zealand

In recent years there have been several instances of the return to Maori of *taonga* by individuals, museums, and other institutions, both from inside New Zealand and from abroad. The term "repatriation" has no precise legal meaning, but it is usually refers to an end result or remedy that involves the

---

[90] Section 4(1) of the act provides for a single Maori member on the trust board of the museum. Despite it not being the national museum that Te Papa is, the Auckland Museum's Maori collection is the largest in New Zealand.

[91] Auckland War Memorial Museum Act 1996, §16(1). *See also* Merata Kawharu, *Indigenous Governance in Museums: A Case Study, the Auckland War Memorial Museum*, *in* The Dead and Their Possessions: Repatriation in Principle, Policy and Practice 293 (Cressida Fforde, Jane Hubert & Paul Turnbull eds., 2002).

[92] *Id.*

[93] *See* Butts, *supra* note 83, at 234–39.

transfer of an object or some concession regarding it by the present possessor (such as an agreement to lend or make a copy of an object).[94]

Returns from foreign institutions to New Zealand Maori have mainly involved ancestral remains and are discussed above. Returns of artifacts held abroad have occurred but are less common and normally depend on a voluntary return being agreed to by a foreign museum or collector.

There is no national law or policy on the return of *taonga* in New Zealand akin to that provided by the Native American Graves Protection and Repatriation Act in the United States.[95] Some New Zealand museums have, however, developed their own repatriation policies, and *ad hoc* repatriations have occurred. It appears, however, that repatriation, as it affects Maori collections in New Zealand museums, has been subsumed under other legal and policy developments, such as the policy of biculturalism outlined above.

The Collection Management Policy of Te Papa contains the following provision under the heading "Deaccession."

> Deaccessioning of items is guided by the Collections Development Policy of the Museum. The process of deaccession is an extension of collection maintenance and reflects the appropriate conservation requirements and cultural sensitivities of the items being deaccessioned. Deaccession involves appropriate modification of the documentation, including database record, relating to the item being deaccessioned. Items are deaccessioned before they are donated as gifts to, or exchanged for other material from, other institutions.
>
> Deaccessioning of items of the Maori, Art and History collections requires authorization from the Board. Deaccessioning of items of the Natural Environment collection requires authorization from the Director.

The implication of the language in the Museum of New Zealand Te Papa Tongarewa Act 1992, together with the Crown Entities Act 2004, is that property in the museum's collections vests in its board. No provision in the law, however, explicitly limits the scope to repatriate *taonga* to Maori.

Some New Zealand museums have seen themselves as having a role that focuses on *taonga* from their particular region. For example, the new Puke Ariki Museum in New Plymouth sees its mission as focusing on Maori culture from the Taranaki region. Thus, *taonga* from the South Island have been returned by Puke Ariki to the Otago Museum in Dunedin. However, like many New Zealand museums, the Taranaki Museum has no distinct written policy regarding such returns.[96]

---

[94] For a survey of different approaches towards repatriation in a variety of contexts, see *Material Culture in Flux: Law and Policy of Repatriation of Cultural Property*, U.B.C. L. Rev. (Special Issue 1995); Repatriation Reader: Who Owns American Indian Remains? (Devon A. Mithesuah ed., 2000).

[95] Pub. L. No. 101-601, 104 Stat. 3048.

[96] Interview of Kelvin Day (Mar. 18, 2004), Puke Ariki, New Plymouth.

The Auckland Museum has distinguished the different ways that artifacts in its collection were acquired. One of these—"inappropriate acquisition"—is based on evidence of theft or other inappropriate method of acquisition. In such cases the Maori advisory committee at the museum will entertain a request for return, but it must be brought forward at the *marae* because there is perceived to be an enhanced obligation to speak truthfully in that context. The Auckland Museum has decided to be proactive in relation to past acquisitions it considers may have been inappropriate by actively seeking out appropriate Maori representatives in such cases.

The first major example of the return of *taonga* to Maori in recent times concerned a Maori meeting house (*wharenui*) located in the Otago Museum in Dunedin and involved lengthy negotiations between the Crown and the Bay of Plenty, North Island, Maori tribe of Ngati Awa.[97] *Mataatua* is a meeting house built by the Ngati Awa Tribe between 1872 and 1875 at Whakatane on the North Island. In 1879, the New Zealand government asked the Ngati Awa chiefs to allow the house to be sent to Australia for exhibition. From Australia, it was sent to London and reassembled in 1924 for display at the Wembley Exhibition. In 1925, *Maatatua* returned to New Zealand for display at the Dunedin South Seas Exhibition that year. The house was then given by the government on permanent loan to the Otago Museum in Dunedin, where it remained. It seems that the removal of *Mataatua* is 1879 was done without consensus amongst the Ngati Awa. Its carvers protested the removal of *Mataatua,* and Maori women objected to it being dismantled for travel.

In 1983, a request for the return of the house from the Otago Museum was made by the Ngati Awa people. The government asked the tribe to negotiate directly with the trustees of the Otago Museum and also suggested that the tribe include the house among issues affecting it that were already before the Waitangi Tribunal. Renewed negotiations began in 1995 between the Ngati Awa and the Minister of Justice. In 1996, the Waitangi Tribunal recommended to the New Zealand government that *Mataatua* be returned. Eventually a written return agreement was concluded. The government agreed to pay the Otago Museum $N.Z.1.75 million for the house. Simultaneously, a deed of settlement and a covenant were signed between the government and Ngati Awa that vested title to *Mataatua* in the tribe. Ngati Awa also received $NZ2 million from the government to help repair and reinstate the house and intend to create a major culture center surrounding *Mataatua.*

Another major return by a museum involved the Auckland Museum's return of a great *taonga,* a very large wood carving of a Te Arawa ancestor named *Pukaki.*[98] *Pukaki* had attracted international interest when he toured the United States as part of the Te Maori exhibition.[99] *Pukaki* subsequently

---

[97] *See* Hirini Moko Mead, *The Mataatua Declaration and the Case of the Carved Meeting House Mataatua,* 69 U.B.C. L. REV. (Special Issue 1995); Ngapine Allen, *Maori Vision and the Imperialist Gaze, in* COLONIALISM AND THE OBJECT: EMPIRE, MATERIAL CULTURE AND THE MUSEUM 144 (T. Barriger & T. Flynn eds., 1998).

[98] *See* Paul Tapsell, *Partnership in Museums: A Tribal Maori Response to Repatriation" in* THE DEAD AND THEIR POSSESSIONS, *supra* note 91, at 284.

[99] *See* PAUL TAPSELL, PUKAKI: A COMET RETURNS (2000).

attained the status of a national icon when his image was reproduced on a commemorative New Zealand coin. What had remained obscure was the history of how *Pukaki* had originally made his way into the Auckland institution that housed him. Dr. Paul Tapsell has uncovered this history, which revealed that *Pukaki* had been given to an Auckland Museum official who was conducting land negotiations with the Ngati Whakaue. These negotiations had failed, but the official kept *Pukaki* and donated him to the Auckland Museum in the late 1870s. The uncovering of this provenance led Ngati Whakaue elders to contact the museum, which acknowledged Ngati Whakaue as the owners of *Pukaki*. In 1997, Auckland Museum officials and Ngati Whakaue descendants met *Pukaki* and escorted him back to Rotorua from where he had traveled to Auckland over a century earlier. *Pukaki* was then properly gifted to the Crown, represented by the governor general, and placed in the Rotorua district council buildings. A memorandum of understanding was later signed on October 2, 1997, between the New Zealand government, Ngati Whakaue elders, and the museum—detailing the reasons for the return of *Pukaki* and his future protection and maintenance. *Pukaki* is now cared for by the Pukaki Trust, formed pursuant to the memorandum, which includes representatives of the various parties to this symbolic return of *taonga*.

These two examples of domestic repatriation show that, in the absence of legislation and formal principles, New Zealand museums can still effect the return of *taonga* in appropriate circumstances. The partnerships between Maori and non-Maori that frequently now characterize the management of New Zealand museum collections will serve to make future returns more expeditious in appropriate circumstances. As the level and effectiveness of these partnerships increases, so should the instances of meaningful returns such as the two just described. There has been, to the writer's knowledge, no formal discussion of the need for legislation expressly dealing with repatriations of *taonga Maori*, but written museum repatriation guidelines continue to be developed by individual institutions.

As to *koiwi tangata Maori* (Maori ancestral remains), including *toi moko* (tattooed heads), in New Zealand museum collections, while the overall focus has been on retrieval of ancestral remains in foreign museums, there have also been concerns about the proper handling and storage of such remains in New Zealand museums.[100] At Te Papa, Maori ancestral remains held within the museum are not regarded as part of its collection and are subject to a separate policy. At the Auckland Museum, all of the North Auckland remains previously held at the museum have been returned to Maori for re-burial. The general policy among New Zealand museums in regard to ancestral remains is that they should be returned to Maori descendants whenever possible. In other cases, where the provenance of remains is unknown, they will remain in consecrated facilities and strict protocols will apply to their management.

The South Island Ngai Tahu Tribe has been the most active regarding *koiwi tangata Maori* held by museums in the territory of the tribe. Ngai Tahu

[100] *See* Robin J. Watt, *Museums Can Never Own The Remains of Other People But They Can Care for Them*, U.B.C. L. Rev. 77 (Special Issue 1995).

developed its own *koiwi tangata* policy after consultation with its tribal members. This policy asserts that tribal authority is granted by the Treaty of Waitangi for Ngai Tahu to manage its ancestors' remains. Pursuant to this policy, Ngai Tahu has negotiated agreements with museums in its territory regarding appropriate storage of ancestral remains. Among other things, any access to ancestral remains requires the approval of the tribal council.[101]

L. CONCLUSION

This survey of the laws and practices surrounding Maori cultural heritage in New Zealand is designed to provide a basis for comparison with similar situations elsewhere. No system is innately superior to any other, but many of the improvements that have been introduced or discussed in New Zealand have been matched by similar changes in countries such as Canada, Australia, and the United States. One of the most unique aspects of the New Zealand context is the law-making role of the reports of the Waitangi Tribunal. While Canadian Aboriginals, for example, must wait for change through an attenuated treaty process or costly litigation, the Waitangi Tribunal has furnished a focused venue for Maori concerns to be listened to, reported on, and, in many instances, expeditiously addressed through new laws and policies (including those surrounding cultural heritage). Since the Treaty of Waitangi now actively informs the development of New Zealand law, we can expect a continued level of enhanced protection of *taonga Maori.* The forms that this protection takes will continue to be of relevance to similar changes relating to the cultural heritage of indigenous populations elsewhere.

---

[101] *See* Butts, *supra* note 83, at 240; Robert K. Paterson, *Ancestral Remains in Institutional Collections: Proposals for Reform, in* PROTECTING FIRST NATIONS CULTURAL HERITAGE; LAWS, POLICY AND REFORM 155–80 (Catherine Bell & Robert Paterson eds., 2009).

GLOSSARY OF MAORI TERMS

hapu	sub-tribe
iwi	a nation or people (tribe)
kaihautu	Leader
kaumatua	Elder
koiwi tangata Maori	Maori ancestral remains
marae	meeting place of iwi, hapu, or whanau
matauranga Maori	Maori intellectual property (knowledge)
tangata whenua	local Maori (people of the land)
tangi	mourning and funeral ceremony
taonga Maori	Maori treasures (anything highly prized)
taonga tuturu	taonga Maori as defined in the Protected Objects Act 1975
tapu	under religious restriction (sacred)
te reo Maori	Maori language
toi iho	Maori made mark
toi moko	preserved tattooed heads
tuahu	a designated sacred area comprising a marked mound
urupa	burial ground
wahi tapu	sacred places
waka	canoe
whanau	extended family
whare-nui	large house (meeting house)

PART II

LEGACY OF INTERNATIONAL CONQUEST AND COLONIZATION

CHAPTER 5
CULTURAL HERITAGE LAW: RECENT DEVELOPMENTS IN THE LAWS OF WAR AND OCCUPATION

Sabine von Schorlemer

A. INTRODUCTION

The idea to spare cultural heritage from both the direct and indirect effects of armed conflict has been gaining more and more influence since the 19th century. We have faced a dynamic evolution of the laws of war and occupation from a status of complete lawlessness of the civilian population and property in such territories to a rather elaborate system of humanitarian law, including cultural heritage norms applicable in armed conflict.

Existing regulations, which are relevant in this respect, start with the Lieber Code of 1863,[1] as the earliest regulation, and the Declaration of Brussels of 1874.[2] Both documents have exercised a considerable influence on the Hague Regulations Respecting the Laws and Customs of War on Land, annexed to Convention No. II of 1899 and to Convention No. IV of 1907 (Hague Regulations).[3] Further rules have been developed: among others, the Treaty on the Protection of Artistic and Scientific Institutions and Historic Monuments (the so-called Roerich Pact)[4] which is considered to still be in force, and the 1954 Hague Convention (Hague Convention for the Protection of Cultural Property in the Event of Armed Conflict)[5] together with the First Protocol for

---

[1] *Reprinted in* Dietrich Schindler & Jiri Toman Eds., Laws of Armed Conflicts: A Collection of Conventions, Resolutions and Other Documents 737 (1988).

[2] Project of an International Declaration Concerning the Laws and Customs of War, adopted by the Conference of Brussels, Aug. 27, 1874, *reprinted in* 1 Am. J. Int'l L. 96–103 (Supp. 1907).

[3] Convention (II) With Respect to the Laws and Customs of War on Land and Its Annex: Regulations Concerning the Laws and Customs of War on Land (The Hague, July 29, 1899), *reprinted in* 32 Stat. 1803, 1 Bevans 247, 26 Martens Nouveau Recueil (ser. 2) 949, 187 Consol. T.S. 429; Convention (IV) Respecting the Laws and Customs of War on Land and Its Annex: Regulations Concerning the Laws and Customs of War on Land (The Hague, Oct. 18, 1907), *reprinted in* 36 Stat. 2277, 1 Bevans 631, 205 Consol. T.S. 277, 3 Martens Nouveau Recueil (ser. 3) 461.

[4] *Reprinted in* Dietrich Schindler & Jiri Toman Eds., Laws of Armed Conflicts: A Collection of Conventions, Resolutions and Other Documents 737 (1988).

[5] 249 U.N.T.S. 240.

the Protection of Cultural Property in the Event of Armed Conflict (First Hague Protocol)[6] and the Second Protocol (SP) to the Hague Convention for the Protection of Cultural Property in the Event of Armed Conflict.[7] Some other important developments are to be found in the Fourth Geneva Convention Relative to the Protection of Civilian Persons in Time of War and in the First[8] and Second[9] Additional Protocols to the Geneva Conventions of August 12, 1949 (1977). Finally, recent evolution of the law of individual responsibility (criminal law) for violations of humanitarian law is reflected in the Statute of the International Criminal Tribunal for the former Yugoslavia[10] (ICTY) and the 1998 Rome Statute of the International Criminal Court[11] (ICC).

The following chapter will highlight some important recent developments concerning the safeguarding of cultural heritage in situations of armed conflict. It will start with an outline of specific dangers for cultural heritage in wartime and analyze reasons for non-compliance with humanitarian law. It will then investigate to what extent the *jus in bello* is applicable to private actors, as this has been particularly controversial in the case of the Iraq War beginning in 2003 and its effect on the National Museum in Baghdad. Recent evolutions pertaining to criminal jurisdiction (ICTY, ICC, national law) demonstrate that national and international criminal jurisdiction is of critical importance in the enforcement of humanitarian law norms. The chapter will conclude with a summary of recent developments in the United Nations and its specialized agencies, particularly UNESCO, regarding the safeguarding of cultural heritage in armed conflict.

B. RECENT DEVELOPMENTS IN THE HAGUE AND GENEVA LAW REGARDING CULTURAL HERITAGE

1. Specific Dangers for Cultural Heritage in Wartime

The tremendous cultural losses in the Iraq War in 2003 made it clear that not only is the moment of attack crucial for the safeguarding of cultural items, but also the hours, days, weeks, and months before and after an invasion. James

---

[6] 249 U.N.T.S. 358. The purpose of the First Protocol was to prohibit the exportation of cultural objects from occupied territories. State parties must also take custody of cultural property imported into their territory from an occupied territory.

[7] 75 U.N.T.S. 287. Neither the United States, China, France, Japan, Russia, nor the United Kingdom is party to the protocol which was adopted on March 26, 1999, 38 I.L.M. 769 (1999); the Second Protocol set up a new definition of military necessity, introduced a category of "enhanced protection," had a new focus on internal conflict, and established the principle of criminal responsibility; for details, see Sabine von Schorlemer, *Legal Changes in the Regime of the Protection of Cultural Property in Armed Conflict*, 9 ART, ANTIQUITY & L. 43 (2004); Jean-Marie Henckaerts, *New Rules for the Protection of Cultural Property in Armed Conflict: The Significance of the Second Protocol to the 1954 Hague Convention for the Protection of Cultural Property in the Event of Armed Conflict*, 835 INT'L REV. RED CROSS 593 (1999).

[8] 1125 U.N.T.S. 3. Particularly relevant is Article 53 of the First Protocol, which prohibits the commission of any hostile acts "directed against the historic monuments, works of art or places of worship which constitute the cultural or spiritual heritage of peoples."

[9] 1125 U.N.T.S. 609. The United States is a signatory of both protocols but has not ratified them.

[10] U.N. Doc. S/25704 (May 3, 1993), *reprinted in* 32 I.L.M. 1192 (1993).

[11] 37 I.L.M. 1002 (1998).

Nafziger outlines four main threats to cultural heritage in armed conflict: "(D)eliberate attack, incidental damage, pillage, and outright theft."[12] According to Rüdiger Wolfrum, Director of the Max Planck Institute for Comparative Public Law and International Law in Heidelberg, Germany, destruction or damage of cultural property in armed conflict "may be the result of having been made a military target or the result of collateral damage."[13] However, he rightly underlines that there may be "other risks" during periods of armed conflict: as the conflict in former Yugoslavia showed, cultural objects may be destroyed "with the intention of erasing the manifestation of the adversary's religious or ethnic identity,"[14] for example as a preparatory element or part of ethnic cleansing. Many of these acts occur during foreign territory occupation.

As Hans-Peter Gasser, former senior legal advisor to the International Committee of the Red Cross (ICRC) in Geneva, stated, there is a "new relevance of international law of occupation."[15] Territories occupied in the Middle East, Kuwait, Somalia, Bosnia,[16] Kosovo, East Timor, and Iraq may serve as recent examples of foreign occupation. It is important to note that the obligations imposed on an occupying power apply once its foreign force is actually in a position to control the territory and to exercise authority over the population.[17] The condition of "actual control" is essential—that is a fact, an actuality—not the motives for the foreign troops' presence. An occupying power must comply with international obligations and exercise authority over the population as soon as it occupies foreign territory in accordance with the meaning of Article 42 of the Hague Regulations.[18] This also means that controversy about the status of a territory is irrelevant for the application of international humanitarian law, including cultural heritage law norms.

The basis for safeguarding during fighting and occupation is that cultural heritage is civilian in nature, and it forms part of the cultural or spiritual heritage of mankind. Cultural heritage is of general interest to humanity.[19] Francesco

---

[12] James A.R. Nafziger, *Protection of Cultural Heritage in Time of War and Its Aftermath*, 6 IFAR J. 1 (2003).

[13] Rüdiger Wolfrum, *Protection of Cultural Property in Armed Conflict*, 32 Isr. Y.B. Hum. Rts. 307 (2003); *see also* Karen J. Detling, *External Silence: The Destruction of Cultural Property in Yugoslavia*, 17 Md. J. Int'l L. & Trade 41 (1993).

[14] *Id.*

[15] Hans-Peter Gasser, *From Military Intervention to Occupation of Territory: New Relevance of International Law of Occupation*, *in* Krisensicherung und Humanitärer Schutz—Crisis Management and Humanitarian Protection, Festschrift für Dieter Fleck, at 139 (Horst Fischer et al. eds., 2004).

[16] *Cf.*, *e.g.*, András J. Riedlmayer, *Destruction of Cultural Heritage in Bosnia-Herzegovina, 1992–1996: A Post-War Survey of Selected Municipalities* (2002), *available at* http://hague.bard.edu/reports/BosHeritageReport-AR.pdf (last visited May 30, 2008).

[17] Gasser, *supra* note 15, at 141; concerning the current challenges to the law of occupation, compare Daniel Thürer, speech delivered, 6th Bruges Colloquium, Oct. 20–21, 2005 (ICRC Official Statement, Nov. 21, 2005), *available at* http://www.icrc.org/web/eng/siteeng0.nsf/html/occupation-statement-211105 (last visited May 31, 2008).

[18] *Id.* Article 42 of the Hague Regulations reads as follows: "Territory is considered occupied when it is actually under the authority of the hostile army. The occupation extends only to the territory where such authority has been established and can be exercised."

[19] *Cf.* Robert O´Keefe, *World Cultural Heritage: Obligations to the International Community as a Whole?*, 53 Int'l Comp. L.Q. 189 (2004).

Francioni argues that although the protection of cultural heritage does not figure in the present category of *erga omnes* obligations, "the contribution of UNESCO to this field consists precisely in its constant commitment to developing a notion of cultural heritage that forms a constituent part of the general interest of humanity."[20] Therefore, in the formulation of the ICRC on the occasion of the 50th anniversary of the 1954 Hague Convention for the Protection of Cultural Property in the Event of Armed Conflict, "cultural property is to be respected and protected in its own right, as part of humanity's common heritage and irrespective of the cultural tradition to which it belongs."[21]

2. The Question of Compliance With the *Jus in Bello*

With regard to the legacy of destruction and looting during wars all over the world, an important question is, what makes a government respect and comply with the rules of cultural heritage law?

When it comes to laws of war and occupation and to the safeguarding of cultural heritage in those conflicts in particular, we realize that the compliance rate risks ranking rather low. As Sir Hersch Lauterpacht emphasized, "(i)f international law is, in some ways, at the vanishing point of law, the law of war is, perhaps even more conspicuously, at the vanishing point of international law."[22] Regarding the fundamental question of the appropriateness of the laws pertaining to armed conflict, the ICRC sees the real problem arising "from a failure to respect its most fundamental rules."[23] Germany is such a case. The International Military Tribunal of Nuremberg qualified the main regulations of the Hague Regulations as customary international law. Thus, independent from the controversial question of the "all party clause" of Article 2 of the Convention Respecting the Laws and Customs of War on Land[24]—not all adversaries of Germany had ratified the Hague Regulations—Germany was bound by their provisions. However, the main problem was that Germany did not *want* to respect the Hague Regulations and therefore looted so many objects in the countries occupied in the East and the West.[25]

---

[20] Francesco Francioni, *A Dynamic Evolution of Concept and Scope: From Cultural Property to Cultural Heritage, in* Abdulqawi A. Yusuf ed., Standard-Setting in UNESCO, Vol. I, Normative Action in Education, Science and Culture 222 (2007).

[21] Francois Bugnion, *The Origins and Development of the Legal Protection of Cultural Property in the Event of Armed Conflict: 50th Anniversary of the 1954 Hague Convention for the Protection of Cultural Property in the Event of Armed Conflict* (2004), *available at* http://www.icrc.org/ (last visited May 30, 2008); *see also* Pierre-Marie Dupuy, *The Impact of Legal Instruments Adopted by UNESCO on General International Law, in* Abdulqawi A. Yusuf Ed., Standard-Setting in UNESCO, Vol. I, Normative Action in Education, Science and Culture 351–63 (2007).

[22] Hersch Lauterpacht, *The Problem of the Revision of the Law of War,* 29 Brit. Y.B. Int'l L. 382 (1952); *see also* B. Kessler, *The Duty to 'Ensure Respect' Under Common Art. 1 of the Geneva Conventions: Its Implications in International and Non-International Armed Conflicts,* 44 Ger. Y.B. Int'l L. 498 (2001).

[23] International Committee of the Red Cross, Annual Reports 2002, at 29 (2003).

[24] Article 2 of the Convention Respecting the Laws and Customs of War on Land (Oct. 18, 1907) sets forth as follows: "The Provisions contained in the Regulations . . . do not apply except between Contracting Powers, and then only if all the belligerents are parties to the Convention."

[25] Tono Eitel, *Beutekunst—Die letzten deutschen Kriegsgefangenen, in* Weltinnenrecht, Liber Amicorum Jost Delbrück 194 (Klaus Dicke et al. eds., 2005).

Armed conflicts in modern times do not even show respect for the integrity of schools and hospitals, so why spare churches and mosques, which are all too often symbols of the cultural identity of the adversary? The wars in the Balkans in the 1990s, but also the outrageous destruction of the fourth- and fifth-century Buddha statues in the Bamiyan Valley in March 2001 by the Taliban Regime[26] during an internal conflict, which was right below the armed conflict threshold, made us well aware that our hopes to civilize conflict by international norms are particularly fragile when cultural objects are concerned.

However, there are some encouraging examples. From what has appeared of the Iraq conflict in 2003, the U.S.- and U.K.-led forces refrained from attacking Iraqi cultural heritage, even in those instances where Iraqi armed forces were using such items for military purposes. Nor did there appear to be extensive collateral damage to cultural property.[27] Some authors ascribe this positive fact to modern technology that enables military objectives to be targeted more accurately than in the past.[28] This explanation of why cultural heritage law was respected is rather technical in nature. There may be other reasons.

If a treaty or treaty norm reflects preexisting interests, compliance may be treaty induced. For example, military necessity—and the possibility of waivers—is firmly enshrined in international humanitarian law, and no further deviation is allowed. Also, reciprocity is certainly relevant in this context. Governments might be well aware that the preservation of the integrity of the *jus in bello* as *corpus juris* is important because—at a later point in history—other law norms than those regarding cultural heritage might become relevant for them, for example, for rules governing the treatment of prisoners of war. Thus, the usual *quid pro quo* approach of implementation on the basis of treaty law might further respect for cultural heritage in armed conflict.

Compliance may also relate to exogenous factors that are unrelated to treaty. Non-state actors—for example, experts, scientists, non-governmental organizations, the media—or international organizations—ICRC, UNESCO, and others—come into play and may influence the level of compliance by state actors. In addition, awareness of the specific vulnerability of cultural heritage and the willingness to engage for its safeguard in the interest of common generations is important: this is a question not only of law, but also of moral responsibility. The looting of the National Museum in Baghdad on April 10–12, 2003, by Iraqi citizens certainly was a shocking example for many international lawyers, as it showed that despite current attempts to protect cultural heritage in armed conflict, massive destruction occurs nonetheless. When U.S. Defense Secretary Donald Rumsfeld was asked at a Pentagon news briefing on April 1,

---

[26] *See* Franceso Francioni & Federico Lenzerini, *The Destruction of the Buddhas of Bamiyan and International Law*, 14 EUR. J. INT'L L. 619 (2003).

[27] Kevin Chamberlain, *The Protection of Cultural Property in Armed Conflict*, 8 ART, ANTIQUITY & L. 237 (2003).

[28] *Id.*

2006, about the looting, he was reported as saying this "happens."[29] Obviously, U.S. forces were not ordered to safeguard the Iraqi National Museum and archaeological sites from looting during the invasion or subsequent occupation, a fact that ignited harsh criticism. As Mary Ellen O'Connell sets forth, "Lawfully invading and occupying Iraq required a *commitment* to protecting civilians and their property during fighting and in the subsequent occupation."[30] And James Nafziger rightly concludes, "Generally, the problems in protecting cultural heritage do not reflect an inadequacy of the law of war itself, but rather a lack of civic responsibility and inadequate commitment and training of military personnel, particularly in paramilitary operations and in time of civil war."[31]

For that reason, peace-time education is a decisive factor in effecting the compliance with humanitarian law. Not only the provisions of *jus in bello*, that is, laws of war and occupation, but also the 1970 UNESCO Convention on the Means of Prohibiting and Preventing the Illicit Import, Export and Transfer of Ownership of Cultural Property, adopted by the UNESCO General Conference on November 14, 1970 (1971), become relevant here. For the

> 1970 UNESCO Convention on Illegal Trafficking in Cultural Property, to which the United States *is* a party, prohibits importation and acquisition of stolen material. This treaty obligation is a reminder that the protection of cultural heritage in the event of war and its aftermath depends on implementation in times of peace, especially efforts to increase public awareness and ensure education of military personnel.[32]

Dissemination of international humanitarian law in the future should not only address dissemination to soldiers, but also to insurgents and civilians. Private actors play an increasing role, as the Iraqi case shows.[33] Factors to be taken into account in addressing private actors should be, among others, the

[29] United States Department of Defense, *DoD News Briefing—Secretary Rumsfeld and Gen. Myers* (Apr. 15, 2003), *available at* http://www.defenselink.mil/transcripts/transcript.aspx?transcriptid=2413 (last visited May 30, 2008).

[30] Mary Ellen O'Connell, *Occupation Failures and the Legality of Armed Conflict: The Case of Iraqi Cultural Property* (3 OSU Moritz College of Law Working Paper Series 1, 2004; emphasis added).

[31] Nafziger, *supra* note 12, at 1.

[32] *Id.* at 3; see also the Second Protocol [hereinafter SP] to the 1954 Convention for the Protection of Cultural Property in the Event of Armed Conflict, which provides examples of what measures have to be taken during peacetime, for example, preparation of inventories, planning of emergency measures, preparation of removal of movable cultural property, designation of competent authorities, etc.; *see* art. 3 SP. The SP also provides for a fund to provide financial or other assistance for contracting parties to safeguard their cultural property; *see* art. 29 SP.

[33] *Cf.* von Schorlemer, *supra* note 7; Wolfrum, *supra* note 12; O'Connell, *supra* note 30; Andrea Cunning, *The Safeguarding of Cultural Property in Times of War and Peace*, 11 TULSA J. COMP. & INT'L L. 238 (2003–2004); Victoria A. Birov, *Prize or Plunder? The Pillage of Works of Art and the International Law of War*, 30 N.Y.U. J. INT'L L. & POL. 201(1997/1998); Wayne Sandholtz, *The Iraqi National Museum and International Law: A Duty to Protect*, 44 COLUM. J. TRANSNAT'L L. 185 (2005); *see also* Chip Colwell-Chanthaphonh & John Piper, *War and Cultural Property: The 1954 Hague Convention and the Status of U.S. Ratification*, 10 INT'L J. CULT. PROP. 217 (2001) [hereinafter Colwell & Piper] for the historic overview.

level of education, the claims of the group, as well as its political and religious ideology.[34]

In summary, governmental compliance with the *jus in bello* appears to be a multi-faceted issue that deserves specific attention in the academic world when it comes to cultural heritage.

3. The Application of the *Jus in Bello* to Private Actors

As international law generally applies between states, an important question is whether the laws of war and occupation are suitable to address wrongful acts committed by individuals. This question gained particular importance during the Iraq War of 2003.

The answer is "yes" as far as the principle of individual criminal responsibility for violations of cultural heritage law in armed conflict is concerned. Criminal responsibility of private actors has been firmly established as part of the international law system. The answer is more difficult when it comes to the "laws of war and occupation," that is, the material obligations of the *jus in bello*. International law is not only related to states, it is also governed by states. Generally, states are obligated to implement international treaties they have ratified and may sanction individuals who violate their rules.

However, in the Iraq War (2003) the question was, is the United States responsible for the looting of the National Museum in Baghdad by Iraqi *civilians*? Apparently, there was little if any U.S. resistance to the looting due mainly to a lack of security and inadequate safeguarding by Iraqi authorities, who had not anticipated the country's cultural objects would be looted by its own people. In particular, international criticism was leveled at the Bush administration for its failure to station troops at the museum during the fighting in Baghdad.

The peculiarity of this case is that the discriminate act, namely looting, was perpetrated by the *civilian* population of the defender—not by the combatants of the defender or the combatants of the invading power. Neither the U.S. forces nor the Iraqi forces looted the museum. Thus, we face a situation of the rights and obligations (United States) with regard to private actions, a situation we know from similar contexts, for example, the responsibility of states for law-infringing acts of private military companies or the responsibility of states for terrorist activities of private actors.

What answer does the *jus in bello* give regarding cultural heritage?

According to Article 56 of the Hague Regulations, the United States as the invading power was bound to refrain from seizing, destroying, or willfully damaging the works of art contained in the National Museum. However, Article 56 does not require a state party to protect cultural property from seizure, destruction, or willful damage by anyone other than itself. As Sasha Paroff emphasized, "Had the United States military looted the museum, the 1907

[34] Gauthier de Beco, *Compliance With International Humanitarian Law by Non-state Actors*, 3 J. Int'l L. Peace & Armed Conflict 197 (2005).

Hague Convention would be an appropriate vehicle to hold the United States responsible."[35]

Furthermore, the United States had signed, but not ratified, the 1954 Hague Convention for the Protection of Cultural Property in the Event of Armed Conflict and was consequently not a party to it.[36] Most authors, however, argue convincingly that the 1954 Hague Convention was binding for the United States at the moment of the invasion of Iraq because it stipulates existing customary international law.[37]

Still it is not quite clear whether the 1954 Hague Convention addresses the obligations of states in the event of looting and destruction by *non-state actors.* Generally, the combatant, but also the party that keeps a territory occupied, is bound to prohibit, prevent and, if necessary, put an end to any theft, pillage, confiscation, or other misappropriation of, and any acts of vandalism directed against cultural property (Article 4(3), 1954 Convention). The crucial question is whether this provision is also applicable when force is applied by private actors. There are good arguments on both sides:

Some authors support the legal viewpoint that there is *no obligation* to prohibit, prevent, and put a stop to looting by private parties to be found in Article 4(3) of the 1954 Hague Convention. Their underlying assumption seems to be that Article 4(3) has never been interpreted as an affirmative obligation to prevent looting by non-state actors and therefore may not be applied in those situations in the future. Sasha Paroff, for example, underlines the fact that the Hague Convention, even with Article 4(3) "has not been universally construed to apply to nonstate actors."[38] Furthermore, Victoria A. Birov argues, the "main difference is that the wartime conventions apply only to conduct by armed forces personnel or persons acting under the authority of the state, while the peacetime conventions also regulate private conduct."[39] "Contextually it

---

[35] Sasha P. Paroff, *Another Victim of the War in Iraq: The Looting of the National Museum in Baghdad and the Inadequacies of International Protection of Cultural Property*, 53 Emory L.J. 2048 (2004); generally and with further references, compare Dieter Fleck, *Humanitarian Protection Against Non-State Actors, in* Jochen Abr. Frowein, Klaus Scharioth, Ingo Winkelmann & Rüdiger Wolfrum eds., Verhandeln für den Frieden—Negotiating for Peace, Liber Amicorum Tono Eitel 70 (2003).

[36] On January 6, 1999, however, after six years of consideration, President Clinton forwarded the Hague Convention to the U.S. Senate with the recommendation that it ratifies the Hague Convention and part of the First Protocol. The U.S. Senate consented to send the treaty to the Committee on Foreign Relations, which has not acted since then; for details, *see* Colwell & Piper, *supra* note 33, at 235. Still, the authors hope that the United States will "revitalize the Convention"; *id.* at 237.

[37] Amy Miller, *The Looting of Iraqi Art: Occupiers and Collectors Turn Away Leisurely from the Disaster*, 37 Case W. Res. J. Int'l L. 49, 68 (2005), with further references to Joshua Katzenberg et al.; *see also* Sandholtz, *supra* note 33, at 227; *see* David A. Meyer, *The 1954 Hague Convention and Its Emergence into Customary International Law*, 11 B.U. Int'l L.J. 356 (1993); Guido Carducci, *L'obligation de restitution des biens culturels et des objets d'art en cas de conflit armé: droit coutumier et droit conventionel avant et après la Convention de La Haye de 1954: L'importance du facteur temporel dans les rapports entre les traités et la coutume*, 2 Rev. Gén. Droit Int'l Pub. 289 (2000).

[38] Paroff, *supra* note 35, at 2049.

[39] Birov, *supra* note 33, at 223.

seems that Article 4.3. speaks to a State Party's obligation to prohibit, prevent, and if necessary, put a stop to any form of theft, pillage, misappropriation, or destruction of cultural property by its *own troops*."[40] Also Karl-Josef Partsch interpreted Article 4(3) narrowly. According to him, this provision "is mainly addressed to the powers with custody of objects in their jurisdiction or in the territories occupied by them."[41] In the case of the Iraqi Museum, custody by the U.S. forces, it may be argued, was not yet clearly established when the private looting occurred. On the other hand, when U.S. troops reached the center of Baghdad on April 10, and looters pillaged the National Museum on April 12,[42] there was certainly enough time to establish custody, even if fighting continued in some suburbs of Baghdad. The problem was rather that of a lack of political will to take objects into custody in a crisis situation. The fact that the subsequent amendment brought about by the Second Protocol established jurisdiction for prosecution of individuals may also be cited as an argument against the application of Article 4(3) on private acts.[43] However, this argument is not very convincing either, as the Second Protocol does not explicitly address such a situation as private looting. It only refers to criminal protection for private action in Articles 10–21.

Other authors prefer a broader interpretation, partially derived from the idea that in an emergency situation, Article 4(3) of the 1954 Hague Convention contains *an obligation* to also stop residents of the defendant state from looting. Several arguments are brought forward in order to substantiate the obligation of the combatant or occupying Power to stop private parties from looting on the basis of an extensive interpretation of Article 4(3).

First of all, it must be noted that Article 4(3) of the Hague Convention contains an open wording. As Paroff maintains, the "plain language of Article 4.3 seems to have obligated the United States to prohibit, prevent, and put a stop to the Iraqi civilian's misappropriation of cultural property."[44] Wayne Sandholtz emphasized that the language of Article 4(3) "repeating the word 'any,' indicates a duty to prevent or put a stop to the prohibited acts, regardless of who is committing them."[45] Commanders of military forces would, accordingly, have an obligation to prevent looting by their own soldiers *and* by the civilian population.

Secondly, the genesis of the provision shows that there was no manifest opposition to the application of Article 4(3) on private actors at the time of its drafting. Its application under these circumstances was at least not ruled out at the time the provision was adopted. The records of the 1954 Conference at

---

[40] Paroff, *supra* note 35, at 2050.

[41] Karl J. Partsch, *Protection of Cultural Property, in* HANDBOOK OF HUMANITARIAN LAW IN ARMED CONFLICT 389 (Dieter Fleck ed., 1999).

[42] As to the chronology of events, see U.S. Department of Defense, *Iraq Museum Investigation: 22APR–8SEP03* (Sept. 2003), *available at* http://www.defenselink.mil/news/Sep2003/d20030922fr.pdf (last visited May 30, 2008).

[43] Paroff, *supra* note 35, at 2051.

[44] *Id.* at 2049.

[45] Sandholtz, *supra* note 33, at 215.

The Hague do not provide any indication that negotiating parties intended Article 4(3) to apply only to state actors.[46]

Thirdly, the obligation of Article 4(3) to prohibit, prevent, and, if necessary, put a stop to any form of theft, pillage, or misappropriation of cultural property and any acts of vandalism directed against it, cannot be waived, not even for reasons of imperative military necessity.[47] This means that Article 4(3) is considered to be one of the most important provisions of the 1954 Convention, which, accordingly, should be fully implemented under all circumstances.

Finally, the purpose of the 1954 Convention and the determination of the concluding parties that "the preservation of the cultural heritage is of great importance for all peoples of the world" and that it "should receive international protection"[48] should be recalled. In order to achieve these goals, it seems indispensable that in emergency situations that have been caused by one party, the looting of private actors must also be prevented by that party. Kevin Chamberlain takes a similar view: he states that Article 4(3) of the 1954 Hague Convention extends not just to prohibiting and preventing theft, pillage, and the like on the part of forces under the command of a party to the conflict, but also to such acts committed by the civilian population, for example, "where there is a breakdown in law and order in the territory occupied by a party to the conflict."[49] Amy Miller suggests that although this body of law does not explicitly state that a state's omission is equivalent to a commission, an affirmative duty on an occupying power exists to prevent residents of an occupied state from looting cultural property.[50]

Thus, it may be said that there is a general tendency in international law, including—as will be shown—recent practices of the U.N. Security Council,[51] to take into consideration rule-violating behavior of private actors. This certainly is an important step forward towards better safeguarding of cultural heritage during armed conflict and foreign occupation.

C. RECENT DEVELOPMENTS IN THE FIELD OF INTERNATIONAL CRIMINAL JURISDICTION

Addressing the "legacy" of conquest is not possible without referring to recent developments in the field of criminal jurisdiction.[52] Where international heritage law cannot be imposed during a conflict, it has to be judicially enforced

---

[46] *Id.*; *see* Intergovernmental Conference on the Protection of Cultural Property in the Event of Armed Conflict, Records of the Conference Convened by the United Nations Educational, Scientific and Cultural Organization (UNESCO), Held at The Hague From April 21 to May 14, 1954 (Staatsdrukkerijen Uitgeverijbedrijf 1961).

[47] Jiri Toman, The Protection of Cultural Property in the Event of Armed Conflict 70 (1996).

[48] *See* Preamble to the 1954 Hague Convention paras. 2 and 3.

[49] Kevin Chamberlain, War and Cultural Heritage: An Analysis of the 1954 Convention for the Protection of Cultural Property in the Event of Armed Conflict 39 (2004).

[50] Miller, *supra* note 37, at 69.

[51] *See infra* Section D.2.

[52] M. Cherif Bassiouni, *Reflections on Criminal Jurisdiction in International Protection of Cultural Property*, 10 Syracuse J. Int'l L. & Comm. 281 (1983).

once the armed conflict has ended. Criminal jurisdiction generally takes on a retrospective perspective—that is, sanctioning war crimes that have been committed by individuals in the past; but it has also an impact on future aspects of international obligations, for example, to deter unlawful acts. Consequently, judicial condemnation of crimes perpetrated on cultural objects is an important way to address the legacy of international conquest. The statutes of the ICTY and ICC are recent examples.

1. The Statutes of the ICTY and the ICC

The Statute of the ICTY, adopted by U.N. Security Council Resolution 827 (1993), mentions as crimes that fall under the jurisdiction of the Court, *inter alia*: "(S)eizure of, destruction or willful damage done to institutions dedicated to religion, charity and education, the arts and sciences, historic monuments and works of arts and science."[53] The prosecution by the ICTY of cultural property crimes[54] is considered important because it aims at overcoming the traditional distinction between crimes against persons and crimes against property.[55] Indeed, the ICTY views a crime against property potentially as a grave breach of the Geneva Convention of 1949, a violation of the laws or customs of war and a crime against humanity.

Most important is Article 8(2)(b)(xiii) of the Rome Statute of the ICC, dated July 17, 1998, which establishes "destroying or seizing the enemy's property" as a war crime, unless such destruction or seizure is imperatively demanded by the necessities of war. Article 8(2)(b)(xvi) makes the pillaging of a town or a place, even when taken by assault, a punishable act. Most important is Article 8(2)(b)(ix) establishing that "(i)ntentionally directing attacks against buildings dedicated to religion, education, art, science or charitable purposes, historic monuments" are war crimes, provided they are not military objectives.[56] According to the provisions of the Rome Statute, every intentional attack on important cultural property in the meaning of the Hague Convention of 1954 is a war crime. By making the destruction of cultural heritage a war crime, the ICC, it has been argued, "has provided a means of enforcing customary law, which seems to be outpacing Hague law."[57]

In this respect it is important to note, for example, that "military necessity," which generally may suspend protection,[58] is of no relevance for the criminal

---

[53] Statute of the ICTY, art. 3(d), U.N. Doc. S/RES/827 (May 25, 1993), Annex, *reprinted in* 32 I.L.M. 1992 (1993).

[54] The ICTY has indicted a number of persons for crimes against cultural property; for details; *see* Sandholtz, *supra* note 33, at 223; Hirad Abtahi, *The Protection of Cultural Property in Times of Armed Conflict: The Practice of the International Criminal Tribunal for the Former Yugoslavia*, 14 Harv. Hum. Rts. J. 1 (2001).

[55] *Id.* at 31.

[56] Rome Statute of the ICC, arts. 8(2)(b)(ix) (international conflict), 8(2)(e)(iv) (non-international conflict); for details, compare Knut Dörmann (with contributions by Louise Doswald-Beck & Robert Kolb), Elements of War Crimes under the Rome Statute of the International Criminal Court: Sources and Commentary (2003).

[57] Cunning, *supra* note 33.

[58] *See* 1954 Hague Convention, arts. 4(2), 11(2)

responsibility of those acts before the ICC. All objects within the meaning of Article 1 of the Hague Convention of 1954, fulfilling the definition of Article 8(2)(b)(ix) of the Rome Statute—which normally is the case—are not allowed to become military objectives. Even if, from a military point of view, it may be seen as "necessary" to attack buildings dedicated to religion, education, art, science, and historic monuments, this will not be allowed. On the contrary, if this rule is violated, the act will be pursued as a war crime. Thus, the provisions of the 1954 Hague Convention and the Second Protocol were strengthened by the Rome Statute.

An important development has also taken place with regard to conflicts of a non-international character: acts such as intentional attacks against cultural property, destruction or seizure of the enemy's property, and pillaging of towns and places committed in non-international conflicts are punishable now as war crimes under Article 8(2)(f) of the Rome Statute.

To conclude, there is a chance that crimes against cultural heritage perpetrated in international armed conflict will be punished more often in the near future, provided that reluctant states follow the example set by European and other states in joining the Rome Statute and are willing to cooperate with the ICC.[59]

2. Evolution of National Criminal Jurisdiction: The Case of Germany

Generally, it is very important that parties establish their national jurisdiction over offences that are either committed on their territory, by their nationals or, in some circumstances, when the alleged offender is present on their territory.[60] In former times, the Hague Convention of 1954 had required states to take, within the framework of their ordinary jurisdiction, all necessary steps to prosecute and impose penal or disciplinary sanctions upon those persons, of whatever nationality, who commit or give orders to commit a breach of the 1954 Convention. However, the provision was of almost no relevance because it did not explain which violations would require criminal sanction. The Second Protocol to the Hague Convention in 1954, adopted in 1999, clarified the situation: Article 15 Second Protocol now defines five acts that constitute serious violations requiring criminal sanctions if committed intentionally and in

[59] As of February 6, 2007, 104 countries are state parties to the Rome Statute of the ICC; *see also* Sabine von Schorlemer, *ICC—The International Criminal Court, in* A CONCISE ENCYCLOPEDIA OF THE UNITED NATIONS 275 (Helmut Volger ed., 2002); Robert J. Johansen, *The Impact of U.S. Policy Toward the International Criminal Court on the Prevention of Genocide, War Crimes, and Crimes Against Humanity*, 28 HUM. RTS. Q. 301 (2006); Adrian Jones, *Continental Divide and the Politics of Complex Sovereignty: Canada, The United States and the International Criminal Court*, 39 CAN. J. POL. SCI. 227 (2006); Jamie Mayerfeld, *Who Shall Be Judge?: The United States, the International Criminal Court, and the Global Enforcement of Human Rights*, 25 HUM. RTS. Q. 93 (2003); Jason Ralph, *International Society, the International Criminal Court and American Foreign Policy*, 31 REV. INT'L STUD. 2744 (2005); PHILIP MEISSNER, THE INTERNATIONAL CRIMINAL COURT CONTROVERSY: AN ANALYSIS OF THE UNITED STATES' MAJOR OBJECTIONS AGAINST THE ROME STATUTE (2005).

[60] For a discussion of the expanding role of universal jurisdiction, *see* HENRY STEINER & PHILIP ALSTON, INTERNATIONAL HUMAN RIGHTS IN CONTEXT: LAW, POLITICS, MORALS: TEXT AND MATERIALS 1021 (1996).

violation of the 1954 Hague Convention or the Second Protocol. For example, if cultural heritage, for which an entry on the List of Cultural Property has been made, is used for military purposes, this amounts to a serious violation of the Second Protocol. Also, extensive destruction, appropriation, theft, pillage, or misappropriation or acts of vandalism directed against cultural heritage protected under the 1954 Convention will bear serious consequences for the perpetrator. Moreover, state parties must extradite or submit persons to their competent authorities provided they committed a serious violation of the Second Protocol, that is, they

(1) either attacked or used an object under enhanced protection in support of military action;
(2) committed an extensive destruction or appropriation of or attack against objects protected under the Hague Convention on the Protection of Cultural Property in Armed Conflict (1954) and the Second Protocol;
(3) committed a theft, pillage or misappropriation of, or acts of vandalism against cultural property protected under the Convention of 1954.[61]

Germany, in contrast to some other states,[62] adopted a Code of Crimes Against International Law (CCAIL/Völkerstrafgesetzbuch), which has been in force since June 30, 2002.[63] It provides part of a "normative infrastructure for the application of humanitarian law," as Michael Bothe puts it.[64] The German CCAIL certainly has a positive effect on the evolution of cultural heritage law in armed conflict. In particular, the provisions on war crimes (Sections 8–12) are relevant. As those provisions are applicable in international and non-international armed conflicts, the role of jus in bello in civil war is higher than provided for in the Rome Statute. Another important issue of the German CCAIL is its focus on methods of warfare.[65] In contrast to the Rome Statute, the prohibition of an attack on civil, non-military objects is expanded to non-international armed conflict. Here again, we find Germany's considerable strengthening of cultural heritage law.

Unfortunately, no progress on the national level was made with respect to the issue of military use of cultural objects. Despite the fact that the Second Protocol to the Hague Convention in 1954 prohibits the use of a civil object and

---

[61] Art. 15(1) SP.

[62] Comparing different forms of implementation in different legal systems: Carsten Stahn, *Die Umsetzung des Rom-Statuts in nationales Recht—Ein erster rechtsvergleichender Überblick*, 1 Humanitäres Völkerrecht 200 (2000).

[63] Bundesgesetzblatt (BGBl.) 2002 I, Nr. 42, at 2254; the Court has dealt with the following cases so far: Nikola J. (OLG Düsseldorf), Judgment Sept. 26, 1997; Novislav D. (BayObLG München), Judgment May 23, 1997; Maksim S. (OLG Düsseldorf), Judgment Nov. 29, 1999 (BGH Judgment Feb. 1, 2001); Djuradi K. (BayObLG München), Judgment Dec. 15, 1999 (BGH Decision Feb. 2001). For further details, see http://www.bundesanwaltschaft.de/de/voelker.php (last visited May 30, 2008).

[64] Michael Bothe, *Neue und alte Konzepte der Durchsetzung des humanitären Völkerrechts, in* Brücken bauen und begehen, Festschrift für Knut Ipsen zum 65. Geburtstag 30 (Volker Epping ed., 2000).

[65] *See* Section 11(1), no. 2, which was formulated according to art. 8(2)(b)(ii), (ix), and (e)(iv) of the ICC Statute.

its surroundings in support of military action,[66] neither the Rome Statute nor the German CCAIL characterizes the fact that civil objects are used for military purposes as a war crime. This is regrettable, and we certainly need to intensify our efforts to prosecute the military abuse of cultural objects (*zivilisatorische Schutzschilde*).

D. RECENT DEVELOPMENTS IN THE UNITED NATIONS CONCERNING THE SAFEGUARDING OF CULTURAL HERITAGE IN ARMED CONFLICT AND FOREIGN OCCUPATION

Various organs of the United Nations, namely the General Assembly, the International Court of Justice, the Security Council, and various U.N. subcommissions along with the U.N. Secretary-General are actively promoting international humanitarian law. The United Nations, as "guardian" of international peace and security, also plays an increasingly active role in dealing with the legacy of armed conflict, paying special tribute to cultural heritage issues.

1. The General Assembly

In the preamble to Resolution 3187 (XXVIII) of December 18, 1973, the General Assembly deplores the removal of works of art without payment as a result of colonial or foreign occupation. However, the restitution of cultural objects lost during World War II and other armed conflicts was neither dealt with in this resolution nor in similar resolutions during the years afterwards. Property lost in armed conflict did not play a role in the General Assembly until the late 1990s.

In Resolution 46/10, adopted by the General Assembly at its 35th plenary meeting, October 22, 1991, and similarly in subsequent resolutions,[67] the relevance of the return of irreplaceable cultural heritage to those who had created it and consequently the need to fully implement the 1970 UNESCO Convention on the Means of Prohibiting and Preventing the Illicit Import, Export and Transfer of Ownership of Cultural Property was emphasized.

In 1999, upon the initiative of Greece, a new draft was introduced, supported by 41 states. The draft was adopted without a formal vote.[68] Experts, such as the German diplomat Thomas Fitschen, highlighted that this resolution set a new focus on the dangers of cultural objects in armed conflict.[69] As a matter of fact, in paragraph 3 in its preamble, the General Assembly resolution recalled the relevance of the Hague Convention (1954). Furthermore, it expressed "concern about the loss, destruction, damage, removal, theft, pillage or misappropriation of and any acts of vandalism directed against cultural property in areas of armed conflict and territories that are occupied."[70] For

---

[66] *See* art. 12 SP and also art. 8(2)(b) of the ICC Statute.

[67] G.A. Res. 48/15, U.N. Doc. A/RES/48/15 (Nov. 11, 1993); G.A. Res. 50/56, U.N. Doc. A/RES/50/56 (Feb. 2, 1996); and G.A. Res. 52/24 U.N. Doc. A/RES/52/24 (Jan. 23, 1998) referred back to previous recommendations.

[68] G.A. .54/190, U.N. Doc. A/RES/54/190 (Feb. 17, 2000).

[69] Thomas Fitschen, *30 Jahre, "Rückführung von Kulturgut,"* 2 Vereinte Nationen 50 (2004).

[70] U.N. Doc. A/RES/54/190, pmbl., para. 9.

the first time, the General Assembly called upon states to ratify the 1954 Convention and the Second Protocol.[71] Similarly, for the first time only the U.N. system and inter-governmental organizations were asked to address the issue of return or restitution of cultural property to the countries of origin and to accordingly provide appropriate support.[72] In former resolutions, states were held responsible for return and restitution.[73]

Another General Assembly resolution, Resolution 56/97 of December 14, 2001, repeated the need to adhere to the 1954 Hague Convention and the Second Protocol.[74] Again, it expressed concern regarding damage directed against cultural property in areas of armed conflict and territories that are occupied, adding that this shall be irrespective of "whether such conflicts are international or internal."[75] Furthermore, the resolution showed a new focus on practical measures, for example, by the newly established International Fund for the Return of Cultural Property to Its Countries of Origin or Its Restitution in Case of Illicit Appropriation, which was launched in November 2002.

General Assembly Resolution 58/17 of December 3, 2003, showed an even higher participation rate (65 submitting states). Here, for the first time the relevance of the First Protocol of the 1954 Hague Convention for the Protection of Cultural Property in the Event of Armed Conflict was emphasized in the preamble.[76] Again, states were called upon to ratify the 1954 Hague Convention and the Second Protocol.[77] A new focus on armed conflict was to be seen by the acknowledgment of the work of UNESCO for the safeguarding of cultural heritage of countries in conflict including safe return to those countries.[78]

Consequently, the focus of the General Assembly on the protection of cultural property in situations of armed conflict, including occupation, and being irrespective of the nature of the conflict (international or internal), was expanded. This new point of attention for the U.N. plenary organ certainly was related to the Iraq crisis: the General Assembly mentioned not only Security Council Resolution 1483 (2003),[79] in particular paragraph 7 relating to the restitution of the cultural property of Iraq, but also the Declaration of the General Conference of UNESCO on the "Destruction of Cultural Heritage" (2003).

In sum, the recent attention by the General Assembly given to cultural heritage in wartime and during occupation is an important devel-opment as it reflects the strong consensus on the global level to protect cultural heritage in danger.

---

71 *Id.*, paras. 2 and 3.
72 G.A. Res. 54/190, para. 5, U.N. Doc. A/RES/54/190/5 (Feb. 17, 2000).
73 For more details, see Fitschen, *supra* note 69, at 50.
74 *Id.*, paras. 2 and 3.
75 G.A. Res. 56/97, pmbl, para. 13, U.N. Doc. A/RES/56/97 (Jan. 30, 2002).
76 *Id.*, para. 4.
77 *Id.*, paras. 4 and 5.
78 *Id.*, para. 6.
79 S.C. Res. 1483 (2003) was adopted on May 22, 2003; *see infra* note 81.

2. The Security Council

Recently, the U.N. Security Council has also actively endorsed the safeguarding of cultural heritage in armed conflict. In Resolution 1483 (2003), the U.N. Security Council resolved under Chapter VII[80] that the United Nations should play a vital role in humanitarian relief and the reconstruction of Iraq. It stressed the need for respecting the archaeological, historical, cultural, and religious heritage of Iraq, and the continued protection of archaeological, historical, cultural, and religious sites, museums, libraries, and monuments.

Furthermore, the Security Council established a binding trade ban on items that have been illegally removed from Iraq. The Security Council decided that all member states "shall take appropriate steps to facilitate the safe return to Iraqi institutions of Iraqi property and other items of archaeological, historical, cultural, rare scientific and religious importance illegally removed from the Iraqi National Museum, the National Library, and other locations in Iraq."[81] Finally, in the same paragraph, UNESCO was called upon to assist in the implementation of the trade ban. As Catherine Phuong stated, the aim of the trade prohibition was "to strangle the international market for stolen cultural objects stolen since 1990."[82] Given the fact that there is no universal membership in the 1970 UNESCO Convention—there were 95 states parties at that time—and given the danger for Iraqi cultural heritage, UNESCO itself had pushed for the adoption of a Security Council resolution. Indeed, the legal importance of Security Council Resolution 1483, which had been sponsored by Spain, the United Kingdom, and the United States, is considerable: First of all, the Security Council contributed substantially to the development of cultural heritage law by requesting all U.N. member states to cooperate closely in order to ensure the recovery and restitution of stolen Iraqi cultural property. *Ratione materiae,* we find a broad scope of application. Second, *ratione temporis,* the Security Council did not only act on the occasion of an isolated event, for example, a crisis, but in a larger time frame of more than a decade from August 1990 to May 2003. Third, the trade prohibition imposed by the Security Council on U.N. member states is rather extensive in substance, including items where reasonable suspicion exists that they have been illegally removed. This means there is a general presumption that many, if not all, Iraqi cultural objects that have been exported from Iraq since 1990 have been illegally removed. Considering the scale of the looting that has taken place over the last few years, this seems to be a realistic assumption. Fourth, the Security Council

[80] The Security Council has the means to enforce its decisions under Chapter VII of the U.N. Charter, provided that it determines the existence of a threat to international peace and security under Article 39. Generally, the Security Council acts under Chapter VII in situations of crisis or armed conflict; *cf.* BEN F. KLAPPE, ACTING UNDER CHAPTER VII OF THE CHARTER OF THE UNITED NATIONS, FESTSCHRIFT FÜR DIETER FLECK, at 329 et seq. (Horst Fischer et al. eds., 2004).

[81] S.C. Res. 1483, para.7, U.N. Doc. S/RES/1483 (May 22, 2003). The binding resolution refers to illegal removal of material "since the adoption of Resolution 661 (1990) of 6 August, 1990, including by establishing a prohibition on trade in or transfer of such items and items with respect to which reasonable suspicion exists that they have been illegally removed."

[82] Catherine Phuong, *The Protection of Iraqi Cultural Property,* 53 INT'L COMP. L.Q. 985 (2004).

resolution—as was indicated previously—has imposed *ad hoc* binding force on all U.N. member states. As it had done before with Resolution 1373 (2001)—and later with Resolution 1540 (2004)[83]—the Security Council obviously wished to seize an opportunity to complement existing treaty law with a new binding provision. The advantage of these proceedings is that the Security Council resolutions enter into force immediately and among all U.N. member states, even those that do not adhere to the UNESCO Convention of 1970. Even though there are some problems of implementation, Security Resolution 1483 and the legislation adopted to implement it are therefore to be seen as "the primary legal measures dealing with cultural property which was illegally removed from Iraq."[84]

In another resolution (Security Council Resolution 1546 of June 8, 2004), the Security Council stressed again the "need for all parties to respect and protect Iraq's archaeological, historical, cultural, and religious heritage." Thus, there are signs that in recent years the Security Council has become increasingly aware of the need to protect cultural heritage in armed conflict. It adopted a new role in legislating a worldwide trade ban in order to safeguard the endangered cultural heritage of U.N. member states. Even if binding acts of the Security Council with implications for cultural heritage law may be more the exception than the rule, they nevertheless reflect the strong support of the international community for preserving cultural heritage to the benefit of future generations.

3. UNESCO

UNESCO is the most influential international organization in the field of cultural heritage law. These efforts are primarily reflected in classical cultural heritage treatymaking, which is traditionally the "turf" of UNESCO. By adopting the Second Protocol to the 1954 Hague Convention in 1999, for example, UNESCO complemented existing provisions of the Convention.

Moreover, as recent conflicts have shown, UNESCO found a new role as "trouble shooter" in crisis situations, being able to react on short notice when cultural heritage of a country is in danger as in the Iraq War. As Francesco Francioni and Federico Lenzerini have noted, the authority of UNESCO for adopting sanctions against member states is rather limited;[85] however, UNESCO has established several institutions, which may exert influence on domestic policies and, as such, certainly have an impact on the development of international humanitarian law as well.

---

[83] With further references, *see* Georges Abi-Saab, *The Security Council as Legislator and as Executive in its Fight Against Terrorism and Against Proliferation of Weapons of Mass Destruction. the Question of Legitimacy*, *in* RÜDIGER WOLFRUM & VOLKER RÖBEN EDS., LEGITIMACY IN INTERNATIONAL LAW 108 et seq. (2008), with comments by Erika de Wet (*id.*, 131 et seq.).

[84] Phuong, *supra* note 82, at 985, 995 (2004), with references to Iraq (U.N. Sanctions); the Dealing in Cultural Objects (Offenses) Act 2003 of the United Kingdom; the Emergency Protection for Iraqi Cultural Antiquities Bill of the United States; the EU Council Regulation No. 1210/2003 of July 7, 2003; *see* Regulation No. 2465/96, 2003 O.J. (L 169) 6.

[85] Franceso Francioni & Federico Lenzerini, *The Destruction of the Buddhas of Bamiyan and International Law*, 14 EUR. J. INT'L L. 639 (2003).

For example, the World Heritage Committee, the body established by the UNESCO Convention Concerning the Protection of the World Cultural and Natural Heritage (1972),[86] can act on its own initiative and place sites on a "red list," making them eligible for assistance from the World Heritage Fund.[87] This may become relevant in situations of armed conflict, for the "outbreak or threat of armed conflict" constitutes a "potential danger"[88] within the meaning of the criteria for the inscription of properties on the List of World Heritage in Danger.

Another body was set up by the General Conference of UNESCO in 1980: The Intergovernmental Committee for Promoting the Return of Cultural Property for Its Countries of Origin or Its Restitution in Case of Illicit Appropriation (the Return and Restitution Committee).[89] Today, it comprises

---

[86] 1037 U.N.T.S. 151.

[87] *Cf.* UNESCO World Heritage in Danger List, *available at* http://whc.unesco.org/pg.cfm?cid=86 (last visited May 31, 2005); in accordance with Article 11(4), of the World Heritage Convention, the committee may inscribe a property on the List of World Heritage in Danger when the following requirements are met: the property under consideration is on the World Heritage List; the property is threatened by serious and specific danger; major operations are necessary for the conservation of the property; assistance under the convention has been requested for the property ("message of concern"). Such assistance may be requested by any committee member or the secretariat; *see Operational Guidelines for the Implementation of the World Heritage Convention*, UNESCO Doc. WHC.08/01, para. 177 (Jan. 2008); as to the legal relevance of the Operational Guidelines, *see* DIANA ZACHARIAS, THE INTERNATIONAL REGIME FOR THE PROTECTION OF WORLD CULTURAL AND NATURAL HERITAGE 23 et seq. (2007).

[88] *Operational Guidelines for the Implementation of the World Heritage Convention*, UNESCO Doc. WHC.08 /01, para. 179(b)(v) (Jan. 2008).

[89] Art. 2 of the Statutes of the Return and Restitution Committee; according to Article 4 of the Statutes of the Committee, it is responsible for

(1) seeking ways and means of facilitating bilateral negotiations for the restitution or return of cultural property to its countries of origin when they are undertaken according to the conditions defined in art. 9. Correspondingly, the committee may also submit proposals with a view to mediation or conciliation to the member states concerned, it being understood that mediation implies the intervention of an outside party to bring the concerned parties to a dispute together and assist them in reaching a solution, while under conciliation, the concerned parties agree to submit their dispute to a constituted organ for investigation and efforts to effect a settlement, provided that any additional, necessary funding shall come from extra-budgetary resources. For the exercise of the mediation and conciliation functions, the committee may establish appropriate rules of procedure. The outcome of the mediation and conciliation process is not binding on the member states concerned, so that if it does not lead to the settlement of a problem, it shall remain before the committee, such as any other unresolved question which has been submitted to it;

(2) promoting multilateral and bilateral cooperation with a view to the restitution and return of cultural property to its countries of origin;

(3) encouraging the necessary research and studies for the establishment of coherent programs for the constitution of representative collections in countries whose cultural heritage has been dispersed;

(4) fostering a public information campaign on the real nature, scale, and scope of the problem of the restitution or return of cultural property to its countries of origin;

(5) guiding the planning and implementation of UNESCO's program of activities

22 member states of UNESCO and acts in an advisory capacity. After bilateral negotiations have failed, member states may submit requests to the Return and Restitution Committee. Since 1999, the committee has also been dealing with disputes concerning cultural objects displaced in relationship to World War II. Following Recommendation 7 of the Return and Restitution Committee, the Director-General was invited to convene a working group of experts. At one of the meetings, which took place in Paris on May 29–31, 2000, eight principles were considered.[90] According to Recommendation 4 of the Return and Restitution Committee, the draft principles were submitted for consideration by the 33rd session of the UNESCO General Conference. Following a resolution of the General Conference,[91] the Director-General convened an inter-governmental meeting on the preparation of a Declaration of Principles concerning displaced objects during World War II. The resolution states that the subject of cultural objects displaced in connection with the Second World War should be subject to a non-binding Declaration of Principles. In pursuance of this resolution, the Director-General submitted a draft of this declaration to the General Conference at its 34th session in 2007.[92]

With regard to special crisis situations, UNESCO improved its capacity to react. Already in the Balkan wars, UNESCO urged parties to respect heritage law and organized emergency assistance, for example, for the city of Dubrovnik, Croatia.[93] In Afghanistan, however—at times when there was no armed conflict—UNESCO failed to prevent the atrocious crimes committed against the Buddha statutes in the Bamiyan Valley because of the intransigence of the Taliban regime. Today, UNESCO has a clear mandate for the rehabilitation

---

with regard to the restitution or return of cultural property to its countries of origin;

(6) encouraging the establishment or reinforcement of museums or other institutions for the conservation of cultural property and the training of the necessary scientific and technical personnel;

(7) promoting exchanges of cultural property in accordance with the Recommendation on the International Exchange of Cultural Property;

(8) reporting on its activities to the General Conference of UNESCO at each of its ordinary sessions.

With further detail, compare Sabine von Schorlemer, *UNESCO Dispute Settlement*, *in* ABDULQAWI A. YUSUF ED., STANDARD-SETTING IN UNESCO, VOL. I, NORMATIVE ACTION IN EDUCATION, SCIENCE AND CULTURE 101 et seq. (2007).

[90] *See* UNESCO Doc. CLT-2002/CONF/602/3 (Feb. 24, 2003). The principles had been originally proposed by Dr. Lyndel V. Prott, the Director of the International Standards Unit of the Division of Cultural Heritage of UNESCO during a Symposium in New York entitled "The Spoils of War—World War II and its Aftermath: The Loss, Reappearance and Recovery of Cultural Property" (Jan. 1995).

[91] UNESCO Doc. 33 C/Res. 45, adopted on the Report of Commission IV at its 20th Plenary Meeting, on Oct. 20, 2005.

[92] *See* UNESCO, General Conference, 34th sess., Paris, 2007, *Draft Declaration of Principles Relating to Cultural Objects Displaced in Connection With the Second World War*, Annex I, UNESCO Doc. 34 C/22 (Sept. 5, 2007) UNESCO, Executive Board, 177th sess., *Report by the Director-General on the Preparation of a Draft Declaration of Principles Relating to Cultural Objects Displaced in Connection With the Second World War*, UNESCO Doc. 177 EX/17 (Sept. 17, 2007).

[93] *See* UNESCO, *Envoys Leave for Dubrovnik to Assess Damage*, AGENCE FRANCE PRESSE, Nov. 28, 1991.

of Afghanistan's cultural heritage and undertakes manifold efforts to enhance cultural heritage conservation.[94] In 2002, UNESCO created the International Coordination Committee for the Safeguarding of Afghanistan's Cultural Heritage ("International Coordination Committee") to coordinate all international efforts for the safeguarding of cultural heritage. At its first meeting, which was held at UNESCO headquarters in Paris, June 16–18, 2003, the International Coordination Committee adopted recommendations for future action.[95]

In the course of the Iraq War (2003) UNESCO reiterated the relevant international norms and took measures for recovering missing items. Within days after the looting of the National Museum, UNESCO organized a consultative expert meeting that called on the Coalition Forces "to observe the principles of the 1954 Hague Convention for the Protection of Cultural Property in the Event of Armed Conflict and its two Protocols."[96] UNESCO also called on states that had not ratified the convention to comply with its provisions, especially as to ensure the return of cultural property already illicitly removed and/or exported from Iraq. On May 16–20, 2003, only a short time after the invasion, the first UNESCO Cultural Heritage Mission to Baghdad took place.[97]

In September 2003, UNESCO created the International Coordinating Committee to Safeguard the Cultural Heritage of Iraq ("International Coordinating Committee, Iraq") under the auspices of the Iraqi Culture Ministry, in order to coordinate international assistance and international activities aiming at safeguarding the Iraqi cultural heritage.[98] It is composed of 25 international experts, including six from Iraq and nine observers from UNESCO partner organizations, including the Getty Conservation Institute. At the first meeting, which was held at UNESCO headquarters in Paris, May 24–25, 2004, seven objectives were adopted, *inter alia*, to "coordinate international action and channel international aid—both bilateral and multilateral—with a view to ensure the implementation of the strategy for the safeguarding of the cultural heritage in Iraq and assess its overall monitoring based on the recommendations adopted by the [International Coordinating Committee, Iraq]."

---

[94] *See* Christian Manhart, *UNESCO's Mandate and Recent Activities for the Rehabilitation of Afghanistan's Cultural Heritage*, 86 Int'l Rev. Red Cross 401 (2004).

[95] UNESCO, *First Plenary Session of the International Coordination Committee For the Safeguarding of Afghanistan's Cultural Heritage (ICC)*, June 16–18, 2003, Paris, Recommendations, *available at* http://whc.unesco.org/uploads/activities/documents/activity-245-1.doc (last visited May 30, 2008). *See* Christian Manhart, *UNESCO's Role in the Rehabilitation of Bamiyan in Afghanistan*, 1(4) J. Int'l Consortium Landslides (2004), *available at* http://www.springerlink.com/content/hude62e6yaab55x2/fulltext.html (last visited May 30, 2008).

[96] *See* UNESCO, *Final Report: First Expert's Meeting on Iraqi Cultural Heritage* (Apr. 17, 2003), http://portal.unesco.org/culture/en/files/8511/10716551167Final_Report_1st_Expert_Meeting.pdf/Final_Report_1st_Expert_Meeting.pdf (last visited May 30, 2008).

[97] John M. Russell, *A Personal Account of the First UNESCO Cultural Heritage Mission to Baghdad* (Aug. 2003), *available at* http://www.archaeological.org/pdfs/papers/J_Russell_IraqA5S.pdf (last visited May 30, 2008).

[98] The Executive Board of UNESCO approved at its 167th session (Decision 9.2) the establishment of the International Coordinating Committee, Iraq.

The second meeting was held in Paris, June 22–23, 2005. The third UNESCO Experts' Meeting on the Safeguarding of the Iraqi Cultural Heritage, which took place in Tokyo on August 1, 2003, discussed the results of the two previous UNESCO assessment missions to Iraq and dealt specifically with issues related to the National Museum in Baghdad. UNESCO projects concerned, among others, the refurbishing of the conservation laboratories of the National Museum, a new database for the archiving and management of collections, photogrammetry equipment, and training.

UNESCO also organized the Cultural Forum for Iraq that, at its first meeting at UNESCO headquarters on May 26–27, 2004, in the presence of Iraqi Minister for Culture Moufid Al Jazairi, adopted an appeal that demanded, among other things, the safeguarding of the cultural heritage. The forum also recommended the establishment of an inventory of architectural and urban heritage.[99]

In summary, it may be said that we have numerous "best practices" that reflect the fact that in recent years UNESCO managed to strengthen international cooperation for the protection and rehabilitation of both tangible and intangible cultural heritage in armed conflict. This is a very important development, in particular because such cooperation helps to establish "early reaction" instruments that prevent damage and loss of irreplaceable cultural heritage in situations of armed conflict.

E. CONCLUSION

There is clear progress in the development of laws and rules of war and occupation regarding the safeguarding of cultural property in armed conflict. As has been shown, efforts are constantly being undertaken to improve the legal foundations and their implementation. As Wayne Sandholtz rather optimistically puts it with regard to the evolution of cultural heritage law, there is a "development of international rules in the direction of a duty to protect."[100]

An important aspect concerns the application of cultural heritage law provisions to private actors, which, as has been shown, is still a controversial issue. Another important development is the evolution of criminal jurisdiction for violating cultural heritage law provisions applicable in armed conflict. International criminal law nowadays constitutes a body of norms the purpose of which is to enforce an important part of international humanitarian law,[101] cultural heritage included. In reaction to the adoption of the Rome Statute of the ICC in The Hague, many countries improved their capacity to undertake

---

[99] *See* UNESCO, *Motion of the Participants to the First Cultural Forum for Iraq* (May 27, 2004), *available at* http://portal.unesco.org/culture/en/files/20797/10857502303Iraq_Motion.pdf/Iraq%2BMotion.pdf (last visited May 30, 2008).

[100] Sandholtz, *supra* note 33, at 188; *see generally* Sabine von Schorlemer, *The "Responsibility to Protect" as an Element of Peace,* (Development and Peace Foundation 2007), *available at* http://www.sef-bonn.org (last visited May 30, 2008).

[101] Michael Bothe, *The Historical Evolution of International Humanitarian Law, International Human Rights Law, Refugee Law and International Criminal Law, in* KRISENSICHERUNG UND HUMANITÄRER SCHUTZ—CRISIS MANAGEMENT AND HUMANITARIAN PROTECTION, FESTSCHRIFT FÜR DIETER FLECK, at 44 (Horst Fischer et al. eds. 2004).

national criminal jurisdiction. This may also give a fresh impetus to the application of cultural heritage law provisions in the future.

Moreover, it has become obvious that there are some important and most interesting recent developments within the United Nations, especially in the Security Council, General Assembly, and UNESCO. Let us hope that the combined efforts of all U.N. institutions may help to ensure a "better world" for future generations by conserving the marvelous beauty of the cultural heritage of mankind.

CHAPTER 6

UNRAVELING HISTORY: RETURN OF AFRICAN CULTURAL OBJECTS REPATRIATED AND LOOTED IN COLONIAL TIMES

Folarin Shyllon

A. INTRODUCTION

Collecting objects from foreign countries and cultures flourished during the 19th century, especially after European powers were more firmly in control in Africa and Asia. Colonialism coincided with the development of new academic disciplines such as anthropology and archaeology. The material evidence of the newly discovered cultures was studied, catalogued, and displayed in European museums to illustrate the greatness of the colonial empire.

B. A LACK OF MUSEUMS

In Africa, the establishment of museums could have prevented or reduced the wholesale removal of cultural objects from the colonies to the Western European metropolis. The attitude of colonial officials, however, could at best be described as indifferent. Consequently, museums sprang up either as a result of the sustained effort and enthusiasm of a few colonial officials or in order to cater for the pastimes of settlers and colonial officials. The museum as an institution had been formalized, however, in Europe well before the scramble for Africa: for example, the Ashmolean Museum in 1683, the Dresden Museum in 1744, the British Museum in 1753, the Vatican Museums in 1784,[1] the Louvre in 1793, and the Prado in 1819. In Kenya what is now the National Museums of Kenya started in 1910 by colonial settlers and naturalists who needed a place to keep and preserve their collections. In Nigeria, the National Museum was established in Jos in 1952, but it was not until 1957 that the National Museum in Lagos was opened. Both Kenneth Murray and E.H. Duckworth, who worked tirelessly for the establishment of a museum in Nigeria, drew attention to the fact that many priceless objects such as Ife bronze heads unearthed in 1938 had left the country because of the absence of a museum. What was true of the Nigerian experience was probably also true of many other countries without

[1] The founding of *Musei Vaticani* (Vatican Museums) can be traced back more than 500 years to 1503, when the newly elected Pope, Julius II della Rovere, placed a statue of Apollo in the internal courtyard of the Belvedere Palace built by Pope Innocent VIII, http://www.christurex.org/www1/vatican/0-Musei.html.

museums. Meanwhile, museums in Europe were holding many African cultural objects. A typical example is the Royal Museum for Central Africa (RMCA) in Tervuren, Belgium.

The RMCA was founded in 1897 by King Leopold II of Belgium as a "window on Central Africa" for the Belgian people. It boasts on its homepage that the "museum is home to some truly remarkable collections. Its collection of ethnographic objects from Central Africa is in fact the only one of its kind in the world" numbering some 500,000 African objects.[2] The largest African museums have an average of 5,000 objects.

C. CULTURAL HEMORRHAGING

It was during the colonial period that cultural hemorrhaging started. Losses were sustained in four main ways. First, as a result of the intrusion and imposition of foreign religions (Christianity and Islam), Africans simply destroyed or left to decay what were once important objects of veneration. If the objects were not destroyed or left to decay, they were removed as curios to museums and private homes in the countries from which the Christian missionaries and colonial administrators came. The second basis of cultural hemorrhaging was through gifts, either as a mark of hospitality or in exchange for knick-knacks or gewgaws. The third basis was through sheer plunder. One of the most infamous exampled is connected with the Benin pillage of 1897. The fourth way in which losses were sustained has been through research workers who have removed art pieces, claiming that they were meant for study collections, or that they would help to publicize the art of Africa around the world.[3]

D. HISTORY AND HERITAGE IN CAPTIVITY

1. The Ethiopian Experience

An article in *The Economist* of July 10, 1999, captioned "Let's Have Our Treasure Back, Please," opened with the following account of the plunder of Ethiopia's cultural treasures in 1868:

> It took 15 elephants and 200 mules to carry off the loot from Ethiopia's old capital, Magdala. The brutal sacking of the mountain-top city in 1868, Britain's revenge on Emperor Tewodros for taking the British consul and a few other Europeans hostage, razed the city to the ground. The hostages were released unharmed but the battle turned into a massacre and treasure hunt. Tewodros committed suicide and British soldiers stripped his body naked for souvenirs. They carted off

[2] *See* http://www.africamuseum.be/museum/about. The museum comprises, for example, 250,000 rock samples, 56,000 wood samples, 8,000 musical instruments, 180,000 other ethnographic objects, and 350 archives; http://www.africamuseum.be/museum/about/histobuildings/histocollection.

[3] Well after the end of colonialism in Africa during the disastrous famine in Ethiopia in the 1980s, it has been alleged that individuals who came to save lives ended up as collectors of cultural objects. Ethiopia's cultural objects were bartered for small amounts to enable their owners to survive.

his library and the treasures from a Coptic Christian church nearby. For £4, Richard Holmes, the British army's "archaeologist," acquired the crown of the Abun, the head of the Ethiopian church and a solid gold chalice from a soldier who had looted them. The booty was collected and auctioned off near Magdala. Holmes bought 350 illuminated bibles and manuscripts for the British Museum. Other books went to the royal library at Windsor and libraries at Oxford and Cambridge. They are still there, though odd treasures have been returned—usually the less valuable one—as gestures, whenever the British needed to court Ethiopia.[4]

Yohannes IV, who emerged as Emperor after Tewodros' death, barely half a year after his coronation on August 10, 1872, dispatched letters to Queen Victoria and the British foreign secretary, Earl Grenville, requesting the return of a manuscript and icon, both of which had been removed from Magdala. The manuscript, a *Kebra Nagast*, or "Glory of Kings," which embodied the legend of the Ethiopian ruling dynasty's origin, was of particular importance, for it appears to have been the volume containing "historical notices and other documents relating . . . to the city of Aksum and its church," as Dr Dieu, an official of the British Museum, was later to record. The British government was at that time anxious to remain on good terms with Yohannes, who had cooperated with the British forces during the Magdala campaign. The Foreign Office accordingly informed the British Museum that it would be a "gracious and friendly act" to comply with the Ethiopian ruler's request. The museum, which possessed two looted copies of the *Kebra Nagast*, agreed to return one—a rare example of the British Museum returning an acquisition.[5]

The question of the booty from Magdala came to the fore again a generation or so later, in 1924, when the then Ethiopian regent, Tafari Makonnen (later Emperor Haile Selassie), undertook a state visit to England. On that occasion King George V presented him with Tewodros' crown, another item from Magdala that had been housed in the Victoria and Albert Museum. Tafari later remarked in his autobiography that though the loss of the crown did not affect Ethiopian sovereignty, its presence in a foreign country "did not please" him. Finally, Queen Elizabeth II, on the eve of her departure during a state visit to Ethiopia in 1965, presented Emperor Haile Selassie in Asmara with two items that had been kept at Windsor Castle for nearly a century: Tewodros' cap and an imperial seal. She explained that she was returning these items "as a token of our gratitude and esteem."[6]

2. The Nigerian Experience

The plunder of Benin by British forces took place in 1897. In that year, a British expedition led by Consul James R. Phillips tried to reach Benin City in today's Nigeria at a time when the king of Benin was performing the most

---

[4] THE ECONOMIST, July 10, 1999, at 53.

[5] Richard Pankhurst, *Restitution of Cultural Property: The Case of Ethiopia*, 149 MUSEUM (UNESCO) 58, 59 (1986).

[6] *Id.* at 59–60.

important religious rite of the year. During this period, the king is not allowed contact with foreign elements, including persons. The expedition was advised accordingly, but Consul Phillips still tried to force his way through to the city. One of the king's aides, acting without the king's knowledge, caused seven out of nine members of the expedition to be killed. The British reaction was swift. The city was invaded, and the palace, where some tens of thousands of works of art in wood, ivory, and bronze were kept, was looted and eventually burnt down. The king was banished. The thousands of art pieces were first removed to London as spoils of war, from which they were dispersed throughout the world.

Among the objects captured is an exquisitely crafted ivory pendant mask now at the British Museum. In 1977, Nigeria requested the loan of the ivory mask for a pan-African cultural festival centered in Lagos, which had chosen the mask as its emblem. The British Museum initially requested an insurance bond of £2 million for the mask but then argued that it was too delicate to be moved from its carefully controlled environment. In any event, the mask was not lent, thereby leading to Nigeria's displeasure.[7] The companion piece of the ivory pendant mask is now at the Metropolitan Museum of Art in New York, where, according to Philippe de Montebello, it is "one of the museum's prized possessions."[8]

An earlier unsuccessful appeal for the return of the Benin objects had been made to the world at large in 1968, when a National Museum was planned for Benin City. The authorities of the Department of Antiquities were faced with the problem of finding exhibits that would be shown to reflect the position that Benin holds in the world of art history. An appeal was made through International Council of Museums (ICOM), at its General Assembly in Paris in 1968, asking for donations of one or two pieces from those museums with large stocks of Benin works. The resolution was converted into a general appeal for restitution or return and then adopted. When the Nigerian delegation returned to the country, it circulated the adopted resolution to the embassies and high commissions of countries known to have large Benin holdings, but no reaction was received from any quarter. The museum was therefore left to display lesser objects and mere casts and photographs of the pieces that once belonged to Benin.[9] The government of Nigeria had to compete at auctions in Europe to buy back for £50,000 all but one of the Benin bronzes that used to be on display in the Benin gallery in the National Museum in Lagos. Later, in 1980, the government of Nigeria spent £800,000 at Sotheby's in London to buy five Nigerian works of art, including three Benin bronzes. Still, the country can boast of fewer than 100 pieces of the famous objects. The legacy of colonization means that Nigeria has the smallest collection of the Benin bronzes after

[7] Folarin Shyllon, *Cultural Heritage Legislation and Management in Nigeria,* 5 INT'L J. CULTURAL PROP. 235 (1996); Folarin Shyllon, *One Hundred Years of Looting of Nigerian Art Treasures,* 3 ART, ANTIQUITY & LAW 253 (1998).

[8] P. de Montebello, "Foreword" to Kate Ezra, *Royal Art of Benin: The Perls Collection* vii (Metropolitan Museum of Art, Exhibition Catalogue 1992).

[9] E. Eyo, "Nigeria, " *in Return and Restitution of Cultural Property: Viewpoints,* 31 MUSEUM (UNESCO) 19, 21 (1979).

Germany (Dahlem in Berlin 4,000 pieces), United Kingdom (British Museum, 700 pieces; Pitt Rivers Museum, Oxford University, 393 pieces), and United States of America (Metropolitan Museum of Art, New York, about 200 pieces). Nigeria thus has only a *minority* holding of its own art.[10]

In the run-up to the centenary of the plunder of the Benin artworks, the November 11–17, 1991, issue of the weekly magazine *West Africa*, in a story captioned "Treasure Hunt," reported that the Oba (king) of Benin, Omo N'Oba Erediauwa had launched a strong campaign for the recovery of thousands of art treasures taken to Britain in 1897. The Oba was collecting as many as 1 million signatures worldwide. The account noted that previous efforts to recover the treasures had failed. Posters were printed and widely circulated both within and outside Nigeria that depicted some of the plundered bronzes with the inscription, "We Want Our Treasures Back." Again nothing came of this enterprise.

From February 17–23, 1997, activities were held in Benin City, the capital of Edo State, in the south-south region of Nigeria to mark the centenary of the events of 1897. The Oba of Benin in his opening address alluded to the threat of some Bini to take the U.K. government to the International Court of Justice over the pillage of 1897. The objective would be a judgment ordering the British government to repatriate the looted works of art. While appreciating the good intention of such Benin people, he cautioned against taking the issue to the International Court of Justice or any court of law, even if those contemplating it were be able to finance such actions. Pointing out that success has been achieved in many international issues through quiet diplomacy, the Oba, a Cambridge trained lawyer, added, "At this very moment, I am happy to say, I am in contact with some eminent people in London who are supportive to our cause and seriously helping."[11]

It is important to point out that the Benin bronzes are not merely cultural objects but part of the history of Nigeria. The 160 bronze heads taken away by the Benin punitive expedition amongst other items are the Benin equivalent to chronological records. Since each head represented an Oba, they recorded dynasties back to the 12th century. When an Oba died, a formal head was cast in bronze to furnish an altar erected to his memory.[12] The refusal to return such cultural objects is tantamount to keeping a people's history and heritage in captivity. And there is no doubt that the colonial powers knew the import and the devastating effect of the removal of irreplaceable cultural heritage. The story of the British seizure of the Golden Stool of the Ashantehene of the then Gold Coast (now Ghana) also illustrates this fundamental point.

E. ASHANTEHENE'S GOLDEN STOOL

The Ashanti had built their strength on gold trade with the Western Sudan: they were one of the sources of the gold that moved north through the

---

[10] Shyllon, *Cultural Heritage Legislation, supra* note 7, at 243.

[11] *The Great Benin Centenary* 30(3), Afr. Arts 28, 33 (1997).

[12] Jeanette Greenfield, The Return of Cultural Treasures 121 (2d ed. 1996).

Sudanese trading empires to North African markets. Not for nothing was the office of their kings symbolized by a Golden Stool that, in Ashanti tradition, "came down from Heaven" and alighted gently on the knees of their hero-founder Osei Tutu in about 1695. The British, in an effort to break up the unity of the Ashanti, seized the Golden Stool.[13]

The Golden Stool is sacred to the Ashanti; it is believed that the Golden Stool contains the spirit or soul of the Ashanti people. Just as man cannot live without soul, so the Ashanti would cease to exist if the Golden Stool were to be taken from them. The Golden Stool is not just sacred; it is a symbol of nationhood, a symbol that binds or unifies all Ashanti. The British knew the significance of the Golden Stool to the Ashanti. Because it represented so much to the Ashanti, the Golden Stool was the one object the British colonial administration especially coveted. The British governor of the Gold Coast, Frederick Hodgson, in a rash act of political triumphalism, demanded the Golden Stool so that he could sit on it—just as Queen Victoria sat on the throne of England. This insult caused the Ashanti to rise up. They inevitably lost the battle and the Golden Stool. The Golden Stool was returned to the people of Ashanti in 1935.

The failure to secure the return of a token few of the Benin cultural objects is not surprising, for even where there is a legal obligation to do so, the sanctity of legal agreements entered into by sovereign states has been ignored. Take, for example, Italy's retention of the obelisk of Aksum and other precious objects from Ethiopia. The story is well known how Mussolini's army in 1935–36 invaded Ethiopia and carried off truckloads of booty to display in Rome, including the statue of the Lion of Judah as a sign of submission. The Italians also took the 2,000-year-old obelisk of Aksum, from the center of Ethiopian Christianity, and dozens of other monuments, ecclesiastical crosses and crowns, manuscripts, and paintings. Although the Treaty of Peace with Italy of 1947 at the end of the Second World War specified that Italy should return "within eighteen months" all cultural property looted from Ethiopia, it was only after much pressure that the Italians agreed to it. As a result, the Ethiopian government archives, the paintings from the Parliament, and the Lion of Judah statue were at last returned, though the latter was not, in fact, sent back until 1969. Another especially culturally significant piece, the throne of Melenik II, was only returned by Italy to Ethiopia in 1982. Only in 1997 did Italy agree to return the obelisk that Italian authorities had placed outside the Food and Agricultural Organization in Rome. It was not until April 2005 that the obelisk was finally returned to Ethiopia.

The appropriation of a nation's art treasures has always been regarded as a trophy of war that adds to the glory of the victor and the humiliation of the vanquished. The practice has often been condemned in the past. As early as 1812, Sir Alexander Croke had a collection of prints and paintings returned to the Philadelphia Academy of Arts on the grounds that the arts and sciences are recognized by all civilized countries as forming an exception to the strict laws of war. It was recognized even then that to return items would therefore

---

[13] Basil Davidson, African Kingdoms 107 (1967); John Addison, Ancient Africa 87–88 (1970).

be in conformity with the law of nations, as practiced by all civilized countries. During the wars following the French Revolution, the booty of war included *objets d'art* and scientific objects. Restitution was made by Great Britain in 1815 of some of the items received as booty, when the Duke of Wellington declared that these annexations had been contrary to the practice of war between civilized nations.[14]

F. UNRAVELING HISTORY

We saw earlier how the British Museum prevaricated and dissembled over the lending of the Benin ivory pendant for a Pan-African and black cultural festival in Lagos, Nigeria in 1977. The final reason given was that the mask was too fragile to leave the museum. In 2001, in an interview in the London *Times*, Robert Anderson, the director of the British Museum, came clean and justified the refusal on two grounds. He said there was never a chance of a loan, as visitors "expect to see these things on display in the British Museum." "History could not be unraveled," he added.[15]

The British Museum continues to hold on firmly to other nations' cultural objects collected from the field of conquest or in colonial situations. It is argued that, legally, the museum is not allowed to alienate objects by act of Parliament. How-ever, it emerged recently that in the 1960s and 1970s, the British Museum had sold more than 30 of the controversial Benin pieces for as little as 75 pounds sterling each. The sale was stopped in 1972. Most of the plaques were bought by Nigeria. The details of the sales emerged when the *Art Newspaper* had a British Museum file on the affair declassified. This file revealed how pairs of superb centuries-old plaques, bought by the museum in 1898, were sold by the British Museum. The museum's African specialist, Dr. Nigel Barley, admitted that the decision to sell was unfortunate.[16] Rarely can such an eminent institution have seen its arguments so thoroughly undermined.

Because of colonialism, Africa lacks not only hundreds of objects of "irreplaceable cultural heritage" to borrow a phrase from UNESCO Director-General M'Bow's "A Plea for the Return of an Irreplaceable Cultural Heritage" in 1978, but thousands of other important antiquities. These are generally found in the countries of former colonizers who are refusing to contemplate the issue of significant loans or restitutions. Thus, the "retentive nationalists" are not the African countries who seek to have access to their treasures, but rather the former colonizers who granted independence but are refusing to let go of what they now consider to be part of their national patrimony.

More than 60 years ago Kenneth Murray, the founding father of the museum movement in Nigeria, highlighted the anomaly in this thinking when he remarked that "the needs, indeed, for a collection of Nigerian art in Europe

[14] JIRI TOMAN, THE PROTECTION OF CULTURAL PROPERTY IN THE EVENT OF ARMED CONFLICT 6–7, 336–37 (1996).

[15] TIMES (London), Dec. 7, 2001, at 11.

[16] BBC News, Mar. 27, 2002, *available at* http://news.bbc.co.uk/2/hi/entertainment/1896535.stm.

cannot be as vital as the need for one in Nigeria. In Europe it would chiefly have an academic purpose, but in Nigeria it is wanted for the cultural life of the country itself."[17] Cultural objects are not simply minerals or other resources that can be exploited; they represent and remain the very essence of the lives of their owners. However, Paul Bator in a seminal essay at the time considered cultural objects as exploitable commodities: "The Elgin marbles are part of England's national patrimony. All such works of art are part of the national capital: they generate income (by attracting tourists, etc.) and they can produce social and psychological benefits for a country and its inhabitants."[18]

"Retentive nationalism," "cultural nationalism," and "cultural internationalism" are not neutral terms after all. As, Greenfield asked, "Is it possible that arguments about 'internationalism' may merely disguise nationalism"?[19] The Bator thesis, stoutly defended by Robert Anderson of the British Museum (visitors "expect to see these things on display in the British Museum"), ignores the fact that the best and most sensitive of Africa's cultural heritage objects are in the West. While the Bator thesis accommodates the "social and psychological benefits" of those who retain the objects, it ignores the social and psychological dysfunction the situation creates for those whose forbearers made the objects. This dysfunction can be gauged from Nigeria's reaction to the British Museum's refusal to release on loan the Benin ivory mask. A Nigerian James Bond-type film called *The Mask* was made in 1980, which indicated that the only way of achieving its return was theft from the museum.[20] When the Nigerian government paid £800,000 in 1980 to buy five objects, it was done "as a matter of national honor and interest,"[21] thereby confirming the assertion of Theo-Ben Guirab, the foreign minister of Namibia, that "the lapse of time did not diminish ownership or the need for restitution."

The commoditization of culture as posited by Paul Bator contradicts one of the profound insights in his essay, in which he observed that although the internationalization of culture may produce benefits, there is also a general human interest in retaining differences. We would surely all be the poorer, he argued, if we could not by travel come upon, not just different works of art, but also a sense of being in a wholly different culture, a different artistic world. Indeed, there is a kind of natural economy in having Mexico specialize in Mexican art and France specialize in French art. He concluded, "The values of diversity and specialization have a powerful claim in the realm of art."[22] The recently adopted UNESCO Convention on the Protection and Promotion of the Diversity of Cultural Expressions[23] confirms Bator's view. The UNESCO

---

[17] Kenneth Murray, *Art in Nigeria: Need for a Museum*, 41 J. Royal Afr. Soc'y 241 (1942).

[18] Paul Bator, *An Essay on the International Trade in Art*, 34 Stan. L. Rev. 275 (1982).

[19] Greenfield, *supra* note 12, at 312.

[20] *Id.* at 141.

[21] Emmanuel Arinze, *The Punitive Expedition 1897*, *in* The Lost Treasures of Ancient Benin (Exhibition Catalogue; Institute of African Studies, University of Ibadan, Nigeria, 1984).

[22] Bator, *supra* note 18, at 306.

[23] UNESCO Doc. CLT-2005, Oct. 20, 2005, entered into force Mar. 18, 2007, http://www.unesco.org/culture/en/diversity/convention.

resolution on the repatriation of African art[24] argued strongly that the repatriation of African art will promote the economic self-sufficiency of African nations and encourage their cultural, economic, and social development.

John Merryman has recently observed that

> no thoughtful person would seriously argue that everything should be returned or that everything should be retained, but there is little agreement on the criteria for deciding whether a particular object presently in the collection of a certain museum should be returned or kept, or whether some other disposition of the object is desirable.[25]

The concluding part of this article looks at issues relating to these criteria and the possibilities for other dispositions of culturally significant objects.

G. CONCLUSION

First, it may be possible to split possession and ownership of cultural objects that were expropriated in the colonial period. We are accustomed to the idea of a "British Institute" in Rome, a "German Archaeological Institute" in Rome, an "American School" in Athens, an "American University" in Beirut, and so on. Why not have branches of the British Museum in Lagos and Benin City, a branch of Tervuren in Kinshasa, and a branch of New York's Metropolitan Museum of Art in Benin City, just as there is a Guggenheim branch in Bilbao, Spain, and so on? In this way, the former colonized country would have possession, and the former colonizer would retain ownership and control. The adoption of this suggestion would introduce a new vocabulary into the discourse, namely "relocation." Return, repatriation, and restitution have now acquired a strong emotive connotation that we can usefully focus on relocation so that, as Thurstan Shaw observed, original works of art could be studied and understood in the milieu that gave them birth.[26]

The enumeration of criteria for restitution and return of objects to countries of origin may not be as difficult as it appears on first consideration. The following criteria are suggested: the object has great symbolic value; the object has great ritual importance; and the object is of great historical importance or value. The criteria leave out M'Bow's "irreplaceable masterpieces" and de Montebello's "a museum's most prized possession."

Instead, the focus would be on symbolic value, and ritual importance or historical importance. In this way, history can be unraveled by showing a little sensitivity in a matter that touches the soul and spirit of formerly colonized people. Finally, it is submitted that what is unique is appropriate for return to its motherland. The birthplace is the first place of life.

The Afo-A-Kom from Cameroon is a good example of an object of great symbolic value, while the 160 bronze heads taken away by the 1897 punitive

---

24 Http://www.worldmun.org/2006/archives/03res/UNESCO.pdf.

25 John Henry Merryman, Imperialism, Art and Resistution 3 (2006).

26 Thurstan Shaw, *Whose Heritage?* 149 Museum (UNESCO) 46–48, 48 (1986).

expedition in Benin represent very good examples of objects of great historical value since they are the Benin equivalent of chronological records. The Benin bronzes were and are so important in the artistic cultural heritage of Nigeria because they presented a record of important events. Thus, the lower house of Nigeria's parliament, the House of Representatives, recently passed a resolution for the return of the Benin bronzes by the British Museum to Nigeria.[27] And before the Italians at last returned the obelisk of Aksum, the parliament of Ethiopia passed a resolution calling for its return. Thus, as the UNESCO resolution on the repatriation of African art argued, the repatriation of African art will promote the economic self-sufficiency of African nations and encourage their cultural, economic, and social development. This is the justification for the unraveling of history and the return of African cultural objects repatriated in colonial times.

[27] "Nigeria Demands Treasures Back," BBC News, Jan. 24, 2002, *available at* http://news.bbc.co.uk/2/hi/entertainment/1779236.stm.

CHAPTER 7
COLONIZATION AND ITS EFFECT ON THE CULTURAL PROPERTY OF LIBYA

Nancy C. Wilkie

Numerous episodes of colonization characterize the history of the territory now included in the modern nation-state of the Libyan Arab Jamahiriya (State of the Masses), from the establishment of Phoenician trading emporia early in the first millennium B.C.E. to the most recent period of Italian domination at the beginning of the 20th century.[1] Although colonies in Libya have been of many different types, Gil Stein's definition of a colony as "an implanted settlement established by one society in either uninhabited territory or the territory of another society . . . [that is] both spatially and socially distinguishable from the communities of the indigenous polity or peoples among whom it is established" is broad enough to encompass them all.[2]

A. HISTORY OF COLONIZATION IN LIBYA

1. Garamantes, Phoenicians, Greeks, and Romans

Early in the first millennium B.C.E., the Garamantes, one of the tribal groups that eventually settled in Libya, came into Fezzan, the southwestern region of Libya (see Figure 1), and took control of the caravan routes that cross the desert there. A short time later, the first Carthaginian colonists arrived in Tripolitania,[3] establishing settlements at coastal sites to facilitate their seaborne trade in the western Mediterranean. After the total destruction of Carthage by the Romans at the end of the Third Punic War in 146 B.C.E., control of Tripolitania was handed over to the Numidians, a tribal group that occupied much of modern Tunisia. One hundred years later, in 46 B.C.E., Tripolitania

[1] For a brief history of Libya, see Library of Congress, *Country Studies: Libya* (1987), *available at* http://countrystudies.us.

[2] Gil Stein, *Colonies Without Colonialism: A Trade Diaspora Model of Fourth Millennium B.C. Mesopotamian Enclaves in Anatolia, in* The Archaeology of Colonialism 30 (C. Lyons & J. Papadopoulos eds., 2002).

[3] Tripolitania is named after the three major ancient cities in the region: Sabratha, Oea (modern Tripoli), and Lepcis Magna. Lepcis is an exact transliteration of the Punic Lpqy, which is found on coins and inscriptions from the site until the fourth century C.E. The adjective Magna was added in the middle of the first century C.E. to distinguish the city from Lepti Minus on the Tunisian coast. Most Italian scholars continue to use the Latinized form Leptis Magna. Ginette Di Vita-Evrard, *Lepcis, in* Libya. The Lost Cities of the Roman Empire 46 (Antonino Di Vita et al. eds., 1999).

was annexed to Rome as part of the Roman province of Africa Nova following upon Julius Caesar's defeat of his rival, Pompey, in the battle of Thapsus and the subsequent death of the Numidian king, Juba I.[4]

Cyrenaica (see Figure 1), on the other hand, was more closely allied with Greece, since the first colony there was founded in 631 B.C.E. by settlers from the Aegean island of Thera, today's Santorini.[5] In time, five major Greek cities arose in Cyrenaica, hence the name Pentapolis by which the area also was known. After the death of Alexander the Great, Cyrenaica came under the rule of the Ptolemies, where it remained until 74 B.C.E., when Ptolemy Apion bequeathed Cyrene to Rome, and the region became a part of the Roman province that also included the island of Crete.

2. Arabs and Ottomans

Throughout the period of Roman control, the cities of Cyrenaica and Tripolitania maintained much of their original Greek and Roman character, but this situation was to change with the Arab conquests of Cyrenaica (642 C.E.), Tripolitania (647 C.E), and Fezzan (663 C.E.) (see Figure 1). For the Arabs as well as their successors, the Normans and the Ottomans, control of Cyrenaica and especially Fezzan was difficult. Except for the period from 1711–1835 when the Karamanlis held power in Tripolitania, the Ottomans were able to maintain control over at least portions of Libya until 1911.

3. Italian Conquest and Colonization

Shortly after the unification of Italy in the 1860s, the Italians began to contemplate the colonial conquest of Libya. Their first move was to undertake a policy of "spontaneous colonization," that is, colonization based on individual or group initiative rather than government planning, as well as "pacific economic penetration."[6] In 1910, however, the Italians followed in the footsteps of the other major European powers—England, France, and Germany—and decided that their reputation and influence would be greatly enhanced if they acquired an empire. Some even argued that Italy, as the heir to the Roman Empire, had an historical right, even a divine right, to dominance in the Mediterranean and in particular to the possession of Libya.

Consequently, on September 30, 1911, Italy declared war on the Ottoman Empire, and on November 5, 1911, it formally annexed the territories of Tripolitania and Cyrenaica. Nearly a year later, Italy and Turkey signed the Treaty of Ouchy, which granted Cyrenaica and Tripolitania "independence" under Italian sovereignty. The Italians met unexpected resistance to their rule, however, and in 1922, they were forced to initiate the "reconquest" of Libya. Shortly thereafter, when the Fascists came into power, the pace and brutality of the campaign accelerated. Not until 1932 did all of Libya come under Italian

---

[4] Susan Raven, Rome in Africa 53–54 (3d ed. 1993).

[5] Herodotus, The Histories, bk. 4, 150–59, provides an account of the founding of Cyrene. *See also* SEG ix 3 for the so-called Foundation Decree of Cyrene.

[6] Ronald S. Cunsolo, *Libya, Italian Nationalism, and the Revolt Against Giolitti*, 37 J. Mod. Hist. 186 (1965).

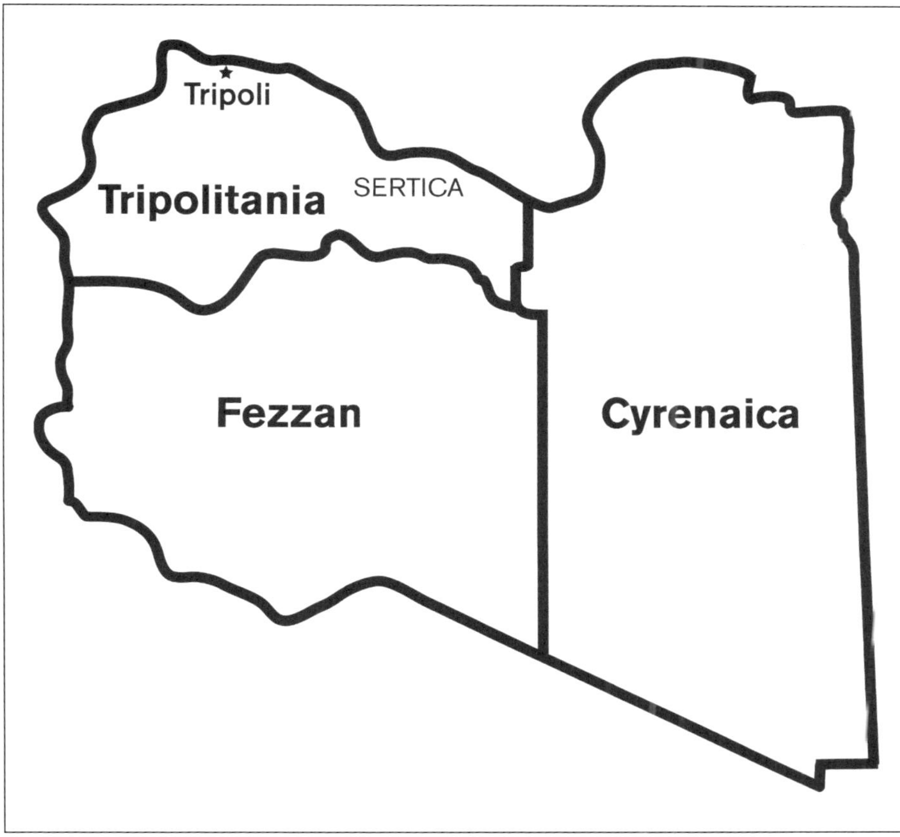

Figure 1. Geographical Regions of Libya.

control. Two years later, the Italians created the colony of Libya, reviving the name the ancients had used for all of North Africa with the exception of Egypt. In 1939, the coastal provinces were integrated into the Kingdom of Italy, forming what was called the "Fourth Shore" of Italy. The result was that all native Libyans were now living in Italy as virtual immigrants to their own land. The Italian dream of a Fourth Shore came to an abrupt end, however, with the beginning of World War II, when Italian settlements in Cyrenaica were destroyed and many colonists returned home.[7]

4. Independence

Unlike other North African countries, Libya did not achieve its independence through a period of revolutionary war. Rather, following the fall of the Axis powers during World War II, jurisdiction over Libya initially was divided between France and England, with Tripolitania and Cyrenaica coming under British control, while Fezzan was administered by the French. Libya finally

[7] Claudio G. Segrè, Fourth Shore: The Italian Colonization of Libya (1974).

was granted its independence—the first independent state to be created by the United Nations—on December 24, 1951. The Sanusi leader Idris was appointed king, but his rule was not universally accepted, especially by those outside Cyrenaica where, as leader of the Sanusi Order (a conservative Islamic sect), Idris had ruled the inland territories, with Italian support, since 1917. Furthermore, the unification into a single state of the three distinct geographic regions of the Libyan territory—Cyrenaica, Tripolitania, and Fezzan—was not popular, since historically they had been under separate administrative rule.

When a group of young army officers seized power in a bloodless coup on September 1, 1969, and shortly thereafter appointed Colonel Muammar el-Qaddafi commander-in-chief, he became the first Berber, that is, indigenous, ruler of a unified Libya since Septimius Severus, a native of Lepcis Magna who was the first African Roman Emperor (193–211 C.E.). Qaddafi's strong ties to his birthplace, the vast desert between the two coastal areas of Tripolitania and Cyrenaica known as the Sirtica (see Figure 1), help to emphasize that he is indeed an indigenous ruler.

B. EARLY EXPEDITIONS TO LIBYA

1. French Expeditions to Lepcis Magna (1686–1708)

The first "archaeological" activity in Libya began in the 17th century when Claude Le Maire, who twice served as French Consul to the Ottoman Regency in Tripoli, retrieved more than 600 columns of marble from Lepcis Magna between 1686 and 1708. He shipped the columns back to France where he sold them for use in Louis XIV's new palaces at Versailles and Paris. However, he did not have an adequate barge to move three of the huge cipolin marble columns from the Great Hadrianic Baths to the king's store ship, so he abandoned them on the seashore where they remain today. Of the columns that he was able to remove, some were used intact; but many, such as those incorporated into the palace at Versailles, were cut into slabs for use as facing material.[8]

2. British Expeditions to Lepcis Magna (1813–1817)

More than a century later, when Hamner Warrington was appointed British Consul in Tripoli, there was intense rivalry among European museums to augment their collections of antiquities. This desire is evident in one of his letters to the Colonial Office, in which Warrington reported that "a foreign power may be seeking permission from the Pasha of Tripoli to excavate sites 'which in my opinion the influence and the superiority of the British flag entitle us to.'"[9] As a result, he persuaded the British government to fund a number of expeditions to Lepcis Magna in order to search for antiquities that could be brought to England. Warrington gained permission from the Ottomans for this endeavor by persuading the Pasha that "it would be politically expedient to present a gift to the Prince Regent,"[10] who later was to become King George IV.

---

[8] Di Vita-Evrard, *supra* note 3, at 48.

[9] Andrew Lane, *The Ruins at Virginia Water (part 1),* 35 Libyan Stud. 67 (2004).

[10] *Id.* at 68.

When Warrington and Commander W.H. Smyth inspected the ruins at Lepcis Magna in 1816, they found many remains lying on the surface that could be removed without excavation. More importantly, they learned that there was a secure mooring at the site where they could load their ships. When they returned in October 1817 to take the antiquities to England, however, they discovered that many of the best pieces had been removed or destroyed. In particular, many of the granite columns had been sawed up by the locals for use as millstones. Nonetheless, although they were able to load more than 100 architectural fragments from Lepcis aboard the HMS Weymouth, even they could not remove the three large cipolin columns that Le Maire had abandoned more than a century earlier.

When the antiquities arrived in London in 1818, they were delivered to the British Museum, where they remained in the courtyard until August 1826, when they were transferred to Windsor Castle. There they were subsequently installed at Virginia Water, an area at the southeast corner of Windsor Great Park where the royal architect, Sir Jeffrey Wyatville, had been engaged to create "an imaginary Classical ruin" beside a large artificial lake, which he called "The Temple of Augustus."[11] In 1829, four roundels carved with the head of Medusa, also from Lepcis Magna, were incorporated into the King's Landing Stage, and at about the same time a second group of column shafts, probably also from Lepcis Magna, were incorporated into the "ruin."

Because of neglect over the years, portions of the "ruin" are now literally in ruin. Three columns have fallen down, several sections of the entablature have been displaced, and most of the column shafts have weathered substantially from exposure to the harsh British climate. Of the inscribed stones inventoried among Warrington's shipment from Lepcis Magna and initially installed at Virginia Water, three are now in the British Museum, while the fourth is in the Ure Classics Museum at Reading University.[12] A fifth remains partially buried on the site.[13] On the other hand, the whereabouts of five roundel fragments and other smaller sculptural fragments is unknown, and the pieces are presumed to be lost.[14] In time, the origin of the ruins was forgotten, and by the middle of the 19th century, some thought they belonged among the marbles brought to England from Athens by Lord Elgin.[15]

C. ARCHAEOLOGICAL EXPEDITIONS TO CYRENAICA

1. British and French Expeditions

No further large-scale excavations were undertaken by the British at Lepcis Magna after the removal of the architectural remains used in the construction

---

[11] *Id.* at 71; *see also* G.E. Chambers, *The "Ruins" at Virginia Water*, 54 BERKSHIRE ARCHAEOLOGICAL J. 49 (1953–54); JANE ROBERTS, ROYAL LANDSCAPE. THE GARDENS AND PARKS OF WINDSOR 459 (1997).

[12] Lane, *supra* note 9, at 77; Chambers, *supra* note 11, at 50.

[13] Roberts, *supra* note 11, at 461.

[14] Lane, *supra* note 9, at 77.

[15] Roberts, *supra* note 11, at 460.

of Virginia Water. Instead, the British turned their attention to Cyrene, where Warrington's son, George, supervised excavations in the Sanctuary of Apollo in 1827.[16] The objects recovered from his excavations subsequently found their way into the British Museum.

No fewer than 28 expeditions were organized by European and American explorers and archaeologists in Cyrenaica between 1706 and 1911, a period of "free-lance exploration,"[17] when Cyrenaica was only nominally under the control of the Ottomans. Many of these expeditions resulted in the expropriation of antiquities that made their way into major European collections. For example, a fourth-century B.C.E. funerary bust now in the Musée du Louvre (Ma 1777) was acquired in 1852, following French excavations in the western necropolis of Cyrene conducted by Vattier de Bourville during 1848.

Somewhat later, during 1860 and 1861, another British expedition led by Lieutenant Robert Murdoch Smith and Commander Edwin Porcher conducted excavations at Cyrene,[18] returning with numerous sculptures and sculptural fragments that are now part of the British Museum's collection.[19] Chief among them is a second century C.E. colossal marble statue of Apollo Citharedus (GR 1861.7-25.1), found in 121 pieces (or 123 pieces, according to Smith and Porcher who cite both numbers) in the precinct of the Temple of Apollo, near the pedestal on which it originally stood.[20] The statue apparently was broken when the Temple of Apollo was burned during the Jewish Revolt of 115–116 C.E. Once excavated, the fragments faced the possibility of further destruction by the armed local Arab population, since to them they were symbols of the pagan past. To prevent this possibility, Smith and Porcher took the precaution of re-burying the sculptural finds in one of the many rock-cut tombs at Cyrene, where they had set up camp, until they could transport the pieces to England where the statue subsequently was restored.

Other objects now on display in the British Museum from the Smith and Porcher expedition include a rare bronze portrait of a man from Cyrene (GR 1861.11-27.13) dating to about B.C.E. that was found in the same location as the statue of Apollo; a marble portrait sculpture of a veiled woman of the mid-second century C.E. (GR 1861.11-27.32) found just north of the Temple of Apollo; and a second-century C.E. bas-relief of the Nymph Cyrene strangling a lion while the goddess Libya crowns her, beneath which there is a dedicatory inscription (GR 1861.11-27.30).[21]

---

[16] Lane, *supra* note 9, at 78; Donald White, *Stranger in a Strange Land: The Untold Story of the 1909 Bates Expedition to Cyrene,* 35 J. Am. Res. Center in Egypt 164 (1998); J.C. Thorn, *Warrington's 1827 Discoveries in the Apollo Sanctuary at Cyrene,* 24 Soc'y Libyan Stud., Ann. Rep. 57–76 (1993).

[17] White, *supra* note 16, at 163–64.

[18] R.M. Smith & E.A. Porcher, History of the Recent Discoveries at Cyrene (1864).

[19] Janet Huskinson, Roman Sculpture From Cyrenaica in the British Museum (1975).

[20] *Id.* at 6; Peter Higgs, *The Cyrene Apollo,* 44 Hist. Today 50 (1994).

[21] For a catalog of Roman sculptures and sculptural fragments from Cyrenaica now in the British Museum, *see* Huskinson, *supra* note 19.

2. American Expeditions

Americans were the last to work at Cyrene immediately prior to the outbreak of the war between Italy and Turkey on September 29, 1911. In 1904, Richard Norton (son of Charles Eliot Norton, the first president of the Archaeological Institute of America) accompanied David Hogarth and A.W. Van Buren on an exploratory expedition to Apollonia and Cyrene. In 1909, Norton returned with Oric Bates, and it is reported that during their visit some members of the expedition appropriated objects from Apollonia, the ancient port of Cyrene. Some years later Norton offered to sell some of these items to the Boston Museum of Fine Arts, apparently without success.[22] When Norton returned to Cyrene in 1910, it was as the head of an ill-fated expedition. The epigrapher for the expedition, Herbert De Cou, was murdered by a group of Arabs on March 11, 1911, probably after being mistaken for Norton.[23] The expedition ended soon thereafter, shortly before the outbreak of the Italo-Turkish War. In 1913, without admitting complicity in De Cou's murder, Italy paid a "voluntary" indemnity of $25,000 to the Archaeological Institute of America, which, along with the Boston Museum of Fine Arts, had sponsored Norton's expedition.[24]

D. ITALIAN EXCAVATIONS IN LIBYA

After the Italian takeover of Libya, archaeological work focused almost exclusively on the remains of the Roman period, to the detriment of those of later periods. When Italo Balbo became Governor of Libya in 1934, he encouraged archaeological excavation at two major Roman sites, Lepcis Magna and Sabratha, with the ostensible goal of turning the sites into tourist attractions for Italians from the homeland. The primary objective, however, was to justify the Italian occupation of Libya by revealing the ancient Roman Empire's role in the development of North Africa, while at the same time ignoring the fact that many of the greatest architectural monuments of the Roman period in Libya were erected not by Romans but by "Romanized" local citizens. This adoption of Roman architecture was especially true during the reign of Septimius Severus, a Libyan from Lepcis Magna and the first African Roman Emperor (193–211 C.E.). Thus, archaeology was used to perpetuate the Italian colonialist ideology, which deprived the indigenous people of Libya of their cultural history, and created an image of Africans "either as passive recipients of superior culture or as nomadic and lawless people incapable of self-government."[25]

---

[22] White, *supra* note 16, at 175.

[23] Richard Goodchild, *Death of an Epigrapher: The Killing of Herbert De Cou*, 8 MICH. Q. REV. 149–54 (1969); James Russell, *From the President: Tales from the Archives*, 46(3) ARCHAEOLOGY 6 (1993).

[24] Goodchild, *supra* note 23, at 153–54. Goodchild notes that Norton accused the Italian consul in Benghazi of instigating De Cou's murder in order to drive the Americans from the country, but there is no evidence to support this allegation.

[25] David J. Mattingly & R. Bruce Hitchner, *Roman Africa: An Archaeological Review*, 85 JRS 169 (1995).

Initially, many of the Italian excavations, especially those outside the major archaeological sites in Tripolitania, were conducted by members of the military who discovered ancient remains, mainly mosaics from the floors of Roman villas and farmhouses, during the construction of roads and fortifications. Among the most notable of these chance finds are the mosaics from the Villa of the Nile Mosaic at Lepcis Magna, which were uncovered by soldiers searching for building stones to construct a new road but were later properly excavated by Italian archaeologists. Similarly, at Dar buc Ammèra, about two kilometers west of Zliten, officers of the 50th Infantry Regiment uncovered most of a Roman villa in 1913. A year later, systematic excavations began, and in 1929 restoration of the villa was initiated.[26]

At Cyrene the first Italian excavations also were undertaken by the military. On December 27, 1913, a thunderstorm washed away soil from the Sanctuary of Apollo, exposing a fourth-century B.C.E. statue of Aphrodite Rising from the Bath (commonly known today as the Venus of Cyrene; see Figure 2).[27] The Italian army, which was camped at Cyrene at the time, proceeded to excavate the site, although they required the protection of a fortified wall to do so.[28] The statue subsequently was taken to Rome, where it was placed on display in the Museo Nazionale delle Terme and later removed to the Vatican for safekeeping during World War II.[29] A cast of the statue was exhibited in the Italian pavilion at the Paris Colonial Exhibition of 1931, along with many other plaster reproductions of sculptures unearthed in the course of Italian excavations in Cyrenaica and Tripolitania from 1913 onwards.[30]

E. REPATRIATION OF LIBYAN CULTURAL PROPERTY

1. Venus of Cyrene

Negotiations for the return of the Venus of Cyrene have been ongoing for many years. In August 2002, the Italian Minister of Culture, Giuliano Urbani, signed an order for its return. That same year, during his visit to Tripoli, Prime Minister Silvio Berlusconi also referred to its planned restitution, stating that the return of the statue would not be "an act of restitution, but a 'gift'."[31] This statement was a clear reference to the fact that Italy was not under a treaty obligation to return the statue, since there were no provisions for the return of cultural material in the conditions for the Italian withdrawal from Libya. This situation is not unusual, since most treaties concluded during decolonization did not address the issue of state succession to cultural material and archives, a

---

[26] SALVATORE AURIGEMMA, ARCHAEOLOGICAL DISCOVERIES, 1911–1943, TRIPOLITANIA. ITALY IN AFRICA: [SCIENTIFIC AND CULTURAL SERIES] (Anthony Luttrell trans. 1960).

[27] Ernest A. Gardner, *The Aphrodite from Cyrene*, 40(2) J. HELLENIC STUD. 203–205, plates IX–X (1920).

[28] JAMES AZEMA, LIBYA HANDBOOK 169 (2000).

[29] *Sanctuary*, TIME MAGAZINE, July 17, 1944, *available at* http://www.time.com/time/magazine/article/0,9171,775149,00.html.

[30] R. MICACCHI, SCULPTURES ANTIQUES EN LIBYE (1931).

[31] Krystyna von Henneberg, *Monuments, Public Space, and the Memory of Empire in Modern Italy*, 16 HIST. & MEMORY 74 (2004).

Figure 2. The Venus of Cyrene (JHS 40:2 [1920] Plate IX).

reflection of the power that museums and former colonizing states continued to wield.[32]

Yet today the offer of the return of the statue remains just that—an empty offer—since the statue continues to reside in Italy following a court challenge by an Italian non-governmental organization, Italia Nostra, and there are no prospects for its immediate return.[33] In fact, many Italians have protested the return of the statue, arguing that "such gestures could easily empty the museums of Europe,"[34] an argument frequently made on behalf of the major art museums of Europe and the United States. The president of the Rome municipality, Giuseppe Lobefaro, invoked an even more unsettling rationale for Italy's retention of the Capitoline Venus when he stated, "It is truly disconcerting that an important museum of Rome's historic center should lose a piece of such high worth and value amidst the most absolute indifference of the authorities charged with conserving our cultural and archaeological valuables."[35]

Such sentiments are in direct opposition to the provisions of a communiqué signed on July 4, 1999, by the Great Socialist People's Libya Arab Jamahiriyah and the Republic of Italy. In it, Italy apologized for its colonization of Libya and the miseries that it caused and pledged "to return all manuscripts, archives, documents, artefacts and archaeological pieces transferred to Italy during and after the Italian occupation of Libya in accordance with the UNESCO convention of 14th November 1970 on banning illegal export and transfer of cultural properties."[36] In addition, the two countries agreed "to cooperate to determine these manuscripts, documents, artefacts and archaeological pieces and their whereabouts."[37] Yet according to Giuma M. Anag, chairman of Libya's Department of Antiquities, despite the fact that seven years have elapsed since the signing of the agreement, neither the Italians nor the Libyans have produced an inventory of the items removed from Libya during the period of colonial rule.[38]

2. Venus of Lepcis Magna

On December 1, 1999, a few months after the agreement between Italy and Libya, left-wing Prime Minister Massimo D'Alema paid a brief visit to Libya, during which he offered apologies to the Libyan people while visiting a monument commemorating a Libyan revolt against Italian rule.[39] He

---

[32] Ana Filipa Vrdoljak, International Law, Museums and the Return of Cultural Objects 200 (2006).

[33] Giuma Anag, personal communication, Aug. 11, 2006.

[34] von Henneberg, *supra* note 31, at 74.

[35] *Id.* at 85 n.53. Recently an Italian court ruled that the statue was not part of Italy's cultural heritage and ordered that it be returned to Libya, yet no date was set for its return. David Ariel, *Italy to Return Ancient Statue to Libya* (April 24, 2007), *available at* www.washingtonpost.com.

[36] *Libya Says Italy Apologizes for Colonial Occupation* (July 10, 1998), *available at* http://news.bbc.co.uk. For reference to the agreement, see also U.N. Press Release GA/9678 (Dec. 7, 1999), http://www.un.org.

[37] *Id.*

[38] Anag, *supra* note 33.

[39] von Hennenberg, *supra* note 31, at 72.

also returned a second-century C.E. copy of the Capitoline Venus (*la Venere capitolina;* see Figure 3) by Praxiteles, which was found in 1924 in the Hadrianic Baths at Lepcis Magna. It had been given to the Nazi German Air-Marshall, Herman Goering, during his 1939 visit to Libya, by Italo Balbo, the Fascist governor-general of Libya, who himself was a leading figure in Italian aviation.[40] Although the statue had been taken as war booty to Moscow, after its return to Germany from Moscow in 1958 its whereabouts were unknown for many years. Eventually, however, it was located in the warehouse of the Pergamon Museum in Berlin. According to Mario Bondioli-Osio, the president of the Italian Inter-Ministerial Commission for the Recovery of Art, Germany's decision to return the statue to Italy was in the spirit of the Wiesbaden Manifesto, in which the looting of art was denounced as a war crime.[41]

The statue was returned to Italy in a ceremony at the Pergamon Museum on July 22, 1999,[42] but it did not remain there for long, since the Libyans had already staked a claim to it in 1965.[43] Its ultimate return to Libya a few months later was due in part to direct intervention by the Libyan Leader Muammar Qaddafi.[44] He stated that the statue was merely the beginning of the restitution of "spoiled" works of art and archaeology, since Libya would demand the return of all objects previously taken by the German and Italian governments.[45] Today the Venus statue is on prominent display in the Jamahiriya Museum in the Tripoli castle.

According to Prime Minister D'Alema, "by getting the statue back from Berlin, restoring it, and then giving it back to Libya, Italy has attempted to heal a wound."[46] Others, however, have suggested that "the return or removal of material markers of memory—in this case statues—does not erase the past so much as reposition Italy's leaders as agile and ambitious spokesmen for a recovered nation."[47] In fact, there is an element of historical expediency underlying these public gestures of restitution and reconciliation, since "restitution is not only intended as a gesture of atonement, but as a way of clearing extant claims against Italy,"[48] presumably with the aim of protecting the flow of trade between Libya and Italy. Indeed, Libya currently supplies 25 percent of Italy's oil and is also the main market for Italy's exports.[49]

3. Current Libyan Demands for Repatriation

Recently Libya has openly demanded the return of archaeological objects from Turkey, France, and England. When the Libyan secretary of culture met

---

[40] *Libya: News and Views* (Dec. 3, 1999), http://www.libyanet.com.

[41] Philip Willan, *Looted Venus Returns to Italy* (July 23, 1999), *available at* http://www.guardian.co.uk.

[42] *Pressemitteilung. Die Stiftung Preußischer Kulturbesitz gibt im Zweiten Weltkrieg aus Italien nach Deutschland verbrachte Kunstwerke zurück* (July 22, 1999), www.hv.spk-berlin.de/deutsch/projekte/einzefaelle/19990722_beutekunst.pdf.

[43] *Id.*

[44] Anag, *supra* note 33.

[45] *Libya: News and Views* (Dec. 7, 1999), http://www.libyanet.com.

[46] von Hennenberg, *supra* note 31, at 84 n.48.

[47] *Id.* at 74.

[48] *Id.* at 73.

[49] *Supra* note 40.

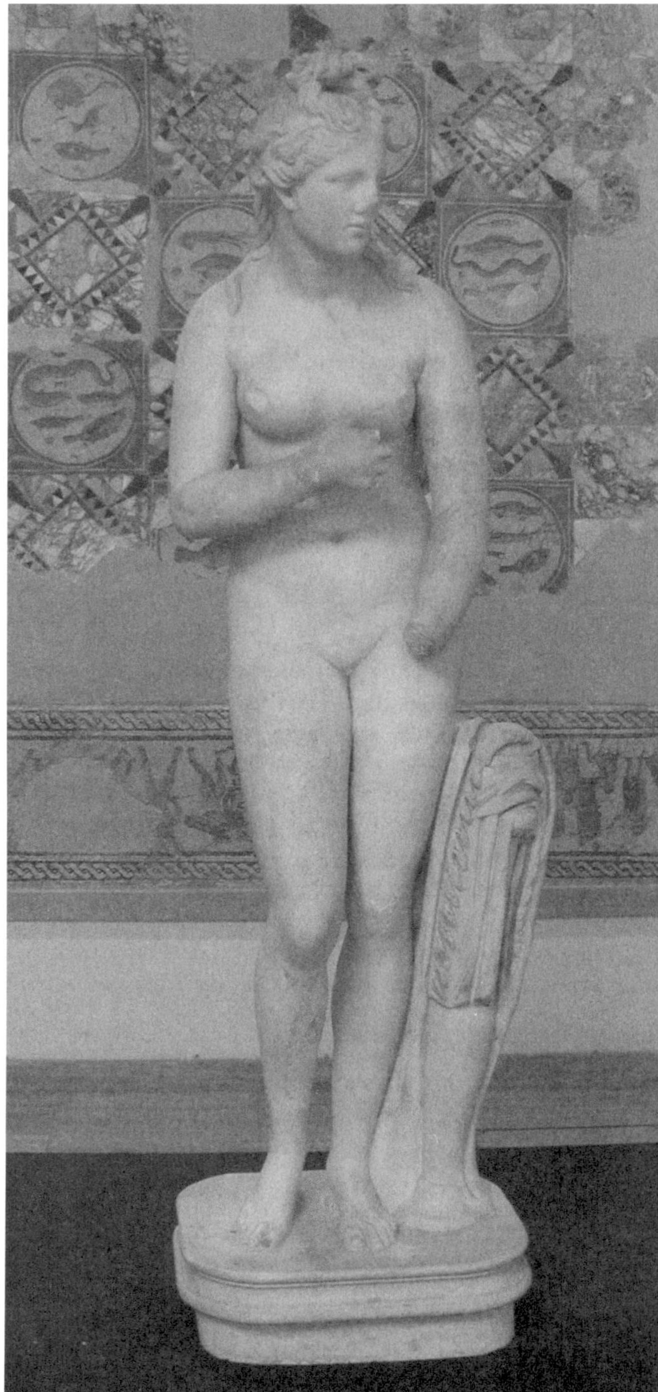

Figure 3. Capitoline Venus (Jamahiriya Museum, Tripoli, Libya). Photo by N. Wilkie.

the French ambassador to Libya on November 2005, he handed the ambassador a leaflet illustrating pieces said to be stolen from Libya and removed to France.[50] Earlier in the same year, representatives of the Libyan Department of Antiquities reached an agreement with Cambridge University regarding the return of material that Professor McBurney had excavated at Haua Fteah and removed to England for study more than 50 years ago.[51]

More recently, it was announced that the Libyan Office for Documentation and Manuscripts had brought 15,000 documents back to Libya from the Ottoman Empire archives. This was said to be a "first step for the repatriation of documents now on exhibit in Turkish museums."[52] Archaeological objects are certain to follow, since, for example, bas-reliefs from tombs of the Roman period at Ghirza, along with sculpture and other movable objects, were taken to Istanbul by the Ottomans early in the 20th century.[53]

Although Libya has been a signatory to the 1970 UNESCO Convention on the Illegal Import, Export and Transfer of Cultural Property since 1973, diplomatic efforts rather than legal means have had the greatest influence to date on the return of its cultural property from abroad. The 1970 UNESCO Convention does not specifically address the return of cultural patrimony removed during periods of colonial occupation, although Article 11 does reaffirm a provision of the 1954 Hague Convention, to which Libya is a signatory, stating that "the export and transfer of ownership of cultural property under compulsion arising directly or indirectly from the occupation of a country by a foreign power shall be regarded as illicit."[54]

Colonel Qaddafi continues to be a strong advocate for the return of Libyan as well as all African antiquities from Western museums. In a recent statement he said,

> the Europeans must return all the antiquities and treasures they stole from us, and which are absolutely essential if we are to develop our tourism industry for the benefit of our own people—as well as all the profits which they accrued from stealing the antiquities, ancient scrolls and other treasures of Africa which have curiously found their way to the museums of the countries that colonized us. There they have served as a lucrative spectacle for intruders, tourists, scientists and archaeologists in the countries that colonized us. These are African treasures and must be returned to Africa. Western museums have made fat profits out of them, but these treasures justly belong to us.[55]

---

[50] *Libya: News and Views* (Nov. 17, 2005), http://www.libyanet.com.

[51] Karen Dabrowska, *Society for Libyan Studies Welcomes Easier Access to Archaeological Sites* (Dec. 5, 2005), http://mathaba.net.

[52] *Libya: News and Views* (June 25, 2006), http://www.libyanet.com.

[53] AZEMA, *supra* note 28, at 131.

[54] Convention on the Means of Prohibiting and Preventing the Illicit Import, Export and Transfer of Ownership of Cultural Property (Nov. 14, 1970), *available at* http://portal.unesco.org/en/ev.php-URL_ID=13039&URL_DO=DO_TOPIC&URL_SECTION=201.html.

[55] Gamal Nkrumah, *Confidence in Ourselves,* AL AHRAM WEEKLY, Apr. 6–12, 2000, *available at* http://weekly.ahram.org.eg.

F. CONTINUING THREATS TO LIBYAN CULTURAL PROPERTY

Recently, officials in Libya's Department of Antiquities have complained that lack of funding hampers their efforts to provide security for museums and archaeological sites, resulting in widespread thefts.[56] Officially the number of stolen objects stands at 90, but the actual number is far greater because most thefts are the result of unauthorized excavations. It is thought that the thefts are part of a larger network of international organized crime, as the discovery of a number of stolen Libyan antiquities in Egypt suggests. [57] For example, some of items stolen from the Sabratha museum were seized at the Egyptian border in 2003. However, they still remain in the custody of the Egyptians, since the Libyans have not been able to provide the necessary proof of ownership to facilitate their return.[58] Several of the 15 stone heads stolen in late 1999 or early 2000 from storerooms at Cyrene, where the objects from the University of Pennsylvania Museum's excavations were deposited, also are thought to have reached the European art market through Egypt. [59] Because the Cyrene sculptures were well documented, it was possible to locate two of them shortly after they were stolen, but the others remain missing. In addition, a statue of Hades from Cyrene, put up for auction at Maastricht, was returned to Libya following a tip from an American.[60] These thefts underscore the need for thorough registration of the holdings of Libyan museums. Ideally this recording should be done according to the international descriptive standard set forth by Object ID and endorsed by UNESCO, since the program is compatible with most art theft databases and has been adopted by major law enforcement agencies worldwide.[61]

In Libya, archaeological sites, as well as museums, are in need of greater protection. This is especially true for the rock art of Libya, which is endangered by the rapid increase in oil exploration and tourism in the Saharan Desert.[62] Although the rock art sites of Tadrart Acacus were inscribed on the World Heritage List in 1985,[63] more vigorous measures are required if the remaining

---

[56] Rana Jawad, *Libya Fears for its Stolen Heritage* (Apr. 28, 2006), *available at* http://news.bbc.co.uk.

[57] *Tourism. Libya. Officials Have Warned of the Dangers Facing Historical Artifacts at the Country's Main Attractions.* 43 Afr. Res. Bull.: Econ., Fin. & Technical Series 16990C-16991A (July 2006)

[58] *Supra* note 56.

[59] Donald White, *Stolen Sculptures from Cyrene, available at* http://www.cyrenethefts.org. *See also* Mark Rose, *Stolen Sculptures from Cyrene, Libya* (Jan. 30, 2001), *available at* http://www.archaeology.org.

[60] Andrew Solomon & Giuma Anag, *Conversations. Saved by Sand: The Challenge of Preservation in Libya,* 59(6) Archaeology 14 (Nov./Dec. 2006). More recently it was reported that a Roman relief stolen in 1999 from an antiquities storeroom in Shahat (ancient Cyrene) was recovered from an auction held in Paris. The piece was handed over to Libyan authorities in a ceremony on February 22, 2008. *Stolen Piece of Antiquity Retrieved* (Feb. 23, 2008), http://www.mathaba.net/news/?x=583012.

[61] Robin Thornes et al., Object ID: Guidelines for Making Records That Describe Art, Antiques, And Antiquities (1999), *available at* http://www.object-id.com. *See also,* Unesco Handbook, Legal and Practical Measures Against Illicit Trafficking in Cultural Property 17–35 (2006), *available at* http://portal.unesco.org.

[62] Giuma Anag et al., *Environment, Archaeology, and Oil: The Messak Settafet Rescue Operation (Libyan Sahara),* 19 Afr. Arch. Rev. 70–73 (2002).

[63] *Libyan Arab Jamahiriya,* http://whc.unesco.org.

rich archaeological heritage of the region is to be protected from further destruction.[64]

Finally, although Libya became a signatory to the 1970 UNESCO Convention on April 9, 1973, it has yet to request a bilateral agreement with the United States under the terms of the Cultural Property Implementation Act.[65] The chairman of the Department of Antiquities, Giuma Anag, has stated that Libya is anxious to enter into such an agreement, so it is possible that the process will begin soon.[66]

G. THE COLONIAL LEGACY

Today the major archaeological museum in Libya is housed in the Turkish castle in Tripoli, where both the building and its contents are a constant reminder of foreign domination. Excavation of many classical sites remains in the hands of foreign archaeologists, and many Libyan archaeologists continue to be trained abroad. The Libyans thus face the challenge of viewing their ancient monuments and cultural property as part of their own history rather than as reminders and manifestations of their colonial past.[67] Only by taking "ownership" of these monuments, physically, intellectually, *and* emotionally, will the Libyans succeed at incorporating them into their history and thus take an active interest in their preservation.

Colonel Qaddafi has criticized archaeologists for continuing to concentrate on the excavation and restoration of classical sites, following the pattern set during the Italian occupation when the Italians pointed to the remains of the Roman period both as symbols of long-standing European superiority in Libya and as monuments that celebrated Italian colonization, which also could be used to promote tourism.[68] This legacy of the colonial period has been difficult to shake, since even after liberation and independence, archaeology in Libya continued to be dominated by foreign archaeologists. Not only did these foreign archaeologists dictate policy in the Antiquities Service, but they also set the research agenda for Libyan scholars, whose degrees were from European rather than North African universities.[69]

If, as Colonel Qaddafi has suggested, archaeologists begin to use their resources to carry out research that is relevant to the needs and interests of modern-day Libya, there could be long-term benefits. No longer would the cultural heritage of one period be given preferential treatment over others. Furthermore, archaeology would cease to be yet another form of colonialism that defines, systematizes and controls the past.[70]

---

[64] *Supra* note 62, at 72.

[65] Pub. L. No. 97-446, 96 Stat. 2329 (Jan. 12, 1983).

[66] *Supra* note 60.

[67] David J. Mattingly, *From One Colonialism to Another: Imperialism and the Magreb*, *in* ROMAN IMPERIALISM: POST-COLONIAL PERSPECTIVES; PROCEEDINGS OF A SYMPOSIUM HELD AT LEICESTER UNIVERSITY IN NOVEMBER 1994 53 (1996).

[68] *Id.* at 52.

[69] *Id.* at 60–61.

[70] Michael Dietler, *The Archaeology of Colonization and the Colonization of Archaeology*, *in* THE ARCHAEOLOGY OF COLONIAL ENCOUNTERS 48 (Gil J. Stein ed., 2005).

CHAPTER 8

LEGAL AND ILLEGAL ACQUISITION OF ANTIQUITIES IN IRAQ, 19TH CENTURY TO 2003

McGuire Gibson

Mesopotamian antiquities became a focus of international interest in the 19th century, when British and French commercial representatives and diplomats began to explore Iraq (see Figure 1), map it, and try to identify sites that were known from biblical and classical sources.[1] Claudius James Rich, a young representative of the British East India Company, correctly identified and mapped Babylon and Nineveh, and visited numerous other sites before his death in 1821. Several other British visitors mapped and described sites in Iraq in the ensuring years, but the real start of excavation and extraction of antiquities began in earnest in 1842, when Paul Emil Botta, the French consul in Mosul, began to explore Assyrian palaces at Khorsabad (ancient Dur Kurigalzu) and Nineveh, sending back to the Louvre shipments of huge winged bulls and wall slabs decorated with the exploits of the Assyrian kings. The British diplomat, Austen Henry Layard began excavations in Nimrud (ancient Kalhu) in 1845 and worked until 1851 at this site and Nineveh, sending back to the British Museum many reliefs and other objects. In some years, the French and British were in unfriendly competition to extract objects, sometimes from the same site. Working with Layard was an Assyrian, Hormudz Rassam, who later carried out major digging at a number of sites in the north and south of Iraq on contract from the British Museum. Where the French and British were systematic insofar as they followed the edges of walls, made plans of the buildings, and drew the scenes on the stone slabs in the palaces, even when they did not remove them, Rassam merely trenched and tunneled, gathering up thousands of cuneiform tablets and other objects.

Once it became clear that there was a monetary value in antiquities, and that limestone reliefs, for instance, had a greater value as objects to be sold to foreigners than just as a source for lime, local Iraqis began to dig on their own, removing thousands of objects, especially cuneiform tablets, from sites. Especially important were the digging at Babylon and other sites in the south, especially Umma (see Figure 2) and Drehem, where very ancient layers containing Sumerian material were to be found right at the surface of the mounds rather than meters below, as at Babylon.

[1] See H. Hilprecht, Explorations in Bible Lands During the 19th Century (1903) for a history of exploration.

Figure 1. Map of Iraq With Major Sites Indicated.

By the 1870s, however, the Ottoman government had also realized the importance of antiquities and had promulgated an antiquities law. Shortly after this, excavations were being carried out by scholars rather than by diplomats and commercial agents, although the digging methods were no better than before. The mining by de Sarzec of Tello (ancient Girsu) yielded masses of very important material but with virtually no context recognized or recorded. The first American expedition in Iraq, sponsored by the University of Pennsylvania at Nippur (1888–1900), was almost as chaotic, but it was important for supplying to the scholarly world a wealth of cuneiform documents that allowed the construction of ancient history, the continued understanding of the Akkadian language, and the decipherment of Sumerian. In the notes, letters, and publications of that expedition,[2] it is clear that the expedition's staff as well as scholars from other institutions in the United States and Europe were buying objects from dealers in Turkey, Baghdad, Hilla, and other places, and doing so by sneaking around the Ottoman authorities, including official representatives

[2] H. Hilprecht, The So-Called Peters-Hilprecht Controversy 45 *passim* (1908).

Figure 2. Umma, Photograph of Large Hole Made by Looters Prior to 2001, Probably as Early as the Late 19th Century. Photo by Mark Altaweel.

who accompanied them. The trade was brisk, and many thousands of tablets and seals found their way to museum and university collections. The Ottoman attempts to control the trade were quite inadequate, and only the shipping of an expedition's excavated finds to Istanbul seems to have been accomplished with any regulation. Although all antiquities were the property of the state, expeditions and even individual scholars could receive a portion of the finds once the Ottoman officials had inspected them. It is interesting to note that the individual members of at least the Nippur expedition thought nothing of buying antiquities clandestinely for themselves or for institutions other than Pennsylvania, which was sponsoring the excavations.[3] The ethics and economics of such practices were not debated. That the Ottoman authorities cared about the loss of antiquities can be shown by the case of Edgar James Banks, a very bright American who had studied in Germany and was hired by the University of Chicago to dig at Adab in 1904–05. Banks was caught trying to smuggle objects out of Iraq and was banned from digging further. Chicago fired him, and then he spent the rest of his life buying and selling antiquities. He bought a very large number of objects just prior to the First World War, and with these in hand he began to send letters to institutions and individuals across America. If you go to almost any public library, university, college, or museum in the United States, you have an excellent chance of finding a few clay tablets (often from Umma and Drehem) and even some cylinder seals. He continued to trade

[3] *Id.*, 311 *passim.*

well into the 1930s, with the letters often stating that the price had to be raised because the new restrictions of the Kingdom of Iraq had made it hard to get fresh supplies. I have seen several of these collections and the accompanying papers, and although Banks's letters imply or even state clearly that these objects came out of Iraq without the permission of the authorities, there is never a hint that the buying institutions had any hesitation to make the purchase.

The German expedition to Babylon, from 1899 until 1917, finally brought an orderly system into the excavation of Mesopotamians sites. German operations here and at Assur and Samarra, as well as other sites, laid the groundwork for the training not only of archaeologists but of local workmen as well. Captured objects from Babylon, Assur, and Samarra became the focus of a policy debate within the British government and among Britain, Germany, and Portugal after the war.[4] When the British forces arrived at Babylon, they found crates of objects that the excavator Koldewey had intended to send to Berlin under a special agreement with the Ottoman government. Those crates and others with objects from Samarra were impounded by the British forces, and there ensued a long discussion in which the Foreign Office, the India Office, the occupying authorities, the British Museum, and other parties debated the merits of keeping the objects as war booty as against returning them to the Germans or the newly independent Iraq. Portugal became a party to the debate because a ship with Assur objects was sequestered in Lisbon. Gertrude Bell, echoed by the Foreign Office, wanted the materials returned to the projected Iraq Museum. Most other parties wanted the objects for England. Most of the material was sent to Britain where eventually it was divided among 17 institutions in Europe, North America, and the Near East, the British Museum and the Berlin Museum receiving the best pieces. Some of the collection of Assur objects in Lisbon eventually found their way to Berlin.

With the founding of the Iraq Museum and the Iraqi Antiquities Service in 1922, Gertrude Bell, the first director, oversaw the adoption of an antiquities law patterned after the Ottoman one. Criticized by some as favoring foreign expeditions in the division of objects found, the law ensured the very swift building up of a collection for the Iraq Museum at little expense to the kingdom. When the division was made in strict adherence to the law, the museum had the choice of the best objects. There were instances in which British directors, especially Richard Cooke who was caught smuggling objects, were not scrupulous in the divisions. An American archaeologist, Richard Starr, apparently innocently became involved as a receiver of the objects sent out by Cooke.[5]

The illegal excavation and sale of objects was still continuing through the 1930s, with the department officials being unable to do much about it. In fact, one of the British directors of antiquities, Sidney Smith, in 1930 issued a memorandum to all expeditions about the purchase of antiquities. He was not so much concerned with the buying as with making sure that the objects

[4] M. Bernhardsson, Reclaiming a Plundered Past: Archaeoogy and Nation Building in Modern Iraq 57–92 (2005).

[5] *Id.* at 159–60.

came from the immediate area of the expeditions' concessions. Such objects could then be included in the official registers of the digs and would be eligible for the division.[6] This practice led to the acceptance of dealers' provenience designations, introducing false certainty into the art historical analyses of Mesopotamian styles.

With the end of the British Mandate, and the independence of the kingdom in 1932, there was a decided change in the official attitude toward antiquities. Especially after the adoption of a new, stricter antiquities law in 1936, in which all antiquities and antiquities sites became the property of the state, the relationship of foreign scholars and expeditions to the Iraqi directorate general of antiquities was altered significantly. It was in this decade that the Iraqis began to do their own digs, initially at Islamic sites. It was also the time in which young scholars were sent abroad, on government fellowships, for graduate degrees. The problems with illicit digging still continued, but the gradual consolidation of the Antiquities Service, with representatives in all the provinces, began to curb the practice. The glorious past of Iraq was seen as a means to bolster national identity and as a potentially important source of revenue from tourism.

The Second World War was a watershed for Iraqi archaeology. With all the foreign expeditions gone, and with newly trained Iraqi archaeologists and philologists back from abroad, the directorate general began to sponsor important excavations in prehistoric and pre-Islamic sites, although still with the aid of a British advisor, Seton Lloyd.

The production of oil in a major way after the war led to increased budgets for antiquities, coinciding with the return of foreign expeditions with improved methods of digging and recording. There was still some illicit digging and smuggling out of antiquities, but at a reduced rate.

Governmental changes after the revolution of 1958 brought about the virtual elimination of illicit digging. From this point until 1990, there was very strong control over the antiquities sites of Iraq. With the oil boom of the 1970s, and the great increase in funding, the Antiquities Service could hire many more staff, including site guards and regional representatives, and enforce the law strictly. A few items might still come onto the international antiquities market, especially coins. An important factor was the construction of the new Iraq National Museum, opened in 1967, and museums in all provinces during the 1970s. Iraq had by now developed the best Antiquities Service in the Middle East and was one of the best countries anywhere in terms of protecting its cultural heritage.

That situation changed drastically in the aftermath of the First Gulf War, 1991. In the chaos that accompanied the uprisings in the south and north of the country, 13 of the 19 regional museums were looted, and more than 5,000 objects were taken.[7] One could take these events as merely the overenthusiastic

---

6 *Id.* at 158.

7 M. Gibson & A. McMahon, Lost Heritage: Antiquities Stolen from Iraq's Regional Museums (1992).

actions of people reacting to years of oppression, but there is a more nuanced context that has to be laid out.

Two events occurred in the late 1980s that were important for Iraqi antiquities as well as those of other countries. One was the collapse of the stock market in the United States and elsewhere, leading investors to seek other fields for profits. At about the same time, the Erlenmeyer Collection, formed in the 1920s and 1930s and largely published, was put on sale in major auctions in Europe and the United States.[8] Because this collection was so old, it did not come under the strictures of the 1970 UNESCO convention,[9] which many museums and universities had agreed to observe. Because it was "clean," this collection could be bid on with a clear conscience, and the bidding was very spirited. Objects that would have fetched a few hundred dollars before this in the shadowy international market brought thousands of dollars. Tablets and cylinder seals were especially sought and set new records. This set of auctions raised the prices for Mesopotamian antiquities in general, and many new people became collectors. In 1990, I saw copies of the Erlenmeyer catalogues in a rug merchant's shop in Baghdad. Although there were no antiquities dealers, per se, in Iraq, there were dealers in antiques and rugs who were interested in antiquities, if not already involved in the trade. The objects that were looted from the regional museums in 1991 found ready buyers in Baghdad, and they were sent on into the international market. The sale of the Moore Collection, another well-known and published collection from well before the UNESCO convention, sent the prices up even more, with four seals fetching more than $100,000.[10] Becoming aware of the prices, dealers in Baghdad began to encourage the illicit digging of sites, especially those that were in the desert to the south between the Tigris and Euphrates. Especially popular were those sites that had furnished museums with tablets, even in the 1880s, for instance Umma. By the late 1990s, cylinder seals often began to fetch more than $100,000, and one Neo-Assyrian royal seal (presented as a product of a supposed Iranian kingdom) even reached $400,000.[11] At the same time, fake seals and other antiquities began to be produced in quantity, with some showing great creativity.

A third event, beginning in 1990, affected the cultural heritage of Iraq. This

---

[8] Christie's, Ancient Near Eastern Texts from the Erlenmeyer Collection, Which Will Be Sold at Christie's Great Rooms on Tuesday 13 December 1988 (1988); Christie's, The Erlenmeyer Collection of Ancient Near Eastern Stamp Seals and Amulets. The Property of the Erlenmeyer Stiftung, Which Will Be Sold at Christie's Great Rooms on Tuesday 6 June 1989 (1989); Sotheby's, Western Asiatic Cylinder Seals and Antiquities (Part I) From the Erlenmeyer Collection. The Property of the Erlenmeyer Stiftung (A Foundation for Animal Welfare): Day of Sale, Thursday 9th July 1992 at 10.30 a.m. and 2.30 p.m. in the Conduit Street Gallery (1992).

[9] Convention on the Means of Prohibiting and Preventing the Illicit Import, Export and Transfer of Ownership of Cultural Property (Nov. 14, 1970), *available at* http://portal.unesco.org/en/ev.php-URL_ID=13039&URL_DO=DO_TOPIC&URL_SECTION=201.html.

[10] Sotheby's, The Ada Small Moore Collection of Ancient Near Eastern Seals. December 1 (1991).

[11] Christie's, The Surena Collection of Ancient Near Eastern Cylinder Seals Monday, 2 PM, June 11, 2001 No. 526 (2001).

was the economic sanctions regime imposed on Iraq and enforced by the no-fly zones declared by the United States. The sanctions were most keenly felt by the poorest of the Iraqis, many of whom were in the south. Probably beginning as a means to find something to sell to feed their families, men began to go out to isolated sites and dig. It is not known if they were induced to do this by dealers, but it was clear as early as 1994 that there was major illicit excavation going on at sites such as Umma (see Figure 3), Umm al-Hafriyat (near Nippur), Adab, Isin, and other mounds in the south of Iraq. The evidence for this activity was a flood of object reaching dealers in London and other centers of the trade, and the quick building up of collections in Europe, the United States, Japan, and the Persian Gulf. One major collector in New York was overhead commenting that this is the golden age of collecting.[12] This is the golden age of collecting." It is important to note that whereas other Iraqi products were forbidden entry into the United States by the sanctions, the antiquities of Iraq were allowed to be bought and sold freely.

The routes by which antiquities were being smuggled varied, insofar as it could be determined. Anecdotal evidence, mainly from employees of the Antiquities Service, indicated some of those routes. In at least one case, a diplomatic car was being used to export objects through the Jordanian border point. The objects were confiscated and returned to the Iraq Museum. Border police patrolling the Iraq-Saudi border intercepted a pickup truck belonging to a *bedu* and seized sacks containing cuneiform documents. The museum mounted a small, short-term exhibition of these seized objects. The driver of the pickup had been contracted to take the objects to Saudi Arabia, where he was to hand them over to someone who would ship them by air to London. Other objects went overland to Iran by various routes or to Turkey, via the Kurdish area, which was no longer under Iraqi government control. Iraqi antiquities were surreptitiously sold in the antique shops of Damascus and Aleppo, so there was at least one route to Syria. And some shops in Amman were also dealing in them. A result of such dealing in Iraqi material was the sharp increase in illegal digging on sites in Syria and Jordan.

Regardless of the route by which an antiquity reaches the markets in Europe and America or Japan, there are several methods by which the smugglers and dealers "legitimize" the object. False papers give somewhat plausible proveniences, and even though everyone in a transaction knows that the provenience papers mean little, they can pretend that they dealt in or bought the piece in good faith. Often, the papers say that an object has been in a European (preferably Swiss) collection for some time before the 1970 UNESCO convention. Or there are faked government papers that authorize the export of the object; the favorite country for such documents seems to be Jordan, although anyone who is knowledgeable about Mesopotamian antiquities knows that they could not be from Jordan, and also knows that Jordan would not have agreed to the export anyway. One very important inscribed object that was the subject of

---

12 *See* Thomas H. Maugh II, *A Plea for Treasures of Civilization,* L.A. Times, Mar. 24, 2003, *available at* http://articles.latimes.com/2003/mar/24/news/war-archeology24.

Figure 3. Photograph of Umma Taken in 2001 Showing Illicit Digging Done in the 1990s. Photo By Mark Altaweel.

much excitement and quiet discussion in the 1990s was the trunk of a black stone statue that had a long historical inscription on the back. The upper and lower portions of the statue had been broken away. A London dealer sent large-format, glossy photographs to some cuneiform scholars, who showed them around an American Oriental Society meeting. I was not at the meeting, but I was shown the photographs shortly thereafter. The excitement was caused by the fact that this object recorded a rebellion by most of the cities of southern Babylonia against Samsuiluna, the son and successor of King Hammurabi of Babylon. The rebellion was led by "the king of Sumer," a title not used in many years. Although there had been some references to a rebellion in other texts, this inscription gave great detail and was of high historical importance. When it was first being offered for something like $400,000, it had papers that said it had been in a Swiss collection for years. There were no buyers. Everyone who learned of the inscription knew that the provenience was impossible, since a text of this importance would have been shown to a cuneiformist when it entered that collection so that there could be a publication for the scholar and an increase in value for the collector. A year or so after the first appearance, another dealer in the United States was said to be showing the pictures once again, but now the value was in the vicinity of $40,000, and the papers said that it had been exported from Jordan with the permission of the Antiquities

Department of that country. Again, no one believed the provenience. Even at the reduced price, there was no buyer because the inscription was already readable in the photographs, and the value of the piece was greatly devalued because it was only a fragment of a statue and would not likely be displayed in a museum. It is not clear where the item is now, although I have heard a rumor that it is in an Italian private collection. Thus far, no one has published the text, although many scholars know of its content. It is unfortunately the case that there is cooperation between scholars, mainly philologists and art historians, who translate, analyze, and authenticate items for collectors and dealers. They do not look beyond the dealers to see the smugglers and looters who supply the traffic, but they justify their actions by citing the loss of information for scholarship if they do not read the inscriptions or analyze the artworks. And they say that if they did not record the items, they would go underground and never be seen again. Clearly, some scholars are in an ethical dilemma here.[13] In contrast, those scholars who primarily identify themselves as archaeologists rather than art historians or epigraphers want to preserve objects in their original findspots so that the invaluable information on context can give greater information on the meaning of the object, and the object can inform on the nature of the findspot.

Museum curators are in another kind of bind, because normally their museums have signed the 1970 UNESCO convention, and they are unable to buy items that have unsure proveniences. This has not, however, prevented them from exhibiting objects "from the collection of Mr. X or Mrs. Y," thus authenticating them and giving them greater monetary value. Unfortunately, antiquities have long been a mark of sophistication and taste, and social status can be conferred by accumulation of museum-quality objects. Often the collectors are major donors to the museums, and this fact colors the judgment of curators and museum directors. In time, the donation by collectors of large sums to name a museum hall or a wing, or to subvert an archaeological excavation, or the donation of the collection to a museum serves to erase the memory of the acquisition trail and the destruction caused to cultural heritage by the suppliers of such an insatiable demand. When collectors are also major donors to political campaigns, or have other levers of power, it is virtually impossible to prosecute them for their part in the criminal acts that lie behind their collections. A few smugglers, dealers, and curators may be prosecuted, and the poor farmers who do the digging just to make a living in very difficult times may be beaten, but the consumers at the root of the trade will escape. They excuse their actions by citing their superior appreciation of the objects, the greater safety of the objects in their possession or in the possession of a Western museum, rather than in the countries of origin. In fact, until the destruction by two wars visited on Iraq by Western powers, that country had a better record of protecting its artifacts and sites than most countries in the world. Artifacts are safest in the ground, awaiting their careful exposure by trained archaeologists,

[13] A. Lawler, *Looted Tablets Pose Scholar's Dilemma, Rencontre Assyriologique Internctionale Meeting*, 309 Sci. 869 (2005).

who can give much greater information on them through an analysis of the context in which they reside.

The mechanisms of the illicit antiquities market are sometimes easy to see, for instance in the cleaned-up part of the trade—the antiquities shops on Madison Avenue in New York or other chic addresses in other cities. Usually conveniently located near the major museum, these establishments have a symbiotic relationship not only with collectors and curators, but also with art historians and philologists who authenticate the objects. Important to the entire trade are the well-illustrated catalogues of antiquities auctions, which have proliferated and grown in size since 1990. These catalogues serve to advertise the goods and let the world, even rug dealers in Baghdad and Aleppo, know the going rate of ancient objects. Despite the fact that at present there is said to be virtually no antiquities flow into the United States because of a presidential decree against dealing in Iraqi cultural property, there is plentiful supply abroad. The Gulf Emirates have become a new marketplace for antiquities from Iraq, often using the Internet for sales, and some major new collections are being accumulated there. I have a suspicion that many of the objects are being held for dealers and collectors in warehouses in the Near East and Europe. Back in the 1990s, it was much easier and simpler. For instance, London dealers sent cylinder seals to at least one New York collector on approval, just like stamps. The buyer was to choose which of the dozens of seals he might want and send the rest back.

During the 1990s, when the looting in Iraq began on a large scale, the no-fly zone in the south was essential to the trade. Without helicopter surveillance, it was very difficult for the Iraqi authorities to control the countryside. They could hold the towns, but they had limited ability to police the country, especially the desert areas that are difficult of access. Even when antiquities representatives could get the local police to go out to investigate a report of looting, the diggers could see the dust from approaching convoys of vehicles and be gone from the site long before they arrived.

Because the market in London and other places in Europe were being flooded with texts from Umma in the 1990s, I advised a writer/photographer, who was being sent by an American magazine to do an archeological story on Iraq in the mid-1990s, to ask to see that *tell* to check on the situation. With a lot of difficulty, she was escorted there and found the site badly damaged by looters. The antiquities officials who accompanied her were able to use the information they gathered to gain emergency funding to conduct salvage excavations at Umma, Umm al-Aqarib, and several other nearby sites, effectively putting an end to looting in that vicinity from 1998 until 2003. But the looters just shifted their operations elsewhere. One badly looted site was Umm al-Hafriyat, a pottery-making center that I had excavated in 1977. Cuneiform documents from this town were in European and American collections by at least the late 1990s, as I learned from one of the specialists in texts. The great city of Isin, which had been the capital of Babylonia during two periods in the Second Millennium B.C. and had been excavated by a German expedition in the 1970s, was also looted in the 1990s. That site was essentially destroyed by intensified looting after the 2003 war.

In 2001, I visited Iraq for a conference and asked to see the salvage projects at Umma and the other sites. Dr. Donny George took a small group from Baghdad on a one-day trip, taking only about two hours to reach the nearest town on the excellent highways. But it took more almost two hours to travel the 15 kilometers through the desert to Umma and Umm al-Aqarib.[14] It was clear from surface indications that although there had been extensive illicit digging at both, the area affected was relatively concentrated. One very deep hole at Umma was probably the location of much of the looting from the late 19th and early 20th century. The pits from the 1990s were relatively shallow. The excavations by the State Board of Antiquities in the past two years had exposed great buildings (see Figure 4) and had recovered many objects in good context. In order to keep the looters from returning to the *tells*, the expedition had to work throughout the year, even in the heat of summer. At Umma, there were as many as 18 guards, an extraordinary number for a site being excavated. Those guards, and those at the other salvage operations in the vicinity were to prove inadequate. The day the 2003 war started, more than 200 looters went to Umma and the other sites, drove off the guards and began digging once again (see Figure 5).[15] The guards at Nippur were equally powerless in May 2003, when armed men began to loot the northwestern side of the West Mound. They dug for a month before police from the nearby town of Afaj came out to drive them off.

It had been clear by late 2002 that the United States was going to pursue a war with Iraq. I went with a small delegation to the Pentagon and the State Department on January 24, 2003, to try to emphasize the importance of Iraq as the center of the world's most ancient civilization. I pointed to the thousands of important sites and stressed their vulnerability, since they are mounds and, being the highest points on the southern landscape, they would be seen as high ground to be taken and held. I also said that they were probably going to be looted if there was chaos following an invasion. I also emphasized the importance of the Iraq National Museum and said that it was likely to be looted. The Pentagon officials said that they were aware of the museum. I took this to mean that it would not only not be bombed, but that it also would be secured. I was mistaken on the second part. Pentagon officials have stated recently that they thought of the potential for looting only in terms of their own soldiers carrying out the action. They were not thinking about the probability of looting by Iraqis, so they were not prepared for it. I can state, categorically, that I had mentioned the probability of looting by Iraqis not only of the Iraq Museum but also of the archaeological sites during the January meeting, and I repeated the warning in e-mails to the same Pentagon officials several times as the war was in progress.

---

[14] A. Lawler, *Archaeology in Iraq,* 293 Sci. 32–44 (2001).

[15] A. Lawler, *Mayhem in Mesopotamia, News Focus Special Report: A Museum Looted,* 101 Sci. 582–88 (2003); A. Lawler, *Assyrian Gold Safe as Looters Threaten Southern Sites,* 300 Sci. 1488 (2003).

Figure 4. Photograph of Façade of Ur III Temple of the God Shara at Umma, Excavated by Iraqi State Organization of Antiquities in 2001. Photo by Mark Altaweel.

Figure 5. Same Building at Umma, Partially Demolished by Illicit Diggers in May 2003. Photo by Jopanne Farchakh.

Figure 6. Photo of Umma From Helicopter, September 2003. Photo by John Russell © with permission.

The worst that can happen to a museum occurred in Baghdad from April 10 to 12, 2003. The worst that can happen to an archaeological site, looting on a scale that involves virtual destruction of whole cities (see Figure 6), is still occurring in southern Iraq, and there is no prospect of its ending.

CHAPTER 9

GERMAN ARCHAEOLOGICAL INSTITUTE'S PROTECTION OF CULTURAL HERITAGE IN IRAQ AND ELSEWHERE IN THE MIDDLE EAST

Margarete van Ess

The German Archaeological Institute (DAI) emerged 180 years ago out of the Istituto di Correspondenza Archeologica in Rome, which had been founded by friends of academics—scholars, artists, and diplomats—from various countries in Europe. Their purpose was to collect, document, and publish information about ancient objects and sites and thereby foster the flow of correspondence between archaeologists throughout Europe.[1]

For financial reasons, however, the international mission of this circle of friends slowly but surely yielded to an institution with a national character. The primary motive of collegial cooperation among scholars in all countries nevertheless persevered. In 1871, this organization was officially installed as an institution of the Prussian state, that is, the *Deutsches Archäologisches Institut*.[2] A manifestation of this official status today is that the DAI is an independent governmental agency located in the sphere of the Federal Foreign Office. Despite its status as a governmental agency, it is nevertheless solely devoted to academic research, while its structure and ethical guidelines are reflective of German cultural policy. Moreover, representative departments and offices of the DAI are located in most of its host countries: Egypt, Greece, Iran, Iraq, Italy, Spain, Syria, Turkey, and Yemen.

Members of the DAI usually reside in the host countries for many years, where they are integrated among the population. They conduct archaeological research and cultural and historical studies together with local archaeologists, historians, and other scientists. They also take part in the academic programs of the respective countries' universities. Hence, they are actively engaged in fulfilling the charge of the DAI of maintaining, preserving, and fostering the cultural heritage of the particular country. Aside from their scholastic duties,

[1] Friedrich Wilhelm Deichmann, Vom Internationalen Privatverein zur Preussischen Staatsanstalt. Zur Geschichte des Instituto di Corrispondenza Archeologica, *in* 9 Das Deutsche Archäologische Institut. Geschichte und Dokumente [The German Archaeological Institute. History and Documents] (Deutsches Archäologisches Institut ed., 1986).

[2] For the legal structures and changes, see Hans Meyer, *Der Rechtsstatus des Deutschen Archäologischen Instituts, in* Rechtsgutachten, 2004/2 AA, at 155–220 (2005).

members of the DAI also assist and consult in organizing exhibitions at sites and in museums, preparing informative pamphlets and booklets for the public, advising filmmakers, and organizing or assist in guided tours.

The DAI is committed to recognizing the special circumstances that prevail in the various host countries and to working collaboratively with the cultural institutions of each country. The DAI's strong interest in this type of cooperation has led to many collaborative projects that are widely acknowledged in the host countries. In consequence, many of the DAI members are honorary professors in the respective country's universities and academies of science. At present 11 departments of the DAI are engaged in archaeological work in 36 countries, and around 190 projects are maintained worldwide.[3]

This background succinctly describes the Oriental Department of the DAI, which maintains branch offices in Baghdad, Damascus, and Sana'a. The branch office in Baghdad was founded in 1955 shortly after the resumption of German excavations in Uruk following World War II. One of its aims was to serve as an administrative base for German archaeological projects. For many years, excavations in Uruk-Warka, Babylon, and several other sites were carried out by the department.[4] From its very beginnings, this office nevertheless saw itself as a cultural institution, cooperating directly with several Iraqi institutions as well as other foreign institutes in Iraq. For instance, some rooms in the DAI's Baghdad office were used for teaching courses in ancient Near Eastern philology to Iraqi students, until the subject was introduced at the University of Baghdad.

The archaeological work of the DAI in Iraq continued during the Iran-Iraq war in 1980–89 and during the economic embargo imposed by the United Nations on Iraq in 1990–2003, albeit irregularly.[5] This period of time was marked by the increasing difficulty of Iraqi colleagues in maintaining contact with the international scientific community. Because of the war, almost all Iraqi citizens were barred from travel permits; further, because of the embargo, even the import of books and other research materials was greatly constrained. The exchange of literature was also subjected to strict control. Chemicals and other substances for conservation work, photographic supplies for documentation, and technical equipment fell under the restrictions of the embargo. During that time the DAI devoted itself to supporting Iraqi colleagues, and this goal often involved carrying out unspectacular yet not at all easy activities. For example, I was serving as director of the Baghdad office in the spring of 1999 when we learned from staff members of the German Embassy that part of the embassy building would be cleared out. Among other things, many boxes of writing paper with embassy letterhead were to be thrown away. At that time, the income of the Iraqi populace had decreased drastically, to an average three to five U.S.

[3] Archäologische Entdeckungen. Die Forschungen des Deutschen Archäologischen Instituts im 20. Jahrhundert (Deutsches Archäologisches Institut ed., 2000). *See also* the Web site of the DAI at http://www.dainst.de.

[4] 50 Jahre Forschungen im Irak 1955–2005—50 Years of Research in Iraq 1955–2005 (Deutsches Archäologisches Institut—Orient-Abteilung. Aussenstelle Baghdad ed., 2005).

[5] During that period Prof. Dr. Rainer Michael Boehmer (until 1996) and Dr. Margarete van Ess (since 1996) have headed the branch office in Baghdad.

dollars a month. As a result of the embargo, the price of a package of paper had become higher than a professor's monthly salary. Because students could not afford to buy paper, they even wrote their notes and lessons on the blank page-rims of newspapers. We collected the discarded writing paper and spent hours cutting off the embassy's letterhead from every single piece of paper. It was a moving occasion when we delivered about one car-trunk full of this cleared paper to the College of Arts at the University of Baghdad.

Other supportive endeavors of the DAI branch in Baghdad included regularly importing photographic films, for those Iraqi colleagues who were working on excavations, and archaeological publications for libraries, so that Iraqi colleagues could gain at least some information about current developments in archaeology. We were and continue to be concerned about our ability to guarantee punctual payment of salaries for the local employees of the DAI and for the guards at our archaeological sites.

In 2000, the DAI entered into a long-planned contract of cooperation with the Department of Archaeology in the College of Arts at the University of Baghdad to introduce students to advanced techniques of archaeology and documentation as well as to facilitate exchange of publications and scholars. In special agreements with the Iraqi State Board of Antiquities and Heritage, similar measures were planned for projects at the traditional German excavation site of Uruk-Warka, such as joint surveys within and outside of Uruk, restoration work of already excavated buildings, and the installation of a site museum for tourists. Yet, the efforts of the Institute's Baghdad branch were hindered or even thwarted by the immense effects of the embargo and, in 2003, by the outbreak of the war.

The embargo can only be described as a moral crime against humanity, for it destroyed the basic social structures of the country's human population without affecting those in power very much. On the one hand, the wealth of those actively collaborating with the government as well as their close relationship increased all the more. On the other hand, the severely impoverished population could do nothing to counter this situation except to withdraw from public life. Corruption, which had not been a major problem in daily life, emerged at all levels, and networks of the black market were created and gradually expanded, including the practice of illegal trafficking of antiquities. The plundering of ancient sites and the looting of antiquities became commonplace. With the weakening of the Iraqi state since 2003, these networks reached all areas of the country, and looting became a major, and in some regions, well-accepted way to gain a basic income.

Since the war in 2003 the activities of the DAI in Baghdad have changed considerably. Although the branch as such is still operative and would be able to continue work on sites in Iraq as soon as political stability improves, archaeological field work is at present out of the question, as is the presence of German archaeologists in the country. The terror of kidnapping, daily crime, and bomb attacks brought life in the scientific community and elsewhere to a nearly complete halt. Just the presence of foreign scholars would draw the attention of terrorists to those Iraqi scholars engaged in international cooperation and would thus irresponsibly expose them to economic pressure and endanger their personal security. As the embargo has already disrupted the social structure, it is still threatened with collapse, and intellectuals are leaving the country by the thousands.

Projects of the DAI in Iraq thus comprise supplying Iraqi colleagues and institutions from abroad; sending books to the universities and subject material like cupboards, scanners, and acid-free materials for archival work to the Iraqi State Board of Antiquities and Heritage; and logistically supporting and safeguarding archaeological sites. Furthermore, within the framework of its regular grant program, every year the DAI extends several invitations to Iraqi scholars for a one- or two-month research sojourn in Germany. It also assists in coordinating projects between the German universities and the German Federal Foreign Office while lobbying for an increase of opportunities for vocational training and advanced studies in Germany.

In view of the ongoing and extensive plundering of archaeological sites in Iraq, however, the DAI's main efforts now are aimed at awakening an awareness among the public of the immeasurable value that ancient civilizations in Iraq and elsewhere represent for world cultural heritage.[6] In this context the DAI is engaged, for instance, in advising the German government to conform its legislation on cultural preservation to the international standards that have been established in recent decades. The DAI's institutional connection with the German Foreign Office makes it easier to address proposals concerning cultural issues and official DAI comments directly to those in executive positions.

The DAI informs German customs officials about the specific properties and features of archaeological objects. It has also helped German customs officials by converting into concrete guidelines a paragraph in U.N. Resolution 1483 on Iraq, which the European Union (EU) implemented in Iraq Ordinance 1210/2003.[7] This measure protects cultural objects from Iraq. So far, any positive practical impact of this ordinance is scarcely noticeable. Because so many special aspects of German trade law must be taken into consideration, the DAI has worked with a legal specialist in studying and publishing the German law pertaining to cultural goods illegally exported out of Iraq, with reference to embargo stipulations, the aforementioned Iraq ordinance, and the foreign trade laws in Germany.[8] The publication offers legal advice on how to handle the highly complex questions should litigation occur.

---

[6] See, for example, the joint statement by the German Archaeological Institute, the Institute of Archaeology of the Russian Academy of Sciences and the American Institute of Archaeology, *available at* http://www.dainst.org/medien/de/Joint-Statement2007.pdf.

[7] Iraq Ordinance 1210/2003, *available at* http://eur-lex.europa.eu/LexUriServ/LexUriServ.do?uri=CELEX:32003R1210:EN:HTML.

[8] Margarete van Ess & Susanne Schoen, *Das VN-Handelsverbot von 2003 für irakisches Kulturgut: Folgenlos in Deutschland?*, 2006/1 AA, at 73–95, and *in* Kunstrechtsspiegel 1/2008, 7–24, *available at* http://ifkur.de/images/dokumente/kunstrechtsspiegel-01-08.pdf.

Another recent task was advisory work for the ratification of the 1970 UNESCO Convention on the Means of Prohibiting and Preventing the Illicit Import, Export and Transfer of Ownership of Cultural Property ("1970 UNESCO Convention"), to which Germany was not yet a party.[9] Until ratification was eventually announced on April 20, 2007,[10] German laws provided for a general ban of trade in stolen goods only, supported by restrictions on the purchase of cultural objects in good faith. These laws, however, do not fully apply to auctions[11] and generally concern only objects stolen *in* Germany. The import of cultural objects from other countries into Germany is legal as long as its customs regulations are complied with. An exception involves objects from member states of the EU, to which its own legislation applies. The EU law has been brought into force in Germany's "Act Implementing Directives of the European Communities on the Return of Cultural Objects Unlawfully Removed from the Territory of a Member State" of October 15, 1998.[12] Otherwise, until 2007, at least, it has not been difficult in Germany to acquire cultural objects that have been stolen or looted from non-EU states. The return of such objects to the country of origin was only possible through complicated civil litigation or acts of good will. Hence, the implementation since 2007 of the 1970 UNESCO Convention should at least facilitate the return of *stolen* objects. It will be instructive to consider the history of this initiative in Germany.

At the beginning of 2006 a bill to implement the 1970 UNESCO Convention as German legislation was introduced in the German Cabinet.[13] Such legislation is necessary for the ratification of any convention by Germany. After several political discussions and hearings in 2006, the bill was approved by the German Bundestag[14] on February 1, 2007, the Bundesrat[15] on March 9, 2007,[16] and the president of the Federal Republic of Germany on May 18, 2007.[17]

---

[9] UNESCO Convention on the Means of Prohibiting and Preventing the Illicit Import, Export, and Transfer of Ownership of Cultural Property (Nov. 14, 1970), *available at* http://portal.unesco.org/en/ev.php-URL_ID=13039&URL_DO=DO_TOPIC&URL_SECTION=201.html.

[10] *Available at* http://www.bgbl.de/Xaver/start.xav?startbk=Bundesanzeiger_BGB1, under "Bundesgesetzblatt Teil II, No. 12 (Apr. 25, 2007).

[11] Anette Hipp, Schutz von Kulturgütern in Deutschland 155–61 (2000) (chapter on the national legal situation in Germany).

[12] Federal Law Gazette 1008, pt. I, no. 70, at 3162 (Oct 21, 1998), *available at* http://www.bgblportal.de/BGBL/bgbl1f/b198070f.pdf.

[13] Drucksache 16/1371 (May 4, 2006), *available at* http://www.bundestag.de/ausschuesse/a22/berichte/unesco-uebereinkommen_kulturgut/Gesetzentwurf_2.pdf and approval: http://dip.bundestag.de/btd/16/041/1604145.pdf.

[14] The lower house of the German Parliament and the representative body of the Federal Republic of Germany.

[15] The upper house of the German Parliament, representing the Lands of the Federal Republic of Germany.

[16] *Available at* http://www.bundesrat.de/cln_050/nn_8336/SharedDocs/Drucksachen/2007/0001-0100/92-07_28B_29,templateId=raw,property=publicationFile.pdf/92-07(B).pdf.

[17] Published in the Federal Law Gazette: Bundesgesetzblatt Jahrgang 2007, Teil I Nr. 21, ausgegeben zu Bonn am 23. Mai 2007, *available at* http://217.160.60.235/BGBL/bgbl1f/bgbl107s0757.pdf.

Ratification of the 1970 UNESCO Convention on April 20, 2007, together with the implementation act, brought the convention into force.[18]

As is well known, however, the 1970 UNESCO Convention focuses only on known, important, and listed cultural material. A number of important elements for an effective cultural heritage regime were not yet apparent at the time when the convention was completed. To respond to these developments the UNIDROIT Convention on Stolen or Illegally Exported Cultural Objects was opened for signature in 1995.[19] Germany has not yet considered the implementation of this important convention because it does not foresee further implementation under national legislation since parts of the convention conflict with existing German legislation, thereby requiring major alterations in German jurisprudence that would be difficult to explain to the German public and political bodies.

In the face of cultural catastrophes in Afghanistan, the Balkans, Iraq, and elsewhere, the German implementation act was amended to add a few paragraphs exceeding the requirements of the 1970 UNESCO Convention. One of these amendments addressed the case of looted, previously unknown archaeological objects.[20] The act allows parties to the 1970 UNESCO Convention to officially list and claim important stolen items within one year after the state is informed of their theft and, in the case of states affected by armed conflict, this deadline starts only after the conflict has abated to a point where states are capable maintaining claims.[21] On the other hand, the implementation act distinguishes between cultural objects from EU and non-EU states. For EU states, in the case of claims of other EU states for return of objects, the act refers to established lists of objects by categories that are specified in the EU legislation.[22] Non-EU states, however, must publish their listed cultural goods in an official German gazette[23] as approved by the cabinet on September 24, 2008. This presents a problem for non-EU states that are parties to the 1970 UNESCO Convention because the implementation act does not recognize their right to formulate the lists according to the respective national definitions of cultural goods. Instead, the German law requires the listing of individually identifiable objects. A proposal by the DAI to omit the differentiation between EU- and non-EU states by relying on the EU category lists for all member states has unfortunately not been accepted.

---

[18] Deposited at UNESCO on Nov. 30, 2007. Officially announced in Germany on Feb. 28, 2008, and in force since Feb. 29, 2008.

[19] UNIDROIT Convention on Stolen or Illegally Exported Cultural Objects, June 24, 1995, *reprinted in* 34 I.L.M. 1322.

[20] Art. 1, § 3, para. 6(2).

[21] Art. 1, § 3, para. 6(2a).

[22] Article 1, Section 3, paragraph 6(1), referring to EU Council Directive 93/7/EEC of March 15, 1993, on the return of cultural objects unlawfully removed from the territory of a member state with changes by EU Council Directive 2001/38/EG from June 5, 2001. *See* http://eur-lex.europa.eu/LexUriServ/LexUriServ.do?uri=CELEX:31993L0007:EN:HTML and http://eur-lex.europa.eu/LexUriServ/LexUriServ.do?uri=CELEX:32001L0038:EN:HTML.

[23] Art. 1, § 3, para. 6(2), cl. 3 and § 4, para. 14. The procedure has been defined in a decree, *available at* http://www.geseize-im-internet.de/bundesrecht/kultgvv/gesamt.pdf.

Another proposal by several German cultural institutions, including the DAI,[24] has likewise been unsuccessful. It would amend the implementation act to provide that although some important cultural goods, such as paintings and major works of art, are easily defined and listed, other scientifically important cultural goods of limited economic value, such as many archaeological objects, are not so easily defined. In order to strengthen the fight against illicit excavations, the proposal therefore was made to add a special paragraph specifically pertaining to archaeological objects, as already had been formulated and accepted in 1992 in the European Convention on the Protection of the Archaeological Heritage[25] that was signed in Malta.

Unfortunately, at the last moment of consultations about the proposal, an initiative of the art and antiquities dealers was accepted for the law: although art and antiquities dealers are now required under German law to collect information about the identity of an object, its origin (if known) and the name and address of the seller, the buyer and the client, this requirement only applies if the value of the object exceeds 1,000 Euros. Most archaeological objects will therefore not be covered by this paragraph. Yet, the 1970 UNESCO Convention is not adequate in itself to solve such problems nor deter illicit excavations It is therefore incumbent on German cultural institutions to encourage the German government to ratify the 1995 UNIDROIT convention.

In the course of analyzing these legal issues, especially as they pertain to Iraq, the DAI has referred constantly to the larger international legal framework and tries to advise executive bodies. For example, the armed forces in Iraq are bound by the long-established and well-known rules and principles of the 1907 Hague Convention on War on Land[26] as well as customary international law. They therefore must provide for the protection of the cultural heritage and assume liability for injuries caused by violations of the law of armed conflict. Also, the famous *Naulilaa* arbitral award against Germany, which was decided on July 31, 1928, established the customary rules for reprisal measures, including damages for injuries, which provide guidance in the circumstances of Iraq although they do not apply directly to the conflict.[27] In this case, Portugal claimed that Germany, based in Southwest Africa (now Namibia), had caused a revolt of Angolans against Portugal by invading the Portuguese colony. All injuries caused by the revolt were understood to be in direct causal connection to the invasion including those resulting from the foreseeable breakdown of public order. Germany therefore had to pay reparations to Portugal. This legal understanding may apply to claims arising out of the Iraqi conflict, as several German specialists in international law emphasize.[28]

---

[24] *Available at* http://www.bundestag.de/ausschuesse/a22/anhoerungen/UNESCO/Stellungnahmen/16_22_051.pdf; *see* page 8.

[25] European Convention on the Protection of the Archaeological Heritage, May 6, 1969, E.T.S., No. 66, *reprinted in* 8 I.L.M. 736.

[26] Convention with Respect to the Laws and Customs of War on Land, Oct. 18, 1907, 36 Stat. 2277, T.S. No. 403.

[27] 2 U.N.R.I.A.A. 1011–33, especially 1014, 1031. 1032 (1928).

[28] M. Kaltenborn, *Die Plünderung des Irakischen Nationalmuseums und das Völkerrecht:*

Despite this attention to international law, the DAI is not an institution fundamentally involved with jurisprudence, but rather one devoted to cultural history. Therefore, it normally follows ethical principles without focusing on the legal aspects first. Indeed, the DAI maintains that laws are only effective when they are understood and accepted by society. The DAI, therefore, seeks to promote the value of preserving culture regardless of its origin. It is the DAI's goal to preserve the invaluable contributions of different cultures, a heritage embracing all peoples, each in its own way and equal in worth. The DAI therefore fully supports international bodies, such as UNESCO, the International Council of Museums (ICOM), the International Council on Monuments and Sites (ICOMOS), the International Center for the Study of the Preservation and Restoration of Cultural Property (ICCROM), and others, which constantly lobby for international recognition of the diversity of cultures, make known the contribution of these cultures to global civilization, and are committed to a strong legal framework that will help peoples to preserve their cultural heritage.

The DAI's focus is, of course, on archaeological, historical, and ethnographic aspects of cultural heritage. As historians, we marvel at the achievements of other civilizations in other times, and we trace the influence that they have exerted upon their neighbors, as well as on how they might have influenced events in history. We justify the existence of our academic field insofar as we can find traces of this influence in modern society and thereby better measure and correlate society's progress or change. Only after contemplating the multitude of different forms of co-existence through history and space does it become clear where the value of one's own culture lies and how interdependent it is with other older or neighboring societies.

Yet, we also have observed and documented that societies sharing cultural roots have taken on divergent ways of life, coming to different conclusions of cultural significance after the same events. It is precisely this multi-faceted aspect of human existence as seen in religion, art, and culture—think only of cooking recipes, for example—that must be preserved. When the modernization of traditional ways of life is disturbed from within a society, historians are professionally obliged to observe and document the traditions. Only through close and unbiased cooperative work with people and scholars in host countries does an approach from different worlds of understanding seem promising, an approach that may provide different answers to the same or similar inquiries. Indeed, appreciating the core of different views and interpretations is a necessary stimulus of scientific analysis. Ultimately, enriched with this understanding, the preservation of different and diverse cultures is the charge of everyone.

Zu den Rechtsgrundlagen des Schutzes von Kulturgütern in internationalen bewaffneten Konflikten, Kunstrecht und Urheberrecht Heft 4, 5. Jahrgang July/Aug. 2004, 97–128.

PART III

PROTECTING CULTURAL HERITAGE TODAY AND TOMORROW (KEYNOTE LECTURES)

CHAPTER 10
WHOSE CULTURE IS IT, ANYWAY?

Kwame Anthony Appiah*

It's a great honor to have been asked to start off this conference. If you are going to have an inter-disciplinary discussion of cultural property—which involves law and art history and museology—it seems only fitting to begin with someone who is a specialist in none of them. I want to talk, today, as a philosopher, about some questions that arise when you begin to think about the ownership of culture: and, since I have no relevant disciplinary expertise, I should like to start by being as clear as I can about the framework within which I do—and I believe we should—think about such things.

Excitement about the variety of human cultural artifacts is one of the two key elements of the tradition of cosmopolitanism, which stretches back to the Cynics of the fourth century B.C.E., who first coined the expression *cosmopolitan*, "citizen of the world." Cosmopolitanism starts with that metaphor of universal citizenship. We are all responsible for one another. But this second, equally important, element, offers a sort of commentary on what it takes to be a moral community: Cosmopolitans think that we can accept responsibility for one another while still living very different lives. In fact, cosmopolitans revel in the range and variety of the ways people live and the things they make and do. And so, unlike many people who think of the world as a moral community, cosmopolitans don't want to change everyone else to fit our own mold. We—I might as well admit at the start that I count myself among the cosmopolitans—we are interested in human social, cultural, and individual variety.

So you might suppose that cosmopolitans should side with those who are busy around the world "preserving culture," resisting "cultural imperialism," salvaging "cultural patrimony." But behind these slogans you often find some curious assumptions. Take "preserving culture." It's one thing to provide people with help to sustain arts they want to sustain. I am all for festivals of Welsh bards in Llandudno funded by the Welsh Arts Council; long live the Ghana National Cultural Center in Kumasi, where you can go and learn traditional Akan dancing and drumming, especially since its classes are spirited and overflowing. Restore the deteriorating film stock of early Hollywood movies; continue the preservation of Old Norse and early Chinese and Ethiopian manuscripts; record, transcribe, and analyze the oral narratives of Malay and Maasai and Maori: all these are a valuable part of our human heritage.

* This text is largely drawn from material in COSMOPOLITANISM: ETHICS IN A WORLD OF STRANGERS (2006).

But preserving *culture*—in the sense of cultural artifacts, broadly conceived—is different from preserving *cultures*. And the preservationists of cultures often pursue the latter, trying to ensure that the Huli of Papua New Guinea (or even Sikhs in Toronto) keep their "authentic" ways. What makes a cultural expression authentic, though? Are we to stop the importation of baseball caps into Vietnam, so that the Zao will continue with their colorful red headdresses? Why not ask the Zao? Shouldn't the choice be theirs?

"They *have* no real choice," the cultural preservationists say. "We have dumped cheap Western clothes into their markets; and they can no longer afford the silk they used to wear. If they had what they really wanted, they'd still be dressed traditionally." But this is no longer an argument about authenticity. The claim is that they can't afford to do something that they'd really like to do, something that is expressive of an identity they care about and want to sustain. This is a genuine problem, one that afflicts people in many communities: they're too poor to live the life they want to lead. If that's true, it's an argument for trying to see whether we can alleviate their poverty. But if they do get richer and they still run around in T-shirts, that is their choice. Talk of authenticity now just amounts to telling other people what they ought to value in their own traditions.

Not that this is likely to be a problem in the real world. People who can afford it mostly *like* to put on traditional garb—at least, from time to time. I was best man once at a Scottish wedding where the bridegroom wore a kilt and I wore kente cloth. Andrew Oransay, who piped us up the aisle, whispered in my ear at one point, "Here we all are then, in our tribal gear." In Kumasi, people who can afford them love to put on their kente, especially the most "traditional" ones, woven in colorful silk strips in the town of Bonwire, as they have been for a couple of centuries. (The prices are high in part because demand outside Asante has risen. A fine kente for a man now costs more than the average Ghanaian earns in a year. Is that bad? Not for the people of Bonwire.) But trying to find some primordially authentic culture can be like peeling an onion. The textiles most people think of as traditional West African cloths are known as java prints, as in the Indonesian island of Java, once a Dutch colony; they arrived with the Javanese batiks sold, and often milled, by the Dutch. The traditional garb of Herero women in Namibia derives from the attire of 19th-century German missionaries, though it's still unmistakably Herero, not least because the fabrics they use have a distinctly un-Lutheran range of colors. And so with our kente cloth: the silk was always imported, traded by Europeans, produced in Asia. This tradition was once an innovation. Should we reject *it* for that reason as untraditional? How far back must one go?

Cultures are made of continuities *and* changes, and the identity of a society can survive through these changes. Societies without change aren't more authentic; they're just dead. Pious talk of the authentic is often, in any case, wonderfully misdirected. Someone told me the other day the story of a collector of recipes who arrived in a Cambodian village yearning for authentic local cuisine. "Here's a dish" one of the locals began. "You take smoked tongue of water ox . . . well, if you can't get smoked water-ox tongue you can use shrimp." "No, no," the visitor said, "I want to follow exactly your authentic recipe." "Really," said the Cambodian, "we only use water-ox tongue because we can't get shrimp." I told this story not long ago to a friend of mine and he reminded me of a conversation he'd had with my octogenarian mother some years ago in Ghana—she was probably only in her seventies then. He had noticed that she could still bend down from her hips, keeping her back perfectly straight to pick things off the ground. "I imagine you learned that from living among Asante women, who have such wonderful posture." "Actually," my mother said, "It's because F.M. Alexander was our lodger in London when I was a young woman." F.M. Alexander being, of course, the Tasmanian inventor of the Alexander Technique, which is, as the Alexander Trust puts it on their Web site, "a method of mental and physical re-education, taught individually, which has the effect of reducing unnecessary tension in all human activity."[1]

Cosmopolitans don't need to endorse every appeal to cultural preservation; preserving culture—in the sense of artifacts—is one thing, preserving cultures is quite another. But my main topic today is another modern shibboleth: cultural patrimony. Given the history of empires, much of the culture we want to preserve lives now far away from the cultures that created it. And it's that fact that raises the issues I want to discuss.

Let me begin my story at home in Kumasi, the town in Ashanti where I grew up. In the 19th century, the kings of Asante—like kings everywhere—gathered objects from all around their kingdom and around the world, in part to enhance their own glory. When the British general, Sir Garnet Wolseley, destroyed Kumasi in a "punitive expedition" in 1874, he authorized the looting of the palace of the Asante King Kofi Karikari. At the treaty of Fomena, a few months later, Asante was required to pay an "indemnity" of nearly a ton and a half of gold, much of which was delivered in the form of jewelry and other regalia. A couple of decades later, a Major Robert Stephenson Smyth Baden-Powell (yes, you know him as the founder of the Boy Scouts) was dispatched once more to Kumasi, this time to demand that the new king, Prempeh, submit to British rule. Baden-Powell described this mission in his book, *The Downfall of Prempeh: A Diary of Life with the Native Levy in Ashanti, 1895–6.*

Once the king and his Queen Mother had made their submission, the British troops entered the palace, and, as Baden-Powell put it, "the work of collecting valuables and property was proceeded with." He continued:

> There could be no more interesting, no more tempting work than this. To poke about in a barbarian king's palace, whose wealth has been reported very great, was enough to make it so. Perhaps one of the most striking features about it was that the work of collecting the treasures was entrusted to a company of British soldiers, and that it was done most honestly and well, without a single case of looting. Here was a man with an armful of gold-hilted swords, there one with a box full

[1] *See* http://www.alexandertrust.org.uk.

of gold trinkets and rings, another with a spirit-case full of bottles of brandy, yet in no instance was there any attempt at looting.[2]

This boast will strike us as almost comical, but Baden-Powell clearly believed that the inventorying and removal of these treasures under the orders of a British officer was a legitimate transfer of property. It wasn't looting; it was *collecting*. In short order, Nana Prempeh was arrested and taken into exile at Cape Coast. More indemnities were paid.

The modern market in African art, indeed in art from much of the global south, is often a dispiriting sequel to these earlier imperial expropriations. Many of the poorest countries in the world simply do not have the resources to enforce the regulations they make. Mali can pass a law against digging up and exporting the wonderful sculpture of Djenne-jeno. But it can't enforce the law. And it certainly can't afford to fund thousands of archaeological digs. The result is that many fine Djenne-jeno terracottas were dug up anyway in the 1980s, after the publication of the discoveries of the archaeologists Roderick and Susan McIntosh and their team. They were sold to collectors in Europe and North America who rightly admired them. Because they were removed from archaeological sites illegally, much of what we would most like to know about this culture—much that we could have found out by careful archaeology—may now never be known.

Now, once the governments of the United States and Mali, guided by archaeologists, created laws specifically aimed at stopping the smuggling of the stolen art, the open market for Djenne-jeno sculpture largely ceased. But people have estimated that, in the meantime, perhaps a thousand pieces—some of them now valued at hundreds of thousands of dollars—left Mali illegally. Given these enormous prices, you can see why so many Malians were willing to help export their "national heritage."

Modern thefts have not, of course, been limited to the pillaging of archaeological sites. Hundreds of millions of dollars worth of art has been stolen from the museums of Nigeria alone, almost always with the complicity of insiders. And Ekpo Eyo, who once headed the National Museum of Nigeria, has rightly pointed out that dealers in New York and London have been less than eager to assist in their retrieval. Since many of these collections were well known to experts on Nigerian art, it shouldn't have taken the dealers long to recognize what was going on. Nor is such art theft limited to the Third World. Ask the government of Italy.

Given these circumstances—and this history—it has been natural to protest against the pillaging of "cultural patrimony."[3] Through a number of declarations from UNESCO and other international bodies, a doctrine has evolved concerning the ownership of many forms of cultural property. It is that, in simplest terms,

[2] Major Robert Stephenson Smyth Baden-Powell, *The Downfall of Prempeh: A Diary of Life with the Native Levy in Ashanti, 1895–6* 128–29 (1898).

[3] I owe a great deal to the cogent (and cosmopolitan!) outline of the development of the relevant international law in John Henry Merryman's classic article, *Two Ways of Thinking About Cultural Property,* 80 Am. J. Int'l L. 831 (1986).

cultural property be regarded as the property of its culture. If you belong to that culture, such work is, in the suggestive shorthand, your cultural patrimony.[4] If not, not.

Part of what makes this grand phrase so powerful, I suspect, is that it conflates, in confusing ways, the two primary uses of that confusing word "culture." It's the confusion we saw when we were thinking about preserving culture. On the one hand, cultural patrimony refers to cultural artifacts: works of art, religious relics, manuscripts, crafts, musical instruments, and the like. Here "culture" is whatever people make and invest with significance through the exercise of their human creativity. Since significance is something produced through conventions, which are never individual and rarely universal, interpreting culture in this sense requires some knowledge of its social and historical context. On the other hand, "cultural patrimony" refers to the products of a culture: the group from whose conventions the object derives its significance. Here the objects are understood to belong to a particular group, heirs to a trans-historical identity, whose patrimony they are. The cultural patrimony of Nigeria, then, is not just Nigeria's contribution to human culture—its voices in our noisy human chorus, its contribution, as the French might say, to the civilization of the universal. Rather, it is all the artifacts produced by Nigerians, conceived of as a historically persisting people: and while the rest of us may *admire* Nigeria's patrimony, it belongs, in the end, to them.

But what does it mean, exactly, for something to belong to a people? Most of Nigeria's cultural patrimony was produced before the modern Nigerian state existed. We don't know whether Nok sculptures were commissioned by kings or commoners; we don't know whether the people who made them and the people who paid for them thought of them as belonging to the kingdom, to a man, to a lineage, to the gods. One thing we know for sure, however, is they didn't make them for Nigeria.

Indeed, a great deal of what people wish to protect as "cultural patrimony" was made before the modern system of nations came into being, by members of societies that no longer exist. People die when their bodies die. Cultures, by contrast, can die without physical extinction. So there's no reason to think that the Nok have no descendants. But if Nok civilization came to an end, and its people became something else, why should those descendants have a special claim on those objects, buried in the forest and forgotten for so long? And, even if they do have a special claim, what has that got to do with Nigeria, where, let us suppose, a majority of those descendants now live?

---

[4] Someone at the conference suggested that "patrimony" was not a word frequently used in UNESCO discussions. Actually, you can find it quite often on the official Web site. But there's a reason why it doesn't occur more often: the standard U.N. translation of the French *patrimoine* (and its Spanish cognate) is "heritage." But this is somewhat misleading, I think, since *patrimoine* has the sense of inheritance and not just of heritage. Only an Anglophone who spent all her time at UNESCO meetings with earphones on during French and Spanish contributions could think patrimony a non-UNESCO word!

Perhaps the matter of biological descent is a distraction: proponents of the patrimony argument would surely be undeterred if it turned out that the Nok sculptures were made by eunuchs. They could reply that the Nok sculptures were found on the territory of Nigeria. And it is, indeed, a perfectly reasonable property rule that where something of value is dug up and nobody can establish an existing claim on it, the government gets to decide what to do with it. It's an equally sensible idea that the object's being of cultural value places on the government a special obligation to preserve it. Given that it is the Nigerian government, they will naturally focus on preserving it for Nigerians (most of whom, not thinking of themselves as heirs to Nok civilization, will probably think it about as interesting as art from anywhere else). But if it is of cultural value—as the Nok sculptures undoubtedly are—it strikes me that it would be better for them to think of themselves as trustees for humanity. While the government of Nigeria reasonably exercises trusteeship, the Nok sculptures belong in the deepest sense to all of us. "Belong" here is a metaphor, of course: I just mean that the Nok sculptures are of potential value to all human beings.

That idea is expressed in the Preamble of the Convention for the Protection of Cultural Property in the Event of Armed Conflict of 1954, which came out of a conference called by UNESCO, as follows:

> Being convinced that damage to cultural property belonging to any people whatsoever means damage to the cultural heritage of all mankind, since each people makes its contribution to the culture of the world.[5]

Framing the problem that way—as an issue for *all* mankind—should make it plain that it is the value of the cultural property to people and not to peoples that matters. It isn't peoples who experience and value art; it's men and women. Once you see that, then there's no reason why a Spanish museum couldn't or shouldn't preserve a Norse goblet, legally acquired, let us suppose at a Dublin auction, after the salvage of a Viking shipwreck off Ireland. It's a contribution to the cultural heritage of the world. But at any particular time it has to be in one place. Don't Spaniards have a case for being able to experience Viking craftsmanship? After all, there's already an awful lot of Viking stuff in Norway. The logic of "cultural patrimony," however, would call for it to be shipped back to Norway (or, at any rate, to Scandinavia): that's whose cultural patrimony it is.

And, in various ways, we've inched closer to that position in the years since the Hague Convention. The Convention on the Means of Prohibiting and Preventing the Illicit Import, Export and Transfer of Ownership of Cultural Property, adopted by the UNESCO General Conference in Paris in 1970,[6]

---

[5] Convention for the Protection of Cultural Property in the Event of Armed Conflict, pmbl. (May 14, 1954), *available at* http://portal.unesco.org/en/ev.php-URL_ID=13637&URL_DO=DO_TOPIC&URL_SECTION=201.html.

[6] UNESCO Convention on the Means of Prohibiting and Preventing the Illicit Import, Export, and Transfer of Ownership of Cultural Property (Nov. 14, 1970), *available at* http://portal.unesco.org/en/ev.php-URL_ID=13039&URL_DO=DO_TOPIC&URL_SECTION=201.html.

stipulated that "cultural property constitutes one of the basic elements of civilization and national culture, and that its true value can be appreciated only in relation to the fullest possible information regarding its origin, history and traditional setting"; and that "it is essential for every State to become increasingly alive to the moral obligations to respect its own cultural heritage." A state's cultural heritage, it further decreed, included both work "created by the individual or collective genius of nationals of the State" and "cultural property found within the national territory." The convention emphasized, accordingly, the importance of "prohibiting and preventing the illicit import, export and transfer of ownership of cultural property." A number of countries now declare all antiquities that originate within their borders to be state property, which cannot be freely exported. In Italy, private citizens are free to own "cultural property," but not to send it abroad.[7]

Plainly, special problems are posed by objects, like Nok art, where there is, as the lawyers might say, no continuity of title. If we don't know who last owned a thing, we need a rule as to what should happen to it now. Where objects have this special status as a valuable "contribution to the culture of the world," the rule should be one that protects that object and makes it available to people who will benefit from experiencing it. So the rule of "finders, keepers," which may make sense for objects of less significance, will not do. Still, a sensible regime will reward those who find such objects and give them an incentive to report not only what they have found but where and how they found it.

For an object from an archaeological site, after all, value comes often as much from the knowledge to be gleaned by knowing where it came out of the ground, what else was around it, how it lay in the earth. Since these articles usually don't have current owners, someone needs to regulate the process of removing them from the ground and decide where they should go. As I have said, it seems to me reasonable that the decision should be made by the government in whose soil they are found. But the right conclusion for them is not obviously that they should always stay exactly where they lay. Many Egyptians—overwhelmingly Muslims who regard the religion of the Pharaohs as idolatrous—nevertheless insist that all the antiquities ever exported from its borders are really theirs. You do not need to endorse Napoleon's depredations of North Africa to think that there is something to be said for allowing people in other countries the chance to see close up the arts of one of the world's great civilizations. And it's a painful irony that one reason we've lost information about cultural antiquities is the very regulation intended to preserve it. If, for example, I sell you a figure from Djenne-jeno with evidence that it came out of the ground in a certain place after the regulations came into force, then I am giving the authorities in the United States, who are committed to the restitution of objects taken illegally out of Mali, the very evidence they need.

Suppose that, from the beginning, Mali had been encouraged and helped by UNESCO to exercise its trusteeship of these Djenne-jeno terracottas by licensing digs and training people to recognize that objects removed carefully

[7] James Cuno, *U.S. Art Museums and Cultural Property*, 16 Conn. J. Int'l L. 189 (2001).

from the earth with accurate records of location are worth more, even to collectors, than objects without this essential element of provenance. Suppose they had required that objects be recorded and registered before leaving and stipulated that if the national museum wished to keep an object, it would have to pay a market price for it, and the acquisition fund had been supported by a tax on the price of the exported objects. The digs encouraged by this regime would have been worse than proper, professionally conducted digs by accredited archaeologists. Some people would still have avoided the rules. But mightn't all this have been better than what actually happened? Suppose, further, that the Malians had decided that in order to maintain and build their collections, they should auction off some works they own. The cultural patrimony purists, instead of praising them for committing needed resources to protecting the national collection, would have excoriated them for betraying their heritage.

The problem for Mali is not that it doesn't have enough Malian art. The problem is that it doesn't have enough money. In the short run, allowing Mali to stop the export of a good deal of the art in its territory does have the positive effect of making sure that there is some world-class art in Mali for Malians to experience. But an experience limited to Malian art—or, anyway, art made on territory that's now part of Mali—makes no more sense for a Malian than it does for anyone else. New technologies mean that Malians can now see, in however imperfectly reproduced a form, great art from around the planet. If UNESCO had spent as much effort to make it possible for great art to get into Mali as it has done to stop great art getting out, it would have been serving better the interests that Malians, like all people, have in a cosmopolitan aesthetic experience.

How would the concept of cultural patrimony apply to cultural objects whose current owners acquired them legally in the normal way? You live in Ibadan, in the heart of Yorubaland in Nigeria. It's the early sixties. You buy a painted carving from a guy—an actor, painter, sculptor, all-round artist—who calls himself "Twin Seven Seven." Your family thinks it's a strange way to spend money. Time passes, and he comes to be seen as one of Nigeria's most important modern artists. More cultural patrimony for Nigeria, right? And if it's Nigeria's, it's not yours. So why can't the Nigerian government just take it, as the natural trustees of the Nigerian people, whose property it is?

Now the Nigerians would not in fact exercise their power in this way. (When antiquities are involved, though, a number of other states will do so.) They are also committed, after all, to the idea of private property. Of course, if you were interested in selling, they might provide the resources for a public museum to buy it from you (though the government of Nigeria, at least, probably thinks it has more pressing calls on its treasury). So far, cultural property is just like any other property. Suppose, though, that they didn't want to pay. There's something else they could do. If you sold your artwork, and the buyer, whatever his nationality, wanted to take the painting out of Nigeria, they could refuse permission to export it. The effect of the international regulations is to say that Nigerian cultural patrimony can be kept in Nigeria. An Italian law (passed, by the way, under Mussolini) permits her government to deny export to any artwork currently owned by an Italian, even if it's a Jasper John painting of the American flag. But then most countries require export licenses for significant cultural property (generally excepting the work of living artists). So much for being the cultural patrimony of humankind.

Such cases are particularly troublesome, because Twin Seven Seven wouldn't have been the creator that he was if he'd been unaware of and unaffected by the work of artists in other places. If the argument for cultural patrimony is that the art belongs to the culture that gives it its significance, most art doesn't belong to a national culture at all. Much of the greatest art is flamboyantly international; much ignores nationality altogether. Early modern European art was court art, or it was church art. It was made not for nations or peoples but for princes or popes or *ad majorem gloriam dei*. And the artists who made it came from all over Europe. More importantly, in the line often ascribed to Picasso, good artists copy, great ones steal; and they steal from everywhere. Does Picasso himself—a Spaniard—get to be part of the cultural patrimony of the Republic of the Congo, home of the Vili, one of whose carvings the Frenchman Matisse showed him at the home of the American Gertrude Stein?

The problem was already there in the Preamble to the 1954 Hague Convention that I quoted a little while back: "*each people* makes its contribution to the culture of the world."[8] That sounds like whenever someone makes a contribution, his or her "people" makes a contribution, too. And there's something odd, to my mind, about thinking of Hindu temple sculpture or Michelangelo and Raphael's frescos in the Vatican as the contribution of a people rather than the contribution of the individuals who made (and, if you like, paid for) them. I know that Michelangelo made a contribution to the culture of the world. I've gazed in wonder at the ceiling of the Sistine Chapel. I will grant that Their Holinesses Popes Julius II, Leo X, Clement the VIII, and Paul III, who paid him, made a contribution, too. But which *people* exactly made that contribution? The people of the Papal States? The people of Michelangelo's native Caprese? The Italians?

This is clearly the wrong way to think about the matter. The right way is to take not a national but a trans-national perspective—to ask what system of international rules about objects of this sort will respect the many legitimate human interests at stake. The point of many sculptures and paintings, the reason they were made and bought, was that they should be looked at and lived with. Each of us has an interest in being able, should we choose, to live with art; and that interest is not limited to the art of our own "people." Now, if an object acquires a wider significance, as part, say, of the oeuvre of a major artist, then other people will have a more substantial interest in being able to experience it and to the knowledge derived from its study. The object's aesthetic value is not fully captured by its value as private property. So you might think there was a case for giving people an incentive to share it. In America such incentives abound. You can get a tax deduction by giving a painting to a museum. You get social kudos from lending your art to shows, where they can be labeled

[8] *See supra* note 5.

"from the collection of. . . ." And, finally, where an object is a masterpiece, you can earn a good sum by selling it at auction, while both allowing the curious a temporary window of access and providing for a new owner the pleasures you have already known. If it is good to share art in these ways with others, the cosmopolitan asks, why should the sharing cease at national borders?

When we're trying to interpret the concept of cultural property, we ignore at our peril what lawyers, at least, know: property is an institution, created largely by laws, which are best designed by thinking about how they can serve the human interests of those whose behavior they govern. If the laws are international laws, then they govern everyone. And the human interests in question are the interests of all of humankind. However self-serving it may seem, the British Museum's claim to be a repository of the heritage not of Britain but of the world seems to me exactly right. The current director of the museum is rightly fond of reminding the British that Sir Hans Sloane left the 71,000 or so objects in his collection, his herbarium, and his library to George II for the nation, on condition that they paid £20,000 to his heirs. If they didn't, Sloane's will said, it should be offered to learned academies in other European countries. Sloane was clear, then, from the start, that his cosmopolitan collection was held in trust by the British—and could equally as well have been held in trust by the Prussian or the Russian academies—for all of humankind. Part of the obligation, though, is to make those collections more widely available not just in London but elsewhere, through traveling collections, through publications, and through the World Wide Web.

It has been too easy to lose sight of the global constituency. The distinguished legal scholar John Henry Merryman—whose work anyone who thinks about cultural property surely knows—once offered a litany of examples of how laws and treaties relating to cultural property have betrayed a properly cosmopolitan (he uses the word "internationalist") perspective. "Any cultural internationalist would oppose the removal of monumental sculptures from Mayan sites where physical damage or the loss of artistic integrity or cultural information would probably result, whether the removal was illegally or legally, but incompetently, done," he writes. "The same cultural internationalist, however, might wish that Mexico would sell or trade or lend some of its reputedly large hoard of unused *Chac-Mols*, pots and other objects to foreign collectors or museums." And though we readily deplore the theft of paintings from Italian churches, "if a painting is rotting in a church from lack of resources to care for it, and the priest sells it for money to repair the roof and in the hope that the purchaser will give the painting the care it needs, then the problem begins to look different."[9]

So when I lament the modern thefts from Nigerian museums or Malian archaeological sites or the imperial ones from Asante, it's because the property rights that were trampled upon in these cases flow from laws that I think are reasonable. I am not for sending every object "home." Much Asante art now in Europe, America, and Japan was sold or given by people who had the right to alienate them under the laws that then prevailed, laws that, as I say, were

[9] Merryman, *supra* note 3, at 852.

perfectly reasonable. The mere fact that something you own is important to the descendants of people who gave it away does not generally give them an entitlement to it. (Even less should you return it to people who don't want it because a committee in Paris has declared it their patrimony.) It is a fine gesture to return things to the descendants of their makers—or to offer it to them for sale—but it certainly isn't a duty. You might also show your respect for the culture it came from by holding on to it because you value it yourself. Furthermore, because cultural property has a value for all of us, it can be reasonable to insist that those to whom it is returned are in a position to take trusteeship; repatriation of some objects to poor countries whose priorities cannot be with their museum budgets might just lead to their decay. Were I advising a poor community pressing for the return of many ritual objects, I might urge them to consider whether leaving some of them to be respectfully displayed in other countries might not be part of their contribution to the cosmopolitan enterprise of cross-cultural understanding as well as a way to ensure their survival for later generations.

To be sure, there are various cases where repatriation makes sense. We won't, however, need the concept of cultural patrimony to understand them. Consider, for example, objects whose meaning would be deeply enriched by being returned to the context from which they were taken—site-specific art of one kind and another. Here there is an aesthetic argument for return. Or take objects of contemporary ritual significance that were acquired legally from people around the world in the course of European colonial expansion. If an object is central to the cultural or religious life of a community, there *is* a human reason for it to find its place back with them. The communities in question are almost never national communities; still, the states within which they lie may be their natural representatives in negotiating their return. Such cases are bound to be messy: it will often be unclear if a work is site-specific or how an outsider should judge whether something is central to a community's religious life. Law, whether national or international, may well not be the best way to settle these questions.

But the clearest cases for repatriation are those where objects were stolen from people whose names we often know; people whose heirs, like the King of Asante, would like them back. As someone who grew up in Kumasi, I confess I was pleased when some of this stolen art was returned, thus enriching the new palace museum for locals and for tourists. (A hearty Asante thank you—yé dase pee—to His Royal Highness Prince Charles.) One of the many symbols that recurs regularly in Asante iconography is a little bird, with its head turned back to pick at the feathers between its wings, a bird called sanköfa, which means, literally, "Go back and get." There's a Twi proverb that says:

> Woto twene na wosan köfa a, yénkyiri.
> If you throw (something) away and you go back and take it, it is not taboo.

The proverb, which you hear often, can be used to say, of course, that it is good to retrieve what you need from the past. Still, I don't think we should demand everything back, even everything that was stolen, not least because we haven't the remotest chance of getting it. Don't waste your time insisting on getting what you can't get. There must be another Twi proverb with that message.

There is, however, a more important reason: I actually want museums in Europe to be able to show the riches of the society they plundered in the years when my grandfather was a young man. I'd rather that we negotiated as restitution not just the major objects of significance for our history—things that make the best sense in the palace museum at Manhyia—but a decent collection of art from around the world. Because perhaps the greatest of the many ironies of the sacking of Kumasi in 1874 is that it deprived my hometown of a collection that was, in fact, splendidly cosmopolitan. As Sir Garnet Wolseley prepared to loot and then blow up the *Aban*, the large stone building in the city's center, European and American journalists were allowed to wander through it. The British *Daily Telegraph* described it as "the museum, for museum it should be called, where the art treasures of the monarchy were stored." The London *Times's* Winwood Reade wrote that each of its rooms "was a perfect Old Curiosity Shop." "Books in many languages," he continued, "Bohemian glass, clocks, silver plate, old furniture, Persian rugs, Kidderminster carpets, pictures and engravings, numberless chests and coffers . . . With these were many specimens of Moorish and Ashantee handicraft." The *New York Herald* augmented the list: "yataghans and scimitars of Arabic make, Damask bed-curtains and counterpanes, English engravings, an oil painting of a gentleman, an old uniform of a West Indian soldier, brass blunderbusses, prints from illustrated newspapers, and, among much else, copies of the *London Times* . . . for 17 October 1843."

We shouldn't become overly sentimental about these matters. Many of the treasures in the *Aban* were no doubt war booty as well. Still it will be a long time before Kumasi has a collection as rich both in our own material culture and in works from other places as those destroyed by Sir Garnet Wolseley and the founder of the Boy Scouts. The *Aban* had been completed in 1822. It was a prize project of the Asantehene Osei Bonsu. And how had this Asante king hit upon the project in the first place? Apparently, he had been deeply impressed by what he'd heard about the British Museum.[10]

Cosmopolitanism starts with what is human in humanity. So we understand the urge to bring these objects "home." We, too, feel what Walter Benjamin called the "aura" of the work of art, which has to do with its uniqueness, its singularity. In this age of mechanical reproduction, Benjamin noticed, where we can make good facsimiles of anything, the original has only increased in value. It is relatively easy nowadays to make a copy of the Mona Lisa so good that merely looking at it—as you would look at the original in the Louvre—you could not tell the copy from the original. But only the original has the aura: only it has the connection with the hand of Leonardo. That is why millions of people, who could have spent their plane fare on buying a great reproduction,

[10] The quotations from the *Daily Telegraph, London Times,* and *New York Herald,* as well as the information about Osei Bonsu are all from Ivor Wilks, Asante in the Nineteenth Century: The Structure and Evolution of a Political Order 200–01 (1975).

have been to the Louvre. They want the aura. It is a kind of magic; and it is the same kind of magic that nations feel towards their history. A Norwegian thinks of the Norsemen as his ancestors. She wants not just to know what their swords look like but to stand close to an actual sword, wielded in actual battles, forged by a particular smith. Some of the heirs to the kingdom of Benin, the people of South West Nigeria, want the bronze their ancestors cast, shaped, handled, wondered at. They would like to wonder at—if we will not let them touch—that very thing. The connection people feel to cultural objects that are symbolically theirs, because they were produced from within a world of meaning created by their ancestors—the connection to art through identity—is powerful. It should be acknowledged. The cosmopolitan, though, wants to remind us of other connections.

One connection—the one neglected in talk of cultural patrimony—is the connection not *through* identity but *despite* difference. We can respond to art that is not ours; indeed, we can only fully respond to "our" art if we move beyond thinking of it as ours and start to respond to it as art. But equally important is the human connection. My people—human beings—made the Great Wall of China, the Chrysler Building, the Sistine Chapel: these things were made by creatures like me, through the exercise of skill and imagination. I do not have those skills, and my imagination spins different dreams. Nevertheless, that potential is also in me. The connection through a local identity is as imaginary as the connection through humanity. The Nigerian's link to the Benin bronze, like mine is, indeed, a connection made in the imagination; but to speak of these connections as imagined isn't to pronounce them unreal. They are surely among the realest connections we have.

CHAPTER 11
THIEVES OF BAGHDAD: THE SEARCH FOR IRAQ'S STOLEN HERITAGE

Colonel Matthew Bogdanos*

A. INTRODUCTION

As the head of the investigation into one of the greatest art crimes in recent memory—the looting of the Iraq Museum in 2003—I have spent more than five years attempting to recover and return to the Iraqi people their priceless heritage.[1] I have spent almost as much time, however, attempting to correct the almost universal misconceptions about what happened at the museum in those fateful days in April 2003, to increase awareness of the continuing cultural catastrophe that is represented by the illegal trade in stolen antiquities, and to highlight the need for the concerted and cooperative efforts of the international community to preserve, protect, and recover the shared cultural heritage of all humanity.

Indeed, in more than 200 speeches in more than 130 cities in 15 countries—in venues ranging from universities, museums, and governmental organizations to law enforcement agencies, Interpol (the International Criminal Police Organization) and both houses of the British Parliament—I have urged a more active role for governments, international organizations, cultural organizations and foundations, and the art community. I have not been very successful. Most governments have their hands full combating terrorism, with few resources left to spare for tracking down stolen artifacts. Most international organizations are content to issue proclamations, preferring to hit the conference center rather than the streets. Many cultural organizations and foundations are equally content to issue a call for papers rather than a call to action. As for the art community, some members wash their hands of unpleasant realities and argue that, while technically illegal, the market in purloined antiquities is benign—victimless—as long as it brings the art to those who can properly protect it and appreciate it (namely, themselves).

* Parts of the following chapter are adapted from MATTHEW BOGDANOS, THIEVES OF BAGHDAD: ONE MARINE'S PASSION TO RECOVER THE WORLD'S GREATEST STOLEN TREASURES (2005). Reprinted by permission of Bloomsbury USA. All his royalties from *Thieves of Baghdad* go to the Iraq Museum.

[1] *See* Matthew Bogdanos, *The Casualties of War: The Truth about the Iraq Museum*, 109 AM. J. ARCHAEOLOGY 477, 477–79 (2005).

And as the investigation continues, much has happened to reinforce the core lesson we learned in the back alleys of Baghdad: the genteel patina covering the world of antiquities rests atop a solid base of criminal activity. Witness the events that have taken place in the United States alone since 2003. In New York, the Metropolitan Museum of Art (the "Met") accepted what amounted to a plea bargain with Italian authorities—agreeing to return 21 antiquities that the Italian government said were stolen, including one of the Met's most prized items: The Euphronios krater, a sixth-century B.C.E. Greek vase.[2] In Missouri, the St. Louis Art Museum broke off negotiations with Egypt over the museum's possession of a 13th-century B.C.E. pharaonic mask that Egyptian authorities claimed was stolen and smuggled illegally out of their country.[3] In California, the director of the J. Paul Getty Museum agreed to recommend to its trustees that the Getty return antiquities the Greek government says were stolen—while Marion True, the Getty's longtime curator for ancient art, resigned and is currently on trial in Rome on charges of conspiracy to receive a completely different set of stolen artifacts.[4] More trials are sure to follow.

I am delighted that nations are moving to reclaim their patrimony. I am also delighted to see media attention beginning to illuminate certain well-appointed shadows where money changes hands and legitimate—but inconvenient—questions of the provenance (origin) of the object are too frequently considered outré.

But shadows remain. In March 2006, for example, private collector Shelby White donated $200 million to New York University to establish an ancient studies institute, prompting one of the university's professors to resign in protest over what he considered the questionable acquisition practices of the donor.[5] Ms. White and her late husband, Leon Levy, have generated considerable debate since at least 1990, when the Met (of which Ms. White is a trustee) presented a major exhibition of 200 of their artifacts from Greece, Rome, and the Near East.[6] The Met did so despite the fact that a study later published in the *American Journal of Archaeology* determined that more than 90 percent of those artifacts had no known provenance whatsoever.[7] As with the Euphronios krater, Italian authorities have consistently maintained that they can prove many of the antiquities in the Levy-White collection were illegally excavated (in other words, stolen) and smuggled out of their country.[8]

---

[2] *See* Randy Kennedy & Hugh Eakin, *The Met, Ending 30-Year Stance Is Set to Yield Prized Vase to Italy*, N.Y. TIMES, Feb. 3, 2006, at A1.

[3] *See* Malcolm Gay, *Out of Egypt*, RIVERFRONT TIMES (St. Louis, Mo.), Feb. 15, 2006.

[4] *See* Christopher Reynolds, *The Puzzle of Marion True*, L.A. TIMES, Oct. 31, 2005, at E1.

[5] *See* Elisabetta Povoledo, *Top Collector is Asked to Relinquish Artifacts*, N.Y. TIMES, Nov. 29, 2006, at E1.

[6] *See id.*

[7] *See* Kate Taylor, *Shelby White in Center Court at the Met*, N.Y. SUN, May 1, 2007, at 3. *See generally* Christopher Chippindale & David W.J. Gill, *Material Consequences of Contemporary Classical Collecting*, 104 AM. J. ARCHAEOLOGY 463 (2000). In this ground-breaking study, the authors analyzed seven celebrated collections and exhibitions in terms of their provenance (as defined in terms of an object's origins, or find spot, and its history since its unearthing) and concluded that the overwhelming majority had no declared or credible find spots and simply surfaced as orphans without history.

[8] *See* Povoledo, *supra* note 5.

Not only did the Met proudly display that collection, dubious provenance notwithstanding, but it also (coincidentally?) celebrated the opening of its new Leon Levy and Shelby White Court for Hellenistic and Roman antiquities on April 15, 2007.[9] Other institutions continue to hold out one hand while covering their eyes with the other. In 2000, Cornell University accepted a gift from well-known collector Jonathan Rosen of 1,679 cuneiform tablets from Ur.[10] They said, "Thank you very much," despite reports of widespread looting at Ur after the 1991 Persian Gulf War and despite the fact that the provenance of 10 percent of the tablets consisted of the phrase "uncertain sites."[11] Harvard University has done equally well in neglecting to ask awkward questions—witness its Shelby White-Leon Levy Program for Archaeological Publications.[12]

But this is nothing new. In 1994, a decade before its current imbroglio, the Getty displayed a major exhibition of classical antiquities owned by Lawrence and Barbara Fleischman.[13] Like the Met, the Getty proudly held this exhibit despite the fact that 92 percent of the objects in the Fleischman collection had no provenance whatsoever, and the remaining 8 percent had questionable provenance at best.[14] To put it in starker terms, of 295 catalogued entries, not a single object had a declared archeological find spot and only three (1 percent) were even described as coming from a specific location. Sometimes, however, the questionable practices extend beyond merely willful ignorance. Consider the following. Prior to the exhibition in 1994, the Fleischman collection had never been published. Thus, the first catalogue for, and hence first publication of, the Fleischman exhibit was the Getty's—of which Ms. Fleischman was a trustee. Fewer than two years later, the Getty purchased part of that collection for U.S.$20 million.[15] But the Getty had a stated policy of not purchasing objects unless they have been previously displayed in published collections.

How, then, could they possibly have justified the acquisition? Easy: the Getty was quick to point out that the collection had been published just two years earlier—by themselves. Further sweetening the deal, while the collection had been purchased originally at a much lower price, it was valued at U.S.$80 million at the time of the sale to the museum.[16] Tax laws use the fair market value at the time of the sale rather than the original purchase price in determining the value of a bequest. As a result, the difference between the 1996 valuation of U.S.$80 million and the U.S.$20 million sale price to the Getty would be deemed a gift of U.S.$60 million—affording a $60 million tax deduction for the Fleischmans. Under these terms, the gift to the Getty,

---

9 *See* Taylor, *supra* note 7, at 3.

10 *See* Martin Gottlieb & Barry Meier, *Ancient Art at the Met Raises Old Ethical Questions*, N.Y. Times, Aug. 2, 2003, at A1.

11 *See id.*

12 *See* Robin Pogrebin, *US$200 Million Gift Prompts a Debate Over Antiquities*, N.Y. Times, Apr. 1, 2006, at A1.

13 *See* Jason Felch & Ralph Frammolino, *The Return of Antiquities a Blow to Getty*, L.A. Times, Aug. 2, 2007, at A1.

14 *See* Chippindale & Gill, *supra* note 7.

15 *See* Felch & Frammolino, *supra* note 13.

16 *See id.*

therefore, was actually financed by U.S. taxpayers. Enron's accounting team could not have done a better job.

In many respects, then, we have advanced very little since the imperial 19th century, when Lord Elgin could haul away the Parthenon Sculptures (now in the British Museum and commonly referred to as the "Elgin Marbles"), and Henry Layard could haul away the Nineveh reliefs (now in the Met). Despite the hue and cry of the last several years, the Met's current policy is to require documentation covering only the last ten years of an object's history.[17] This, even though most institutions view 1970—the year of the landmark UNESCO convention[18] to regulate the transfer of antiquities—as the cut-off date for requiring proof that an antiquity was not illegally looted.[19]

The imposition of a firm date (here, 1970) is crucial in stopping the trade in illegal antiquities. As each year passes, it becomes less and less likely that a previously unpublished (and hence unknown) antiquity can appear on the market and be legal—either in the sense of having come from a properly sanctioned excavation or from some ancient collection that was assembled before the imposition of any requirement of documentation. To put it another way, as each year passes, it becomes increasingly certain that previously unpublished items are stolen.

Thus, the Met's policy of requiring documentation covering only the last ten years of an object's history becomes more unsupportable as each year passes. For example, in May of 2013, the Met could begin to buy items stolen from the Iraq Museum in April 2003 without violating its stated policy. All it need do is not ask where it comes from before the ten-year window. As if to flaunt the Met's policy of "see no evil," Philippe de Montebello, the museum's director, told the *New York Times* in February 2006 that the context in which an artifact is found is virtually meaningless; in his opinion, it accounts for less than 2 percent of what we can learn from antiquity.[20] His position is as absurd as the equally unreasonable view of some purists that context is everything.[21]

But far from this world of museum receptions and limos waiting at the curb, however, there has been an even more troubling development. In June 2005, U.S. Marines in northwest Iraq arrested five insurgents holed up in underground bunkers filled with automatic weapons, ammunition stockpiles, black uniforms, ski masks, and night-vision goggles. Along with these tools of their trade, were 30 vases, cylinder seals, and statuettes that had been stolen from the Iraq Museum. Since then, the scenario has been repeated many times. It does not take a counter-terrorism expert to detect the sinister adjustment that

---

[17] *See generally* The Metropolitan Museum of Art, http://www.metmuseum.org (last visited Feb. 25, 2008).

[18] Convention on the Means of Prohibiting and Preventing the Illicit Import, Export and Transfer of Ownership of Cultural Property, Nov. 14, 1970, 823 U.N.T.S. 231.

[19] *See* Pogrebin, *supra* note 12.

[20] Randy Kennedy & Hugh Eakin, *Met Chief, Unbowed, Defends Museum's Role*, N.Y. Times, Feb. 28, 2006, at E1.

[21] *See id.*

has taken place. In 2003, when pursuing leads to recover antiquities, we usually came across weapons and links to violent groups. Now, as security forces pursue leads for weapons and insurgents, they find antiquities. In a modern-day version of the old "molasses to rum to slaves" triangle trade of pious New England ship captains and owners who sang hymns and offered prayers while getting rich off human misery, the cozy cabal of academics, dealers, and collectors who turn a blind eye to the illicit side of the trade is, in effect, supporting the insurgents who are killing coalition troops in Iraq.

This is not surprising. As the National Commission on Terrorist Attacks Upon the United States ("the 9-11 Commission") noted, international law enforcement has aggressively attacked traditional means of terrorist financing by freezing assets and neutralizing charities that had previously served as fronts for jihadists.[22] But terrorists are nothing if not adaptive. In late 2005, the German newspaper *Der Spiegel* reported that 9/11 conspirator Mohammed Atta had approached a professor at the University of Goettingen trying to sell Afghan antiquities to raise money to buy an airplane.[23] While nothing came of that inquiry, times have changed. Like the Taliban in Afghanistan who have learned to finance their activities through opium, insurgents in Iraq have discovered a new source of income in Iraq's cash crop: antiquities.

We do not have hard numbers—the traffic in art for arms is still too recent a phenomenon, and some of the investigations remain classified because of the connection to terrorists. But this illicit trade has become a growing source of revenue for the insurgents, ranking just below kidnappings for ransom and "protection" money from local residents and merchants. Iraq is a war zone, but it is also the cradle of civilization, with more than 10,000 poorly guarded archaeological sites.[24] Among the most prized items from those sites are cylinder seals, intricately carved pieces of stone about the size of a piece of chalk, which can sell for $250,000, enabling an insurgent to smuggle millions of dollars in his pocket. Given this almost limitless supply of antiquities, the insurgency appears to have found an income stream sufficiently secure to make any chief financial officer sleep well at night. As a result, the desert night is filled with the roar of bulldozers ripping into the ancient mounds of clay that were once thriving cities.

All the while, the situation in Iraq in the years following 2003 deteriorated dramatically, seemingly descending into chaos and causing most of the international community and many in the United States to call for equally dramatic—if not complete—withdrawal of forces from Iraq. Even in 2008—and despite the fact that most knowledgeable participants and observers recognize significant advances in Iraq since the onset of the much heralded surge in U.S. combat forces—a majority of the U.S. electorate seems increasingly reluctant to risk American blood to save Iraqi lives. So it is a pretty tough sell to ask people

---

[22] *See* Col. Matthew Bogdanos, Op-Ed., *The Terrorist in the Art Gallery*, N.Y. TIMES, Dec. 10, 2005, at A15.

[23] *See Art for Financing Terrorism?*, DER SPIEGEL (F.R.G.), July 18, 2005, at 20.

[24] *See* Bogdanos, *supra* note 22, at A15.

to care about a bunch of old rocks with funny writing. Finding the political will to divert resources to saving cultural artifacts, no matter how precious, seems like cutting funding for police and fire in order to expand the public library. There might be a case for it, but when? After all, looting has always been a cottage industry in Iraq, the region that gave birth not just to agriculture, cities, the wheel, and pottery, but to war and conquest as well.

The argument for protecting artifacts takes on added strength when we recognize that we are where we are today, not just because of our failure to provide sufficient security to overcome the long-festering tribal and religious animosities, but also because of our continuing failure to appreciate the importance Iraqis place on the preservation of their history. This failure to protect a rich heritage going back to the dawn of civilization has convinced many in Iraq and the Middle East that we do not care about any culture other than our own. And their belief is continually reinforced: five years after the initial looting—and despite having recovered almost 6,000 antiquities since then—we cannot keep pace with the artifacts that are being looted every day.

B. PROTECT ARCHAEOLOGICAL SITES

Based on my experience in both counter-terrorism and law enforcement—and as a result of the time I have spent in Iraq and throughout the world in tracking down the stolen antiquities—I submit that the first order of business in addressing this catastrophe must be to protect the archaeological sites. Some of these, such as Babylon and Nimrud, require several hundred guards and support staff for protection around the clock. The math is daunting: country-wide, more than 50,000 personnel are required, along with the necessary vehicles, radios, weapons, and logistical needs. But there is an immediate solution.

In other contexts, the United Nations and the North Atlantic Treaty Organisation (NATO) have acted to address catastrophic situations. In Bosnia, Cyprus, and Afghanistan, for example, many countries have provided contingents for specific missions under United Nations or NATO auspices. But not in Iraq. The reasons are much-argued, and I will not revisit them here.

Recalling Voltaire's observation that "every man is guilty of all the good he didn't do," I will focus instead on what we can do now.

So who might act? In the past, most archaeological excavations in Iraq have had foreign sponsorship—the Germans at Babylon and Uruk, the British at Ur and Nimrud, the French at Kish and Lagash, the Italians at Hatra and Nimrud, the Americans at Nippur and Ur.[25] Leveraging this history, I propose that these (and eventually other) countries provide forces to protect Iraq's archaeological sites until a professional Iraqi security force dedicated to the sites can be recruited, equipped, and trained.

Under this proposal—with the permission of the Iraqi government, facilitated by the U.S. military, and under the authority of the United Nations or NATO—each country would "adopt" a site.

---

[25] *See* Col. Matthew Bogdanos, Op-Ed., *Fighting for Iraq's Culture*, N.Y. TIMES, Mar. 6, 2007, at A21.

After sending an assessment team to the assigned sites to determine the precise numbers and type of personnel and equipment required, each donor nation would then draft and sign bilateral status of forces agreements with Iraq, outlining the rules of engagement, funding, billeting, and the standard logistical issues. Then, each country would deploy its security forces (military, police, private contractors, or a combination of all three) to the agreed-upon archaeological sites around the perimeter and around the clock.

Upon arrival, each country's contingent would also be assigned a group of Iraqi recruits (who would live and work with them) to train at their chosen site. Once those Iraqi security forces were fully trained—that ordinarily takes six months—the donor nation would recall (or reassign) its forces on a site-by-site basis. In half a year, every archaeological site of consequence in Iraq could be completely protected from the looters. Mesopotamia's cultural patrimony would be safe, Al-Jezeera television would have to find other ways to show Western indifference to Arab culture, and the terrorists would have to find another income source.

Unfortunately, neither NATO nor the United Nations has such plans in the works. NATO opened a training center in Iraq in 2005, but it has trained only 1,500 Iraqi security personnel, none of whom have been assigned to archaeological sites. The United Nations has never trained guards for the sites. Even the U.N.'s cultural arm, UNESCO has failed to act. Despite the fact that UNESCO already has a somewhat similar contingency program, under Italian leadership, for the rescue and protection of cultural heritage at risk, UNESCO has established no such program in or for Iraq, claiming it has no such mandate from its member nations. Assuming that to be true, UNESCO ought to convince its member nations to support such an initiative. It is time for the United Nations to seize the mantle of international leadership and convince its members to support such a plan. As our best hope, UNESCO ought to step into the vacuum of international leadership, seize the bully pulpit, and become relevant again. Man "should share the passion and action of the time," former Supreme Court justice Oliver Wendell Holmes, Jr. once noted, "at peril of being judged not to have lived."[26]

Individual countries are also slow to respond. Only the Italians, Danes, Dutch, and Poles have joined the Americans and British in protecting these sites. Succumbing to political pressures at home, most have already left Iraq—soon there will be none. Other countries have argued that the level of violence does not permit deployment of their forces. The circular nature of this rationalization is underscored by the fact that it is the failure to protect these sites that is partly funding those who are creating the unsafe environment. "If you were to take account of everything that could go wrong," Herodotus advised long ago, "you would never act."[27] Of course there is risk. I know this first-hand. But the risks of the failure to act are far worse: more money for the insurgents, more propaganda for Al-Jezeera, and the loss of these extraordinary testaments to our common beginnings.

---

[26] Oliver Wendell Holmes, Memorial Day Address, Keene, N.H. (May 30, 1884).

[27] Herodotus, The Histories bk. 7, ch. 50.

Equally risky are the politics: most elected officials view involvement in Iraq as political suicide. But an internationally coordinated contribution of personnel would not be a statement about the war or the Bush administration's policies in Iraq. It would be a humanitarian effort to protect a cultural heritage rich with a common ancestry that transcends the current violence.

Real leaders should have no difficulty convincing their electorate of the distinction between politics and culture. It is, of course, the very definition of leadership to educate, inform, and motivate into action those who might otherwise be inclined to do nothing.

C. THE NEXT STEPS: A FIVE-POINT ACTION PLAN

The incomparable works of art unearthed in the land between the rivers pre-date the split between Sunni and Shiite. They pre-date the three competing traditions that have brought so much bloodshed to the Middle East—Judaism, Christianity, and Islam. Attending to this cultural heritage from the very dawn of civilization reminds us of our common humanity, our common aspiration to make sense of life on this planet. I have seen these pieces of alabaster and limestone with funny writing on them work their magic through a language that is both immediate and universal, visceral and transcendent.

While protecting the archaeological sites in Iraq is a vital beginning, much more needs to be done. To stop the rampant looting and the black market that funnels money into terrorist hands, we must adopt a comprehensive global strategy using all of the elements of international power. Toward this end, I propose a five-step plan of action to combat the global traffic in illegal antiquities.

1. Mount a Public Relations Campaign for Mainstream Society

The cornerstone to any comprehensive approach must take into account that real, measurable, and lasting progress in stopping the illegal trade depends on increasing public awareness of the importance of cultural property and of the magnitude of the current crisis. First, then, we must develop and communicate a message that resonates with mainstream society—not just with academics. We must create a climate of universal condemnation, rather than sophisticated indulgence, for trafficking in undocumented antiquities.

But this call to arms needs to avoid the sky-is-falling quotes so beloved by the media, while steering clear of the debilitating rhetoric of red state vs. blue state politics. It also has to keep the discussion of the illegal trade separate from broader issues such as repatriation of objects acquired prior to 1970 and the question of whether there should be any trade in antiquities at all. The Parthenon Sculptures are in the British Museum, but their return is a diplomatic or public relations issue, not a matter for the criminal courts. Similarly, there is a legal trade in antiquities that is completely fair, regulated, and above board. And it is simply unproven (and unfair) to argue that the legal trade somehow encourages an illegal trade. Most dealers and museums scrupulously do avoid trading in antiquities with a murky origin.

Repatriation for pre-1970 transfers and the question of whether all trade in antiquities should be banned are legitimate issues, but they are not my issues. Every time the discussion about stopping the illegal trade in antiquities veers off into these broader realms, we lose focus, we lose the attention of mainstream society, and it makes the job of recovering stolen antiquities that much harder.

2. Provide Funding to Establish or Upgrade Antiquities Task Forces

Although several countries—including the United States, Britain, Italy, and Japan—have pledged millions of dollars to upgrade the Iraq Museum, to improve its conservation capacity, and enhance the training of the Iraq State Board of Antiquities and Heritage's archaeological staff, not a single government, international organization, or private foundation anywhere in the world has provided additional funding for investigative purposes. Still operating under anachronistic, but nonetheless firmly held prejudices and reluctant to be seen cooperating with police and military forces, many cultural leaders and organizations seem oblivious to the fact that a stolen artifact cannot be *restored* until it has been *recovered*. To put it more clearly, money for conservators is pointless without first providing the money to track down the missing objects to be conserved. This ivory-tower distortion of priorities affects investigative efforts worldwide. Interpol can afford to assign only two officers to its Iraqi Antiquities Tracking Task Force—and both have other responsibilities as well.[28] Scotland Yard's art and antiquities squad has four officers covering the entire world—and in January of 2007, their budget was slashed in half.[29] The U.S. Federal Bureau of Investigation's (FBI) Rapid Deployment National Art Crime Team has just eight people.[30] Regardless of the exceptional dedication and talent of these personnel, no law enforcement agency can operate effectively at such levels.

Thus, as a second component, all countries—but most especially the countries of origin, transit, and destination—must establish robust, specialized art and antiquities task forces, with particular attention paid to the borders and the ports of entry. Where such forces already exist, we must increase their size and scope, with cultural foundations providing art-theft squads with vehicles, computers, communications equipment, and training.

3. Create a Coordinated International Law Enforcement Response

Among the many dirty secrets of the looted antiquities market is that "open" borders are as profitable as they are dangerous. Many countries, especially those with free ports or free-trade zones, generate sizeable customs and excise fees from shipping and—despite their public protestations to the contrary—are not eager to impose any increase in inspection rates that might reduce such revenue. Even if willing, the sheer tonnage passing through certain international ports and free-trade zones makes 100 percent inspection

[28] *See* Bogdanos, *supra* note 22.

[29] *See id.*

[30] *See id.*

rates impossible. Nor does the improved technology installed as a result of September 11 solve the problem: devices that detect weapons and explosives do not detect alabaster, lapis lazuli, and carnelian. Further exacerbating the problem, most high-end smugglers are simply too sophisticated and the questionable acquisition practices of some dealers, collectors, and museums, too entrenched to be defeated by improved border inspections and heightened public consciousness alone.

The *sine qua non* for effective interdiction, then, is an organized, systematized, and seamlessly collaborative law enforcement effort by the entire international community. We need coordinated simultaneous investigations of smugglers, sellers, and buyers in different countries. And—just as important—prosecution and incarceration need to be credible threats. Thus, as a third component, the United Nations, through UNESCO, should establish a commission to continue the Iraq Museum investigation, expanding it to include other pillaged countries as well. Interpol, the International Criminal Police Organization, must also become more active, entering into agreements with its 191 member nations stipulating that each country forward to them immediately, along a secure network (that already exists), a digital photograph and the particulars (who, what, when, and where) of all antiquities encountered by law enforcement or military forces anywhere in the world—including those items that were seized, as well as those that were inspected and not seized because there was insufficient evidence of criminality at the time of the inspection.

The global criminal enterprise that is antiquities smuggling must be defeated globally through international cooperation (promoted by UNESCO) and real-time dissemination of information (enabled by Interpol). The consequent ability to conduct monitored deliveries of illegal shipments to their destinations (a tactic long used against drug smugglers) would enable legal authorities to incriminate and thereafter prosecute each culpable party along the trail. It would also serve as a deterrent to those collectors or curators who could never be sure that the next shipment was not being monitored by law enforcement officials.

4. Establish a Code of Conduct for Trading in Antiquities

Museums, archaeologists, and dealers should establish and observe a strict and uniform code of conduct. Similar to ethics rules for lawyers and doctors, this code of conduct would clarify the documentation and diligence required for an artifact to change hands legally. If they refuse such self-regulation, then Congress should impose regulation. Although many argue that the interests of dealers, collectors, museums, and archaeologists differ from each other so dramatically that any single code of conduct acceptable to all is impossible, I point out that the differences within the art world are no greater than those existing between prosecutors and criminal defense attorneys. Yet, the American Bar Association has adopted and actively enforces a single code of ethics applicable to every attorney admitted to the bar.[31] Until then, I continue to urge

[31] *See, e.g.*, Model Code of Professional Responsibility (1980).

academics, curators, and dealers to abandon their self-serving complacency about—if not complicity in—irregularities of documentation.

5. Increase Cooperation Between the Cultural Heritage Community and Law Enforcement

Finally, the art community must break down barriers and assist investigators by serving as law enforcement's eyes and ears. We need scholars and knowledgeable dealers as on-call experts to identify and authenticate intercepted shipments and to provide crucial in-court expert testimony. They should also request appropriate law enforcement personnel (depending on country and focus) to provide detailed, factual briefings at every conference purporting to address art or antiquities smuggling. The call for up-to-date investigative facts should become as standard as the call for papers.[32] But the education and information exchange should run in both directions. In 2004, Dr. C. Brian Rose, then first vice-president (and currently president) of the Archaeological Institute of America, developed and conducted cultural-awareness training in half a dozen pilot locations around the country for military personnel scheduled to deploy to Iraq or Afghanistan. The program should be expanded to include every unit deploying overseas. A similar program should be offered to the FBI and the Department of Homeland Security on a regular basis. Such cooperation between the art and archaeological communities, on the one hand, and the law enforcement and military communities, on the other, presents a real chance of winning a fight we cannot afford to lose.

D. FUTURE MILITARY CONFLICTS

The U.S. military has lessons to be learned as well. Looking to the future, we must never again cede the moral high ground on issues of cultural sensitivity and national patrimony. Thus, before the U.S. military takes action in any country, our commanders must clearly articulate our recognition of that country's proud cultural heritage and our intent to protect such property, to the extent possible, during the conflict and post-conflict stage. Not just the message, but the actions that flow from it, must convince the world that the

[32] With this insistence on facts must come a recognition of the dangers of presenting non-fact-based speculations under the guise of "expert opinion." The worst offenders were those archaeologists (none of whom had any legal or investigative experience) who immediately after the looting of the Iraq Museum presented often-creative and always-conspiratorial theories of how the looting took place. While most have been more responsible since then, there are still counter-productive lapses into conjecture. For example, in early 2008 and in response to one of the central theses in this article, Antonia Kimbell, a manager at the Art Loss Register in London, said she had yet to see concrete evidence connecting the trade in illegal antiquities and insurgent financing, while Laurent Levi-Strauss, chief of the cultural objects and museums section at UNESCO, also weighed in, noting that the "market is totally secret, so we don't know . . . who is buying them or where the money is going." Elena Becatoros, *Artifact Smuggling Aids Iraq Insurgents,* Assoc. Press, Mar 19, 2008. The illegal market *is* secret, of course; and perhaps it is "totally secret" to those who have witnessed the trade only through press reporting and without benefit of first-hand investigative facts, confidential informants, and eyewitnesses. But to trained investigators who have had such benefits, the evidence is undeniable.

United States and, in particular, the U.S. military are committed to honoring and preserving the heritage of all nations and religious traditions.

To do so, military leaders must plan before any action for the protection of cultural property in the proposed area of operations. This protection must go beyond merely putting the site on the no-strike list. It must include the securing of significant sites (as identified by members of the archaeological community) and the immediate deployment, if needed, of on-call security forces (identified in advance of the operation) upon reports of looting. Where such forces already exist, U.S. military forces should assist by providing them with vehicles, radios, and training. Where no such forces exist, the U.S. military must protect the sites until trained forces are available. Such preparation would enable planners to identify shortfalls and—where appropriate—attempt to fill such needs from international organizations or coalition countries before the conflict.

Diverting resources to save cultural artifacts during a time of war may seem trivial considering the human cost of war. But some of our best soldiers have seen the wisdom. "Inevitably, in the path of our advance will be found historical monuments and cultural centers which symbolize to the world all that we are fighting to preserve," said General Dwight D. Eisenhower, just before D-Day during the deadliest war of the last one hundred years, one that threatened our nation's existence. "It is the responsibility of every commander to protect and respect these symbols whenever possible."[33]

E. CONCLUSION

More than five years after the looting of the Iraq Museum, the list of missing pieces is still far too long—and still includes the one that breaks my heart. It is the piece that is on the cover of my book, *Thieves of Baghdad*: the Lioness attacking a Nubian Boy, an extraordinary eighth-century B.C.E. chryselephantine ivory plaque inlaid with lapis and carnelian and overlaid with gold (see Figure 1)). It is, in my view, the single most exquisite and historically significant piece that is still missing, which is why it is on the cover—a painful reminder to me that my journey has only just begun.

On my first tour in Iraq, our mission was to track down illegal arms and terrorist networks. My decision to expand our mission to include investigating the looting of the Iraq Museum and tracking down the stolen artifacts was characterized by many as a distraction. I regret that I did not pursue that distraction even more.

Antiquities trafficking will never merit the same attention or resources as terrorism, drugs, human trafficking, or violent street crime. But, at the very least, it deserves to be on the same list. From government corridors, precinct headquarters, and media newsrooms to faculty lounges, museum boardrooms, and galleries on Madison Avenue, this cultural catastrophe must be confronted and debated. We must expose those who engage in the illegal trade for what they are: criminals.

---

[33] OWEN J. ROBERTS, REPORT OF THE AMERICAN COMMISSION FOR THE PROTECTION AND SALVAGE OF ARTISTIC AND HISTORIC MONUMENTS IN WAR AREAS 102 (1946).

Colonel Bogdanos considers the figure of a Lioness Attacking a Nubian boy (shown here on the cover of his book) to be the single most exquisite and historically significant piece that is still missing.

PART IV

LEGACY OF COMMERCE IN THE FRAMEWORK OF INTERNATIONAL LAW

CHAPTER 12
MYTHOLOGY OF THE ANTIQUITIES MARKET

Ricardo J. Elia

A. INTRODUCTION

When the Metropolitan Museum of Art in New York ("the Met") signed an agreement with the Italian Ministry of Culture on February 21, 2006, to transfer title to Italy of a group of 21 antiquities, including the controversial Euphronios krater, in return for long-term loans of "equivalent beauty and importance,"[1] it seemed like a new era of cooperation and harmony had dawned in the hotly contested international debate over cultural property. Armed with evidence that the antiquities in question had been looted from archaeological sites in its territory, Italy had pursued the Met along with other American art museums and private collectors. The Met's director, Philippe de Montebello, said in a statement that the return to Italy was "the appropriate solution to a complex problem, which redresses past improprieties in the acquisitions process through a highly equitable arrangement."[2] The pact also affirmed the Met's commitment "to the responsible acquisition of archaeological materials and ancient art according to the principle that all collecting be done with the highest criteria of ethical and professional practice."[3]

But even as the Met and Italy were basking in the glow of mutual cooperation, there were ominous signs that perhaps little would actually change. In an interview published barely a week before he signed the accord, Mr. de Montebello sounded not only unrepentant but downright belligerent, claiming that "a resurgence of nationalism and misplaced patriotism" was behind the Italians' effort to recover antiquities from the Met. "The world is changing," he said, "and you have to play by the rules." The Italians would probably exhibit the Euphronios krater as a "trophy of conquest," he opined, despite acknowledging that the vase had come to the Met in a "completely improper way—through machinations, lies, clandestine night digging."[4]

---

[1] Metropolitan Museum of Art, *Statement by the Metropolitan Museum of Art on Its Agreement with Italian Ministry of Culture,* (Feb. 21, 2006), http://www.metmuseum.org/Press_Room/full_release.asp?prid=%7BF9704AC3-297B-4704-999B-111ACC8E6804%7D. For the story of the Euphronios krater, see T. Hoving, Making the Mummies Dance. Inside the Metropolitan Museum of Art 307–40 (1993).

[2] Metropolitan Museum of Art, *supra* note 1.

[3] Agreement between the Italian Ministry of Culture and the Metropolitan Museum of Art (February 21, 1996), *available at* http://www.elginism.com/20060224/339/http://www.elginism.com/20060224/339/.

[4] D. Solomon, *Stolen Art? Interview with Philippe de Montebello,* N.Y. Times, Feb. 19, 2006,

The whole event evoked a sense of déjà vu. The Met was involved in a similar scandal involving ancient artifacts acquired in the 1960s. In 1993, following a six-year legal contest, the museum agreed to return the so-called Lydian Hoard, a collection of gold, silver, and bronze antiquities that had been looted from tombs in Turkey in the 1960s. Legal documents in the case indicated that Met staff members were aware that the objects had likely been looted from Turkey.[5] Mr. de Montebello, director at the time, acknowledged that the "Turkish authorities did provide evidence that most of the material in question may indeed have been removed clandestinely from tombs."[6] One might have expected the Met to have changed its acquisition policies for antiquities after the return of the Lydian Hoard, but I know of no evidence for such a change and, in any event, the Met certainly continued to acquire antiquities of questionable provenance after that case, including two ceramic vessels that were included in the 2006 agreement with Italy.[7] Given this recent history, it is difficult to be optimistic that museums like the Met will significantly change their acquisition policies for antiquities following the Italian scandal.

B. ARCHAEOLOGISTS ARE FROM MARS; COLLECTORS ARE FROM VENUS

Collectors and archaeologists have such different attitudes towards the collecting of antiquities that they might as well come from different planets. As an archaeologist I find this polarization unsettling. To me the causal relationship between collecting and the looting of archaeological sites is painfully clear: I see the holes in the ground; I read site reports that document the devastation caused by looting; I see photographs of pillaged areas in Peru, Iraq, and Italy that look like lunar landscapes. I also observe that each year, thousands of antiquities surface on the market and are purchased by collectors, the vast majority of which have no documentation as to findspot or previous owners and must come from countries that have strict laws aimed at preventing looting and illegal export. There is no doubt that these two activities—looting and collecting—are linked. In fact the antiquities market is an economic system based on elementary principles of supply and demand: Collectors (both private and institutional) create the demand, and looters create the supply through the intermediary of the dealers. The market drives the looting and the looting destroys the sites.

This basic outline of how the antiquities market works as an economic system has been well known for almost four decades. The adoption of the UNESCO cultural property convention in 1970 brought the topic of looting

---

available at http://www.nytimes.com/2006/02/19/magazine/19wwln_q4.html?_r=1&oref=slogin.

[5] L.M. Kaye & C.T. Main, *The Saga of the Lydian Hoard: From Usak to New York and Back Again, in* ANTIQUITIES TRADE OR BETRAYED: LEGAL, ETHICAL & CONSERVATION ISSUES 150 (Kathryn W. Tubb ed., 1995).

[6] C. Vogel, *Metropolitan Museum to Return Turkish Art,* N.Y. TIMES, Sept. 23, 1993, *available at* http://query.nytimes.com/gst/fullpage.html?res=9F0CE5D91431F930A1575AC0A965958260.

[7] Laconian kylix, 1999.527 and red-figured psykter, 1996.250; *see* Metropolitan Museum of Art, *supra* note 1.

and the illicit trade to the world's attention.[8] In the 1970s a series of books exposed the looting-collecting nexus, including Dora Jan Hamblin's *Pots and Robbers* (1970), Karl Meyer's *The Plundered Past* (1973), and Bonnie Burnham's *The Art Crisis* (1975). A steady spate of articles, conference proceedings, and books has followed, including several detailed case studies of looting as well as of efforts to assess the problem of looting from a quantitative perspective.[9] Based on all the information that has been readily available in the last few decades, no informed, rational person can deny that market demand, and therefore collecting is directly responsible for the looting of the world's cultural heritage.

Yet as a group, the dealers, collectors, and curators who participate in the antiquities market almost never acknowledge this basic fact. Instead they offer denial, obfuscation, blame, and self-justification. Demand does not cause looting; the nationalistic, retentionist laws of the source countries do. Collectors are not responsible for archaeological site destruction; they are the saviors and custodians of ancient art treasures. Looting is not as bad as the archaeologists think; most of the cultural objects on the market are from old collections or chance finds. What accounts for this disconnect between the well-documented reality of the antiquities market and the mentality of collectors?

Clemency Coggins has described the fundamental differences in values and interests between the "two basic cultures" of the antiquities market and the archaeologists and source countries that oppose the current system.[10] Collectors and dealers prize ancient objects primarily as works of art and beauty, while archaeologists value them as artifacts embedded in archaeological contexts capable of yielding meaningful information about the ancient culture and society that produced them. According to Professor Coggins, these two perspectives "might be described as scientific versus humanistic, but they are closer to cultural versus aesthetic."[11] Another approach to sorting out the different values that are ascribed to cultural objects has been articulated by William D. Lipe, who sets out four basic values—informational, associative/

---

[8] Convention on the Means of Prohibiting and Preventing the Illicit Import, Export and Transfer of Ownership of Cultural Property (Nov. 14, 1970), *available at* http://portal.unesco.org/en/ev.php-URL_ID=13039&URL_DO=DO_TOPIC&URL_SECTION=201.html; *see also* P.J. O'Keefe, Commentary on the UNESCO 1970 Convention on Illicit Traffic (2000).

[9] *See, e.g.*, C. Chippindale & D.W.J. Gill, *Material Consequences of Contemporary Classical Collecting*, 104 Am. J. Archaeology 463–511 (2000); Stealing History: The Illicit Trade in Cultural Material (N. Brodie, J. Doole & P. Watson eds., 2000); R. Atwood, Stealing History: Tomb Raiders, Smugglers, and the Looting of the Ancient World (2004); P. Watson & C. Todeschini, The Medici Conspiracy: The Illicit Journey of Looted Antiquities from Italy's Tomb Raiders to the World's Greatest Museums (2006); N. Brodie, M.M. Kersel, C. Luke & K.W. Tubb eds., Archaeology, Cultural Heritage, and the Antiquities Trade (2006). For a useful listing of relevant sources, see the online "Looting Question" bibliography, in H. Jarvis, *The "Looting Question" Bibliography: Web and Literary Resources on the Archaeological Politics of Private Collecting, Commercial Treasure Hunting, Looting, and "Professional" Archaeology* (2008), http://wings.buffalo.edu/ anthropology/Documents/lootbib.shtml.

[10] C.C. Coggins, *United States Cultural Property Legislation: Observations of a Combatant*, 7 Int'l J. Cultural Prop. 52, 57 (1998).

[11] *Id.*

symbolic, aesthetic, and economic.[12] Using Professor Lipe's scheme, we may characterize the primary value of cultural objects for archaeologists as informational, while that of collectors is aesthetic, although there is certainly overlap among the various values. Archaeologists, for example, while ranking the informational value as paramount, do not ignore the aesthetic value of artifacts. Source countries regard antiquities as important elements of their cultural heritage or cultural identity—Lipe's associative/symbolic value—as a primary value, but the informational and aesthetic values are also important to them. Collectors privilege the aesthetic value above all others, but many are also be sensitive to the economic value of their collections in terms of an eventual sale or charitable donation (which could yield tax benefits).

The cultural property debates, then, are about competing values. If a collector only cares about the beauty of an ancient object and not its archaeological context (where it came from, what it was found with, what it can tell us about ancient society), then it does not matter whether it was excavated archaeologically or acquired through other means. The object is what counts. The antiquities market generates a supply of mostly undocumented cultural objects; this system satisfies the aesthetic and economic interests of collectors and dealers. Unfortunately the market's principal source is looted archaeological sites, and looting destroys both the informational value of cultural objects by destroying archaeological sites as well as their associative/symbolic values by alienating them from their countries of origin. The archaeological process, on the other hand, preserves the informational, associative/symbolic, *and* aesthetic values by recovering cultural objects and their contexts. It also preserves the economic value, in the sense of allowing potential revenues from cultural tourism as opposed to sale of the objects.

C. FIVE MYTHS OF THE ANTIQUITIES MARKET

The fundamental difference between the perspectives of archaeologists and collectors is striking. What is unclear is how the collecting community manages to hold fast to its view that collecting is a noble pursuit in the face of overwhelming evidence for the destructive consequences of collecting. How can private collectors, museums, and dealers continue to avoid responsibility for the role they play in stimulating the looting of archaeological sites? How can they argue that collecting of undocumented antiquities is in the public interest if it is based upon a foundation of plunder?

I would like to suggest that the collector community operates on the basis of a particular mythology that explains, justifies, and validates the collecting of antiquities. The essential elements of this mythology have been in place for the better part of half a century and constitute a bulwark against outside criticism and an increasingly inconvenient corpus of facts; in this sense, the mythology

[12] W.D. Lipe, *Value and Meaning in Cultural Resources*, *in* Approaches to the Archaeological Heritage: A Comparative Study of World Cultural Resource Management Systems (H. Cleere ed., 1984). In addition to the values identified by Lipe, we might add a value related to the enhancement of social status or prestige through the collection of antiquities.

of the antiquities market offers a fundamentalist alternative to the reality of looting, theft, and smuggling. In a recent commentary, I sketched the outlines of this mythology:

> For decades the antiquities market has promoted a unitary vision of how objects come to the market. This vision acts as a mythology that sanctions the collection of antiquities, blames the victims, and denies the reality of archaeological site looting. It is a fantasy world where source countries are repressive villains and collectors are heroes, where the economic forces of supply and demand have no effect, and where every one of the thousands of museum-quality antiquities that appear on the market each year comes from old collections or chance finds made by poor peasants. In the fantasy world of the antiquities market, systematic looting by criminal gangs does not exist, archaeologists are dreary Philistines who don't appreciate beauty, and archaeological context does not matter.[13]

In the following discussion I offer some thoughts on why I believe that the intransigent views of collectors and dealers—the community that participates in the antiquities market—may be explained in terms of a mythological view of the world of collecting. I also identify and describe five myths that form the core of this mythology.

My mythographical exploration of the antiquities market employs a functional (or socio-functional) perspective that analyzes how myths articulate the needs, goals, and worldview of a society or a particular subgroup of a society,[14] in this case the specialized and fairly restricted group of people who buy, sell, and collect antiquities. Among the founders of the functionalist study of myth were Emile Durkheim and Bronislaw Malinowski. In a classic formulation, Malinowski articulated the importance of myth in reflecting society's standards and confirming social order:

> Myth fulfills in primitive culture an indispensable function: it expresses, enhances, and codifies belief; it safeguards and enforces morality; it vouches for the efficiency of ritual and contains practical rules for the guidance of man. Myth is thus a vital ingredient of human civilization; it is not an idle tale, but a hard-worked active force: it is not an intellectual explanation or an artistic imagery, but a pragmatic charter of primitive faith and moral wisdom.[15]

Myth means "story" in Greek, and myths are stories about the world. They explain how the world works and offer guidance to people negotiating the complexities of social relationships. For specific social groups within a society, such as collectors, myths serve to validate the behavior of the group, justifying

---

[13] R.J. Elia, *Comment on "Irreconcilable Differences?": Scholars for Sale,* 18 Papers from the Inst. of Archaeology 16–18, 16 (2007).

[14] W.G. Doty, Mythography: The Study of Myths and Rituals 125–56 (2d ed. 2000).

[15] B. Malinowski, Magic, Science and Religion and Other Essays 101 (1954, rep. ed. 1954).

its activities and strengthening its cohesion and self-identity, even in the face of outside opposition or criticism. My analysis of the world of collectors has convinced me that its members share a number of pervasive myths that, viewed from a socio-functionalist perspective, may be seen to shape and validate the worldview of the collector community. They do so by offering a scenario whereby antiquities appear on the market without having been looted, by glorifying collectors as saviors of the past, and by blaming the victims (source countries) for any looting or smuggling that does occur. Below I describe five essential myths of the antiquities market: (1) the Myth of the Old Collection, (2) the Myth of the Chance Find, (3) the Myth of the Reputable Dealer, (4) the Myth of the Collector as Guardian of the Past, and (5) the Myth of the Guilty Source Country. Significantly, each of these myths offers a plausible explanation of a situation that is fraught with controversy or conflict; they are self-sustaining, just-so narratives that allow collectors and dealers to justify their activities without requiring them to engage in critical, serious inquiry.

1. The Myth of the Old Collection

This myth is the first of two foundational myths that explain how antiquities surface on the market. Together with the second, the Myth of the Chance Find, it provides a convenient alternative to the charge that the bulk of antiquities comes from looted archaeological sites. Each myth is plausible: some objects in the market certainly do come from old collections, and chance finds of antiquities certainly do occur. Together they function as origin or creation myths that describe how the world (of antiquities collecting) is created.

The narrative of the Myth of the Old Collection is straightforward:

> Let us consider the old collections first. As the great private collections of yesterday are broken up and dispersed, owing to social and economic upheavals, antiquities of every description continue to be thrown onto the market.[16]
>
> * * *
>
> Antiquities have been collected for thousands of years—for example, the Romans were avid collectors of Greek sculpture—and in this time, the number of pieces coming on to the market ran to millions.[17]

There is no doubt that antiquities collecting has been going on for a long time, especially for certain areas such as Greek and Roman art but less so for other areas that have become popular more recently, such as pre-Columbian artifacts or West African terracotta figures. Material from old collections should be able to be documented as such, although some of the provenances may be lost in time.[18] Yet the percentage of antiquities in modern collections or on the contemporary market that have documented *ex collection* provenances is surprisingly low. For

[16] H. Hoffman, Collecting Greek Antiquities 228 (1971).

[17] J. Ede, *Ethics, the Antiquities Trade, and Archaeology,* 7 Int'l J. Cultural Prop. 128, 129 (1998).

[18] *Id.*

example, by my reckoning, material stated to be from older collections accounts for the following percentages in several important modern collections: Zollman (pre-Columbian), 8 percent; Fleischman (Classical), 8 percent; Leon Levy and Shelby White (Classical), 17 percent; Ortiz (Classical, Old World), 21 percent; Alsdorf (Indian, Himalayan, Southeast Asian), 0 percent; Eilenberg (Indian and Southeast Asian), 5 percent.[19] To cite an example from market sources, my study of Apulian red-figure vases (a type of pottery that has been collected since the middle of the 18th century) revealed that of the 1,550 Apulian red-figure vases auctioned by Sotheby's in the period 1960–98, previous owner/collector information is recorded for only 15 percent of the objects.[20]

Old collection provenances are notoriously untrustworthy; in fact, they have become something of a joke since Karl Meyer exposed them back in 1973 in *The Plundered Past* as a convenient way for dealers to "launder" objects that are in fact looted and smuggled.[21] Forgeries of provenances have become as commonplace as forged antiquities. I cite only a few well-known recent examples: the Getty Kouros;[22] looted Moche artifacts from Sipán, Peru;[23] and looted Egyptian sculpture in the Frederick Schultz case.[24] Unless an old collection attribution can be verified, it is prudent to remain skeptical. As Thomas Hoving, former director of the Met admitted in 1990, "Deep down, you just know that every antiquity . . . you are being offered could not have come from a private collection over fifty years old."[25]

2. The Myth of the Chance Find

Because old collections cannot account for anything like a majority of the antiquities that circulate on the market, collectors commonly point to another source (other than looting)—accidental or chance finds. Like the Myth of the Old Collection, the Myth of the Chance Find functions as a kind of creation myth, a primal account of how the world produces antiquities. Its archetypal nature is evidenced by the frequency with which it is adduced, the remarkable regularity and recurrence of its narrative elements, and the fact that it can never be disproved (or proved, for that matter) because it relies on anecdotal information. As a validating "charter" for collecting, the myth operates on several levels: It denies the causal connection between collecting and looting; it places the blame on the source countries; and it glorifies the collectors who "rescue" endangered art. The Myth of the Chance Find is so prevalent among

---

[19] Percentages are based on my tabulations of stated provenances from published collections: Zollman coll., Parsons, Carlson, and Joralemon 1988; Fleischman coll., True and Hamma 1994; Levy/White coll., von Bothmer 1990; Ortiz coll., Ortiz 1994; Alsdorf coll., Pal 1997; Eilenberg coll., Lerner and Kossak 1991. *See also* Chippindale & Gill, *supra* note 9.

[20] R.J. Elia, *Analysis of the Looting, Selling, and Collecting of Apulian Red-figure Vases: A Quantitative Approach, in* TRADE IN ILLICIT ANTIQUITIES: THE DESTRUCTION OF THE WORLD'S ARCHAEOLOGICAL HERITAGE 150 (N. Brodie, J. Doole & C. Renfrew eds., 2001).

[21] K. MEYER, THE PLUNDERED PAST: THE TRAFFIC IN ART TREASURES 15, 40, 90 (1973).

[22] M. True, *The Getty Kouros: Background on the Problem, in* THE GETTY KOUROS COLLOQUIUM 13 (1993).

[23] Atwood, *supra* note 9, at 84.

[24] *Id.* at 162.

[25] T. Hoving, *Should You or Shouldn't You?,* CONNOISSEUR 119 (Jan. 1990).

dealers, private collectors, and curators that I quote several versions of it below, from different dates and sources. First, the collector J. Paul Getty from 1965 made the following statement:

> An Italian farmer excavating the foundations of a new barn might accidentally unearth a marble bust or a bronze statue. If he is sophisticated and unscrupulous enough, he will not report his find to the authorities, but will slip the object to some dealer no more scrupulous than himself. The dealer will, in turn, either offer it "under the counter" to some especially avid or particularly gullible collector, or will smuggle the object out of the country and sell it abroad.
>
> To buy any object from such dubious sources is obviously risky. In the first place, the buyer is contravening, or at least conspiring to contravene the law, and is liable to penalties ranging from heavy fines to actual imprisonment.[26]

Dealers frequently cite the Myth of the Chance Find.[27] For example, here is the myth as related by the antiquities dealer André Emmerich in 1976:

> How are these old graves found? They're often found when very heavy rains cause graves to collapse, leaving a hole in the ground. More often such discoveries occur when a highway, housing development, or new barn is built, or a well is sunk. Then the archaeological service should be notified; they'll put up a fence, stop your work, and the site will eventually be excavated. Of course, in these poor countries, the archaeological services are underfinanced and very slow. In the meantime the police will come and grill you and your staff, demanding to know what you have stolen already.[28]

This example is from James Ede, a London-based dealer:

> The problem of chance finds also deserves consideration. It is inevitable that a large proportion of excavated material will be found during the course of normal agricultural and economic activity. Draconian laws result in the destruction of the archaeological record unless a proper system of reward exists, since the finder will usually channel such objects into the illicit market. Anecdotal evidence suggests the penalties for doing so are now so severe that finders are deliberately destroying pieces rather than run the risk of being caught with them. This is an absurd situation.[29]

---

[26] J.P. Getty, The Joys of Collecting 21 (1965).

[27] Several examples appear in S.R.M. Mackenzie, Going, Going, Gone: Regulating the Market in Illicit Antiquities 163–69 (2005).

[28] A. Emmerich, Comments, *Proceedings of the Panel on the U.S. Enabling Legislation of the UNESCO Convention on the Means of Prohibiting and Preventing the Illicit Import, Export, and Transfer of Ownership of Cultural Property,* 4 Syracuse J. Int'l L. & Com. 106, 109 (1976).

[29] Ede, *supra* note 17, at 130.

This version of the myth comes from a museum curator:

> Many important pieces are chance finds. Most of these are reported and go to regional museums, but for the farmer who has a large family to feed and no money it is a temptation to sell. Often the governments seize material without recompensing the finder, or simply have no money to pay him.[30]

My final example is from the prominent art historian John Boardman:

> Most new antiquities on any market are come by through accident, not design, and a great many are virtually heirlooms, whether documented or not. All products of such activity are now to be treated on a par with the results of deliberate plunder, the most important of which never reach any open market at all, and so are immune to antiquities legislation and seem often immune to laws concerning theft . . . If current legislation is truly effective, anyone anywhere who now comes on a hoard of coins or Roman silver will do best simply to melt them down. What good does that do for scholarship and the heritage of humanity?[31]

I suspect, although I cannot prove, that the Myth of the Chance Find originated among antiquities dealers as a convenient story to tell their clients. Certainly it provides a comfortable explanation for collectors who rely on the expertise of "reputable dealers" (see below) to shield them from unsavory and possibly illegal transactions. Finds appear accidentally, almost magically, and certainly not as a result of targeted plunder. The Myth of the Chance Find also puts the blame squarely on the source countries, which will treat an innocent finder as a thief, or will confiscate a farmer's land, and in any case will not offer a reasonable incentive for the finder to report the find. Finally, the myth validates the collecting enterprise, because given the unfavorable situation in the source country, the finder may be tempted to destroy the object or site; in these cases the collector becomes the savior by placing a value on chance finds that result in their being rescued from oblivion.

As a foundational myth, a charter for collectors, the Myth of the Chance Finds conveniently skirts around several facts. First, while chance finds do occur, there is overwhelming evidence that looting is a systematic and organized criminal activity conducted in many source countries on a vast scale. There are simply too many fresh antiquities surfacing on the market to be accounted for by accidental finds. Nor do chance finds account for the fact that the popularity of specific types of antiquities peak at different times, such as Luristan bronzes in the 1960s or South Italian red-figure pottery during the 1980s and 1990s. Of

---

[30] G.G. Griffin, *Collecting Pre-Columbian Art, in* The Ethics of Collecting Cultural Property: Whose Culture? Whose Property? 109 (P. Mauch Messenger ed., 1989).

[31] J. Boardman, *Archaeologists, Collectors, and Museums, in* Who Owns Objects? The Ethics and Politics of Collecting Cultural Objects 37 (E. Robson, L. Treadwell, & C. Gosden eds., 2006).

course, chance finds do occur, but while the discovery of the first grave or two of an ancient necropolis may be accidental, the cleaning out of the rest of the necropolis is more likely to be from looting.

In addition to minimizing the problem of looting, the Myth of the Chance Find also implicitly condones several crimes relating to archaeological sites and objects. First is the legal requirement that most countries of origin have to report chance finds. The myth condones contravention of this requirement by claiming that source countries would subject the finder to unfair treatment. Most source countries also make it illegal for individuals to sell or otherwise dispose of unreported antiquities. Many source countries assert title to antiquities, including those found on private property, and treat unauthorized disposal as theft. Finally, if the illegally acquired chance find is taken out of the country of origin, then the crime of smuggling (illegal export) is also being condoned by the Myth of the Chance Find.

3. The Myth of the Reputable Dealer

This myth offers another way for collectors to assure themselves that they are not participating in any illicit activity involving the purchase of antiquities. The main concern is to avoid buying a forgery or a work that may have been stolen from a museum or private collection or may otherwise have questionable title that may be contested after purchase by a collector. According to J. Paul Getty, "To all intents and purposes, the modern-day collector of ancient Greek and Roman art must confine himself to buying from one or another of two sources—well established and highly reputable dealers or other collectors."[32]

In my experience, the notion of the "reputable dealer" has led to considerable confusion because the general public and the media tend to assume that there are two distinct types of dealers: bad dealers, those who sell looted antiquities, and reputable dealers, those who do not. In fact both illicit and legal aspects are combined in the antiquities market. Oscar White Muscarella[33] and Bonnie Burnham[34] clarified this point in the 1970s by showing that the term "reputable dealer" does not mean someone who will not deal in cultural objects that have been illegally excavated or illegally removed from source countries. As Muscarella points out, "It must be understood that the use of the honorific adjectives mentioned with regard to dealers does not speak to the methods used by the latter to acquire their material, methods that more often than not involve not only the destruction of archaeological monuments, but smuggling and bribery to remove the object from the country of origin."[35]

Dealers may draw the line when it comes to buying or selling objects illegally taken from museums or other public institutions, or from protected archaeological sites; these they regard as "stolen" cultural objects. But they

[32] GETTY, *supra* note 26, at 21.

[33] O. White Muscarella, *Unexcavated Objects and Ancient Near Eastern Art, in* MOUNTAINS AND LOWLANDS 160 (L.D. Levine & T.C. Young, Jr. eds., 1977).

[34] B. BURNHAM, THE ART CRISIS 93 (1975).

[35] Muscarella, *supra* note 33.

generally oppose source country laws that aim to protect antiquities buried in unprotected, or unregistered, archaeological sites throughout the country; nor do they favor recognition of source countries' export laws that prohibit the unauthorized removal of antiquities. Objects that enter the market in those cases are not regarded as "stolen" but merely "illegally exported."[36] This ethical position allows the dealers, in effect, to handle looted antiquities as long as they can assure themselves that they were not "stolen" in the sense noted above. If collectors wish to avoid purchasing objects that may have been looted, then they must not place their faith in the notion of the reputable dealer. As I have said before, in this context "reputable dealer" is an oxymoron.[37]

4. The Myth of the Collector as Guardian of the Past

Many antiquities collectors take pride in their passion for art and the care they bestow on their collections. They view collecting not only as a passion but also as a beneficial activity because they make their collections accessible to scholars and members of the public. I have already shown above that the Myth of the Chance Find promotes the notion that collectors are rescuing objects that might otherwise be destroyed or lost. The Myth of the Collector as Guardian of the Past reinforces that message by stressing the role of collectors as custodians of ancient art. At the same time, by privileging the aesthetic value of the object above all other values, this myth conveniently ignores or minimizes the loss of archaeological sites, objects, and knowledge resulting from the looting that brings antiquities into the hands of collectors.

Leon Levy and Shelby White, prominent collectors of Classical antiquities, have described their roles as collectors: "We know our objects have had many caretakers—for when you are a collector a caretaker is what you become. We know, too, that we are just links in a very long chain and that our treasures will someday have new homes in new places."[38] In a later article, Shelby White elaborated as follows: "As collectors, we believe we are preserving and expanding knowledge of the past . . . over the years, we have built a collection of interest to scholars as well as the general public."[39] Gillett G. Griffin, a museum curator, expressed a similar view: "I feel that I am not the owner, but only the custodian of the works which I have assembled, and my goal has been to pass them on to the world in an ordered way, so that they will add to the knowledge of present and future generations."[40]

Because the myths of the antiquities market always function to sever the causal link between collecting and looting, they allow collectors to avoid

---

[36] *E.g.*, P. Marks, *The Ethics of Art Dealing*, 7 INT'L J. CULTURAL PROP. 116–27 125 (1998); Ede, *supra* note 17, at 129–30; P.J. O'KEEFE, TRADE IN ANTIQUITIES: REDUCING DESTRUCTION AND THEFT 47–51 (1997); MACKENZIE, *supra* note 27, at 75–88.

[37] R.J. Elia, *The World Cannot Afford Many More Collectors With a Passion for Antiquities*, 41 THE ART NEWSPAPER 19 (Oct. 1994).

[38] S. White & L. Levy, *Introduction*, *in* GLORIES OF THE PAST: ANCIENT ART FROM THE SHELBY WHITE AND LEON LEVY COLLECTION x (Dietrich von Bothmer ed., 1990).

[39] S. White, S, *A Collector's Odyssey*, 7 INT'L J. CULTURAL PROP. 170, 170 (1998).

[40] Griffin, *supra* note 30, at 114.

taking responsibility for the destruction that accompanies looting. They may take pride in preserving a treasure from the past without thinking about the destruction that may have taken place in order to obtain that treasure in the first place. Looters seeking Greek pots, for example, will dig through ancient graves, destroying all the archaeological and contextual information that might inform us about the people who were buried there; even the very location of the grave or cemetery may be lost. But the loss is not just informational; the looters also discard or maliciously destroy anything that is not marketable: human remains, undecorated vessels, fragile organic materials, and metal objects that would require expensive conservation. Moreover, the clandestine nature of the looting and trade often results in damage to recovered objects or even their destruction. To take one recent example, we may consider the fate of the Judas Gospel, which has recently been published: it was looted from an unknown archaeological site; its archaeological context was destroyed; it was smuggled out of its country of origin and handled by several dealers over a period of more than two decades; it was allowed to deteriorate in a bank vault without climate control; it was freeze dried by one dealer; and pages of the codex were removed and sold separately. The wonder is that it survived at all.[41] One also wonders how many similar ancient documents have been lost completely through looting and the antiquities market. Yet the dealer who ended up with the Judas Gospel has been hailed for "rescuing" the codex.[42]

The Myth of the Collector as Guardian of the Past sometimes employs a clever analogy, which I term the Orphan Analogy, to sidestep any responsibility for the means of acquisition and focus on the custodial benefit of the acquisition itself. Mr. de Montebello recently used the Orphan Analogy to defend museum collecting:

> As archaeologists have said, these unprovenanced objects are orphans, as their parentage, through absence of a known find spot, is lost. But would these same archaeologists abandon a shivering orphaned child on the cold rainy day in the street? We museums are the orphanage of these objects.[43]

This version of the Orphan Analogy manages to equate museums with caring for "shivering orphaned" children while implicitly criticizing archaeologists for being so unfeeling that they would abandon an orphan "on the cold rainy day in the street." It also allows no linkage between lost "parentage" and the orphan: parentage (archaeological find spot) is simply lost, and an orphan (art object) is created; no one is to blame, and therefore rescuing the orphan is the right thing to do. The moral of the story is simple: looting just happens, and collecting is noble.

---

[41] H. Krosney, The Lost Gospel: The Quest for the Gospel of Judas Iscariot (2006).

[42] R. Kasser, The Gospel of Judas Together with the Letter of Philip, James, and a Book of Allogenes from Codex Tchacos 15 (*Critical Edition* 2007).

[43] R. Berman, *Met Chief Defends Museums' Pursuit of Antiquities,* N.Y. Sun, Apr. 18, 2006, *available at* http://www.nysun.com/article/31135.

A more appropriate analogy would take into account the causal relationship between collecting and looting:

> These unprovenanced objects are orphans. Their parents have been murdered by slave traders and the orphaned children kidnapped and sold abroad. Museums and collectors stimulate the slave trade by paying high prices for the orphans.

In my version of the analogy, the museums and collectors are responsible for the slave (antiquities) trade because they create a market for orphans (unprovenanced objects), which causes the murder of the parents (looting).

The Myth of the Collector as Custodian of the Past is also reinforced by arguments that promote the aesthetic value of antiquities and minimize the informational value that derives from the archaeological process. This aspect of the myth is frequently accompanied by a peculiar use of symbolic or magical numbers involving percentages greater than 90 percent; those who quote these percentages give the impression of speaking with statistical authority even though the figures are always unverifiable and often patently ridiculous. For example, Mr. de Montebello recently scoffed at what can be learned from archaeology: "Ninety-eight percent of everything we know about antiquity we know from objects that were not out of digs."[44] He cited the Euphronios krater as an example: "How much more would you learn from knowing which particular hole in—supposedly Cerveteri–it came out of? Everything is on the vase."[45] Professor Boardman, presumably referring to the same vase, claimed that the interest in the piece "is 98 per cent in its sheer existence (we know who made it, when and where) with only a 2 per cent loss in knowledge of what Etruscan grave it came from."[46] Since we have no idea what site the vase came from, or what the site contained, how can Professor Boardman assign an exact figure of 2 percent for the lost archaeological context?

Another example of pseudo-statistics is the statement of a New York dealer interviewed for Mackenzie's recent study of the antiquities market. Referring to looters as "diggers," the dealer stated, "The archaeological sites, for guided or proper archaeological digs, in general, have always been found, I would say up to 90%, have always been found by diggers."[47] Another dealer, Jerome Eisenberg, also denigrates the value of archaeology: "Although most archaeologists are loath to admit it, probably 99 per cent or more of the objects now being uncovered do not lead to any further significant insight into our past history or knowledge of ancient art."[48]

A final example comes from Carlos Picón, curator of Greek and Roman

---

[44] Randy Kennedy & Hugh Eakin, *Met Chief, Unbowed, Defends Met's Role,* N.Y. Times, Feb. 28, 2006, *available at* http://www.nytimes.com/2006/02/28/arts/28mont.html?_r=2.

[45] *Id.*

[46] Boardman, *supra* note 31, at 39.

[47] Mackenzie, *supra* note 27, at 173.

[48] J.M. Eisenberg, *Ethics and the Antiquity Trade. in* Antiquities Trade or Betrayed: Legal, Ethical and Conservation Issues 220 (K.W. Tubb ed., 1995).

art at the Met. In a recent interview, Picón left no doubt about his view of archaeologists ("deadly dull," "demented," people who "only care about dirt") and archaeology ("I don't care about the bones, and the person buried there. . . . What can you know about them, anyway?").[49] Referring to his museum's Classical holdings, Picón said, with a numerological flourish, "Ninety-nine-point-nine-nine-nine per cent of what we have bought in the last generation has been absolutely and straightforwardly documented,"[50] a statement that says precisely nothing about the quality of documentation available for pieces acquired by the museum. Mr. Picón might have provided another statistic in the 90 percent range. This one, unlike the others cited above, is verifiable: According to the Met's new catalog of its Classical collection, 92 percent of the Classical antiquities acquired by the museum during the period of Mr. de Montebello's tenure as director (1977–2006) lacks a stated provenance.[51]

5. The Myth of the Guilty Source Country

The final myth is unusual because it is the only one that explicitly acknowledges the existence of looting as a means of obtaining antiquities. In this sense it contradicts the other myths, which tend to exclude or at least ignore the phenomenon of looting, and one would expect it to have at least a disquieting effect on the acceptance of the other myths by collectors. I have not observed this to be the case, however, but instead I have noticed a tendency for this myth to be discussed in a very circumscribed manner, which is primarily to assign blame for looting on the laws of the source countries. Ironically, the fact that looting is acknowledged as a problem does not seem to have eroded belief in the other myths, as far as collectors are concerned.

The basic outline of the Myth of the Guilty Source Country is conveyed in this statement by the dealer Charles Ede:

> More recently, and very properly, export controls in such countries as Egypt, Greece and Italy have become increasingly tight, but a certain amount of material is still dug illicitly and smuggled out. It is, indeed, sad that the very strictness of some countries' rather chauvinist laws has defeated its own object. An embargo on the export of very minor pieces has in effect created a sufficient turnover to support sizeable tomb-robbing and smuggling industries, which could not have existed on such a scale had it been limited to handling major finds only.[52]

Arts correspondent Geraldine Norman (1995) also blamed the looting problem on the countries of origin in an article titled "Bad Laws Are Made to Be Broken." Calling export bans for antiquities "contrary to human nature," Norman

---

[49] R. Mead, *Den of Antiquity: The Met and the Antiquities Market,* New Yorker, April 9, 2007, at 55, 61.

[50] *Id.* at 55.

[51] The figure is based on my tabulation of data from C.A. Picón, J.R. Mertens, E.J. Milleker, C.S. Lightfoot & S. Hemingway, Art of the Classical World in the Metropolitan Museum of Art. Greece. Cyprus. Etruria. Rome (2007).

[52] C. Ede, Collecting Antiquities: An Introductory Guide xiv (1976).

candidly asserted that "in deed, if not in word, the whole of the antiquities trade and most museum curators condone antiquities smuggling for the reasons that have been adumbrated—the laws in the countries of origin make no sense."[53] Interestingly, while she talks of tomb robbers and peasants finding valuable objects, Norman never mentions the losses to archaeology or the fact that what makes objects valuable in the first place is market demand.

Proponents of the antiquities market criticize source countries for having retentionist, chauvinistic policies that include legal bans on the export of antiquities. According to this view, these restrictive policies effectively create a black market in looted artifacts. Source countries, of course, claim the right to protect archaeological sites and the antiquities in them as their cultural heritage. The disagreement is not merely philosophical because if one does not respect the protective legislation of source countries, then it is an easy step to condone the looting of archaeological sites and the smuggling of antiquities out of source countries.

The Myth of the Guilty Source Country allows those who benefit from the looting—the dealers and collectors—to shift the responsibility for looting onto the victims of the looting. While acknowledging that looting exists, this myth denies any causal connection between collecting and looting. It also opens the door for efforts to convince the source countries to open up the trade in antiquities. The dealer James Ede, for example, argues that restrictive laws encourage looting and "have the opposite effect to that which was intended. Adjustment to encourage the legitimate trade would go a long way toward restricting the smuggling routes on which illicit trade depends."[54]

The idea that the legal restrictions of source countries are actually responsible for the looting seems plausible enough on its face; one might consider, for example, the impossibility of enforcing a ban on alcohol during the Prohibition era, a comparison often cited in this context.[55] What makes the Myth of the Guilty Source Country succeed as a functional myth for the collecting community, and the reason why I have identified it as a myth in the first place, is the fact that like all of the other myths, it offers a believable narrative that explains why looting exists without requiring any admission of culpability on the part of collectors. It may be that the passage of certain laws results in a greater willingness on the part of some people to break those laws, but the myth still begs the basic question: Why are people trying to obtain antiquities in the first place? The answer is obvious—demand by collectors. Now, if source countries enact laws that try to protect their archaeological, cultural, and artistic heritage, the question becomes: Why should collectors have the right to finance, no matter how indirectly, the looting of that heritage, especially when it would involve the destruction of the archaeological and cultural heritage in return for the preservation of some portion of the artistic heritage?

---

[53] G. Norman, *Bad Laws Are Made to Be Broken, in* ANTIQUITIES TRADE OR BETRAYED: LEGAL, ETHICAL & CONSERVATION ISSUES 143 (K.W. Tubb ed., 1995).

[54] Ede, *supra* note 17, at 130.

[55] *E.g.*, Marks, *supra* note 36, at 123.

Fortunately for collectors, the Myth of the Guilty Source Country allows them to avoid having to answer that question. There is another basic flaw in the formulation of this myth. The claim that source country laws are causing the looting is simply that, a claim. Those who argue this point offer no evidence to back it up; like all the other myths this one is a just-so story that relies on little more than apparent plausibility and reasonableness. On the one hand, it is true enough that if source countries opened up their markets, then more antiquities would be able to leave legally; but that is rather like a bank robber telling a bank that if it opened its vaults, the robber would not have to steal from them. Where is the evidence that a liberalized market would diminish looting? For one thing, no source country would be likely to permit important pieces to leave the country, and that is precisely the kind of material that museums and major collectors demand, so there would always be a market for high-end objects that could only be satisfied by looting. Second, opening up markets might actually increase demand rather than decrease it, by encouraging new collectors to enter the field; source countries do not have a limitless amount of material that could be exported, and a diminishing supply would eventually encourage looting. Third, even if source countries tried to regulate a more liberal flow of antiquities, there is no reason to assume that looters would not continue to operate outside the law in order to circumvent government regulations and fees.

Regarding this last point, we may cite the experience of several countries that have operated a legal commerce in antiquities. We should expect to see little looting in these countries, yet their actual experience indicates exactly the opposite. In the United States, for example, where fully two-thirds of the landmass is private property, and there is little or no regulation on the trade in antiquities (with a few exceptions such as objects from federal lands, Native American reservations, and sites containing Native American human remains), looting on both private and public property has been a long-standing problem.[56] In Israel, where a legal antiquities market has operated for years, looting is rampant.[57] Historical examples, such as Egypt in the 1920s, show the same pattern: looting was a pervasive problem there despite a legal market for antiquities and a healthy system of sharing of artifacts (partage) from archaeological excavations.[58]

D. CONCLUSION

In this chapter I have suggested a way to account for the intransigence of collectors and dealers who seem to be in denial about the reality of the

[56] F.P. McManamon & S.D. Morton, *Reducing the Illegal Trafficking in Antiquities, in* Cultural Resource Management in Contemporary Society: Perspectives on Managing and Presenting the Past 259–63 (F.P. McManamon & A. Hatton eds., 2000).

[57] O. Blum, *The Illicit Antiquities Trade: An Analysis of Current Antiquities Looting in Israel,* 11Culture Without Context (2002), http://www.mcdonald.cam.ac.uk/projects/iarc/culttturewithoutcontext/issue11/blum.htm.

[58] J. Hankey, A Passion for Egypt: A Biography of Arthur Weigall 45–46, 62–63, 75–79 (2001); A. Khater, Le Régime Juridique des Fouilles et des Antiquités en Égypte 165–71, 242–47 (1960).

looting problem. In trying to understand how the proponents of the art market can continue to deny their basic responsibility for stimulating the looting of archaeological sites, I have explored the notion that they have embraced a mythology that insulates them from the destructive reality of the antiquities market. This mythology creates a comfortable, if fanciful, world view that allows dealers and collectors to explain how antiquities surface (mostly, in their view, through recycled collections and chance finds); how they are legitimately conveyed to collectors (by reputable dealers); how those collectors act (as noble stewards of the past); and how, if by chance some antiquities do surface through looting, then it is the fault of the source countries (which should liberalize their laws). I am confident that further mythographical study of the attitudes of the private collectors, museum curators, and dealers who make up the antiquities market would reveal additional beliefs and values that may be organized around mythical narratives like the five myths I have described here.

Throughout this chapter, I have taken the comments of dealers, collectors, and curators at face value. I am not, of course, in a position to assess the degree to which any individual actually believes the opinions he or she expressed. I do have doubts, however, about the veracity of the members of the dealer and museum communities who espouse the myths described above. Because dealers are, in effect, the middlemen between the looters and the collectors, and because they frequently claim specialized expertise vis-à-vis their clients, especially private collectors, they are in a unique position to provide false or misleading information about matters such as the provenance of antiquities that they are selling. Many museum curators, likewise, are art historians who have ready access to the abundant literature pertaining to looting; like the dealers, they also should be completely familiar, as a matter of professional competence, with the facts about the nature and extent of looting and its relationship to the market.

The fact these dealers and curators, who should know better, continue to parrot the Myths of the Antiquities Market is shocking, and I frankly wonder how genuinely they believe them. My personal view is that most antiquities dealers and museum curators—shall we say 99 percent?—are well aware of the fact that collecting causes looting. They know that most of the antiquities they handle have been looted, and they simply do not care. They purvey these myths to their clients, the private collectors, out of self-interest. After all, dealers wish to sell antiquities to them and curators to acquire antiquities from them. If my suspicions are correct, then technically speaking, while the Myths of the Antiquities Market may genuinely function as myths among private collectors, for most dealers and curators they are not myths at all, but rather lies. Either way, as long as the Myths of the Antiquities Market continue to be promoted by the collector community without serious challenge, I remain skeptical that we are likely to see any major changes in the way that antiquities are acquired.

CHAPTER 13
UNESCO INTERNATIONAL FRAMEWORK FOR THE PROTECTION OF THE CULTURAL HERITAGE

Lyndel V. Prott

A. INTRODUCTION

Of all the organizations of or connected to the United Nations, the U.N. Educational, Scientific and Cultural Organization (UNESCO) is the one mandated to deal with preservation of the cultural heritage. Specifically UNESCO's Constitution provides that it will "contribute to peace and security by promoting collaboration among the nations through education, science and culture in order to further universal respect for justice, for the rule of law and for the human rights and fundamental freedoms"[1] and will therefore *inter alia,*

> *(c)* Maintain, increase and diffuse knowledge:
>
> By assuring the conservation and protection of the world's inheritance of books, works of art and monuments of history and science, and recommending to the nations concerned the necessary international conventions.[2]

It has therefore fallen to UNESCO to provide the legal framework for heritage protection, a function that is central to preservation around the world, but has sometimes been lost sight of, among the demands for operational work, for example, on heritage sites. It is notable, however, that such operations are not mentioned in UNESCO's Constitution, and the organization has never been adequately funded for them, having been conceived of as fundamentally working "upstream" to provide the framework for international collaboration rather than work on the ground. The change in emphasis, dating from the 1960s and UNESCO's very successful campaign to mobilize international action to save the Nubian monuments from the rising waters of Egypt's Aswan Dam, has led to a change, and some would even argue a distortion, of its purpose.

B. RESPONSE TO PROBLEMS OF CONQUEST

There is no doubt that one of UNESCO's first major tasks after its establishment in 1946 was to respond to demands for an appropriate international

[1] UNESCO Constitution art. I(1), *available at* http://portal.unesco.org/en/ev.php-URL_ID=15244&URL_DO=DO_TOPIC&URL_SECTION=201.html.

[2] *Id.*, art. I(2)(c).

convention to give details on how to implement and enforce the prohibition on destruction of cultural property during conflict, as established by the Hague Convention IV on the Laws and Customs of War on Land, 1907 ("Hague Convention on Land Warfare 1907").[3]

UNESCO's work on the draft of this new convention drew the Soviet Union into the international organization. Until then, it had refrained from joining the international organizations under the aegis of the United Nations, which it saw as dominated by the United States and hostile to its interests. Although it was a founding member of the United Nations in 1945, it did not become a member of UNESCO until 1954—the very date of the Hague Convention for the Protection of Cultural Property in the Event of Armed Conflict 1954 ("1954 Hague Convention").[4] The intentional devastation of Slav heritage had left an indelible impression in Slav areas, and the need for international cooperation to prevent future events of this kind was evident even to the Moscow skeptics. (That the USSR was holding massive amounts of looted material from Germany as well as other countries was not then known.)

The obligations created by the convention, regulations and protocols can be summarized as follows:

- A duty to safeguard cultural property (1954 Hague Convention, Articles 2 and 3);
- A duty to respect cultural property (1954 Hague Convention, Articles 2 and 4);
- A duty to train the military in the principles of the convention (1954 Hague Convention, Article 7); and
- A special series of duties on occupying powers (1954 Hague Convention, Article 5; Regulations Articles 2 and 19; Protocol (1954) Articles 1 and 4).

Since its adoption, the 1954 Hague Convention, which now has 118[5] states parties, has been in and out of favor. Although signatories in 1954, the United States and United Kingdom have not yet ratified. President Clinton sent the convention to the Senate for approval in 1999, and in 2004, the United Kingdom announced that it would ratify. The United States used its influence in the late 1950s, during the intensifying chill of the Cold War, to persuade other English-speaking states not to ratify—thus Australia ratified only in 1984 and Canada as late as 2005.[6] It is to be noted, however, that all the major states on the European

---

[3] Hague Convention (IV) respecting the Laws and Customs of War on Land (Oct. 18, 1907), *available at* http://www.icrc.org/ihl.nsf/FULL/195?OpenDocument.

[4] Hague Convention for the Protection of Cultural Property in the Event of Armed Conflict (May 14, 1954), *available at* http://www.icrc.org/ihl.nsf/FULL/400?OpenDocument.

[5] Participation numbers in all the legal instruments mentioned in this chapter have been updated to June 2008. In addition, on March 13, 2009, the United States deposited its instrument of acceptance.

[6] The reason was the fear held in the Pentagon that, should a "hot war" break out, it would be inhibited from bombing the Kremlin, a historic and cultural complex that was also the headquarters of military planning for the Soviet Union. The fear was ungrounded because of the provision that use of such a monument or collection of monuments, even where

continent, which had suffered so much damage to and destruction and loss of their cultural heritage, signed and promptly ratified the convention.

Apart from that initial reluctance to ratify, there was also a feeling in the 1970s that the advent of the inter-continental ballistic missile had made the 1954 Hague Convention's provisions somewhat meaningless. What point was there in marking a site with the protective emblem of the convention when those firing the weapon could not even see the country that they were aiming at from over the horizon, let alone a particular monument in it? Since then, however, the pendulum has swung back again, owing to the increasing accuracy of targeting. With the outbreak of conflict both in Iraq and Yugoslavia in 1991, the focus was suddenly on the convention once more.

Two factors of dissatisfaction are now apparent: one is the problem of "occupation" and the other is the increasing difficulty of applying the 1954 Hague Convention to small local conflicts and those involving irregular forces not under state control.

1. Occupation

To meet the concerns arising out of the conflicts of the 1990s, a Second Protocol to the 1954 Hague Convention ("Second Protocol") was adopted in 1999.[7] The United Kingdom and the United States, as signatories to the convention, asked to be included in the negotiations and in fact played an active role in them. The fact that, nine years after its adoption, they have still not ratified the 1954 Hague Convention (and cannot, therefore, ratify its protocols) is therefore extremely disappointing.

The problem of occupation continues to be worrying. The Hague Convention on Land Warfare, 1907,[8] in the first two articles of Section III ("Military Authority over the territory of the hostile State") provides that

> Territory is considered occupied when it is actually placed under the authority of the hostile army.
>
> The occupation extends only to the territory where such authority has been established and can be exercised [Article 42].
>
> The authority of the legitimate power having in fact passed into the hands of the occupant, the latter shall take all the measures in his power to restore, and ensure, as far as possible, public order and safety, while respecting, unless absolutely prevented, the laws in force in the country [Article 43].

---

under "special protection," in support of the military effort, deprives it of its immunity (1954 Hague Convention, arts. 9 and 11).

[7] Second Protocol to the Hague Convention of 1954 for the Protection of Cultural Property in the Event of Armed Conflict (March 26, 1999), *available at* http://portal.unesco.org/en/ev.php-URL_ID=15207&URL_DO=DO_TOPIC&URL_SECTION=201.html. The Protocol to the Convention for the Protection of Cultural Property in the Event of Armed Conflict (May 14, 1954; "First Protocol") related to movables and consists of articles abstracted from the main convention in order to appease states who argued that these provisions dealt with private law matters and were therefore unacceptable to them in the main convention.

[8] *Supra* note 3. Currently there are 35 states parties to this convention.

The present difficulty is in applying such a concept of occupation. Apart from the fact that insurgency and guerilla warfare relies for the most part in keeping unclear from the other side the extent and degree of control by the insurgent forces, the doctrine of "surgical strikes" may lead to traditionally organized armies choosing not to prepare for control of the territory over which they range or misjudging what will necessary. This was clearly the case in Iraq in 2003. It is also clear in that instance, since the report on Babylon,[9] that the rules as to "respect" of cultural property have not been observed. Furthermore, questions have been raised about U.N. peacekeepers. It is generally the case that they have minimal resources for their operational task in any theater of war and that physically they often have barely enough for minimal control. In addition, they are there with the agreement of the governments concerned and are therefore not "occupiers" in the traditional sense.

These questions were raised during negotiations for the Second Protocol and resulted in Article 9 on the "Protection of cultural property in occupied territory":

> 1. Without prejudice to the provisions of Articles 4 and 5 of the Convention, a Party in occupation of the whole or part of the territory of another Party shall prohibit and prevent in relation to the occupied territory:
>   a. any illicit export, other removal or transfer of ownership of cultural property;
>   b. any archaeological excavation, save where this is strictly required to safeguard, record or preserve cultural property;
>   c. any alteration to, or change of use of, cultural property which is intended to conceal or destroy cultural, historical or scientific evidence.
>
> 2. Any archaeological excavation of, alteration to, or change of use of, cultural property in occupied territory shall, unless circumstances do not permit, be carried out in close co-operation with the competent national authorities of the occupied territory.

2. Insurgency

As for insurgents, the 1954 Hague Convention does provide in Article 5 as follows:

> Any High Contracting Party whose government is considered their legitimate government by members of a resistance movement, shall, if possible, draw their attention to the obligation to comply with those provisions of the Convention dealing with respect for cultural property.

[9] *Available at* http://www.thebritishmuseum.ac.uk/iraqcrisis/reports/Babylon%20Report04.pdf; www.newscientist.com/article.ns?id=dn6888-42k; http://www.guardian.co.uk/world/2005/jan/15/iraq.arts1. John Curtis, keeper of the museum's Ancient Near East department and an authority on Iraq's many archaeological sites, found "substantial damage": cracks and gaps where somebody had tried to gouge out the decorated bricks forming the famous dragons of the Ishtar Gate; a 2,600-year-old brick pavement crushed by military vehicles, archaeological fragments scattered across the site, and trenches driven into ancient deposits.

Article 19 also provides as follows:

Conflicts Not of an International Character

> 1. In the event of an armed conflict not of an international character occurring within the territory of one of the High Contracting Parties, each party to the conflict shall be bound to apply, as a minimum, the provisions of the present Convention which relate to respect for cultural property.

While the Second Protocol reiterates this provision (Article 22(1)), it adds the not very helpful words that

> This Protocol shall not apply to situations of internal disturbances and tensions, such as riots, isolated and sporadic acts of violence and other acts of a similar nature.

The formlessness of many current international conflicts, where insurgent groups may not be under the control of any other government, or may be related more to an ideological movement rather than a national one, as well as the blurred lines between insurgency, civil war, and national liberation movements, may make it more difficult to realize controls under the 1954 Hague Convention.

The 1954 Hague Convention and its protocols deal with very difficult subjects, and their drafters knew that, like humanitarian law in general, they can never be completely effective, but only set standards that should minimize destruction as much as possible. Such instruments are difficult to negotiate and difficult to apply. Nevertheless, the great stride forward in their implementation is the inclusion of provisions based on their texts in the statutes of specific war crimes tribunals and of the International Criminal Court. Thanks to that now established practice, two senior officers held responsible for the damage to Dubrovnik are now in jail in the Netherlands.[10]

C. RESPONSE TO COLONIALISM AND PARALLEL PHENOMENA

UNESCO's response to issues generated by colonialism has been much more tortuous. Despite pleas for a convention to regulate the return of objects taken during colonial times, the holding states have never agreed to this demand. Rather surprisingly, the states seeking return have not sought to rely on the rules of state succession, which would appear to give a clear answer in a number of disputed cases.

---

[10] International Tribunal for the Prosecution of Persons Responsible for Serious Violations of International Humanitarian Law Committed in the Territory of the Former Yugoslavia Since 1991, Prosecutor v. Jokic, Case No. IT-01-42/1-S 2005 (seven years' prison sentence confirmed by Appeals Chamber 2005); Prosecutor v. Strugar, Case No. IT-01-42-T 2005 (sentenced to eight years in jail, appeal by Strugar dismissed July 17, 2008).

1. Action in the United Nations

During the 1960s, increasingly strong demands emerged within the United Nations as the states released from colonial ties became independent. An echo of this concern is found in the Convention on the Means of Prohibiting and Preventing the Illicit Import, Export and Transfer of Ownership of Cultural Property 1970 ("1970 Convention")[11] where it is provided that states parties to the convention

> shall respect the cultural heritage within the territories for the international relations of which they are responsible, and shall take all appropriate measures to prohibit and prevent the illicit import, export and transfer of ownership of cultural property in such territories [Article 12].

While the holding states were prepared to negotiate an agreement for the future, now embodied in the 1970 Convention, they were adamant that it would not apply to past events.

The Conference of Heads of State or Government of Non-Aligned Countries may be credited with having started the whole debate about dispossession in colonial, rather than wartime, situations. Reference was made to a resolution of the Fourth Conference of that body, held at Algiers in 1973, in the Preamble of G.A. Resolution 3187 (XXVIII)[12] entitled "Restitution of Works of Art to Countries Victims of Expropriation" which spoke of the desire of these countries "to safeguard their own personality, to revive and enrich their cultural heritage."

Resolution 3187 also referred in its Preamble to the Declaration on the Granting of Independence to Colonial Countries and Peoples (G.A. Resolution 1514 (XV)[13]). This resolution deplored "the wholesale removal, virtually without payment, of *objets d'art* from one country to another, frequently as a result of colonial or foreign occupation" and stated that "the restitution of such works would make good the serious damage suffered by countries as a result of such removal."

It was decided that UNESCO, the specialized agency of the United Nations responsible for cultural matters, would be the proper place for work on these problems. Nonetheless, since 1973 the U.N. General Assembly has considered the question every two years and has passed a series of resolutions on the subject.

2. UNESCO Action

In response to G.A. Resolution 3187,[14] the 18h General Assembly of UNESCO in 1974 passed a resolution inviting the Director-General to contribute to the work of restitution

---

[11] Convention on the Means of Prohibiting and Preventing the Illicit Import, Export and Transfer of Ownership of Cultural Property (Nov. 14, 1970), *available at* http://portal.unesco.org/en/ev.php-URL_ID=13039&URL_DO=DO_TOPIC&URL_SECTION=201.html.

[12] G.A. Res. 3187 (XXVIII) (Dec. 18, 1973).

[13] G.A. Res. 1514 (XV) (Dec. 14, 1960).

[14] *See supra* note 12.

> by defining in general terms the most suitable methods, including exchanges on the basis of long-term loans, and by promoting bilateral arrangements to that end [Resolution 3.428].

In 1978, Amadou M'Bow (director-general of UNESCO) issued a "A Plea for the Return of an Irreplaceable Cultural Heritage to those who Created It." This appeal tries to keep a balance but puts the case clearly for those states that resented the refusal of holding states to deal with historical injustices.[15]

That same year, following advice from the International Council of Museums, the UNESCO Intergovernmental Committee for Promoting the Return of Cultural Property to its Countries of Origin or its Restitution in Case of Illicit Appropriation was established. Despite this, the committee has been used very little. After 14 sessions of the committee, there have only been eight cases formally submitted to it. Two cases have been settled; another was resolved by litigation in the courts of the holding country; one has not been proceeded with; one resulted in a return; and one has only just been submitted. Two are still outstanding. The most notorious of these is that of the Parthenon marbles held by the British Museum. Only three of the eight cases are arguably colonial type situations (two between Turkey and each of the two former German Republics and between Greece and the United Kingdom). In neither case was there a direct colonial relationship between the countries concerned: there was, however, in both a powerplay between a colonial power and a developing country, which gave the country of origin of the objects little real freedom of choice. The sphinx from Hattusha, the ancient capital of the Hittite kingdom (modern Boguskoy) was taken to Germany in 1917. The Parthenon marbles were taken to the United Kingdom in 1806, over 170 years before the setting up of the committee.

In recent years, there has been a general acceptance that formal limitation periods should not prevent return in cases of spoliation during the Second World War. The UNESCO committee would have jurisdiction in such cases. In the early 1990s, when the emergence of some independent states from the Soviet Union and the change of philosophy in others led to renewed claims about cultural property missing since the Second World War, UNESCO made it discreetly known to those states making and receiving claims that it was ready to assist and that the committee would have jurisdiction to handle such disputes. Without exception, they all replied that they would prefer first to seek to resolve such claims at the bilateral level.

It is clear that the UNESCO committee is not being used to facilitate solutions in the cases where it has jurisdiction. This is true of objects taken by the colonizing state during the colonial period as well as objects in cases that may technically not have concerned a colonizing and a colonized country, but nonetheless where the local people were unable to prevent transfers of cultural

---

[15] This important document foreshadows many of the arguments being raised by ex-colonial and other states at present. The full text is available from the UNESCO Web site and should be consulted; http://www.unesco.org/culture/laws/pdf/PealforReturn_DG_1978.pdf.

property that never had their real consent. Examples are those where cultural objects were taken during punitive raids, such as the removal of the Benin bronzes by a British expeditionary force in 1897, the looting of the Ethiopian capital, Maqdala, by British forces in 1868, and the taking of over 170 volumes of the Korean national archives by French naval forces in 1866.

A particularly difficult issue is that of human remains. Institutions in the West have holdings of skulls, mummified bodies, and bones that have in the past been used for display, as well as for medical and other scientific research. Some people, particularly indigenous and tribal groups, view such scientific research as desecration of their ancestors. They maintain that the only solution is for human remains to be returned and re-buried. Clearly such claims are in a special position: respect for other cultures, a fundamental tenet of cultural interchange enshrined in Article 1 of UNESCO's 1966 Declaration of the Principles of International Cultural Cooperation,[16] requires that practices with regard to human remains deriving from another culture should not be offensive to that culture. Indigenous peoples in Australia, Canada, New Zealand, and the United States have had their claims recognized, and material has been returned to them. They have also made claims at the international level, though with less success.

However this is a situation where the UNESCO committee is unlikely ever to be requested to act. First, the very name of the committee—UNESCO Intergovernmental Committee for Promoting the Return of Cultural *Property* [emphasis added] to its Countries of Origin or its Restitution in Case of Illicit Appropriation—is abhorrent to most claimants, as they do not regard human remains as property and, indeed, find that quite unacceptable. Secondly, the groups most concerned do not have a direct right of access to the committee, since only member states of UNESCO can make requests. This means that they first have to persuade their national states to make such requests on their behalf.

To summarize, UNESCO's response to the legacy of colonialism has not been as successful as its response to the legacy of conflict. It has no convention on the subject owing to the strong opposition of holding states, and the director-general's plea has been, at least until very recently, largely ignored. Although the UNESCO committee has jurisdiction to receive requests for return, it does not have a mandate to decide between states but can only mediate. It is not being used by the former colonies for their claims.

D. COMMERCE

UNESCO's interest in this aspect of heritage protection relates to the damage caused to cultural heritage by criminal activity in many countries and its tolerance, and indeed, as shown by recent litigation in the United States[17]

[16] Declaration of Principles of International Cultural Cooperation (Nov. 4, 1966), *available at* http://portal.unesco.org/en/ev.php-URL_ID=13147&URL_DO=DO_TOPIC&URL_SECTION=201.html.

[17] United States v. Schultz, 333 F.3d 393 (2d Cir. 2003), *cert. denied*, 124 S. Ct. 1041 (2004).

and Italy,[18] endorsement and even instigation, by trading interests in wealthy states.

1. The 1970 Convention

The history of the 1970 Convention[19] against illicit trafficking is enlightening. Although it was a difficult negotiation, it was adopted by the General Conference of UNESCO with only one negative vote and eight abstentions. The United States became a party in 1983, but it was many years until any other major art trading state followed suit. Countries that had interests both of protection and of trade, such as Argentina in 1973, Canada and Italy both in 1978, Australia in 1989, and "victim" states did ratify. The arguments against the 1970 Convention by the art trade states were that it was against free trade principles, that its principles were acceptable but its mechanisms were not, in one case that it was contrary to the Agreement on the Importation of Educational, Scientific and Cultural Materials 1950 (the "Florence Agreement"),[20] and, in another case, that the government concerned "saw no advantage" for that country in adopting it. Several pronouncements were made that it was a failure.[21] Nonetheless, in every year since its adoption, it continued and still continues to achieve new participations.

UNESCO continued its efforts to persuade and to elucidate. The 1970 Convention now has 115 states parties (France in 1997, the United Kingdom in 2002, Switzerland in 2003, and Germany in 2007). Other European states with substantial collecting and dealing interests, such as the Scandinavian states, have also ratified. The Netherlands has passed legislation in the lower house of Parliament and is expecting passage through the upper house shortly, meaning a ratification is probable in 2008 or 2009. Belgium announced in 2005 that it would become party to the convention "as quickly as possible."[22] Japan also became a party to the convention in 2002, though it is doubtful whether its legislation adequately implements the convention.[23]

The drafting of the 1970 Convention is not entirely satisfactory and has given rise to divergent interpretations. Regarded as radical in its day, 39 years later, 1970 has become the watershed date for assessments of provenance,

---

[18] Tribunale di Roma, Decision Dec. 13, 2004, against Giacomo Medici (currently subject to appeal) and current prosecution of Robert Hecht (dealer) and Marion True (until 2005 Curator of Antiquities at the Getty Museum in California). Both cases are discussed in detail in P. Watson, P. & C. Todeschini, The Medici Conspiracy (2006).

[19] *See supra* note 11.

[20] Agreement on the Importation of Educational, Scientific and Cultural Materials (June 17, 1950), *available at* http://portal.unesco.org/en/ev.php-URL_ID=12074&URL_DO=DO_TOPIC&URL_SECTION=201.html.

[21] Notably by John Merryman, *The Nation and the Object*, 3 Int'l J. Cultural Prop. 61, 63 (1994), *reprinted in* J.H. Merryman, Thinking About the Elgin Marbles: Critical Essays on Cultural Property, Art and Law 158–73 (2000).

[22] UNESCO Press Release, Feb. 2, 2005, "Official visit by UNESCO Director-General Koichiro Matsuura" to Belgium. Belgium deposited its instrument of ratification on March 31, 2009.

[23] P.J. O'Keefe, Commentary on the 1970 Convention 124–28 (2d ed. 2007).

as is shown by the following guidelines[24] for museums issued by the British Department for Culture, Media, and Sport with respect to intended acquisitions of foreign origin:

The museum must either:

- be certain and have evidence that the item was in the United Kingdom before 1970 and have no reason to suspect it was illegally exported from its country of origin or
- be certain that the item was out of the country of origin (but not in the United Kingdom) before 1970 and have evidence that its subsequent export to the United Kingdom was in line with the regulations of the country from which it was exported to the United Kingdom or
- be certain that the item was in its country of origin after 1970 and have evidence that it was legally exported in line with the regulations of the country of origin.

Clearly the 1970 Convention has not only changed the obligations of states at the international level but has influenced the practice of states that have not become party to it. The Association of Art Museum Directors (AAMD) in the United States recently produced a report stating that its members "normally should not acquire a work unless research substantiates that the work was outside its country of probable modern discovery before 1970 or was legally exported from its country of probable modern discovery after 1970."[25]

2. The 1995 UNIDROIT Convention

The failure of the 1970 Convention[26] to deal with the very difficult issues of limitation and good faith acquisition led UNESCO, starting from its proposal in 1985, to work with UNIDROIT to develop a convention dealing with these aspects of private law. The resulting UNIDROIT Convention on Stolen or Illegally Exported Cultural Objects, 1995 ("1995 UNIDROIT Convention")[27] would certainly not have been achieved without the change in public attitudes affected by the 1970 Convention. The 1995 UNIDROIT Convention is regarded as complementary to the 1970 Convention and is promoted by UNESCO at the same time.

The UNIDROIT Convention currently has 29 states parties, and another nine states have signed but not yet ratified. It too dealt with very difficult aspects of law, where there was a considerable diversity of legal regulation and philosophy. It will not, therefore, have a rapid accession or ratification rate. On

---

[24] *Combating Illicit Trade: Due Diligence Guidelines for Museums, Libraries and Archives on Collecting and Borrowing Cultural Material* (2005), *available at* http://www.culture.gov.uk/SearchResults.aspx?_SRH_SearchString=museum%20guidelines (last visited June 30, 2008).

[25] *See* http://aamd.org/newsroom/documents/2008ReportAndRelease.pdf.

[26] *See supra* note 11.

[27] UNIDROIT Convention on Stolen or Illegally Exported Cultural Objects (June 24, 1995), *available at* http://www.unidroit.org/english/conventions/1995culturalproperty/1995culturalproperty-e.htm.

the other hand, it does resolve what have been heretofore intractable problems that enable stolen and other illegally traded objects relatively easy entrance into the legal trade, thus fueling damage and destruction of sites and theft of movables. It is also very well drafted and therefore less liable to flights of imaginative interpretation to avoid serious obligation. Finally, after 13 years of the UNIDROIT Convention's existence, 29 of the 61 member states of UNIDROIT are party to this convention, nearly half of its members. After 13 years of existence, the 1970 Convention (in 1983) there were 50 states parties to the 1970 Convention, less than one-third of its then 163 member states (currently it has 115 states parties of the 193 member states of UNESCO). The UNIDROIT Convention is, of course, open to any state to join. It is likely to be a significant function of UNESCO over the next 20 years to convince states of the importance of the 1995 UNIDROIT Convention and to persuade them to join this demanding international network of obligations.

3. The 2001 Convention

Finally, the battle to cleanse the art trade was the major motivation behind the Convention on the Protection of the Underwater Cultural Heritage, 2001 ("the 2001 Convention").[28] The severe restrictions on the trading of artifacts from unauthorized underwater activities have certainly drawn criticism.[29] This degree of control is, however, a natural response to a totally unregulated situation, which has led to commercial salvage of, and treasure hunts for, historic shipwrecks. The unregulated situation resulted, in many cases, in the complete destruction of the historic shipwrecks and no cultural benefit for any of the peoples associated with it (by history, location, origin of ship, origin of cargo). There was therefore a consensus at the negotiations that the lack of regulation had created a situation of such dire emergency that further commercial exploration was likely to wreck the last vestiges of an irreplaceable archaeological resource. Interestingly enough, this provision and the rules of the annex, which spell out this principle in detail, were accepted by the end of the third session of the negotiations by every delegation without exception. The United States, which is unlikely to ratify the 2001 Convention at present, went to the extent of expressing its complete accord with these provisions while voting against the adoption of the 2001 Convention at the UNESCO General Conference.

UNESCO has persistently responded to the problem of damage to the cultural heritage from improper handling by working to exclude from commerce any objects that have been illicitly trafficked. It is painstaking work, but no other organization in the world has done anything like the amount of important standard-setting in this area as has UNESCO.

---

[28] Convention on the Protection of the Underwater Cultural Heritage (Nov. 6, 2001), *available at* http://unesdoc.unesco.org/images/0012/001260/126065e.pdf.

[29] Described as "breath-taking" by John Merryman, in *Cultural Property Internationalism*, 12 INT'L J. CULTURAL PROP. 25 (2005).

E. THE CURRENT POLITICAL CONTEXT

While UNESCO's standard-setting on heritage protection for its first half century could be seen as a response to the legacy of conquest, colonization, and commerce, its most recent two conventions do not fall easily into those categories. The earlier conventions are based on the need for technical rules designed to bind all states into a protective network and were established at the request of a significant number of states prepared to accept serious adjustments to their existing legal obligations. The Convention for the Safeguarding of the Intangible Cultural Heritage, 2003,[30] and the Convention on the Protection and Promotion of the Diversity of Cultural Expressions, 2005,[31] seem more truly to respond to the desire of certain states who wish to popularize a particular view of heritage and to provide ammunition to defend interests that are considered to be under attack in other international fora.

1. The World Heritage Convention

The UNESCO Convention concerning the Protection of the World Cultural and Natural Heritage, 1972 ("World Heritage Convention")[32] was perhaps a precursor of this other approach to the making of conventions. Its text was the result of a consolidation of two separate texts. One was prepared by the International Council for Monuments and Sites (ICOMOS) as a response to the problem of state-initiated major works projects likely to destroy or irrevocably alter sites of extreme importance in cultural development, along the lines of the UNESCO Recommendation concerning the Preservation of Cultural Property Endangered by Public or Private Works, 1968.[33] The other was an initiative of the United States working through the International Union for the Conservation of Nature (IUCN—now the "World Conservation Union"). The United States wanted to mark the 100th anniversary of the establishment of the world's first natural reserve, Yellowstone National Park, in 1872, and was initially only interested in natural sites. Here lies the germ of that treatment of the World Heritage Convention as a kind of international endorsement of national pride in heritage. The putting together of these two different kinds of heritage preceded the current understanding of the mutual dependence of the cultural and natural aspects of sites and, indeed, of humanity and its achievements in relation to its natural context. It possibly also led to some confusion as to the aim of the World Heritage Convention.

---

[30] Convention for the Safeguarding of the Intangible Cultural Heritage (Oct. 17, 2003), *available at* http://unesdoc.unesco.org/images/0013/001325/132540e.pdf.

[31] Convention on the Protection and Promotion of the Diversity of Cultural Expressions, (Oct. 20, 2005), *available at* http://portal.unesco.org/en/ev.php-URL_ID=31038&URL_DO=DO_TOPIC&URL_SECTION=201.html.

[32] UNESCO Convention concerning the Protection of the World Cultural and Natural Heritage (Nov. 16, 1972), *available at* http://portal.unesco.org/en/ev.php-URL_ID=13055&URL_DO=DO_TOPIC&URL_SECTION=201.html.

[33] Recommendation concerning the Preservation of Cultural Property Endangered by Public or Private Works (Nov. 19, 1968), *available at* http://portal.unesco.org/en/ev.php-URL_ID=13085&URL_DO=DO_TOPIC&URL_SECTION=201.html.

An international convention sets up reciprocal obligations between states. If these are not met, then the state not conforming to its obligations has violated international law and could be the object of a legal or arbitral claim by another state party to the convention. We have seen the kind of claims that could be made under the Hague Convention on Land Warfare, 1907, and 1954 Hague Conventions[34]—indeed, the specialized tribunals for war crimes now sitting in The Hague and elsewhere (such as those for Yugoslavia and Rwanda), as well as the new statute for the International Criminal Court, are specifically foreseen to enforce obligations under those conventions.

A striking feature of the World Heritage Convention is that the major obligations set out in Articles 3 to 5 are not easy for another state party to enforce. They seem more in the nature of declarations of intent than legal obligations to another state, especially since they are all performed on a state's own territory. Note that the wording of Articles 4 and 5 requires a state "to do all it can, to the utmost of its own resources" and uses phrases such as "in so far as possible and as appropriate for each country." These give a wide latitude for subjective judgment.

Article 6(3) might be seen as a more solid obligation, since a state party agrees "not to take any deliberate measures which might damage directly or indirectly" the cultural heritage of another state party. There was discussion in the intergovernmental World Heritage Committee about a mining project on part of the world heritage site of Mount Nimba, jointly nominated by Guinea and Côte d'Ivoire. Leaving aside the issue of the *nominating* states' obligations, should the French government have stopped the French mining company from acting contrary to the conditions on which the site had been listed as world heritage? The issue was resolved without answering that question by excising the area of the mine from the world heritage site.

Perhaps the contribution to the World Heritage Fund (Articles 5–18) is a well-defined legal obligation. Notably, the World Heritage Convention leaves open the possibility of making an optional, rather than a compulsory, contribution to the fund (Article 16(2)). Probably the fluid nature of the convention's wording explains why very few legal scholars have written about the convention and that the first detailed commentary on its articles appeared only in 2008.[35]

Apart from the very general duties of protection imposed on the states parties by the World Heritage Convention, there is also the phrasing of Article 6(1). This clause did not appear in the preliminary draft on the protection of monuments, groups of buildings, and sites that was prepared by UNESCO in June 1971 and was the basis of much of the convention. However, its insertion was a key point for some delegations, such as the United States, and it was one of the last clauses to have its text finalized in the drafting process.

---

34 *See supra* notes 3 and 4.

35 F. Francioni & F. Lenzerini, The 1972 World Heritage Convention: A Commentary (2008).

> 6(1) Whilst fully respecting the sovereignty of the States on whose territory the cultural and natural heritage mentioned in Articles 1 and 2 is situated, and without prejudice to property right provided by national legislation, the States Parties to this Convention recognize that such heritage constitutes a world heritage for whose protection it is the duty of the international community as a whole to co-operate.

So, does Article 6(1) mean that a state can avoid its obligations under the convention by arguing that a matter raised by the World Heritage Committee or another state party relating to a violation of the convention is within its sovereignty and therefore outside the reach of the convention? If so, then what is the point of having the convention? I will come back to this point in Section E.3 below.

The nature of the obligations of the states parties has been analyzed in Australia, the only legal system where litigation has resulted in a detailed and extensive examination of the World Heritage Convention by the supreme tribunal in the country (the High Court of Australia).[36] In 1982, the "Tasmanian Wilderness," a site of over 1 million hectares in the island state south of the Australian continent, was inscribed on the World Heritage List. In 1983, the federal government made regulations prohibiting the making of a dam on the site. Tasmania argued before the Australian High Court that the World Heritage Convention imposed no obligation on the Commonwealth to pass the laws it had made, because the convention was no more than a statement of general political accord to pursue broad objectives that leaves it to each state party to determine its course of action concerning the world heritage. Nation-states should not be assumed to be willing to surrender the regulation of heritage in their territory to an international regime and hence to restrict their freedom of action.[37]

The court did not accept this view. In the robust view of Judge Deane,

> However loosely such obligations may be defined, it is apparent that Australia, by depositing its instrument of ratification, bound itself to observe the terms of the Convention and assumed real and substantive obligations under them . . . Unless one is to take the view that over seventy nations have engaged in the solemn and cynical farce of using words such as "obligation" and "duty" where neither was intended or undertaken, the provisions of the Convention impose real and identifiable obligations and provide for the availability of real benefits at least in respect of those properties which have . . . been indisputably made the subject of those obligations and identified as qualified for those benefits by being entered, upon the nomination of the states in which they are situated, on the World Heritage List.[38]

[36] Commonwealth v. Tasmania [1983] H.C.A. 21, (1983) 158 C.L.R. 1, 13.

[37] Arguments reported *id.* at 478, 526, 546.

[38] *Id.* at 546.

The integrity of the World Heritage Convention, as an international legal instrument of solemn reciprocal state relations, was preserved by this interpretation. But the High Court of Australia is so far the only tribunal that has been called on to decide this question.

2. The 2003 and 2005 Conventions

The two latest conventions of UNESCO relating to the cultural heritage, the Convention for the Safeguarding of the Intangible Cultural Heritage, 2003 ("2003 Convention"),[39] and the Convention on the Protection and Promotion of the Diversity of Cultural Expressions, 2005 ("2005 Convention"),[40] might equally give rise to questions about the purpose of their adoption. Is it really "to impose real and identifiable obligations"[41] on states or, as Tasmania argued, to make "a statement of general political accord to pursue broad objectives"[42] without restricting their freedom of action?

The 2003 Convention is virtually a copy of the World Heritage Convention,[43] and the opportunity to avoid the weaker interpretation of the convention (which in Judge Deane's view would have made it "a solemn and cynical farce") by more precise language has not been taken, despite expert criticism emerging from 30 years experience with that convention. The motivation behind the 2003 Convention was to provide states whose cultural energies are best read from their living cultural traditions, rather than from their artifacts, with international recognition similar to that endowed by inscription on the World Heritage List. An international convention was not necessary to do this, any more than it was necessary in 1972, had that then been the sole intention of that convention. In the case of the intangible heritage, there was already a process established by UNESCO in 1997, the Proclamation on Masterpieces of the Oral and Intangible Heritage, to list and thus publicize and endorse national examples of such heritage. Such proclamations were made in 2001 and 2003, clear evidence from UNESCO's own practice that a convention was not necessary for this purpose.

In the 2003 Convention, there are, once again, no enforcement provisions, and the obligations on states to contribute assistance funding are optional. The existing items currently on the three Proclamations of Masterpieces of the Oral and Intangible Heritage of Humanity are to be incorporated into the Representative List of the Intangible Cultural Heritage of Humanity established by the 2003 Convention (Article 31). As a result, more than one expert may assume that the purpose of the 2003 Convention was to endorse national policy without creating new and serious inter-state obligations. While states with a rich

---

[39] Convention for the Safeguarding of the Intangible Cultural Heritage (Oct. 17, 2003), *available at* http://unesdoc.unesco.org/images/0013/001325/132540e.pdf.

[40] Convention on the Protection and Promotion of the Diversity of Cultural Expressions (Oct. 20, 2005, *available at* http://portal.unesco.org/en/ev.php-URL_ID=31038&URL_DO=DO_TOPIC&URL_SECTION=201.html.

[41] *See supra* note 38.

[42] *See supra* note 36.

[43] *See supra* note 32.

intangible heritage may feel satisfied with such a result, international lawyers may well feel some disquiet about the use of a convention for such a purpose.

The 2005 Convention arose, in particular, out of a view held strongly by some states that "artistic expressions" (now phrased as "cultural expressions"), should be exempted from certain trade rules. France and Canada, in particular, have sought to preserve the "cultural exception" in international trade law from efforts to delete it by the United States, which would like to see these markets for film, television, and print more open to competition from other states. France and Canada, however, fear "dumping" by foreign commercial interests into their markets, thus destroying their distinctive national voice in such products. This concern could be seen as the basis of their efforts to establish the 2005 Convention, and this possible view is supported strongly by the vigorous debate created over Article 20 of the 2005 Convention.

That provision reads as follows:

Article 20—Relationship to Other Treaties: Mutual Supportiveness, Complementarity and Non-Subordination

1. Parties recognize that they shall perform in good faith their obligations under this Convention and all other treaties to which they are parties. Accordingly, without subordinating this Convention to any other treaty,
   (a) they shall foster mutual supportiveness between this Convention and the other treaties to which they are parties; and
   (b) when interpreting and applying the other treaties to which they are parties or when entering into other international obligations, Parties shall take into account the relevant provisions of this Convention.
2. Nothing in this Convention shall be interpreted as modifying rights and obligations of the Parties under any other treaties to which they are parties.

Once again, some may question whether the 2005 Convention does more than state a shared policy without creating new and serious inter-state obligations. The speed from first draft to adoption of these two conventions (two years) does not reassure. It is also notable how much more popular and readily ratified are conventions that have relatively weak or minimal obligations. Thus, the recent 2003 and 2005 Conventions already have 95 and 83 parties, respectively, and the World Heritage Convention has 185. This is an indication that states have little to change—probably no legislation is required and little study made as the text seems undemanding. The Annex to this chapter provides a chart showing participation in the various conventions.

3. The Value of These Conventions

It is notable that the last five of UNESCO's cultural heritage treaties (the World Heritage Convention, the Second Protocol, the 2001 Convention, the 2003 Convention, and the 2005 Convention) have all provided for the establishment of intergovernmental bodies to supervise the working of the treaty. The committees have various functions—in relation to the World Heritage List and Representative List of Intangible Cultural Heritage, the principal function is the vetting of nominations and decisions on inscriptions and the granting of financial assistance. In other cases, it may be to have a general supervisory role in the conventions' working. While such bodies are very popular with states, one has to inquire whether they provide good value for their cost. With the relatively small budget allocated for heritage law within UNESCO,[44] a good deal of it will be taken up with simply administering these committees, consequently lessening the amount available for assistance to states with drafting of legislation and implementation of the conventions. (The burden of translation and interpretation alone is immense.) Furthermore, taking these sorts of functions away from the secretariat makes the implementation of the treaty far more political. Finally, action by such supervisory bodies might indeed have represented a serious intergovernmental commitment, if it were not the case that they have no real power to address violations and that, in some instances, these intergovernmental bodies have themselves ignored or contradicted the views of the expert bodies responsible for assessments. Such committees may, however, provide a useful forum for discussion of the best management principles, later embodied in substantial guidelines.[45]

The lack of serious legal commitment in these instruments reflects a cynicism on the part of states parities about UNESCO's law-making process, which is disturbing. These suspicions gain weight when one looks at the wording of these instruments. Consider the following "definitions" (emphasis added to show the circularity of these formulations):

> The "intangible *cultural* heritage" means the practices, representations, expressions, knowledge, skills—as well as the instruments, objects, artefacts and cultural spaces associated therewith—that communities, groups and, in some cases, individuals recognize as part of their *cultural* heritage. This intangible cultural heritage, transmitted from generation to generation, is constantly recreated by communities and groups in response to their environment, their interaction with nature and their history, and provides them with a sense of identity and continuity, thus promoting respect for cultural diversity and human creativity. For the purposes of this Convention, consideration will be given solely to such intangible cultural heritage as is compatible with existing international human rights instruments, as well as with the requirements

[44] The 2008–2009 budget of UNESCO allocated $13,750,200 for activities to implement the heritage conventions. This amounts to less than 2.2 percent of the regular budget of $621 million. Even including staff costs for the cultural heritage conventions, the total is still only about 6.5 percent of the total budget. It should be noted that other funds are raised by voluntary donations from states. It should also be borne in mind that the total budget of UNESCO covers, besides standard-setting and operational measures for preservation of cultural heritage, major programs in education (which takes by far the biggest slice (17 percent) of the budget), sciences (natural and social), as well as communication and information.

[45] *See infra* note 47.

> of mutual respect among communities, groups and individuals, and of sustainable development [(Article 2(1), 2003 Convention].
>
> "*Cultural* diversity" refers to the manifold ways in which the *cultures* of groups and societies find expression. These expressions are passed on within and among groups and societies. Cultural diversity is made manifest not only through the varied ways in which the cultural heritage of humanity is expressed, augmented and transmitted through the variety of cultural expressions, but also through diverse modes of artistic creation, production, dissemination, distribution and enjoyment, whatever the means and technologies used [Article 4(1), 2005 Convention].
>
> "*Cultural* content" refers to the symbolic meaning, artistic dimension and *cultural* values that originate from or express cultural identities [Article 4(2), 2005 Convention].
>
> "*Cultural* expressions" are those expressions that result from the creativity of individuals, groups and societies, and that have *cultural* content [Article 4(3), 2005 Convention].

All of these "definitions" are circular, since they contain the same concept both in the term being defined and in its meaning, and the first three are also descriptive rather than definitive.

Another problem is the use of non-mandatory language. Consider the following examples (emphasis added):

> To ensure the safeguarding, development and promotion of the intangible cultural heritage present in its territory, each State Party shall *endeavour* to:
> (a) *adopt* a general policy aimed at promoting the function of the intangible cultural heritage in society, and at integrating the safeguarding of such heritage into planning programmes;
> (b) *designate or establish one or more competent bodies* for the safeguarding of the intangible cultural heritage present in its territory;
> (c) *foster* scientific, technical and artistic studies, as well as research methodologies, with a view to effective safeguarding of the intangible cultural heritage, in particular the intangible cultural heritage in danger;
> (d) *adopt appropriate* legal, technical, administrative and financial measures. [Article14, 2003 Convention].
>
> Within the framework of its safeguarding activities of the intangible cultural heritage, each State Party *shall endeavour to ensure* the widest possible participation of communities, groups and, *where appropriate*, individuals that create, maintain and transmit such heritage, and to involve them actively in its management [Article 15, 2003 Convention].
>
> Within the framework of its cultural policies and measures as defined in Article 4.6 *and taking into account its own particular circumstances and*

> *needs*, each Party *may* adopt measures aimed at protecting and promoting the diversity of cultural expressions within its territory. [Article 6(1), 2005 Convention].
>
> Parties *shall endeavour* to strengthen their bilateral, regional and international cooperation for the creation of conditions conducive to the promotion of the diversity of cultural expressions . [Article 12, 2005 Convention].

Contrast this language, for example, with that of the European Convention for the Protection of the Architectural Heritage, 1985:[46]

Article 4

Each Party undertakes:

1. to implement appropriate supervision and authorisation procedures as required by the legal protection of the properties in question;
2. to prevent the disfigurement, dilapidation or demolition of protected properties. To this end, each Party undertakes to introduce, if it has not already done so, legislation which:
   a. requires the submission to a competent authority of any scheme for the demolition or alteration of monuments which are already protected, or in respect of which protection proceedings have been instituted, as well as any scheme affecting their surroundings;
   b. requires the submission to a competent authority of any scheme affecting a group of buildings or a part thereof or a site which involves:
      - demolition of buildings,
      - the erection of new buildings,
      - substantial alterations which impair the character of the buildings or the site;
   c. permits public authorities to require the owner of a protected property to carry out work or to carry out such work itself if the owner fails to do so;
   d. allows compulsory purchase of a protected property.

Article 5

Each Party undertakes to prohibit the removal, in whole or in part, of any protected monument, except where the material safeguarding of such monuments makes removal imperative. In these circumstances the competent authority shall take the necessary precautions for its dismantling, transfer and reinstatement at a suitable location.

---

[46] European Convention for the Protection of the Architectural Heritage (Mar. 10, 1985), *available at* http://conventions.coe.int/Treaty/en/Treaties/Html/121.htm.

Then there is the insertion of a "national sovereignty" clause, already discussed in relation to Article 6 of the 1972 World Heritage Convention and replicated in the 2005 Convention:

> The Parties, . . . *reaffirm their sovereign right* to formulate and implement their cultural policies and to adopt measures to protect and promote the diversity of cultural expressions and to strengthen international cooperation to achieve the purposes of this Convention [Article 5(1), 2005 Convention].

Of course, conventions do have a very important educational effect—seen from the history of the 1954, 1970, and 1972 Conventions. But this should not be their sole function: there are other methods of education that may be superior, and a convention alone is certainly not sufficient to educate. It is also true that the very limited amounts of financial assistance available from the World Heritage Fund have been used as seed money to attract much more substantial funding from other bodies, although such a fund can, of course, be set up without the need for a convention.

Despite these benefits, the doubts sown by sloppy language, inadequate definitions, and "permissive" rather than precise language, tend not only to discredit the convention in question, but to raise skepticism about the other existing UNESCO conventions, which may have taken very many years to negotiate and are regarded by their states parties as entailing very serious reciprocal and justiciable obligations.

Thus, the current political context of heritage lawmaking within UNESCO may be seen by many as not conducive to good heritage lawmaking by that body.

F. IMPLEMENTATION AND THE ART OF THE POSSIBLE

None of the issues that UNESCO has been asked to deal with are easy to solve, and opinions are divided on its success. Nonetheless, it is the only international organization with a mandate for lawmaking at the universal level for cultural heritage,[47] and it has been responsible for a considerable body of international law on the subject. Besides the six conventions and the two protocols, its very important work in soft law should not be forgotten. Apart from the declarations,[48] the plea mentioned in Section C.2, and the guidelines,[49]

[47] There are, of course, some regional organizations such as the Council of Europe, and more recently the European Union, as well as the Organization of Andean States, which have such a mandate for a more restricted number of states.

[48] Declaration of Principles of International Cultural Cooperation, 1966, *supra* note 16; UNESCO Universal Declaration on Cultural Diversity (Nov. 2, 2001), *available at* http://portal.unesco.org/en/ev.php-URL_ID=13179&URL_DO=DO_TOPIC&URL_SECTION=201.html; UNESCO Declaration concerning the Intentional Destruction of Cultural Heritage (Oct. 17, 2003), *available at* http://portal.unesco.org/en/ev.php-URL_ID=17718&URL_DO=DO_TOPIC&URL_SECTION=201.html.

[49] Standard Form concerning Requests for Return or Restitution of Cultural Property adopted by the UNESCO Intergovernmental Committee for Promoting the Return of Cultural Property to its Countries of Origin or its Restitution in Case of Illicit Appropriation in

UNESCO has been responsible for 13 recommendations that set the standards of best practice for the protection of cultural heritage. These are as follows:

- Recommendation on International Principles Applicable to Archaeological Excavations, 1956;
- Recommendation concerning the most Effective Means of Rendering Museums Accessible to Everyone, 1960;
- Recommendation concerning the Safeguarding of the Beauty and Character of Landscapes and Sites, 1962;
- Recommendation on the Means of Prohibiting and Preventing the Illicit Import, Export and Transfer of Ownership of Cultural Property, 1964;
- Recommendation concerning the Preservation of Cultural Property Endangered by Public or Private Works, 1968;
- Recommendation concerning the Protection, at National Level, of the Cultural and Natural Heritage, 1972;
- Recommendation on Participation by the People at Large in Cultural Life and their Contribution to It, 1976;
- Recommendation concerning the Safeguarding and Contemporary Role of Historic Areas, 1976;
- Recommendation concerning the International Exchange of Cultural Property, 1976;
- Recommendation for the Protection of Movable Cultural Property, 1978;
- Recommendation for the Safeguarding and Preservation of Moving Images, 1980;
- Recommendation concerning the Status of the Artist, 1980; and
- Recommendation for the Protection of Folklore and Traditional Culture, 1989.[50]

It is notable that there have been no standard-setting recommendations on cultural heritage since 1989. This suggests that their useful persuasive functions have been pushed into the form of conventions. Such conventions may, however, as we have seen, have been reduced by linguistic softening and have little more effect than if they were recommendations.

The recommendations in some respects are more successful than the conventions: they are more likely to be based on technical expertise (such as advice from the International Council of Museums (ICOM) or ICOMOS) and are somewhat less likely for their text to be highjacked at the negotiating stage by extraneous political factors that slow down negotiations by the need to study

1983; Guidelines for the Use of the Standard Form Concerning Requests for Return or Restitution of Cultural Property adopted by that Committee in 1985; and Operational Guidelines for the Implementation of the World Heritage Convention first adopted in 1977 with a total of 28 paragraphs, revised 17 times and now with 290 paragraphs and nine annexes running to a total of 161 pages.

[50] *See* http://portal.unesco.org/en/ev.php-URL_ID=13649&URL_DO=DO_TOPIC&URL_SECTION=-471.html.

new draft provisions that have little to do with the substance of the text.[51] On the other hand, although member sates of UNESCO have a legal obligation to bring their provisions to the notice of the relevant national authorities and to report on their implementation or the reasons why they are not being implemented, many states not only ignore these obligations, but seem even unaware of the recommendations' existence, even though they provide very useful principles on which to base satisfactory heritage policy.

Some of the recommendations have been extremely influential. Some of the more important are as follows: the Recommendation on International Principles Applicable to Archaeological Excavations, 1956, which, though regarded as radical in its day, has become the basis of the majority of national legislation on the subject; the Recommendation concerning the Safeguarding of the Beauty and Character of Landscapes and Sites, 1962; the Recommendation concerning the Preservation of Cultural Property Endangered by Public or Private Works, 1968; and the Recommendation concerning the Safeguarding and Contemporary Role of Historic Areas, 1976.

On the other hand, some "soft law" is adopted simply because it is too difficult to negotiate hard law on the subject. Thus, at least three recommendations were the precursors of conventions: the Recommendation on the Means of Prohibiting and Preventing the Illicit Export, Import and Transfer of Ownership of Cultural Property, 1964; the Recommendation concerning the Protection, at National Level, of the Cultural and Natural Heritage, 1972; and the Recommendation for the Protection of Folklore and Traditional Culture, 1989. These deal with action to be taken at the national level. It is therefore somewhat surprising to find statements about action at the national level in the subsequent conventions in addition to apparently international content. Generally states have always wanted to reaffirm the inappropriateness of including, in international treaties, obligations that relate only to their domestic practice. If they are found there, it is often with additional assertions of "sovereignty," which in effect negate the international context. The texts of all three conventions omit provisions that states are not prepared to accept unequivocally in an international treaty and in that respect the contents of the conventions are frequently a shadow of those of the Recommendations on the same subject.

Similarly the principles of the Universal Declaration on Cultural Diversity, 2001, are more detailed and far broader in scope than the provisions of the 2005 Convention, while the Declaration concerning the Intentional Destruction of Cultural Heritage, 2003, states no more than existing law, and some might therefore argue that it even weakens it. Why re-state in a declaration what is already mandatory?

---

[51] For example, an interest in changing the status of warships, which was left undetermined by the U.N. Convention on the Law of the Sea (Dec. 10, 1982), *available at* http://www.un.org/Depts/los/convention_agreements/convention_overview_convention.htm, was a major concern of Russia and the United States during the negotiations for the 2001 Convention, and Germany had a particular interest at the same negotiations in securing additional jurisdiction for the Hamburg tribunal established under the U.N. 1982 convention. Arguments on these issues took up a great deal of time.

There are a number of factors that would lead to more satisfactory heritage lawmaking by UNESCO. First, UNESCO itself should devote more resources to this work. It is usually completed by a tiny secretariat, swelled perhaps for the actual negotiating meetings, but generally inadequate for the importance of the task. Secondly, it should not succumb to uninformed views that the principal function of a convention is to popularize a subject. An international convention is a serious inter-state set of obligations that reciprocally bind states. Dressing up as a convention, an agreed policy, which is not intended or expressed as an obligation, and which has no enforcement procedures, makes a mockery of international lawmaking and discredits those conventions that do make serious changes in international law by pushing existing regulation further and where state compliance, or lack of it, can be readily judged.

Thirdly, member states themselves should take this law-making function more seriously. For example, while it is understood that a state will probably reserve its most efficient negotiators for the most serious and crucial tasks such as arms control, they should make sure that their negotiating teams are more than competent, very knowledgeable in the subject and fully briefed by their governments.[52]

The states should also take the trouble to coordinate the views of different ministries and national interest groups before they enter into treaty negotiations in UNESCO. It is of no help to other delegations to know that different views are held within a delegation and that a view expressed in a working group may later be contradicted after that group has reached a conclusion with the apparent agreement of all its members. Most importantly, states must make the effort to ensure that their country speaks with the same voice on the subject when it is raised in UNESCO and in other intergovernmental organizations—it is not at all uncommon to find the delegates of a country expressing a view in another international organization that is inconsistent with views expressed by its delegates (staffed by a different ministry) in UNESCO. Such behavior contributes enormous confusion to the subject. For example, delegates from a Ministry of Trade working on topics in the International Trade Organization should see that their views do not contradict those of delegates of the Ministry of Culture of the same country speaking in UNESCO.

States should also refrain from seeking to shore up their political views by embedding them in an instrument termed a "convention" when it in fact is little more than soft law that can be perfectly, and much more appropriately, embodied in a recommendation or declaration.

Further, a state that hosts the diplomatic conference, which is intended to finalize the text, should allow sufficient time for a thorough last negotiating session. The two weeks for the Second Protocol and two weeks for the UNIDROIT final sessions led to thoroughly exhausted (and thus less efficient) delegates, rushed compromise provisions, and the dropping of certain draft

---

[52] For further comments on this issue, see the *Report on Heritage Law Creation of the Cultural Heritage Committee of the International Law Association,* 67th Conference (Helsinki) 325, at 330–32 (1996).

articles, simply to ensure that the instrument as a whole could be adopted. This is not a satisfactory way of dealing with important issues, though one understands that the huge volume of international negotiating taking place today burdens the budget and personnel of all foreign ministries of hosting countries. Since UNESCO's voted budget for standard-setting in its Culture Sector (including its advocacy work and the running of the intergovernmental committees), is so small, having states offer to host the diplomatic conference for the finalization of a convention text is a very important contribution to the work of the organization.

Finally, and most importantly of all, states must refrain from dragging extraneous political issues into negotiations that are focused on heritage. This is easier said than done, because heritage in many countries is a highly visible indicator of national identity, and other issues of national identity are therefore often easily imported into such negotiations, particularly when this ensures populist success at home. Insistence on a particular phrasing for a national interest and interpretation, which has little to do with the purpose of the convention, is often responsible for convoluted language in some instruments. An example here would be Article 10(4) of the 2001 Convention, which is not even in good English, but which one delegation insisted was essential to its participation with no amendments acceptable, even to the punctuation.[53]

It is to be hoped that the 21st century will see a continuation and maturing of international lawmaking on cultural heritage and that UNESCO's success in pioneering this field will be better recognized and supported.

[53] See the discussion of this provision in P.J. O'Keefe, Shipwrecked Heritage: A Commentary on the UNESCO Convention on Underwater Cultural Heritage 92–93 (2002).

Annex
State Parties to UNESCO's Heritage Conventions as at 30 July 2008

		1954	Protocol 1954	2nd Prot. (1999)	1970	UNIDROIT 1995	1972	2001	2003	2005
1.	Afghanistan				*	*	*			
2.	Albania	*	*		*		*		*	*
3.	Algeria				*		*		*	
4.	Andorra						*			*
5.	Angola				*		*			
6.	Antigua and Barbuda						*			
7.	Argentina	*	*	*	*	*	*	*	*	*
8.	Armenia	*	*	*	*		*		*	*
9.	Australia	*			*		*			
10.	Austria		*	*			*			*
11.	Azerbaijan		*	*	*	*	*		*	
12.	Bahamas				*					
13.	Bahrain						*			
14.	Bangladesh	*	*		*		*			*
15.	Barbados	*			*		*			
16.	Belarus	*	*	*	*		*		*	*
17.	Belgium	*	*				*		*	
18.	Belize				*		*		*	
19.	Benin						*			*
20.	Bhutan				*		*		*	
21.	Bolivia	*			*	*	*		*	*
22.	Bosnia and Herzegovina	*	*		*		*			
23.	Botswana	*					*			
24.	Brazil	*	*	*	*	*	*		*	*
25.	Brunei Darussalam									
26.	Bulgaria	*	*	*	*		*	*	*	*
27.	Burkina Faso	*	*		*		*		*	*
28.	Burundi						*		*	
29.	Cambodia	*	*		*	*	*	*	*	*
30.	Cameroon	*	*		*		*			*
31.	Canada	*	*	*	*		*			*
32.	Cape Verde						*			
33.	Central African Republic				*		*		*	
34.	Chad						*			
35.	Chile						*			*
36.	China	*	*		*	*	*		*	*
37.	Colombia	*	*		*		*		*	
38.	Comoros						*			
39.	Congo						*			
40.	Costa Rica	*	*	*	*		*		*	
41.	Côte d'Ivoire	*			*		*		*	*
42.	Croatia	*	*	*	*	*	*	*	*	*

		1954	Protocol 1954	2nd Prot. (1999)	1970	UNIDROIT 1995	1972	2001	2003	2005
43.	Cuba	*	*		*		*	*	*	*
44.	Cyprus	*	*	*	*	*	*		*	*
45.	Czech Republic	*	*	*	*		*			
46.	Democratic People's Republic of Korea				*		*			
47.	Democratic Republic of the Congo	*	*		*		*			
48.	Denmark	*	*		*		*			*
49.	Djibouti						*		*	*
50.	Dominica						*		*	
51.	Dominican Republic	*	*		*		*		*	
52.	Ecuador	*	*	*	*	*	*	*	*	*
53.	Egypt	*	*	*	*		*		*	*
54.	El Salvador	*	*	*	*	*	*			
55.	Equatorial Guinea			*						
56.	Eritrea	*					*			
57.	Estonia	*	*	*	*		*		*	*
58.	Ethiopia						*		*	
59.	Fiji						*			
60.	Finland	*	*	*	*	*	*			*
61.	France	*	*		*		*		*	*
62.	Gabon	*	*	*	*	*	*		*	*
63.	Gambia						*			
64.	Georgia	*	*		*		*		*	
65.	Germany	*	*		*		*			*
66.	Ghana	*	*				*			
67.	Greece	*	*	*	*	*	*		*	*
68.	Grenada				*		*			
69.	Guatemala	*	*	*	*	*	*		*	*
70.	Guinea	*	*		*		*		*	*
71.	Guinea-Bissau						*			
72.	Guyana						*			
73.	Haiti						*			
74.	Holy See	*	*				*			
75.	Honduras	*	*	*	*		*		*	
76.	Hungary	*	*	*	*	*	*		*	*
77.	Iceland				*		*		*	*
78.	India	*	*		*		*		*	*
79.	Indonesia	*	*				*		*	
80.	Iran (Islamic Republic of)	*	*	*	*	*	*		*	
81.	Iraq	*	*		*		*			
82.	Ireland						*			*
83.	Israel	*	*				*			
84.	Italy	*	*		*	*	*		*	*
85.	Jamaica						*			*

	1954	Protocol 1954	2nd Prot. (1999)	1970	UNIDROIT 1995	1972	2001	2003	2005
86. Japan	*	*	*	*		*		*	
87. Jordan	*	*		*		*		*	*
88. Kazakhstan	*	*				*			
89. Kenya						*		*	*
90. Kiribati						*			
91. Kuwait	*	*		*		*			*
92. Kyrgyzstan	*			*		*		*	
93. Lao People's Democratic Republic						*			*
94. Latvia	*	*				*		*	*
95. Lebanon	*	*		*		*	*	*	
96. Lesotho						*			
97. Liberia						*			
98. Libyan Arab Jamahiriya	*	*	*	*		*	*		
99. Liechtenstein	*	*							
100. Lithuania	*	*	*	*	*	*	*	*	*
101. Luxembourg		*	*			*		*	*
102. Madagascar	*	*		*		*		*	*
103. Malawi						*			
104. Malaysia	*	*				*			
105. Maldives						*			
106. Mali	*	*		*		*		*	*
107. Malta						*			*
108. Marshall Islands						*			
109. Mauritania				*		*		*	
110. Mauritius	*			*		*		*	*
111. Mexico	*	*		*		*	*	*	*
112. Micronesia (Federated States of)						*			
113. Monaco	*	*				*		*	*
114. Mongolia	*			*		*		*	*
115. Montenegro	*	*	*	*		*			
116. Morocco	*	*		*		*		*	
117. Mozambique						*		*	*
118. Myanmar	*	*				*			
119. Namibia						*		*	*
120. Nauru									
121. Nepal				*		*			
122. Netherlands	*	*	*			*			
123. New Zealand				*	*	*			*
124. Nicaragua	*	*	*	*		*		*	
125. Niger	*	*	*	*		*		*	*
126. Nigeria	*	*	*	*	*	*	*	*	*
127. Niue						*			
128. Norway	*	*		*	*	*		*	*
129. Oman	*			*		*		*	*
130. Pakistan	*	*		*		*		*	
131. Palau						*			

	1954	Protocol 1954	2nd Prot. (1999)	1970	UNIDROIT 1995	1972	2001	2003	2005
132. Panama	*	*	*	*		*	*	*	*
133. Papua New Guinea						*			
134. Paraguay	*	*	*	*	*	*	*	*	*
135. Peru	*	*	*	*	*	*		*	*
136. Philippines						*		*	
137. Poland	*	*		*		*			*
138. Portugal	*	*		*	*	*	*	*	*
139. Qatar	*		*	*		*			
140. Republic of Korea				*		*		*	
141. Republic of Moldova	*	*		*		*		*	*
142. Romania	*	*	*	*	*	*	*	*	*
143. Russian Federation	*	*		*	*	*			
144. Rwanda	*			*		*			
145. Saint Kitts and Nevis						*			
146. Saint Lucia						*	*	*	*
147. Saint Vince & Grenadines						*			
148. Samoa						*			
149. San Marino	*	*				*			
150. Sao Tome and Principe						*		*	
151. Saudi Arabia	*	*	*	*		*		*	
152. Senegal	*	*		*		*		*	*
153. Serbia	*	*		*		*			
154. Seychelles	*			*		*		*	
155. Sierra Leone						*			
156. Singapore									
157. Slovakia	*	*	*	*	*	*		*	*
158. Slovenia	*	*	*	*	*	*			*
159. Solomon Islands						*			
160. Somalia									
161. South Africa	*			*		*			*
162. Spain	*	*	*	*	*	*	*	*	*
163. Sri Lanka	*			*		*		*	
164. Sudan	*					*			
165. Suriname						*			
166. Swaziland						*			
167. Sweden	*	*		*		*			*
168. Switzerland	*	*	*	*		*			
169. Syrian Arab Republic	*	*		*		*		*	*
170. Tajikistan	*	*	*	*		*			*
171. Thailand	*	*				*			

	1954	Protocol 1954	2nd Prot. (1999)	1970	UNIDROIT 1995	1972	2001	2003	2005
172. The former Yugoslav Rep. of Macedonia	*	*	*	*				*	
173. Timor-Leste									
174. Togo						*			*
175. Tonga						*			
176. Trinidad and Tobago						*			
177. Tunisia	*	*		*		*		*	*
178. Turkey	*	*		*		*		*	
179. Turkmenistan						*			
180. Tuvalu									
181. Uganda						*			
182. Ukraine	*	*		*		*	*		
183. United Arab Emirates						*		*	
184. United Kingdom				*		*			*
185. United Republic of Tanzania	*			*		*			
186. United States of America				*		*			
187. Uruguay	*	*		*		*		*	*
188. Uzbekistan	*			*		*		*	
189. Vanuatu						*			
190. Venezuela	*			*		*		*	
191. Viet Nam				*		*		*	*
192. Yemen	*	*				*		*	
193. Zambia				*		*		*	
194. Zimbabwe	*			*		*		*	*
TOTAL	118[1]	97	48	115**	29[2]	185**	17**	95**	83**
As of May 2009	123	100	52	117	29	186	25	112	97

One hundred ninety-two (192) members of the United Nations, with the addition of the Holy See and Niue (not listed among U.N. members BUT members of UNESCO) are listed.

The following seven states are not party to any of the UNESCO heritage conventions: Brunei Darussalam, Equatorial Guinea, Nauru, Singapore, Somalia, Timor-Leste, Tuvalu.

**UNESCO Conventions are adopted by the General Conference and signed by the president of the conference and the Director-General. Thereafter they are ratified (by states that were member states of UNESCO at the date of signature) or acceded to.

[1] Andorra, Ireland, New Zealand, the Philippines, the United Kingdom, and United States, signed but have not yet ratified this convention. Following general international treaty practice, The Hague Convention and Protocols were signed at the time of adoption of the texts by individual states who intended to ratify.

[2] Nine states signed the UNIDROIT Convention but have not yet ratified. Following general international practice, The Hague Convention and Protocols and the UNIDROIT Conven-tions were signed at the time of its adoption by individual states who intended to ratify.

CHAPTER 14

2001 UNESCO CONVENTION ON THE PROTECTION OF THE UNDERWATER CULTURAL HERITAGE

Tullio Scovazzi*

A. AN UNEXPECTED OBSTACLE

On November 6, 2001, the Convention on the Protection of the Underwater Cultural Heritage (CPUCH)[1] was signed in Paris during the General Conference of UNESCO. It entered into force on January 12, 2009, and applies to "all traces of human existence having a cultural, historical or archaeological character which have been partially or totally under water, periodically or continuously, for at least 100 years."[2]

The CPUCH, which is the outcome of lengthy negotiations, was adopted by vote (87 states in favor, 4 against[3] and 15 abstentions[4]). However, the lack

* This chapter is based on T. Scovazzi, *The Protection of Underwater Cultural Heritage: Article 303 and the UNESCO Convention*, *in* DAVID FREESTONE, RICHARD BARNES & DAVID ONG EDS., THE LAW OF THE SEA—PROGRESS AND PROSPECTS 120 (2006). Some updates have been made.

[1] Convention on the Protection of the Underwater Cultural Heritage (Nov. 6, 2001), *available at* http://unesdoc.unesco.org/images/0012/001260/126065e.pdf [hereinafter CPUCH]. On this convention, see PATRICK O'KEEFE, SHIPWRECKED HERITAGE: A COMMENTARY ON THE UNESCO CONVENTION ON UNDERWATER CULTURAL HERITAGE (2002); Roberta Garabello, *The Negotiating History of the Provisions of the Convention on the Protection of the Underwater Cultural Heritage*, *in* ROBERTA GARABELLO & TULLIO SCOVAZZI EDS., THE PROTECTION OF THE UNDERWATER CULTURAL HERITAGE—BEFORE AND AFTER THE 2001 UNESCO CONVENTION 89 (2003).

[2] CPUCH, *supra*, note 1, art. 1, para. 1(a). The CPUCH entered into force after the deposit of the 20th instrument of ratification or accession (art. 27).

[3] The Russian Federation, Norway, Turkey, and Venezuela. The observer delegate of the United States, who was not entitled to vote (the United States not being a member of UNESCO at that time), regretted that his delegation could not accept the CPUCH because of objections to several key provisions relating to jurisdiction, the reporting scheme, warships, and the relationship of the convention to the U.N. Convention on the Law of the Sea (Dec. 10,1982), *available at* http://www.un.org/Depts/los/convention_agreements/convention_overview_convention.htm [hereinafter UNCLOS]. The negative vote of Turkey and Venezuela was due to disagreement on the CPUCH provisions on peaceful settlement of disputes (art. 25) and reservations (art. 30).

[4] Brazil, Czech Republic, Colombia, France, Germany, Greece, Iceland, Israel, Guinea-Bissau, Netherlands, Paraguay, Sweden, Switzerland, United Kingdom, and Uruguay. The abstentions were based on different, and sometimes opposite, reasons. For instance, the Greek delegate stated, *inter alia,* that "despite the fact that throughout the negotiations at UNESCO the majority of governmental experts were in favour of extending coastal rights over underwater cultural heritage on the continental shelf, the Draft Convention does not even mention the term 'coastal State.'" According to the French delegate, "la France est en désaccord

of consensus at the moment of its adoption should not be considered as an irreparable flaw. Not only did the great majority of developing countries vote in favor, but also several among the industrialized countries and maritime powers were satisfied with the final outcome of the negotiations.[5]

Explaining the merits of the CPUCH requires a preliminary consideration. Any attempts to deal with the cultural heritage at sea must inevitably face an unexpected obstacle, that is, Article 303 of the United Nations Convention on the Law of the Sea (UNCLOS).[6] This provision is not only incomplete, but also counter-productive. Indeed, it can be interpreted to undermine the very objective of protecting the underwater cultural heritage. Such a clear-cut assumption about the deficiencies of Articel 303 requires some elaboration.

B. THE UNCLOS REGIME

The UNCLOS regime relating to the underwater cultural heritage is based on the following scheme.

1. Two General Obligations

Article 303, paragraph 1, sets forth two very general obligations of protection and cooperation that apply to all archaeological and historical objects, wherever at sea they are found:

> States have the duty to protect objects of an archaeological and historical nature found at sea and shall co-operate for this purpose.

Due to its rather broad content, Article 303, paragraph 1, does not say very much. Nevertheless, some legal consequences can be drawn from it. A state that knowingly destroyed or allowed the destruction of elements of the underwater cultural heritage would be responsible for a breach of the obligation to protect it. Likewise, a state that persistently refused any request by other states to establish some forms of cooperation aiming at the protection of the underwater cultural heritage could also be held responsible for an internationally wrongful act. An obligation to cooperate is not devoid of legal meaning. It implies a duty to act in good faith in pursuing a common objective and in taking into account the situation of the other interested states. As the International Court of Justice remarked in its judgment of February 20, 1969, in the *North Sea Continental Shelf* cases,

---

avec le projet sur deux points précis: le statut des navires d'Etat et les droits de juridiction, dont nous considérons qu'ils sont incompatibles avec les dispositions de la Convention sur le droit de la mer."

[5] For example, Australia, Canada, China, Japan, New Zealand, the Republic of Korea voted in favor. Among the member states of the European Community (at that time), Austria, Belgium, Denmark, Finland, Ireland, Italy, Luxembourg, Portugal, and Spain voted in favor, while France, Germany, Greece, the Netherlands, Sweden, and the United Kingdom abstained.

[6] *See supra* note 3. On the UNCLOS regime of underwater cultural heritage, see LUIGI MIGLIORINO, IL RECUPERO DEGLI OGGETTI STORICI E ARCHEOLOGICI SOMMERSI NEL DIRITTO INTERNAZIONALE (1984); ANASTASIA STRATI, THE PROTECTION OF THE UNDERWATER CULTURAL HERITAGE: AN EMERGING OBJECTIVE OF THE CONTEMPORARY LAW OF THE SEA (1995).

> the parties are under an obligation to enter into negotiations with a view to arriving at an agreement, and not merely to go through a formal process of negotiation as a sort of a prior condition for the automatic application of a certain method of delimitation in the absence of agreement; they are under an obligation so to conduct themselves that the negotiations are meaningful, which will not be the case when either of them insists upon its own position without contemplating any modification of it.[7]

2. Cigarette Smugglers, Clandestine Immigrants, and Infectious Patients

While underwater cultural heritage located within internal maritime waters, archipelagic waters, and the territorial sea is subject to the jurisdiction of the coastal state,[8] Article 303, paragraph 2, UNCLOS specifically relates to archaeological and historical objects located within the 24-mile zone (the contiguous zone) set forth in Article 33 of UNCLOS:

> In order to control traffic in such objects, the coastal State may, in applying article 33, presume that their removal from the sea-bed in the zone referred to in that article without its approval would result in an infringement within its territory or territorial sea of the laws and regulations referred to in that article (namely, customs, fiscal, immigration or sanitary laws and regulations).

Article 303, paragraph 2, does give some rights to the coastal state. But the content of these rights is far from clear because the wording of the provision gets entangled in mysterious complications. As provided for in Article 33, in the contiguous zone, which is located between the external limit of the territorial sea (12 nautical miles, in the case of most states) and 24 nautical miles, the coastal state may exercise control for customs, fiscal, immigration, or sanitary purposes. If literally understood, paragraph 2 suggests that the removal of archaeological and historical objects located in the contiguous zone can determine a violation of domestic provisions relating to matters that have little or nothing to do with the cultural heritage, such as smuggling, public health, and immigration. Under the UNCLOS logic, it is only as a consequence of the

---

[7] 1969 I.C.J. para. 85, Judgment. According to the arbitral award rendered on November 16, 1957, in the *Lake Lanoux* case (France v. Spain), the obligations to negotiate an agreement "take very diverse forms and have a scope which varies according to the manner in which they are defined and according to the procedures intended for their execution; but the reality of the obligations thus undertaken is incontestable and sanctions can be applied in the event, for example, of unjustified breaking off of the discussions, abnormal delays, disregard of the agreed procedures, systematic refusals to take into consideration adverse proposals of interests, and, more generally, in cases of violation of the rules of good faith"; 24 I.L.R. 128 (1957).

[8] The question of the regime of state vessels and aircraft will not be discussed here. According to certain states, such as the United States, the flag state retains title indefinitely to its sunken craft, wherever it is located, unless title has been expressly abandoned or transferred by it. Other states believe that there is no reason to envisage two different kinds of underwater cultural heritage. On the question, with special reference to the Spanish galleons, see Mariano Aznar Gomez, La protección international del patrimonio subacuático con especial referencia al caso de España (2004).

competences that it can already exercise in dealing with cigarette smugglers, clandestine immigrants, and infectious patients that the coastal state can exercise other competences for the protection of the underwater cultural heritage located within 24 nautical miles from the shore. The wisdom of such a logic, which implies that underwater cultural heritage cannot be protected per se, is not fully convincing, to say the least.

Other problems arise from the wording of Article 303, paragraph 2, if literally understood. The coastal state, which is empowered to prevent and sanction the "removal from the sea-bed" of objects of an archaeological and historical nature, is apparently defenseless if such objects, instead of being removed, are simply destroyed in the very place where they have been found.[9] Again, it is difficult to subscribe to the logic of such a conclusion.

All the textual complications of Article 303, paragraph 2, are probably due to the obsession of the drafters of the UNCLOS to avoid any words that might give the impression of an extension of coastal state jurisdiction beyond the territorial sea—a *horror jurisdictionis*, so to speak. Rather than laying down a substantive regime to deal with a new concern, such as the protection of the underwater cultural heritage, the UNCLOS seems more interested in paying tribute to abstractions, such as the attachment of some states to the almost theological dogma of freedom of the seas.

In any case, even if the spectre of cigarette smugglers, clandestine immigrants, and infectious patients does not seem the ideal way to transmit the message, from Article 303, paragraph 2, the conclusion may be drawn that the coastal state can establish a 24-mile so-called archaeological zone where it can apply its legislation for the aim of protecting the relevant objects.[10]

3. The Benefit of Mankind as a Whole

A specific provision of the UNCLOS (Article 149) deals with the underwater cultural heritage found on the seabed and ocean floor beyond the limits of national jurisdiction (the so-called Area):

> All objects of an archaeological and historical nature found in the Area shall be preserved or disposed of for the benefit of mankind as a whole, particular regard being paid to the preferential rights of the State or country of origin, or the State of cultural origin, or the State of historical and archaeological origin.

Article 149 appears rather vague in its content and devoid of details that could ensure its practical application. It shows a preference however for those uses of archaeological and historical objects that promote the "benefit of mankind as a whole." Private interests, such as the search for and use of the objects for trade and personal gain, are given little weight, if any.

---

[9] For example, destroyed by a company holding a license for oil exploitation.

[10] In fact, a number of countries have already created such a zone.

Some categories of states, which have a link with the objects, namely, the state of cultural origin, the state of historical and archaeological origin, the state or country of origin *tout court*,[11] are given preferential rights, although Article 149 does not specify the content of these rights nor the manner in which they should be harmonized with the concept of "benefit of mankind as a whole."

4. A Legal Vacuum

While specific UNCLOS provisions apply to the space within 24 nautical miles, on the one hand, and to the Area, on the other, UNCLOS does not define a regime relating to the archaeological and historical objects found on the continental shelf or in the exclusive economic zone,[12] which is the space located between the 24-mile limit of the archaeological zone and the Area. It is clear, however, that the rights of the coastal state on the continental shelf are limited to the exploration and exploitation of the relevant "natural resources," as explicitly stated in Article 77, paragraph 1, of UNCLOS, and cannot be easily extended to man-made objects,[13] such as those belonging to the underwater cultural heritage.[14]

This legal vacuum greatly threatens the protection of cultural heritage, as it brings into the picture the abstract idea of freedom of the seas.[15] It could easily

---

[11] The imprecise wording of Article 149 gives rise to some textual doubts. Must the state of historical origin be at the same time also the state of archaeological origin in order to get preferential rights? What is the meaning of the word "country" in the expression "state or country of origin"? Why is "country" not used in the cases of cultural, historical, and archaeological origin?

[12] The reference to the exclusive economic zone seems redundant (and will be hereinafter omitted), as the objects of archaeological or historical nature are more likely to lie on the seabed than to float in the waters of the exclusive economic zone. However, during the negotiations for the CPUCH, the highly hypothetical example was made of a bottle containing a message by the Italian national hero, Giuseppe Garibaldi, which is later found floating in the exclusive economic zone of the United States or Uruguay, countries where Mr. Garibaldi had lived in certain periods of his life. Embarking on another effort of imagination, one could also think of an ancient little statue that has been eaten by a fish or cetacean swimming in the exclusive economic zone.

[13] As also stated by the International Law Commission in the commentary to the relevant provision of the draft convention on the continental shelf, "It is clearly understood that the rights of the coastal State do not cover objects such as wrecked ships and their cargos (including bullion) lying on the seabed or covered by the sand and the subsoil" (2 Y.B. INT'L L. COMM'N 298 (1956)).

[14] It seems too eccentric to assume that archaeological and historical objects that are found embedded in the sand or encrusted with sedentary living organisms can be likened to natural resources. But this approach is followed in the Abandoned Shipwreck Act (43 U.S.C. §§ 2101 2106) adopted by the United States on 1987.

[15] UNCLOS, *supra* note 3, art. 59 (*Basis for the resolution of conflicts regarding the attribution of rights and jurisdiction*), which is the provision on the so-called residual rights in the exclusive economic zone, should also be taken into consideration. Under Article 59, "in cases where this Convention does not attribute rights or jurisdiction to the coastal State or to other States within the exclusive economic zone, and a conflict arises between the interests of the coastal State and any other State or States, the conflict should be resolved on the basis of equity and in the light of all the relevant circumstances, taking into account the respective importance of the interests involved to the parties as well as to the international community as a whole." In fact, the CPUCH regime could be seen as the application of UNCLOS Article 59, as far as the under-

lead to a "first come, first served" approach. Availing himself of the principle of freedom of the sea, any person on board any ship could explore the continental shelf adjacent to any coastal state, bring any archaeological and historical objects to the surface, become their owner under a domestic legislation (in most cases, the flag state legislation[16]), carry the objects into certain countries, and sell them on the private market. If this were the case, there would be no guarantee that the objects are disposed of for the public benefit rather than for private commercial gain or personal benefit. Nor could a state that has a direct cultural link with the objects prevent the continuous pillage of its historical heritage. The danger of freedom of fishing for underwater cultural heritage is far from being merely theoretical.[17]

During the negotiations for the UNCLOS, some countries were ready to extend, under certain conditions, the jurisdiction of the coastal state to the underwater cultural heritage found on the continental shelf. For instance, an informal proposal submitted in 1980 by Cape Verde, Greece, Italy, Malta, Portugal, Tunisia, and Yugoslavia provided as follows:

> The Coastal State may exercise jurisdiction, while respecting the rights of identifiable owners, over any objects of an archaeological and historical nature on or under its continental shelf for the purpose of research, recovery and protection. However, particular regard shall be paid to the preferential rights of the State or country of origin, or the State of cultural origin, or the State of historical and archaeological origin, in case of sale or any other disposal, resulting in the removal of such objects out of the Coastal State.[18]

The rejection of this kind of proposal, due to the already mentioned fear of creeping jurisdiction by coastal states (*horror jurisdictionis*),[19] led to the legal vacuum resulting from the present UNCLOS regime.

5. An Invitation to Looting

The danger of uncontrolled activities is aggravated by Article 303, paragraph 3, UNCLOS, which subjects the general obligations of protection of archaeological and historical objects and international cooperation to a completely different set of rules:

---

water cultural heritage within the exclusive economic zone is concerned. *See* Luigi Migliorino, *Submarine Antiquities and the Law of the Sea, in* MARINE POLICY REPORTS 1 (1982).

[16] In this regard, the problems posed by flags of convenience must be taken into consideration.

[17] See, as regards the story of the expeditions made by Mr. Ballard in the Mediterranean and the various stories of Spanish galleons looted by treasure hunters, Tullio Scovazzi, *The Application of Salvage Law and Other Rules of Admiralty to the Underwater Cultural Heritage, in* GARABELLO & SCOVAZZI, *supra* note 1, at 20, 38.

[18] Informal proposal by Cape Verde, Greece, Italy, Malta, Portugal, Tunisia, and Yugoslavia, U.N. Doc. A/CONF.62/C.2/Informal Meeting/43/Rev. 3 (Mar. 27, 1980).

[19] *Id.* at § B.2.

> Nothing in this article affects the rights of identifiable owners, the law of salvage and other rules of admiralty, or laws and practices with respect to cultural exchanges.

In fact, salvage law and other rules of admiralty are given an overarching status by the UNCLOS. If there is a conflict between the objective to protect the underwater cultural heritage, on the one hand, and the provisions of salvage law and other rules of admiralty, on the other, the latter prevail, as they are not affected by any of the paragraphs of Article 303.[20]

UNCLOS does not clarify the meaning of "the law of salvage and other rules of admiralty." In many countries, the notion of salvage (*sauvetage*, in French) is only related to the attempts to save a ship or cargo from imminent marine peril on behalf of its owners. But it was never intended to apply to submerged archaeological sites or to ancient sunken ships that, far from being in peril, have been definitively lost.

On the contrary, in a minority of common law countries, the concept of salvage law has been enlarged by some court decisions to cover activities that have very little to do with the traditional sphere of salvage. For example, the U.S. Court of Appeals for the Fourth Circuit in a decision rendered on March 24, 1999,[21] stated that the law of salvage and finds is a "venerable law of the sea." It was said to have arisen from the custom among "seafaring men" and to have "been preserved from ancient Rhodes (900 B.C.E.), Rome (Justinian' *Corpus Juris Civilis*) (533 C.E.), City of Trani (Italy) (1063), England (the Law of Oleron) (1189), the Hansa Towns or Hanseatic League (1597), and France (1681), all articulating similar principles."[22] Coming to the practical result of such a display of legal erudition, the law of finds seems to mean that "a person who discovers a shipwreck in navigable waters that has been long lost and abandoned and who reduces the property to actual or constructive possession becomes the property's owner." The application of the law of salvage, which is something different from the law of finds, is also hardly satisfactory, as it gives the salvor a lien (or right *in rem*) over the object. Yet the expression "the law of salvage and other rules of admiralty" simply means the application of a first-come-first-served or freedom-of-fishing approach that can only serve the interest of private commercial gain.

The fact remains that the body of "the law of salvage and other rules of admiralty" is today typical of a few common law systems but remains a complete stranger to the legislation of other countries. Because of the lack of corresponding concepts, the very words "salvage" and "admiralty" cannot be properly translated into languages different from English. In the French official text of the UNCLOS, they are rendered with expressions (*droit de*

[20] Luckily enough, the drafters of the UNCLOS did not subject to salvage law and other rules of admiralty the heritage found in the Area which falls under Article 149.

[21] R.M.S. Titanic, Inc. v. Haver, 171 F. 3d 943 (4th Cir. 1999).

[22] 1999 I.L.M. 807. For the details of the judicial "saga" of the Titanic, see Scovazzi, *supra* note 17, at 60. On the application of salvage law to the underwater cultural heritage, see James Nafziger, *The Evolving Role of Admiralty Courts in Litigation Related to Historic Wrecks*, 44 HARV. INT'L L.J. 251 (2003).

récupérer des épaves et (. . .) autres règles du droit maritime), which have a broader and different meaning. No Italian lawyer (with the laudable exception of a few scholars) would today know what the "law of salvage and finds" is, despite the fact that the cities of Rome and Trani, which are said to have contributed to this body of "venerable law of the sea," are located somewhere in the Italian territory. Nor is it clear how a "venerable" body of rules, which is believed to have developed in times when nobody cared about the underwater cultural heritage, could provide today any sensible tool for dealing with the protection of the heritage in question. All the almost theological expressions employed by the supporters of the law of salvage and the law of finds ("return to the mainstream of commerce," "admiralty's diligence ethic," "venerable law of the sea," etc.) are doubtful euphemisms.

This worsens the already sad picture of Article 303 of the UNCLOS. Does this provision, while apparently protecting the underwater cultural heritage, strengthen a regime that results in the destination of much of this heritage for commercial purposes? Does Article 303 give an overarching status to a body of rules that cannot provide any sensible tool for the protection of the heritage in question? The doubt is far from being trivial.[23]

6. Prospects for a Better Regime

It would be difficult to find so many obscurities and contra-dictions as can be found in the UNCLOS regime of the underwater cultural heritage.[24] If the protection of the underwater cultural heritage is to be achieved "for the benefit of mankind as a whole" (as stated in Article 149), why are salvage law and the other rules of admiralty, which only serve the purpose of private benefit and commercial gain, granted an overarching status (as stated in Article 303, paragraph 3)? If the underwater cultural heritage is to be protected everywhere (as stated in Article 303, paragraph 1), why is an evident gap left open as regards the heritage located on the continental shelf?[25]

---

[23] In recent decades treasure salvage has been added as an element of marine salvage under admiralty law. From an archaeological perspective, salvage law is a wholly inappropriate legal regime for treating underwater cultural heritage. Salvage law regards objects primarily as property with commercial value and rewards its recovery, regardless of its importance and value as cultural heritage. It encourages private-sector commercial recovery efforts, and is incapable of ensuring the adequate protection of underwater cultural heritage for the benefit of mankind as a whole."

The Archaeological Institute of America, *Comments on the UNESCO/UN Division on Ocean Affairs and the Law of the Sea Draft Convention on the Protection of the Underwater Cultural Heritage, in* LYNDEL PROTT & IENG SRONG EDS., BACKGROUND MATERIALS ON THE PROTECTION OF THE UNDERWATER CULTURAL HERITAGE 176 (1999). For other critical remarks about the results of the application of this body of law, see Peter Throckmorton, *The World's Worst Investment: The Economics of Treasure Hunting with Real Life Comparisons, reprinted in* PROTT & SRONG, *supra* at 181. But see the different views expressed by Barbara Hoffmann, *Sailing on Uncharted Waters: The U.S. Law of Historic Wrecks, Sunken Treasure and the Protection of Underwater Cultural Heritage, in* TULLIO SCOVAZZI ED., LA PROTEZIONE DEL PATRIMONIO CULTURALE SOTTOMARINO NEL MARE MEDITERRANEO 297 (2004).

[24] "The regimes for underwater archaeology resulting from the Convention are complicated and not complete." MYRON NORDQUIST, SHABTAI ROSENNE & LOUIS SOHN, UNITED NATIONS CONVENTION ON THE LAW OF THE SEA 1982—A COMMENTARY 161 (1989).

[25] The fact that the UNCLOS regime is far from being satisfactory seems implicitly ac-

As a further surprise, it may be added that prospects to find some remedy to the unsatisfactory regime of the UNCLOS could be drawn from Article 303, paragraph 4, itself. Accordingly, Article 303 does not prejudice "other international agreements and rules of international law regarding the protection of objects of an archaeological and historical nature."[26] There is no reason why future agreements, such as the CPUCH, should not be covered by this provision. In other words, the UNCLOS itself seems to allow the drafting of more specific treaty regimes that can ensure a better protection of the underwater cultural heritage. The UNCLOS itself seems to encourage filling in the gaps and eliminating the contradictions that it has generated.

C. THE CPUCH AS A DEFENSIVE TOOL

The CPUCH may be seen as a reasonable defense against the results of the contradictory and counter-productive regime of the UNCLOS. The basic defensive tools are three: the elimination of the undesirable effects of the law of salvage and finds; the exclusion of a "first come, first served" approach for the heritage found on the continental shelf; and the strengthening of regional cooperation.

1. The Rejection of the Law of Salvage and Finds

While most countries participating in the negotiations for the CPUCH concurred in rejecting the application of the law of salvage and finds to underwater cultural heritage, a minority of states were not prepared to accept an absolute ban. To achieve a reasonable compromise, Article 4 (*Relationship to law of salvage and law of finds*) of the CPUCH provides as follows:

> Any activity relating to underwater cultural heritage to which this Convention applies shall not be subject to the law of salvage or law of finds, unless it:
> (a) is authorized by the competent authorities, and
> (b) is in full conformity with this Convention, and
> (c) ensures that any recovery of the underwater cultural heritage achieves its maximum protection.

This provision is to be understood in connection with Article 2, paragraph 7, of the CPUCH ("underwater cultural heritage shall not be commercially exploited") and with the rules contained in the annex, which form an integral part of the CPUCH. In particular, under Rule 2 of the annex,

---

knowledged in the declaration made by the Netherlands on June 28, 1996, on ratification of the UNCLOS:

> Jurisdiction over objects of an archaeological and historical nature found at sea is limited to articles 149 and 303 of the Convention. The Kingdom of the Netherlands does however consider that there may be a need to further develop, in international cooperation, the international law on the protection of the underwater cultural heritage.

[26] Under paragraph 3, Article 303 does not affect salvage law and other rules of admiralty. Under paragraph 4, Article 303 is without prejudice to other international agreements regarding the protection of objects of an archaeological and historical nature. If there is a conflict between salvage law and an international agreement covered by paragraph 4, which one would prevail? Article 303 is entirely silent about the issue.

> the commercial exploitation of underwater cultural heritage for trade or speculation or its irretrievable dispersal is fundamentally incompatible with the protection and proper management of underwater cultural heritage. Underwater cultural heritage shall not be traded, sold, bought or bartered as commercial goods.

While not totally excluding the application of law of salvage and law of finds, the CPUCH regime has the practical effect of preventing all the undesirable effects of this kind of rules. Freedom of fishing for archaeological and historical objects is definitely banned. This important compromise seemed generally acceptable to all the states participating in the UNESCO negotiations.

2. The Exclusion of a "First Come, First Served" Approach for the Heritage Found on the Continental Shelf

The majority of the countries participating in the negotiations were ready to extend the jurisdiction of the coastal state to the underwater cultural heritage found on the continental shelf or in the exclusive economic zone. However, a minority of states assumed that the extension of the jurisdiction of coastal states beyond the limit of the territorial sea would have altered the delicate balance embodied in the UNCLOS between the rights and obligations of the coastal state and those of other states. Such a difference of positions proved to be a thorny question.

During the negotiations, the chairman of Working Group 1 of the Group of Governmental Experts, trying to find a way out of the deadlock,[27] undertook to produce a tentative proposal.[28] It was based on a three-step procedure: reporting of planned activities or discoveries; consultations on how to ensure the effective protection of the underwater cultural heritage; and provisional protection measures. The coastal state was entitled to coordinate the consultations among the states that declared their interest,[29] unless it invited another state to act as coordinating state. Pending the outcome of the consultations, all states parties had to comply with the provisional protection measures adopted by the coordinating state.

During the same session, a "non-paper" was proposed by three unnamed delegations as a basis for discussion. Although different in several aspects from

---

[27] *See* Final Report of the Third Meeting of Governmental Experts on the Draft Convention on the Protection of Underwater Cultural Heritage, UNESCO Doc. CLT-2000/CONF.201/CLD.7, para. 4 of Annex 1 [hereinafter Final Report].

[28] UNESCO Doc. WG1-NP3 (July 6, 2000), *reprinted in* Final Report, *supra* note 27.

[29] To avoid the ghost of jurisdiction (*horror jurisdictionis*), the coastal state was not called coastal state but was given a special responsibility as a coordinating state under the following wording:

> Taking into account its interest in avoiding unjustified interference with the exercise of sovereign rights and jurisdiction in its exclusive economic zone or on its continental shelf in accordance with international law, a State Party has a special responsibility for the co-ordination of activities directed at the underwater cultural heritage and for the protection of any discoveries made in its exclusive economic zone or on its continental shelf (Article D, paragraph 2, of the tentative proposals of the chairman of Working Group 1).

the proposal of the chairman of Working Group 1, the non-paper was also based on reporting and consultation.[30] It introduced two important elements: the states entitled to participate in the consultations were those that had a "verifiable link" with the underwater cultural heritage concerned, and the coastal state[31] was entitled to impose requirements not in its own interest but on behalf of all states parties as a whole.

Both proposals were inspired by a spirit of compromise and showed an effort to bring solutions to problems rather than problems to solutions. Without insisting on a mere extension of the jurisdiction of the coastal state, a procedural mechanism was envisaged that would involve the participation of all the sates linked to the heritage. Both proposals led to the present Articles 9 and 10 of the CPUCH, which were accepted by the majority of the states engaged in the negotiation. It is regrettable that, despite all the efforts to reach a reasonable compromise, a consensus could not be achieved.

It would be a difficult task to dwell upon all the nuances of provisions such as Articles 9 and 10 that resulted from a stratification of proposals, counter-proposals, last-minute changes, and "constructive ambiguities," which produced something less than an easily readable text. The essence of the regime is the three-step procedure (reporting, consultations, urgent measures) it sets forth.[32]

As regards *reporting*, the CPUCH bans secret activities or discoveries.[33] States parties must require their nationals or vessels flying their flag to report activities or discoveries to them. If the activity or discovery is located in the exclusive economic zone or on the continental shelf of another state party, the CPUCH sets forth two alternative solutions:

> (i) States Parties shall require the national or the master of the vessel to report such discovery or activity to them and to that other State Party;
>
> (ii) alternatively, a State Party shall require the national or master of the vessel to report such discovery or activity to it and shall ensure the rapid and effective transmission of such report to all other States Parties.[34]

While the wording leaves a certain margin of ambiguity, the "State Party" mentioned in sub-paragraph (ii) is to be understood as the state to which

[30] UNESCO Doc. WG.1/NP.1 (July 5, 2000), *reprinted in* Final Report, *supra* note 27.

[31] Again, the expression "coastal state" was not used in the "non-paper" either.

[32] Under Articles 11 and 12 of the CPUCH, a similar, though not identical, three-step procedure applies to the underwater cultural heritage found in the Area.

[33] For obvious reasons, the principle of transparency of information is limited to the competent authorities of states parties:

> Information shared between States Parties, or between UNESCO and States Parties, regarding the discovery or location of underwater cultural heritage shall, to the extent compatible with their national legislation, be kept confidential and reserved to competent authorities of States Parties as long as the disclosure of such information might endanger or otherwise put at risk the preservation of such underwater cultural heritage. (CPUCH, *supra* note 1, art. 19, para. 3.)

[34] CPUCH, *supra* note 1, art, 9, para. 1(b). On depositing its instrument of ratification, acceptance, approval, or accession, a state party shall declare the manner in which reports will be transmitted. *Id.*, art, 9, para. 2.

the "national" belongs or the state of which the "vessel" flies the flag.[35] This interpretation is in conformity with the preparatory works of the CPUCH.[36]

States parties must also notify the director-general of UNESCO who must promptly make it available to all states parties.

As regards *consultations,* the coastal state is bound to consult all states parties that have declared their interest in being consulted on how to ensure the effective protection of the underwater cultural heritage in question.[37] The CPUCH provides that any state party may declare such an interest and that this "declaration shall be based on a verifiable link, especially a cultural, historical or archaeological link, to the underwater cultural heritage concerned."[38]

The coastal state[39] is entitled to coordinate the consultations, unless it expressly declares that it does not wish to do so, in which case the states parties that have declared an interest in being consulted shall appoint another coordinating state. The coordinating state must implement the measures of protection that have been agreed by the consulting states and may conduct any necessary preliminary research on the underwater cultural heritage.

As regards *urgent measures,* Article 10, paragraph 4, of CPUCH provides as follows:

> Without prejudice to the right of all States Parties to protect underwater cultural heritage by way of all practicable measures taken in accordance with international law to prevent immediate danger to the underwater cultural heritage, including looting, the Coordinating State may take all practicable measures, and/or issue any necessary authorizations in conformity with this Convention and, if necessary prior to consultations, to prevent any immediate danger to the underwater cultural heritage, whether arising from human activities or any other cause, including looting. In taking such measures assistance may be requested from other States Parties.

---

[35] The ambiguity lies in the fact that the "State Party" in question could also be understood as the coastal state.

[36] A draft resolution submitted by the Russian Federation and the United Kingdom and endorsed by the United States tried to clarify the point by proposing the following wording: When the discovery or activity is located in the exclusive economic zone or on the continental shelf of another State Party: (i) a State Party shall require its national or the master of a vessel flying its flag to report such discovery or activity to it and to that other State Party; (ii) alternatively, a State Party shall require its national or the master of a vessel flying its flag to report such discovery or activity to it and shall ensure the rapid and effective transmission of such reports to all other States Parties. (UNESCO Doc. 31 C/COM.IV/DR.5 (Oct. 26, 2001).)

The draft resolution was not adopted, however.

[37] CPUCH, *supra* note 1, art. 10, para. 3 (a), and art. 9, para. 5. Here and everywhere else, the CPUCH avoids the words "coastal State" (because of the already mentioned *horror jurisdictionis*) and chooses other expressions, such as the "State Party in whose exclusive economic zone or on whose continental shelf" the activity or discovery is located.

[38] No attempt was made to define what is a "verifiable link."

[39] *See supra* note 37.

The right of the coordinating state to adopt urgent measures is an important aspect of the CPUCH regime. It would have been illusory to subordinate this right to the conclusion of consultations that are normally expected to last for some time. It would also have been illusory to grant this right to the flag state, considering the risk of activities carried out by vessels flying the flag of non-parties or a flag of convenience.[40] By definition, in a case of urgency a determined state must be entitled to take immediate measures without losing time in procedural requirements.[41]

The CPUCH clearly sets forth that in coordinating consultations, taking measures, conducting preliminary research, and issuing authorizations, the coordinating state acts "on behalf of the States Parties as a whole and not in its own interest."[42] Any such action shall not in itself constitute a basis for the assertion of any preferential or jurisdictional rights not provided for in international law, including the UNCLOS.

In any case, "a State Party in whose exclusive economic zone or on whose continental shelf underwater cultural heritage is located has the right to prohibit or authorize any activity directed at such heritage to prevent interference with its sovereign rights or jurisdiction as provided for by international law including the United Nations Convention on the Law of the Sea."[43] This could mean that the coastal state can exercise broader rights if, for instance, a wreck is embedded in the sand or is encrusted with oysters, mollusks, or other sedentary living resources over which it already exercises sovereign rights under the UNCLOS provisions on the continental shelf.[44]

3. The Strengthening of Regional Cooperation

The CPUCH devotes one of its provisions (Article 6) to bilateral, regional or other multilateral agreements:

> 1. States Parties are encouraged to enter into bilateral, regional or other multilateral agreements or develop existing agreements, for

[40] The difficulty of regulating fishing by vessels flying flags of convenience and engaging in so-called IUU (illegal, unreported, unregulated) fishing demonstrates this risk.

[41] On the contrary, the draft resolution submitted by the Russian Federation and the United Kingdom and endorsed by the United States, *supra* note 36, subordinated the right to adopt measures to prevent immediate danger to a specific condition: "but in any event prompt assistance shall be requested from the State Party that is the flag State of the vessel engaged in such activities."

[42] CPUCH, *supra* note 1, art. 10, para. 6.

[43] *Id.*, art. 10, para. 2.

[44] The majority of states participating in the CPUCH negotiations rejected the assumption, put forward by the United States on the basis of several judicial decisions, that the only possibility for the coastal state to protect the underwater cultural heritage was based on its right to prevent interferences with its sovereign rights or jurisdiction as provided for by international law. This assumption is in principle unacceptable, as it implies that oysters and other equally respectable living resources are more important than the cultural heritage. It is also dangerous, as it can be interpreted in the sense that the salvor can retain the wreck after having given all the oysters to the coastal state!

> the preservation of underwater cultural heritage. All such agreements shall be in full conformity with the provisions of this Convention and shall not dilute its universal character. States may, in such agreements, adopt rules and regulations which would ensure better protection of underwater cultural heritage than those adopted in this Convention.
>
> 2. The Parties to such bilateral, regional or other multilateral agreements may invite States with a verifiable link, especially a cultural, historical or archaeological link, to the underwater cultural heritage concerned to join such agreements.[45]

Article 6 opens the way to a multiple-level protection of underwater cultural heritage. This corresponds to what has already happened in the field of the protection of the natural environment where treaties having a world sphere of application are often reinforced by treaties concluded at the regional and sub-regional level. The key to coordination between treaties applicable at different levels is the criterion of the better protection, in the sense that the regional and sub-regional treaties are concluded to ensure better protection than the protection granted by those adopted at a more general level.

The possibility to conclude regional agreements should be carefully considered by the states bordering enclosed or semi-enclosed seas that are characterized by a particular kind of underwater cultural heritage, such as the Mediterranean, the Baltic, or the Caribbean. For instance, in a declaration adopted in Siracusa, Italy, on March 10, 2001,[46] the participants to an academic conference stressed that "the Mediterranean basin is characterized by the traces of ancient civilisations which flourished along its shores and, having developed the first seafaring techniques, established close relationships with each other" and that "the Mediterranean cultural heritage is unique in that it embodies the common historical and cultural roots of many civilizations." They consequently invited the Mediterranean countries to "study the possibility of adopting a regional convention that enhances cooperation in the investigation and protection of the Mediterranean submarine cultural heritage and sets forth the relevant rights and obligations." This suggestion has not been followed so far.

D. GOING BEYOND THE UNCLOS

It is not likely that any sensible prospects for protecting the underwater cultural heritage may be drawn from the contradictory and counter-productive regime embodied in the UNCLOS, at least if it were literally read. The drafters of the UNCLOS could not forecast the subsequent progress in underwater technologies and the diffusion of treasure hunting activities in many seas of the world. They probably did not feel that the protection of the underwater cultural heritage was to be considered an urgent need.

---

[45] Under CPUCH, *supra* note 1, Article 6, paragraph 3, the CPUCH "shall not alter the rights and obligations of States Parties regarding the protection of sunken vessels, arising from other bilateral, regional or other multilateral agreements concluded before its adoption, and, in particular, those that are in conformity with the purposes of" the CPUCH.

[46] *Reprinted in* GARABELLO & SCOVAZZI, *supra* note 1, at 274.

For its innovative and pragmatic character, the CPUCH is a major step forward in the progressive development of international law. It has been criticized for the reason that, irrespective of Article 3,[47] it departs from the regime embodied in the UNCLOS. Perhaps it partially departs. But the fact remains that the UNCLOS regime is so insufficient that it was impossible to protect the underwater cultural heritage without partially departing from it.

Variations from the UNCLOS regime are not a novelty. After the adoption of the UNCLOS, two multilateral treaties have been concluded that apparently "implement" the UNCLOS, namely, the 1994 Agreement Relating to the Implementation of Part XI of the UNCLOS[48] and the 1995 Agreement for the Implementation of the Provisions of the UNCLOS Relating to the Conservation and Management of Straddling Fish Stocks and Highly Migratory Fish Stocks.[49] In fact, as both agreements depart from the UNCLOS, the politically prudent label of "implementing agreements" can be considered as a euphemism for the substantively more accurate word "amendment." The reality is that, as it is itself a product of time, the UNCLOS cannot stop the passing of time. It is therefore subject to a process of evolution in the light of subsequent international practice.

The establishment of an effective protection regime for the underwater cultural heritage cannot be seen as an encroachment on the principle of the freedom of the sea. Nor is it the creation of other jurisdictional zones. It is difficult to see how rules and entitlements on the underwater cultural heritage found on the continental shelf could affect navigation in the superjacent waters. The concept of freedom of the sea is today to be understood not in an abstract way, but in the context of the present range of marine activities and in relation to the other potentially conflicting uses and interests. Also, the idea that the coastal state can exercise rights on the oil found on its continental shelf corresponded, when it was initially proposed,[50] to an encroachment on the freedom of the high seas. Evident encroachments on the freedom of fishing on the high seas are also apparent in the 1995 Straddling and Highly Migratory Fish Stocks Agreement. It introduces the innovative idea that states that persistently undermine the measures agreed upon by the others can be excluded from an activity taking place on the high seas. In this case, a new regime was considered

---

[47] Nothing in this Convention shall prejudice the rights, jurisdiction and duties of States under international law, including the United Nations Convention on the Law of the Sea. This Convention shall be interpreted and applied in the context of and in a manner consistent with international law, including the United Nations Convention on the Law of the Sea.

[48] 1994 Agreement Relating to the Implementation of Part XI of the UNCLOS, G.A. Res. 48/263 (July 28, 1994), *reprinted in* 33 I.L.M. 1309.

[49] 1995 Agreement for the Implementation of the Provisions of the UNCLOS Relating to the Conservation and Management of Straddling Fish Stocks and Highly Migratory Fish Stocks, U.N. Doc. A/CONF.164/37 (Dec. 4, 1995), *reprinted in* 34 I.L.M. 1542.

[50] See the presidential proclamation Policy of the United States with Respect to the Natural Resources of the Subsoil and Seabed of the Continental Shelf, adopted on September 28, 1945 (the so-called Truman Proclamation), Proclamation No. 2667, 3 C.F.R. §§ 1943–1948, 10 Fed. Reg. 12303.

a necessary tool to promote the conservation and sound management of living marine resources and, as such, was found reasonable by the great majority of States. Abstract principles and fears of creeping jurisdiction (*horror jurisdictionis*) were not sufficient to prevent the evolution of international law of the sea and the drafting of reasonable legal responses to emerging needs.

Similarly, effective solutions are today required with respect to the underwater cultural heritage. The protection of the underwater cultural heritage is endangered by an increasing number of unreported and unregulated activities that are the consequence of the improvement of underwater instruments and technologies. Should a freedom-of-fishing approach govern underwater objects of an archaeological and historical nature? Do they deserve less protection than fish? The CPUCH provides sensible negative answers to both questions.[51]

Sadly enough, the message coming from the CPUCH has not yet been followed by many states. In particular, it is really disappointing to see that in 2004 the U.N. General Assembly urged

> all States to cooperate, directly or through competent international organizations, in taking measures to protect and preserve objects of an archaeological and historical nature found at sea, in conformity with article 303 of the Convention [the UNCLOS].[52]

Not only did the General Assembly fail to mention the CPUCH, but Article 303 of the UNCLOS; that is, the provision that includes the invitation to looting (paragraph 3), is emphasized as a model!

Fortunately in the following year, the General Assembly took a more balanced approach. In Resolution 60/30 on oceans and the law of the sea, adopted on November 29, 2005, it did not refrain from mentioning the CPUCH, noting

> the effort made by the United Nations Educational, Scientific and Cultural Organization with respect to the preservation of underwater cultural heritage, and notes in particular the rules annexed to the 2001 Convention on the Protection of the Underwater Cultural Heritage that address the relationship between salvage law and scientific principles of management, conservation and protection of underwater cultural heritage among parties, their nationals and vessels flying their flag.[53]

The resolution also implies some doubts that the "venerable" salvage law is the best way to protect the underwater cultural heritage, as the General Assembly urges

---

[51] In fact, Article 30, paragraph 1 (d), of the International Convention on Salvage (London, 1989) allows states parties to make a reservation in order to not apply the Convention "when the property involved is maritime cultural property of prehistoric, archaeological or historic interest and is situated on the sea-bed."

[52] G.A. Res. 59/24 (*Oceans and the Law of the Sea*), para. 4, U.N. Doc. A/RES/59/24 (Nov. 17, 2004).

[53] G.A. Res. 60/30, para. 8, U.N. Doc. A/RES/60/30 (Nov. 29, 2005). The same wording is repeated in G.A. Resolution 61/222 on "Oceans and Law of the Sea," U.N. Doc. A/RES/61/222 (Dec. 20, 2006).

> all States to cooperate, directly or through competent international bodies, in taking measures to protect and preserve objects of archaeological and historical nature found at sea, in conformity with the Convention [LOSC], and calls upon States to work together on such diverse challenges and opportunities as the appropriate relationship between salvage law and scientific management and conservation of underwater cultural heritage, increasing technological abilities to discover and reach underwater sites, looting and growing underwater tourism.[54]

The word "looting," which makes its appearance in the resolution, points at the most serious danger.

---

54 *Id.*, para. 7.

CHAPTER 15

INCREASING EFFECTIVENESS OF THE LEGAL REGIME FOR THE PROTECTION OF THE INTERNATIONAL ARCHAEOLOGICAL HERITAGE

Patty Gerstenblith

A. INTRODUCTION

Controlled, scientific excavation of archaeological sites allows for maximum retrieval of historical and cultural information and is crucial to our ability to reconstruct and understand the past. Archaeological sites consist of a complex of ancient artifacts and other material remains of the past preserved in a contextual relationship. This context is key not only to recovering ancient artifacts, but also to understanding all aspects of past human life. Ethnographic studies in such disparate parts of the world as Peru, Turkey, Israel, Italy, and Iraq[1] have now demonstrated that the looting of archaeological sites has become a well-organized business with an international network of local looters, middlemen at transit points, and traders and buyers in the destination markets. The international movement of artworks is often viewed as a positive force for increasing cross-national understanding and globalization. However, when cultural objects have been obtained through the looting of sites, internationalism and globalization take on a different meaning because of the negative effects imposed on society through the loss of scientific, historical, and cultural information.

Because most looting of archaeological sites is motivated by profit, the rate of looting will respond to the basic economic law of supply and demand. If demand for a commodity is reduced, then the looting that is motivated by the demand should also be reduced. If collectors (both private and public) in

[1] Morag K. Kersel, License to Sell: The Legal Trade of Antiquities in Israel (2006) (unpublished Ph.D. dissertation, Cambridge University) (copy on file with author) (Israel and West Bank); Peter Watson & Cecilia Todeschini, The Medici Conspiracy: The Illicit Journey of Looted Antiquities (2006) (Italy); Roger Atwood, Stealing History: Tomb Robbers, Smugglers, and the Looting of the Ancient World (2004) (Peru); Joanne Farchakh, Mesopotamia Endangered: Witnessing the Loss of History, Lecture delivered at the University of California, Berkeley (Feb. 7, 2005), *available at* http://webcast.berkeley.edu/event_details.php?webcastid=10048 (Iraq); C.H. Roosevelt & C. Luke, *Looting Lydia: The Destruction of an Archaeological Landscape in Western Turkey*, *in* Archaeology, Cultural Heritage and the Antiquities Trade 173 (N. Brodie, M.M. Kersel, C. Luke, & K. Walker Tubb eds., 2006) (Turkey) [hereinafter The Antiquities Trade].

the market nations refuse to buy undocumented artifacts, then incentives for the looting of artifacts will diminish.[2] The law should therefore aim to impose a cost on those who contribute directly or indirectly to the looting of sites by punishing the handling, selling, and buying of looted antiquities. This chapter will first examine the structure of the legal regime that is used to preserve the international archaeological heritage and then consider the means for improving the effectiveness of this legal regime.

B. THE LEGAL REGIME FOR PROTECTING THE ARCHAEOLOGICAL HERITAGE

1. Specialized Laws

The law in the United States may be examined as an example of a market nation's attempt to control the market in antiquities. Two aspects of the legal regime have developed in the United States that are concerned with the protection of the archaeological heritage—laws specifically designed to protect archaeological heritage and laws of general application that have been used increasingly for this same purpose. The first laws enacted at the federal level to protect the archaeological heritage were primarily concerned with preservation of the United States' own domestic heritage. The first such law was the Antiquities Act of 1906, which vested control and ownership of objects of antiquity found on federal land in the federal government.[3] As it pertains to archaeological sites and artifacts, the Antiquities Act was supplemented and largely superseded by the Archaeological Resources Protection Act of 1979 (ARPA).[4] While ARPA, like the Antiquities Act, is primarily concerned with sites and artifacts found on federally owned or controlled land, ARPA also prohibits trafficking in inter-state or foreign commerce of any archaeological resource[5] excavated, removed, sold, purchased, exchanged, transported, or received in violation of state or local law.[6]

The first legislation to be concerned exclusively with the international trade in looted or dismembered archaeological materials was the Importation of Pre-Columbian Monumental or Architectural Sculpture or Murals Act, enacted in 1972.[7] This act prohibits the import into the United States of any pre-Columbian

[2] While there are other causes of damage to archaeological sites, including natural processes, such as floods and erosion, agricultural activities and development, intentional looting is the one activity that can be controlled and that bears no countervailing positive social effects.

[3] Antiquities Act of 1906, 16 U.S.C. §§ 431–433 (2008). Other sections of the act gave the U.S. president the authority to declare national monuments without seeking Congress's consent. The Ninth Circuit declared parts of the Antiquities Act unconstitutional because it viewed the term "object of antiquity" in the statute to be unconstitutionally vague. United States v. Diaz, 499 F.2d 113, 115 (9th Cir. 1974). It is interesting to note that one of the motivating factors for enactment of the Antiquities Act was the activity of looters who were selling archaeological artifacts abroad.

[4] 16 U.S.C. §§ 470aa–470gg (2008).

[5] ARPA cured the vagueness of the Antiquities Act by offering a clear definition of archaeological resources as "any material remains of past human life or activities which are of archaeological interest" and that are at least 100 years old, 16 U.S.C. § 470bb(1).

[6] 16 U.S.C. § 470ee(c).

[7] 19 U.S.C. §§ 2091–2095 (2008).

architectural or sculptural pieces or fragments without an export license from the country of origin. By allowing only seizure and forfeiture of artifacts whose import has violated the statute, the Pre-Columbian Act established a pattern of handling the international trade primarily at the border and primarily through forfeiture, rather than criminal prosecution. Thus, while representing the first effort of the United States to deal with the problems of the international trade in looted artifacts, it nonetheless set a minimalist standard for confronting this problem and for the legal consequences imposed for a violation.

The 1970 UNESCO Convention on the Means of Prohibiting and Preventing the Illicit Import, Export and Transfer of Ownership of Cultural Property ("1970 UNESCO Convention")[8] was the first international attempt to control the market in cultural objects.[9] Although this convention was slow in gaining acceptance among the market nations,[10] the U.S. Senate voted unanimously to ratify it in 1972 but with the understanding that it would not be self-executing. In 1983, the United States enacted the Convention on Cultural Property Implementation Act (CPIA),[11] implementing two sections of the 1970 UNESCO Convention.[12]

The CPIA prohibits the import into the United States of stolen cultural property that had been documented in the inventory of a public religious or secular institution in another state party.[13] The CPIA also grants the president the authority to impose import restrictions, pursuant to either a bilateral agreement or an emergency action, on designated categories of archaeological and ethnological materials that are subject to pillage in another state party.[14] The other state party must submit a request for a bilateral agreement to the United States. The request is reviewed by the Cultural Property Advisory Committee,

---

[8] UNESCO Convention on the Means of Prohibiting and Preventing the Illicit Import, Export, and Transfer of Ownership of Cultural Property (Nov. 14, 1970), 823 U.N.T.S. 231.

[9] The 1970 UNESCO Convention was preceded by the first convention to address the exclusive subject of cultural property, the 1954 Hague Convention on the Protection of Cultural Property in the Event of Armed Conflict. The text of the convention and its protocols is available at http://portal.unesco.org/en/ev.php-URL_ID=13637&URL_DO=DO_TOPIC&URL_SECTION=201.html.

[10] Most of the other major market (or destination) nations are now also parties to the UNESCO Convention including Switzerland, the United Kingdom, France, Germany, Belgium, and Japan. A list of states parties may be found at http://portal.unesco.org/la/convention.asp?KO=13039&language=E&order=alpha. The U.K. implementing legislation, Dealing in Cultural Objects (Offences) Act 2003, may be found at http://www.opsi.gov.uk/acts/acts2003/20030027.htm. The Swiss implementing legislation, the Federal Act on the International Transfer of Cultural Property, may be found at http://www.kultur-schweiz.admin.ch/arkgt/files/kgtg2_e.pdf.

[11] 19 U.S.C. §§ 2601–2613 (2008).

[12] 1970 UNESCO Convention, arts. 7(b) and 9.

[13] This provision prohibits the import of any "cultural property documented as appertaining to the inventory of a museum or religious or secular public monument or similar institution in any State Party which is stolen from such institution." 19 U.S.C. § 2607. The definition of "cultural property" tracks that given in Article 1 of the 1970 UNESCO Convention and is very broad. 19 U.S.C. § 2601(6).

[14] 19 U.S.C. §§ 2602–2603.

which recommends whether the four statutory criteria are satisfied.[15] The president has delegated the final decision-making authority as to whether the United Sttes should enter into an agreement to a State Department official. If the circumstances warrant it, the United States can impose import restrictions unilaterally (but only after a request has been submitted for a bilateral agreement) under an emergency action.[16] Import restrictions under an emergency action may last for five years and may be renewed for a final three years. An agreement can last for up to five years but may be renewed an indefinite number of times.[17] The CPIA provides only for civil forfeiture of the cultural materials at stake and has no criminal penalties.[18]

Perhaps the most interesting law that applies specifically to the cultural and archaeological heritage is the Sentencing Guideline for Cultural Heritage Resource Crimes, adopted by Congress in 2002 ("Sentencing Guideline").[19] Sentencing Guidelines are used to determine the punishment (both fines and incarceration time) for those who have been convicted of a crime. Because crimes involving stolen or illegally imported cultural objects are considered to be property crimes, in the past, the sentence was determined by the market value of the property involved in the crime. However, this meant that those convicted of similar crimes might receive very different sentences because the value of antiquities from different parts of the world may have very different market values. Furthermore, punishment based on market value fails to take into consideration the intangible values of knowledge and heritage that are

---

[15] The four determinations are (1) whether the cultural patrimony of the requesting nation is in jeopardy from the pillage of archaeological or ethnological materials, (2) whether the state party has taken internal measures consistent with the 1970 UNESCO Convention to protect its cultural patrimony, (3) whether U.S. import restrictions would be part of a multilateral action taken by other states with an import market in the same materials, and (4) whether import restrictions are in the interest of furthering cultural interchange. 19 U.S.C. § 2602 (a)(1)(A)–(D). There is an exception to the third criterion when U.S. restrictions alone would be of substantial benefit in deterring the situation of pillage. 19 U.S.C. § 2602(c)(2).

[16] The CPIA defines an emergency situation as one in which any archaeological or ethnological material of any state party meets one of the three following criteria:

> (1) a newly discovered type of material which is of importance for the understanding of the history of mankind and is in jeopardy from pillage, dismantling, dispersal, or fragmentation;
>
> (2) identifiable as coming from any site recognized to be of high cultural significance if such site is in jeopardy from pillage, dismantling, dispersal, or fragmentation which is, or threatens to be, of crisis proportions; or
>
> (3) a part of the remains of a particular culture or civilization, the record of which is in jeopardy from pillage, dismantling, dispersal, or fragmentation which is, or threatens to be, of crisis proportions.

19 U.S.C. § 2603(a).

[17] A list of current and expired import restrictions is available on the State Department Web site, http://www.exchanges.state.gov/culprop/.

[18] 19 U.S.C. § 2609. However, St. Hilaire suggests that a knowing violation of a CPIA import restriction would constitute a criminal violation under 18 U.S.C. Section 545 (2008), which prohibits importation of goods contrary to law. Ricardo A. St. Hilaire, International Antiquities Trafficking: Theft by Another Name (unpublished paper presented at the Feb. 26, 2007 meeting of ICOM-CC, Issues in the Conservation of Cultural Heritage) (copy on file with author).

[19] 18 U.S.C. App. § 2B1.5 (2008).

destroyed through the looting of archaeological sites.[20] For crimes involving a cultural heritage resource,[21] the new Sentencing Guideline uses valuations based on commercial value, cost of restoration and repair, and archaeological value[22] in appropriate circumstances. It also provides for an increased offense level for crimes involving specially protected places[23] or specially protected objects.[24] This Sentencing Guideline represents Congress's most recent and explicit expression of intent to protect cultural heritage both within the United States and internationally as well as to establish an understanding of the intangible value inherent in the cultural heritage.

2. Laws of General Application

a. Theft From Known Collections

In addition to these specialized laws, there are many statutes and legal principles of general application that apply to the international trade in stolen

---

[20] The Sentencing Commission wrote in its explanation of the new Sentencing Guideline:

> Because individuals, communities, and nations identify themselves through intellectual, emotional, and spiritual connections to places and objects, the effects of cultural heritage resource crimes transcend mere monetary considerations. Accordingly, this new guideline takes into account the transcendent and irreplaceable value of cultural heritage resources and punishes in a proportionate way the aggravating conduct associated with cultural heritage resource crimes.

Reason for Amendment, *id.*

[21] Cultural heritage resources are defined to include the following: historic property and historic resources, defined by the National Historic Preservation Act, 16 U.S.C. Section 470w(5) (2008); archaeological resources, defined by ARPA, 16 U.S.C. Section 470bb(1), as "any material remains of past human life or activities which are of archaeological interest" and are at least 100 years of age; cultural items, as defined by the Native American Graves Protection and Repatriation Act, 25 U.S.C. Section 3001(3), to include human remains, associated funerary objects, unassociated funerary objects, sacred objects, and objects of cultural patrimony; commemorative work, as defined by 40 U.S.C. Section 8902(a)(1) (2008), and any national monument or national memorial; objects of cultural heritage, defined as any object that is more than 100 years old or worth more than $100,000, 18 U.S.C. Section 668(a)(2) (2008); designated ethnological material, defined as the product of a nonindustrial or tribal society, which is "important to the cultural heritage of a people because of its distinctive characteristics, comparative rarity, or its contribution to the knowledge of the origins, development, or history of that people" and whose import is prohibited under either a bilateral agreement or an emergency action pursuant to the CPIA, 19 U.S.C. Sections 2601(2)(ii), 2601(7), and 2604. 18 U.S.C. App. § 2B1.5, Application Note 1.

[22] The Sentencing Guideline defines "archaeological value" as "the cost of the retrieval of the scientific information which would have been obtainable prior to the offense" from research design to publication of results "as would be necessary to realize the information potential." 18 U.S.C. App. § 2B1.5, Application Note 2(C)(i).

[23] Specially protected places include sites listed on the World Heritage List; a national monument, park, cemetery, memorial, or marine sanctuary; a National Historic Landmark, and a museum (including museums in both the United States and abroad). 18 U.S.C. App. § 2B1.5(b)(2).

[24] Specially protected objects are those specifically covered by federal legislation, including: human remains, a funerary object, cultural patrimony, or a sacred object, as defined by an object of Native American Graves Protection and Repatriation Act (NAGPRA; 25 U.S.C. §§ 3001–3013 (2008)); archaeological or ethnological materials designated under the CPIA; cultural property as defined by the CPIA; or a pre-Columbian monumental or architectural sculpture or mural. 18 U.S.C. App. § 2B1.5(b)(3).

or looted archaeological objects. Both state laws and the National Stolen Property Act (NSPA) criminalize the knowing transport, receipt, and possession of stolen property. The NSPA specifically applies to stolen property worth more than $5,000 that has crossed a state or international boundary.[25] An individual who knowingly engages in this conduct can be criminally prosecuted. The stolen property can be seized and forfeited with or without an accompanying criminal prosecution.

The original owner can also recover stolen property in a private civil action in replevin. In countries that follow the common law of property, like the United States, a thief can never convey title to stolen property even if the property is sold to a good faith purchaser.[26] This contrasts with the rule of many civil law nations (such as on the European continent) in which a good faith purchaser can obtain title under certain circumstances despite a theft in the object's history.[27] Although in common law countries a thief cannot transfer title to stolen property, the original owner may be barred from recovering the property by a statute of limitation if the claim is not brought within a specific time period.

Statutes of limitation generally provide fairly short time periods for the recovery of stolen personal property, including artworks and cultural objects, from the time that the theft occurs.[28] Because of the ease of hiding and transporting artworks and other cultural objects, most courts that have confronted cases of stolen artworks delay the accrual of the cause of action until the original owner learns the location of the artwork and demands its return from the current possessor (New York)[29] or delay the accrual so long as the original owner is searching diligently for the stolen work.[30] California has enacted a specific statute of limitation to delay accrual of the cause of action in cases involving "any article of historical, interpretive, scientific, or artistic significance."[31] Through adoption of these statutory interpretations that delay

---

[25] National Stolen Property Act, 18 U.S.C. §§ 2314–2315 (2006) (prohibiting the interstate or international transport of stolen property and the receipt, transfer, and possession of stolen property that has been transported across state or international boundaries, worth more than $5,000, and known to have been stolen).

[26] *See, e.g.*, the Uniform Commercial Code codified by state law in the United States, U.C.C. § 2-403(1) (stating "[a] purchaser of goods acquires all title which his transferor had or had power to transfer").

[27] See the discussion of the good faith purchaser doctrine of Switzerland in *Autocephalous Greek-Orthodox Church of Cyprus and the Republic of Cyprus v. Goldberg & Feldman Fine Arts, Inc.*, 717 F. Supp. 1374, 1400 (S.D. Ind. 1989).

[28] The statutory time period is determined by state law and, for recovery of stolen property, generally ranges from two to six years. The time period runs from the time the cause of action accrues, which is normally considered to be the time when the injury that is the basis for the lawsuit occurred.

[29] *See, e.g.*, Kunstsammlungen zu Weimar v. Elicofon, 678 F.2d 1150 (2d Cir. 1982) (applying the "demand and refusal" rule). New York courts also apply the equitable defense of laches and may bar the claim if the plaintiff's unreasonable delay caused prejudice to the defendant. Solomon R. Guggenheim Found. v. Lubell, 569 N.E.2d 426 (N.Y. 1991).

[30] *See, e.g.*, Autocephalous Greek-Orthodox Church of Cyprus, 717 F. Supp. 1374, 1388–89 (S.D. Ind. 1989).

[31] Cal. Code Civ. Proc. § 338(c) (2008).

accrual of the cause of action until the victim of art theft has had a realistic opportunity to learn the location of stolen art and cultural objects, U.S. courts have demonstrated their concern for the unique cultural value of such works and their idiosyncratic relationship to the true owner.

b. Archaeological Theft

In addition to theft from known collections, there is a particular form of theft that applies exclusively to archaeological objects that are looted directly from the ground. Such objects may be particularly appealing to the international art market because their existence is undocumented so that there is no record of a theft. It is therefore extremely difficult to trace such objects through normal law enforcement methods and to establish their true origin. So long as the international market is willing to trade in antiquities without known provenance history, there will continue to be an incentive to loot sites to supply the market with undocumented artifacts.

To combat this form of theft, many nations have enacted laws that vest ownership of undiscovered archaeological objects in the state. These ownership laws apply to any objects discovered or excavated after the effective date of the statute. If an object is excavated (or looted) after this date and removed from the country without permission, then the object is stolen property and it retains this characterization even after it is brought to the United States.[32] Such artifacts are included in the NSPA's prohibition on interstate and international transport. Depending on the factual circumstances and the proof available to the government, the stolen property may be seized and forfeited and the individual may be subject to criminal prosecution.

This doctrine was tested in the 2001 prosecution of the prominent New York antiquities dealer, Frederick Schultz, for conspiring to deal in stolen property in violation of the NSPA.[33] Until shortly before his indictment, Schultz was president of the National Association of Dealers in Ancient, Orienta, and Primitive Art. Schultz was indicted on one count of conspiring to deal in antiquities stolen from Egypt in violation of Egypt's national ownership Law 117, which was enacted in 1983.[34] Schultz's co-conspirator, the British restorer Jonathan Tokeley-Parry, plastered over ancient Egyptian sculptures, including a head of the Egyptian pharaoh Amenhotep III, to make them look like cheap tourist souvenirs and then exported them to England. There, Tokeley-Parry

---

[32] The United Kingdom followed this legal rule in the conviction of Jonathan Tokeley-Parry, R. v. Tokeley-Parry, [1999] Crim. L.R. 578 (1998) (stating that "all antiquities in Egypt are the property of the state and if held by an individual without a licence or removed from Egypt, are stolen."), and more recently in a civil recovery action, Government of the Islamic Republic of Iran v. The Barakat Galleries Ltd., [2007] EWCA Civ. 1374 (2007). This rule has also been incorporated into the U.K. statute creating a new criminal offense, although the statute applies only in the case of thefts that occurred after the date of its enactment, December 2003. Dealing in Cultural Objects (Offences) Act, 2003 ch. 27, *available at* http://www.opsi.gov.uk/acts/acts2003/20030027.htm.

[33] *See supra* note 25.

[34] United States v. Schultz, 178 F. Supp. 2d 445 (S.D.N.Y. 2002), *aff'd*, 333 F.3d 393 (2d Cir. 2003).

restored the sculptures to their original appearance, after which he and Schultz attempted to sell them in the United States and England. To this end, the two of them fabricated a fake "old" collection, attributed to a relative of Tokeley-Parry who had traveled in Egypt in the 1920s. Schultz and Tokeley-Parry reportedly soaked labels in tea and microwaved them to make them appear old. Nonetheless, Tokeley-Parry was eventually discovered by Scotland Yard and convicted in England of handling stolen property. Schultz's prosecution followed not long after.

Schultz's prosecution relied on an earlier case, *United States v. McClain*,[35] in which several dealers were convicted for conspiring to deal in antiquities stolen from Mexico, which also has a national ownership law.[36] Schultz argued that the Egyptian law was not a true ownership law and, further, that the *McClain* decision should no longer be accepted, in part because it had been superseded by enactment of the CPIA. The court examined the Egyptian law, concluding that it was a true ownership law, both because it plainly stated that it was and because it was internally enforced within Egypt.[37] The court also held that the CPIA and this application of the NSPA could co-exist. While recognizing that there might be circumstances in which both the CPIA and the NSPA might apply to the same conduct, the court held that this did not pose an inherent conflict because of differences in their nature (the CPIA being civil in nature and the NSPA being criminal) and in the elements of proof required for a violation.[38] The court concluded by stating,

> Although we recognize the concerns raised by Schultz and the amici about the risks that this holding poses to dealers in foreign antiquities, we cannot imagine that it "creates an insurmountable barrier to the lawful importation of cultural property into the United States." Our holding does assuredly create a barrier to the importation of cultural property owned by a foreign government. We see no reason that property stolen from a foreign sovereign should be treated any differently from property stolen from a foreign museum or private home. The mens rea requirement of the NSPA will protect innocent art dealers who unwittingly receive stolen goods, while our appropriately broad reading of the NSPA will protect the property of sovereign nations.[39]

In addition to criminal prosecution and forfeiture actions that the government can bring, the original owner (most typically the foreign government) can bring a replevin claim in a U.S. court to recover its stolen property. Basing its right to

---

[35] 545 F.2d 988 (5th Cir 1977). *McClain* was preceded by United States v. Hollinshead, 495 F.2d 1154 (9th Cir. 1974), which was decided on the same principle of national ownership.

[36] The defendants' conviction on the substantive counts was reversed because the Fifth Circuit held that Mexico's earlier laws regulating archaeological remains were not true vesting statutes. Only Mexico's 1972 law was truly a vesting statute, so the defendants' conviction on the conspiracy count was affirmed. United States v. McClain, 593 F.2d 658 (5th Cir. 1979).

[37] United States v. Schultz, 333 F.3d 393, 398–402 (2d Cir. 2003).

[38] *Id.* at 408–09.

[39] *Id.* at 410–11.

ownership on national vesting laws, as recognized in the *McClain* and *Schultz* decisions, a foreign state can recover antiquities looted and removed without permission after the effective date of its national ownership law. Many such successful claims have been brought, including Turkey's recovery of the 360 objects in the Lydian hoard from the Metropolitan Museum of Art in New York and its recovery of the Elmali coin hoard from private collectors.[40] This is also the legal theory on which the recent successes of Italy and Greece in recovering artifacts from the Metropolitan Museum of Art in New York, the Boston Museum of Fine Arts, the J. Paul Getty Museum in Malibu, the Cleveland Museum of Art, and the Princeton University Art Museum, as well as from the dealer Jerome Eisenberg and the private collector Shelby White, were premised.[41]

c. *Illegal Importation*

The third aspect of illegal conduct is illegal importation or smuggling. While goods that have been illegally exported from one country are not generally regarded as contraband once they enter another country (absent an additional agreement, such as a bilateral agreement under the CPIA, or the status of the property as stolen), illegal import renders the goods subject to seizure and forfeiture under the customs laws. The U.S. customs statute prohibits the entry into the United States of goods imported contrary to law.[42] Application of this provision is based on a variety of laws, ranging from the NSPA (in the case of stolen property) to statutes that require declaration of the country of origin and value of the goods to be imported.

Illegal import often results from improper declaration of the goods upon entry into the United States. This is illustrated by the 1999 decision, *United States v. An Antique Platter of Gold*,[43] which involved a late fourth-century B.C. phiale that was imported into the United States for purchase by the New York collector, Michael Steinhardt. The dealer had seen the bowl in Sicily where it had been found. The dealer received the bowl at the Swiss-Italian border, carried it through Switzerland and, from there, brought it to the United States. The customs declaration forms, however, stated that the country of origin of the bowl was Switzerland (rather than Italy) and misstated the value of the bowl

---

40 Republic of Turkey v. OKS Partners, 797 F. Supp. 64 (D. Mass. 1992); Lawrence M. Kaye & Carla T. Main, *The Saga of the Lydian Hoard: Uşak to New York and Back Again*, *in* ANTIQUITIES TRADE OR BETRAYED: LEGAL, ETHICAL & CONSERVATION ISSUES 150, 153–54 (Kathryn W. Tubb ed., 1995).

41 *See* Agreement between the Ministry for Cultural Heritage and Activities of the Italian Republic and the Metropolitan Museum of Art (Feb. 21, 2006) (copy on file with author); Agreement between the Boston Museum of Fine Arts and Italy and objects returned, *available at* http://www.mfa.org/collections/index.asp?key=2656; Elisabetta Povoledo, *Boston Art Museum Returns Works to Italy*, N.Y. TIMES, Sept. 29, 2006, at B25; Hugh Eakin, *Getty Museum Agrees to Return Two Antiquities to Greece*, N.Y. TIMES, July 11, 2006, at B1.

42 18 U.S.C. § 545; 19 U.S.C. § 1595a(c).

43 18 U.S.C. §§ 542, 545. United States v. An Antique Platter of Gold, 184 F.3d 131 (2d Cir. 1999) (holding that the country of origin of an ancient gold phiale was Sicily, where it was excavated, rather than Switzerland, as declared by the importer, through which it was transported en route to the United States).

by close to $1 million. The court allowed the forfeiture of the bowl because it was imported into the United States by means of false declarations.

The court's decision implicitly held that the country of origin of archaeological objects is the place where they are found or excavated in modern times. A growing body of law supports this interpretation of the "country of origin" requirement for customs declarations as applied to archaeological artifacts. The Importation of Pre-Columbian Monumental or Architectural Sculpture or Murals Act defines "country of origin" as "the country where such sculpture or mural was first discovered."[44] The U.S. government forfeited several Buddha statues and other antiquities from Pakistan because the importer stated their country of origin to be Dubai, the transit country through which the artifacts passed en route to the United States.[45] In another case, the dealer declared the country of origin as Syria for a silver rhyton that was discovered in Iran. The dealer, Hicham Aboutaam, pled guilty to a misdemeanor for the false declaration and the artifact was forfeited.[46] Much of the legal regime that aims to protect the archaeological heritage, including both the import restrictions enacted under the CPIA and the application of the NSPA to cases of archaeological theft, depends on the particular modern country in which the artifact was discovered. A definition of country of origin as the place of discovery of the artifact in modern times is crucial to the effectiveness of the legal regime.

C. INCREASING THE DETERRENT EFFECT OF THE LEGAL REGIME

While the legal regime has developed several sophisticated legal rules for deterring the trade in stolen and looted antiquities, several shortcomings of the law render these rules less effective than they might otherwise be. In particular, although the new Sentencing Guideline was devised to increase criminal penalties for those convicted of a cultural heritage resource crime, the risks of detection and punishment do not seem adequate to fully deter illegal conduct. As the criminologist Simon McKenzie has recently pointed out in his study of the market in antiquities as a criminal enterprise, "[j]ust as justice must not only be done but be seen to be done, so antiquities must not only be licitly excavated and traded, but must be seen to be licitly excavated and traded."[47] This is very difficult to accomplish in a market in which a large proportion of the antiquities that are traded have an undocumented background. Many of these artifacts most likely were not legally excavated but may still be legally traded because of several aspects of the legal system and, most importantly, because of the large numbers of antiquities on the market without a documented history.

---

[44] 19 U.S.C. § 2095(4).

[45] U.S. Immigration and Customs Enforcement Press Release, Department of Homeland Security Returns Rare Artifacts to the Pakistani Government, Jan. 23, 2007, *available at* http://www.ice.gov/pi/news/newsreleases/articles/070123newark.htm.

[46] U.S. Attorney for the Southern District of New York, Press Release, Art Dealer Pleads Guilty in U.S. Court to Customs Violation in Iranian Antiquity Case, June 24, 2004, *available at* http://www.usdoj.gov/usao/nys/pressreleases/June04/aboutaampleapr.pdf.

[47] S.M.R. MACKENZIE, GOING, GOING, GONE: REGULATING THE MARKET IN ILLICIT ANTIQUITIES 21 (2005).

In the absence of documentation and because the burden of proving illegal background falls on the government or claimant, the proof may be inadequate to establish that an undocumented antiquity is an illegally traded one. There are several reasons why the legal regime, as currently constructed, may not offer adequate risk of detection and severity of punishment for illegal activity in the international antiquities market, but most of these reasons hinge on the fact that undocumented antiquities are frequently traded on the international market and are accepted by purchasers. There are some indications that this situation may be changing, but it is necessary to examine why the risks of violating the law sometimes do not serve as an adequate deterrent to trading in looted artifacts.

The burden of proof falls on the government in criminal prosecutions and civil forfeiture actions and on a private claimant in a suit to recover stolen property. The elements that need to be proven vary with the type of legal action, as does the standard for the burden of proof. For example, in criminal prosecutions, the government must prove the elements of the crime and knowledge or intent on the part of the defendant beyond a reasonable doubt. In a civil suit, the claimant must prove the right of ownership or possession under the normal civil standard of more likely than not. In a civil forfeiture action, the government must prove the required elements under the normal civil standard or a lower civil standard of probable cause.[48] Because of the high burden of proof required in criminal prosecutions, such prosecutions have been few. Civil forfeitures, with the lowest burden of proof, are the most common such actions, but the importer or possessor of the artifact then loses only the monetary value of the artifacts and does not risk any more severe punishment, such as fines or incarceration. Because the mark-up in the value of antiquities from their "source" at an archaeological site, to the transit points, and finally to the destination market is so great,[49] the loss of the artifact does not generally impose a significant cost on the trader in a market country. Market participants not only have relatively little financial investment at risk, but they can recoup their losses through other sales when they lose only the value of a particular object.

Mackenzie points out that those who participate in white-collar crime, including the illegal aspects of the international trade in antiquities, are highly influenced by the risk of detection and the severity of punishment, as well as social factors.[50] The high numbers of unprovenanced antiquities in the market

---

[48] The standard that applies in a civil forfeiture action depends on whether the forfeiture action is taken under Title 19 (the customs statute) of the United States Code or under some other statutory provision. In the case of violations of the CPIA and other customs provisions, the standard the government must meet is the lower standard of probable cause. Civil Asset Forfeiture Reform Act, 18 U.S.C. § 983 (2008).

[49] *See* Patty Gerstenblith, *Collecting Antiquities in the International Market: Philosophy, Law and Heritage*, *in* 2007 Y.B. CULTURAL PROP. L. 139 (Sherry Hutt ed., 2007).

[50] MACKENZIE, *supra* note 47, at 205–26 (analyzing the practical balance sheet, the moral balance sheet, and the social balance sheet in the context of the antiquities trade). There is some indication that the public auction houses, whose catalogues and sales are usually subject to public scrutiny, are sensitive to social factors such as reputation. For example, fol-

and the lack of any requirement to affirmatively establish provenance mean that it is difficult to prove that a market participant *knew* that a particular antiquity was stolen property with the consequence of insufficient risk of criminal prosecution.[51]

The most effective change in the law would be to reverse the burden of proof in legal proceedings so as to require the current possessor of an archaeological artifact to prove legitimate background. This has been done, to a limited extent, in the United Kingdom, with respect to cultural materials illegally removed from Iraq after August 1990 pursuant to U.N. Security Council Resolution 1483.[52] There is some indication that this measure, requiring the possessor to demonstrate that he or she did not have reason to know that cultural materials were illegally removed from Iraq, seems to have had an effect on the London market in Mesopotamian artifacts.[53] However, it is unlikely that such a reversal of the burden of proof would or could, within the bounds of the Constitution, be enacted in the United States for criminal prosecutions or even civil forfeitures and private replevin claims.[54]

While little beyond the traditional bounds of the law can be done to influence private participants in the market, museums in the United States may be more susceptible to additional regulation. Through indirect regulation, the government can adopt requirements that would essentially shift the burden of proving the legitimate background of archaeological artifacts that museums acquire or accept as gifts.[55] The bases for this indirect regulation would be

---

lowing the exposé of Sotheby's practices by the British journalist Peter Watson, SOTHEBY'S: THE INSIDE STORY (1997), Sotheby's closed its antiquities department in London.

[51] The prosecution in *Schultz* was feasible because the major participants kept copious written records and Schultz's co-conspirator, Jonathan Tokeley-Parry, was willing to testify against Schultz. United States v. Schultz, 333 F.3d 393, 396–98 (2d Cir. 2003). The prosecution in *McClain* succeeded because of an undercover operation. United States v. McClain, 593 F.2d 658, 660–63 (5th Cir. 1979).

[52] Iraq (United Nations Sanctions) Order, Statutory Instrument 2003 No. 1519, *available at* http://www.hmso.gov.uk/si/si2003/20031519.htm; Section 8(3) states, "Any person who deals in any item of illegally removed cultural property [from Iraq] shall be guilty of an offence . . . , unless he proves that he did not know and had no reason to suppose that the item in question was illegally removed Iraqi cultural property."

[53] Neil J. Brodie, *The Plunder of Iraq's Archaeological Heritage, 1991–2005, and the London Antiquities Trade, in* THE ANTIQUITIES TRADE, *supra* note 1, at 206, 217–18.

[54] The one circumstance in which the current possessor of a cultural object has the initial burden of proof is at the moment of importation. Under the CPIA, 19 U.S.C. Section 2606, the importer must present documentation of lawful export or other satisfactory evidence, as defined in this section. In the case of importation of any commercial goods, the importer has the obligation to declare the country of origin, the value of the goods, and possibly other information before proceeding to a forfeiture.

[55] I have written elsewhere of the potential liability of museum trustees who breach their fiduciary duty of care by wasting corporate assets when a museum acquires antiquities without an assurance that the museum is receiving legal title to the antiquity. The state attorney general is the sole party with the standing to enforce this fiduciary obligation and hold trustees accountable. Patty Gerstenblith, *Acquisition and Deacquisition of Museum Collections and the Fiduciary Obligations of Museums to the Public*, 11 CARDOZO J. INT'L & COMP. L. 409, 453–62 (2003). In addition to a possible breach of the trustees' fiduciary obligation, the museum that acquires undocumented antiquities and may therefore be contributing to the destruction of

(1) through federal, state, and local funding provided to museums and (2) through the tax deduction that is given to donors of artworks to museums.

Because of the deductibility of donations to American museums that are organized as charitable institutions, the American private collector can afford to pay a premium when buying artwork on the international market.[56] American museums and private collectors therefore play a significant role in the international art market. While some American museums have taken voluntary steps to restrict their acquisitions through codes of ethics and acquisitions, not enough of the art-acquiring museums have publicly accessible acquisitions policies that demonstrate that these museums are adequately distancing themselves from the contemporary looting of archaeological sites. Not only must these museums have codes of practice that dictate the measures that a museum will take to avoid acquiring recently looted artifacts, they must also be seen to be avoiding such acquisitions by publicly announcing their new acquisitions and making the provenance history of such artifacts available to the public.

Some museums have voluntarily adopted acquisitions policies stating that the museum will not acquire an archaeological artifact unless its history can be documented back to a particular date or that is known to have been exported legally from its country of origin.[57] However, until recently, neither of the two major museum associations in the United States had formulated guidelines that specifically pertained to the acquisition of ancient art and artifacts. In 2004, the Association of Art Museum Directors (AAMD) issued guidelines to address specifically the acquisition of ancient art and artifacts. This policy was much criticized, in particular, because it adopted a ten-year rolling limitation—

---

archaeological sites and knowledge about the past is arguably violating the purpose for which it receives tax-exempt and charitable status under the Internal Revenue Code. *See infra* note 78. Greater oversight by the Internal Revenue Service (IRS) to determine whether museums are contributing to the destruction of knowledge and by state attorneys general to enforce the fiduciary obligations of museum trustees would also help to fill the gaps in law enforcement. One indication of possible increased scrutiny by the IRS and other government agencies came in the raids in January 2008 on four Southern California museums that seem implicated in an alleged scheme to defraud the government in connection with inflated charitable deductions for smuggled and looted antiquities from China and Thailand. *See, e.g.*, Edward Wyatt, *Museum Workers are Called Complicit*, N.Y. TIMES, Jan. 26, 2008, at A17.

[56] Shelby White, the owner of one of the largest collections of antiquities in the United States, wrote that the extent of public subsidy when artworks are donated to museums from larger estates is approximately one-fourth of the art's fair market value. Shelby White, *Building American Museums: The Role of the Private Collector*, *in* WHO OWNS THE PAST? CULTURAL POLICY, CULTURAL PROPERTY, AND THE LAW 165, 174 (Kate Fitz Gibbon ed., 2005).

[57] Often the cut-off date selected is 1970, the year when the UNESCO Convention on the Means of Prohibiting and Preventing the Illicit Import, Export and Transfer of Ownership of Cultural Property was promulgated. The J. Paul Getty Museum adopted such a policy in October 2006, *available at* http://www.getty.edu/about/governance/pdfs/acquisitions_policy.pdf. The policy of the Field Museum of Natural History in Chicago on accessions states that "the museum and staff 'shall be in full compliance with laws and regulations, both domestic and foreign, governing transfer of ownership and movement of materials across political boundaries.'" Willard L. Boyd, *Museums as Centers of Cultural Understanding*, *in* IMPERIALISM, ART AND RESTITUTION 47, 50 (John Henry Merryman ed., 2006).

that is, museums could acquire artifacts once they were known to have been out of their country of origin for a ten-year period.[58] Only in 2008 did the AAMD and the American Association of Museums (AAM) issue new guidelines, which share many similarities but also differ in some of their important and more interesting details.[59]

The most significant feature of these guidelines is the adoption of a fixed cut-off date of 1970. In addition, both the AAM and AAMD guidelines require that a museum make its acquisitions policy publicly available and that it make information about new acquisitions, including provenance, background, and an image, publicly accessible, although the policies do not require this information to be posted on the Internet. Both sets of guidelines permit exceptions to the 1970 requirement.

In the case of the AAMD guidelines, an acquisition can proceed based on the museum's informed judgment, a factor which leaves much to the discretion of the individual museum. This discretion is to be informed by balancing the potential financial and reputational harm to the museum against the benefit of acquiring the object. It is unfortunate that the AAMD sought only to balance two different interests of the museum against each other and did not see fit to incorporate into the calculation concerns for the rights of the country of origin and the potential harm to the world's cultural heritage and historical record.

In a somewhat novel step, the AAMD has established an online registry where any object, whose provenance history cannot be traced back either to 1970 or to legal export from the country of origin, must be posted with available documentation and an image.[60] Apparently modeled on the databases of art works identified in museum collections that may have been looted during the Holocaust, this registry seems designed to facilitate eventual restitution of archaeological objects to their rightful owner. The AAMD approach thus focuses on ownership rights rather than on preservation of original contexts. However, close to a year after creation of the registry, only one object has been listed—a ganesh stele, possibly from India, acquired by the Portland Art Museum. The only provenance history known about this piece is that it was sold at Sotheby's in 2000. It is difficult to draw any conclusion at this time about the efficacy of either the AAMD's new policy or the registry in deterring acquisition of poorly provenanced works.

While sharing several similarities, the AAM standards focus not just on restitution of newly-acquired objects but also on facilitating restitution claims for artifacts that are already in an institution's collection by calling on museums

---

[58] Report of the AAMD Task Force on the Acquisition of Archaeological Artifacts and Ancient Art, *available at* http://aamd.org/papers/documents/TaskForceReportwithCoverPage_Final.pdf. For a more detailed analysis of the 2004 AAMD guidelines, see Gerstenblith, *supra* note 49.

[59] AAMD New Report on Acquisition of Archaeological Materials and Ancient Art, *available at* http://aamd.org/newsroom/documents/2008ReportAndRelease.pdf; AAM Standards Regarding Archaeological Material and Ancient Art, available at http://www.aam-us.org/museumresources/ethics/upload/Standards%20Regarding%20Archaeological%20Material%20and%20Ancient%20Art.pdf.

[60] AAMD Object Registry is *available at* http://aamdobjectregistry.org.

to examine their existing collections. The AAM standards thus represent a more holistic approach to the problem of looted antiquities and indicate a willingness to examine past conduct in an attempt to return antiquities to their rightful owner and make meaningful restitution.

In two other particularly contentious areas concerning museum collections of cultural objects, museums have adopted more stringent policies, either voluntarily or through government regulation. These two areas involve artworks looted during the Holocaust and Native American human remains and cultural objects. In 1990, Congress enacted the Native American Graves Protection and Repatriation Act (NAGPRA).[61] Utilizing authority based on the provision of federal funding, Congress required museums[62] to create inventories of Native American human remains and associated funerary objects[63] and less detailed summaries of unassociated funerary objects, sacred objects, and objects of cultural patrimony.[64] NAGPRA thus requires museums to examine the Native American cultural items already in their collections, provide notice to the affected Indian tribes of the inventory,[65] or provide access to the summaries,[66] and to make the cultural items available for restitution to lineal descendants or culturally affiliated tribes under certain circumstances.[67]

In the case of artworks looted during the Holocaust, Congress was considering enacting legislation to regulate museums,[68] but the museum associations promulgated voluntary regulations, thereby heading off new legislation.[69] These voluntary codes both require museums to examine the artworks currently in their collections[70] and to make lists of those artworks with suspicious backgrounds publicly available.[71] Museums are also to apply strict criteria so as to avoid

[61] 25 U.S.C. §§ 3001–3013 (2008).

[62] *See* 25 U.S.C. § 3001(8) (defining "museums" as "any institution or State or local government agency (including any institution of higher learning) that receives Federal funds").

[63] 25 U.S.C. § 3003.

[64] 25 U.S.C. § 3004. These terms are defined in 25 U.S.C. § 3001(3).

[65] 25 U.S.C. § 3003(d).

[66] 25 U.S.C. § 3004(a).

[67] 25 U.S.C. § 3005.

[68] Judith Dobrzynski, *Capitol Hill Looks at Issue of Art Stolen in Wartime*, N.Y. Times, Feb. 15, 1998, § 1, at 17. Additional impetus was provided by the Washington Conference Principles on Nazi-Confiscated Art, *available at* http://www.state.gov/www/regions/eur/981203_heac_art_princ.html.

[69] The Report of the AAMD Task Force on the Spoliation of Art during the Nazi/World War II Era (1933–1945) and guidelines are available at http://www.aamd.org/guideln.shtml [hereinafter AAMD Task Force]. The AAM Guidelines Concerning the Unlawful Appropriation of Objects During the Nazi Era are available at http://www.aam-us.org/museumresources/ethics/upload/ethicsguidelines_naziera.pdf [hereinafter AAM Guidelines].

[70] AAMD Task Force, *supra* note 69, Section II Guidelines, A (1)–(3) (Research regarding Existing Collections), D (Discovery of Unlawfully Confiscated Works of Art), and E (Response to Claims Against the Museum). The AAM Guidelines are similar except that they acknowledge that museums may want to waive available defenses "in order to achieve an equitable and appropriate resolution of claims." AAM Guidelines, *supra* note 69, para. 4(-).

[71] AAMD Task Force, *supra* note 69, Section II Guidelines, C (Access to Museum Records). The AAM has now made publicly available a list with over 25,000 objects in 154 participating museums available at its Nazi-Era Provenance Internet Portal Project with links to each museum's Web site, *available at* http://www.nepip.org/. *See also* AAM Press Release, "AAM Testifies

acquiring new works of suspicious background.[72] It is clear that ongoing public and congressional concern has caused museums to change their practices with respect to specific categories of cultural objects. In the case of both artworks that were possibly looted during the Holocaust and Native American indigenous cultural items, museums are now required to examine the artworks and artifacts in their collections and to take steps to avoid acquiring new works that fit into these particularly problematic categories.

Museums receive many forms of financial subsidies, both direct and indirect, from the federal and state governments. These subsidies include exemption from income tax,[73] below-market rate leases of the land on which they are located, direct subsidies to the museum's operating budget,[74] and funding of specific projects and exhibitions.[75] In exchange for these financial benefits, the government should require that museums affirmatively search their collections of antiquities. Museums should then publish catalogues with those antiquities of questionable background and make the catalogues available on the Internet. Museums should also be required to make their policies publicly available, announce new acquisitions with their provenance background and avoid acquiring antiquities with a background that cannot be objectively documented back to a particular date, such as 1970.[76] Failure to comply with these requirements could be punished through civil penalties, as in the case of NAGPRA violations.[77]

The second legal context in which the burden of proof could be reversed would involve donations of antiquities to museums. When an artwork is donated to a museum, the taxpayer receives a deduction from income tax in the amount of the work's fair market value.[78] If the deduction claimed is more than $5,000,

---

Before Congress: U.S. Museums Making Significant Strides Addressing Nazi-Era Loot: (July 27, 2006), *available at* http://www.aam-us.org/pressreleases.cfm?mode=list&id=109.

[72] AAMD Task Force, *supra* note 69, Section II Guidelines, B (Future Gifts, Bequests, and Purchases).

[73] 26 U.S.C. § 501(c).

[74] For example, the Metropolitan Museum of Art in New York and the Brooklyn Museum lease the land on which they are located from New York City at nominal rents and receive direct subsidies for their operating budgets. *See* Brooklyn Inst. of Arts and Sci. v. New York, 64 F. Supp. 2d 184, 187–90 (E.D.N.Y. 1999).

[75] *See, e.g.*, the grants given by the National Endowment for the Arts in FY2007 to museums, *available at* http://www.nea.gov/grants/recent/disciplines/Museums/07museums.html. Museums are eligible for many of the grants administered by the National Endowment for the Humanities (NEH), including NEH support for exhibitions; *see* http://www.neh.gov/projects/et-index.html.

[76] The new Getty policy includes all three of these key elements, *see supra* note 57.

[77] 25 U.S.C. § 3007 (allowing the Secretary of the Interior to assess civil penalties for a museum's failure to comply with NAGPRA requirements).

[78] Donations to organizations that qualify as charitable organizations, defined as "[c]orporations, and any community chest, fund, or foundation, organized and operated exclusively for religious, charitable, scientific, testing for public safety, literary, or educational purposes," 26 U.S.C. Section 501(c)(3), may be deducted from the income of the donor (both individuals and corporations) for income tax purposes. 26 U.S.C. § 170(a); *see also* 26 U.S.C. § 642(c) (allowing a deduction from the income of an estate or trust); 26 U.S.C. § 2055 (allowing a deduction in the valuation of an estate for estate tax purposes); 26 U.S.C. § 2522 (allowing an exemption from payment of gift tax for *inter vivos* gifts).

then the fair market value must be substantiated by an independent appraisal; with higher value works, a panel established by the Internal Revenue Service (IRS) may review the fair market value appraisal.[79] Along with establishing fair market value, the taxpayer should also bear the burden of establishing legal title. If the donor cannot convey title to the antiquity to the museum, then the museum is not receiving anything of value.[80] Further, any uncertainty as to title should be an element in determining the fair market value of the donated work because there is now market evidence that legitimate title is an important factor in fair market value.[81] However, the IRS art advisory panel, as currently constituted, is composed of dealers, who have an interest in inflating the market value of artworks and in de-emphasizing the significance of title concerns. Dealers thus have a conflict of interest in evaluating the title to antiquities and should not be determining whether the donor is able to convey title to artworks. Rather, the question of title should be reviewed by an independent advisory panel composed of individuals with knowledge and expertise concerning the questions of title that are unique to antiquities. The key element, however, is that the burden should be placed on the donor-taxpayer to establish title and, if the burden is not satisfied, then the donor should be denied the deduction.

D. CONCLUSION

The law has continued to develop in significant ways over the past few years as a tool for preventing trade in looted archaeological artifacts. Despite this progress and the increasing number of cases brought under the existing legal regime, the disincentive to trade in undocumented artifacts still does not seem to be an adequate deterrent. Although the relevant laws could be expanded, particularly in the availability of criminal punishment, this seems unlikely because those involved in the antiquities market in the United States wield significant political power. Additional means of deterring trade in undocumented antiquities must therefore be found within existing legal structures.

One such means is through greater oversight of the practices of U.S. museums—both their acquisitions by purchase and their acceptance of gifts from private collectors. This greater oversight can be achieved through careful scrutiny of the taxpayer deduction for those who donate antiquities to museums and through government requirements, imposed through the financial support

---

[79] *See* IRS Form 8283.

[80] See also *supra* note 55 for discussion of increased IRS scrutiny of alleged donations of looted antiquities with inflated fair market values.

[81] Within six months, Sotheby's set two records for sales of antiquities. In June 2007, Sotheby's auctioned a sculpture, *Artemis and the Stag*, for $27 million, the highest amount paid at public auction for an antiquity and the highest amount paid for a sculpture of any date. The sculpture had been on display at the Albright-Knox Museum in Buffalo since the 1930s. John Sullivan, *Buffalo: Museum Raises Millions in Auction*, N.Y. TIMES, June 15, 2007 at B6. In December 2007, this record was broken when Sotheby's auctioned the Guennol Lioness for $57 million. The Lioness was acquired in Baghdad in 1931 and had been on display at the Brooklyn Museum since 1948. Carol Vogel, *The Lioness Commands Many Millions*, N.Y. TIMES, Dec. 6, 2007, at E2. Market observers attribute at least some of these high prices to the security of title that comes with a well-known and well-documented work of ancient art.

given by federal, state, and local governments, for greater transparency in, and stricter adherence to, acquisition policies and practices. When the museum or taxpayer is seeking a government benefit, they, not the government, should bear the burden of proving legitimate ownership and a documented history that excludes the possibility that these antiquities are the product of recent site looting. The goal of such additional regulation is increased preservation of archaeological sites so that we, and future generations, can learn from and enjoy the past.

PART V

ROLE OF GOVERNMENTS

CHAPTER 16
PRESERVATION OF CULTURAL HERITAGE: A TOOL OF INTERNATIONAL PUBLIC DIPLOMACY

Maria P. Kouroupas

A. INTRODUCTION

The Bureau of Educational and Cultural Affairs ("the Bureau") of the U.S. Department of State ("the Department") is a pillar of the Department's international public diplomacy mission. For generations, the Bureau's long-standing academic and professional exchange programs have enriched Americans and foreign participants, who return to their home countries better equipped to assume positions of leadership. The Cultural Heritage Center ("the Center"), which resides within the Bureau, supports the foreign affairs functions of the Department that relate to the protection and preservation of cultural heritage. In recent years, the rising tide of interest in cultural preservation has made it a palpable element of public diplomacy, particularly with respect to movable cultural property and the built environment that represent the development of mankind.

A primary function of the Center is to administer the responsibilities of the Department relating to the 1970 UNESCO Convention on the Means of Prohibiting and Preventing the Illicit Import, Export and Transfer of Ownership of Cultural Property ("the 1970 UNESCO Convention").[1] For example, the Department provides technical and administrative support to the Cultural Property Advisory Committee ("the Committee"), which is appointed by the president of the United States to carry out specific statutory functions.[2] The president has designated the Department to consider the Committee's recommendations and other relevant information and carry out the statutory decision-making responsibilities related to entering into agreements with other countries to assist with mitigating the pillage that endangers those countries' cultural patrimony. Additional discussion of this responsibility occurs later in this chapter.

[1] UNESCO Convention on the Means of Prohibiting and Preventing the Illicit Import, Export, and Transfer of Ownership of Cultural Property (Nov. 14, 1970), *available at* http://portal.unesco.org/en/ev.php-URL_ID=13039&URL_DO=DO_TOPIC&URL_SECTION=201.html.

[2] The Convention on Cultural Property Implementation Act, 19 U.S.C. Section 2601 et seq., sets out the specific statutory functions carried out by the Committee.

The other principal responsibility of the Center is the U.S. Ambassadors Fund for Cultural Preservation (AFCP). The AFCP, which was created by Congress in 2001, enables American ambassadors in developing countries to support local projects to preserve sites, collections of objects, or forms of traditional expression. The AFCP offers an opportunity for the United States to demonstrate its respect for the cultural heritage of other countries. The program has enjoyed great success and a consistent 80 percent response rate from ambassadors. The AFCP has supported over 500 projects worldwide, including technical support for the preservation of historic sites; assessment of museum collections and their conservation; archaeological conservation; documentation to save threatened traditional crafts; preservation of archives and manuscripts; recording of oral history; and documentation of music, dance, and language.

In recent years the Center has chaired an Interagency Working Group on the Preservation of Iraq's Cultural Heritage to coordinate support for Iraq among executive branch agencies such as the National Endowment for the Humanities, the Institute of Museum and Library Services, the Library of Congress, and the National Science Foundation. The Center administers the Department's special projects supporting the Iraq National Museum and other initiatives to safeguard Iraq's heritage. Congress has noted its concern about the site looting and illicit trafficking in cultural property from Iraq and Afghanistan and has asked the Department to focus greater attention on problems in these countries and throughout the world. To that end, the Department has supported the development, production, and distribution of a Red List of Iraq Antiquities at Risk and a Red List of Afghanistan Antiquities at Risk.[3] Red Lists are produced by the International Council of Museums (ICOM) as part of its commitment in the fight against illicit traffic of cultural property. Also, in coordination with the Department of Homeland Security, the Department of State anticipates the implementation of a special law authorizing the president to impose import restrictions on all cultural property originating in Iraq.[4]

B. BACKGROUND

The cultural property protection work of the Department is directed largely at implementing U.S. responsibilities under the aforementioned 1970 UNESCO Convention. The convention was adopted by UNESCO member states in response to worldwide concern over wanton pillage in countries rich in archaeological resources and the appearance in market countries of large quantities of objects of unknown provenience. Although the Senate unanimously ratified the convention in 1972, it was not until President Ronald Reagan signed the Convention on Cultural Property Implementation Act ("the Act")[5] into law in 1983 that the United States became a state party to the 1970

[3] Red Lists have also been developed for Peru, Cambodia, Mexico, and Central America. Others are in the planning stages.

[4] Emergency Protection for Iraqi Cultural Antiquities Act of 2004, Pub. L. No. 108-429, tit. III, 118 Stat. 2599. Import restrictions were announced on April 30, 2008.

[5] 19 U.S.C. §§ 2601–2613 (2008).

UNESCO Convention. The United States is one of 117 countries that have ratified the convention, including the so-called market countries of France, Switzerland, the United Kingdom, Japan, Denmark, Sweden, Belgium, and Germany. The ratification process is currently underway in the Netherlands.

The United States does not specifically regulate the acquisition of archaeological and ethnological material from other countries. Laws that apply to the movement of cultural objects govern, broadly speaking, theft, smuggling, and fraud. In addition, the United States may impose specific import restrictions.[6] Such import restrictions fall under the Civil Code and are not punitive in nature. The Act, it should be noted, is salutary legislation that gives the president broad discretion in applying it. Thus, it is a remedial agent in safeguarding endangered cultural property.

The basis for the United States' adherence to the 1970 Convention is found in the U.S. Senate report accompanying the enabling legislation that Congress adopted at the end of 1982:

> There has been an expanding trade in . . . artifacts deriving from clandestine activities and excavations that result in the mutilation of ancient centers of civilization. . . The appearance in the United States of important art objects of suspicious origin has often given rise to outcries and urgent requests for return. The United States considers that, on grounds of good foreign relations and motivated by ethical and moral principles, it should render assistance.[7]

The report further noted the importance of promoting "U.S. leadership in achieving greater international cooperation towards preserving cultural treasures that not only are of importance to the nations [from which] they originate, but also to greater international understanding of our common heritage."[8] The report also drew a distinction between cultural objects—non-renewable cultural resources—and products of mass production by noting that

> unlike other commodities, increased or new production of these articles cannot rise to meet the demand. Instead, the increased supply results from the sales of known artifacts and those newly recovered from archaeological sites. The unique origin and character of these articles raises serious trade issues distinct from the normal concerns of reciprocal trade agreements or U.S. trade law.[9]

From testimony and other documentation received by Congress, the report concluded as follows:

> the demand for cultural artifacts has resulted in the irremedial destruction of archaeological sites and articles [of cultural property],

---

[6] Examples of import restrictions include those applied under the 1972 Pre-Columbian Monumental or Architectural Sculpture or Murals Act (19 U.S.C. §§ 2091–2095 (2000)) and restrictions imposed on categories of cultural objects pursuant to the U.S. Convention on Cultural Property Implementation Act.

[7] S. Rep. No. 97-564, at 23 (1982).

[8] *Id.* at 21.

[9] *Id.* at 22–23.

> depriving . . . countries of their cultural patrimony and the world of important knowledge of its past. Further, because the United States is a principal market for articles of archaeological or ethnological interest and of art objects, the discovery here of stolen or illegally exported artifacts in some cases severely strains our relations with the countries of origin.[10]

Finally, the report weighed the following consideration:

> the interest of the United States . . . extends beyond our import market and our interest in fostering the careful study of foreign cultures. . . . The increasing interest in Native American, Hawaiian, and Alaskan artifacts concomitantly has spurred the pillaging of U.S. historic sites. The[ir] destruction . . . and the disappearance of the historic record . . . has given rise to a profound national interest in joining other countries to control the trafficking of such articles in international commerce."[11]

The U.S. enabling legislation implements two principal articles in the 1970 UNESCO Convention. Article 7b requires a state party "to prohibit the import of cultural property *stolen* from a museum or a religious or secular public monument or similar institution in another State Party . . . provided that such property is documented as appertaining to the inventory of that institution."[12] In this context, cultural property is broadly defined as material that is important "for archaeology, prehistory, history, literature, art or science."[13] Thus, the Act provides for a standing U.S. import restriction on material *stolen* from any of the other parties to the 1970 UNESCO Convention. Over the years, there have been numerous recoveries pursuant to the relevant section of the U.S. implementing legislation, 19 U.S.C. Section 2607. Most recently, a Colonial period painting from Peru was recovered while on consignment at an auction house, and a magnificent Colonial period hand-carved altarpiece, also from Peru (Challapampa), was located in Santa Fe, New Mexico, and has been repatriated. Another Colonial period painting that was stolen from a church in Hidalgo, Mexico, eventually found its way to the San Diego Museum of Art where it was recovered with the full cooperation of the museum and repatriated to Mexico.

C. ARTICLE 9 IMPLEMENTATION

Implementation of Article 9 of the 1970 UNESCO Convention, however, is most central to the United States' treaty obligations under the convention. It is a window through which the United States and other countries can engage with each other to mitigate pillage and illicit trafficking. Article 9 invites any state party to the convention whose cultural patrimony is in jeopardy from pillage of archaeological or ethnological materials to call upon other state parties for assistance.[14] Therefore, pursuant to Article 9 and the U.S. implementing

---

[10] *Id.* at 23.

[11] *Id.*

[12] 1970 UNESCO Convention, art. 7b, *supra* note 1 (emphasis added).

[13] *Id.*, art. 1.

[14] *Id.*, art. 9.

legislation, a state party may petition the United States for import restrictions on cultural property that is either archaeological and ethnological and that remains today in its country of origin. This material, particularly archaeological objects *in situ,* which cannot be documented, is the most vulnerable to pillage and illicit movement across international borders. This material often becomes the source for fresh supplies of cultural property in international commerce, feeding a large clandestine trade that brings high yield with little risk to its participants. Although most countries restrict the export of their cultural property, such export controls are not enforceable in the United States. Through the Act, the United States has the authority to impose import restrictions, but only on a country-by-country basis, and only if requested pursuant to Article 9 of the convention.

A state party's request for U.S. import restrictions should inform the United States about the following statutory criteria:[15] (1) that the national cultural patrimony is in jeopardy from pillage; (2) that internal protective measures have been put into place; (3) that action by the United States would be of benefit if applied in concert with similar steps implemented or to be implemented by other importing nations;[16] and (4) that U.S. import restrictions would be in the best educational, cultural, and scientific interests of the international community. Initial findings on these criteria are made by the Committee and final determinations are made by the Department. Additional research and analysis pertinent to the criteria is conducted by the Center, and relevant outside comments are invited to further enlighten the advisory and decision-making process.

D. U.S. IMPORT RESTRICTIONS

At the end of the process described above, if an import restriction is granted, it is applied prospectively and becomes an instrument for reducing future losses to the archaeological or ethnological record. A Designated List of categories of objects that are restricted is published in the U.S. *Federal Register* by the Department of Homeland Security, where the U.S. Customs Service is now administered. To assist the collecting community in identifying categories of restricted objects, the Department of State has created a Web-based image database.[17] The term *restriction* is the statutory language used in the Act. Lawmakers chose *restriction* over such terms as *embargo* or *ban* because restricted categories of objects actually are permitted to enter the United States if accompanied by an export certificate issued by the country of origin. Furthermore, a restriction does not apply to objects in circulation outside the country of origin at the time the Designated List is published if there is verifiable documentation that such objects left the country of origin prior to the import restriction.

---

[15] *See* 19 U.S.C. § 2602(a).

[16] This criterion is further governed by language in 19 U.S.C. Section 2602(c)(1)–(2), which broadens the decisionmaker's discretion in entering into an agreement.

[17] *See* https://exchanges.state.gov/culprop.

The enabling legislation, therefore, accommodates a legitimate trade in appropriately documented objects. The type of documentation needed to substantiate the provenance of traded objects (not to be confused with *provenience*, the find spot of an object) would substantiate historical information about previous transactions and possession of the object, forming the basis for more scrupulous trading and collecting practices. However, the practice of non-disclosure, often associated with assertions of ignorance, has long served as a veil of convenience in transactions involving antiquities. In adopting the Act, Congress understood that the absence of appropriate documentation impedes the ability to distinguish material that is grandfathered by the U.S. cultural property legislation from material newly looted to supply the marketplace. Once the ability to draw this distinction becomes the norm, a licit trade in cultural property has a chance to flourish.

E. ADVISORY AND DECISION-MAKING PROCESS

The Department is the executive branch agency largely responsible for implementing U.S. participation in the 1970 UNESCO Convention. As noted before, the Department administers the Committee and carries out the president's responsibilities under the U.S. enabling legislation. Foreign government requests for United States' protection pursuant to Article 9 of the 1970 UNESCO Convention have been received from Canada, El Salvador, Honduras, Guatemala, Nicaragua, Peru, Bolivia, Colombia, Mali, Cambodia, Cyprus, Italy, and China.

Requests are reviewed by the Committee whose 11 members, appointed by the president, include representatives of museums and the general public, experts in the international sale of art, and archaeologists. Once appointed, members of the Committee become Special Government Employees (SGEs) who must undergo an ethics review by the Office of the Legal Adviser of the Department of State as well as a security clearance conducted by the Department's Office of Diplomatic Security. They are expected to maintain confidentiality and abide by conflict-of-interest laws, obligations, and restrictions that pertain to public service.

Meetings of the Committee, which are called by the Department on an as-needed basis, are held to review a new foreign government request submitted under Article 9 of the 1970 UNESCO Convention, or to review the extension of an existing agreement as proposed by the Department, or to conduct an interim review of an existing agreement. The Department publishes notifications of Committee meetings in the *Federal Register*. Although the Department is under no requirement to do so, open sessions of the Committee are held to allow for oral comments from outside interested parties. Such comments are expected to relate to the statutory criteria for which the Committee must make findings as it reviews a particular country's request.[18] The Committee's deliberations on these criteria are closed:[19]

---

[18] The criteria are set forth in the Act, 19 U.S.C. § 2602.

[19] *See* 19 U.S.C. § 2605(h) (2008) (special exemption to disclosure requirements). *See also* Federal Advisory Committee Act (Public Law No. 92-463, 86 Stat. 770); 5 U.S.C. (Appendix I) (2008) (exemptions to disclosure requirements).

> [T]he provisions of the Federal Advisory Committee Act shall apply to the Committee *except that* the requirements of subsections (a) and (b) of section 10 and section 11 of such Act (relating to open meeting, public notice, public participation, and public availability of documents) shall not apply to the Committee, whenever and to the extent it is determined by the President or his designee that the disclosure of matters involved in the Committee's proceedings would compromise the Government's negotiating objectives or bargaining positions on the negotiations of any agreement authorized by this title.[20]

F. CULTURAL PROPERTY AGREEMENTS

The Committee's findings and recommendations are submitted to the president's designee, the Assistant Secretary for Educational and Cultural Affairs, who renders a decision after considering the Committee's views and any other relevant information. A favorable decision by the president's designee leads to an agreement to restrict certain categories of objects. However, it also sets forth certain goals to be accomplished during the effective period of the agreement. These goals are contained in a special section of any agreement—Article II—discussed below. All agreements are available on the Department's Web site, where one can find image databases of representative examples of the cultural object categories that are restricted.[21]

It is difficult to measure the success of U.S. implementation of the 1970 UNESCO Convention through cultural property agreements entered into with those countries that have sought them. Some may wish to define success as interdictions at ports of entry. But the scale of border crossings and entries at ports is daunting, and one cannot begin to imagine that every crate, parcel, and person is examined for contraband artifacts. However, interdictions of restricted cultural property do occur with regularity, and the Department of Homeland Security has assigned greater priority to the issue. New search technologies, a law enforcement community more knowledgeable about illicit cultural property trafficking, and increased vigilance at the borders of the United States will likely yield more recoveries.

Success might also be measured by how well the programmatic elements of a cultural property agreement—embedded in Article II of an agreement—are being implemented. An agreement is not solely about the imposition of an import restriction on designated categories of cultural property. Article II of each agreement sets forth long-term goals for improving the safeguarding of the partner country's cultural patrimony, such as museum development, documentation and inventory of collections and sites, technical training in conservation, professional development, research, and exchanges. While, on the one hand, import restrictions are intended to reduce the incentive for further pillage, on the other hand, provisions in Article II can and do open the way to improved and sustainable strategies for protecting a country's national patrimony.

---

[20] 19 U.S.C. § 2605(h) (emphasis added).

[21] *See* https://exchanges.state.gov/culprop.

By way of example, the agreement with El Salvador extends well beyond the imposition of U.S. import restrictions on El Salvador's pre-Hispanic archaeological resources. Among other things, it calls for technical assistance in cultural resources management and security to El Salvador. The agreement represents a pledge by El Salvador to expedite the registration of cultural property in public and private collections and to educate the public about its laws and the importance of protecting archaeological sites. The initial five-year agreement also secured a pledge that El Salvador would use its best efforts to re-establish its national museum, which was destroyed by an earthquake. At the time, El Salvador was the second poorest country in the western hemisphere, but the first order of business to which Salvadoran cultural officials tended after entering into the agreement with the United States was to obtain funding from the legislative assembly to rebuild the nation's museum. Completed within five years, the museum not only showcases exhibits of material representing El Salvador's pre-Columbian heritage, but also digitizes its collection and maintains a central site database inventory. (Ironically, the new museum briefly served as a temporary safe haven for Salvadoran legislators to assemble in the aftermath of yet another earthquake that de-stabilized their government building.)

Similarly, under the terms of its agreement with the United States, Peru has set in motion public education initiatives, customs training workshops, institutional participation in a special conservation internship program established by the American Embassy in Lima, and stepped up law enforcement—all part of carrying out good-faith pledges under Article II of the cultural property agreement with the United States.

When the agreement with Italy was negotiated, the interests of the U.S. museum community figured prominently. Mindful of museum concerns about Italy's limitations on loans to exhibitions abroad, Department negotiators succeeded in obtaining a pledge from the Italian government to make loans of antiquities available to American museums for periods longer than their statutory limit of one year. To facilitate the implementation of this provision, the Department sponsored meetings between Italian curators and their American counterparts to explore ideas for exhibitions. The first exhibition, "In Stabiano: Exploring the Ancient Seaside Villas of the Roman Elite," went on view at the Smithsonian Institution in April 2006 and immediately attracted the interest of other museums. After being viewed in Washington, DC, by more than 3 million visitors, the show has traveled to a dozen other venues throughout the United States. Moreover, the Italian government passed a new law extending the legal limit for foreign loans to four years. Provisions in Article II of the United States–Italy cultural property bilateral agreement are echoed in the recently negotiated accord between the Ministry of Culture of Italy and the Metropolitan Museum of Art.[22]

Cultural property agreements have been an effective means of establishing benchmarks that promote long-term approaches for the sustainable protection

[22] Italy has entered into similar accords with the Boston Museum of Fine Arts, the Cleveland Museum of Art, the J. Paul Getty Museum of Art, and the Princeton Museum of Art.

of cultural property. As it carries out its advisory responsibilities, the Committee devotes considerable attention to matters such as public education, conservation, research, exhibition exchange, and the development of local, regional, and national museum systems. Provisions that relate to these areas of concern, similar to those in the El Salvador agreement, are routinely recommended by the Committee to the Department for negotiation in agreements. In turn, the Department attaches considerable importance to them as it negotiates and concludes agreements.

G. CONCLUSION

The climate today with respect to the movement of cultural property has changed from what it was 30 years ago. More market countries have ratified the 1970 UNESCO Convention, making it today a more viable instrument for deterring further depredation to the cultural heritage. Increasingly, source countries have shown that they are no longer timid about pursuing claims for the recovery of their patrimony where it can be shown that wrong-doing has occurred. New alliances are being formed, and there is growing international public support for protecting and preserving the cultural heritage, a non-renewable resource. Increased media attention heaped on egregious acts of pillage and high-profile antiquities cases have provided the public-at-large with a far greater understanding about pillage and its consequences and about the operations behind the illicit movement of cultural objects across boundaries.

In addition to law enforcement, there is growing attention to other ways of mitigating the twin problems of looting and illicit trafficking of cultural property. For example, greater collaboration between U.S. institutions, particularly museums, and those abroad is needed more than ever in order to engender trusting professional relationships in which the safe and legal interchange of cultural property can occur regularly. Especially helpful would be capacity-building collaborations with developing countries that would include the transfer of knowledge in museum management, curatorial practices, conservation, and education programs. Opportunities already exist through a program administered by the American Association of Museums, with funding from the Department's Bureau, which also supports cultural specialists and short-term visiting scholars, whose expertise is needed abroad. Worth noting is the recent paradigm of a successful grant proposal submitted by the Cincinnati Art Museum to the Bureau. In collaboration with other American museums, Cincinnati undertook a phased educational and training program for staff from the Jordanian Department of Antiquities. The Jordanian visitors participated in the development of a major loan exhibition while learning about standard museum practices. The Walters Art Museum in Baltimore is planning a similar collaboration with the Sudan National Museum in Khartoum. The collaboration would train the latter's staff in exchange for loans to a major exhibition that the Walters Art Museum is mounting.

The U.S. cultural property implementing legislation is a compromise among trade interests, museum interests, and archaeology interests, which addresses some but not all of the concerns of each of these groups. From any one of these perspectives, therefore, it is not an ideal piece of legislation. Most of all, the legislation is not the sole solution to the problem of pillage and illicit trade. However, together with the 1970 UNESCO Convention, it creates a framework of cooperation for instituting import restrictions as a deterrent to further looting, thereby enhancing opportunities for scientific research of still undisturbed sites and improving the ability of indigenous groups to protect and utilize objects of traditional and ceremonial importance. As previously noted, the very bilateral agreements that set forth import restrictions also identify strategies for safeguarding cultural heritage. Thus, the U.S. implementing legislation is not only an instrument for stabilizing situations of pillage, but also an agent for advancing the steps necessary to secure the foundations of sustainable heritage stewardship. As a result, future generations will be in a better position to fulfill their duty as stewards of the non-renewable universal past.

CHAPTER 17
CULTURE AND DEVELOPMENT: THE ROLE OF GOVERNMENTS IN PROTECTING AND PROMOTING CULTURE

Anastasia Telesetsky

A. INTRODUCTION

The protection and promotion of both tangible and intangible culture are not priorities for economic development. Culture is neglected by policymakers as a source of hope, consolation, community, and empowerment to those who struggle most to meet basic sustenance needs. Yet culture has the potential to generate opportunities even for the most impoverished. Both development aid donors and development aid recipients need to create new linkages between the protection and promotion of culture and those international development goals designed to create livelihood opportunities for the most vulnerable sectors of societies. In this chapter, the terms "culture" and "cultural" are used broadly to refer to shared creative processes that may include painting, handicrafts, literature, oral history, music, rituals and festivals, architecture, drama, dance, visual arts, and indigenous knowledge of the natural world.

B. CREATING A CULTURE AND DEVELOPMENT PARADIGM

On one level, the abstract goal of protecting and promoting culture seems extraneous if viewed in the context of specific quantitative development goals of electrifying so many villages, harvesting so much wheat, or vaccinating so many children. Governments and market-motivated development experts generally view culture as a set of luxury goods and services, not as an intrinsic component of all human experience. For example, cultural studies scholar Elazar Barkan argues,

> Heritage is for the rich. The poor may wish for it or dream about it, but often they cannot afford to preserve their own cultural heritage. For the poor, in most instances, cultural property becomes significant only when it enhances their prosperity or independence . . . privileging cultural heritage over progress and prosperity is feasible only after a minimum level of affluence has been achieved.[1]

---

[1] Elazar Barkan, *Amending Historical Injustices: The Restitution of Cultural Property*, *in* Claiming the Stones—Naming the Bones, at 35 (Elazar Barkan & Ronald Bush eds., 2002).

Reality, however, belies Barkan's argument that culture worth protecting belongs only to the province of the rich. For example, in the town of Lijiang, China, it was ironically the poverty in this community that preserved the ancient village. With limited livelihood opportunities and a large number of families living below the Chinese poverty line, Lijiang homeowners simply could not afford to modernize their traditional homes and became instead inadvertent preservationists.

As a concept, economic development is generally synonymous with modernization and not with preserving the traditional past unless the past can be commodified and marketed. Lijiang is beloved by the Chinese national and the Yunnan provincial governments because it has miraculously generated tremendous growth for a relatively remote and economically impoverished area. Yet commodification comes with its own costs including continued wealth disparities and the marketing of the unauthentic. The newfound wealth has not benefited the vulnerable members of the local population whose families have been responsible for the generations spent preserving and maintaining the old city. It has instead benefited outside economic opportunists. For example, of the current shopkeepers running businesses in the old city, only one-fourth of the entrepreneurs are local. Regarding authenticity, Lijiang's old town has become its own simulacrum. Not only is the historic old town devoid of actual villagers since the former residents were relocated to reduce the population density, but the government has also removed historic buildings in order to create new "historic" buildings that the government officials conceived of as better capturing the traditional atmosphere.[2]

Government intervention that is intent on promoting large-scale tourism can be dangerous. It promotes institutionally imagined versions of national culture at the expense of community-based localized culture. When tourism is prioritized as the core component of a neoclassical growth strategy, it falsely raises local expectations for job creation and income generation. Depending on consumer whims, such government-promoted or incentive-driven tourism may or may not satisfy community expectations. Pandering to consumer whims may result in a tragedy of place where a previously vibrant community becomes nostalgia for both visitors and residents. Relying exclusively on tourism as a holistic development strategy to protect and create expressions and experiences of tangible and intangible culture can backfire. A strategy tied to outside consumers is too vulnerable to the vagaries of random market forces and inexplicable trends.

Contrary to the current practice, culture needs not be developed for end markets in order to become part of a nation's development strategy. Rather, the practice of protecting and creating culture can become a long-term catalyst for economic development as part of a government-funded job creation scheme.

[2] International Council for Monuments and Sites (ICOMOS) 15th General Assembly and Scientific Symposium October 17–21, 2005, Fan Li and Yong Shao, *The Impact of Tourism on Core Area and Buffer Zone: Heritage Management in the Old Town of Lijiang China*, at 2–8, *available at* http://www.international.icomos.org/xian2005/papers.htm.

Such "employer of last resort" schemes have historically proven invaluable to combat nationwide systemic poverty. Joblessness is generally concentrated among the sectors of societies most vulnerable to chronic poverty including minorities, youth, elderly, women, and uneducated individuals. Examples of successful "employer of last resort" include the United States' Works Progress Administration (WPA), Argentina's Jefes de Hogar ("Heads of Household") program, and India's National Rural Employment Guarantee Act of 2005. Each of these programs provided or provides income-generating work for individuals at a fixed wage.

Job creation is particularly critical for regions such as Africa and Asia. Presently, 87.2 percent of working South Asians and 78.6 percent of working Africans earn less than $2 a day, a sum that is insufficient to sustain a family as basic food prices continue to increase.[3] The International Labor Organization predicts a decline in poverty for Africa, but while the percentage of people living on less than $2 a day will decline, the overall number of individuals living on barely $2 will increase.[4] Unemployment of youth is particularly problematic. In South Africa, for example, 60 percent of the youth are unemployed.[5] Keynesian economic growth focused on creating demand may not be enough to kickstart African economies such as Zimbabwe, the Central African Republic, and Guinea-Bisseau that have been experiencing negative gross domestice product (GDP) growth.[6]

An examination of a nation's tangible and intangible culture could generate a combination of low-skill and high-skill jobs. For example, there are roles not only for artists to create art but also, as the current crisis in Iraq has demonstrated, for protecting cultural monuments from armed looters and vandals. The U.S. program during the Great Depression generated an array of low-skill and high-skill culture jobs. Acting as an "employer of last resort," the Public Works of Art Program, the Treasury Department Program of Sculpture and Painting, and most importantly, the WPA's Federal Art Program ("F.A.P.") generated numerous culture-based jobs. The F.A.P. successfully created thousands of paid jobs. Not all of the jobs went to professionally trained artists. For example, the Milwaukee Handcraft Project begun in 1935 employed over the course of eight years nearly 5,000 workers who were considered unemployable because of age or disability. These workers earned income by making rugs, draperies, furniture, wall hangings, and toys to be purchased by public institutions such as hospitals and schools for the cost of the materials.[7]

C. CULTURE AND DEVELOPMENT RHETORIC

Linking culture with development is gaining traction with policymakers, and the idea of "culture and development" is beginning to enter the rhetoric of

---

[3] International Labour Organisation, African Employment Trends, at 13 (2007).

[4] *Id.* at 16.

[5] *Id.* at 10.

[6] *Id.* at 18.

[7] Lois M. Quinn, John Pawasarat & Laura Serebin, *WPA Milwaukee Handicraft Program in* History of Jobs for Workers on Relief in Milwaukee County 1930–1994, at 22–26 (Feb. 1995, at 22–26), *available at* http://www.uwm.edu/Dept/ETI/wpamilw.htm.

policy. The early linkages do not however require governments to systematically apply culture, heritage, or development aid to creating new livelihood opportunities. Without creating a linkage between jobs and culture, the idea of "culture and development" becomes a feckless concept.

The government rhetoric does suggest a shift in thinking about how to accomplish development goals. For example, Norway has designed cooperative development policies that recognize culture as a foundation for development. In 2005, the Norwegian Ministry of Foreign Affairs published their "Strategy for Norway's Culture and Sport Co-operation with Countries in the South" as a "new approach to development." The strategy emphasizes the value of cultural exchanges and commits Norway to cooperating with developing countries to "ensure better access to cultural goods" and to "encourage the use of cultural heritage as a resource for the sustainable development of society."[8]

While some European nations seem to be forging some formal connection between culture and development, few aid recipient countries have recognized cultural heritage and cultural creation as part of a broader development approach. In a 2004 evaluation, the Swedish International Development Cooperation Agency (SIDA) commissioned a group of researchers to analyze 16 "poverty reduction strategy" papers produced by governments in Latin America, Africa, Asia, and Europe in response to World Bank and International Monetary Fund requirements.[9] The Swedish researchers observed that discussion of culture as a component of government poverty reduction strategy was relatively sparse. While some linkages were drawn in the poverty reduction strategy papers between heritage tourism and economic growth, cultural property protection and creation of culture have not been systematically incorporated into poverty reduction strategies.

Organizations including the U.N. Conference on Trade and Development (UNCTAD) have criticized "poverty reduction strategy" papers as prioritizing short-term stabilization over long-term development and ignoring the reality that certain countries do not have the necessary pre-conditions for economically competitive markets.[10] While the disconnect between culture and development in the strategy papers may signify nothing in terms of long-term policy, there are encouraging trends in aid-recipient countries that link cultural industries with poverty reduction. For example, as of 2006, Uganda, one of the countries in the 2004 SIDA analysis had undertaken a linkage between culture and poverty reduction. The Ugandan government drafted and publicized a national policy to promote cultural industries such as "local literature [books, magazines,

---

[8] Norwegian Ministry of Foreign Affairs, Strategy for Norway's Culture and Sport Co-operation with Countries in the South, at 19 (2005), *available at* http://www.regjeringen.no/upload/kilde/ud/rap/2005/0022/ddd/pdfv/265661-culture.pdf.

[9] Cecilia M. Ljungman et al., *SIDA's Work with Culture and Media, in* SIDA Evaluation 04/38, at 15–20 (2004).

[10] United Nations Conference on Trade and Development, UNCTAD Proposes Alternative Approach to Improve Poverty Reduction Strategies in LDCs (June 18, 2002), http://www.unctad.org/Templates/webflyer.asp?docid=2450&intItemID=1528&lang=1.

newspapers], audio-visual tapes of music and drama, arts and crafts" as possible employment opportunities for the poor.[11]

D. PRACTICAL ROLE FOR GOVERNMENTS IN PROMOTING CULTURE AND DEVELOPMENT

Governments can play an important role in pursuing long-term development strategies by means of cultural protection and promotion. This is true for both aid donor and recipient countries. For example, Mongolia discovered that physically re-building some of its cultural heritage that had been destroyed during the rule of the Soviet Union has proven to be a unifying force that has "paved the way for a more healthy development process."[12]

Once governments accept that culture is a powerful qualitative tool for furthering the quantitative goals of development, they may wish to pursue a number of practical strategies to link culture with economic development. A number of strategies are discussed below. While not all of these strategies are appropriate for all governments, each of the selected strategies is included because it has the potential to increase both access to culture and to enhance the availability of economic opportunities for communities. The strategies described below do not include either international or domestic tourism as desirable economic development schemes. Much has been written on the benefits of heritage tourism as an economic strategy. Most governments are eager to become a destination for tourists because tourism is perceived as a growth industry requiring low government inputs and accruing substantial immediate benefits for the governments such as taxes and fees on visitor services. Yet, tourism is unlikely to be sustainable in terms of creating jobs for the most vulnerable of the poor because tourism depends on the development of certain infrastructure such as electricity and the mastering of certain skills such as learning a foreign language.

1. Job Creation

For a government that is committed to the dual objectives of creating the conditions for equitable economic development and protecting and promoting culture, government resources need to be primarily channeled into job creation. As described earlier in this chapter, the government can and in some circumstances should serve as an "employer of last resort." Job creation does not need to be responsive to a perceived market such as tourist services. Post-Keynesian economists such as Hyman Minksy argue that allocating government resources for job creation provides conditions for greater economic development than simply training workers for jobs that may never materialize.[13]

---

[11] Ministry of Gender, Labor, Industry and Social Development, Uganda National Cultural Policy, at 19 (Dec. 2006), *available at* http://www.ocpa.irmo.hr/resources/policy/Uganda_Culture_Policy-en.pdf.

[12] *Millennium Development Goals and Cultural Heritage*, International Centre for the Study of the Preservation and Restoration of Cultural Property Newsletter 12 (2006).

[13] L. Randall Wray, *The Employer of Last Resort Programme: Could It Work for Developing Countries?*, Economic & Labour Market Papers, at 5 (Aug. 2007).

For a government seeking to reduce chronic unemployment, there are two options for generating jobs. Jobs will be created through indirect job creation by giving private sector incentives such as tax breaks to create jobs, or by the government acting as an "employer of last resort."[14] The advantage of an "employer of last resort" program is that it can be tailored to meet certain particularly vulnerable individuals. For example, the Argentinean Jefes de Hogar (Heads of Household) program limited the participation to one head of each household with dependent children and to four hours a day in order to provide more job opportunities to more individuals.[15]

In spite of being primarily economic development programs, the "employer of last resort" programs have also been successful in building new community networks based on trust and loyalty. In fact, even though the Jefes de Hogar program has been officially terminated because the government did not deem the production of goods and services efficient enough, many individuals who are eligible to collect monthly benefits without working under the new social services system are still returning to their former workplace to provide services on a volunteer basis.[16]

"Employer of last resort" programs are particularly valuable for poor communities because they target key populations such as families with young children and provide services and infrastructure for geographic areas that are traditionally overlooked. Culture as a source of possible employment becomes not simply a luxury good. Rather, culture is an important tool for disadvantaged communities to make contributions of self-expression both within and outside their community. Through these programs, poor communities may become empowered to seek greater accountability from the government for how development aid is spent.

While such programs do require financial resources to ensure their viability, the expenses of the programs are relatively modest when compared to other government programs. For example, the Jefes de Hogar program's spending was equal to about 1 percent of the GDP.[17] Guaranteeing 100 hours of paid work for every adult in the rural area, the Maharashtra Employment Guarantee Scheme costs India about 10–14 percent of its total development budget.[18] Some of the most important advantages of making a government employment program available to the chronically poor are difficult to quantify. For example, the Jefes de Hogar program and the Maharashtra program reduced social unrest while protecting the basic human rights of some of society's most vulnerable populations.[19] The Indian program is credited for having improved nutrition and provided wage income for women who would otherwise have no access to wage-earning employment. [20]

---

[14] *Id.* at 7.

[15] *Id.* at 10.

[16] *Id.* at 33.

[17] *Id.* at 32.

[18] *Id.* at 33.

[19] *Id.* at 35.

[20] S. Mahendra Dev, *India's Employment Guarantee Scheme, in* EMPLOYMENT FOR POVERTY RE-

As the cultural sector has been progressively employing more individuals, there is a wider recognition of the role that culture plays in sustaining communities and nations. In the United Kingdom, 4.5 percent of the jobs are considered cultural jobs in the creative industries including museums, performing arts, fairs, architecture, fashion, graphic arts, and industrial design.[21] Cultural jobs that might be generated through an "employer of last resort" scheme include handicraft cooperatives, musical troupes, traditional construction, or cultural historian work. The advantage of having cultural jobs as a component of an "employer of last resort" scheme is that such jobs can draw on a wide variety of skills that do not necessarily require a high level of formal education.

As described above, in order to generate jobs, culture need not be considered a precursor for widespread tourism. Culture does not need an external market. When the U.S. government established the WPA, 7 percent of the WPA jobs were cultural jobs targeted at writers, artists, musicians and actors who were out of work. These WPA employees focused on creating "public goods" for consumption by the American public. Under the F.A.P., artists created murals and sculptures for post offices, schools, and other public buildings. The Federal Music Project hired musicians to perform community concerts. The Federal Theatre Project created theatrical touring companies that performed plays in remote areas. The Federal Writers Project undertook folklore and oral history interviews.[22] While the WPA was eventually terminated because jobs were created by industries in response to World War II, the WPA had provided several thousand jobs and have documented an important and difficult era in American history.

While the WPA's art programs may not have tackled chronic poverty, the programs bolstered system-wide employment and boosted morale by providing opportunities beyond menial work. In conjunction with creating society-wide infrastructures (discussed in Section D.3 below), the government as an "employer of last resort" has the potential to provide individuals with the ability to feed both their bodies and their imaginations.

2. Creating a Market for Professional Artists Through Regional Cooperation

Promoting culture by protecting and creating opportunities for cultural expression has the potential to transcend traditional ethno-political divides and create new social alliances for regional development. In general, aid recipient governments have not sought regional opportunities to promote culture across borders. One project that could serve as a regional model for linking cultural protection with development goals is the Sahel Opera. Sponsored by the Prince Claus Fund for Culture and Development, the Government of Mali, and

---

DUCTION AND FOOD SECURITY 127–28 (Joachim von Braun ed., 1995), *available at* http://www.ifpri.org/pubs/books/vonBraun95/vonBraun95ch05.pdf.

[21] ORGANISATION FOR ECONOMIC CO-OPERATION AND DEVELOPMENT, CULTURE AND DEVELOPMENT, at 16 (2005).

[22] LIBRARY OF CONGRESS, NEW DEAL PROGRAMS: SELECTED LIBRARY OF CONGRESS RESOURCES, http://www.loc.gov/rr/program/ bib/newdeal/index.html (last visited May 1, 2008).

a French theater, the Sahel Opera is an African opera production composed and performed by people from Europe and the various Sahel communities in Africa. The Opera has served quantitative development goals by creating a number of employment opportunities for artists. But equally important, the opera has also achieved qualitative culture goals by creating a network of skilled regional individuals with the motivation to build new collaborative projects in the region on issues that are relevant to the population.[23]

Governments can seek out regional opportunities to build cultural knowledge capacities in South-South partnerships. While developing countries may struggle with the challenges of educating their primary school children, there are unmet needs to create vocational secondary schools and academies that would target talented youth who show promising skills in the visual arts. Presently, artists in many developing countries have extremely limited opportunities to develop their creative or technical skills because they lack access to basic artistic supplies or to any mentorship. Governments in a specific geographic region, such as East Africa or Indochina, could collaborate to build the infrastructure for an art institute, to provide a combination of internationally and regionally notable artists as teachers, and to seek funding for promising students from vulnerable communities. To help fund the operation of the schools, American, Japanese, European, Arab, or successful expatriate collectors could provide full scholarships to promising artists residing in vulnerable communities such as refugee camps or famine-prone regions. Recruitment of scholarship candidates could be done by working through networks of non-governmental organizations and humanitarian aid organizations to find a selection of talented students who might be able to create a long-term career after enrollment in a vocational school. In return for their philanthropic investment, these collectors would have the first opportunity to purchase works from the graduating art students for their collections. Even if students are not able to live from selling their fine art or being commissioned to make public art, these students may be able to translate their new skills into other creative income-generating fields such as stock photography, film crew, graphic arts, product design, fashion, advertising, architectural drafting, or fine arts teaching. Even though art institutes will not generate large numbers of jobs, graduates from such institutes may help to generate a wider social interest in art by creating new local markets for their skills.

There are a number of promising models to explore for best practices. In Egypt, architect Ramses Wissa Wassef founded an art center in 1951 near the Pyramids to teach 12 low-income Egyptian village youth how to create pottery and tapestries based on personal creative expression. His personal philosophy was that

> One cannot separate beauty from utility, the form from the material, the work from its function, man from his creative art. A child is artistically gifted provided he is not inhibited by his circumstances of life

[23] *See generally* The Sahel Opera Project, http://www.sahelopera.com (last visited May 15, 2008).

and education, with the help of a sensitive teacher, the child's innate creative energies could be released."[24]

At the art center, Ramses also re-taught local builders the art of building indigenous Egyptian architecture such as adobe domes and vaults, forms that were being replaced by Western modernist cube buildings. Even though Wassef has passed on, his school has left a legacy with many of his former students still creating art as part of their livelihood and transmitting their skills to future generations of weavers, potters, and builders.

While the Wassef Art Centre is a privately funded effort, governments have provided funding for similar models such as the Madaba Institute for Mosaic Art and Restoration in Jordan. This project was originally started in 1993 with funding from the Italian government in cooperation with the Department of Antiquities. The intent was in part to develop the cultural heritage potential of the area as a tourism destination by building local capacity for archaeological restoration work. As of 2007, the project had grown beyond providing basic skills in mosaic art training to local Jordanian high school students to providing professional college diplomas to Middle Eastern students for training in mosaic art and stonework restoration and production.

Programs such as the Wassef Art Centre and the Madaba Institute serve multiple development functions. They create employment opportunities, build local capacity in the traditional arts, and create a generation with a new appreciation for high quality artisan work that in turn generates a potential domestic market.

3. Constructing Cultural Infrastructure

Blessed by relatively easy access to world culture, Americans and Europeans take for granted much of the cultural infrastructure that has been built by the civic minded individuals of preceding generations. Governments can further a cultural protection and promotion agenda by dedicating resources to building and financing cultural infrastructure that will provide citizens with more opportunities to fully participate in their nation's cultural life.

Depending on the country, needed cultural infrastructure includes performance halls, art workshops, galleries, museums, and movie centers. Building an integrated cultural infrastructure can result in limited job creation for both professionals as well as low-skill workers. Skilled professionals can work as architects, teachers, performers, museum curators, conservation experts, and historical interpreters. Lower-skilled workers can be construction workers on the site, building security, or janitorial staff. In order for these projects to benefit more low-income individuals, some of the jobs for building security and cleaning could be offered on a rotating basis to individuals from communities that are economically disadvantaged such as indigenous communities, certain isolated rural communities, and groups of slum dwellers, orphans, or refugees.

---

[24] Wissa Wassef Art Centre, http://www.egyptvoyager.com/artcrafts_wissawassef_mainpage.htm (last visited May 1, 2008).

One possible model for how the creation of cultural infrastructure might achieve culture and development goals is the Museum of Returned African Art in Grand-Popo, Benin. "Returned Art" refers to art that was either removed forcibly from a country during, for example, a punitive expedition or smuggled from a country in contravention of national laws. This museum is being designed jointly by African and Finnish architects and financed by private sponsors and the Finnish government with a $120,000 starting operational budget.[25] The organizers are focused on acquiring, through the cooperation of international museums, missionary societies, and private collectors, at least 500 works of art to be displayed in the museum by 2008 by means of virtual exhibits, long-term loans of art, and potential property acquisitions. Some of the works will be acquired from burgeoning African art markets in Gabon, Cameroon, Senegal, Tanzania, Congo, Mozambique, and South Africa.[26] Eventually, the project organizers intend to organize touring exhibitions of the returned art throughout Africa in order to build up awareness of Africa's cultural history. The project is promising on a number of levels: it champions replacing cultural property within the cultural context of its source nations, facilitates the dual goals of culture and development, and reinforces the idea of access to culture as a human right.

4. Trade and Custom Regulations

Governments exert sizable control over what goods enter and leave their borders and what services are available within their borders. While numerous nations have strong protectionist policies to protect industries with domestic lobbies such as agriculture, there are few to no protections on certain products such as contemporary handicrafts and artwork. In fact, the United States levies no duty on certain categories of goods such as baskets and leather goods originating in countries that are granted dispensation under the generalized system of preferences. Ideally, a government's office of trade would coordinate with the government's development aid office to identify what countries have existing cottage industries that might benefit from access to a tariff free market and what goods would benefit most from being tariff free. For example, presently, clothing that is certified as having been hand-loomed and other clothing-related "folklore products" are assessed a duty rate of 11.8 percent from all countries except Bahrain, Canada, Chile, Israel, Jordan, Mexico, Dominican Republic, Singapore, and those Caribbean nations participating in the Caribbean Basin Initiative.[27] Whatever the political reasons are for maintaining this tariff, it seems that the tariff may be counter-productive for enhancing development goals when the creation of hand-loomed cloth is one of the cottage industries available to communities with few resources.

---

[25] *New Museum for Looted Artifacts*, AFR. RES. BULL., at 16736 (July 1–31, 2006).

[26] Saska Snellmanm, *African Art Pillaged by Colonial Masters to Get New Home*, HELSINGIN SANOMAT (Dec. 1, 2005), *available at* http://www.hs.fi/english/article/African+art+pillaged+by+colonial+masters+ to+get+new+home/1135218386586.

[27] *See generally* Official Harmonized Tariff Schedule of the United States, Chapter 62 "Articles of apparel and clothing accessories, not knitted or crocheted" (Apr. 16, 2008), http://www.usitc.gov/tata/hts/bychapter/index.htm.

Perhaps more urgent than reform of tariffs in countries such as the United States is reforming how customs and excise taxes are collected and processed in developing countries. While certain regions have incorporated best practices, such as Uganda and Kenya, with their launch of the Revenue Authorities Digital Data Exchange to electronically exchange customs information among revenue authorities, the reality is less propitious for trade in other regions. Janet Nkubana's experience is instructive.[28] Working with her sister, Ms. Nkubana employs 3,200 Hutu and Tutsi women across Rwanda who work together in weaving communities to create baskets while also creating a culture of reconciliation. While the business does over $300,000 of business in exporting duty-free "peace baskets" to the United States and is the fifth largest tax payer in Rwanda, the task of getting the baskets out of land-locked Rwanda has proven to be both frustratingly time consuming and expensive with average shipments taking 47 days to clear the customs authorities.

Eliminating bureaucratic obstacles and providing duty-free exports for cultural products produced by certain economically vulnerable communities could create income-generating jobs among the poor by establishing the necessary conditions that would allow for motivated but not cash-rich communities to enter previously unavailable regional or international markets.

5. Funding: Offer Incentives for the Private Cultural Sector to Create Job Opportunities for Vulnerable Groups or Levy Specific Taxes on the Private Cultural Sector to Provide Aid for Creating Cultural Jobs

Governments have the authority to levy taxes and to provide sizable tax breaks to private institutions and companies that agree to assist in poverty-reduction strategies that link culture and development. Such strategies may assist a nation in meeting specific development goals like creating more long-term employment opportunities for the poor or reducing the number of families living off $1 or $2 a day. Possible projects that would qualify for a tax break might include private sponsorship for a traditional art school or start-up costs for a performing art troupe with members from disadvantaged communities.

Developing countries could also fund culture and development aid programs through selective taxation of large cultural industries such as Christie's, Sotheby's, Sony Pictures, and Warner Brothers. All of these companies make their profit by creating economic value from the creation or sale of cultural expression. The amount of money in the private cultural sector is vast—Christie's and Sotheby's together sold $12.5 billion of art.[29] Certain taxes are already collected from cultural goods sold including sales tax in the United States and value added taxes in the United Kingdom. Additional fees have been levied on occasion including royalty fees collected under the EU Artist's Resale Right Directive that provides living artists a resale royalty each time their artwork is

---

[28] *Weaving Peace in Rwanda*, *in* WORLD BANK, DOING BUSINESS: WOMEN IN AFRICA, at 7–11 (2007).

[29] Deborah Brewster, *Art Sales Soar as Boom Rolls On*, FIN. TIMES, Jan. 19, 2008, *available at* http://www.ft.com/cms/s/0/4c091fa2-c61c-11dc-8378-0000779fd2ac.html?nclick_check=1.

sold in the United Kingdom. Governments could seek to levy additional taxes from multi-national cultural industries doing more than a billion dollars of worldwide business. These taxes would be collected by the cultural industries in order to provide funding for both domestic government-funded culture programs and an International Fund for Culture that could be modeled after the Global Fund for AIDS, Tuberculosis, and Malaria where no money from donors goes to overhead expenses,[30] all programs are proposed by countries rather than the fund, and funding is based on certain development performance targets. The Cultural Fund would be available to provide funding to any developed or developing country that can identify discrete cultural promotion or protection programs for socio-economically vulnerable communities living below country-based poverty lines. Funds could provide financing for many of the projects described previously in this chapter such as the job-creation programs or art schools.

E. OBSTACLES TO GOVERNMENTS LINKING CULTURE AND DEVELOPMENT

Linkages between culture and development make sense where development practices are understood as trying to satisfy self-actualization needs. However, this linkage is problematic for governments that are not interested in free expression or pursuit of happiness. A government's best interest does not necessarily coincide with a citizen's best interest especially when citizens come from minority, marginalized, or disenfranchised groups. Generating job opportunities that allow individuals payment for communication through oral history, painting, sculpture, or dance may be dangerous for a government that seeks to control the content of expressions. Clashes between government-sponsored ideas of culture and the local communities' experience of its own culture can spark fundamental conflicts, especially where culture has become politicized.

Attitudes about the value of different aspects of culture have serious implications for culture and development projects. For example, in 2005, Italy returned the ancient Axum obelisk to Axum, Ethiopia, a small city located in the Tigray region of Northern Ethiopia that is considered one of the holiest cities for Ethiopian Orthodox Christians. For some Ethiopians especially Tigrayans, it was an occasion to celebrate. Critics of the return considered it either a glorification of Ethiopian Tigrayan culture to demonstrate the power of the ruling government party or a massive waste of foreign aid that could have been better spent on food security.[31]

Objects of culture and expressions of culture do not mean the same thing across all strata of society. Culture and development programs are not apolitical. Such programs have the potential to prioritize certain forms of expression and silence other forms. Taken in the abstract, "employer of last resort" programs that promote culture make sense because they provide jobs that may have value beyond the generation of income by giving communities a space for expression.

---

[30] Overhead expenses are funded by income from investments held in trust.

[31] Ian Limbach, *The Axum Obelisk Returns, But Some Still Grumble*, 58 ARCHAEOLOGY 4 (July/Aug. 2005), *available at* http://www.archaeology.org/0507/etc/specialreport.html.

In non-democratic societies, government-run cultural employment may end up co-opting rather than encouraging new voices. For example, if you are an ethnic minority from a group seeking self-determination, and you accept a job from the government to produce public art, how much freedom is there to express views that criticize positions taken by the government?

For governments, actively protecting and promoting culture can mean opening a Pandora's box of citizen woes. Just as culture can be used to protect ruling interests by creating pedigrees and hierarchies, it can also be used as a source of protest. This unpredictable quality of culture threatens those governments who insist on converging divergent opinions. In regimes where voices are most heavily repressed, it is not uncommon for development standards to be stunted by the high rates of infant mortality, hunger, and employment. Would programs linking culture and development merely become another government shield to deeper systemic social problems, or could groups strategically use government programs to meet the recurring personal needs for self-expression?

A related question is whether governments will allow cultural constructs, such as traditional customary laws, to prevent an effective linkage of culture and development. For example, in Swaziland, even though the king approved a Constitution providing for gender equality, Swazi customary law prevails and women are prevented from opening bank accounts without approval from men. Swazi businesswoman Zoë Dean-Smith understands the practical implications of this situation as the executive director for a fair trade craft business.[32] Even though exporting crafts with Swazi cultural designs overseas helps the women artisans earn a fair trade income, these women are thwarted by other aspects of Swazi culture since they cannot manage their income money for their family, and the money is often spent by men on their own perceived needs and not for food or educational fees.

Linking culture and development in a fair and equitable manner so as to achieve basic development goals remains, in large part, connected to the greater challenge of good governance, accountability, and full implementation of international human rights obligations.

F. CREATING SYNERGIES BETWEEN CULTURAL PRACTICE AND DEVELOPMENT POLICIES

This chapter has proposed governments as social actors creating a synergy between development policy and cultural promotion policy. Heritage tourism is not a panacea for poverty especially chronic poverty. Creating more livelihood opportunities is essential to fighting chronic poverty. This chapter has proposed a number of programs that a government can promote, which could provide both new livelihood and cultural opportunities for the most vulnerable communities. The "employer of last resort" schemes are promising models for targeting wage-generating opportunities for the poorest of the poor. Creating jobs in the cultural sector provides the classical win-win situation:

[32] *Gone Rural*, *in* World Bank, *supra* note 28, at 25–30.

individuals receive money for being creative and productive while the public sector receives an infusion of new energy and vision into public art and cultural infrastructure. Governments can invest regionally in cultural capacity by building projects such as art schools that may create new professions and new markets. Addressing trade and custom barriers will ensure that those artists who are most in need will have access to markets. Finally governments should seek creative financing to provide more equitable access to cultural resources.

Culture can serve an important counter-point to the poverty, war, and recurring environmental disasters plaguing so many poor communities. In the context of job creation schemes, politically and economically disempowered individuals might find work that offers not just income but also hope in the form of a connection to a longer legacy of artistic creation and expression. While public art exhibitions and restoration of traditional architecture may not seem to be high priorities as eradicating debilitating diseases or planting high-yield crops, the concept of culture becoming an integral part of development offers a more holistic view of people and their needs. To be fulfilled we need more than simply to meet our survival needs. Government programs that link culture and development may prove more successful than traditional development programs that continue to emphasize the logic of survival needs over the irrational yet compelling need to participate in some form of self-expression.

Norwegian author Erik Fosnes Hansen captures the potential value of a long-term investment in a culture and development strategy.

> Working with culture can be an ungrateful task, in that it is often difficult to produce practical results or to demonstrate its usefulness. It is a path of many tiny steps. In a way one might say that it follows the principles of homeopathy: It works, strongly distilled, some times invisibly. But every step, every drop counts.[33]

[33] Norwegian Ministry of Foreign Affairs, *supra* note 8, at 31.

PART VI

AVOIDANCE AND RESOLUTION OF CULTURAL HERITAGE DISPUTES

CHAPTER 18

RECOVERY OF ART LOOTED DURING THE HOLOCAUST

Lawrence M. Kaye*

A. INTRODUCTION

The Nazi program for confiscating art has been called the greatest displacement of art in human history.[1] The volume of artworks stolen by the Nazis during World War II from both museums and private collections throughout Europe is astounding. This wholesale pillaging was an official Nazi policy and not a mere byproduct of war. Much of the looted art was intended to fill the Führermuseum that Adolf Hitler was planning to build in his hometown of Linz, Austria.[2] The U.S. government has estimated that German forces and other Nazi agents before and during World War II seized or coerced the sale of approximately *one-fifth* of all Western art then in existence.[3] If one adds books, manuscripts, and other cultural artifacts, the number of items of stolen property runs into the millions.[4] The value of the looted art alone exceeded the total value of all artwork in the United States in 1945: it has been estimated to have been $2.5 billion at the time or approximately $20.5 billion in today's values.[5] It is said that more than 100,000 artworks stolen by the Nazis have still not been located.[6]

---

* Mr. Kaye and his firm currently represent the heir of Jacques Goudstikker in her efforts to recover Nazi-looted art, the heirs of Kazimir Malevich in *Leonard Malewicz, et al. v. City of Amsterdam*, 362 F. Supp. 2d 298 (D.D.C. 2005), and the heirs of Lea Bondi in *United States v. Portrait of Wally*, 2002 U.S. Dist. LEXIS 6445 (S.D.N.Y. Apr. 11, 2002), all of which are discussed in this chapter and some of which are currently pending. Mr. Kaye would like to thank Mari-Claudia Jiménez and Frank K. Lord IV for their assistance in the preparation of this chapter.

1 *See* Michael J. Bazyler, Holocaust Justice: The Battle for Restitution in America's Courts 202 (2003) [hereinafter Bazyler].

2 *See* Howard N. Spiegler, *Ownership and Protection of Heritage: Cultural Property Rights for the 21st Century: Recovering Nazi-Looted Art: Report from the Front Lines*, 16 Conn. J. Int'l L. 297 (2001) (*passim*); *see* Kelly Diane Walton, *Leave No Stone Unturned: The Search for Art Stolen by the Nazis and the Legal Rules Governing Restitution of Stolen Art*, 9 Fordham Intell. Prop., Media & Ent. L.J. 549, 557 (1999) [hereinafter Walton].

3 *See* Kelly Ann Falconer, Comment, *When Honor Will Not Suffice: The Need for a Legally Binding International Agreement Regarding Ownership of Nazi-Looted Art*, 21 U. Pa. J. Int'l Econ. L. 383, 383–84 (2000).

4 *See id.* at 383. It is well known that throughout history art and cultural items have been captured as war booty; the size and scope of the Nazis' looting of cultural property, however, was unprecedented. *See id.*

5 *See* Bazyler, *supra* note 1, at 202.

6 *See* Barbara J. Tyler, *The Stolen Museum: Have United States Art Museums Become Inadvertent*

Unfortunately, very few claims have been made and resolved in the United States, although many of the stolen pieces did ultimately end up in museums and private art collections here. Given that information concerning the ownership of these pieces is just now coming to light, the number of claims unquestionably will increase.

There is a growing recognition in international law and among the members of the international community that *cultural property wrongfully taken from its rightful owners should be returned.* This is the guiding principle at the heart of the development of a favorable body of law in the United States. These sentiments were embodied in the Washington Conference principles that were endorsed as a result of a 1998 conference in which 40 countries participated in the Washington Conference on Holocaust Era Assets ("Washington Conference").[7]

The experts at the conference considered and debated the many issues raised by the continuing discovery of Nazi-looted assets, including artworks. The conference promulgated 11 principles concerning Nazi confiscated art; among them that pre-war owners and heirs should be encouraged to come forward to make their claims known and, once this happens, steps should be taken expeditiously to develop "fair and just claims procedures" with liberal rules of evidence so that the art can be returned to its rightful owners.[8] Since then, some governments have researched art with questionable provenance and developed the requisite legal regimes, and many auction houses, museums, and collectors have shunned art with gaps in provenance between 1933 and 1945. While much good therefore has come out of the Washington principles, Stuart Eisenstadt, the force behind the Washington Conference, recently reported that unfortunately more often than not, the principles are being ignored.[9] Many others who practice in this field continue to experience great frustration throughout the world, especially in the former Eastern European nations, but even in the United States and Western Europe.

B. THE *GOUDSTIKKER* CASE

The case of the looted Goudstikker collection is a microcosm of the restitution world since the Washington Conference. Jacques Goudstikker was the foremost Jewish dealer in the Netherlands before World War II. His collection, which contained more than 1,200 works of art, mostly Dutch, Flemish, and Italian Old Master paintings, was looted by the Nazis following their invasion of Holland in 1940. My firm has been privileged to represent Marei von Saher, Jacques' daughter-in-law, and her children in their Herculean efforts to restore

---

Fences for Stolen Art Works Looted by the Nazis In World War II?, 30 RUTGERS L.J. 441, 449 (1999).

[7] *See* U.S. Department of State, *Washington Conference on Holocaust-Era Assets*, http://www.state.gov/www/regions/eur/wash_conf_material.html.

[8] *See* Commission for Looted Art in Europe, *Washington Conference Principles on Nazi-Confiscated Art*, http://www.lootedartcommission.com/Washington-principles.

[9] *See Testimony on the Status of Art Restitution Worldwide by Stuart E. Eizenstat, Subcommittee on Domestic and International Monetary Policy, Trade, and Technology Committee on Financial Services, U.S. House of Representatives, Washington, DC, July 27, 2006*, http://financialservices.house.gov/media/pdf/072706see.pdf.

one of the most extraordinary pre-war collections looted by the Nazis. The Goudstikker saga of recovery aptly illustrates how some cultural property disputes can be avoided and how others, unfortunately, are destined to follow a long and bitter path of adversarial battle before their resolution.

The story of Jacques and Desi Goudstikker is a panoramic saga.[10] Jacques Goudstikker was the most prominent Jewish art dealer in the Netherlands prior to World War II. He married the beautiful Austrian opera singer, Desi von Halban Kurz. They lived in grand style and were the toast of Amsterdam society; their parties at Jacques' Nijenrode Castle were legendary. There was no equal to Jacques in the art field. He had a great eye that helped him amass one of the great collections of his time. He not only was a dealer but also was generally recognized as a tastemaker and innovator, known to put on exhibitions that museums simply were not able to mount.

In May 1940, the Goudstikkers' life took a tumultuous turn. On May 10, the moment that had long been feared in the Netherlands finally arrived: Nazi forces entered and quickly overran the country. On May 15, the Netherlands became the first country in Western Europe to capitulate. Jacques, Desi, and their two-year old son, Eduard (Edo), were at their country home, Ostermeer, when the Germans invaded. The day before the capitulation, Jacques and his family made their way to Amsterdam, where they were met by his elderly mother, Emilie, and Jacques' staff at the Goudstikker Gallery.

Although the full scope of the atrocities committed by the Nazis would not become clear until years later, the Goudstikkers were well aware that, as a prominent Jewish family (in addition to Jacques' fame as the premier dealer in Old Master paintings in the Netherlands and Desi's renown as an opera singer), they were at great risk. They decided to try to escape the country by sea, but even though she understood and approved of the decision, Emilie refused to leave with them. Desi would later recall that, as they fled to the port town of Ijmuiden, Rotterdam burned and German paratroopers fell from the sky.

When they reached the port, they managed to secure passage on the S.S. Bodegraven, which was heading to South America after stopping in England. But tragedy struck nevertheless. On the night of May 15, Jacques went up on deck for a bit of fresh air. In the dark, he did not see an open hatch on the deck. It was only hours later, after a desperate search of the ship by Desi and others, that his body was found. Within 48 hours of his flight to freedom, Jacques Goudstikker had broken his neck in an accidental fall and died. His body was taken ashore at Falmouth where he was buried. She and her son sailed across the Atlantic, eventually settling in New York, where they remained for the duration of the war.

The Goudstikker family had been able to take with them only a few personal belongings. Jacques' most valuable assets, the more than 1,200 artworks from his collection, were left behind. Shortly after the Nazi invasion, Reichsmarschall Hermann Goering, second in command of the Third Reich, looted paintings,

---

[10] *See generally* Pieter den Hollander, De Zaak Goudstikker (The Goudstikker Affair) (1998).

drawings, antiquities, and other works of art from the Goudstikker Collection in typical Nazi fashion. Under explicit warnings that her property and that of her son would be confiscated—and worse, that she would be "deported"—Emilie was persuaded to vote her minority block of shares in the Gallery for a "sale" of its assets to Göring and his henchman, Alois Miedl, at a small fraction of their value. But Desi, who together with Edo inherited the majority of the outstanding shares in the Gallery upon Jacque's death, specifically *refused* to consent to the proposed "sale" when contacted by her husband's former employees. The forced "sale" went forward nonetheless.

Göring took some 800 of the most valuable artworks looted from the Goudstikker Collection to Germany, where they were displayed in his several residences, including Karinhall, his country estate near Berlin. Miedl began operating his own art dealership out of Jacques' gallery, using its remaining stock, its former employees, its infrastructure and the good will of the Goudstikker name to do so. Approximately 200 of the artworks looted by Göring and taken to Germany were discovered there by the Allied forces during the liberation of Germany in 1945 and were sent to the Munich Central Collecting Point. These and other artworks that had been stolen from the Netherlands were returned there to be held in trust by the Dutch government for their lawful owners. This was accomplished pursuant to the established policy of the Allies, which flowed from the 1943 London Declaration,[11] to return all the property recovered from the Nazis to the governments of the countries of origin so that they could be returned to the original owners.[12]

Desi returned to the Netherlands in 1946 with the expectation that she would be able to reclaim her stolen property. She was met instead with great hostility by the post-War Dutch government having to confront a "restitution" regime that did everything in its power to make it difficult for Jews actually to recover their property.[13] Indeed, although the Netherlands purported to establish a sensible restitution system as contemplated by the London Declaration, the system actually adopted by the Dutch government did not accomplish the task. Indeed, the post-war Dutch government, which was extremely concerned that Jews would play too large a role in the post-War Dutch economy, did everything

---

[11] On January 5, 1943, the Allies, including the Netherlands, issued the "Inter-Allied Declaration Against Acts of Dispossession Committed in Territories under Enemy Occupation or Control," now commonly known as the "London Declaration." The declaration warned that the Allies reserved "all their rights to declare invalid any transfers of or dealings with, property, rights and interests of any description whatsoever . . . whether such transfers or dealings have taken the form of open looting or plunder, or of transactions apparently legal in form even when they purport to be voluntarily effected."

[12] Assets were restituted once the country of origin could be identified, and missions sent by other governments helped to identify assets that were subject to restitution. In cases where assets were restituted in this manner, the recipient government bore the responsibility to locate the rightful owner and to restitute the property turned over to it by U.S. authorities.

Presidential Advisory Commission on Holocaust Assets in the United States, Plunder and Restitution: The U.S. and Holocaust Victims' Assets 8 (2000).

[13] *See generally* Isaac Lipschits, De Kleine Sjoa. Joden in Naoorlogs Nederland (2d ed. 2001).

in its power to prevent Jews from reclaiming their positions and playing a significant role in the new business community.[14] One result of this policy was that Desi could not recover the works stolen by Göring and returned to the Netherlands after the war. The Dutch government simply kept the works in the National Collection, never obtaining title to them. There, most of them remained for almost 60 years.

Both Desi and Edo died in 1996. Following their deaths, Marei von Saher learned about the Goudstikker works in the possession of the Dutch government from a Dutch journalist, Pieter den Hollander who had been researching the Goudstikker story and shortly thereafter published a book on the case.[15] In January 1998, she presented a claim to the State Secretary in charge of cultural affairs for the return of the Goudstikker works that remained in the custody of the Dutch government. Her application was denied, and she also lost several different proceedings to overturn that decision. In 2002, after years of defeat and frustration, the Dutch government adopted new restitution guidelines in response to the Washington Conference that gave Marei some hope. She filed an application under those guidelines in 2004 and spent two more years fighting the case in the Netherlands. This effort culminated in a hearing before the Dutch Restitutions Committee, which issued a recommendation in December 2005 substantially in Marei's favor. As a result, in a decision issued on February 6, 2006, the then State Secretary of Cultural Affairs announced that she was restituting to Marei the 200 Goudstikker works looted by Göring and returned to the government after the war that were still in the possession of the Dutch government.

A great story with a happy ending? Yes, although Jacques and Desi and their son, Edo, were not present to witness this historic development.

But there is more to the Goudstikker saga. More than 1,000 of the looted works were not found by the Allies and remain missing. The family is also committed to locating and recovering these assets, although they are apparently spread throughout the world. To this end, the family has engaged noted art recovery specialists who are conducting a massive research project in archives throughout Europe and the United States to identify and locate the missing works. Their effort, reported in the *New York Times*[16] and numerous other publications, is one of the most comprehensive research initiatives ever to track down a single-owner art collection stolen by the Nazis; and it is the family's goal to find—and recover—every single work.

They have been aided in their work by a little black book—a meticulous inventory of Jacques' collection that contains notations in his own hand—which he had with him at the time he died and which Desi retrieved. But this

---

[14] *Id.*

[15] *See generally* DEN HOLLANDER, *supra* note 10.

[16] *See* Alan Riding, *Dutch to Return Art Seized by Nazis*, N.Y. TIMES, Feb. 7. 2006, *available at* http://www.nytimes.com/2006/02/07/arts/design/07rest.html; *see also* Alan Riding, *Göring, Rembrandt, and the Little Black Book*, N.Y. TIMES, Mar. 26, 2006, *available at* http://www.nytimes.com/2006/03/26/arts/design/26ridi.html.

is only the beginning of the team's work. They then have to find out what the works looked like, and this task of "visualizing" the black book is a large part of the endeavor. Working in photograph archives and on the Internet, they have already identified 60 percent of the works. But, of course, identifying is not the same as finding, and finding is not the same as recovering. To date, though, more than 100 of the works have been located, leading to more than 30 restitutions. Let me recount some of the successes resulting from a joint effort among the heirs, historians, and lawyers.

The first restitution came in the spring of 2002, when Jan de Cock's *Temptation of St. Anthony* was returned. The painting was discovered as part of an estate sale at Christie's, which was then notified by the London-based Art Loss Register about the painting's Goudstikker provenance. After being approached by Christie's, the estate restituted the work to Marei von Saher. Also that year, the Art Loss Register discovered that a Van Dyck painting, *Mary Magdalene,* was scheduled to be included in the Old Masters auction at Van Ham Fine Art Auctions of Cologne in April 2002. They alerted von Saher. The Van Dyck painting, after being identified as a lost Goudstikker painting, was removed from the auction by Van Ham. With its assistance, discussions began between the Goudstikker family's representatives and the consignor of the Van Dyck, a private collector who asked to remain anonymous. As a result, the consignor and the Goudstikker family were able to reach an agreement for restitution of the painting to the Goudstikker family.

In the summer of 2004, the Staatsgalerie Stuttgart, one of Germany's largest museums, paid an undisclosed sum to compensate the family for yet another looted work, a still life by the renowned Belgian expressionist painter, James Ensor. The work was found by the Goudstikker research team, which then approached the museum. At first the museum was skeptical, but after being persuaded by the claim, it agreed to a cash restitution that recognized the historical injustice but permitted the piece to remain on public display. In 2005, the Israel Museum in Jerusalem restituted a charcoal drawing by Edgar Degas, which had been donated to the museum in the 1970s. The museum had taken the claim for return of the drawing very seriously. Working with the Goudstikker research team, which presented photographic research they had located, the museum was able to determine that the drawing was indeed the missing Goudstikker work and not another example of Degas' image. As the museum stated at the time, it is critically important to address the subject of restitution in an appropriate fashion, noting that it was gratified to have been able to respond effectively to von Saher's claim and expressing the hope that its positive response to the claim would support the ongoing effort to set standards for the field.

In early 2006, the resolution of von Saher's claim to an extraordinary terracotta relief of the *Madonna and Child* by Donatello demonstrated the new global partnership that has developed in recent years to stop the traffic in Nazi-looted art and make sure that just results are achieved. The relief, a rare work that had been in the Goudstikker collection in 1940, when it was looted by the Nazis and then disappeared, was offered to Sotheby's New York for sale. Sotheby's, recognizing it as a possibly looted Goudstikker work, told the consignor that it must get in touch with me as the representative of the family. When it did, with the good will of all involved, the claim was fairly resolved and the piece was sold by von Saher with the Goudstikker provenance duly noted.[17]

We have recently obtained many more restitutions for the Goudstikker family including works by Palmezzano, Fernhout, Palamedesz, Dirck Hals, Lundens, Teniers, de Gelder, de Keyser, Salomon van Ruysdael, and Rachel Ruysch, among others. The Ruysch restitution is noteworthy because it shows what can happen when a public institution, confronted with a claim for displaced cultural property, focuses not on legal or moral defenses, but rather on the pure notion that such displacement is a crime not just against the original owners, but against humankind. *Still Life with Flowers*, dating from 1690, by one of the few female Old Masters, Rachel Ruysch, was identified by the Goudstikker research team in the Old Master's Picture Gallery of the Dresden Art Museum. A Goudstikker label on the back of the picture confirmed its provenance, although it had been looted 65 years earlier.[18] We contacted the museum, which took the Goudstikker claim very seriously. Choosing to "do the right thing" and not wanting looted Nazi art in its collection under any circumstances, the museum quickly returned the work to von Saher without the need for legal action.

In these successful restitutions, the museums and galleries in possession of the looted art did not force the Goudstikker heir to prove her claim in court, did not defend on the ground that the statute of limitations barred the claim, and did not argue that returning the painting would open the floodgates to myriad claims against museums about their collections. Rather, upon discovering the presence of Nazi looted art in their collections, the possessors took the matter seriously, did the requisite research, negotiated in good faith, and ultimately did the right thing. Unfortunately, the Goudstikker family has been less successful in resolving claims against U.S. and Canadian museums, which have been much less cooperative than their Western European counterparts when presented with claims, often coming up with reasons and excuses for not dealing with the issue.[19]

C. OTHER CASE HISTORIES AND ISSUES

Of course, it is not always possible to settle Holocaust claims without litigation; and the burdens faced by Holocaust claimants when they seek restitution of their art in the United States and Europe can be daunting and, at times, insurmountable. Any claim for the recovery of Nazi-looted art in the United States is predicated on a fundamental rule that is at the core of all cultural

[17] *See* Kimbell Art Museum, *Collection*, https://www.kimbellart.org/Collections/Kimbell-Collections.aspx.

[18] *See* Alan Riding, *The Art of Solving 1,000 Nazi Thefts*, SCOTLAND ON SUNDAY, Apr. 2, 2006, *available at* http://scotlandonsunday.scotsman.com/index.cfm?id=507012006; *see also* Staatliche Kunstsammlungen Dresden Press Release on the Ruysch Restitution, *available at* http://www.skddresden.de/de/presse/pressearchiv.html?id=199.

[19] *See* Konstantin Akinsha, *Restitution: Unfulfilled Promises*, ARTNEWS, Dec. 2006, at 131.

property cases: no one, not even a good faith purchaser, can obtain good title to stolen property. This uncomplicated rule is accepted and applied as a basic tenet of property and tort law in the United States.[20] Thus, the owner of stolen property has the right to reclaim that property from anyone, unless barred by the statute of limitations or similar doctrines. Litigation concerning Holocaust artwork, however, can also involve a vast array of legal and factual issues, ranging from simple property concepts to complex questions of international law. The core concerns can be grouped into three basic categories.[21]

1. Locating the Artwork

After the war, the Allies began the colossal task of sorting the millions of pieces of art, cultural artifacts, and other items systematically stolen by the Nazis. Those works were dispersed across Europe, often far from their countries of origin.[22] While some collections were found intact, the contents of many others were scattered in warehouses or buried in rubble, mines, or bombed-out churches.[23] Also, during the war, art galleries and dealers, particularly French, Swiss, Dutch, and German ones, collaborated with the Nazis to sell many artworks, reaping enormous profits.[24] In many instances, the art simply disappeared through theft.[25]

The end result was that many pieces of art could not be located. But in the last ten years, claims have started to surface, in part because of the publicity generated by the Washington Conference and the seizure in 1998 of Egon Schiele's *Portrait of Wally* by Robert Morgenthau, the District of Attorney of New York County.[26] Also, books written on the subject, such as *The Lost Museum*

---

[20] *See* W. Page Keeton et al., Prosser and Keeton on the Law of Torts § 15, at 93–94 (5th ed. 1984); *see also* Autocephalous Greek Orthodox Church of Cyprus v. Goldberg & Feldman Fine Arts, Inc., 717 F. Supp. 1374, 1398 (S.D. Ind. 1989), *aff'd*, 917 F.2d 278 (7th Cir. 1990).

[21] *See generally* Lawrence M. Kaye, *The Future of the Past: Recovering Cultural Property*, 4 Cardozo J. Int'l & Comp. L. 23 (1996); *see also* Howard N. Spiegler & Lawrence M. Kaye, *American Litigation to Recover Cultural Property: Obstacles, Options and Proposal, in* Trade in Illicit Antiquities: The Destruction of the World's Archeological Heritage 121 (Neil Brodie, Jennifer Doole & Colin Renfrew eds., 2001).

[22] *See* Walton, *supra* note 2, at 562. For example, many of the most precious artworks were transferred to Austria when the Allied bombings began and were discovered in abandoned salt mines near Alt Aussee in Austria (citing Hector Feliciano, The Lost Museum: The Nazi Conspiracy to Steal the World's Greatest Works of Art 16 (Tim Bent & Hector Feliciano trans., 1997) [hereinafter Feliciano])).

[23] *See* Walton, *supra* note 2, at 562–63 (citing Lynn H. Nicholas, The Rape of Europa: The Fate of Europe's Treasures in the Third Reich and the Second World War (1994) [hereinafter Nicholas]).

[24] *Id.* at 563–64 (citing Feliciano, *supra* note 22, at 344). For example, French, Swiss, and German dealers who visited the Jeu de Paume in Paris to pick through the looted art apparently knew where the artworks had come from and the fact that they were illegally acquired. *Id.* Art prices continued to rise throughout the war, and dishonest gallery owners took advantage of the Nazis' disdain for modern, so-called "degenerate art" by reaping exorbitant profits from the exchange of works highly valued by the Nazis. *Id.*

[25] *See id.* at 563. Many works of art entered the black market after being falsely claimed at collecting points or passing through the hands of multiple thieves. *Id.* at 563 (citing Nicholas, *supra* note 23, at 344).

[26] It is extremely ironic that the *Schiele* case (to be discussed later), which is credited

by Hector Feliciano and *The Rape of Europa* by Lynn Nicolas, have been instrumental because of their comprehensive examination of the large number of works looted during the war. *The Lost Museum* furnishes a good example.[27] One famous litigation involving a Holocaust-looted artwork, a Matisse painting called *Odalisque,* arose when the heirs of the owner, Paul Rosenberg, discovered the whereabouts of their painting because it was cited by Feliciano as having been in their family's collection and then looted by the Nazis.[28] The heirs demanded that the painting be returned by the Seattle Art Museum, which initially rejected mediation of the dispute and reportedly decided to defend in court in what it called a "test case."[29] Finally, a year later, it agreed to return the painting to the Rosenberg heirs after obtaining the findings of a research study that concluded that the *Odalisque* had indeed been stolen by the Nazis from Rosenberg.[30] The Seattle Museum of Art then sued Knoedler & Co., the gallery responsible for selling the painting, for $11 million, representing the loss of the painting and legal fees. In an out-of-court settlement, the Seattle Art Museum dropped its suit against the gallery in return for one or more works from Knoedler's inventory. The gallery also agreed to reimburse the museum for legal fees and other related costs.[31]

In addition to books such as those of Feliciano and Nicholas[32] and a general

---

with bringing attention to Holocaust claims, is still pending and unresolved. *See, e.g.*, Diane Haithman, *Watching the Detectives: Scholars at Area Museums Face an Enormous, Often Tedious Task: Searching Out Records to Trace the Nazi-Era Ownership of Their Works*, L.A. TIMES, Sept. 3, 2000, at 8; *Dispute Over the Ownership of a Painting that the Nazis Took from a Jewish Art Dealer in 1938 Vienna* (National Public Radio: Morning Edition, Aug. 31, 2000), *available at* 2000 WL 21481433; Mark Hamblett, *Seized Painting Ruled No Longer 'Stolen'; Path Cleared for Portrait's Return to Austria,* N.Y.L.J., July 20, 2000, at 1; Jay Rayner, *The Full List of Art Treasures Looted by the Nazis Has Been Suppressed for 50 Years. Finally It's Been Published. And Now the Trouble Really Begins,* THE OBSERVER, Jan. 17, 1999, at 1.

[27] See FELICIANO, *supra* note 22, for a details on the plundering of Jewish-owned artwork during World War II, tracing five Jewish families in Europe who were targeted by the Nazis because of their extensive and valuable art collections.

[28] *See* BAZYLER, *supra* note 1, at 222. Paul Rosenberg, Paris's most important art dealer, was forced to leave his home, as were other Jews when the Nazis invaded Paris. *Id.* In 1941, Rosenberg was informed that the Nazis had plundered his collection of over 300 paintings, which included works by Renoir, Cezanne, Pissaro, Monet, and Delacroix. *Id.* He had stored one particular painting, Matisse's "Odalisque," in a French bank vault, which Hitler ordered his top aide Herman Goering to seize in 1941. *Id.* The "Odalisque," like many others, was sent to the Jeu de Paume where it was bartered and traded until it found its way to a New York gallery. *See id. See also* Stephanie Cuba, Note, *Stop the Clock: The Case to Suspend the Statute of Limitations on Claims for Nazi-Looted Art,* 17 CARDOZO ARTS & ENT. L.J. 447, 447–48 (1999) [hereinafter Cuba].

[29] *See* BAZYLER, *supra* note 1, at 224.

[30] *Id.* "In June 1999, the Holocaust Art Restitution Project ('HARP'), after receiving funding from the Seattle Art Museum to conduct research, released findings that confirmed that the Museum's 'Odalisque' was the same work that the Nazis had stolen from Paul Rosenberg. That same year, without resorting to litigation, a French museum agreed to return to the Rosenberg heirs a Monet masterpiece valued at 7.5 million dollars." *Id.* at 174. *See* Spiegler, *supra* note 2, at 20, citing Joanna Massey, *Heirs Reclaim Plundered Monet,* BOSTON GLOBE, Apr. 30, 1999, at B4; *see also* BAZYLER, *supra* note 1.

[31] Raphael Rubinstein, *Seattle Lawsuit Resolved—Seattle Art Museum and M. Knoedler and Company Inc. Settle Case Over Matisse Painting,* 88(12) ART IN AMERICA 31 (Dec. 2000).

[32] *See generally* Nicholas, *supra* note 23; KONSTANTIN AKINSHA ET AL., BEAUTIFUL LOOT: THE

renewal of awareness of Nazi-looted art, records and other documentation are now available for public review for the first time.[33] During the Cold War, the Nazi confiscation lists and records compiled by the Allied art-recovery troops were classified, and access to Soviet archives was of course impossible.[34] It is only over the last 15 years or so, after the political changes in Russia and other countries, that these documents have begun to be declassified and archives opened up. For example, the National Archives in Washington, DC, and records in Switzerland and Germany are being unsealed and declassified to allow individuals and organizations to trace the ownership of Nazi-looted art.[35] But searching through this multitude of documents is difficult even for the expert researcher.[36] Thus, many governments are funding further archival research, with the stated intention of completing art registries listing inventories of Nazi-looted art.[37] In addition, major museums in the United States and elsewhere are beginning publicly to identify artworks in their collection with gaps in provenance between 1933 and 1945 and placing images of the artworks on

---

SOVIET PLUNDERS OF EUROPE'S ART TREASURES (1995); PETER HARCLERODE & BRENDAN PITTAWAY, THE LOST MASTERS. WORLD WAR II AND THE LOOTING OF EUROPE'S TREASURE HOUSES (1999); JONATHAN PETROPOULOS, ART AS POLITICS IN THE THIRD REICH (1996); JONATHAN PETROPOULOUS, THE FAUSTIAN BARGAIN: THE ART WORLD IN NAZI GERMANY (2000).

[33] *See* Cuba, *supra* note 28, at 448–50. The declassification of governmental archives in France, Germany, the former Soviet Union, and Switzerland has spurred a reawakening of claims from Holocaust victims and their heirs. *Id.*

[34] *Id.* at 449.

[35] *Id.* The meticulous inventories and catalogs kept by the Nazis listing the works of art they looted and a report compiled by the U.S. Office of Strategic Services after the war that includes a "Biographical Index of Individuals Involved in Art Looting" are extremely valuable. *Id.* at 449 n.21. The index lists more than 2,000 people who handled works of art that were looted by the Nazis and can be viewed at http://docproj.loyola.edu. *Id.* at 449 n.21. However, many governments and institutions have not opened up their archives. "Therefore, it remains extremely difficult for individuals to research and establish their claims. For example, the Vatican has refused to open its archives, and many believe that they could be instrumental in proving the provenance of many works of art." *See id.* at 463. Funding for this work also presents a problem. The U.S. Presidential Advisory Commission on Holocaust Assets has been constructing a database of claims made immediately after World War II for missing works of art. "These records, numbering over 300,000, detail Nazi looting of fine art, furniture, household effects, rare books, and other collections. As of now, the records are stored in the National Archives. The database would allow potential claimants to easily access and search these records. The project is about to run out of funding, however, and unless Congress allocates additional money, the database will not be completed." *See Spiegler, supra* note 2, at n.24, citing Ron Grossman, *Key to Art Nazis Stole May Be Locked Away: Commission's Plan to Publish Postwar Loss Claims in Peril*, CHI. TRIB., Dec. 17, 2000, at 1.

[36] As the head of the department of curatorial records at the National Gallery of Art in Washington, DC, noted,

> The very nature of World War II provenance research is interdisciplinary. It requires knowledge of art history, politics, the history of collections, and the locations of archival materials that document the movement of art, in addition to historical provenance research, a fairly specialized methodology in its own right.

Nancy H. Yeide, *Behind the Lines: Lessons in Nazi-Era Provenance Research*, MUSEUM NEWS, Nov./Dec. 2000, at 49; *see Spiegler, supra* note 2, at n. 25.

[37] *See, e.g.*, Martin Bailey, *Report on the Vilnius Forum on Holocaust-Era Looted Art: Christie's and Sotheby's to Help with Provenance Research*, http://www.theartnewspaper.com/news/article.asp?idart=3714.

their Web sites.[38] Slowly but surely, stolen artworks are coming to light, and the families of Holocaust victims are recognizing them and beginning to make claims. But in a survey recently conducted by the Jewish Claims Conference regarding the response of U.S. Museums to the Washington Conference, of 332 museums in the United States, 118 did not respond.[39]

2. Establishing the Right to Make a Claim

Locating the looted art is just the beginning of the recovery process. The next step is to establish the claimant's ownership rights to the satisfaction of the possessor and, if necessary, a court. Often that is a difficult and complicated task. Given the Nazis' systematic elimination of their victims, and the passage of time since the war, the original owners are rarely available to establish ownership. The claim therefore must be asserted by an heir, perhaps a distant descendant, who is not likely to have direct personal knowledge of the painting's ownership and provenance.

Hence, personal family records must be examined including, where available, insurance policies or even old photographs identifying the art in the original owner's home. In addition, government archives may provide documentation concerning the ownership of the artwork. Possible sources include U.S. archival records of recoveries by Allied forces and the archives of the European governments that were involved in the confiscation and recovery of Nazi-looted art. Catalogues raisonnés or contemporaneous exhibition catalogs can also assist in identifying the owners.[40]

One Holocaust art recovery case, *Goodman v. Searle*,[41] illustrates the problems that claimants may have in finding and then establishing their ownership of Nazi-looted art.[42] The case involved *Landscape with Smokestacks,* an 1890 painting by Edgar Degas that Friedrich and Louise Gutmann, a Dutch couple who had converted to Christianity from Judaism, purchased in 1932. In 1939, with the war fast approaching, Gutmann allegedly sent it to an art dealer in Paris for safekeeping. The dealer placed it in storage to protect it from seizure by the Nazis along with other works owned by the Gutmanns that were being stored for the same purpose. The Degas later disappeared.[43] Meanwhile, the Gutmanns died in Nazi concentration camps in 1944. Their two children attempted to find their parents' artworks after the war but were unsuccessful.[44] In 1994, the Degas was finally discovered in the United States by a Gutmann grandson, Simon Goodman.[45] The family, believing that the Degas had been taken by Soviet troops to Russia, had hoped to find information about it after 1991 when

---

[38] *See* Celestine Bohlen, *Museums Accept Stronger Role in Search for Looted Art,* N.Y. TIMES ABSTRACTS, Nov. 30, 2000, at *1, *available at* 2000 WL 30522019.

[39] *Nazi Era Stolen Art and U.S. Museums: A Survey, available at:* http://usmuseumsurvey.claimscon.org/.

[40] *See* Cuba, *supra* note 28, at 458 n.90.

[41] N.D. Ill. July 17, 1996 (No. 96-6459).

[42] *Id. See also* BAZYLER, *supra* note 1, at 215.

[43] *Id.*

[44] *See id.*

[45] *Id.*

the Soviet Union collapsed and its archives were newly opened. As it turned out, however, when Goodman was simply leafing through art books at the U.C.L.A. art library, he came upon a photo of the Degas, which indicated that it was in the collection of Daniel Searle, the Chicago pharmaceutical magnate, who had purchased it in 1987 for $850,000.[46]

The Gutmann heirs demanded that Searle return the piece to them and Searle refused. Suit was then commenced by the Gutmanns' daughter, then in her mid-70s, and two grandchildren. Searle claimed that Gutmann had sold the Degas when he was suffering financially during the war, but apparently no bill of sale or other proof existed. Searle also argued that the plaintiffs' claims were barred by the statute of limitations on the basis that if they had been more diligent, they would have learned of the whereabouts of the Degas well before Searle bought it.[47] These issues were never resolved, however, since the parties settled the case on the eve of trial but only after *four* years of litigation. The terms of the settlement are interesting: Searle and the Goodmans agreed to share ownership of the Degas. Searle then donated his one-half interest to the Art Institute of Chicago, where he is a trustee, and the institute agreed to purchase the Goodmans' one-half interest based on independent appraisals of the painting.[48]

3. Overcoming the Summary Passage of Time: The Statute of Limitations

a. Summary

In virtually all cases of stolen art, the specter of the statute of limitations must be confronted. This poses a host of potential problems for claimants of Nazi-looted art, in particular, with claims now coming more than 60 years after the theft. A statutory limitations period begins to run when the cause of action accrues. U.S. statutes specify the length of the limitations period. The definition of when a cause of action accrues, however, has been left for the most part to the discretion of the courts. With respect to stolen art in the possession of good faith purchasers, the courts have fashioned accrual rules that allow a plaintiff to make a claim for the recovery of art stolen years before. For example, New York applies a "demand and refusal" rule under which the limitations period does not begin to run against a good faith purchaser until the owner makes a demand for the return of the property and the possessor refuses. In *Menzel v. List*,[49] one of the earliest reported U.S. cases to address the question of restituting Nazi-plundered art, the plaintiffs tried to reclaim a Chagall painting that had been

---

[46] *Id.* at 217–19.

[47] *Id.* at 219. Searle argued that the Goodmans should have known about the Degas' presence in the United States because of the publication of two books (in 1968 and 1974), which included information regarding it, and because of three exhibits at college museums (in 1965, 1968, and 1974), which featured it. *See id.* at 219. The plaintiffs claimed that they reported the loss of the artwork immediately after the war to the Allied forces, government officials in Germany, France and Holland, Interpol, art experts, and the International Foundation for Art Research. *See id.*

[48] *Id.* at 221.

[49] 267 N.Y.S.2d 804, 809 (N.Y. Sup. Ct. N.Y. County 1966).

seized by the Nazis in 1941 in Brussels.[50] Eighteen years after the war ended, they finally located the painting in the collection of the defendant, who had purchased it in 1955 from a reputable New York art gallery.[51] In response to their lawsuit to recover the painting, the defendant argued that the action was barred by New York's three-year statute of limitations because, he contended, the cause of action accrued when the painting was stolen in 1941 or, at the latest, when he purchased the painting in 1955.[52] Holding that the cause of action arises "not upon the stealing or the taking, but upon the defendant's refusal to convey the chattel upon demand," the court concluded that the plaintiffs were the rightful owners of the painting.[53]

Years later, the New York Court of Appeals reaffirmed the demand-and-refusal rule in a case in which the Guggenheim Museum was seeking to recover a painting stolen some 20 years earlier.[54] The question before the court was whether the museum's alleged failure to take certain steps to locate the painting was relevant to the application of the demand-and-refusal rule. The state's highest court declined to impose any duty of diligence on the owner in this statute of limitations context.[55] Many commentators have criticized New York's "demand-and-refusal" rule as really being no statute of limitations at all. They argue that it is unfair because many years, even decades, may pass before the owner locates the art and makes its demand that, when refused, sets the statute of limitations in motion.[56] But the rule has been defended, justifiably I believe, on the ground that as between the two victims—the owner who was deprived of the property and the buyer who acquired it innocently—the claimant needs the greater protection because the buyer has means at its disposal to avoid the purchase in the first place.

The courts in *Guggenheim* did, however, rule that the diligence of the plaintiff—and the vigilance of the defendant—would come into play when assessing the equitable defense of laches, which may operate to bar the claim if the defendant can show that the claimant unreasonably delayed pursuing its rights to the prejudice of the defendant.[57] Laches generally involves a case-by-case analysis of the circumstances, including whether or not the defendant would be prejudiced by the delay in bringing the claim. Examples of prejudice are the death of witnesses, the loss of evidence, and so on. In some cases

---

[50] *Id.* at 804–06.

[51] *Id.* at 806.

[52] *Id.* at 806–09.

[53] *Id.* at 809.

[54] *See* Solomon R. Guggenheim Foundation v. Lubell, 550 N.Y.S.2d 618 (1st Dep't 1990), *aff'd,* 77 N.Y.2d 311 (1991) [hereinafter *Guggenheim*]. The Guggenheim Museum sought to recover a 1912 Chagall gouache worth an estimated $200,000 that was allegedly stolen in the mid 1960s. The plaintiff discovered the defendant's possession of the painting in August of 1985 and demanded its return the following January. *See id.* at 619.

[55] *Id.*

[56] *See, eg.,* Alexandre A. Montagu, *Recent Cases on the Recovery of Stolen Art—The Tug of War Between Owners and Good Faith Purchasers Continues,* 18 COLUM.-VLA J.L. & ARTS 75, 101 (1993–1994).

[57] *Guggenheim, supra* note 54.

following *Guggenheim,* New York courts have started to use the equitable doctrine of laches to offset what is perceived by some as a limitations rule too favorable to claimants.[58] Laches has even been used in Holocaust cases,[59] although rarely, and a well-represented plaintiff with a valid claim should be able to resist a laches defense if efforts to locate the stolen work were made or would have been futile. And many states other than New York, which as noted earlier may have different statute of limitations rules, do not even allow a laches defense to be asserted in a replevin action.[60]

A majority of states in the United States, however, employ a different rule, imposing a duty of diligence on the plaintiff that requires an affirmative showing that appropriate steps have been taken to locate the property.[61] In these states, the limitations period begins to run when the plaintiff discovers, or after the exercise of reasonable diligence should have discovered, the whereabouts of the stolen art.[62] This so-called "discovery rule" has also been criticized for its imposition of a burdensome duty on the owners of stolen art.[63] Not only do most individuals lack the knowledge, resources, and experience necessary to successfully locate art, but in the particular case of Nazi-plundered art, information concerning the pieces stolen is just now coming to light. In addition, even if an owner or heir had identified an artwork after the war, there is historical evidence that the atmosphere in post-war Europe was such that claimants often justifiably feared an adverse result if they made claims, and many survivors and heirs believed that making a claim after the war was a largely a futile effort.[64] One would hope that a court applying the discovery rule would permit the admission of such historical evidence and not hold this type of delay against claimants now.

At least one state concluded that claims for the recovery of Nazi-looted art implicate unique policy concerns that required a unique legislative response. The state of California therefore enacted a special statute that extends the statute of limitations for actions that seek to recover Holocaust-era artwork from any museum or gallery in the state of California until December 31, 2010 (that is, ten years from the date of its enactment).[65]

In contrast to the statute of limitations laws in the United States, which are generally favorable to plaintiffs seeking the recovery of artworks, the experience in civil code countries is quite different. As I noted previously, in the United States (and other common law jurisdictions), a good faith purchaser cannot acquire good title to stolen property no matter how long the stolen

[58] *See, e.g.*, Wertheimer v. Cirker's Hayes Storage Warehouse, Inc., 300 A.D.2d 117 (N.Y. App. Div., 1st Dep't 2002).

[59] *Id.*

[60] San Francisco Credit Clearing House v. Wells, 196 Cal. 701 (1925).

[61] *See* Cuba, *supra* note 28, at 456–61. *See generally* Marilyn E. Phelan, *Scope of Due Diligence Investigation in Obtaining Title to Valuable Artwork*, 23 PUGET SOUND L. REV. 631 (2000).

[62] *Id.*

[63] *See id.*

[64] *See, e.g.*, Andrew Decker, *A Legacy of Shame*, ARTNEWS, Dec. 1984, at 55, 67–71.

[65] *See* CAL. CODE CIV. PROC. § 354.3 (2006).

property had been in his possession. But civil codes in effect in most European countries are far less favorable to the owner, and a good faith purchaser of stolen property can get good title with the passage of time, often a short period, and sometimes immediately, as in Italy.[66] While good faith must be shown in civil code jurisdictions, this is an amorphous standard at best.

Although, as noted earlier, there have not yet been a large number of Holocaust cases in the United States, those Holocaust claims that have reached the courts aptly demonstrate how the foregoing factors can play an important role in the determination of looted art cases in U.S. courts. Also, sovereign immunity from the jurisdiction of courts has proven to be an important issue.

b. Examples

i. United States v. Portrait of Wally[67]

Based on recent experiences, it is fair to say that claimants seeking the return of Nazi-looted art in the United States should be prepared for litigation—perhaps long drawn-out litigation—to reclaim their property. By way of example, one rather famous case, which my firm is handling, involves the claim of the heirs of Lea Bondi to *Portrait of Wally*, painted by Egon Schiele. The case has been litigated for more than seven years against two museums that have aggressively fought not only the claim of a Holocaust victim's heirs but the government of the United States as well as the New York City district attorney, all in order to prevent the restitution of a painting stolen by a Nazi agent over sixty years ago.[68]

Lea Bondi was a Jewish art dealer in Vienna who was forced to sell her gallery to a Nazi named Friedrich Welz pursuant to recently adopted Aryanization laws in Austria that prohibited Jewish business ownership. Bondi owned a painting by Egon Schiele called *Portrait of Wally* that she maintained in her private art collection in her apartment. Shortly before Bondi and her husband were to flee to England, Welz came to their apartment to discuss the gallery's transfer. Upon spotting *Wally*, he insisted that she give it to him. Out of fear for what Welz could do if she refused, she turned it over. After the war, the U.S. armed forces transferred the painting to the Austrian government authority, but the painting was erroneously shipped to an Austrian national museum. Upon discovering that her painting was hanging in the Austrian National Gallery, Bondi told Dr. Rudolph Leopold, an Austrian collector, that she was the true owner of the painting and asked him to help her recover it. Dr. Leopold, however, acquired the painting for himself.[69]

---

[66] *See* 3 P.J. O'Keefe & L.V. Prott, Law and the Cultural Heritage 408 (1989).

[67] 2002 U.S. Dist. LEXIS 6445 (S.D.N.Y. 2002).

[68] Because my law firm represents the heirs, my comments will necessarily be limited to a description of what is contained in the public record.

[69] *See Second Amended Verified Complaint at 2–17,* United States v. Portrait of Wally, A Painting by Egon Schiele, 105 F. Supp. 2d 288 (S.D.N.Y. 2000) (No. 99-9940).

In 1994, Leopold's art collection, which included *Portrait of Wally*, became part of the newly formed Leopold Museum, where Leopold himself is director for life. In late 1997, *Wally* was loaned by the Leopold Museum to the Museum of Modern Art (MoMA) in New York for an exhibition of Schiele's artworks. Upon learning that the painting was being exhibited at MoMA, Bondi's heirs demanded that it hold the work pending the resolution of the heirs' claim to ownership of the painting. MoMA refused, citing its contractual obligation to return the painting to the Leopold Museum at the end of the exhibition. New York District Attorney Morgenthau commenced a criminal investigation into the matter and directed MoMA not to return the painting to the Leopold Museum, but his action was eventually reversed by the state's highest court a year later.[70] Within hours of that decision, the U.S. Customs Service, acting under federal law, obtained a warrant of seizure of the painting, and the United States Attorney commenced an action to remove the property permanently from the Leopold Museum.

The Leopold Museum made an application to the Federal District Court for the Southern District of New York to terminate the action without going to trial. In addition, it made an application to dismiss the Bondi heirs' claim, contending that they did not properly represent the Bondi estate, as well as on statute of limitations grounds, and even claimed that *Wally* was not really stolen from Lea Bondi by the Nazi Welz since she had handed it to him when he demanded it. The court granted the Leopold Museum's motion to dismiss the case. The basis of its decision was simply that *Wally* was not stolen property within the meaning of the applicable National Stolen Property Act.[71]

The court ruled that after *Wally* had been recovered by U.S. forces, it was no longer "stolen property." It based its decision on the so-called "sting cases" where the police recovered stolen property, then used the property to trap the next criminal up the line, usually called "the fence." In such cases. our courts have ruled that the "fence" cannot be convicted of receiving stolen property because that property, often televisions or cars, is no longer considered stolen once the police having recovered the property, are then deemed to be acting as agents for the true owner in recovering the property at that time.[72] Thus, the court in *Wally* concluded that when the painting was recovered from Welz by the U.S. forces after the war, it was no longer stolen because they had discovered it as agents for Lea Bondi, even though they did not know her name or that the painting was hers.[73]

Happily, the court eventually reversed itself when the government's complaint was amended to allege, among other things, that at the time they recovered the property, U.S. forces did not even know the painting had been

---

[70] *See, e.g., In re* Grand Jury Subpoena Duces Tecum Served on the Museum of Modern Art, 677 N.Y.S.2d 872 (N.Y. Sup. Ct. N.Y. County 1998) (granting museum's motion to quash based on N.Y. Arts & Cult. Aff. Law § 12.03), *rev'd, In re* Grand Jury Subpoena Duces Tecum, 253 A.D.2d 211 (N.Y. App. Div. 1999).

[71] *See* United States v. Portrait of Wally, 105 F. Supp. 2d 288 (S.D.N.Y. 2000).

[72] *Id.*

[73] *Id.*

stolen by Welz; the Allies unlike the police in "sting cases," were under no obligation to turn over *Wally* to the true owner but only to return the confiscated property to the Austrian government without the need for any authority from the owner or imputed agency relationship with the owner.[74] Finally, the court held that Leopold had wrongfully converted the painting so that it was stolen all over again. Cross motions for summary judgment have been filed, and a decision on those motions is likely later in 2009.

ii. Republic of Austria v. Altmann[75]

In 2004, the U.S. Supreme Court considered the quest of 89-year-old Maria Altmann to reclaim five paintings by Gustav Klimt, then in the Austrian National Gallery, which had been confiscated from her family in Vienna by the Nazis during World War II. Altmann alleged the Klimt paintings had been wrongly expropriated from her family by the Nazis and later the Austrian government in violation of international law. The issue under review was whether the U.S. Foreign Sovereign Immunities Act of 1976 (FSIA)[76] should be applied retroactively to permit an action to proceed that challenged the illegal confiscation of Jewish property during the Nazi era. In filing suit in the Central District of California, not Austria, Mrs. Altmann relied on the FSIA's expropriation exception to a defense of sovereign immunity, which expressly exempts from immunity all cases involving property taken in violation of international law (so long as the property has a commercial connection to the United States, and the agency or instrumentality that owns the property is engaged in the commercial activity here). Austria and the Austrian Gallery, concededly an instrumentality of the republic, filed a motion to dismiss, raising, among other defenses, sovereign immunity.[77] They claimed that as of 1948, when much of the alleged wrongdoing took place, they would have enjoyed absolute immunity from suit in the United States and argued that nothing in the FSIA should be construed to divest them of that immunity retroactively. The district court and, on appeal, the Ninth Circuit Court of Appeals both rejected the sovereign immunity defense.[78] The district court concluded both that the FSIA applied to pre-1976 conduct and that the expropriation exception extended to Mrs. Altmann's specific claims. The Supreme Court limited its review to the first issue only.

In July 2004, the U.S. Supreme Court issued a landmark decision on this issue in *Republic of Austria v. Altmann*,[79] The Court ruled that the FSIA, which permits lawsuits in the United States against foreign governments under certain limited circumstances, applies even to actions that occurred prior to its enactment in 1976. Despite "friend of the court" briefs filed by the United States and several foreign governments in support of Austria's position that the suit should be dismissed because the FSIA should not be applied retroactively,

[74] *See* United States v. Portrait of Wally, 2002 U.S. Dist. LEXIS 6445 (S.D.N.Y. 2002).
[75] 541 U.S. 677 (2004).
[76] 28 U.S.C. §§ 1330, 1602–1611 (2000).
[77] Altmann v. Republic of Austria, 142 F. Supp. 2d 1187 (D. Cal. 2001).
[78] *Id.*
[79] *Id.*

the Court held that the date of the expropriation was essentially irrelevant.[80] It is not an understatement to suggest that the Supreme Court's decision in *Altmann* came as something of a surprise; almost all commentators were predicting the apposite outcome. The *amicus curiae* brief submitted by the State Department contained some very strong language suggesting that if the FSIA could be applied to conduct that occurred long ago, it would have disastrous effects on the ability of the executive branch of the United States to conduct foreign policy. Nevertheless, the Court upheld the decision of the courts below but on very different grounds.

The case was then returned to the District Court in California to be heard on the merits, but the case in California was voluntarily terminated in favor of arbitration in Austria.[81] In January 2006, the Austrian arbitration panel unanimously ruled in favor of Mrs. Altmann in a landmark decision.[82] The works, including an extraordinary portrait of Adele Bloch-Bauer, Mrs. Altmann's aunt, which many say is the greatest portrait of the 20th century, were quickly returned to Mrs. Altmann in California and went on display in the Los Angeles County Museum of Art. The Neue Galerie in New York, through its president, Ronald Lauder, acquired the *Portrait of Adele Bloch-Bauer I* (for one of the highest prices ever paid).[83] I was privileged to handle the transaction for our client, Neue Galerie. The remaining restituted Klimt works were sold by Christie's at auction in November 2006 for approximately $190 million.[84]

iii. Leonard Malewicz et al. v. City of Amsterdam[85]

The FSIA is being used more often to facilitate claims in the United States against foreign governments. In a recent case in the Federal District Court in Washington DC, *Leonard Malewicz et al. v. City of Amsterdam,* which did not seek the recovery of Holocaust loot, the court denied a foreign sovereign's attempt to dismiss the case, thereby allowing the claimants to pursue their case against a foreign museum that was holding their stolen artworks.[86] The interesting issue here is that the works, on loan to two U.S. museums, had been granted immunity from seizure under one U.S. law, while they were in the United States, but the court ruled that their presence in the United States was nevertheless a sufficient basis for jurisdiction in an action against the foreign sovereign to recover the works. While not a Holocaust case, Holocaust groups have applauded the decision below because it will apply with equal force to Holocaust claims against foreign sovereigns.

---

[80] *Id.*

[81] Altmann v. Republic of Austria, 335 F. Supp. 2d 1066, 1067 (D. Cal. 2004).

[82] *See* Richard Bernstein, *Austrian Panel Backs Return of Klimt Works,* N.Y. TIMES, Jan. 17, 2006, *available at* http://www.nytimes.com/2006/01/17/arts/17klim.html?_r=1&scp=2&sq.

[83] *See* Carol Vogel, *Lauder Pays $135 Million, a Record, for a Klimt Portrait,* N.Y. TIMES, June 19, 2006, *available at* http://www.nytimes.com/2006/11/09/arts/design/09christies.html?_r=1&oref=slogin.

[84] *See* Carol Vogel, *$491 Million Sale Shatters Art Auction Record,* N.Y. TIMES, Nov. 9, 2006, *available at* http://www.nytimes.com/2006/11/09/arts/design/09christies.html?scp=1&sq.

[85] 362 F. Supp. 2d 298 (D.D.C. 2005).

[86] *Id.*

iv. United States v. Femme en Blanc[87] *(and Related Cases in Federal and State Courts in Illinois and California)*

Last year, a lawsuit by the heirs of a Holocaust victim to recover *Femme En Blanc* by Pablo Picasso was settled, reportedly for $6.5 million.[88] In that case, Thomas Bennigson, the grandson of a German woman who owned the 1922 Picasso oil painting before it was confiscated by the Nazis in 1940, sought to recover the work from Marilyn Alsdorf, a private collector in the United States.[89] Ms. Alsdorf and her husband had purchased the painting around 1975, allegedly unaware that it had been looted by the Nazis. The pre-war owner was Carolota Landsberg of Berlin, who had entrusted it to a well-known art dealer in Paris. After the Nazis invaded France in 1940, the painting disappeared. In 2002, 27 years after purchasing it, Ms. Alsdorf, then a widow and the sole owner of the painting, consigned the painting to a Los Angeles-based art dealer. The L.A. art dealer sent the painting to Switzerland to be viewed by a potential purchaser. The prospective buyer, in turn, contacted the Art Loss Registry in London, which identified the painting as having been looted by the Nazis. After the painting was returned to Los Angeles, Bennigson attempted to negotiate for its release or a settlement payment. Initial settlement talks failed, however, and litigation then ensued in California, where Mr. Bennigson and the painting were located, and in Illinois, where Ms. Alsdorf lives. After extensive, multi-state litigation, the case was eventually settled with the assistance of the U.S. Attorneys' Office and a federal magistrate judge.[90]

v. Adler v. Taylor[91]

Adler v. Taylor underscores that not all claims will be honored on the mere *ipse dixit* that the owners were victims of the Holocaust. In this case, four descendants of a German woman whose possessions were confiscated by the Nazis in the 1930s sued actress Elizabeth Taylor to recover a painting by Vincent van Gogh, which had been appraised at $10–$15 million. The heirs charged that Taylor's father, who purchased the painting at Sotheby's in 1963, failed to review the provenance of *View of the Asylum of Saint-Remy* before acquiring it. In February 2005, a U.S. federal judge granted Taylor's motion to dismiss the lawsuit after finding that the suit against Taylor was barred by the statute of limitations. The court held that the case clearly did not fit under the California law that gives heirs until the year 2010 to sue galleries and museums for the return of Nazi looted artworks.[92] Thus, not every case brought for the return of Nazi-looted art is a good one. Often, there are procedural or jurisdictional

---

[87] 362 F. Supp. 2d 1175 (C.D.Cal. 2005).

[88] *See* Howard Reich, *$6.5 Million Settlement Reached Over Picasso Looted by Nazis*, CHI. TRIB., Aug. 10, 2005, at 16.

[89] *See* Nanette Asimov, *Oakland Man Claims a Picasso: Grandmother's Painting Now Worth $10 million, Was Looted*, S.F. CHRON., Dec. 27, 2002, *available at* http://www.sfgate.com/cgi-bin/article.cgi?file=/c/a/2002/12/27/BA127626.DTL; *see also* Reich, *supra* note 88.

[90] *Id.*

[91] Adler v. Taylor, 2005 U.S. Dist. LEXIS 5862 (D. Cal. 2005).

[92] *Id.*

barriers that make it impossible to win some claims. Other times, claims are unwarranted and lacking in substance.

vi. Cassirer v. Kingdom of Spain et al.[93]

The *Cassirer* case revolves around a Camille Pissaro painting that was extorted from its Jewish owner in 1939 as a condition to issuing her an exit visa. After World War II, the painting changed hands several times, ultimately ending up in the hands of the Baron Thyssen-Bornemisza. In 1988, the Baron loaned his art collection to Spain under contract, and Spain spent millions of dollars refurbishing a state-owned palace in Madrid and providing it at no charge as the home for a museum to display the collection. Spain then paid the Baron $50 million for a ten-year lease of the collection and in 1993 paid an additional $327 million to enable the Thyssen-Bornemisza Collection Foundation to be able to buy the collection. In 2000, the original owner's grandson, a California resident, discovered that it was part of the collection of the Thyssen-Bornemisza Museum allegedly the first indication he had had of the painting's whereabouts since it was taken in 1939.

In 2001, Cassirer petitioned Spain's then Minister of Education, Culture, and Sports for the paintings return, but this request was refused. When, in July 2003, the Minister of Culture again refused the request after being petitioned by five U.S. congressmen writing on Cassirer's behalf, he filed suit in the United States, seeking recovery of the painting and a variety of other remedies. Spain and the Thyssen-Bornemisza Collection Foundation, which runs the museum, moved to dismiss the action on the basis of the FSIA stating that the court lacked subject matter jurisdiction over the dispute and stating that the court lacked personal jurisdiction and that the Central District of California was not a proper venue for the lawsuit. The court focused on the FSIA—and the issue of whether the court should assert jurisdiction over the dispute under the "expropriation" or "takings" exception to it for cases involving property expropriated in violation of international law. The court concluded that the plaintiff had supported with jurisdictional discovery a "non-frivolous" claim under the expropriation exception to the FSIA so that the court did have subject matter jurisdiction over the case as to both defendants. The case is currently on appeal.

D. CONCLUSION

In conclusion, it is clear that efforts to restitute Nazi-looted artworks to their rightful owners are finally beginning to gain momentum. Governments across the world are slowly beginning to address the need to do something about Nazi-looted art and right historical wrongs. While it is unfortunate that it has taken many years, marked by international conferences and seminal cases, the world has now been awakened, and everyone on every side of the issue is starting in large and small ways to address this 60-year-old problem.

---

[93] 461 F. Supp. 2d 1157 (C.D.Cal. 2006).

CHAPTER 19

RESOLVING MATERIAL CULTURE DISPUTES: HUMAN RIGHTS, PROPERTY RIGHTS, AND CRIMES AGAINST HUMANITY

Robert K. Paterson

A. INTRODUCTION

Artworks stolen from victims of the Nazis, along with the material cultural heritage of many indigenous peoples removed during colonialism, have both been the subject of a significant literature in recent years.[1] Few writers, however, seem to have attempted to compare these two categories with each other. This may partly be explained by the scarcity of reported judicial decisions concerning claims for the return of indigenous material, in comparison to the relatively large number of cases brought to recover artworks stolen by the Nazi regime. This chapter will first endeavor to explore whether these two types of claims should be treated according to similar principles or whether they present differences that warrant contrasting approaches. It will then discuss appropriate strategies, besides litigation, for resolving disputes involving both types of claims.

B. THE AMERICAN CASES ON RECOVERY OF NAZI-ERA ART

Though claims by owners or their heirs seeking to recover Nazi-seized art have been brought before courts in several countries, American judges have decided by far the largest number of such cases.[2] The earliest example of these was *Menzel v. List*, where the Belgian owners of a Marc Chagall painting that had

[1] In the case of the 1933 to 1945 period in Europe, see, for example, L.H. Nicholas, The Rape of Europa (1994); Hector Feliciano, The Lost Museum: The Nazi Conspiracy to Steal the World's Greatest Works of Art (1997); Jonathan Petropoulos, Art as Politics in the Third Reich (1996); Elizabeth Simpson, The Spoils of War: World War II and its Aftermath (1997). In respect of indigenous material culture during colonialism, see, for example, Tim Barringer & Tom Flynn, Colonialism and the Object: Empire, Material Culture and the Museum (1998); Cressida Fforde et al., The Dead and Their Possessions: Repatriation in Principle, Policy and Practice (2001); Nicholas Thomas, Entangled Objects: Exchange, Material Culture and Colonialism in the Pacific (1991).

[2] *See* Michael J. Bazyler, Holocaust Justice: The Battle for Restitution in America's Courts (2003); Michael J. Bazyler & Roger P. Alford, Holocaust Restitution: Perspectives on the Litigation and its Legacy (2006).

been seized by the German authorities in 1941 sued its subsequent purchaser in a replevin action.[3] The original owners had inadvertently discovered the whereabouts of their painting in 1962 when they saw a reproduction of it in an art book along with the name of its current possessor. Litigation ensued. Significantly, the trial court dismissed arguments that the Menzels had abandoned the painting, that its seizure by the Nazis be seen as war booty, and that the Act of State Doctrine precluded the court investigating the acts of the German government.[4] The dismissal of the latter argument was based on a finding that the seizure was not by a foreign sovereign government but by an organ of the Nazi party.[5] The seizure of the painting was, therefore, treated as being equivalent to outright theft, and the court dismissed a statue of limitations argument by the good-faith purchaser based on what is now known as the "Demand and Refusal" rule. Under this rule, the statute of limitations does not start to run until the true owner discovers the whereabouts of his or her stolen property, and the person in possession refuses the owner's demand for its return.[6]

It is the issue of whether Nazi-looted art claims, like the one in *Menzel,* are statute-barred that has been the preoccupation of American courts asked to resolve such cases. As Lawrence Kaye, who has been actively involved in bringing claims on behalf of victims of the Holocaust, points out, the "Demand and Refusal" rule favors protection of the true owners of stolen property over that of honest purchasers.[7] The rule has been followed in New York State—not just in respect of Holocaust-looted art but for stolen property in general. Given the stature of New York City as a world art market capital, the rule has significant scope for application in stolen art cases.

In most American jurisdictions, however, another approach to the application of limitation periods has developed. The so-called "Discovery Rule" replaces the owner-favoring "Demand and Refusal" rule with an approach that seeks to assess the relative equities of the parties.[8] In *Autocephalous Greek-Orthodox Church of Cypress et al. v. Goldberg, etc.*, a well-known case involving Byzantine antiquities looted from Cyprus, the U.S. Court of Appeals for the Seventh Circuit opined "[c]entral to . . . the discovery rule. . . . is the determination of the plaintiff's diligence in investigating the potential cause of action . . . if [the] plaintiff was not reasonably diligent in discovering fraud the statute will run from the time discovery ought to have been made."[9]

---

[3] Menzel v. List, 253 N.Y.S.2d 43 (1st Dep't 1964), 267 N.Y.S.2d 804 (Sup. Ct. N.Y. 1966), *modified on other grounds,* 279 N.Y.S.2d 608 (1st Dep't 1967), *modification rev'd,* 298 N.Y.S.2d 976 (1969).

[4] Menzel v. List, 267 N.Y.S.2d 804, 810–16 (Sup. Ct. N.Y. 1966).

[5] *Id.* at 815.

[6] For an outline of the rule, see Patty Gerstenblith, Art, Cultural Heritage and the Law: Cases and Materials 394–401(2004).

[7] Lawrence Kaye, *The Statute of Limitations in Art Recovery Cases: An Overview,* 1 IFAR J. 22 (1998).

[8] *See* Gerstenblith, *supra* note 6, at 401–13.

[9] Autocephalous Greek-Orthodox Church of Cyprus v. Goldberg & Feldman Fine Arts, Inc., 917 F.2d 278, 288 (7th Cir. 1990), *cert. denied,* 112 U.S. 377 (1991).

This test assesses the potential loss to each party if the stolen property is awarded to the other. It resembles another basis for denying a right to recover the possession of stolen property—the equitable doctrine of laches. *Guggenheim v. Lubell* involved an artwork stolen from the Guggenheim Museum in New York and purchased two years later.[10] When the museum located its painting in 1985 it brought an action against the purchasers. The court said that if the defendants could show a lack of diligence, on the owner's part, in seeking to discover the whereabouts of its lost work, the balance of equities might justify the art being awarded to the purchasers. The case illustrates that laches could be an important defense in New York State where the operation of the "Demand and Refusal" rule will often exclude a statute of limitations defense.

Despite some success in the courts, many of those concerned with the recovery and return of Holocaust artworks have pursued other venues besides courts to resolve their claims. At conferences and meetings around the world, a movement gained momentum that urged museums and other institutions to open their archives so that the provenance of objects could be examined and requests for restitution made in appropriate cases. These initiatives include the Vilnius Forum Declaration on Holocaust Era Looted Cultural Assets, issued at a conference of European states and non-governmental organizations in October 2000,[11] and the Principles on Nazi-Confiscated Art of the Washington Conference on Holocaust-Era Assets in 1998.[12]

C. NAZI-ERA ART AS THE PROCEEDS OF A CRIME AGAINST HUMANITY

Despite general agreement that artwork stolen by the Nazi regime was wrongfully taken from its owners, there has been relatively little support for the argument that once an object is proven as having been taken in that context, it must be returned regardless of the merits of a claim to its possession by a subsequent purchaser. This arose because all litigated claims have been dealt according to conventional legal remedies for the recovery of stolen property, remedies that do not allow for differentiation between various forms of theft. Another way of looking at such claims would be to regard the artworks involved as the proceeds of crimes against humanity and thus not properly amenable to defenses based on the merits of its retention by others.

A change in the legal principles governing claims for the recovery of property by victims of a crime against humanity would be consistent with ongoing dissatisfaction with the legal regimes applicable to such claims.[13] While this dissatisfaction sometimes applies to the relationship of buyers of stolen art

---

[10] Solomon R. Guggenheim Found. v. Lubell, 550 N.Y.S.2d 618 (App. Div. 1990), *aff'd*, 569 N.E.2d 426 (N.Y. 1991) (finding the defendant was prejudiced by the plaintiff's delay).

[11] International Forum on Holocaust-Era Looted Cultural Assets, Vilnius, Lithuania, Oct. 3–5, 2000.

[12] *Washington Conference Principles on Nazi-Confiscated Art* (Washington, DC, Dec. 3, 1998) (released in connection with the Washington Conference on Holocaust-Era Assets); *see also* Looted Cultural Property, Parliamentary Assembly of the Council of Europe, Resolution 1205, Nov. 4, 1999.

[13] *See* Steven A. Bibas, *The Case Against Statutes of Limitations for Stolen Art*, 103 YALE L.J. 2437 (1994).

to the victims of its theft in general, it is even more compelling in the instance of takings that are not instances of mere theft but a crime of much greater magnitude. Although there have been many efforts and suggestions concerning title claims by Holocaust victims, progress in securing the recovery of artworks has been relatively modest.[14] This suggests that a principle-based solution is not only appropriate, but also necessary.

Clearly the Holocaust represented a crime against humanity.[15] The Charter of the International Military Tribunal, which sat at Nuremberg, represented the first time such crimes were articulated in international law.[16] The Nuremberg Tribunal, however, made clear that it was describing acts that had long been seen as contrary to international law, and its findings merely represented a restatement of the law.[17] Crimes against humanity are included in the Statutes of the International Criminal Tribunal for the former Yugoslavia[18] and the International Criminal Court.[19] While the specific crimes included within the category of crimes against humanity refer to acts against persons (such as torture and deportation), any resultant loss of property to the victims of such crimes must be seen as a direct outcome associated with such crimes against the person. Seen in this way, the proceeds of crimes against humanity should not be (along with the crimes themselves) subject to such defenses as statutes of limitation, whose underlying policy goals (closure and stale evidence) are not properly applicable, given the gravity of the criminal acts committed in connection with the property stolen.[20]

Recognition of an exception to a statute of limitations defense in the case of theft associated with crimes against humanity articulates concerns regarding

---

[14] *See, e.g.,* Robert Schwartz, *The Limits of the Law: A Call for a New Attitude Toward Artwork Stolen During World War II*, 32 Colum. J.L. & Soc. Probs. 1 (1998); Kelly Diane Walton, *Leave No Stone Unturned: The Search for Art Stolen by the Nazis and the Legal Rules Governing Restitution of Stolen Art*, 9 Fordham Intell. Prop. Media & Ent. L.J. 549 (1999).

[15] *See* M. Cherif Bassiouni, Crimes Against Humanity in International Criminal Law (1999); Benjamin Ricci, Crimes Against Humanity: A Historical Perspective (2004).

[16] Charter of the International Military Tribunal (1945), *available at* http://www.law.umkc.edu/faculty/projects/ftrials/nuremberg/NurembergIndictments.html.

[17] *See* Judgment of the International Military Tribunal for the Trial of German Major War Criminals, *available at* http://www.nizkor.org/hweb/imt/tgmwc/judgment/.

[18] *See* Statute of the International Tribunal for the Prosecution of Persons Responsible for Serious Violations of International Humanitarian Law Committed in the Territory of the Former Yugoslavia since 1991, Article 5, U.N. Doc. S/25704 at 36, annex (1993) and S/25704/Add.1 (1993), adopted May 25,1993, UN. Doc. S.RES/827 (1993).

[19] *See* Rome Statute of the International Criminal Court, art. 5(1)(b) (2002), *available at* http://www.icc-cpi.int/library/about/officialjournal/Rome_Statute_120704-EN.pdf; *see also* Statute of the International Tribunal for Rwanda, art. 3, *available at* http://69.94.11.53/ENGLISH/basicdocs/statute.html. The United States informed the U.N. secretary-general on May 6, 2002, that it did not regard itself as having any legal obligations arising from its signature to the Rome Treaty on December 31, 2000. The United Nations has not removed the United States from the list of official signatories.

[20] *See* Convention of the Non-Applicability of Statutory Limitations to War Crimes and Crimes Against Humanity, G.A. Res. 2391, U.N. GAOR, 23d Sess., U.N. Doc. A/7218 (1968); *see also* Rome Statute, *supra* note 19, art. 29; European Convention on the Non-Applicability of Statutory Limitations to Crimes Against Humanity and War Crimes, E 7582, 13 I.L.M. 540 (Jan. 25, 1974).

the morally compelling nature of Holocaust art claims. It also represents a meaningful interpretation of national law that takes into account the current state of international law. The recognition of such a legal principle by national courts would depend on the law seen as applicable to a particular case. In Canada, for instance, customary international law is already seen as part of domestic law, so there is scope for such an approach.[21]

Canada was a major force in the establishment of the International Criminal Court. The provisions of the Rome Statute of the International Criminal Court have been enacted into Canadian law in the form of the Crimes Against Humanity and War Crimes Act ("the Act").[22] Under the Act it is an indictable offense to commit a crime against humanity outside Canada.[23] Furthermore, there are no limitation periods applicable to indictable offenses in Canada.[24] Canadian law also provides for the seizure of any property obtained outside Canada through the commission of what, according to Canadian law, is a crime against humanity. Returns are to be made to persons lawfully entitled to the property concerned.[25] Enforcement is still a major problem in connection with offenses of this nature. So far, Canada has focused on bringing individuals accused of war crimes to justice, but the legal framework is in place for the return of seized Nazi-era artworks that were earlier acquired in the context of crimes against humanity.[26]

---

[21] *See* Hugh M. Kindred et al., International Law Chiefly as Interpreted and Applied in Canada 165–68 (6th ed. 2000).

[22] S.C. 2000, ch. 24.

[23] *Id.* at §. 6. Section 4(3) of the Act defines a "crime against humanity" as meaning: murder, extermination, enslavement, deportation, imprisonment, torture, sexual violence, persecution or any other inhumane act or omission that is committed against any civilian population or any identifiable group and that, at the time and in the place of its commission, constitutes a crime against humanity according to customary international law or conventional international law or by virtue of its being criminal according to the general principles of law recognized by the community of nations, whether or not it constitutes a contravention of the law in force at the time and in the place of its commission.

[24] *See* Sanjeev S. Anand, *Should Parliament Enact Statutory Limitation Periods for Criminal Offences?*, 44 Crim. L.Q. 8 (2000). The only exception is for treason using force or violence.

[25] Criminal Code, R.S.C. 1985, ch. C-46, § 462.32(4.1)

[26] *See* Fifth Annual Report; Canada's Crimes Against Humanity and War Crimes Program, 2001–2002, http://www.cic.gc.ca/english/pub/war2002/section 04.html#d. In 2005, Canada acceded to the two protocols to the 1954 UNESCO Convention for the Protection of Cultural Property in the Event of Armed Conflict. Canada had ratified the convention itself in 1998. Section 36.1 of the Canadian Cultural Property Export and Import Act, R.S.C. 1985, ch. C-51, now makes it an offense for a Canadian citizen or resident to unlawfully remove cultural property (as that term is defined in Article 9(a) of the convention) from an occupied territory of a state party to the Second Protocol contrary to its laws (there are currently 42 parties to the Second Protocol, including Austria and Hungary). In these circumstances, the government of a state party can ask the attorney general of Canada to bring proceedings in Canada to obtain recovery and an order for the return of the property in question. No statutes of limitation apply to proceedings under Section 36.1 (see Section 36.1(10)). *See also* Criminal Code, R.S.C., 1985, ch. C-46, § 7(2.01).

D. SACRED INDIGENOUS MATERIAL CULTURE AS A HUMAN RIGHT

Like Holocaust claims involving cultural property, claims by indigenous peoples respecting material removed in colonial times presents challenging issues for conventional legal analysis.[27] Unlike Nazi-era claims, few indigenous claims have even been heard by domestic courts.[28] The principal reason, apart from a lack of financial resources, is probably the inability to uncover the actual circumstances surrounding the original acquisition of the cultural material involved. While the facts of certain removals are well known, such as the Benin bronzes taken from the territory of what is now Nigeria by the 1897 British Punitive Expedition, the vast majority are not.[29] The scope of such acquisitions was vast, in geographical, ethnic, and numerical scope. Many items were traded or gifted, while others were stolen, obtained by force, misunderstanding, or removed as part of the actions of early missionaries and others.[30] While some argue that the whole process of colonization by European powers represented a kind of genocide analogous to the Holocaust, the events involved are probably too varied and complex to really permit such a generalized evaluation.[31] It is the variety of situations through which indigenous cultural property was obtained that factually most distinguishes such cases from those that occurred as part of the Holocaust. That said, if the circumstances of any acquisition of indigenous cultural material can be shown to constitute a crime against humanity, then the victims of such takings or their descendants should have an unqualified right to the return of any cultural material involved.

Professor James Nafziger has said of the Native American Graves Protection and Repatriation Act (NAGPRA)[32] in the United States that NAGPRA is, first and foremost, human rights legislation. It is *not* property rights legislation. Nor is it a legislative framework for balancing interests, although it was intended to operate within a collaborative framework that included such instruments as the Vermillion Accord.[33] Congress clearly intended the legislation to repair past wrongs and ensure present and future rights. As such, it must be seen and interpreted against the backdrop of modern human rights legislation at both domestic and international levels. NAGPRA also conforms with a general theory for repatriation. Accordingly, it can be fairly described as an instrument of decolonization, self-determination and reparation; as a vindication of Native American religious and other cultural freedoms; as a means of enhancing cultural revival and transmission of cultural knowledge among tribes and Native Hawaiian groups; as a contributor to self-identity and community solidarity; and

---

[27] *See* Catherine E. Bell, *Limitations, Legislation and Domestic Repatriation*, Special Issue UBC L. Rev. 149 (1995).

[28] *See, e.g.*, Mohawk Bands v. Glenbow Alberta Institute, 3 C.N. L.R. 70 (Alta. Q.B. 1988).

[29] *See* Jeanette Greenfield, The Return of Cultural Treasures 141–48 (1989).

[30] *See* Douglas Cole, Captured Heritage: The Scramble for Northwest Coast Artifacts (1985).

[31] This is the conclusion of David B. Macdonald, *Daring to Compare: The Debate About a Maori "Holocaust" in New Zealand*, 5 J. Genocidal Res. 383 (2003).

[32] 25 U.S.C. §§ 3001–3013 (2000).

[33] Vermillion Accord on Human Remains, The World Archaeological Inter-Congress, Jan.y 15, 2006, http://www.wac.uct.ac.za/archive/content/vermillion.accord.html.

as a means for restoring Native American control over pertinent culture.[34]

The enormous advantage of a NAGPRA-like approach to claims by indigenous peoples is that the entitlement of claimants turns less on the provenance of particular material and more on the nature of the objects themselves. While Anglo-American common law has never recognized different categories of personal property based on their cultural significance, some legal systems recognize a separate category of *res sacrae* that because of its sacred or religious character is not subject to the ordinary rules affecting personality.[35] Thus, the Quebec Court of Appeal set aside sales of Roman Catholic 18th-century silver liturgical objects by a parish priest on the basis of their being sacred in character and not alienable without compliance with canon law.[36]

Many indigenous claims involve objects lost before the 1930s. Litigation may therefore raise the same issues concerning the application of statutes of limitation as arise with Nazi-era claims. This issue has been partly addressed in Canada and the United States where courts have suggested that it may be inappropriate to apply statutes of limitation to certain indigenous claims in view of factors such as the fiduciary obligation of the government or the equivocality of limitation statutes themselves.[37] NAGPRA overrides limitations' problems, but it does not address indigenous cultural material outside the United States or that found in private collections. Neither the 1970 UNESCO Convention on the Means of Prohibiting and Preventing the Illicit Import, Export and Transfer of Ownership of Cultural Property nor the UNIDROIT Convention on Stolen or Illegally Exported Cultural Objects applies retroactively to require the return of objects illegally removed before these treaties were in effect.[38] This means most indigenous claims will either be statute-barred or unprovable due to the passage of time, the death of witnesses, and other factual impediments.

Institutionalized and *ad hoc* modes to resolve indigenous material culture claims show a similar pattern respecting which objects are seen as most susceptible to repatriation. Both NAGPRA and the Canadian Task Force Report on Museums and First Peoples present a hierarchical approach that places ancestral remains and sacred objects as the most qualified for return and, conversely, places utilitarian and domestic objects as less qualified.[39] This suggests that there may be an emerging standard that supports the right of

---

[34] James A.R. Nafziger, *Protection and Repatriation of Indigenous Cultural Heritage in the United States*, ch. 2 in this volume.

[35] *See* Kurt Siehr, *International Art Trade and the Law*, 243 Recueil des Cours 64, 64–66 (1993).

[36] *See* Benoit Pelletier, *The Case of the Treasures of L'Ange Gardien: An Overview*, 2 Int'l J. Cultural Prop. 371 (1993).

[37] *See* Oneida, County of v. Oneida Indian Nation, 470 U.S. 226 (1985); Bell, *supra* note 27.

[38] UNESCO Convention on the Means of Prohibiting and Preventing the Illicit Import, Export and Transfer of Ownership of Cultural Property, 10 I.L.M. 189 (1971); 1995 UNIDROIT Convention on Stolen and Illegally Exported Cultural Objects, June 24, 1995, *available at* http://www.unidroit.org/english/conventions/1995culturalproperty/1995cultural property-e.htm.

[39] *See* 25 U.S.C. §§ 3001–3013 (1988); Task Force on Museums and First Peoples, Turning the Page: Forging New Partnerships Between Museums and First Peoples 8–9 (2d ed. 1992).

indigenous peoples to the return of, at least, certain important religious or sacred material. These developments can also be seen as receiving some level of international support in the form of the new U.N. Declaration on the Rights of Indigenous Peoples ("U.N. Declaration"). Article 12 of the U.N. Declaration states as follows:

> 1. Indigenous peoples have the right to manifest, practice, develop and teach their spiritual and religious traditions, customs and ceremonies; the right to maintain, protect, and have access in privacy to their religious and cultural sites; the right to the use and control of their ceremonial objects; and the right to the repatriation of their human remains.
>
> 2. States shall seek to enable the access and/or repatriation of ceremonial objects and human remains in their possession through fair, transparent and effective mechanisms developed in conjunction with indigenous peoples concerned.[40]

The U.N. Declaration is still only evidence of the present state of international law on this subject, but it continues to receive support from the practice of museums in several countries. Recently, the Association of Art Museum Directors (AAMD) in the United States issued a report of its Task Force on the Acquisition and Stewardship of Sacred Objects.[41] The report notes that the most commonly recognized works of art considered to be sacred are those deriving from indigenous cultures. It makes specific reference to First Nation cultures in Canada but notes that very few national or international laws dictate special consideration for such works. The report does not address the question of repatriation directly but mainly concerns itself with raising the consciousness amongst its membership of the special character of sacred cultural material and the complexity of the issues such material presents for museums in terms of acquisition, handling and display.

Another informing aspect of the distinction between Nazi-era and indigenous claims is that the latter involves material that is culturally affiliated with indigenous peoples themselves, whereas the art appropriated by the Nazis and their agents comprised a variety of property, most of which had no specific cultural connection to its owners. In view of this distinction, it seems appropriate that recovery of the latter be based not on the character of the property stolen, but on the actions of the Nazis in taking it. Entitlement to indigenous cultural property, on the other hand, should not depend on the vagaries of the various levels of egregiousness surrounding its acquisition (unless crimes against humanity can be established) but on a human right to claim it based on the

[40] Declaration on the Rights of Indigenous Peoples, G.A. Res. 61/295, U.N. Doc. A/61/PV.107 (Sept. 13, 2007) (Canada and the United States dissented in the vote adopting the resolution); *see* Dean B. Suagee, *Human Rights and the Cultural Heritage of Indian Tribes in the United States*, 8 Int'l J. Cultural Prop. 48, 67 (1999).

[41] *See* Report on the Stewardship and Acquisition of Sacred Objects of the Association of Art Museum Directors (June 1, 2006), http.//www.aamd.org/papers/documents/SacredObjectsReleaseand GuidelinesCombined8.9.06.dated.pdf; Hugh Eakin, *Museums Set Guidelines for Use of Sacred Objects*, N.Y. Times, Aug. 10, 2006, at B3.

religious or cultural significance of the material to the indigenous claimant.

A further difference between Nazi-era and indigenous claims is that while the former are often brought against both institutions and private individuals, the latter almost always concern claims against museums or other public institutions. This is both a result of differences in the character of the objects whose return is sought and the different laws applicable to these two categories. As already mentioned, NAGPRA does not apply to private collectors, and the state of indigenous title law makes claims against them unpredictable at best. Even if one bases repatriation of indigenous cultural material on a human rights argument, it may be harder to make that argument against private parties who, at least in the first instance, are not subject to the same international human rights norms as are states and state instrumentalities.[42] This is not to suggest, however, that the existence of indigenous cultural rights against governments might not have a "chilling effect" on the private collecting of sacred and religious indigenous objects, much as gaps in provenance have affected the private collecting of antiquities.[43]

E. ALTERNATIVE DISPUTE RESOLUTION IN MATERIAL CULTURE DISPUTES

The legal challenges involving the principles that should govern Nazi-era and indigenous claims carry forward into a consideration of the most effective means for resolving such disputes. Both types of claims challenge the ingenuity of courts in adequately responding to the problems of evidence, ethics, and morality that typify these sorts of disputes. Many reported decisions display the awkwardness of applying generic legal rules about property to the unique and serious ethical, moral, and cultural dimensions typically involved. This perception has led many to propose alternatives to litigation in these cases, such as mediation or arbitration.[44]

Although strategies such as treaties and litigation in domestic courts have achieved some success in addressing certain cultural property issues, many experts advocate the need for other innovative types of approaches.[45] To an extent, this anxiety arises from the unique nature of cultural objects and the special feelings they evoke because of their symbolic, religious, historical, and aesthetic qualities. Few laws seem to respond to these sorts of considerations because they often appear to be too elusive to permit of the precise definition lawyers usually seek.

---

[42] *See* Lyal S. Sunga, Individual Responsibility in International Law for Serious Human Rights Violations (1992).

[43] *See* Fred R. Myers, The Empire of Things: Regimes of Value and Material Culture (2001). This has achieved a degree of formal legal recognition in the United Kingdom under the provisions of the Dealing in Cultural Objects (Offences) Act, 2003, ch. 27, http://www.opsi.gov.uk/acts/acts2003/ukpga_20030027_en_1, which criminalizes dealing in "tainted" objects (which includes objects illegally excavated in the United Kingdom or abroad).

[44] *See, e.g.*, Resolution of Cultural Property Disputes: Papers Emanating from the Seventh Permanent Court of Arbitration International Law Seminar, May 23, 2003 vol. 7 (Permanent Court of Arbitration/Peace Palace Papers 2004); Barbara T. Hoffman, Art and Cultural Heritage: Law, Policy and Practice 463–87 (2006).

[45] *See* Resolution of Cultural Property Disputes, *supra* note 44, at 265, 302.

Since 2004, the Committee on Cultural Heritage Law of the International Law Association (ILA) has been working to prepare a set of Principles for Cooperation in the Mutual Protection and Transfer of Cultural Material ("the ILA Principles"), which were adopted at the June 2006 meeting of the International Law Association in Toronto, Canada.[46] The development of the ILA Principles was based on a desire to lessen the level of acrimony that can often surround disputes concerning cultural material. For example, the ILA Principles promote the exploration of alternatives to the outright return of objects, such as long-term loans, exchanges of objects, and the making of copies.

A 2001 agreement between the United States and Italy, which was renewed in January 2006, imposes import restrictions on certain categories of Italian archaeological material.[47] Like other similar agreements to which the United States is a party, the 2001 Agreement obliges the United States to return material improperly exported from Italy in certain specified circumstances.[48] The Italian agreement, however, in a break with precedent, also explores additional options to the outright return of cultural material. The agreement commits both sides to use their best efforts to facilitate contact between their respective museums and institutions and, in particular, increase loans of Italian cultural material to American museums.[49] Italy also agrees to continue to devote more funding to guard its archaeological sites and museums and develop tax incentives for the private support of legitimate archaeological excavation.[50]

This expanded version for a type of agreement more usually concerned solely with the recognition and enforcement of foreign cultural property export controls was followed in 2006 by another high-profile agreement between Italy and the Metropolitan Museum of Art in New York.[51] The Metropolitan Museum agreement focused on the return of several archaeological objects from the museum's collection, including an esteemed fifth-century krater painted by Euphronios. Notably, however, the krater is to remain on loan at the museum

---

[46] Principles for Cooperation in the Mutual Protection and Transfer of Cultural Material, Adopted at the 72d Conference of the International Law Association, held in Toronto, Canada, June 4–8, 2006, *reprinted in* 13 INT'L J. CULTURAL PROP. 409 (2006). *See also* Robert K. Paterson, *The "Caring and Sharing" Alternative: Recent Progress in the International Law Association to Develop Draft Cultural Material Principles*, 12 INT'L J. CULTURAL PROP. 62 (2005).

[47] Agreement Between the Government of the United States of America and the Government of the Republic of Italy Concerning the Imposition of Import Restrictions on Categories of Archaeological Material Representing the Pre-Classical, Classical and Imperial Roman Periods of Italy, Jan. 19, 2001, 40 I.L.M. 1031 (2001) [hereinafter Agreement]. The 2001 agreement has been extended until January 19, 2011 and Article II replaced by the Extension and Amendment to the Agreement between the Government of the United States of America and the Government of the Republic of Italy concerning the Imposition of Import Restrictions on Categories of Archaeological Material Representing the Pre-Classical, Classical and Imperial Roman Periods of Italy (2006), *available at* http://culturalheritage.state.gov/it06agr.html.

[48] *Id.* at art. 1. For the status of import restrictions under the Convention on Cultural Property Implementation Act, see http://exchanges.state.gov/culprop/chart.html.

[49] Agreement, *supra* note 47, at art. II(E)(1).

[50] *Id.* at art. II(B).

[51] *See* Elisabetta Provoledo, *Italy and U.S. Sign Antiquities Accord*, N.Y. TIMES, Feb. 22, 2006.

until 2008, and other loans to the United States are to be arranged from Italy, including items discovered during excavations financed by the Metropolitan Museum or restored by its conservation personnel.

Many recent agreements to return objects acquired under questionable circumstances have required recipients to fund the making of copies of disputed artifacts. When the Stockholm Ethnographic Museum agreed to return a totem pole originally from British Columbia, Canada, the requesting Haisla First Nation agreed to make a replica for the Swedish museum to exhibit in place of the original. Such a solution means that a historical loss is not repeated.[52]

The ILA Principles are designed to be a voluntary basis for parties exploring ways to resolve requests for the return of cultural material in a broad range of situations. Thus, they suggest a sort of minimum standard to which parties can agree in advance. For instance, requests should be in writing, with a detailed description of any cultural material whose return is requested, together with reasons substantiating the request.[53] Recipients of such requests are required to respond in writing with reasons for agreeing or disagreeing to the request, along with a proposed timetable for implementation or further negotiations.[54]

Given the controversy surrounding the suitability of litigation in cases involving the return of cultural material, the ILA Principles contain a separate provision on dispute settlement that advocates the use of some form of alternate dispute mechanism (such as mediation or arbitration) over recourse to national courts.[55] Many museums and other institutions have already established internal repatriation committees to deal with requests for the return of cultural material.[56] These may offer cost savings, privacy, and more flexibility than the alternative of litigation. For instance, agreed-upon ethical and moral standards can be applied to cases where conventional legal principles may be seen to fall short of the parties' needs and expectations.

The ILA Principles do not, however, go so far as to eliminate litigation as an option because it can still sometimes expeditiously and imaginatively resolve difficult cases. One such instance is when a New Zealand court granted probate in respect of the estate of a long-deceased Maori warrior whose preserved tattooed head (toi moko) had been consigned for auction in London.[57] The issuance of letters of administration to an executor facilitated the withdrawal of the head from sale and its return to New Zealand for burial in accordance with indigenous Maori custom.[58]

---

[52] *See* Derah Hansen, *An Emotional Homecoming*, VANCOUVER SUN, Apr. 27, 2006, at B3.

[53] Principles for Cooperation in the Mutual Protection and Transfer of Cultural Material, *supra* note 46, at Principle 2: Requests and Responses to Requests for the Transfer of Cultural Material.

[54] *Id.*

[55] *Id.* at Principle 9: Dispute Settlement.

[56] *See, e.g.*, The Repatriation Guidelines of the Museum of Anthropology at the University of British Columbia, http://www.moa.ubc.ca/pdf/Repatriation_guidelines.pdf.

[57] Re Estate of Tupuna Maori, No. P580/88 (High Court of New Zealand) (unreported case 1988).

[58] Patrick J. O'Keefe, *Maoris Claim Head*, 1 INT'L J. CULTURAL PROP. 393 (1992).

There now seems to be an increased readiness among parties to disputes involving cultural material to experiment with new solutions. The ILA Principles, therefore, seem timely insofar as they confirm established practice and build upon it to develop standards that seek to facilitate non-confrontational outcomes. In a sense, the ILA Principles may even represent evidence of emerging international minimum standards concerning the treatment of certain cultural material and supplement the work of other international institutions such as UNESCO, UNIDROIT, and non-governmental bodies including the International Council of Museums and the World Archaeological Congress. It now seems appropriate to many in the field of international cultural heritage law to move beyond choices that involve either appeasement or intransigence and to attempt enlightened and innovative solutions to these difficult issues.

F. INSTITUTIONAL MEANS TO RESOLVE MATERIAL CULTURAL DISPUTES

Two contemporary examples of institutionalized alternatives to litigation in seeking resolution of repatriation disputes, involving Nazi-era property thefts and indigenous cultural material, respectively, are the Spoliation Advisory Panel in the United Kingdom and the Native American Graves Protection and Repatriation Review Committee in the United States. The following is a brief outline of how these two procedures operate.

1. The U.K. Spoliation Advisory Panel[59]

In February 2000, the United Kingdom established a Spoliation Advisory Panel ("the Panel") to assist both claimants and institutions respecting property lost during the Nazi era and now held in national institutions. The Panel is chaired by a retired Lord Justice of Appeal, the Right Honorable Sir David Hirst, and is intended to provide an alternative to litigation that is not a judicial body. So far the Panel has issued reports on five claims.

The most recent of these claims involved four drawings now in the possession of the British Museum.[60] It was brought on behalf of the heirs of Dr. Arthur Feldmann who had lost the drawings in March 1939 when the Gestapo seized his collection from his villa in Brno, Czechoslovakia. The British Museum subsequently acquired the drawings at an auction in England in 1946, as well as through bequest. Initially the Commission for Looted Art in Europe presented the claim in 2002 on behalf of the claimants. The U.K. attorney general then sought, with the commission intervening with leave of the English court, a decision from the courts on whether the British Museum could lawfully return an object in its collection if it considered itself to be morally obliged to make such a return. The court answered in the negative, based on the language of the British Museum Act, which prohibits the museum disposing of objects in its collections, as being too unequivocal to permit an implied exception.[61]

---

[59] *See* Department for Culture Media and Sport: Spoliation Advisory Panel, http://www.culture.gov.uk/what_w_do/Cultural_property/sap.htm.

[60] *See* Report of the Spoliation Advisory Panel in Respect of Four Drawings Now in the Possession of the British Museum (The Stationery Office 2006), http://www.culture.gov.uk/Reference_library/Publications/archive_2006/sapreport_hc1052.htm.

[61] British Museum Act 1963 (U.K.), 1963, c. 24, as amended by Museum and Galleries

The claimants then revoked the authority of the commission and proceeded to make a joint submission, along with the British Museum, to the Panel. The submission proposed a "preferred solution" that the drawings remain at the British Museum and the claimants receive the full value of the drawings by way of compensation. The Panel's Terms of Reference oblige it to, *inter alia*,

> (c) examine and determine the circumstances in which the claimant was deprived of the object, whether by theft, forced sale, sale at an undervalue, or otherwise; . . .
>
> (e) give due weight to the moral strength of the claimant's case; . . .
>
> (g) consider whether any moral obligation rests on the institution, taking into account in particular the circumstances of its acquisition of the object, and its knowledge at that juncture of the object's provenance;
>
> (h) take account of any relevant statutory provisions, including stipulations as to the institution's powers and duties, including any restrictions on its powers of disposal.[62]

The Panel stated that its duty to give weight to moral considerations was founded on the terms of two international instruments: the 1943 Inter-Allied Declaration Against Acts of Dispossession Committed in Territories Under Enemy Occupation or Control[63] and the 1998 Principles with Respect to Nazi-Confiscated Art Issued by the Washington Conference on Holocaust-Era Assets.[64] It went on to find that, since the parties had not sought a return of the drawings by the British Museum, the only two possible remedies the Panel could recommend were compensation or an *ex gratia* payment. The former was seen as inappropriate given the lack of clear legal entitlement to the drawings on the part of the claimants but that on the strength of their moral claim an *ex gratia* payment of £175,0000 was considered to be appropriate.

Other Panel decisions have shown a consistent and compatible approach to spoliation cases. In respect of a painting by Jan Griffier the Elder, that the claimant contended had been lost by his mother during the war, compensation was sought instead of physical possession of the painting.[65] The Panel examined

---

Act 1992 (U.K.) 1992, ch. 44, s. 11(2), S ch. 8, pt. 1, s. 5(9); *see* Attorney-General v. Trustees of the British Museum [2005] 3 W.L.R. 396 (Ch.).

[62] *See* Spoliation Advisory Panel Constitution and Terms of Reference, para. 7, http://www.culture.gov.uk/NR/rdonlyres/9F0B7A06-16C4-4CBD-B52C-DCDC6805098B/0/SAPConstitutionandTermsofReferenceApril07.pdf.

[63] Inter-Allied Declaration against Acts of Dispossession committed in Territories under Enemy Occupation or Control, http://www.lootedartcommission.com/inter_allied_declaration.

[64] Washington Conference Principles on Nazi-Confiscated Art, endorsed by the Washington Conference on Holocaust-Era Assets (Washington, DC, Dec. 3, 1998), http://www.lootedartcommission.com/Washington-principles.

[65] *See* Report of the Spoliation Advisory Panel in Respect of a Painting Now in the Possession of the Tate Gallery (The Stationery Office 2001), http://www.culture.gov.uk/Reference_library/Publications/archive_2001/sapreport_hc111.htm.

issues of title and limitation periods and concluded that any claim against the Tate Gallery was now statute-barred under English law. Considering the level of diligence on the part of the Tate Gallery surrounding its acquisition of the painting, the Panel recommended an *ex gratia* payment to the claimant of £125,000, together with a recommendation that the Tate Gallery display alongside the picture an account of its history and provenance during and since the Nazi era, with special reference to the interest of the claimant and his family.

In a claim involving a Chardin still-life in the possession of the Glasgow City Council as part of the Burrell Collection, the claimants contended that they had lost possession of the picture in 1936 as a result of a forced sale.[66] The council argued the Panel should recommend an *ex gratia* payment. The Panel was informed, however, that the authenticity of the painting was seriously in question, and since its owners had earlier received what, in retrospect, seemed a fair price when it was sold at auction, the Panel recommended restitution of the painting to the claimants.

Another Panel report dealt with a 12th-century manuscript in the possession of the British Library.[67] Conflicting evidence was presented to the Panel about the provenance of the manuscript, but the Panel concluded it had been looted in Italy between 1943 and the time of its acquisition by a British citizen from a Naples bookseller in 1944. The British Museum acquired the object in 1947, and it was transferred to the British Library in 1973. Since the Panel concluded the manuscript had been spoliated during the 1933–1945 period it found the claim was within its jurisdiction. The Panel then concluded the manuscript should be returned to Benevento Cathedral in Italy. Unfortunately for the Panel, English law prohibited the British Library from making such a return. It recommended that legislation be introduced to allow the deaccessioning of Nazi-spoliated objects. This would still not necessarily permit the Benevento manuscript to be returned as it may have been taken by a British soldier during the occupation of Benevento by the Allies after October 1943. In view of the Panel's recommendations, however, it has been suggested that an exception be legislated to allow the return of this particular item. In the meantime, based on the Panel's recommendations, negotiations are under way to allow the transfer of the manuscript by way of a loan to the Biblioteca Nazionale in Naples.

The Panel's reports illustrate a level of flexibility surrounding the resolution of Nazi-era claims that cannot be achieved through litigation. Through its ability to take into account the moral aspects of claims brought before it, the Panel is able to temper the unequivocality of strictly legal options. The Panel is also not bound by the ordinary rules of the law of evidence so that it can

---

[66] *See* REPORT OF THE SPOLIATION ADVISORY PANEL IN RESPECT OF A PAINTING NOW IN THE POSSESSION OF GLASGOW CITY COUNCIL (The Stationery Office 2004), http://www.culture.gov.uk/Reference_library/Publications/archive_2004/report_spa.htm.

[67] *See* REPORT OF THE SPOLIATION ADVISORY PANEL IN RESPECT OF A 12TH CENTURY MANUSCRIPT NOW IN THE POSSESSION OF THE BRITISH LIBRARY (The Stationery Office 2005), http://www.culture.gov.uk/Reference_library/Publications/archive_2005/rpt_spoliation_advisory_panel.htm.

consider facts that a court might not be able to access. In the claim concerning a painting in the possession of the Glasgow City Council, the Panel supported the claimants wish to remain anonymous (basing this decision on Article 8 of the European Convention on Human Rights).[68] The Panel has also been ready to consider various instruments and codes even though they may not be legally binding in the United Kingdom, such as when the British Library Panel considered principles developed by the National Museum Directors' Conference. The terms of reference for the Panel also explicitly suggest several forms of recommended relief for resolving claims besides outright restitution. These include the ability to recommend *ex gratia* payments and the enactment of legislation to alter the legal powers and duties of institutions.

2. The Native American Graves Protection and Repatriation Review Committee

Any party to a dispute over a request for the return of certain American Indian or Native Hawaiian cultural material or human remains from an American museum or U.S. federal agency can request the Native American Graves Protection and Repatriation Review Committee ("the Committee") to facilitate the resolution of the dispute.[69] Apart from dispute resolution, the Committee also assists in defining ambiguities surrounding the NAGPRA itself and facilitating draft repatriation strategies to avoid disputes arising in the first place. The Committee is comprised of seven members; three nominees from indigenous communities themselves, three nominees of museums and scientific organizations, and one person chosen by the other six. If the Committee agrees to hear a request, it will peruse written documentation and may also hear from the parties. Committee recommendations are non-binding and made to the secretary of the interior.

During its approximately 16-year lifespan, the Committee has met over 25 times and wrestled with many complex issues, including culturally unidentifiable remains and their reburial, the protection of sacred tribal information, and repatriations to federally unrecognized tribes. The recent work of the Committee has focused on dispute avoidance through the development of clearer definitions and principles. This flexible approach has meant that the Committee has been able to effectively respond to the sorts of problems that are unique to indigenous repatriation—such as the contamination of remains and the nature of sacred objects—as well as increase the overall effectiveness of NAGPRA itself and relieve the perception that it presents a rigid and overly legalistic approach to repatriation issues affecting American indigenous peoples.[70]

Determining whether an object is a "sacred object" is a perennial difficulty under NAGPRA. Often the answer is reached after consultation and

[68] European Convention on the Protection of Human Rights and Fundamental Freedoms, Nov. 4, 1950, E.T.S. No. 5, 213 U.N.T.S. 221.

[69] 25 U.S.C. § 3006(c)(4) (2000); *see* C. Timothy McKeown & Sherry Hutt, *In the Smaller Scope of Conscience: The Native American Graves Protection & Repatriation Act Twelve Years After*, 21 UCLA J. Envtl. L. & Pol'y 153, 202–05 (2002–2003).

[70] *See* Nafziger, *supra* note 34.

collaboration between native groups and museums and federal agencies. "Sacred objects" are defined in NAGPRA as "specific ceremonial objects which are needed by traditional Native American religious leaders for the practice of traditional Native American religions by their present day adherents."[71] Who is a traditional religious leader is determined according to a person's recognition by members of an Indian tribe or Native Hawaiian organization as being responsible for cultural duties relating to the ceremonial or religious traditions of the tribe or organization.[72] Thus, in one case, the Committee found that a Hawaiian carved wooden figure was a "sacred object" and recommended its repatriation to Native Hawaiian organizations.[73] The museum responded to this recommendation by filing court proceedings. Subsequently the parties settled their dispute by agreement that the Office of Hawaiian Affairs pay $125,000 to the Providence Museum.[74]

The role and functioning of the Committee continues to provoke controversy and debate. This probably indicates it is doing its job. Many see NAGPRA as involving the repatriation process in radically different ways of understanding culture, history, and ownership.[75] These challenges may be novel and confusing to some, but they also reveal that the role of the Committee is central to the resolution of indigenous American claims for the return of their cultural heritage and it continues to exhibit an ability to develop more flexible solutions than those likely to emerge from litigation.

G. THE FUTURE OF DISPUTE RESOLUTION INVOLVING NAZI-ERA AND INDIGENOUS RESTITUTION CLAIMS

Even as the state of international and national law relating to these sorts of cultural material claims continues to develop greater certainty, there seems to be a consensus that the courtroom is usually not the best place for them to be resolved. Alternative forms of dispute resolution, including institutional (as in the case of NAGPRA and the Panel) or *ad hoc* procedures agreed to between the parties themselves, are increasingly producing realistic and meaningful solutions to what often at first seem to be intractable problems.

The ILA Principles represent the latest attempt at comprehensive guidelines for parties to disputes concerning cultural material. They are not intended to be definitive since the nuances of such cases defy uniform approaches. Not all indigenous communities want or can afford to even initiate claims. It is very unlikely the process of restitution will ever reach its conclusion. The practicalities are that museum collections of indigenous objects will likely continue to exist, and long-lost Holocaust-era art objects will continue to be

---

[71] 25 U.S.C. § 3001(3)(c) (2000).

[72] *See* 43 C.F.R. § 10.2(d)(3).

[73] *See* NAGPRA Review Committee Advisory Findings and Recommendations Regarding a Carved Wooden Figure from the Hawaiian Islands, 62 Fed. Reg. 23, 794–95 (May 1, 1997).

[74] *See* Susan Kreifels, *Hawaiian Spear-Rest Expected Home: An OHA Representative Says a Compromise Will be Worked Out*, HONOLULU STAR-BULL., Mar. 19, 1998.

[75] *See* Robert H. McLaughlin, *The American Archaeological Record: Authority to Dig, Power to Interpret*, 7 INT'L J. CULTURAL PROP. 342 (1998).

discovered. What is important about the ILA Principles is that they nurture the process of negotiating returns by focusing attention on what needs to accompany it—such as the making of inventories, the existence of protocols for the making and receipt of requests, and the notification of newly found material.

H. CONCLUSION

Alongside the evolution of new dispute resolution mechanisms, the norms applicable to the resolution of particularly challenging claims will continue to be refined. In this chapter, I suggest that in at least two instances (indigenous cultural material of a sacred or religious character and property stolen by the Nazi regime as part of the Holocaust) a consensus is emerging about the principles of entitlement. The ordinary rules pertaining to the right to personal property sometimes appear as compromised. In the case of indigenous sacred cultural material, this compromise forms part of the human rights of the peoples themselves. In the case of the property of Jews and others, appropriated by the Nazi regime, a right to restitution should now be seen as premised on the commission of a crime against humanity.

CHAPTER 20
USING UNIDROIT TO AVOID CULTURAL HERITAGE DISPUTES: LIMITATION PERIODS

Patrick O'Keefe

In the year 2000, the minister for the arts in the United Kingdom established an Advisory Panel on Illicit Trade ("the Panel"). Its terms of reference included the following: "To consider how most effectively, both through legislative and non-legislative means, the UK can play its part in preventing and prohibiting the illicit trade, and to advise the government accordingly."[1]

In its report[2] of December 2000, the Panel advised that the United Kingdom should accede to the UNESCO Convention on the Means of Prohibiting and Preventing the Illicit Import, Export and Transfer of Ownership of Cultural Property 1970 ("UNESCO Convention") and against accession to the UNIDROIT Convention on Stolen or Illegally Exported Cultural Objects 1995 ("UNIDROIT Convention").[3] The British government accepted the Panel's advice, and the United Kingdom became party to the UNESCO Convention in 2002. Interestingly, the Culture, Media, and Sport Committee of the House of Commons had recommended exactly the opposite a short time before the publication of the Advisory Panel on Illicit Trade report.[4]

The Panel saw the greatest barrier to adoption of the UNIDROIT Convention as being the provisions on limitation periods, that is, the time within which a legal action must be commenced. Since limitation periods are not addressed

---

[1] Department for Culture, Media, and Sport, Report of Advisory Panel on Illicit Trade, 2 (2000), http://www.culture.gov.uk/NR/rdonlyres/2BF7F816-AA1A-41BC-993F-1161F7E3A42A/0/ Report_AdPanel_Illicit_Trade.pdf.

[2] Department for Culture, Media, and Sport, Report of Advisory Panel on Illicit Trade (2000), http://www.culture.gov.uk/NR/rdonlyres/2BF7F816-AA1A-41BC-993F-1161F7E3A42A/0/ Report_AdPanel_Illicit_Trade.pdf.

[3] UNESCO Convention on the Means of Prohibiting and Preventing the Illegal Import, Export and Transfer of Ownership of Cultural Property (Nov. 14, 1970), 823 U.N.T.S. 231, 10 I.L.M. 289; 1995 UNIDROIT Convention on Stolen and Illegally Exported Cultural Objects, June 24, 1995, *available at* http://www.unidroit.org/english/conventions/1995culturalproperty/1995culturalproperty-e.htm.

[4] Department of Culture, Media, and Sport Committee, *Seventh Report: Cultural Property: Return and Illicit Trade: Volume I* (2000), http://www.parliament.the-stationeryoffice.com/pa/cm199900/cmselect/cmcumeds/371/37109.htm.

in the UNESCO Convention, this results in the continued application of normal national rules. However, when UNIDROIT was being drafted, limitation periods proved a most difficult issue, and the final provisions are the work of long and complex negotiations. The House of Commons Committee had said of these limitation periods, "It is appropriate that special limitation periods should apply to cultural property to reflect the cultural and personal importance of its ownership and the possibilities of unique identification."[5]

UNIDROIT has the capacity to play a significant role in the avoidance and resolution of cultural heritage disputes. It came into force on July 1, 1998. As of September 2006, there were 27 states party to the UNIDROIT Convention, including Argentina, China, Cyprus, Finland, Hungary, Italy, Norway, Portugal, and Spain. Its widespread adoption would establish a uniform standard for dealing with issues of theft and illicit traffic worldwide. The fact that such a significant player in the art market as the United Kingdom is singling out limitation periods as the greatest barrier to adoption of the UNIDROIT Convention is disturbing.

A. THE UNIDROIT CONVENTION

A 1982 report[6] to UNESCO on national legal control of illicit traffic in cultural property recommended that UNESCO take up private law matters arising from such illegal activity with an international body specialized in that branch of law. UNIDROIT was requested by UNESCO to consider a convention to deal with these issues. The ultimate result was the UNIDROIT Convention.[7]

The UNIDROIT Convention consists of five chapters, two of which address limitation periods. Chapter 2 pertains to restitution of stolen cultural objects and contains the specific limitation rules relating to this situation. The third chapter deals with the return of illegally exported cultural objects and contains a less complex set of limitation periods applicable to this situation.

In general, the UNIDROIT Convention is not retroactive. This means that the aforementioned limitation periods will only come into play for transactions dating from July 1, 1998, at the very earliest. Specifically, that date was when the convention was entered into force in accordance with Article 12. At that time, six states were party.

The standard rule in international law is that a convention is not retroactive.[8] However, no simple formula exists to determine how this rule works in everyday practice, as there can be a number of states involved that all become party to the convention at different times. Consequently, the UNIDROIT Convention provides further clarification in Article 10. With respect to stolen cultural

[5] *Id.*

[6] Lyndel Prott & Patrick O'Keefe, *National Legal Control of Illicit Traffic in Cultural Property*, commissioned by UNESCO and discussed at a Consultation of Experts on Illicit Traffic, Paris, UNESCO Doc. CLT/83/WS/16 (1983), http://unesdoc.unesco.org/images/0005/000548/054854eo.pdf.

[7] *See supra* note 4.

[8] Vienna Convention on the Law of Treaties, art. 28 (May 23, 1969), 1155 U.N.T.S. 331.

objects, the state where the claim is brought must be party to the convention at the time of the theft. Moreover, the theft must have occurred within the territory of a contracting state after it became party, or the object must have been located in a contracting state after that state became party. In the first situation, the object must have been stolen after the entry into force of the convention for both states. It is irrelevant whether the object is located in a contracting state at the time the claim is made. Of course, if the object is not located in the state where the claim is brought, there could be problems in enforcing the judgment if the claim is successful. The second situation covers one where the object was stolen from the territory of a non-contracting state. A claim may be made for its recovery if it is located in a contracting state.[9]

With respect to illegally exported cultural objects, the UNDROIT Convention only applies if the object was illegally exported after both the claimant state and the state where the claim is made became party to the convention.[10]

B. LIMITATION PERIODS APPLYING TO STOLEN OBJECTS

The basic rule governing limitation periods states that "a claim for restitution shall be brought within a period of three years from the time when the claimant knew the location of the cultural object and the identity of the possessor." In any case, the claim must be made within 50 years from the time of the theft.[11] This raises issues both substantive and practical.

First, the practical problems. Three years is not very long for many claimants to make a decision to pursue legal remedies, particularly when the theft occurred many years ago. For example, the British Spoliation Advisory Panel[12] recently considered a claim against the British Library for return of a missal taken from a monastery in Benevento, Italy.[13] The library announced its acquisition of the missal in 1952. In September/October 1961, there was an exchange of correspondence between the abbot of the monastery and the assistant keeper of the Department of Manuscripts in the British Museum, the library then being part of the museum. However, nothing further occurred until 1997, 16 years later, when the Italian Institute of Culture made inquiries. Even then there was no claim made. From evidence given during the inquiry by the panel it seems that the existence of the manuscript within the monastery

---

[9] A more detailed analysis of Article 10(1)(b) can be found in LYNDEL PROTT, COMMENTARY ON THE UNIDROIT CONVENTION ON STOLEN AND ILLEGALLY EXPORTED CULTURAL OBJECTS 80–81 (1997).

[10] UNIDROIT Convention, *supra* note 3, art. 10(2).

[11] *Id.* art. 3(3).

[12] This was set up to consider claims from anyone (or their heirs) who lost possession of a cultural object during the Nazi era (1933–1945) where the object is in the possession of a U.K. national collection or another U.K. museum or gallery established for the public benefit. The advisory panel advises the parties what is an appropriate action in response to the claim.

[13] Department for Culture, Media and Sport, *Report of the Spoliation Advisory Panel in Respect of a 12th Century Manuscript Now in the Possession of the British Library* (2005), http://www.culture.gov.uk/Reference_library/Publications/archive_2005/rpt_spoliation_advisory_panel.htm.

library was confused and, in any case, the state of ecclesiastical libraries in Italy was such that Pope John XXIII had ordered a special investigation.

In another inquiry[14] by the panel, the claimant for a small painting held by the Tate Gallery had in fact identified it on a visit to the gallery in 1990. The painting had been sold by his mother for "an apple and an egg" in Belgium during the Second World War. He related its history as he knew it to the assistant keeper of the British Collection at the gallery on January 15, 1991. She made a note of the conversation on the painting's provenance card. At that time, he made no suggestion that the painting should be returned or compensation be paid.

Both the above inquiries concerned claims where any legal right to the objects was barred by the expiration of limitation periods. The claim was a moral one only. Nevertheless, they show that claimants can be very slow to organize or put forward demands—even if they are only of a moral nature. It is true that the Spoliation Advisory Panel did not come into being until February 2000, and so this avenue was not available when the incidents above occurred. However, this does not prevent a moral claim from at least being registered.

Turning to the overall 50-year period, this can pose practical problems for all parties. This is a long period of time, as far as the existence and continuation of evidence is concerned. In the Benevento claim above, the panel accepted that the missal had been in the possession of the Metropolitan Chapter of Benevento at the outbreak of World War I. From then until 1944, there was no reliable evidence as to where the missal was, although there was nothing to suggest that it had left the chapter library. In 1943, the library had been removed to a seminary to escape wartime damage. The seminary itself was then requisitioned by the Allies for use as a military hospital. In 1944, the missal was purchased by a British army captain from a second-hand bookseller in Naples and eventually sold by him to the British Museum. He died in 1994. The panel had absolutely no evidence as to how the missal found its way from the chapter library to the Italian bookseller and then to Captain Ashe. It could have been stolen, lost, or misappropriated. The case does illustrate that after a long period of time there may well be no way of establishing the circumstances of theft—if, indeed, theft did actually occur.

Chamberlain states that in England, it is common for dealers and auctioneers in the art trade to not keep records of transactions going back further than six years.[15] Police records may also be unlikely to exist after 50 years. It is, of course, possible to require by legislation that such records be kept, but who will pay for this? How will they be kept? Paper records can last that long but human nature is such that physical records are misplaced or inadvertently lost. Even

[14] Department for Culture, Media and Sport, *Report of the Spoliation Advisory Panel in Respect of a Painting Now in the Possession of the Tate Gallery* (2001), http://www.culture.gov.uk/Reference_library/Publications/archive_2001/sapreport_hc111.htm.

[15] Kevin Chamberlain, *The Iraq (United Nations Sanctions) Order 2003—Is It Human Rights Act-Compatible?* 8 Art, Antiquity & L. 357, 361 (2003).

electronic storage is no guarantee, as current devices for storage have only a limited life, and the machines for reading them may also disappear.

As already noted, the Advisory Panel on Illicit Trade looked askance at the UNIDROIT limitation rules. It gave as an example the situation where a museum has an object stolen from it but does nothing to determine the location of the object or the identity of its possessor for 48 years. The assumption was made that both these matters could have been ascertained "by elementary means." Having found who has it and where, the museum claims it under the UNIDROIT Convention. According to the scenario set up by the panel, the possessor surrenders it in accordance with the convention but then seeks redress from his vendor of 40 years ago under the English Sale of Goods Act 1979, Section 12(2)(b). This creates a warranty of quiet possession, which runs for six years from the date possession is disturbed (i.e. the vendor may be sued for breach of the warranty).

"Of course the buyer might alternatively seek an indemnity by a claim for compensation from the claimant under Article 4 of the Convention. But this device, even if adopted, may not satisfy the possessor and may leave the vendor vulnerable."[16]

This is a somewhat cavalier dismissal of the right to compensation given under Article 4. The possessor is entitled to compensation, subject to two preconditions. Firstly, he or she must not have known, nor had reasonable cause to know, that the object was stolen. Secondly, the possessor must be able to prove that it exercised due diligence when acquiring the object. Neither of these conditions is unreasonable and indeed fulfills one of the objectives of the UNIDROIT Convention, which is to require greater care on the part of the art trade when dealing in cultural objects.

The limitation rules in the UNIDROIT Convention were not arrived at lightly. In England, the basic rule is that title expires six years following a good-faith conversion (i.e., when the object is sold to an innocent purchaser.)[17] But other states had vastly different rules. In Italy, title passes immediately to a good-faith purchaser; in Switzerland, title passes after five years. In Iran, there were no time limitations applying to stolen cultural property. In New York, there was the demand and refusal rule.[18] The UNIDROIT limitation rules are a compromise in which many states had to give up cherished traditional local methods of resolving the problem of determining how long a title could survive.

The UNIDROIT Convention does not refer to the ultimate effect of the limitation period, for which there are two possibilities. For example, the limitation period may be procedural only (i.e., it bars a claim against a person who has been in undisturbed possession for a certain number of years). Alternatively, at the end of the limitation period, the original title may in fact

---

[16] DEPARTMENT, *supra* note 2, at 24 n.21.

[17] Ruth Redmond-Cooper, *Good Faith Acquisition of Stolen Art*, 2 ART, ANTIQUITY & L. 55 (1997).

[18] *See generally* Stephen E. Weil, *The American Legal Response to the Problem of Holocaust Art*, 4 ART, ANTIQUITY & L. 285, 291 (1999).

be extinguished (i.e., the limitation period has a substantive effect). What happens at the end of a limitation period under the UNIDROIT Convention is left to the relevant national legal system.

Furthermore, the advisory panel does not take account of the possibility that the UNIDROIT limitation periods will improve transparency in the art trade. For example, the Swiss law of obligations in relation to claims on warranty or guarantee due to defects of title to cultural property now imposes an absolute deadline of 30 years for such claims.

> The fact that a purchaser may assert contractual claims over a period of 30 years thanks to the increased statute of limitation will no doubt have a serious impact on the attractiveness of trade with objects of cloudy origins. The latent threat of actions over 30 years means that sellers of cultural property will endeavor to exercise even more diligence for their businesses in the future.[19]

The English Advisory Panel on Illicit Trade was also motivated by what it saw as the absence of any express recognition within the UNIDROIT Convention that the three-year limitation period could be activated by constructive notice on the part of the claimant, as well as by actual knowledge. The panel was concerned that claimants would do nothing to establish the location of the object and the identity of the possessor, and then take advantage of the limitation period when this knowledge fortuitously comes to them. Panel members considered that claimants should be required to take reasonable steps to discover these matters if they were to enjoy the benefits of the limitation period.

Lyndel Prott points out that the phrase "or ought reasonably to have known" was part of earlier formulations; however, following extensive discussion, it was omitted at the Diplomatic Conference.[20] Its omission or inclusion is, of course, a policy decision. Why should claimants be under this obligation? From a jurisprudential point of view, it may contribute to the faster resolution of cases of theft but at the expense of the claimant. If the claimant does not want to actively pursue a theft after having notified the relevant authorities, or is unable for some reason to do so, then surely it is the claimant's choice. It is up to the acquirer to take all possible precautions to ensure that he or she gets a good title. This may result in a more transparent art market, one in which buyers are more careful about their purchases.

It is interesting to note that Article 934 of the Swiss Civil Code, as amended by the Cultural Property Transfer Act 2003, states that cultural property "lost against the will of the owner . . . is subject to a statute of limitations of one year after the owner gains knowledge of the location and the ownership of the cultural property, at the latest, however, 30 years after the property is lost." There is no indication that the claimant must have taken steps to actively seek out the knowledge in question.

---

[19] Andrea Raschèr et al., Cultural Property Transfer 64 (2005).

[20] Prott, *supra* note 9, at 37.

Other questions are likely to arise in practice. For example, in a case discussed later, *City of Gotha v. Sotheby's and Cobert Finance S.A.*,[21] a museum in Germany was approached with an offer to return a stolen painting for a sum of money. Should this be taken as fixing the German government with knowledge sufficient to start the limitation period running? At what level in the government does the knowledge become relevant? What if the person involved does not realize the relevance of the information? What if proceedings are commenced in one country, but it is then realized that this is an inappropriate venue? Does this commence the time running for later proceedings in another jurisdiction?

It is, of course, possible for courts to take the unreasonable delay in seeking to discover the whereabouts of the object or its possessor into account in legal proceedings other than those involving the limitation period. Take, for example, such proceedings as laches (i.e., negligence or unreasonable delay in asserting or enforcing a right).

C. OTHER LIMITATION PERIODS

So far, the discussion has concentrated on the basic UNIDROIT Convention system of limitation periods. However, there are special rules applying to "a cultural object forming an integral part of an identified monument or archaeological site, or belonging to a public collection."[22] Claims to such stolen objects are not subject to the overall 50-year limitation; only the three-year period applies.

However, under Article 3(5), a state party to the UNIDROIT Convention may declare that an overall period of 75 years applies to stolen objects that fit within the categories set out in Article 3(4) "or such longer period as is provided in its law." This declaration must be made at the time the state concerned deposits its instrument indicating it is becoming party to the Convention.[23] If it is not done then, it cannot be done at a later date. The longer period must be "as is provided in its law," which means that there must be some period; there cannot be an indefinite period or no period at all.

The possibility of having an overall 75-year period, or even longer period, was an attempt to deal with issues of inalienability. As is well known, some states (e.g., France), specify that all objects in the national collections are inalienable, meaning that ownership resides in the state and cannot be lost by any legal proceeding such as adverse possession or passage of time. These states would have preferred a provision in the UNIDROIT Convention prohibiting the application of any limitation period to claims for objects from monuments, archaeological sites, or public collections. However, this was unacceptable to other states where there were no inalienable objects. Article 3(5) was a compromise expressed as a long period, which is an exception to the general rule of Article 3(4).

---

[21] [1994] 1 W.L.R. 114.

[22] UNIDROIT Convention, *supra* note 3, art. 3(4).

[23] *Id.*, art. 3(6).

There is an element of reciprocity for such claims. Under Article 3(5), a state that has made a declaration respecting the limitation period will have the same period applied to any claim it makes for restitution of such an object in another contracting state.

The objects must be part of an identified monument or archaeological site, or belong to a public collection. The first would cover the situation that arose in *Autocephalous Greek-Orthodox Church of Cyprus v. Goldberg & Feldman Fine Arts Inc.*[24] There, the mosaics at issue had once been part of the Kanakaria Church in Cyprus until they were ripped out in the aftermath of the Turkish invasion of Northern Cyprus in 1974. However, between 1959 and 1967, the mosaics had been cleaned and restored by, *inter alia*, the Dumbarton Oaks Centre for Byzantine Studies. This body published "an authoritative volume on the Kanakaria Church and its art."[25] There was thus no problem in identifying the mosaics as coming from the church or, in other words, as "being part of an identified monument." Similarly, the stela at issue in *United States v. Hollinshead*[26] had been discovered and recorded by the archaeologist Ian Graham, who recognized it and notified the authorities.[27]

However, not all situations of this nature will be so easily resolved. Many monuments are unrecorded, and clandestine excavation of archaeological sites is rife. Nevertheless, it is interesting to note that legislation has been passed in the United Kingdom making it an offense to dishonestly deal in a cultural object that is tainted while knowing or believing it to be so.[28] A tainted object is one that has been removed in defined circumstances or excavated, and the removal or excavation constitutes an offense. The removal must have been from a building or structure of historical, architectural, or archaeological interest where at any time it formed part of the building or structure, or it had been removed from a monument of such interest. The definition of "monument" further expands the scope of the legislation. It means

- any work, cave or excavation;
- any site comprising the remains of any building or structure or of any work, cave or excavation; or
- any site comprising, or comprising the remains of, any vehicle, vessel, aircraft or other movable structure, or part of any such thing.[29]

Specifically, the building, structure or monument may be above or below ground or underwater. There is nothing in the legislation that causes an object to cease to be tainted.

The third category of material subject only to the three-year period under Article 3(4) is that belonging to a public collection. This is not a term of art,

---

[24] 717 F. Supp. 1374 (1989), *rev'd,* 917 F.2d 278 (1990).

[25] *Id.* at 1378.

[26] 495 F.2d 1154 (1974).

[27] Karl Meyer, The Plundered Past: The Traffic in Art Treasures 32 (1974).

[28] Dealing in Cultural Objects (Offences) Act 2003, ch. 27 (2003) (U.K.). This does not apply to Scotland.

[29] *Id.* at § 2(5).

but it is specifically defined for the purposes of the UNIDROIT Convention. It consists of a group of inventoried or otherwise identified cultural objects owned by

- a contracting state;
- a regional or local authority of a contracting state;
- a religious institution in a contracting state; or
- an institution that is established for an essentially cultural, educational, or scientific purpose in a contracting state and is recognized in that state as serving the public interest.[30]

The first point is that this article requires a "group" of cultural objects (i.e. there must be more than one object). However, two or more objects would be sufficient to constitute a group and thus fulfill the first requirement for a "collection." There is no requirement of a unifying theme in order to constitute the collection. The public collection is then defined by who owns it.

The second point is that the cultural objects must be "inventoried or otherwise identified" as owned by the entities listed. It is well known that inventories are notoriously inaccurate. For example, a major survey of public heritage collections made in Australia in 1991 revealed a significant number of local museums with no inventory and a number of major institutions with inadequate documentation.[31] Of an English collection owned by a company limited by guarantee but registered as a charity, it was said: "When surveyed in 1992, the collection was roughly 60 percent documented, which, given the size and nature of the collections, was pretty good really."[32] Consequently, this requirement of there being an inventory will curtail the volume of material that will be covered by the "public collection" exception to the general rule of Article 3(3). If the object is not inventoried, it will be difficult to "otherwise identify" it in terms of the article. There may be a registration number affixed that is unique to a particular collection, or resort may be made to the memory of curators, but these are unlikely methods of identification.

Paragraphs (a) and (b) of Article 3(7) are relatively straightforward and need no discussion. Whether collections are owned by the contracting state or one of its constituent bodies is a matter for the political structure and law of that state. It is clear that they are public collections. Institutions falling under paragraph (d) may be structured as private bodies (e.g., legally they may be set up as trusts, foundations or, as mentioned above, as companies or whatever other form may be available in the state concerned). However, they must have "an essentially cultural, educational or scientific purpose." Profits may be sought to assist in funding the operation (e.g., restaurant, gift shop) but cannot be the *raison d'etre* of the institution's existence. The institution must also be recognized "in that State" as serving the public interest. The paragraph

---

[30] UNIDROIT Convention, *supra* note 3, art. 3(7).

[31] Margaret Anderson, *Heritage Collection Working Group: Heritage Collections in Australia: Report*, NAT'L CTR. FOR AUSTRALIAN STUDIES 28, 57 (1991).

[32] Peter Cannon-Brookes, *University and Foundation Collections and the Law*, 13 MUSEUM MGMT. & CURATORSHIP 340, 377 (1994).

does not say "by that State." If there is general public recognition that it serves the public interest, that is sufficient. This may be by way of media perception and treatment as a general public benefit. Public funding by the state or one of its organs would indicate a strong presumption that the body concerned serves the public interest. The European Union Council Directive on the Return of Cultural Objects Unlawfully Removed from the Territory of a Member State[33] also refers to "public collections," but emphasizes this financial aspect: the collection must be owned by an institution which is itself "the property of, or significantly financed by, that Member State or a local or regional authority."

Paragraph (c) refers to "a religious institution in a Contracting State." It is much more difficult to envisage why a group of objects owned by such an institution should be regarded as a "public collection." It is true that in some states, the overwhelming proportion of cultural heritage is owned by a religious body—in many cases the Roman Catholic Church. Parts of this are recorded in inventories, but much is not. The church does have places where heritage is exhibited to the public as secular objects, but much of what it possesses is used for devotional purposes, and much is not recorded apart from what exists in parish records or the memory of local pastors. By contrast, in Sweden, legislation requires that every parish of the Church of Sweden and autonomous cathedrals keep a list of church furnishings of historic value. However, there is no central record.

Why should the collections of a religious institution be singled out for special treatment? There is reference to cultural property stolen from a "religious . . . public monument" in Article 7(b)(i) of the UNESCO Convention. At least this restricts the circumstances to theft from a "public monument," which would include a cathedral or church. However, many religious groups of objects are not held in such places. And what of the Miho Museum in Japan? It houses Mihoko Koyama's private collection of Asian and Western antiques, as well as other pieces bought on the world market by the Shumei organization, a spiritual movement.[34] Could at least this part of the collection be said to be a "public collection" in the sense of Article 3(7)(c)? In other words, what is the situation where part of a collection is owned by a religious institution and part not? Moreover, does the collection have to relate to the spiritual activities of the institution in an objective sense? Are all institutions that claim to be religious to be accorded the benefits of Article 3(4)? Schneider states that "the word 'religious' was adopted as representing all faiths."[35] Can a person establish his or her own religion for this purpose? The concept of public collections belonging to religious institutions is very broad and difficult to confine within practicable limits.

---

[33] Council Directive, 93/7/EEC, Mar. 15, 1993 (E.U.), http://europa.eu/scadplus/leg/en/lvb/l11017b.htm.

[34] *See* Souren Melikian, *A Splendid Art Collection Goes on Display in Japan*, INT'L HERALD TRIB., Nov. 6, 1997, *available at* http://iht.com/articles/1997/11/06/museum.t.php? page=1.

[35] Marina Schneider, *UNIDROIT Convention on Stolen or Illegally Exported Cultural Objects: Explanatory Report*, 6 UNIF. L. REV. 512 (2001).

Finally, there is a special provision on limitations when the object stolen is "a sacred or communally important cultural object belonging to and used by a tribal or indigenous community in a Contracting State."[36] These objects are subject to the same time limitations as those from public collections. The provision applies to objects from a broad group of people. Attempts[37] have been made to define the concept of "indigenous," but it is still amorphous. Commonly invoked distinguishing features include original habitation of an area taken over by conquest or colonization and a distinctive culture. Inclusion of tribal groups greatly expands the scope of Article 3(8). Some countries are totally composed of tribal groups. Nevertheless, this article explicitly reflects the reference to the cultural heritage of "tribal, indigenous or other communities" in the preamble to the UNIDROIT Convention.

However, the potential scope is cut down by the requirement that the object must be "sacred or communally important." "Sacred" means there must be a connection with the religion of a tribal or indigenous community. What is "communally important" is a matter for each group but would have to be proven to the satisfaction of a court or the authorities of the state where the claim is being made. Additionally, the object must be used as part of the community's traditional or ritual use. "Ritual" is defined as being "of, with; consisting in, involving, religious rites."[38] In most cases, this should be relatively easy to establish for the type of object that is sufficiently attractive to the market to be stolen. We are not saying that the object must have aesthetic qualities in the Western sense. It may be stolen solely because it has been venerated by an indigenous people, even though it appears to be nothing more than a rock[39] or a piece of twisted wood.

Some of the issues involved are apparent in the *tau tau* statues of Tana Toraja in Indonesia. In 1990, at least 50,000 Toraja practiced the *aluk to dolo* religion (literally "rituals of the ancestors") and even those who had converted to Christianity still had strong respect for the tradition of carving statues of the deceased and placing them in high caves near where the burial took place.

"Displayed for all to see, the statues symbolized for the Toraja the individual status of the deceased, the collective powers and prescience of the ancestors, and the conscious ethnic identity of a minority mountain cultural tradition."[40]

"Discovered" by dealers, many of the statues or their heads were stolen in the years immediately after 1971 and eventually appeared in Western museums.

---

[36] UNIDROIT Convention, *supra* note 3, art. 3(8).

[37] For example, Economic and Social Council, *Discrimination Against Indigenous Peoples*, U.N. Doc. E/CN.4/Sub.2/1994/2 (Apr. 4, 1994).

[38] THE CONCISE OXFORD DICTIONARY 1078 (1st ed. 1964).

[39] For example, the focus of worship to Siva in the Hindu religion is the Siva Lingam, a phallus-shaped piece of stone that was held in *Bumper Development Corp. Ltd. v. Commissioner of Police*, [1991] 1 W.L.R. 1362, [1991] 4 All E.R. 638 (1991), to have the ability to sue in the English courts. *See* unreported decision of Kennedy, J. (copy on file with the author).

[40] Eric Crystal, *Rape of the Ancestors: Discovery, Display, and Destruction of the Ancestral Statuary of Tana Toraja*, *in* FRAGILE TRADITIONS: INDONESIAN ART IN JEOPARDY 29, 31 (Paul Taylor ed., 1994).

This is an example of cultural objects that are both sacred and communally important being used as part of the community's traditional or ritual use.

But what was envisaged by use of the word "traditional"? It must be something else than associated with religion. Moreover, the object must be "communally important." This excludes objects in everyday use by families even though they may be of a traditional nature. It may catch, for example, a loom used for traditional weaving if it is one used by a community and important to that community.

D. LIMITATION PERIODS APPLYING TO ILLEGALLY EXPORTED OBJECTS

There is only one provision on these periods, Article 5(6), and it is relatively straightforward. Any request for return has to be brought within three years from the time when the requesting state knew the location of the cultural object and the identity of the possessor. The various implications of this formulation have already been discussed.

> It should be noted that the limitation periods for theft and illegal export are identical (albeit dealt with in separate provisions)—this is so as to ensure that the (different) length of the limitation period does not become the deciding factor in determining the grounds on which a claim will be brought, for example where unlawfully excavated objects are concerned.[41]

There is also an overall period of 50 years from the time when the object was illegally exported. The problem with this could well lie in establishing just when illegal export occurred. The need for limitation rules such as the above is well illustrated by the following. During debate on Article 3 in the Diplomatic Conference, an Australian representative described a recent case summarized below.

> [I]n Australia where the return of an object that was part of the collection of the Australian National Gallery had been claimed by the Peruvian Government. It had taken the Peruvian Government approximately three years, if not more, after it had knowledge of both the location of the object and the identity of the possessor, to collect all the evidence necessary.[42]

E. DISPUTE SETTLEMENT

The limitation rules in the UNIDROIT Convention can contribute to the avoidance and resolution of cultural heritage disputes by eliminating competing rules. Consider the case of *City of Gotha v. Sotheby's and Cobert Finance S.A.* before Mr. Justice Moses in the English High Court.[43] It concerned a painting of

---

[41] Schneider, *supra* note 35, at 508.

[42] Rosalie Balkin in Presidenza del Consiglio dei Ministri, *Diplomatic Conference for the Adoption of the Draft UNIDROIT Convention on the International Return of Stolen or Illegally Exported Cultural Objects: Rome 7 to 24 June 1995: Acts and Proceedings* 173 (1996).

[43] *City of Gotha, supra* note 21, *available at* http://www.iuscomp.org/gla/judgments/foreign/gotha1.htm.

The Holy Family with Saint John and Elizabeth, by Joachim Wtewael, which had been the property of a foundation in the city of Gotha in the German Land of Thuringia. At the end of the Second World War, it disappeared. The judge concluded that probably it had been taken from a depositary by a Soviet trophy brigade because, in 1986, it surfaced in Moscow. By a long and circuitous route, it came into the hands of the defendant, Cobert Finance S.A., a Panamanian registered company. Cobert conceded at trial that neither it nor anyone else had acquired the painting in good faith.

Judge Moses found that, following various legal proceedings, the painting was owned by the German government, provided its claim was not time barred. He held that the German limitation period of 30 years had not expired at the time proceedings for recovery were commenced. The period began to run in 1987 when there had been a misappropriation.

However, the judge went on to offer his opinion as to what should happen if the German claim were found to be statute barred. This is of course an *obiter dictum*. Judge Moses indicated that, in his opinion, it was possible to identify a "public policy in England that time is not to run either in favour of the thief nor in favour of any transferee who is not a purchaser in good faith."

What would be the situation if both Germany and the United Kingdom were party to the UNIDROIT Convention and the facts were to arise in the future? The painting obviously came from a public collection in terms of Article 3(7). As such, if no declaration had been made under Article 3(5), paragraph 4 would be applicable. Germany would have had three years from the time when it knew the location of the painting and the identity of its possessor. Proceedings were commenced by Germany in 1997 and by the city of Gotha in 1993. From the facts as given in the case, it appears that one of the possessors of the painting approached the museum in Gotha in 1990 with an offer to sell it, but the museum was unable to raise the price asked. The facts are not sufficiently precise to take the matter further. However, if the facts were such that the UNIDROIT Convention could apply, then the issue would have been resolved without the lengthy legal analysis and multitude of legal specialists that were involved.

F. CONCLUSION

The UNIDROIT Convention contains rules on limitation periods that are fair and, in general, of no great complexity. Certainly there are issues that will arise when they are implemented. However, all limitation periods are the result of compromises; all will have defects when viewed by people whose legal systems have taken other directions. The UNIDROIT rules are the result of long and intense negotiation. They deserve respect even when particular national legal systems differ from them. In particular, the rules have been drafted to deal with the peculiarities of the art market, something that most legal systems are only just coming to appreciate. In the words of Richard Crewdson, a leading English authority on cultural heritage law, appearing before the House of Commons Committee on Culture, Media and Sport, "[T]o apply the standard limitation period to cultural property is harsh because each piece of cultural property is unique, and the remedial benefits of insurance cannot provide adequate recompense in the way they do routinely for the loss of consumable durables."[44]

---

[44] Department of Culture, Media and Sport Committee, *supra* note 4, at iv.

PART VII

MUSEUMS AND SITES

CHAPTER 21
PROVENANCE RESEARCH: LITIGATION AND THE RESPONSIBILITY OF MUSEUMS

Lawrence M. Kaye*

Issues regarding the legal and moral responsibilities of museums in connection with the acquisition of antiquities and other cultural properties have been hotly debated over the past several years by museum officials, lawyers, archaeologists, public officials, and other commentators. Indeed, sharp lines have been drawn, and two strikingly disparate points of view have emerged. On one side are many museum advocates who, while conceding that care should be shown and research performed before an acquisition, argue that antiquities can, and should, be acquired even in the absence of clear and convincing evidence that they have not been looted or are of questionable legal status. According to this view, if a problem arises later, then it can be dealt with at that time. On the other side are archaeologists and other commentators who believe that if there is any doubt about the provenance of an antiquity being considered for acquisition, the transaction should not be completed.

One can read in the news nearly every day about the discussions and agreements for the restitution of cultural objects to countries of origin. For example, Italy and Greece have entered into agreement with major museums including the Metropolitan Museum of Art in New York (the "Met"), the J. Paul Getty Museum in Los Angeles (the "Getty") and the Museum of Fine Arts in Boston (the "MFA") on the other, regarding the return of claimed antiquities under a strict set of conditions.[1] Ricardo Elia has suggested such arrangements

* Mr. Kaye and his firm represented the Republic of Turkey in several important matters involving antiquities, including *Republic of Turkey v. The Metropolitan Museum*, 762 F. Supp. 44 (S.D.N.Y. 1990), which is discussed *infra*, and *Republic of Turkey v. OKS Partners*, No. 89-CV-3061, 1998 U.S. Dist. LEXIS 23526, *1 (D. Mass. Jan. 23, 1998). Mr. Kaye would like to thank Frank K. Lord IV and Mari-Claudia Jiménez for their assistance in the preparation of this chapter.

[1] Press Release, The Metropolitan Museum of Art on Its Agreement with Italian Ministry of Culture, New York, Feb. 21, 2006, *available at* http://www.metmuseum.org/press_room/full_release.asp?prid={F9704AC3-297B-4704-999B-111ACC8E6804}; Jason Edward Kaufman, *Metropolitan to Return Antiquities to Italy*, The Art Newspaper, Mar. 9, 2006, *available at* http://www.theartnewspaper.com/article01.asp?id=206&tf_teaser=0%20; Hugh Eakin, *Getty Museum Agrees to Return Two Antiquities to Greece*, N.Y. Times, July 11, 2006, *available at* http://select.nytimes.com/search/restricted/article?res=F10F16FC3A540C728DDDAE0894DE404482;

constitute a new avenue for museums to pursue concerning unprovenanced or questionable artifacts and their policies about the acquisition and retention of antiquities.[2] We will certainly be hearing more about this in the coming years. In fact, just over two years after the announcement of the Met's agreement with Italy, the Cleveland Museum agreed to return 16 artifacts, including a South Italian Medea vase, to that country.[3]

Like all newsworthy events, there is a background story. As many of you know, Italy spent more than ten years in discussions with the Met about the Morgantina silver, and talks about the Euphronius Krater went on for longer than that. Similarly, potential claims against the Getty and the MFA have been pending for years. Why are these issues coming to the forefront now? I would like to think that the lessons learned in the dispute between Turkey and the Met over the Lydian Hoard[4]—in which I represented the government of Turkey and which ended with the unconditional return of the Hoard to Turkey—would perhaps have led the Met and other institutions to settle them, rather than become involved in protracted litigation. That would seem to be especially likely at a time when museums have been focusing on issues about transparency in the area of Nazi-looted art. The dispute between Turkey and the Met can also illustrate what can happen under the microscope of litigation and American-style discovery.

From 1966 to 1970, the Met acquired more than 360 Lydian objects dating from the sixth century B.C.E., including fragments of wall paintings, marble sphinxes, gold, silver and bronze vessels, and gold, silver, and glass jewelry.[5] The artifacts had been looted from tombs in the Uşak region of Turkey in Central Anatolia. They were acquired by the Met in three lots, shortly after they were illegally excavated and smuggled out of Turkey, and they passed through the hands of some New York antiquities dealers. The pre-trial discovery in that case revealed much about the approach taken to acquisitions at that time. One of the curators at the Met described how a dealer spread some of the objects on a table; to the curator they appeared to be some of the most extraordinary examples of the Lydian civilization ever gathered in one place. To paraphrase (with great liberty) from the curator's deposition: Did he ask the dealers where

Press Release, The Museum of Fine Arts, Boston and The Italian Ministry of Culture, Boston, MA, July 27, 2006; Elisabetta Povoledo, *Boston Museum Returns 13 Ancient Works to Italy*, N.Y. Times, Sept. 29, 2006, *available at* http://select.nytimes.com/search/restricted/article?res=F30B1EF83D540C7A8EDDA00894DE404482; and Press Release, Hellenic Republic Ministry of Culture and the J. Paul Getty Trust Issue Joint Statement, Dec. 11, 2006, *available at* http://www.getty.edu/news/press/center/statement06_getty_greek_joint_release_121106.html.

[2] *See* Chapter 12 of this volume.

[3] *See* Suzan Mazur, *Italy Will Contest Medea Vase Now at Cleveland Museum*, Scoop News, Oct. 9, 2006, *available at* http://www.scoop.co.nz/stories/HL0610/S00114.htm; and *Cleveland Museum Agrees to Return 16 Artifacts to Italy*, CBC News, May 9, 2008 *available at* http://www.cbc.ca/arts/artdesign/story/2008/05/09/cleveland-italy.html.

[4] Republic of Turkey v. The Metropolitan Museum, 762 F. Supp. 44 (S.D.N.Y. 1990).

[5] *See generally* Lawrence M. Kaye & Carla T. Main, *The Saga of the Lydian Hoard Antiquities: From Uşak to New York and Back Again*, *in* Antiquities: Trade or Betrayed: Legal, Ethical & Conservation Issues 150–61 (Kathryn Walker Tubb ed., 1995); Knur Özgen & Jean Öztürk, Heritage Recovered: The Lydian Treasure (1996).

the objects came from? The answer—no. Did the dealers offer any information about the origin or history of the objects? The answer—no. This was not an atypical example of how museums and dealers operated in a "don't ask, don't tell" fashion in those days. Not long after he left the Met, Thomas Hoving, who was the museum's director at the time of this acquisition, described it as typical of the "age of piracy" rampant in the museum world at that time.[6] It appears that, in that era, the problem went far beyond whether due inquiry was made. In this case, it became quite clear that museum officials knew full well from where the objects had originated.[7] Perhaps that is why the acquisition of this extraordinary hoard went unheralded until the mid-1980s. And then, after having been stored in the Met's basement for that long period of time, the objects were finally put on permanent display in 1984 but as part of the collection called the "East Greek Treasure."[8] During the course of the litigation, minutes from the Acquisition Committee of the Board of Trustees meetings were produced. These stated that the second of the three purchases "came from the same area of Central Anatolia as the first lot," making it clear that the museum undeniably knew that these antiquities had come from Turkey and had no legitimate provenance. In his 1994 book, *Making the Mummies Dance*, Hoving conceded as much.[9]

Unfortunately, the Lydian Hoard case, which ended in 1993 with the return of the Hoard to Turkey, has made news again. After the Hoard was returned, it was first displayed in the Museum of Anatolian Civilizations, where it enjoyed a successful stay. But internal politics led the Turkish government to move the Hoard to the Uşak Museum so that it could be as close as possible to the tombs from which it originated. This has led to two developments. First, Philipe de Montebello, director of the Met, has blasted Turkey for taking the Hoard back to its source, claiming that only 769 people had visited it in five years.[10] I am sure that is an exaggeration, but it is meant to bolster the position of those who say that artifacts are more accessible in a major international museum and, consequently, should be displayed there. I personally feel that it is perfectly appropriate for the Turkish government—or any other government that recovers looted antiquities—to make its own decision about what should be done with its national property.

But there is more fuel for the fire: it was discovered that one of the "stars" of the collection—a gold brooch in the shape of a hippocamp—had been stolen and replaced with a fake,[11] giving rise to great embarrassment and contributing to a feeding frenzy for those who claim that countries of origin cannot take care of their own treasures. A Marsyas statue that my firm helped return to Turkey

---

[6] Thomas Hoving, Making the Mummies Dance: Inside the Metropolitan Museum of Art 217 (1994).

[7] *Id.*

[8] Kaye & Main, *supra* note 5, at 151.

[9] *Id.*

[10] Sebnem Arsu & Campbell Robertson, *After 27 Centuries, Croesus Riches Still Tempt*, Int'l Herald Trib., May 31, 2006, *available at* http://www.iht.com/articles/2006/05/30/news/turkey.php.

[11] *Id.*

was also stolen a few years ago—but happily was found and restored to the museum from which it was taken.

The good news is that the theft of the brooch created a national outcry, demonstrating the importance of the objects to the Turkish people and that the theft was no joking matter. The issue, of course, is one of limited resources, and I concur that Western museums would be well served by working with countries that are rich in art to improve their cultural institutions and organizations.

But to return to the issue of the stewardship of U.S. museums, it is instructive to look at the transactions underlying a recent breach-of-contract case, *Phoenix Ancient Art, S.A. v. Kimbell Art Foundation*.[12] Let me be clear: I do not wish to single out the Kimbell unfairly. It is an excellent museum that recently returned an important piece of Nazi-looted art. But its conduct in the transactions with Phoenix Ancient Art, a gallery owned by brothers Hicham and Ali Aboutaam, in 2000, is a telling example of museum acquisition problems.[13] Simply stated, the Kimbell decided to purchase a Sumerian statuette from the gallery. After extensive negotiations, including the drafting and re-drafting of complex agreements, the acquisition was completed in December 2000.[14] But surprisingly, about seven months later, the parties executed a written agreement whereby Phoenix Ancient Art bought the statuette back from the Kimbell for the original purchase price.[15] In order to guarantee repayment, the gallery gave the Kimbell a sculpture of a Roman torso to hold until the purchase price was repaid.[16] Subsequently, the museum expressed an interest in buying the torso, but, in the end, Phoenix Ancient Art brought a lawsuit for breach of contract against the Kimbell when that transaction was not completed.[17] The gallery lost that case because the court found that a meeting of the minds had not really occurred.[18]

The more interesting facts of this case, however, concern the aborted purchase of the Sumerian statuette. The Kimbell's decision to change its mind about what it had already purchased generated some lively discussion in the press.[19] One report gave the Kimbell's explanation for its reversal: there were other objects on the antiquities market that the museum was more interested in; however, many noted that reputable museums do not repudiate transactions simply because they later decided to buy something else.[20] It would

---

[12] No. 03 Civ. 1008, 2003 WL 22705119, *1 (S.D.N.Y. Nov. 17, 2003).

[13] *Id.* at *1.

[14] *Id.*

[15] *Id.*

[16] *Id.*

[17] *Id.* at *1–*2.

[18] *Id.* at *3.

[19] Andrew Marton, *Kimbell Negotiating Refund for $2.7 Million Statue*, FORT WORTH STAR-TELEGRAM, Aug. 17, 2001, at News 1; Andrew Marton, *Return of Statue Stirs Art World*, FORT WORTH STAR-TELEGRAM, AUG. 22, 2001, at LIFE & ARTS 1 [hereinafter *Return of Statue*]; *Kimbell Suckered in Ancient Art Scam?* (Aug. 24, 2001), *available at* http://www.artnet.com/magazine/news/artnetnews/artnetnews8-24-01.asp; Andrew Marton, *Statue's Odyssey: Latest Twist in Kimbell Saga*, FORT WORTH STAR-TELEGRAM, May 1, 2002, at Life & Arts 1.

[20] Marton, *Return of Statue, supra* note 19; Marton, *Kimbell Negotiating Refund for $2.7 Million Statue, supra* note 19.

be impossible for museums to continue operating in the marketplace if they treated acquisitions in such a cavalier manner. Although officials vigorously denied it, commentators suggested that it was more likely that the Kimbell learned that the statuette had real problems regarding its ownership and origin, or had turned out to be a forgery.[21] Indeed, the decision to return the piece was apparently made after the museum received inquiries from the Internal Revenue Service about Phoenix Ancient Art, although the museum's director later said that those inquiries were not so specific that they raised serious concerns.[22]

The various press statements and news reports do not shed much light on the circumstances surrounding the purchase and leave serious questions about the Kimbell's original decision to acquire the piece unanswered. But these very issues lead one to doubt that there was a comprehensive acquisition policy in place or that appropriate steps were taken to avoid a problematic purchase. For example, it may be that the pre-acquisition provenance research into the Sumerian statuette was inadequate, perhaps in part because it was cut short when Phoenix offered the museum a $300,000 discount if the transaction was completed by the end of the year.[23] This raises a wholly different issue: there is general agreement that whenever a substantial discount is offered for an antiquity, it should raise a red flag that the antiquity is undervalued because its authenticity or ownership is in question.[24] Also, at the time, experts were quoted as saying that establishing a legitimate provenance for *any* Sumerian object was extremely difficult, as most such objects originated in Iraq.[25] In addition, experts have said "an extremely conservative estimate is that 70% of [Near Eastern] pieces that appear for the first time on the market are stolen or looted" and furthermore would run afoul of the trade embargo imposed in 1991 after the Gulf War.[26]

Thomas Hoving, the former director of the Metropolitan Museum of Art, observed during the controversy,

> If this stuff would come to me, I'd probably just laugh and not really be interested in seeing it, but would then take a quick look if only to know what I think is being smuggled. . . . Look, it's a no-brainer because, unless you know for a fact this Sumerian piece has been in some English Lord's collection for years, you can bet you're probably trading with Sadam Hussein and it's probably all stolen stuff with cooked up, fake provenances. As a museum director, don't even bother with it. Just hands off.[27]

---

[21] *Id.*

[22] Marton, *Statue's Odyssey, supra* note 19.

[23] Marton, *Kimbell Negotiating Refund for $2.7 Million Statue, supra* note 19.

[24] *Id.*

[25] *Id.*

[26] *Id.*

[27] *Id.*

Jerome Eisenberg, a well-known dealer in Near Eastern antiquities, echoed these concerns:

> [T]o verify the authenticity of any piece of Sumerian antiquity, you have to send it to a serious laboratory for examination because, frankly, a panel of experts can argue both sides of its authenticity. Candidly, it is this whole problem of authenticity in very rare Mesopotamian art objects that defies most dealers from working with them.[28]

The Kimbell mounted a strong defense of its conduct, emphasizing that the provenance was thoroughly researched, that archives were checked, and that archaeologists had corroborated the statuette's presence in a private collection in the 1960s,[29] that is, prior to the enactment of the 1970 UNESCO treaty[30] against the trade in looted antiquities. It also appears that the museum reversed its decision to buy the torso that Phoenix had substituted for the Sumerian statuette originally offered after receiving a subpoena from a federal grand jury seeking information regarding Phoenix Ancient Art.[31] The museum immediately cut off discussions, which led to the breach of contract suit.[32]

It does at least seem clear that the matter was mishandled and not conducted with the kind of transparency that should be expected of public institutions. The incident was an embarrassment for the Kimbell, even though it won the lawsuit over the torso. It also raises a number of serious, and larger, questions:

1. Did the Kimbell have a clear acquisition policy? Was it followed?[33]
2. Did the Kimbell really conduct a sufficient examination into the authenticity and provenance of the statuette?
3. Should the Kimbell have listened to those experts who said that, in this day and age, museums should be extremely careful about purchasing any Sumerian antiquity? Did the Kimbell take these concerns into consideration?
4. Although the director stated, in general terms, that they had sufficient evidence that this particular statuette had been in private hands for some 40 years, why did he never publicly disclose the details of its ownership history?
5. What would the outcome have been if the museum had fully and completely investigated the piece and the gallery selling it?
6. If the museum determined the piece was unprovenanced, was returning the statuette to the dealers the best course of action?

---

[28] *Id.*

[29] Marton, *Kimbell Suckered in Ancient Art Scam?*, *supra* note 19.

[30] UNESCO Convention on the Means of Prohibiting and Preventing the Illegal Import, Export and Transfer of Ownership of Cultural Property (Nov. 14, 1970), 823 U.N.T.S. 231, 10 I.L.M. 289.

[31] Phoenix Ancient Art, S.A. v. Kimbell Art Found., No. 03 Civ. 1008, 2003 WL 22705119, at *2 (S.D.N.Y. Nov. 17, 2003).

[32] *Id.*

[33] On acquisitions policies, see Archaeological Institute of America (AIA), *Principles for Museum Acquisitions of Antiquities* (Mar. 2006), *available at* http://www.archaeological.org/pdfs/archaeologywatch/museumpolicy/AIA_Principles_Musuem_Acquisition.pdf.

On this last point, it turns out that the principals of the Phoenix gallery had a number of legal problems. Swiss and Italian authorities reportedly confiscated 70 to 80 terracotta pieces in raids during the period between the initial purchase and the Kimbell's return of the statue.[34] In 2004, one of the principals, Hicham Aboutaam, pled guilty in a Manhattan federal court to a misdemeanor charge for falsely representing that an Iranian silver drinking vessel that he imported into the United States came from Syria. He was sentenced to a year's probation and fined $5,000.[35] The two Phoenix principals were also the subject of an investigative report in the *New York Times* that was not particularly favorable and made a number of assertions about possible illicit activity.[36] Would a diligent investigation by the museum prior to the consummation of the transaction for the Sumerian statuette have uncovered relevant information?

So, in the end, I must profess skepticism.

This brings us to the dichotomy concerning the museum's obligations to develop appropriate policies for the acquisition of cultural property. At the outset, it should be noted that the two sides of this argument agree that museum officials have a duty of due care in deciding whether to acquire antiquities. I think everyone agrees that they must act in good faith and utilize appropriate standards of due diligence. The problem arises when one tries to define what those standards are. On the museum side, a typical view is represented in articles by James Cuno, formerly the director of the Harvard University Art Museums and now director of the Art Institute of Chicago.[37] According to Cuno, a museum should be able to acquire an antiquity without having all the ownership and provenance history it might need as long as certain procedures have been followed.[38] If, after making the acquisition, convincing evidence comes to light proving that the work was illegally excavated in violation of a country's antiquities law, then the museum would be obligated to return the property.[39] He minimizes the fact that museum funds may have been misspent in the initial acquisition, noting that this is simply the "cost of doing business in museums."[40] As Cuno puts it,

> Within the limited period of time preceding acquisition, museums should research the objects thoroughly, inquiring with colleagues into

---

[34] Marton, *Kimbell Negotiating Refund for $2.7 Million Statue, supra* note 19.

[35] Malcolm Gay, *Out of Egypt: From a Long-Buried Pyramid to the Saint Louis Art Museum: The Mysterious Voyage of the Ka-Nefer-Nefer Mask*, RIVER FRONT TIMES, St. Louis, Feb. 15, 2006, *available at* http://www.riverfronttimes.com/2006-02-15/news/out-of-egypt/.

[36] Barry Meier & Martin Gottlieb, *Loot: Along the Antiquities Trail; An Illicit Journey Out of Egypt, Only a Few Questions Asked*, N.Y. TIMES, Feb. 23, 2004, *available at* http://select.nytimes.com/search/restricted/article?res=F60711FE3C580C708EDDAB0894DC404482.

[37] James Cuno, *Ownership and Protection of Heritage: Cultural Property Rights for the 21st Century: U.S. Art Museums and Cultural Property*, 16 CONN. J. INT'L L. 189 (Spring 2001); James Cuno, *Cultural Property: The Hard Question of Repatriation Museums and the Acquisition of Antiquities*, 19 CARDOZO ARTS & ENT. L.J. 83 (2001).

[38] Cuno, *Cultural Property, supra* note 37, at 91.

[39] *Id.* at 96.

[40] *Id.* at 88.

> any problems known or suspected with the objects, the collector, or the dealer in question, and notify the appropriate governmental authorities of the likely country of origin. If nothing discouraging turns up, one is free to acquire such objects. However, the museum is still obligated to research the works further in anticipation of their being published and exhibited.[41]

This is where the two sides begin to differ. In essence, he is saying that just because there is no provenance—or insufficient provenance—the museum need not conclude that the piece has been stolen or illegally excavated. To the contrary, Cuno has written that overly cautious acquisition policies will improperly prevent objects from contributing to the museum's mission to educate, inspire, and protect.[42] For him, museum acquisitions are "in the service of the public good": works of art are transferred "from the private to the public realm, where scholars are more likely to learn of their whereabouts, and students and the general public will be given a chance to study and appreciate them."[43] He thus concludes that museums should continue to acquire works of ancient art, following a common sense approach, so that the past is preserved for the benefit of future generations.[44]

Cuno also injects a subjective standard into this proposed policy. He cites one example regarding Harvard's acquisition of Greek vase fragments.[45] Some of his colleagues opposed the acquisition because the vendor had no evidence to indicate where the fragments came from or whether "they had been legally and ethically acquired."[46] Cuno saw no reason, however, to conclude that the fragments had a suspicious provenance, even though similar fragments had been illegally excavated.[47] Instead, he imposed this subjective standard: the museum should determine how important the objects were to the culture of the state from which they may have been taken.[48] In the case of the vase fragments, he noted that there were undoubtedly "tens of thousands in Italian museums" and, in the absence of evidence that they originated from "a looted archeological site, let alone an important archeological site (as opposed to, say, a farmer's field)," he "had no reason to suspect that . . . acquiring these fragments would jeopardize Italy's cultural patrimony."[49] If, on the other hand, the acquisition had involved Khmer Temple sculptures, one would have been more suspicious of their status.[50]

Certainly, despite diligent research, it is not always possible to know everything about a work's origin, ownership history, and legal standing before

---

41 *Id.* at 91.
42 *Id.* at 92.
43 *Id.*
44 *Id.* at 95–96.
45 *Id.* at 88
46 *Id.* at 89.
47 *Id.*
48 *Id.*
49 *Id.* at 89–90.
50 *Id.* at 90.

acquiring it. If an object has been plundered from a previously unexcavated site, its identification as looted art may not occur until the object is acquired by a museum and publicly displayed, because the authorities in the country of origin never had a chance to examine, study, and record the object there. Sometimes, the thieves who originally plundered the material will be caught and statements will be taken, providing information that can lead to a successful search and identification once it has left the country. But, this is not often the case. The issue, then, is whether the museum should purchase the object if it cannot obtain sufficient provenance information. Museums argue that the absence of provenance does not necessarily point to illicit extraction.[51] Perhaps a piece was sold long ago by authorities in the country of origin or by someone who legally owned the piece either before patrimony laws were implemented or under the terms of enacted laws.

Even when provenance information is available, the question is then how the museum can best evaluate it. In the recent much publicized criminal prosecution of Frederick Schultz, a prominent New York dealer convicted of conspiring to smuggle stolen Egyptian artifacts, the courts observed that Mr. Schultz and his confederates went to great pains to create false provenances for some of the objects at issue, like a sculpture of Amenhotep III.[52] False papers were prepared to suggest that a relative of one of the conspirators had transported this object out of Egypt and had been keeping it in an English collection since the 1920s.[53] A fictional collection to house the piece—"The Thomas Alcock Collection"—was even created; labels carefully counterfeited to appear to be from the 1920s were prepared, and efforts were made to sell the piece with the Alcock Collection story.[54] In another case in which I was involved, affidavits were prepared by individuals attesting to the fact that a certain statue that was allegedly illegally smuggled out of one country had actually been in another country months, even years, before the date of the alleged illegal exportation. To have gone all over the world establishing that each of the affidavits was true would have taken years and probably proved futile. In that case, the museum did not acquire the object. Nevertheless, the question arises as to what extent a museum is obligated to ascertain whether provenance materials and documentation are, in fact, authentic.

Another problem that museums confront in verifying the status of objects presented for acquisition is that without knowing the object's history, it is almost impossible to evaluate its legal status. This is because certain countries have laws that vest ownership in previously undiscovered antiquities in the state, while others do not. Even with respect to those countries that do have statutes—which, in the United States, courts have made clear will be honored in both the civil and criminal context—the object must have been illegally removed from the country at a time when that statute was in effect.[55] Thus, information about

---

[51] *Id.* at 89.

[52] United States v. Schultz, 333 F.3d 393, 396 (2d Cir. 2003).

[53] *Id.*

[54] *Id.*

[55] *See, e.g.,* United States v. McClain, 593 F.2d 658 (5th Cir. 1979); United States v. Schultz, 333 F.3d 393 (2d Cir. 2003).

when the object was removed is critical to the analysis. There are also numerous defenses that can be asserted against the claimant, including, most significantly, the statute of limitations, which is an issue that will generally be impossible to evaluate at the time of acquisition. Obviously, where there is more information available on the object, such as the original context and its provenance, legal advisors can better help museums ascertain whether they are buying material that they will later have to return in response to a claim from a victimized country. This furnishes support for those who would say that museums simply should not acquire any property if their inquiries at the time of acquisition do not reveal enough information to properly evaluate the provenance and legal status of the object.

But this is only the beginning of a list of complicated questions. What kind of inquiry is sufficient? How far does the museum need to go in making its inquiry? If there is some suspicion that the object is tainted, does the museum have an affirmative obligation to examine all available stolen art registers to see if the piece has been reported missing? Certainly, just as appraisers who are members of the Appraisers Association of America (AAA) are guided by their code of ethics not to prepare appraisals for objects that "readily appear to have a doubtful provenance and may be stolen,"[56] museums should not acquire objects that raise those red flags. But the AAA rules continue to state that, if "the appraiser is aware of clear and convincing evidence that the item may be stolen property,"[57] the appraiser has an obligation to contact the authorities.[58] Does a museum have a similar obligation? What constitutes a reasonable inquiry? What is "clear and convincing evidence"? Lawyers and courts grapple with questions like these every day. How are museum officials, even with proper legal advice, supposed to deal with them?

In the absence of complete information, should the museum walk away or purchase the objects and only face these legal questions when a claim is made? I think all would agree that museums should try to get whatever provenance information is available. If after reasonable inquiry, those documents are not forthcoming, should the process stop? What if the dealer trying to sell the objects says that all the records were there, but the warehouse where they were stored burned down years before? Do you proceed? Perhaps the answer is to allow the museum to acquire the object but adopt rules that require it to refrain from asserting technical defenses, like the expiration of the statute of limitations, if a claim is later made.

For every museum official who argues that a good-faith effort to make the necessary inquiries is all that is required, there is an archaeologist who will argue the opposing view that museums simply should not acquire antiquities unless it can be proved that they were legally excavated and exported. Doing otherwise only fosters more pillage and looting, leading to the loss of critically

---

[56] Appraisers Association of America, Inc., Bylaws and Code of Ethics, 19, *available at* http://www.appraisersassoc.org/personal-property-appraiser/fine-art-appraisals/find-an-appraiser/PageId/1/LId/0,1,3/Id/3/Code-of-Ethics.html.

[57] *Id.*

[58] *Id.*

important knowledge about the object and its context. Archaeologists believe that the acquisition of objects with incomplete or no provenance will encourage smugglers and illicit marketers to loot unexcavated sites because there will be a market for their unprovenanced booty.[59] There will always be collectors and dealers who patronize the illicit antiquities market. But museums, which are held to higher standards, should not be players in that game. Professor Patty Gerstenblith of DePaul University, writing on the fiduciary obligations of museums, presents an excellent summary and analysis of the position espoused by many leading archaeologists.[60] She rejects the suggestion by museum officials that they are "performing an act of rescue" when they buy questionable objects and deny responsibility for separating the objects from their archaeological context.[61] She believes that this conduct on the part of museum officials is nothing less than a failure to fulfill their fiduciary obligations.[62] There should be a higher "duty of care in the acquisition context" coupled with a recognition that "the acquisition of decontextualized objects causes historical, cultural and scientific losses."[63] Under the regime that she advocates, the provenance and good title of an object can *never* be assumed unless proven otherwise.[64]

Professor Gerstenblith urges museums, in adopting acquisition policies, to incorporate fundamental concepts of due diligence that should include "demanding documentation from the previous owner of the object, independent research into the background of the object and previous publications, and checking with the computerized databases that now compile records of stolen works of art."[65] Particular scrutiny should be given to "objects that come from areas known to have been the victim of war and civil unrest."[66] Of course, "many of the types of research utilized in the acquisition of most museum objects will not indicate whether a museum can acquire good title to the archeological object."[67]

As I have noted, because objects illegally excavated are not known "to the government of the country of origin until after the object appears on the market or in a museum collection . . . [that] government . . . [will not have been able] to register the archeological object as stolen with a computerized data base,"[68] checking the database, which may be quite useful in a Holocaust-related case, will very often reveal nothing about the background of the object in question. As exemplified in the *Schultz* case, documentation produced by the seller may provide only questionable information and, even worse, may be falsified.

---

[59] AIA, *supra* note 33.

[60] Patty Gerstenblith, *Acquisition and Deacquisition of Museum Collections and the Fiduciary Obligations of Museums to the Public*, 11 CARDOZO J. INT'L & COMP. L. 409 (2003).

[61] *Id.* at 452.

[62] *Id.* at 453.

[63] *Id.*

[64] *Id.* at 454.

[65] *Id.* at 460–61.

[66] *Id.* at 461.

[67] *Id.*

[68] *Id.*

Certainly, holding museums to a high standard of due inquiry in the acquisition of antiquities is not a radical concept. Indeed, in New York, this principle has been applied to art dealers in other contexts for many years. The well-known 1979 case of *Porter v. Wertz*,[69] is instructive. The court ruled that a dealer could not take advantage of a statutory provision permitting him to resist a claim from a true owner, where the latter had placed an object in the hands of a dealer in that kind of object who would have apparent authority to dispose of it.[70] The court found that, having failed to make an appropriate inquiry as to who the seller was, the dealer could not claim to have acted in good faith.[71] If he had made reasonable inquiries, he would have discovered that the seller was, in fact, not an art dealer, but rather a delicatessen employee.[72] Certainly, museums should not be held to a lower standard than the dealer in that case, and they are not.

And so we return to the question I posed earlier: how do you rationalize the conflicting views of museums and archaeologists? While I agree that loose policies will lead to a continued proliferation of the illicit market and the removal of objects from their context, at the same time, I believe that museums provide a valuable and indispensable role in our society and should be encouraged to operate, albeit within reasonable boundaries. As with most difficult issues, compromise is necessary. But what limits should be imposed? Are there rules that can be adopted that satisfy both camps?

Actually, this difficult question has been addressed, beginning in 1970, by the Code of Ethics of the International Council of Museums (ICOM).[73] The Code of Ethics, which was most recently revised in 2004, seeks to provide "a global minimum standard" upon which more specific or rigorous requirements can be built.[74] Section 2 of the Code of Ethics deals directly with the acquisition of illicit material.[75] It states, rather bluntly, that the museum should not acquire any object "by purchase, gift, loan, bequest or exchange" unless valid title is obtained.[76] Similarly, "[e]very effort must be made before acquisition to ensure that . . . [the] object has not been illegally obtained in, or exported from its country of origin or any intermediate country in which it may have been owned legally[.]"[77] Thus, the Code of Ethics states that "[d]ue diligence in this regard shall establish the full history of the item since discovery or production"[78] before acquisition is considered. If the museum has "reasonable cause to believe" that objects' excavation "involved unauthorized or unscientific fieldwork, or intentional destruction . . . of monuments, archaeological or geological sites," or

---

[69] 416 N.Y.S.2d 254 (1st Dep't 1979).

[70] *Id.* at 257–58.

[71] *Id.* at 258–59.

[72] *Id.* at 257.

[73] International Council of Museums, Code of Ethics for Museums (2006), *available at* http://icom.museum/ethics.html [hereinafter Code of Ethics].

[74] *Id.*, Introduction by Geoffrey Lewis.

[75] *Id.* at § 2.

[76] *Id.* at § 2.2.

[77] *Id.* at § 2.3.

[78] *Id.*

involved "a failure to disclose the finds . . . to the proper legal or governmental authorities," the objects should not be acquired.[79]

The Code of Ethics does note, however, that a professional conflict can arise when an acquisition that is highly desired by a museum lacks provenance.[80] It acknowledges that, in very rare cases, "an item without provenance may have such an inherently outstanding contribution to knowledge that would be in the public interest to preserve it," and leaves open the possibility that such an object may be acquired if "specialists in the discipline concerned" think it should be.[81]

Even though the Code of Ethics states that each museum should "adopt and publish a written collection policy,"[82] most museums do not publish their collection policy. Thus, it is difficult to determine whether a museum actually has an adequate policy and, if so, what that policy specifically states. Perhaps a more important issue is whether museums actually follow their own policies. For example, in connection with the recent adoption of new rules by museums concerning claims for Holocaust-related property, museums are encouraged not to assert technical defenses such as the statute of limitations and laches;[83] but in my experience, they still routinely do so.

The Code of Ethics is extremely helpful in that it articulates the position urged by many archaeologists that the acquisition and exhibition of unprovenanced pieces condones the illicit trade in cultural property.[84] Again, ICOM urges that, with respect to collections, a written policy be adopted and museums take steps to ensure that all acquired objects are properly and fully documented, with a complete description of all items, their provenance and sources, and the conditions of acceptance by the museums.[85] Research should be conducted to establish provenance, and publication is encouraged. The rules not only urge that members of the museum profession not authenticate objects they believe may have been illegally acquired, but also urges them "not to act in any way that could be regarded as benefiting such activity."[86] The rules further note that the appropriate authorities should be informed if there is reason to believe, or even suspect, illegal or illicit conduct.[87] If adopted by museums, the acquisition and collection policies urged by ICOM will go a long way to improving the situation.

The ICOM rules do not go as far as Professor Gerstenblith urges, that is, that a museum may not acquire archaeological and ethnological objects unless

---

[79] *Id.* at § 2.4.

[80] *Id.* at § 3.4.

[81] *Id.* at § 3.4.

[82] *Id.* at § 2.1.

[83] *American Association of Museums Guidelines Concerning the Unlawful Appropriation of Objects During the Nazi Era*, approved November 1999, amended April 2001, at 7, *available at* http://www.aam-us.org/museumresources/ethics/upload/ethicsguidelines_naziera.pdf.

[84] Code of Ethics, *supra* note 73, at § 2.4.

[85] *Id.* at § 2.

[86] *Id.* at § 5.1.

[87] *Id.*

their due diligence inquiries result in documentation that shows legitimate origins and provenance. [88] Although that proposition is salutary, in practice, some close calls have to be made—and probably should be. At the same time, museums that act without full documentation should then go forward to adopt and implement policies that seek information regarding the object under a structure similar to what many museums have done with respect to possible retention of Holocaust-related material. An example is the posting by many museums on their Web sites of all acquisitions with any gaps in provenance between 1933 and 1945. This is not a perfect solution, but it is one calculated to elicit claims.

In 2004 the Association of Art Museum Directors (AAMD) issued a *Report on the Acquisition of Archaeological Materials and Ancient Art.*[89] It includes guidelines that urge member museums to "rigorously research the provenance of a work prior to acquisition." The guidelines also set forth a number of elements that must be included in such research, including the "ownership history," "the countries in which the work has been located and when," any exhibition or publication histories that are available, "whether any claims to ownership of the work of art have been made," "whether the work appears in relevant databases of stolen works," and "the circumstances under which the work is being offered."[90] It urges museums to "make a concerted effort to obtain accurate written documentation with respect to the history of the work of art" and asks member museums to "require sellers, donors and their representatives to provide all available information and documentation."[91] The guidelines also urge that, after an acquisition, the "member museums . . . publish promptly . . . an image . . . and relevant provenance information" about the object.[92] The rules press member museums to be familiar with legal developments and seek appropriate advice.[93]

All of this is well and good, but a problem arises when, notwithstanding the research that has been done, the provenance remains incomplete and there is not enough information to adequately determine whether the object being acquired complies with "applicable law and the . . . Guidelines."[94] The AAMD Code says that museums should "use their professional judgment in determining whether to proceed with the acquisition" under these circumstances because, even though there is a chance that the object has a tainted history, its acquisition may be in the best interest of the public and consistent with the museum's mission.[95] Examples given include situations where "the work of art is in danger of destruction or deterioration," when "the acquisition would make the

[88] Gerstenblith, *supra* note 60, at 460–62.

[89] The Association of Art Museum Directors, *Report on Acquisition of Archaeological Materials and Ancient Art,* New York (June 4, 2004), *available at* http://www.artic.edu/aic/collections/TaskForceReport.pdf.

[90] *Id.* at 3.

[91] *Id.*

[92] *Id.*

[93] *Id.* at 4.

[94] *Id.* at 5.

[95] *Id.*

work publicly accessible, providing a singular and a material contribution to knowledge, as well as facilitating the reconstruction of its provenance thereby allowing claimants to come forward."[96] Member museums are also urged to consider other factors, including "whether the work of art has been outside of its probable country or countries of origin for a sufficiently long time that its acquisition would not provide a direct, material incentive to looting or illegal excavation."[97] The AAMD recommends a ten-year period, but the individual museums set their own policy.[98]

I believe that this will pose a significant problem for archaeologists, and even for me. It sounds strikingly similar to the Declaration on the Importance and Value of Universal Museums issued by the directors of a number of well-known international art institutions.[99] That declaration, which was not particularly well received by the archaeological community, suggested that, over time, acquired antiquities become part of the museums that have cared for them and, by extension, part of the heritage of the nations that house them. I do not understand how acquiring an unprovenanced objects that may have been on the illicit market for a long time fails to foster the continuation of that market, as the AAMD guidelines suggest. Indeed, much material that is stolen in the dark of night from unexcavated sites remains underground for many years.[100] In the Lydian Hoard case, as I mentioned, the bulk of the collection sat in the Met's basement storerooms from the late 1960s to the mid 1980s. The rationale is that after so much time has passed, claims will not be made, or, if made, will be much more difficult to sustain because of statutes of limitations, the absence of available proof, and so on. I find it disheartening that the AAMD guidelines seek to perpetuate this sentiment. It is not too radical to suggest that the guidelines, in countenancing this exception, ultimately negate the provisions that seek to protect against the acquisition of unprovenanced or illicit objects.

Even if museums, pursuant to ICOM or on their own initiative, were to adopt codes that included provisions calculated to prevent the acquisition of unprovenanced or tainted objects, there are no enforcement mechanisms to ensure compliance. None of the guidelines include provisions that penalize museums that violate the codes. Without an effective enforcement provision, I fear that the codes only give victimized countries a sense of false security and are probably honored more in the breach.

---

[96] *Id.*

[97] *Id.*

[98] *Id.*

[99] Declaration on the Importance and Value of Universal Museums, ICOM News no. 1 (2004), at 4, *available at* http://icom.museum/pdf/E_news2004/p4_2004-1.pdf.

[100] AIA Statement on Museum Acquisitions and Loans of Antiquities and Ancient Art Works: Response to the AAMD Report on the Loan of Archaeological and Ancient Artworks (Mar. 2006), *available at* http://www.archaeological.org/pdfs/archaeologywatch/museumpolicy/AIA_AAMD_Response.pdf. *See also* Press Release, Archaeologists Recommend Responsible Museum Acquisitions Policies (Feb. 28, 2006), *available at* http://www.archaeological.org/pdfs/archaeologywatch/museumpolicy/AIA_PR_Museum_Acquistion_Policy.pdf.

Professor Gerstenblith, in acknowledging this problem, has urged the enactment of state and federal legislation requiring museums, both public and private, to disclose information about acquisitions and to provide documentation establishing good title for those objects that have been acquired.[101] She points to existing anti-secrecy legislation in Wisconsin, which requires disclosure of "the condition of museums, [and] the articles added to the museum," but such legislation may not be particularly effective because it is not specific enough and may not be adequately enforced.[102] Such legislation is also defective because it only requires disclosure after acquisition, and thus, does not necessarily prevent inappropriate acquisitions.[103]

There are no easy answers, but more attention to these issues is needed. Meanwhile, the problems proliferate. In January 2004, federal authorities seized a marble statue of the Roman Emperor Trajan that was part of an auction at Christie's, claiming that it was stolen six years earlier from a Roman museum.[104] In responding to the seizure, the auction house claimed to have done its due diligence prior to the auction and relied on what it thought was credible provenance information from the consignor.[105]

Compromise, as always, is needed. Perhaps museums are better off acquiring objects when no information can be obtained either way. That will at least get the material off the illicit market, but this approach must be coupled with rules that ensure that when claims are made, they will not be met with technical defenses that lead to years of complex and expensive litigation.

---

[101] Gerstenblith, *supra* note 60, at 462–63.

[102] *Id.*, at 463.

[103] *Id.*

[104] Barry Meier, *U.S. Seizes Portrait of a Roman That Was Sold at Auction*, N.Y. TIMES, Jan. 17, 2004, *available at* http://select.nytimes.com/search/restricted/article?res=FB0712FC34540C748DDDA80894DC404482.

[105] *Id.*

CHAPTER 22

MUSEUMS AS SITES OF RECONCILIATION

Claire L. Lyons

For museums that collect Greek and Roman art, 2006 was a watershed year. Evidence seized during raids on the Swiss warehouses of several prominent antiquities dealers revealed the details of fraudulent business practices, graphically documented by photographs of artifacts, still covered with dirt from freshly plundered sites. Some of these images were matched to objects on display in the galleries of international museums. With these records, Italian prosecutors exposed a global network of traffickers closely tied to auction houses and private collectors—a network that brought works of art to the secondary market and thence to distinguished public institutions.[1] Particularly among North American museums, demands for the restitution of stolen and illegally exported cultural property have had major repercussions, both in terms of negative public perception and the costs of litigation. Jeopardizing the cosmopolitan ideals that museums embrace, the expanding investigations that source countries are pursuing signal that the problem of illicit antiquities from all eras and regions of the world will be resolved neither easily nor soon.

In the wake of the antiquities scandals, however, there have been positive outcomes. Evidence can no longer be waved aside that site looting and the burgeoning commerce in unprovenanced artifacts go hand in hand. Going well beyond the quiet repatriation of stolen works of art, agreements have been forged that entail exchanges between museums as well as other kinds of productive partnerships. The cultural agreements that several U.S. museums have struck with Italy, described below, call for long-term loans, collaboration on exhibitions, and conservation projects. Most importantly, strict policies governing acquisitions of ancient art and other objects that fall under the definition of cultural property have established a "bright line," a date after which the provenance of objects must be documented.

When it comes to antiquities, private collectors and archaeologists have long been at odds over acquisition practices. Globalization and the politics of culture in the 21st century, however, are redefining their public obligations. Making ancient art meaningful and accessible—and bridging the gap between scholars who work in the field and those who work in galleries—demand creative strategies. By acknowledging the multiple values of items previously seen solely

[1] PETER WATSON & CECILIA TODESCHINI, THE MEDICI CONSPIRACY: THE ILLICIT JOURNEY OF LOOTED ANTIQUITIES. FROM ITALY'S TOMB RAIDERS TO THE WORLD'S GREATEST MUSEUMS (2006).

through the lens of fine art, museums can function as sites of reconciliation. This chapter describes some recent developments at the J. Paul Getty Museum, which has been a lightning rod for controversies that have polarized professions as much as nations.

A. THE FRANCAVILLA PROJECT

In 1994, the Getty Museum informed the Italian Ministry of Culture about the presence of a large quantity of artifacts that had been determined to come from a location in South Italy known as Timpone della Motta. Situated close to the Calabrian coastal town of Francavilla Marittima, Timpone is the location of a religious sanctuary, where Italian and Dutch excavators discovered a series of temples in the 1960s and 1970s. Active from about the eighth century B.C.E., the sanctuary was frequented by the inhabitants of a nearby Iron Age settlement. Later it was associated with the Achaian colony of Sybaris, famed in antiquity for its wealth and extravagant lifestyle. When the research priorities of the local archaeological superintendency shifted to Sybaris proper, looters pillaged Timpone, emptying the contents of one or more votive deposits. The deposits contained dedications of terracotta figurines, bronze implements, gold and silver jewelry, and decorated pottery. The haul was clandestinely exported from Italy to Switzerland in the 1970s, with some of the finer pieces ending up in private collections. Quantities of objects emerged on the Swiss art market, from which selections were acquired in 1975–78 by the Ny Carlsberg Glyptotek in Copenhagen. Other artifacts made their way in batches to the J. Paul Getty Museum in Malibu between 1978 and 1982; the remaining pottery finds wound up in the Institute of Classical Archaeology in Bern.

Specific features of the material from the authorized excavations made it plain to the excavators that the Copenhagen, Bern, and Malibu groups all belonged to the Timpone deposit.[2] To date, over 100 joins have been made between museum fragments and freshly excavated materials. Joins with the objects still in situ have also confirmed their common source. These discoveries set into motion a project to study, conserve, and publish the Malibu and Bern groups. Conceived by Marion True and supported by the director of the Archaeological Institute in Bern, Dietrich Willers, the aim of the Francavilla project was to de-accession and amalgamate the dispersed votives, and to relocate the entire collection to the Museo Archeologico Nazionale della Sibaritide, which is the archaeological museum in nearby Sibari (ancient Sybaris).

Rather than a unilateral restitution of looted antiquities, the project seized the opportunity to convene an international team of researchers to inventory and analyze the entire assemblage. The Getty objects were sent to Bern in

[2] Marianne Kleibrink et al., *Water for Athena: Votive Gifts at Lagaria (Timpone della Motta, Francavilla Marittima, Calabria, in* The Object of Dedication, World Archaeology 36.1, 44 (Robin Osborne ed., 2004). The Getty's share had been acquired by a former curator, the late Jiri Frel, who—when presented with corroborating evidence—acknowledged that the find-spot was indeed Timpone. A timeline of events surrounding the Francavilla objects is published on the Getty Web site, in an April 4, 2007, press communication, http://www.getty.edu/news/press/center/francavilla_marittima_timeline.html.

1996 for ongoing study, and in 2001 the exhibition "Irrwege: Antike auf der Rückreise" ("Gone Astray: Antiquities on the Way Home") was mounted to publicize the issues of provenance and original context. A celebratory exhibition in the Sibari museum opened in the summer of 2001, demonstrating the relationships between the repatriated objects and the finds from scientifically controlled excavations. Initially hesitant to return its Francavilla objects outright despite the identification of joining fragments in Copenhagen and Timpone, the Ny Carlsberg Glyptotek has indicated its willingness to negotiate with Italian authorities on this matter.[3] Altogether, more than 5,000 artifacts were returned, making this one of the largest restitutions of looted archaeological materials to date.

The Francavilla project has produced a number of tangible and intangible benefits. Two publications have appeared: a comprehensive study of Greek, colonial and native pottery, and a monograph on the metal artifacts.[4] Exhaustive metallographic analysis determined sourcing, manufacturing processes, and the presence of associated organics such as wood, fiber, and plant debris. The archaeometrical aspects of the project were especially fruitful , as this is one of the few significant groups of metal artifacts from the Mediterranean basin to be analyzed to this degree.[5] The votives witness the presence of a major extra-urban cult, where worshippers offered personal tokens deriving from international centers of production from southern Italy to the Greek mainland. The Francavilla project enabled researchers to connect the original contents of the votive deposit with the construction history of a sequence of temples erected over several centuries. These remains were "reanimated," in a sense, by reconstituting the human dimensions of ritual practice over a long time span. Few votive contexts have been as scrupulously investigated, producing a critical mass of data that informs the ongoing excavations and deepens our understanding of cult practices at Timpone della Motta. Also fruitful was the network of scholars who forged an interdisciplinary collaboration that generated much good will.

Four museums adopted varying but complementary approaches. On the part of the Swiss university museum, the materials were studied, and a public exhibition was mounted to inform audiences of the consequences of looting. The Ny Carlsberg Glyptotek completed a detailed publication of its objects,

---

[3] Jette Christiansen, *in* TOBIAS FISCHER-HANSEN ET AL., CAMPANIA, SOUTH ITALY AND SICILY: NY CARLSBERG GLYPTOTEK, nos. 20–28, 92–94 (1992); Jette Christiansen, *in* FLEMING JOHANSEN ET AL., GREECE IN THE ARCHAIC PERIOD. CATALOG, NY CARLSBERG GLYPTOTEK, nos. 36–37, 68–102, 105–13, 116–19, 121 (1994).

[4] FREDERIKE VAN DER WIELEN-VAN OMMEREN & LUCILLA DE LACHENAL, LA DEA DI SIBARI E IL SANTUARIO RITROVATO. STUDI SUL RINVENIMENTI DAL TIMPONE MOTTA DI FRANCAVILLA MARITTIMA: I, 1 CERAMICHE DI IMPORTAZIONE, DI PRODUZIONE COLONIALE E INDIGENA. BOLLETTINO D'ARTE (2006); JOHN K. PAPADOPOULOS, LA DEA DI SIBARI E IL SANTUARIO RITROVATO. STUDI SUI RINVENIMENTI DEL TIMPONE MOTTA DI FRANCAVILLA MARITTIMA II.1. THE ARCHAIC VOTIVE METAL OBJECTS. BOLLETTINO D'ARTE (2003). Additional publications on the ceramic material and terracotta figurines are anticipated in the near future.

[5] David Scott, *Analytical Studies of the Francavilla Metal Objects*, *in* PAPADOPOULOS, *supra* note 4, at 167.

extended support for ongoing excavations through its foundation, and, as noted earlier, is engaged in negotiations on the ultimate disposition of the Timpone materials. In addition to overall project coordination, the Getty Museum invested heavily in laboratory analysis to extract the maximum information from the finds. As the primary steward, the archaeological museum in Sibari is now better able to fulfill its mandate to conserve artifacts and structures together *in situ* and present them to the public.

Although the results go a considerable distance to compensate for the original loss, it is important to stress that the unfortunate circumstances surrounding Timpone della Motta can never be fully rectified, however well funded and progressive restitution agreements like this may be. Deep looter trenches still scar the Timpone hillsides. Archaeologists will ask how many desirable objects were skimmed off by private collectors, and whether extraneous materials were conflated in the chain from thief, to middleman, to dealer. They will also wonder about the dedications of textiles and other organic finds that could only be detected microscopically. As a model for how to deal *post facto* with an influx of illicit antiquities into museum collections, the project nevertheless was farsighted. In the 1990s, similar long-term exchanges were accomplished, thanks to the pioneering efforts of the director of the Antikensammlung in Berlin, Wolf-Dieter Heilmeyer, to create a network of cooperating museums in Germany, Italy, and Greece.[6] At the Michael C. Carlos Museum, a program known as the "Emory University Museum International Loan Project" (EUMILOP) was launched to bring antiquities out of storerooms and into the public eye. Former director Maxwell Anderson worked with archaeological superintendencies in Rome and Syracuse to organize three exhibitions: "Roman Portraits in Context" (1988), "Syracuse: the Fairest Greek City" (1989), and "Radiance in Stone" (1989). Other U.S. collections are now building similar alliances, as they negotiate with source countries over contested objects, both from recent unauthorized digging and from collecting campaigns conducted in earlier eras.

Timpone was a phenomenal discovery. Gifts of vases, jewelry, and figurines presented to the deity were not, as some would have it, simply minor and repetitive examples of southern Italian material culture, though they may appear so when a few handfuls of attractive objects are singled out in auction catalogues. Half a dozen cult buildings, a stoa, and an altar established on the acropolis represent the earliest temple structures on Italian soil. Cult rituals were practiced continuously from the eighth through the fourth centuries B.C.E., arguably one of the most dynamic periods in ancient Mediterranean history. A temple of Athena was identified from a unique inscribed bronze tablet dedicated by the early sixth-century B.C.E. Olympic victor Kleombrotos of Sybaris. During the half millennium that the sanctuary was active, an evolution of ritual practices can be observed in the changing types of votives. Native Oenotrian worshippers of a wool-working divinity gradually accommodated the

[6] See Wolf-Dieter Heilmeyer & J. Cordelia Eule, Illegale Archäologie. Internationale Konferenz über zukünftige Probleme bei unerlaubtem Antikentransfer, 236–38 (2004), for the Berlin Resolution 2003 crafted by Heilmeyer.

rituals and beliefs of Greek colonists, and the Greek goddess of crafts, Athena, came to be fused with the indigenous deity.[7] Also venerated here was Epeios, the legendary Trojan War hero who carried water for the Greek forces and built the Trojan horse. Finds of many small water pitchers reflect a tradition attested in literary sources, which describe a temple of Athena and Epeios at a south Italian site called Lagaria, confirming the historical name of the Timpone sanctuary. Sites such as Timpone della Motta help us to answer some fundamental questions: the relationship between Greek cities and their overseas neighbors, the Hellenizing influence of epic poetry, the nature of colonialism, and the role religion played in mediating ethnic differences. Conclusions drawn from this site may be relevant for a wide swath of colonial sites on both sides of the Mediterranean. How different cultures found common ground is not an inconsequential issue to ponder in the contemporary world.

B. JUST RETURNS

Restitution of the Francavilla votive deposit was not the first and certainly not the last time that museums have joined forces to return antiquities to their countries of origin. Throughout the 1990s, research brought to light other objects, frequently supplied with forged documentation, which had gone missing from excavation storage or had been illegally exported from private collections. An Etruscan bronze tripod from the Guglielmi collection in Florence was smuggled to Switzerland and sold, contravening regulations that restricted the export of works of art in private hands. When the ministry received inquiries about the tripod prior to purchase, the owner claimed that it had been stolen. The so-called Gladiator from the Giustiniani collection was sold to the Getty Museum as a Mithra from "a nineteenth-century English collection," after the original was altered by cutting off the head, arms, and a lion figure.[8]

Together with the Metropolitan Museum of Art in New York, the Boston Museum of Fine Arts, the Cleveland Art Museum, and the Princeton University Art Museum, the Getty has been immersed in negotiations over the repatriation of additional works of art to Greece and Italy. Four objects were returned to Greece in 2006–2007: a Boeotian gravestone of Athanias, illicitly excavated in the 1990s; a fifth-century relief from Thasos, stolen from the French excavation storeroom in the early 1900s and purchased by J. Paul Getty in 1955; a Hellenistic gold funerary wreath found near Serres in northern Greece in ca. 1990; and a Parian marble torso of a *kore* (maiden), which was simultaneously claimed by both Greece and Italy. The case of the Thasos relief shows that when there is reasonably sound evidence of an illegal transaction, there should be no statute of limitations for making restitutions. Discussions with Italy proceeded at a slower pace due to legal complexities and the scope of the Italian request. Twenty-six objects from a list of 52 were initially identified for restitution, but negotiations

[7] Kleibrink, *supra* note 2; SILVANA LUPPINO, OFFERTE ALLA DEA DI FRANCAVILLA DA BERNA E DA MALIBU (2001).

[8] Marion True, *The Changing Role of Museums: Looking to the Future*, *in* WHO OWNS CULTURE? CULTURAL PROPERTY AND PATRIMONY DISPUTES IN AN AGE WITHOUT BORDERS 79–81 (Richard Brilliant et al. eds., 2001).

faltered over the two most valuable sculptures: a fifth-century B.C.E. marble and limestone cult statue of a female goddess, known as Aphrodite; and a bronze statue of a victorious athlete recovered from the northern Adriatic Sea. Investigations into the "Aphrodite" image pointed convincingly to a Sicilian provenance, a conclusion reached on both stylistic criteria and the sourcing of the limestone in a quarry near Ragusa. Uncertainty over the bronze athlete's precise find spot—whether in national or international waters—and the Italian contention that the piece was illegally exported once it passed through Italian territory, has blocked a resolution to the larger claim.

Commitments to cooperate on joint undertakings are likely the wave of the future. Following the settlement with the Boston Museum of Fine Arts, the Italian Minister of Culture emphasized "cultural projects, not cultural property."[9] More than just a quid pro quo exchange of objects to place in vitrines, arrangements that provide a basis for long-term, open-ended partnerships are the most fruitful. These may entail loan exhibitions, conservation treatment and training, publications, inventory, and data exchanges, all of which should aim to enhance understanding, expertise, and public enjoyment. In the 21st-century economy of knowledge, the provision of skills and resources becomes at least as important as physical possession of art objects. Although the terms of the Getty's cultural agreement with Greece are in discussion, one member of the Greek legal team that visited the Getty remarked optimistically that "things ended up in the best possible way for both parties."[10]

C. ACQUIRING ANTIQUITIES

Acquisition policies for antiquities constitute a thorny topic that has been much discussed, as institutions and museum professional associations revise guidelines and codes of practice that govern how objects are evaluated for purchase or donation. One obvious conclusion from the Francavilla experience is that adequate investigation of an object's background is preferable to remedial research and retroactive compensation. More stringent acquisitions policies and due diligence have been demanded by archaeologists. Part of the Boston Museum of Fine Arts agreement entails greater transparency, with objects of potential Italian origin being brought to the attention of authorities in advance of purchase.[11] Such gestures of cooperation have long been standard practice, and advising possible source countries of the existence of an object is only effective insofar as that object has been previously documented. By their very nature, pillaged antiquities are often excavated from unrecorded sites, and pillagers have no interest in documenting finds and contexts. Checking databanks of stolen art is consequently a well-meaning but fruitless enterprise. The Getty Museum addressed certain loopholes in its 1994 guidelines, which stressed documentation of provenance independent of dealer warranties. This

---

[9] Elisabetta Povoledo, *Boston Art Museum Returns Works to Italy*, N.Y. TIMES, Sept. 29, 2006, at E27; David Gill & Christopher Chippendale, *From Boston to Rome: Reflections on Returning Antiquities*, 13(3) INT'L. J. CULTURAL PROP. 311–31 (2006).

[10] Personal communication.

[11] *See An Agreement with the Italian Ministry of Culture,* http://www.mfa.org/collections/index.asp?key=2656.

policy was effective insofar as acquisitions since then have been few in number and involve objects with a solid pedigree. Imperfect as it may have been, the policy was far stricter than that observed by most museums in the United States.

In practice, procedures for documenting potential acquisitions throughout the Getty have been strengthened continually, not only in the wake of events of the past year, but over the course of the last decade, in order to respond to developing legal and ethical norms. Civil forfeiture proceedings against a gold phiale owned by the collector Michael Steinhardt and the 2002 conviction of the antiquities dealer Frederick Schultz marked key turning points.[12] Legal review of proposed acquisitions involves increasingly arduous research and documentation. Due diligence is carried out not only for museum objects, but also for library materials including drawings, vintage photographs, archives and rare books. Works on paper can fall under the category of cultural property, but because they are usually produced as multiples, they have rarely been subject to the kind of restrictions that surround works of art, except as price and rarity demand. Each acquisition proposal (or donation offer) may require tracking provenance through several generations of owners, dealers, or auctions; requesting proof of import and export; and working to bring art dealers and collectors up to speed with changing guidelines. Most dealers and private collectors have been cooperative, and the minority that are reluctant to disclose sources will need to look elsewhere. While investigations into the history of collecting can produce valuable historical information, occasionally acquisitions cannot go forward for lack of clear origins, especially in the case of private collectors who failed to record the details of every purchase.

Adopted in October 2006, the Getty Museum's revised acquisition policy established stronger criteria for potential acquisitions, applying equally to purchases, gifts, bequests, exchanges, or any other method by which objects enter the collections. Most significantly, the "bright line" for establishing a date before which works of art must be documented was set at 1970, the year in which the UNESCO Convention on the Means of Prohibiting and Preventing the Illicit Import, Export and Transfer of Ownership of Cultural Property went into force.[13] Specifically, the policy requires that

> No object will be acquired that, to the knowledge of the Museum, has been stolen, removed in contravention of treaties and international conventions of which the United States is a signatory, illegally exported from its country of origin or the country where it was last legally owned, or illegally imported into the United States.

---

[12] Claire L. Lyons, *Objects and Identities: Claiming and Reclaiming the Past*, *in* CLAIMING THE STONES/NAMING THE BONES: CULTURAL PROPERTY AND THE NEGOTIATION OF NATIONAL AND ETHNIC IDENTITY 116–37 (E. Barkan & R. Bush eds., 2002); Patty Gerstenblith, *United States v. Schultz*, CULTURE WITHOUT CONTEXT 10, 27–31 (2002).

[13] UNESCO Convention on the Means of Prohibiting and Preventing the Illegal Import, Export and Transfer of Ownership of Cultural Property (Nov. 14, 1970), 823 U.N.T.S. 231, 10 I.L.M. 289.

> In addition, for the acquisition of any ancient work of art or archaeological material, the Museum will require:
>
> a.) Documentation or substantial evidence that the item was in the United States by November 17, 1970 (the date of the UNESCO Convention on the Means of Prohibiting and Preventing the Illicit Import, Export and Transfer of Ownership of Cultural Property) and that there is no reason to suspect it was illegally exported from its country of origin, or
>
> b.) Documentation or substantial evidence that the item was out of its country of origin before November 17, 1970 and that it has been or will be legally imported into the United States, or
>
> c.) Documentation or substantial evidence that the item was legally exported from its country of origin after November 17, 1970 and that it has been or will be legally imported into the United States.[14]

Setting a precedent, the date of the 1970 UNESCO convention was acknowledged in the U.K. Museums Association Code of Ethics, which emphasizes to a greater degree the possibility that acquisitions of archaeological materials lacking complete documentation may be considered in consultation with the presumed country of origin, as follows.[15]

> *5.10* Reject items that have been illicitly traded. Note that the UNESCO Convention (on the Means of Prohibiting and Preventing the Illicit Import, Export and Transfer of Ownership of Cultural Property) was finalised in 1970.
>
> Reject, therefore, any item if there is any suspicion that, since 1970, it may have been stolen, illegally excavated or removed from a monument, site or wreck contrary to local law or otherwise acquired in or exported from its country of origin (including the UK), or any intermediate country, in violation of that country's laws or any national and international treaties, unless the museum is able to obtain permission from authorities with the requisite jurisdiction in the country of origin.
>
> *5.11* Reject any item that lacks secure ownership history, unless there is reliable documentation to show that it was exported from its country of origin before 1970, or the museum is acting as an externally approved repository of last resort, or in the best judgment of experts in the field concerned the item is of minor importance and has not been illicitly traded.

More flexible guidelines were recommended in a policy statement issued by the North-American based Association of Art Museum Directors (AAMD) in 2004. Citing only Article 7b of the 1970 UNESCO convention, it directs member museums not to acquire objects "stolen from a museum, or

---

[14] Excerpt from Board of Trustees of the J. Paul Getty Trust, *Policy Statement: Acquisitions by the J. Paul Getty Museum* (Oct. 23, 2006), http://www.getty.edu/about/governance/policies.

[15] U.K. Museums Association Code of ethics, http://www.museumsassociation.org.

a religious, or secular public monument," or "known to have been part of an *official* archaeological excavation and removed in contravention of the laws of the country of origin" (emphasis added). When sufficient information about an object's history is lacking, the policy allows for acquisition if an object is endangered, would make a significant contribution to knowledge, and has been out of its country of origin for a rolling time period of ten years.[16] As noted in a critical rebuttal by the Archaeological Institute of America, such exceptions are little more than loopholes through which many illicit works of art readily find their way to willing buyers, and ignore the fact that plundered objects usually derive from *unofficial*, previously unknown excavations. Dealers who traffic in such objects would be little inconvenienced by keeping them for a decade. Indeed, there are clear economic advantages to hold material back, and thus the ten-year limit would furnish incentives for obscuring the details of provenance.[17] The Getty's decision to enact a stricter policy has had a ripple effect. Accepted by growing numbers of North American museums, including the Princeton University Art Museum, the 1970 benchmark is now also recommended by the American Association of Museums (AAM).

D. BRIDGING THE GAP

Projects like Francavilla and similar collaborations between researchers in the field, the laboratory, and museums demonstrate how much there is to be gained from working together. Despite the tendency to create a false dichotomy between an object's social history and its aesthetic qualities, archaeologists and art historians hold many ideas about the values of archaeological heritage in common. A realistic middle ground offers ample space for carrying forward the work of preservation, historical awareness, and cultural understanding. In this context, a recent colloquium at which archaeologists and museum professionals met to identify shared interests and objectives is relevant.[18] A series of recommendations emerged that highlight areas of consensus. The principles listed here are a work in progress; some are gaining wider acceptance, while others will still require thoughtful dialogue. While complete agreement may be elusive, an inclusive process for seeking resolutions should be the main objective.

1. The date of the adoption of the 1970 UNESCO convention by the UNESCO General Conference should become the standard benchmark for documenting the provenance of potential acquisitions.
2. The International Council of Museums (ICOM) should establish a list of museums that have specifically indicated their acceptance of and adherence to the ICOM Code of Ethics. A "red-list" of institutions that violate the Code of Ethics should be published.

---

[16] *Report of the AAMD Task Force on the Acquisition of Archaeological Materials and Ancient Art*, Jan. 4, 2004, http://www.aamd.org/papers/.

[17] *Statement on Museum Acquisitions and Loans of Antiquities and Ancient Art Works*, http://www.archaeological.org/pdfs/archaeologywatch/museumpolicy/AIA_AAMD_Response.pdf.

[18] The colloquium *Museums and Archaeologists: Partnerships and Progress in the 21st Century* took place at the Archaeological Institute of America's 2007 annual meeting.

3. Museums should formulate an explicit policy for acquisitions of archaeological objects and ancient art, and should purchase only those antiquities for which a pedigree is provided. An object's history in collections is as important as its history in ancient times and constitutes its cultural biography. From an archaeological perspective, these standards apply equally to works of art and to minor artifacts.
4. Museums and other institutions, as well as private collectors and commercial owners of antiquities, should make all records pertaining to acquisition and provenance publicly available.
5. Loans of archaeological objects between museums should be encouraged as an important means of making known their full cultural, historical, and functional significance. Museums making or receiving loans should adhere to the ICOM Code of Ethics, confirming their adherence in the loan contract. Museums receiving loans of objects without provenance should clearly acknowledge the lack of provenance in both exhibitions and catalogues. Source countries with restrictive loan regulations should revise them to enable international long-term loans.
6. Embracing the highest standards of ethics and legality, institutions and individuals who hold archaeological materials in trust need to move beyond narrow concepts of ownership of archaeological objects. They should be alert to evolving approaches to ancient art, artifacts, and monuments.
7. The issue of how to address undocumented antiquities, acquired after 1970, remains a matter for further consideration. Restitution of objects that can be clearly proven to have been stolen from source countries is justified. Discussion with source countries, either direct or through mediation, is likely to offer the best way forward. Alternatives to restitution should be explored; collaborative research can be effective in achieving "just returns" and promoting beneficial partnerships in the future.
8. Museums that have adopted responsible acquisitions policies should establish a cooperative network for loans, conservation, scholarly programs, and other joint initiatives.
9. The Archaeological Institute of America should work to form closer relationships with the College Art Association, the American Association of Museums, and the AAMD on issues of mutual concern. Efforts need to be made to overcome cynicism on both sides and to seek consensus where it can be most productive.

E. CONCLUSION: A COSMOPOLITAN ETHIC

In his recent book *Cosmopolitanism*, Kwame Anthony Appiah traces the cosmopolitan ethic to ancient philosophical schools that took root in the multicultural communities where Greeks met foreign neighbors.[19] It is no coincidence that throughout history, the colonial ambit has been a seedbed

---

[19] Kwame Anthony Appiah, Cosmopolitanism: Ethics in a World of Strangers (2006).

of cultural contact, hybrid identities, and openness to unfamiliar ideas. Timpone and other sites at the crossroads of cultures represent the essence of cosmopolitanism on the ground, not as a vague ideal, but as an historical actuality. It was here that people of different backgrounds devised new modes of exchange and community through the encounter with strangers. If it is a matter of concern how art and expressions of spirituality created a space for shared values, then protecting sites and the integrity of the objects they yield has to be paramount. Organizing displays of archaic material culture from Magna Graecia for curious onlookers from Denmark to California is not sufficient grounds for rationalizing the cosmopolitan claim. Scattering the fruits of theft in galleries, detached from a rich historical context, falls far short of this ethic. The commodities that are ever more in demand are knowledge and opportunity, not things, and the question should no longer be "who owns culture," but rather how to create the circumstances that enable greater numbers of people to engage in and expand their cultural values. Insofar as they adopt cosmopolitan means-transparency, inclusiveness, and cooperation-museums can realize cosmopolitan ends.

F. POSTSCRIPT

Since the October 2006 conference published in this volume, several disputes over antiquities in American collections have been resolved at an unexpectedly quick pace, and a consensus on standards for documentation of provenance has been achieved by the major American museum organizations. The J. Paul Getty Museum and the Ministry of Culture for the Hellenic Republic concluded discussions for the return of a gold funerary wreath and a Parian marble statue of a kore in February 2007. In August 2007, the Italian Ministry of Culture and the J. Paul Getty Trust finalized an agreement regarding the ministry's claim for objects in the museum's antiquities collection, which entailed the return of forty objects, the adjournment of further discussions on the bronze statue of a victorious youth pending legal proceedings in the Italian courts, and a plan for extensive cultural collaborations including the loan of important works of art, joint exhibitions, research, and conservation projects. Details of these agreements and lists of the objects that were returned are posted on the Getty's Web site (February 7 and August 1, 2007, press releases).[20] The possible origins of the cult statue of a goddess, popularly known as the "Aphrodite of Morgantina," were examined in an international scholarly workshop at the Getty in May 2007. Scholars addressed the phenomenon of pseudo-acrolithic sculpture in Archaic and Classical Greece, the art-historical features of the statue, and its petrographic and micropalaeontological data, as well as surveying soil and pollen residues. The papers were published online.[21] The AAMD issued a revised policy on museum acquisitions of antiquities, accepting the UNESCO 1970 Convention as a "line in the sand," in June 2008. The American Association of Museums followed suit two months later. The Archaeological

[20] Http://www.getty.edu/news/press/.

[21] *Summary of Proceedings from a Workshop Held at the Getty Villa on May 9, 2007,* http://www.getty.edu/museum/symposia/workshop_goddess.html.

Institute of America and AAMD have established a joint task force, to consider a number of outstanding issues, including how to deal with "orphaned" objects (undocumented antiquities in public and private collections, acquired since 1970) and other issues of mutual concern.

INDEX